CONTEMPORARY DISCOURSES ON IE & C THEORY AND PRACTICE

CONTEMPORARY DISCOURSES ON IE &C THEORY AND PRACTICE

THEOPHILUS K. GOKAH
EDITOR

Nova Science Publishers, Inc.
New York

Copyright © 2009 by Nova Science Publishers, Inc.

All rights reserved. No part of this book may be reproduced, stored in a retrieval system or transmitted in any form or by any means: electronic, electrostatic, magnetic, tape, mechanical photocopying, recording or otherwise without the written permission of the Publisher.

For permission to use material from this book please contact us:
Telephone 631-231-7269; Fax 631-231-8175
Web Site: http://www.novapublishers.com

NOTICE TO THE READER

The Publisher has taken reasonable care in the preparation of this book, but makes no expressed or implied warranty of any kind and assumes no responsibility for any errors or omissions. No liability is assumed for incidental or consequential damages in connection with or arising out of information contained in this book. The Publisher shall not be liable for any special, consequential, or exemplary damages resulting, in whole or in part, from the readers' use of, or reliance upon, this material. Any parts of this book based on government reports are so indicated and copyright is claimed for those parts to the extent applicable to compilations of such works.

Independent verification should be sought for any data, advice or recommendations contained in this book. In addition, no responsibility is assumed by the publisher for any injury and/or damage to persons or property arising from any methods, products, instructions, ideas or otherwise contained in this publication.

This publication is designed to provide accurate and authoritative information with regard to the subject matter covered herein. It is sold with the clear understanding that the Publisher is not engaged in rendering legal or any other professional services. If legal or any other expert assistance is required, the services of a competent person should be sought. FROM A DECLARATION OF PARTICIPANTS JOINTLY ADOPTED BY A COMMITTEE OF THE AMERICAN BAR ASSOCIATION AND A COMMITTEE OF PUBLISHERS.

LIBRARY OF CONGRESS CATALOGING-IN-PUBLICATION DATA

Gokah, Theophilus Kofi.
  Contemporary discourses on IE&C theory and practice / Theophilus K. Gokah.
      p. cm.
  ISBN 978-1-60692-360-3 (hardcover)
 1. Information society. 2. Information technology--Social aspects. 3. Mass media in health education.
 4. AIDS (Disease) in mass media. I. Title. II. Title: Contemporary discourses on information education & communication theory and practice.
  HM851.G65 2009
                              303.48'33--dc22
                                                                                          2008049101

Published by Nova Science Publishers, Inc. ✦ *New York*

CONTENTS

Forward		vii
Preface		ix
Editor's Acknowledgment		xi
Section I: IE & C Theoretical Perspectives		1
Chapter 1	Bridging Contested Spaces in IE & C Theory and Practice: An Introduction *Theophilus K. Gokah*	3
Chapter 2	Social Marketing and IE & C: A Misunderstood Partnership *William Smith*	9
Chapter 3	Does Education Provide 'Social Vaccine' Against AIDS? *Peter Badcock-Walters, Michael J Kelly and Marelize Gorgens-Albino*	23
Chapter 4	An Analysis of Population Information Education and Communication (IEC) Projects in Anglophone Africa *Waithira Gikonyo and Isaac Obeng-Quaidoo*	55
Chapter 5	Theory and Practice of IE & C: A Case of the Media and HIV/AIDS *Alex Buertey Puplampu*	69
Chapter 6	Knowledge Management for Public Health Subspecialties Using Diffusion of Innovations Theory and Information and Communication Technology *Theresa C. Norton*	87
Chapter 7	Utilization of Effective Communication Channels for Tuberculosis Control: Emerging Scenario in South India *Rajeswari Ramachandran and M. Muniyandi*	101

Chapter 8	Between Knowledge, Theory and Practice: How Health-Promoting Schools "Happened" in China *Carmen Aldinger, Cheryl Vince Whitman, Zhang Xin-Wei and Jack T. Jones*	113

Section II: IE & C Practice for Social and Behaviour Change — 183

Chapter 9	What Works in IE&C Practice: An Introduction *Theophilus K. Gokah*	185
Chapter 10	Mind the Cross-Cultural Gap *Karamjit S. Gill*	191
Chapter 11	Changing a Harmful Social Convention: Female Genital Mutilation/Cutting *Innocenti Digest, UNICEF and IRC*	221
Chapter 12	Action Media: Consultation, Collaboration and Empowerment in Health Promotion *Warren Parker*	259
Chapter 13	Interlocking Media for Community Education and Training *Theophilus Kofi Gokah*	267
Chapter 14	Uganda Family Planning Programs: Lessons from the Field Partnering with Communities and District Health Teams *Diana DuBois*	283
Chapter 15	Aranya Township, Indore, India: An Experiment for Sustainable Human Habitat *Utpal Sharma*	307
Chapter 16	Evaluation - The What, the Wherefore and the How *John Durant*	331

Epilogue	344
References	349
About the Contributors	377
Index	379

FORWARD

Evidence over the past years has clearly indicated that knowledge acquisition and sharing will be increasingly technology mediated, and information and communication processes will be further revolutionized. In the coming decades the importance of acquiring factual knowledge will decrease. At the same time, the ability to find one's way in complex systems and to find, judge, organize and creatively use relevant information, as well as the capability to learn what to do with it, will become crucially important.

These developments hold many promises for attaining the Education for All (EFA) goals. Subsumed in IE&C methodology in creating knowledge, awareness and possible behaviour change is the role of ICT. Indeed, ICTs have great potential for improving knowledge dissemination, effective learning and the development of more efficient education services. The ICT revolution presents us with a wide range of innovative learning solutions and these technologies hold many promises that learning can also be afforded by people in remote and rural areas. But this potential will not be realized unless these technologies serve rather than drive the implementation of education strategies. To be effective, especially in developing countries, ICT based learning methods must be combined with those that are more traditional. At the same time, there is a strong need to set universal standards for digital learning aids/tools in order to ensure that a content revolution parallels those in ICTs.

Education must reflect the diversity of needs, expectations, interests, languages and cultural contexts. This poses particular challenges under conditions of globalization given its strong tendency towards uniformity. We therefore need to define the best use of ICT for improving the quality of teaching and learning, sharing knowledge and information, introducing a higher degree of flexibility in response to societal needs, lowering the cost of education and improving internal and external efficiencies of the education system.

I am certain that this publication provides a useful contribution to these debates.

Abdul Waheed Khan
Assistant Director-General
Communication and Information, UNESCO

PREFACE

A wide range of views exist on IE&C (Information, Education and Communication) related work and experience in what works continues to be built, as this timely volume demonstrates. IE&C is generally defined as an approach, particularly related to health care, which attempts through a variety of different media and methods to change people's behaviour, or reinforce positive change among a population (WHO 2001). Those involved in IEC are only too well aware that their messages and associated interventions have to compete with an ever burgeoning array of sources of information which may 'drown out' positive health messages.

The press coverage around HIV and AIDS is a case in point. To take one example, on the 10th July 2003 the following headline appeared on the front page of the Hyderabad edition of The Times of India: `AIDS suspect stoned to death in Chief Minister's constituency', the article told how a 32 year old woman had been stoned to death because villages suspected that she was HIV-positive. During the course of the next week the newspaper followed up with articles discussing whether a stoning had or had not occurred and the information this act provided on certain segment's of the population's understanding of the epidemic. Yet, the very headline did little to counter stigma: `AIDS-suspect' suggests someone who is guilty, someone to be blamed, and that is what would have caught the reader's eye. It is not difficult to find dozens of such headlines in the archives of the press throughout the world which promote fear rather than support positive attitudes to people living with HIV. UNAIDS attempt to provide guidelines on terminology has had little impact on such reporting (UNAIDS, 2007). Sensational stories sell newspapers and the popular press thrives on drawing the reader's attention to their content by such means. The stigma that continues to haunt the AIDS epidemic in so many countries not only affects prevention and treatment interventions, it may also affect the mitigation of the impact of the epidemic. As Tallis wrote `the denial, blame and stigma surrounding HIV has silenced open discussions, delayed effective responses, and added to the burden of those living with HIV and AIDS' (2002: 1).

Trevor Cullen (2006) writing on the reporting of the growing AIDS epidemic in Papua New Guinea quotes the words of the then head of World Vision, Don Bradford, published in a Papua New Guinean national newspaper (Post Courier) on 23rd September 2004. Bradford said `we can flood the market place with condoms and all sorts of other programs but if people's hearts and minds do not change—then we are simply wasting our time'. IE&C is bound up in that changing of hearts and minds, and in tackling the often counter-productive messages that may appear in the mass-media, whether in printed form or in the ever increasingly available internet. It is the spread of misinformation, the perpetuation of misleading myths and the whipping up of moral-panic around research results that make their way to the public domain (whether over diet, vaccinations or adverse drug reactions) which have to be tackled through the effective spread of information through channels that can reach the very same audiences. This is no easy task, but as the papers in this book demonstrate, IE&C does work; health communication can foster positive health practices and can bring about change that lasts. However, an important lesson that continues to be learnt is that context and timing are important. Something that worked before may not work again. We need to continue to share examples and lessons, to engage with the evolving discourse and keep abreast of the opportunities that emerge as technology offers new ways to communicate. I welcome this volume's contribution to this endeavour.

Dr. Janet Seeley
School of Development Studies
University of East Anglia
Norwich, UK

EDITOR'S ACKNOWLEDGMENT

Contemporary Discourses on IE&C brings together analysis from parallel fields of action to understand how individuals make sense of development and change processes and the effects of knowledge management or organizational learning approaches. The enormous diversity of ideas expressed in this edited collection provides ways of knowing how IE&C knowledge and social marketing processes influence behaviour and shape advocacy to affect positive social change.

The foundation of this project dates back to my training in IE&C at the UNFPA Regional Population IE&C Training for Anglophone Africa, Nairobi where twenty-three media and communication practitioners had gathered to train as trainers-of-trainers in IE&C. Of course, the knowledge and expertise gained would not have been possible without financial support from UNFPA. My thanks also go to facilitators Dr Waithira Gikonyo and Dr Isaac Obeng-Quaidoo whose leadership was profound. Fond memories go to colleagues on the programme – Donatus Ngandu (Namibia); Benard Mijioni (Malawi); Fiona Gibson (Ghana); Julitha Masanja (Tanzania); Ncamsile Matsebula (Swaziland); Veliphi Hlashwayo (Swaziland); Charles Njanga (Kenya); Mario Marrengula (Mozambique); Kaltoum Totil (Eritrea); Kofi Wellington (Ghana); Crescent Muhandi (Tanzania); Akyoo Simalingi (Tanzania); Mary Mbeyela (Arusha); Joy Masheke (Zambia); Tesfalidet Ghebreyohannes (Eritrea); Papi Foranty (Addis Ababa); Nene Akrasi Korda (Ghana); Mogeus Alembo (Awassa); Eveless Kayanula (Blantyre); Agnes Kamunyu (Nairobi); Hirut Geleta Bodji (Addis Ababa), Joshua Nicole (Sierra Leone), Gladys Kamboo (Namibia) and Constance Mweemba (Lusaka)

I am also grateful to the many contributors in this book project and organisations that agreed for their material to be reproduced in this edition. Without their generous help this book would not have been achieved.

I owe particular debt of gratitude to UNESCO for agreeing to write the forward to this book and also to Dr Jane Seeley of University of East Anglia for writing its Preface.

Editor

Section I:
IE & C Theoretical Perspectives

In: Contemporary Discourses on IE & C Theory and Practice ISBN: 978-1-60962-360-3
Editor: Theophilus K. Gokah © 2009 Nova Science Publishers, Inc.

Chapter 1

BRIDGING CONTESTED SPACES IN IE & C THEORY AND PRACTICE: AN INTRODUCTION

Theophilus K. Gokah

IE&C, information, education and communication involves a systematic process of conveying messages to targeted populations. It is a relatively new concept especially in development practice which requires conceptual understanding into the theory and practice of its implementation. Given the overlap between socio-economic and the political fabric of communities and their livelihood, there is a strong link between community-based management and sustainability within which information, education and communication programmes become the binding cord with which such communities are held together. For programme actors, to plan and implement IE&C programmes require knowledge and understanding of how communication functions; activities and processes, knowledge and understanding of the functioning of various media, community organisations and structures; so that they can tailor their messages more effectively.

Information and communication are key elements that make things happen (Quebral, 2002). Information is data which has been processed and ready to be used. Information can be on anything be it the culture of a people or their behaviour patterns. When the data (information) is available it is then processed to educate the same people from whom the data was collected. This process of educating the people involves communication.

Easy access to information facilitates communication among people; it promotes enlightenment, decision making and action. The more informed people are, the more they get involved in the development process. Unfortunately, not everybody has equal access to information (Rosen, 2002). For example, there is a big gap between developed and developing countries, inter-nationals and intra-national in terms of access to information. Within this circuit of information lag, some receive information late while others do not receive any at all. Thus, it is necessary to build a sound and reliable information system where information can easily be collected and disseminated.

Despite the communication gap that exists, it is essential that communication plays an important role in promoting livelihood and development. Simply having information is not enough; people need to exchange views and information. In other words, communication should be participatory, but the difficulty here is that communicating to the vast majority who may be rural people, who do not have access to feed-back systems, hinders participatory communication. Other communication channels such as folk media and interpersonal channels can be effective in filling this gap (Gokah, 2007). The situation may be less complex in urban areas where various forms of talk-back systems might exist (Manyozo, 2005). Other facilities such as the electronic mail, the availability of postal systems, and the accessibility of transport networks makes it possible for people in urban areas to participate more frequently than those in infrastructure deficient localities (UNDP, 1998). In societies where literacy rates are low access to print media is hindered, and development information is thus limited to a relatively few people (Ford, Abimbola & Renshaw, 2005). The use of modern electronic systems in educating communities can be complex in terms of people's involvement in the process (Rosen, 2002). This is more pronounced in resource challenged areas. Where this is possible the essence of detailed learning and utilisation can be hindered due to inappropriate, confusing or misunderstood terminology. In deed, development information to people is becoming less difficult but as the gap between the 'rich' and 'poor', technological advantaged and disadvantaged keep widening a receiver-centric phenomena tends to grip most populations; a situation where one group of people will be at the mercy of the other, receiving whatever comes likened to 'the donor-recipient syndrome' (McQuail 1983: 97).

Development, for instance, does not occur in a vacuum; there must first be an awareness of need and that awareness should be seen to be created by established systems and communication sources. Arguably, there is no universal path to development which means that other channels may be needed to ensure that development occurs and sustainable lives are ensured (Servaes, 1996: 77). Social structures such as education and the family are known sources of information but the media has the power of exerting greater influence through information dissemination, education, communication and entertainment. In other words, Danladi's (1996:89) assertion that 'information is power' is no longer in contention and that is why liberal democracies places emphasis on the media to arm citizens with adequate quality information so that they can make a rational choice in exercising their power; but, Obeng-Quaidoo and Gikonyo's (1995:70) argument appeals more to the kind of project being undertaken here. They argue that since the field of development endeavours and approaches are numerous and varied, communication facilitating functions also tend to be numerous. For instance, when a new contraceptive is introduced on the market, the general approach is to inform people about the product and work with a segmented population or community to see if the product is part of their need. For the moralist and traditionalist this may or may not augur well for behaviour change (see for instance Schaalma, 2004; Buston, et al 2002; Landry, 1999). Working with segmented groups (described by Roggers, 1962; Servaes and Malikhao 1994 as passive recipients of innovation) in the community through interpersonal communication or folk groups to determine needs is quite different from other forms of disseminating information, i.e. radio, television and print (Obeng-Quaidoo and Gikonyo. op.cit.). This dichotomy between education and information and vice versa becomes clear where information can be said to be a function of education.

The concept of education is seen differently by different scholars, for instance, van Der Veen (2003) describe community development as citizens education. It is also seen in terms of social action (Foley, 1999). When we say education, people think about the teaching side of education and not much attention is paid to the learning side of education. The learning side is equally important because lots of information can be passed on but if the learner does not take the responsibility to learn what has been communicated to him or her, all the effort will be futile. There are useful lessons from Nyirenda (1996: 6) which asserts that 'once a person perceives and understands a challenge and recognise the possibility of a response, that person will act and the nature of his or her action will correspond to the nature of his or her understanding'. Hence, critical understanding of situations leads to critical action.

Education is communicating information from a person who 'supposedly knows' to a person or groups of people who supposedly do 'not know'. This might not always be the case. In deed, there are different ways in which knowledge can be constructed but the definition of 'knowledge' can be conceptually complex. For example when a journalist is writing or broadcasting to an intellectual group, it cannot be said that those intellectuals do 'not know' even though they might be ignorant about the issue under discussion.

Illiteracy has been widely studied (UNESCO, 1994) just as ignorance has been investigated (Feenan, 2007; Frosch, Beaman & Mccloy, 2007). Education equips and motivates people to break that cycle and question issues. Education makes (and must make) people critical so that values that are inimical to personal or national development will be changed. Where the opposite occurs society is placed on the verge of catastrophe.

People do things they normally would not have done. Not until it is pointed out to them they might not know the consequences of their action. For example, some people might enter marriage by impulse without necessarily going through 'traditional' processes of marriage. Others will have children without questioning their readiness. Using IE&C strategies will educate and communicate to such people the implication(s) of their behaviour. Education is not only what is taught but why and how it is taught. This implies that, education must not only enable a person to read and write but to equip him or her to analyse and make decisions, i.e. to become functionally literate (Aro and Olkinuora, 2007). This is the type of education that enhances a sense of personal and cultural identity. Education processes are therefore not neutral. They can either be an instrument of domination (Ginsburg, Espinoza, Popa & Terano, 2003) or liberation (Tarc, 2006). Fraire (1970) puts it in a more succinct way as 'in a culture of silence the masses are 'mute', that is, they are prohibited from creativity, taking part in the transformation of their society and therefore prohibited from being ... even if they are able to read and write because they are taught, they are nevertheless alienated from the power responsible for their silence'.

Education that denies people the power to think for themselves and become architects of their own destinies is not adequate to make a person functional. It does not actually provide people with critical challenges in their own social reality which will enable them to know what must be changed with corresponding action on them. Frarie's ideas on non neutrality of education can be compared to functional literacy because functional literacy, according to Nyirenda (1996) means possession or acquisition of literacy skills which are adequate for carrying out those actions or activities required of a person or society such as reading and writing. Doesn't functional literacy go beyond that? How do the media or IEC strategies make people functional?

Education for development has four objectives: to motivate, to inform, to teach and to change behaviour. This can take three forms: open broadcasting in which regular information and developmental messages are routinely sent out without any organised follow-up. It can also take the radio forum or listening group approach, and third, the campaign approach, using a combination of methods. Appropriate population and development information and education ensure that dissemination is effective. The process is, however, not complete if the media has the information and does not communicate it.

The right to information is a basic human right in most national constitutions but not all people have access to information through modern media. The availability of radio and television sets in some rural communities is limited. Implied in this thinking is the fact that information dissemination through the use of modern media in rural communities may experience some setbacks as compared to large urban cities. Rural communities may however have several alternative communication channels which can be capped under folk media, which are different from modern media. The problem in this pattern of communication, however, is that as the information goes through several people the message gets distorted (Sager, 2006). Unlike communication by word of mouth, written messages might also have problems of reading and understanding its content especially in low literate societies. Written information might also be defaced by improper handling or misplaced by a commercially minded person. Other inter-personal communication channels such as the open forums have also been used and are still in use (see for example Gokah, 2007).

In modern societies where the speed of information dissemination has changed, it is not so easy to cope or adapt; coping with modern communication means keeping abreast with technology and communication consumption patterns. Most developing countries do not have the financial strength to cope with the rate of change (MØller and Dictow, 2002). They will, therefore, have to utilise what is available to them in the most efficient manner. In spite of the difficulty, communication is able to change perceptions even among people who hold firm to one belief or another. This is not to say that communication alone can achieve absolute success in IE&C programmes and activities. Other indicators such as economic and social factors are equally important in achieving IE&C goals.

Some IE&C programmes and projects have failed or have been discontinued after the initial donors have left because their implementers did not initially involve the beneficiaries; they did not listen to the community, respect their local ideas and opinions and mutual trust was not built into activities from the start, a conception first held by Obeng-Quaidoo and Waithira (1995: 72); lack of genuine involvement of target groups lead to blurred objective setting, fuzzy strategies, inconsequential program activities and lack of evaluation in impact terms.

Communication as a tool for development is no longer an assumption to be tested because several researches have proved and tested different paradigms which attest to the role of communication in development (see for example Servaes, 2007; Dutta, 2006; Singhal, & Rogers 2002; Andreason, 1995). In terms of practice UNICEF's Information, Education and Communication (IE&C) intervention in its GOBI strategy (growth monitoring, oral rehydration, breast feeding and immunization) and World Health Organisation's expanded programme on immunisation (EPI), have brought about significant reduction in levels of childhood mortality through immunization against six of the major infectious diseases prevalent in developing countries (Dodoo, Renner, van Grootheest, Labadie, Antwi-Agyei, Hayibor, Addison, Pappoe & Appiah, 2007). These are but few examples of IE&C programmes which support population and family planning awareness programmes and motivation, attitude and behaviour changes, all of which have communication at the centre of their activity.

IE&C discourses have in the past been limited to the health sector. The under utilisation of such a resource is an obvious oversight in the use of IE&C methodology to address other important and equally challenging issues in society. Behaviour change or social change can not be limited to personal health. It is just as important that people change their thinking and behaviour towards the environment and other ecological issues that affect communities and society in general. Knowledge about sustainable poverty reduction, the promotion of social justice and social exclusion can all be addressed using IE&C. In deed, if governments want to close development gaps, at national and local levels or even at regional level, then IE&C is the window of hope; the two areas of this book reflects this ethos.

Less attention has been paid to the resource of social marketing despite the veracity of it being a powerful tool for planned processes of social change. Chapter two thus considers the theory of social marketing and how its discourses play out within IE&C framework with the aim of achieving a much needed behaviour and social change in contemporary society.

In Chapter three, Peter Badcock-Walters et al addresses a critical question about whether education provides social vaccine against HIV/AIDS. The scourge of AIDS is largely a behaviour issue which requires that people change their behaviour for public good. In the eyes of some commentators education should play an important role in achieving that goal. How this works in theory and practice is the preoccupation of Peter Badcock-Walters and his collaborators.

Chapter four is a retrospective review of trainees and their performance on population IE&C projects across Anglophone African. Recommendations proposed by its authors for use in population communication projects to support behavioural change and development is welcome.

Understanding how Media-based IE&C programs to prevent, reduce or minimise the risk and consequences of risk behaviours occupies the attention of Alex Puplampu. Thus, in chapter five, the theory and practice of how media, specifically radio broadcasters, use 'framing' to shape HIV/AIDS news agenda in Ghana is highlighted.

Chapter six leads readers into contemporary media revolution of internet communication technology (ICT) as a way forward in shaping knowledge and social change; Here, Theresa Norton looks at using ICTs to address information action restrictions in fields that need innovative global solutions.

In chapter seven, the central theme in Rajeswari Ramachandran and Muniyandi's paper is that there is a need to plan and implement suitable information, education and communication (IEC) strategies/interventions focusing on the community / patients behaviour from the time of diagnosis till patients complete treatment that needs to be modified to achieve the objectives of a tuberculosis programme.

Chapter eight Carmen et al show fascinating processes of how Health-Promoting Schools happened in China and lessons that can be learnt from them.

The other topics are covered in section two of this book. Through its entire discourses it is hoped that this book will not only unearth spatial elements in IE&C but bridge contested spaces between its theory and practice; rhetoric and application.

Chapter 2

SOCIAL MARKETING AND IE & C: A MISUNDERSTOOD PARTNERSHIP

William Smith

This paper reviews the relationship between social marketing and information, education, and communication strategies. It argues that social marketing is an effective ways to integrate the functions of program design, program delivery and program promotion (IEC) around the needs of citizens and consumers. The lack of this integration, that is the use of IEC where programs are poorly designed or where programs are poorly delivered, not only wastes valuable resources but runs the risk of alienating and frustrating those most in need. This chapter reviews the theory of social marketing as it has been practiced in developing countries, with a special emphasis on Africa and on public health interventions.

Keywords: Social Marketing, IEC, Public health, HIV/AIDS

LESSONS FROM SOCIAL MARKETING TO IEC

Introduction: Social Marketing and IEC

Social Marketing is defined here as:

An organizational function for creating, delivering and communicating value to citizens which benefits both the citizens as individuals and societal needs

Key to understanding the contribution that social marketing can make to IEC is found in the words *create and deliver value*. As we will explore in this chapter the role of IEC is the critical role of communicating value. But we will argue that society change is rooted in behaviour change and people rarely give up traditional behaviours which have served them well because of a message alone. Social marketing is based on the assumption that for people to protect themselves from, say, AIDS, immunize their child, vote in an election, replace abstractive farming with sustainable agriculture, or any one of a number of other complex human behaviours, programs and policy must create value and deliver that value in exchange for what people are now doing (Kotler and Zaltman, 1971). It is not enough to tell people to use a condom; we must make condoms attractive, available and affordable. It is not enough to tell mothers to immunize a child; we must make immunizations programs available at convenient times and ensure that vaccines are safe. It is not enough to tell a farmer to give up clear cutting for firewood; we must give him or her a viable alternative.

All of this is obvious. But we continue to send messages to people they can not accept. We motivate them to try products and services that do not work, or if they are available once through some campaign, they are never available again because funding has cut.

Many of you reading this chapter may say, "But I am an IEC professional. I am not responsible for vaccine safety." I will argue that, Yes you are if you are promoting a message that will go to millions of women who trust you. Yes, you are and you must accept this responsibility. We are responsible for the content of our messages as their format. And social marketing is an approach which integrates the creation; delivery and communication of social change in a single integrative and ethically responsible process (see also Smith, 2006).

Social marketing in much of the West, Britain, America, Canada, and Australia, has focused on creating campaigns to reduce smoking, increase seat belt use, and prevent obesity. The health topics have ranged over a broad spectrum from domestic violence (McKenzie, Burns, McCarthy and Freund, 1998), skin cancer (Everett and Colditz, 1997), to recruiting school teachers (Whitehead and Postlethwaite, 2000). The hallmark of these programs has been IEC messages: carefully developed with segmented audiences; positioned to break through the clutter of advertising saturated markets; and resulting in compelling TV, radio, and print executions which garner their creators fame, if not fortune. Who can forget the crying American Indian, the skeletons of death bowling down helpless Australians, or the unbuckled teenager whose body, flying through the family car, crushes the skull of his unsuspecting mother.

The use of messages as surrogates of social marketing in the West is well documented. Despite all the theory and academic guidance by Kotler, Andreasen and Roberto and the promotion P rules, forty years after Kotler's first article in 1967, a participant on the social marketing list serve asked incredulously "does social marketing sell things"?

Well, the truth is social marketing does sell things. It also designs things to meet the special needs of poor people; it packages them so poor people can use them; it distributes them in places poor people can get them; it prices them so that poor people value them; and yes, it advertises, and educates poor people about why and how to use them.

This chapter focuses on this unique contribution of social marketing, developed out of the necessity to compensate for dysfunctional public systems. Social marketing in the poor countries of the world faces three challenges rarely met by programs in the developed West. First, there is no reliable health system to deliver anything. Second, funding of most health programmes are highly dependent upon the unreliable largesse and political priorities of international donors. Three, there is a desperate need for jobs coupled with the same enormous creativity that exists in the West.

It might be argued that social marketing in the West has served the middle class better than it has served the poor. Health disparities in America, Britain, Canada and Australia continue to be national embarrassment, even where socialized medicine is the standard (Gutzwiller, 2005). It may be that we all have a lot to learn from the experience of developing countries about the power of social marketing, not just to motivate and educate, but to create social systems that serve their peculiar needs. That, at least is the intention of this chapter.

THE SPECIAL CONDITIONS OF DEVELOPING COUNTRIES

Developing countries represent a unique context for social marketing. Government health services are inadequate to meet the health needs of many developing countries (see for example Kapiriri and Douglas, 2007). The private sector health systems (with the exception of some faith-based health centers) service a small minority of the population. The major health problems- reproductive health, infant mortality, HIV/AIDS, and malaria are infectious rather than chronic diseases caused by the lack of basic infrastructure – clean water, adequate sanitation, a reliable food supply, refrigeration and the delivery of basic health services such as immunizations, epidemiology surveillance and effective treatment. The lack of basic education, the exclusion of women, a brain-drain of trained professionals, rapid population growth and political instability compound these problems. Despite these formidable barriers considerable progress has been made in the developing world, although the progress varies widely from one country and one health problem to another.

For the exclusive purposes of this chapter we will define social marketing as:

Any deliberate program of large-scale behaviour change which creates and markets new products and services designed to improve the quality of society, with a specific focus on pubic health.

Our purpose in using this narrow definition is not to re-define the field, but simply place emphasis on the one unique contribution of social marketing to social change – that is, the creation and marketing of physical products and social services for the purpose of societal benefit. We recognize and accept that many social marketing programs in the literature do not create new product or services, but rather use message strategies to realign attitudes towards benefits and barriers based upon a citizen-centered planning model.

This definition makes more specific the importance of product, place and price in the selection of examples and case studies for this chapter. There are hundreds, perhaps thousands of examples of health communication programs which we will not review in this chapter, focussing instead on this narrower and more marketing-centered definition.

We recognize that there is a debate among leading academics as to whether *communication* includes *social marketing*, or *social marketing* includes *communication*. Rice and Paisley in their book *Public Communication Campaigns* (1981), for example, include social marketing as a practice of communication. Marketing textbooks, however, consistently view communication as either an integrated function across product, place, price and promotion, or as a function primarily managed by promotion. This debate is critical in understanding the contributions of social marketing to international development. In the West this debate remains masked by the prevalent practice of describing almost all modern mass communication campaigns as social marketing, so that *campaign* and *social marketing* are synonymous in many practitioners minds.

Both communication and social marketing share important tactical approaches; For example, both emphasize the importance of consumer research to develop programs; both segment audiences; promote benefits; and integrate various media in strategic ways to reach and influence audience segments.

The fundamental differences we focus on in this chapter rests on two areas. First, social marketing *creates environmental changes by creating new products and/or services that make access easier, increase benefits desired by audiences; and reduce barriers audiences consider important. It then uses persuasive communication to promote those changes.* Communication programs focuses principally on the role of *messages in promoting benefits, reducing audience concern over barriers and creating a wide spread sense that social norms are changing in the direction of the desired behaviour change.*

Advocacy approaches to large-scale behaviour change, like social marketing, also focuses on creating new benefits and reducing barriers, but their focus is largely *through legislation, rather than designing and marketing new products and services.* These three approaches, social marketing, communication and advocacy share many tactics in common and are often confused with each other - leading to pointless debates about which is better. What we hope to do here is to avoid that debate about what's better and simply focus on the unique strength of social marketing in a developing country setting to create and market new products and services.

This narrow definition also allows us to include public private partnership as a social marketing model. Here, commercial companies cooperate with public agencies and non-profit organizations to deliver subsidized products to low income markets. Pricing these subsidized products to promote both sustainability and access by the poor is a critical social marketing challenge. Indeed, the sales of subsidized products to the poor has recently attracted criticism from some Western economists who consider these sales to the poor of vital social products such as malaria bed nets both immoral and ineffective. Advocates of social marketing argue, however, that stimulating private sector participation in delivering social services to the poor (a) helps relieve the burden to serve everyone on embattled public sector institutions; (b) increases the likelihood of long-term sustainability in resource scarce environments; and (c) stimulates the creation of businesses and good paying jobs locally.

In the West, the integration of the private sector in social marketing programs has been much less common. Indeed, certain private sector industries, notably the tobacco industry, have been identified as the leading focus of social marketing attacks (see Snell and Bailey, 2005; Fisher and Colditz, 1999). Industry generally has been considered an un-necessary and somewhat suspect partner in the promotion of social good. Internationally, corporations often suffer from the same suspicion, but the practical needs to deliver services in countries where the public sector is weak has helped overcome and innovate in the creation of effective public private partnerships.

EXAMPLES OF SOCIAL MARKETING PRACTICE IN DEVELOPING COUNTRIES

Social marketing emerged in developing countries as one away to address the complex set of barriers to adequate public health. Social marketing was designed to compliment and support a public sector unable to meet the demand made on it. Social marketing programs in countries like India, Bangladesh, Thailand, Brazil, the Philippines, Ghana, and others were created by local talent with little control or aid from Western experts. Although there has been a small cadre of Western organizations active in international social marketing; including AED, The Futures Group, DKT International, and PSI. The largest single funder of social marketing in developing countries has been the United States Agency for International Development (USAID). Beginning with family planning programs in the 1970's, USAID has provided the funds to expand and sustain the application of social marketing to other social problems around the world. Its commitment to measurement has provided our field with some of the most convincing data that social marketing works. The range of products and services successfully promoted in dozens of cultures, under conditions we cannot even imagine here in the West, is the best evidence we have to show the robust and sustainable impact of social marketing on human health and development.

Social marketing in developing countries has focused on the creation of new products, the creative use of unexpected distribution channels, clever pricing of subsidized products, and yes, some compelling and exciting promotional communication as well. From elephants in Thailand, to Carnival floats in Rio de Janeiro, social marketing has been serious business with a funny face. While social marketing has been used for a wide variety of health problems, four health sectors (reproductive health, Infant Mortality, HIV/AIDS and malaria) have received major attention and will form the organizational structure of this chapter. Rather than providing a comprehensive review of each health sector, this chapter will discuss the sectoral issues broadly and provide one or two of the most important and evaluated examples of social marketing in that sector. The four health topics of primary importance are: reproductive health, infant mortality, HIV/AIDS, and malaria.

REPRODUCTIVE HEALTH: INDIA

India has the largest social marketing in the world. It was one of the first countries to introduce social marketing for family planning with sales of condoms today reaching over 1 billion condoms a year. The sophistication and creativity of India's program represents something of the enormous challenge the country faces in providing voluntary alternatives to female sterilization.

India's population growth rate is 1.74%. India accounts for about 20% of all new births worldwide. One-third of India's population is under 15 years of age and 50% are of reproductive age. The norm of a smaller family has been adopted in India with family size down from 6 children in the 1960s to just fewer than 2.85 as of 2008. Condom use account for 3.1% of the contraceptive market, with female sterilization at 34.5% and traditional and natural methods at 5.4%; India's large rural population (70%), the large number of languages and religions, and the traditional beliefs about women's role in society make the distribution, sale and use of condoms an enormous challenge.

Nirodh, India's most widely known condom was begun in 1968 by the Department of Family Welfare. A high quality condom product is manufactured in India and the price subsidized by the government. Social marketing is used to develop innovative distribution channels, organize community action and advertising and promote the brand.

DKT India is one of the India's government social marketing partners in promoting the wide spread use of condoms for both contraception and HIV/AIDS prevention. DKT India works in 18 of India's 29 provinces and reaches some 599 million people. About 30% of condoms sales occur in rural areas of the country. A variety of condom products are offered to meet various segments of the marketing. Packaging emphasizes the sensual qualities of the product and making for attractive desirable products. Prices remain stable at less than $.01 per condom.

Emphasis has been given to developing a local distribution network to meet the special challenges of India's size and complexity. A system of 1 hub, 6 agents, and 500 stock lists and 80,000 retailers provides reliable channels through which to deliver a variety of contraceptive products. Sales representatives not only provided face-to-face promotion to retailers but monitor stocks of contraceptive to ensure consumers have reliable access.

Creative point-of-purchase materials stimulate retailer and consumer interest. Discounts, and contests for consumers provide promotional push for selected products, Communication to doctors, private family planning clinics include meetings, leaflets, and newsletters. Mass media campaigns also play a major role in promoting the brand. And mass media is complimented by community education programs coordinated with government and other players.

Educational activities are conducted in villages at the "Mandi" or weekly market area of the town. Interactive session with married men and women demonstrated condom use. Barbers and adolescents are educated on AIDS awareness as part of the program. Young women serving and dancing in local bars are at particular risk of AIDS. Small groups training sessions provide these women with information, while at the same time sensitizing local bar owners to the need for protection.

The DKT program is one of many which compliment the government's massive family planning effort. Branding, consumer choice, multiple distribution points and systems, and promotion of condoms from multiple sources have been an important key to meting the enormous challenges in India.

INFANT MORTALITY: HONDURAS

In 1978, the World Health Organization, UNICEF, and the U.S. Agency for International Development (USAID) embarked on a crusade to combat infant mortality in the developing world, which during this time averaged more than 200 per 1000 live births. Children in developing countries were dying in large numbers from such preventable diseases and illnesses as diarrheal rehydration, measles, and respiratory infections, all of which had long been under control in the rest of the industrialized world. Inadequate medical resources and facilities and the lack of effective immunization programs in developing countries allowed diseases such as these to persist, and kept infant mortality inordinately high.

The Mass Media and Health Practices project was the first major test of social marketing applied to reduction in infant mortality in developing countries. The project soon outgrew its name and became a full-fledged social marketing program as data poured in from grassroots consumer research pointing out the needs for new products, lower complexity costs and massive teaching of new skills. Mothers were being asked to adopt a new product – an oral rehyderation solution – that required they learn when it was needed, how to find and prepare it, and then how to administer it safely to their child. The product was differentiated in the two test sites, home-mix sugar, salt and water in Africa and pre-package salts in Latin America. In Africa a mass mobilization strategy was taken, driven by the use of a radio course that involved thousands of women learning and then practicing to mix the home-mix safely. In Latin America the program evolved from a package salts to a broader childcare during diarrheal product. In Latin America infant mortality due to diarrheal rehyderation dropped from 47.5% to 25% in the first year. Both programs became models for a decade of child survival programs that successfully attacked infant mortality in a dozen countries around the world.

As part of this movement to significantly reduce infant mortality in developing countries, USAID contracted a number of non-profit development organizations to take the lead in developing and implementing consumer-oriented social marketing programs. One such program was the Mass Media and Health Practices Program initiated by the Academy for Educational Development to address the growing epidemic of acute diarrheal rehyderation in infants in Honduras.

Before the start of the USAID funded program, diarrheal rehyderation accounted for 24 percent of all infant deaths in Honduras and represented the single leading cause of infant mortality. In 1977, the year preceding the program's commencement, diarrheal rehyderation caused the deaths of 1,030 infants. Treatment during this time was expensive and limited both in scope and availability. The only treatment available to Hondurans for diarrheal rehyderation was intravenous (IV) therapy, which requires trained medical personnel and a sterile environment, and was offered exclusively in fixed health facilities serving only a small percentage of the country's rural population.

The existing product of ORT had been developed by UNICEF as a packet of salts, wrapped in a high quality aluminium foil envelop with instructions for its use printed in various languages. Field test of this product in rural areas of Honduras demonstrated that not only were the instructions unintelligible, they were not even recognized by non-literate women as instructions. Mixing test with this packets showed that women mix it intuitively, similar to a familiar packet of headache medicine. They used an 8 oz glass of water rather than the required litre of water. Administration of this dense concentration of salts would lead to severe shock and death.

It was clear another packet design was necessary if ORT was to become recognized as the primary treatment for early onset diarrheal. Extensive field tests were developed using a proto-typing methodology, rather than focus groups or survey research. Here, various formats were shown to women and they were asked to use the new packet to mix the salts. Verbal instructions were kept to a minimum in order to simulate the conditions under which women would use the packets - often alone in their home with a sick child and no coach. Again testing showed that even carefully designed visual instruction went unrecognized as instructions. The culture of illiteracy had accustomed women not to look for instructions on medicines, but rather mix them intuitively.

This insight led to a much more marketing approach than originally anticipated. A series of radio programs were designed to "teach" mother to "look for the instructions – look at the pictures on the packet". Radio messages constantly repeated the mixing volumes, saturating the country with the one litre message.

A second problem was encountered when women said they understood the litre message, but did not believe that a medicine could be given to a small child in a litre volume. It just seemed too much liquid to give. The solution was to market the ORT product as a "tonic" rather than a medicine which fit comfortably into mother's mental model of health product.

The packet was also designed to be colourful and fun – contrasting greatly with the UNICEF look of a serious complex medicine.

The program operated in a carefully chosen site that included a representative population of 400,000 individuals. The campaign began by providing 900 health care workers with four to eight hours of ORT training. The training program concentrated on teaching the proper mixing and administration of ORT salts and instructing other village assistants, who would ultimately have to conduct the same exercises directly with rural families. Using props and training dummies, the program trainees repeatedly practiced each step of the mixing and administration processes. The health workers and village trainees then began instructing mothers and grandmothers in ORT and other health behaviours such as breastfeeding, infant food preparation and person hygiene. When rural families completed their ORT training, a flag was posted at their house to let other mothers in the area know where they could obtain health advice and instruction.

As the training program was being carried out, a media campaign was implemented to reinforce the health care instruction effort. The campaign developed print materials and radio advertisements to issue basic messages related to the diarrheal rehydration therapy and the AED training program. The messages emphasized the correct administration of oral rehydration salts "Litrosol," the continuation of breastfeeding during infant diarrheal periods, and encouraged mothers to seek medical assistance if a child's condition deteriorates. Posters and flipcharts were also created to illustrate ORT and to deliver supporting messages. The radio advertisements were placed in 30 – 60 spot announcements and often included some form of jingle, slogan, or song. Many of the ads included a familiar announcer, Dr. Salustiano, the program's spokesman for technical information, who subsequently became a nationally known figure.

The tone of the campaign was serious, straightforward and caring. It successfully promoted a mother-craft concept, where a mother's current actions and beliefs are supported and the program's health techniques become an added complement to her care-giving regimen. ORT training was presented as a new development in modern medicine: the latest remedy for lost appetite and a recovery aid. With a high rate of literacy (87 percent of each household with at least one literate member), and 71 percent of all households owning a functional radio, the media campaign became an effective communication and education tool.

A year after AED's Mass Media program's implementation, an evaluation conducted by Stanford University to chart the project's impact consisting of a data sample collected from 750 randomly selected families from more than 20 communities, the study showed that the diarrheal rehydration project in Honduras had achieved significant results in both disseminating important health information and in fostering specific changes in behaviour related to treating infant diarrheal.

Decreased mortality: Between 1981 and 1982 mortality rates for children under five years of age had decreased from 47.5 percent to 25 percent.

Significant campaign awareness: After little more than a year of the project's start, 93 percent of the mothers sampled from rural Honduras knew that the program's radio campaign was promoting Litrosol, the brand name of the locally packaged oral rehydration salts (ORS) used to treat diarrheal; and 71 percent could recite the radio jingle used to promote the administration of liquids during diarrheal affliction.

Increased health knowledge and changed behaviour: Of the mothers sampled in the study, 42 percent had knowledge that the use of Litrosol prevented rehydration; and 49 percent had actually used the ORS Litrosol. Of those that had used Litrosol, 94 percent were accurate in describing the correct mixing volume and 96 percent knew that the entire package of ORS was to be used in treatment. Sixteen months after the program's start, 39 percent of all of the cases of diarrheal within the prior two weeks among the sampled families had been treated using Litrosol.

HIV/AIDS: BRAZIL AND THE POWER OF POLICY

Brazil shocked the world when it broke the patient on anti-retroviral drugs (ARVs) and provided anti-retroviral therapy (ART) universally free. The average cost of ART per patient in 1998 was around $4,459 in Brazil. By 2000 Brazil had reduced treatment costs by 72.5% through local manufacture, while prices of imported drugs dropped only 9.6%. The number of death due to HIV/AIDS is reported to have dropped by 80% Some 125,000 people are on treatment, with another 300,000 constantly having HIV levels checked.

But behind this highly publicized political step, the Brazilian national AIDS program has been a model of social marketing. Focusing on the two audiences most at risk, men who have sex with men, and female sex workers, Brazil rejected international funding that required they condemn prostitution. Recognizing that stigma would drive those most at risk underground they launched a consumer-centered program providing these two groups the support they needed to avoid infection. Brazil has criticized countries who preach celibacy and fidelity as the primary means to fight HIV/AIDS.

Prevention campaign among youths

Street youth in Brazil fight a daily battle for survival. These youth live for the day. They have no sense of a future or planning for prevention. They are often rounded up by private police, attacked and sometimes killed (see also Gokah, 2006). They trust few people. Sex is one of their few joys and high-risk sex is all that is open to them. A local non governmental organization working with a team from Porter-Novelli and AED began to think what might be done to help these children protect themselves. Street conversations with the kids showed that condoms were too expensive and not a viable solution to gangs of kids on the move. These children were proud of their ability to survive. They called themselves – or "streetwise rascal". Working with this image, developed a series of T-shirt which promoted non-penetrative sex, masturbation, as the

_____ way to beat AIDS. The _____ beat the system, beat the police, beat all the adults that tried to trap them and now they would beat AIDS by being smart.

This small project is just one example of the enormous creativity of the Brazilian program. Its ability to understand different audiences, create solutions that worked for them and execute the solutions in creative ways was a key to the overall success of Brazil program. If there is one lesson from the Brazil program for social marketers, it is that people know what they need. Social marketing is not only a way to listen to the disenfranchised, but to create services and products that help them within the context of their own reality.

CAMEROON: COMPREHENSIVE MARKETING OF AIDS PREVENTION

The AIDS Control and Prevention (AIDSCAP) program in Cameroon (1992 - 1996) was designed to address unmet needs in HIV prevention. Available HIV prevalence information in 1992 indicated that Cameroon still had a relatively low HIV prevalence rate, estimated between 0.5 and 1 percent of the general population. However, surveillance studies suggested that the epidemic was increasing rapidly among specific populations within Cameroon, specifically, urban youth, commercial sex workers (CSWs), sexually transmitted disease (STD) patients, and the military.

The program focused on improving behaviour change communication (BCC) for select targeted groups at higher risk of HIV and STDs, expanding condom availability and affordability through condom social marketing, and assisting the Ministry of Public Health to establish a national STD control service. It was funded by the United States Agency for International Development (USAID) through a cooperative agreement with Family Health International (FHI).

The AIDSCAP/Cameroon strategy included peer health education, community-based outreach programs, the development and distribution of educational materials, and alternative media such as theatre. The heart of the Cameroon Program was its pioneering behaviour change interventions that have inspired the peer education models currently used around the world. Interventions with the military, university students, STD patients, and CSWs and their clients were implemented by the NACS in collaboration with the ministries of defence, higher education and health. CARE/Canada and Save the Children-USA, two international NGOs, respectively implemented the in- and out-of-school youth project and a community-based intervention project in the East and Far North Provinces of the country. The interventions focused on adoption of risk reduction behaviour, including promotion of abstinence for young adults, fidelity for couples, partner reduction, condom use, and treatment for STDs. The projects used multiple, reinforcing communication channels and information, education, and communication (IEC) activities. Specific approaches included interpersonal counseling and educational techniques, such as formal education sessions, drama, informal chats and one-on-one counseling, and mass and traditional media. The projects also focused on building capacity for sustainability through training, and the development and production of peer health educator manuals for CSWs, the armed forces, youth, and university students. Over the course of the program, AIDSCAP/Cameroon trained over 2,000 peer educators and leaders, who in turn educated more than 700,000 women, men and youth about HIV/AIDS prevention. Over 1.18 million educational materials that reinforced communication activities and behaviour change were produced and distributed as well as radio and television spots.

The strategy was complemented and reinforced by a specific condom social marketing program. Condom programming was implemented by AIDSCAP subcontractor, Population Services International (PSI). Under AIDSCAP, the condom social marketing program expanded countrywide to reach additional target group populations. As part of its strategy, PSI established officially recognized and supervised distributors in all major urban centers using specific marketing techniques and advertising to cover all of Cameroon's ten provinces. Over 9,500 condom sales locations were established for *Prudence* condoms. The program also used peer educators, especially CSWs, to serve as condom sales agents in non-traditional venues while CSM sales staff supplied the more traditional commercial outlets. In Yaoundé alone, CSWs sold over three million condoms. A number of CSWs were as successful as condom sales agents, that they were able to leave the sex work profession. Over the life of the AIDSCAP project, the social marketing program sold over 24 million condoms and distributed close to one million for free.

At the initiation of the AIDSCAP/Cameroon project, no national STD control program existed; AIDSCAP/Cameroon efforts led by an AIDSCAP subcontractor and the Institute of Tropical Medicine (ITM), concentrated on supporting the NACP in the development of national STD guidelines. As a result of these efforts, a national STD control plan and standard diagnosis and treatment guidelines were adopted by the Ministry of Health.

Over the life of the project significant accomplishments were achieved. These include the following:

- The capacity of the Ministry of Health to plan, manage, and evaluate comprehensive STD/HIV/AIDS programs was substantially increased.
- More than 700,000 men, women, and youth were educated about how to protect themselves from HIV/AIDS and STDs.
- Over 2,000 individuals working in professional and/or volunteer capacities were trained in the skills they need to sustain HIV prevention activities in their communities.
- Close to 25 million condoms were distributed; all but one million were sold through the condom social marketing system.
- Over one million educational and promotional materials that reinforce behaviour change communication efforts and condom use were distributed.
- National guidelines for STD diagnosis and treatment were developed and adopted by the Ministry of Health.

The final country program evaluation was completed under a grant with Institut de Recherche et des Etudes de Comportement (IRESCO), a local research institute. IRESCO conducted the end-of-project knowledge, attitudes, beliefs, and practices (KAPB) surveys among all the target groups. **Knowledge of two correct methods of preventing HIV has increased among all the target groups.** One of the most dramatic increases was evidenced among youth in the Eastern Province. In 1993, only 37 percent were able to cite two correct methods of AIDS prevention. By 1996, this had increased to 70 percent. **Reported safer sexual behaviour related to condom use increased among several target groups.** Of the CSWs who reported having ever used a condom, the percentage has risen steadily from 28.3 in 1988 to 65 in 1990, to 68 in 1994, and finally to 88 in 1996. The percentage of clients who reported ever having used a condom also rose significantly, from 55.5 in 1990 to 81 in 1996. Consistent condom use by CSWs with non-regular clients increased from 52 percent in 1994 to 75 percent in 1996 and 63 percent with regular clients. **Reported safer sexual behaviour related to condom use increased among several target groups.** Of the CSWs who reported having ever used a condom, the percentage has risen steadily from 28.3 in 1988 to 65 in 1990, to 68 in 1994, and finally to 88 in 1996. The percentage of clients who reported ever having used a condom also rose significantly, from 55.5 in 1990 to 81 in 1996.

MALARIA: AFRICA WIDE

NetMark is a unique cross-sector partnership created to fight malaria in sub-Saharan Africa where the disease kills more than two million people each year. It was initiated by the United States Agency for International Development (USAID) and developed under the management of the Academy for Educational Development (AED).

NetMark's mandate is to increase demand for and expand the availability of insecticide-treated nets (ITNs), a simple but effective way to prevent the mosquito bites that cause malaria. To accomplish this task, AED has developed a market-based approach of shared risk and investment dubbed Full Market Impact ™ (FMI™), based on the premise that as demand grows within a competitive market, consumers will benefit from improved quality, lower prices, and wider availability.

FMI^{TM} provides an operational model that creates common ground between the private and public sectors. Partners from both sectors agree on common objectives while observing their respective roles across each of the five factors: supply, distribution, affordability demand/appropriate use, and equity / sustainable markets.

NetMark's FMI^{TM} model was intentionally designed to reflect the way businesses thought about the market, thus the model's convergence with the classic "4 Ps" of marketing: product, place, price, and promotion. In this way, FMI^{TM} demonstrates how meeting the needs of the poor can translate into good business that promotes expansion into new market segments. AED believes that FMI^{TM} challenges the way businesses think about market opportunity, taking a broader view of the role their products play and the consumer behaviours they influence, while addressing critical public health issues and serving the needs of the poor.

In its six years, the NetMark project has shown that international and African companies are willing to invest in producing, marketing, and distributing ITNs when working in partnership with the public sector.

Data from household surveys conducted by NetMark in 2004 show considerable gains since the baseline research in 2000 and the first country launch in late 2001. In all NetMark countries, awareness and use of nets and ITNs increased dramatically, and more nets are being treated or purchased pre-treated. For example, the percentage of households that owned a net or ITN in Nigeria rose from 12% in 2000 to 27% in 2004; in Senegal from 34% to 56%; and in Zambia from 27% to 50%. Moreover, NetMark's commercial sector consumers approach resulted in increased use among all socio-economic groups. Net coverage rates are increasing equitably, and vulnerable groups are being reached in both urban and rural areas.

By 2004, ITN sales by NetMark's formal partners neared the 2 million mark. While this represented only 62% of the ambitious projection total made by the various commercial partners for 2004, it did represent a 132% increase over 2003 sales. Progress is being made in a sustainable manner, and the market appears to be poised for rapid growth now that supply issues are being addressed. Overall, commercial sales in NetMark countries have reached 9 million based on reports from partners, and estimates of additional sales made by NetMark based on market research conducted in 2004.

In sum NetMark's impact includes:

- More than US $18 million has been invested by private sector partners in developing the commercial ITN market in Africa
- Nearly 15 million more people are protected from malaria by insecticide-treated bed nets (ITNs).
- More than 100 million people have been educated about malaria, the importance of ITNs and how to use them effectively.
- More than 350,000 pregnant women and children under five have gotten discount vouchers for ITNs, of which 243,000 have been redeemed.
- Treated nets now cost from 30% to 75% less than untreated nets did in 2000 due to competition fostered by NetMark.
- NetMark has increased the supply of ITNs in eight African countries, with the number of ITN distributors increasing from 2 in 1999 to 29 in 2005.

Challenges still lie ahead. Public policy must continue to support ITNs and a role for the commercial sector; free and subsidized ITN programs must be fully targeted to the poorest and not totally undermine commercial investments; NetMark and partner marketing efforts must continue to build sustainable demand; and NetMark's commercial partners must expand their investment in ITNs to replace the support provided by NetMark. Under these conditions, the ITN market will continue to grow while serving the public health fight against malaria.

LESSONS FROM SOCIAL MARKETING TO IEC

There are perhaps three important lessons that can be gleaned from the experience of social marketing to the poor.

1. The poor need more than messages.

To tell a woman to use contraception when she can't find one, afford one, or convince her partner to use one, is nonsense. Social marketing has proven very efficient at listening to the poor, designing contraceptives that meet their needs, making them widely available, pricing them and promoting them in ways that are compelling and credible to people who have little trust of authority.

2. The poor are willing to pay for services they value.

The poor are like everyone, accept they have less money. Like the rest of us, the poor are not all alike. Some know that you don't get much for nothing. For those so poor they have no choice but to depend on hand-outs, they often become trapped in a vicious cycle of dependency. For others, paying as much as 1/3 of their income to a traditional healer is a price they are willing to pay for health services they trust. And for others, they distrust anything free from the government. Social marketing does not meet all the needs of the poor, but the subsidized creation and marketing of useful goods and services to the poor relieves financially stretched governments and provides quality services the poor desperately need.

3. The poor can be just as creative and entrepreneurial as the rich.

Social marketing to the poor is not only about price and subsidized products. It is about understanding who the poor are. It is about understanding that street kids in Brazil are not going to read a pamphlet, see a TV spot, or buy a condom. It understands that many rural women in Africa have come to believe that cleanliness is next to Godliness. Therefore they want to wash the dirt off a malarial bed net that has become infested with dirt and insects. They don't need a lecture on how the insecticide washes off. They need a net that can be washed without ruining it. Social marketing is also about bringing fun into the lives of people with precious little of it. It's about contests instead of lectures; parades instead of pamphlets and participation instead of preaching. Social marketing to the poor has released the inherent creativity of communities across the world and shown that you don't need an MBA to be a business person.

Chapter 3

DOES EDUCATION PROVIDE 'SOCIAL VACCINE' AGAINST AIDS?

Peter Badcock-Walters, Michael J Kelly and Marelize Gorgens-Albino*

In Sub-Saharan Africa, the epicentre of the pandemic, HIV is primarily transmitted sexually. The main approach to preventing its spread has been through HIV education, including the use of mass media such as the radio and TV; institutional media such as schools; and personal media such as social networks. This chapter seeks to understand whether young people who have been exposed to HIV education are more likely to change or mitigate high-risk sexual behaviour, thereby reducing their risk of being infected with HIV. To attempt to confirm this, a meta-analysis of relevant experimental and observational studies was undertaken.

This meta-analysis provided a number of interesting insights. **First**, there is evidence that, over time, *increased education levels* (not necessarily increased HIV education) positively correlate with positive changes in high-risk HIV behaviour. It is likely that the reason for this is that the cognitive and literacy skills required to make informed choices in respect of HIV risk and behaviour change, are substantively based on levels of education and literacy. **Second**, *increased HIV knowledge or literacy* also correlates positively with reductions in high-risk HIV behaviour, although there are a number of other factors (socio-economic, cultural and social norms) that influence decisions about HIV-related sexual behaviour. **Third**, it is *not possible to pinpoint which type of media or which type of message have produced the most positive effect on behaviour change.* The research suggests, unsurprisingly, that knowledge and risk-reducing skills are acquired from a complex network of formal and informal sources, *including* but not limited to the education system. Whereas we cannot statistically attribute the relative contribution of the education system, mass media or other types of information sources, we can say with some measure of certainty that *all* these channels converge and contribute to the internal decision support system upon which every person must ultimately rely.

The chapter concludes that HIV knowledge is an essential HIV prevention mechanism, but that its success depends on *who we communicate to* (including community leaders and traditional leaders, councillors, members of parliament, teachers, learners, parents, etc.); *what kind of message we deliver* (clearly addressing the political, socio-economic and cultural factors that drive HIV transmission, as well as biological and individual behavioural factors); *who does the communicating* (reflecting the importance or standing of persons or authorities communicating the messages); and the *education level of the person receiving the communication*.

INTRODUCTION

"Several decades into the AIDS pandemic, HIV transmission in most of the world remains firmly concentrated among sex workers, men who have sex with men (MSM), injecting drug users (IDUs), and their sex partners. In some parts of Africa, where over two-thirds of infections occur globally, HIV has expanded outside these high-risk groups, creating generalised, predominantly heterosexual epidemics; In nine Southern African countries, more than 12% of adults are infected with HIV" (Potts et al., 2008).

In a field depressed by mounting evidence of HIV and AIDS impact in many countries, the links between education and HIV prevention have been explored, *ad infinitum,* over the years: Not only does it seems intuitively 'right' that education should offer protection against HIV, the idea is central to the concept of a 'window of hope' (World Bank, 2004) in which young people[1] will make better informed decisions about the avoidance of risk. Much of the HIV and education research community, as well as related implementation agencies, have readily assumed that education, in general, will allow those at risk to understand and judge their options better, and that improved retention in school will increase their chances of survival (WFP, 2006). "Schools can provide the best defence against HIV infection. They offer the best mechanism to deliver HIV prevention information, as well as the long term educational and social skills that protect against infection." *(*Carol Bellamy, Executive Director of UNICEF, February 2004).

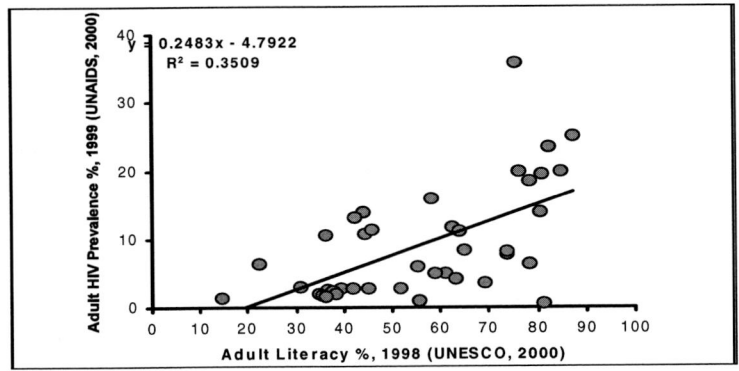

Figure 1: HIV prevalence in adults aged 15-49 years by level of adult literacy for 40 countries in sub-Saharan Africa.
Source: Gregson et al., 2001

---

1 For the purpose of this chapter, young people are defined as those of both genders in the population, between the ages of 15 and 24.

Yet, there is some counter-intuitive evidence about the role of education in HIV transmission risk, as figure 1 illustrates. Without careful interpretation and a thorough understanding of all the facts, Graph 1 could simply be interpreted to suggest that lack of education (i.e. lower literacy rate) is actually protective (at a population level) against HIV infection.

More recently, concerns have been expressed in many circles (Epstein, 2007; Pisani, 2008; Potts et al., 2008; Wilson and Halperin, 2008) that the comparative successes of HIV prevention efforts have not always been rigorously interrogated. For example, modelling results have shown that reductions in intergenerational sex, as well as age of sexual debut, may not have a population-level effect on reducing the number of HIV infections, as women continue to get married later in life (Hallett et al., 2007). Other studies have shown that numbers of sexual partners, levels of commercial sex and HSV-2 infection remain risk factors, even in mature generalised epidemics. Where counter-intuitive evidence has been presented, it has sometimes been disregarded in the face of the 'conventional wisdom' of the AIDS community.

Given these mounting concerns, the somewhat counter-intuitive evidence about the link between HIV and education and the urgent need to prioritise HIV prevention efforts that have been shown to work and address the real drivers of the epidemic (Fraser et al., 2008), we present a summary of all the available evidence (collected through a meta analysis of existing research studies and a primary analysis of DHS results) in an attempt to add clarity and coherence to the messages about HIV and education.

After a brief discussion on risk factors for HIV transmission (which we might expect education to reduce or eliminate altogether over time), we set out in this chapter to demonstrate that:

a) Increased levels of education, not HIV and AIDS education *per se*, has been shown in recent years to correlate with positive changes in high-risk HIV-related behaviour and lower HIV prevalence;
b) That HIV education, in its broadest sense, remains important as an HIV prevention strategy; and
c) That the type of media and messages conveyed all play a role in the outcome of the HIV prevention interventions and therefore on its impact on reducing the incidence of HIV infections.

How Can HIV be Prevented?

Historically, HIV prevention interventions have mostly been based on biomedical and individual behaviour change approaches (Bloom et al., 2004; Fraser, Gorgens-Albino et al, [forthcoming]). Individual behaviour change approaches assume that individuals move from an existing condition of HIV exposure (or, we would add, risk-related activity) to a condition of lower risk by adopting a range of risk-reducing strategies (Parker (2003). The basis for adopting such a range of risk-reducing strategies is sufficient knowledge; the problem is that even if people have the knowledge, they may not have the incentive or power to change their behaviour (Barnett & Whiteside, 2002).

Over time, a general recognition has developed that these biomedical and individual behaviour approaches on their own have not been successful – their impact at an individual level (through randomized control trials) and through population-level studies (through multivariate analysis) have sometimes been disproved (Parker, 2003; Potts et al, 2008; Wilson and Halperin, 2008). Voluntary counselling and testing, the bedrock of many HIV prevention policies, have never been proven – at individual level or population level – to reduce high-risk behaviour or new HIV infections (Calsyn et al., 1992; Wenger et al., 1992; Potts et al., 2008). In fact, a recent RCT showed negative behavioural outcomes for men who tested HIV negative (Corbett et al., 2007). Biomedical and individual behaviour approaches have ignored the community or macro level risk factors that could possibly impact on HIV transmission (Airhihenbuwa, 1999; Bloom et al., 2002; Campbell, 2003).

As more qualitative and quantitative research has become available, different theories have emerged regarding the risk factors that influence the rate of new HIV infections, the relationship between these risk factors, and thus what should be done to minimise the spread of HIV. These theories have often been captured in conceptual frameworks to show the causal chain that leads to HIV infection (see figures 2 and 3 for two of the latest of these models).

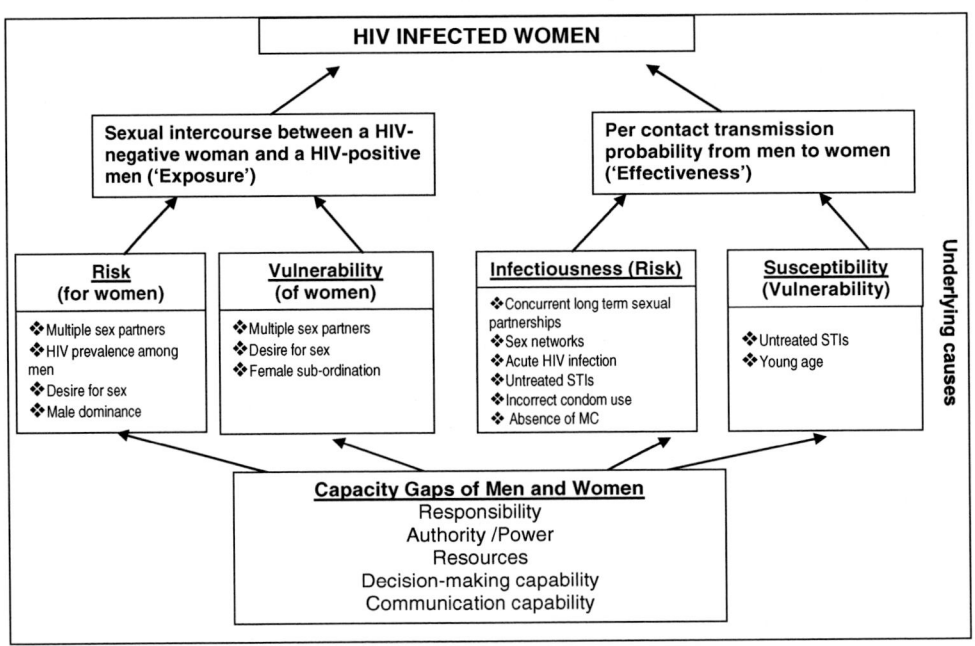

Figure 2. Conceptual Framework for the Vulnerability of Young Women and Girls to HIV infection
Source: Jonsson (forthcoming)

What most of these conceptual frameworks have in common is that they postulate that there are proximate and distal factors that impact on HIV transmission. Fraser et al. (2008), for example, suggests that factors that impact on HIV transmission risk may best be categorised at the individual level (factors within the control of a single individual – e.g. number of sexual partners); at the community level (factors over which a community would have the most control and that an individual cannot control on his/her own – e.g. social norms about the number of sexual partners); and at the structural or macro level (factors over which individual communities do not have control – e.g. laws about the legality of polygamous marriages).

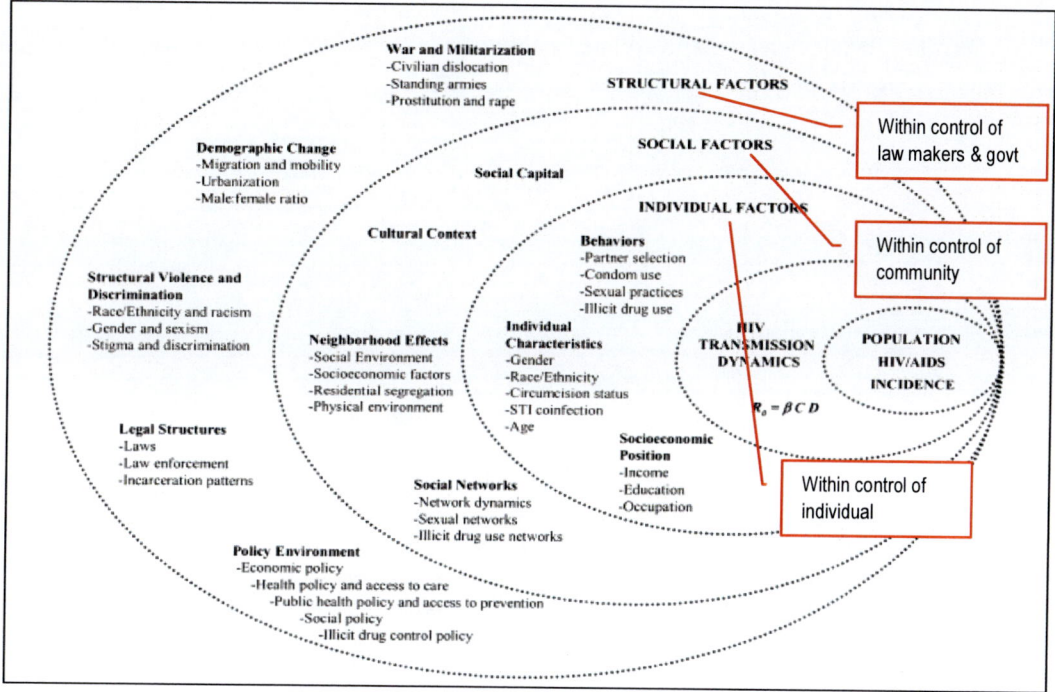

Figure 3. Poundstone's framework for categorizing risk factors for HIV transmission

Notes to Figure 3: (taken from Poundstone et al. 2004), 'A framework for the social epidemiology[2] of HIV and AIDS'. The dotted lines separating the levels illustrate the porous nature of the distinctions made between levels of analysis. In reality, there are extensive linkages between factors at all levels that give rise to observed epidemic patterns. The basic reproductive rate (R_o) is a measure of the potential for growth of an infectious disease epidemic and depends on the pattern of infectious contacts within the host population, the likelihood of infection being transmitted during a contact, and the duration of infectiousness.

What, therefore, has been the role of education, if any, in addressing (or exacerbating) risk factors for HIV at the individual level, community level and structural (macro) level? The next section will consider all available evidence.

---

[2] Social epidemiology is the study of the distribution of health outcomes and their social determinants. The social epidemiology perspective emphasizes social conditions as fundamental causes of disease

HIV-Related Knowledge, HIV-Related Behaviour, and HIV Prevalence: Links with Education Levels

In this section, we consider the relationship, if any, shown between HIV knowledge and HIV education levels; between HIV-related behaviour (i.e. risk factors at the individual level) and education levels; and between HIV prevalence and education levels.

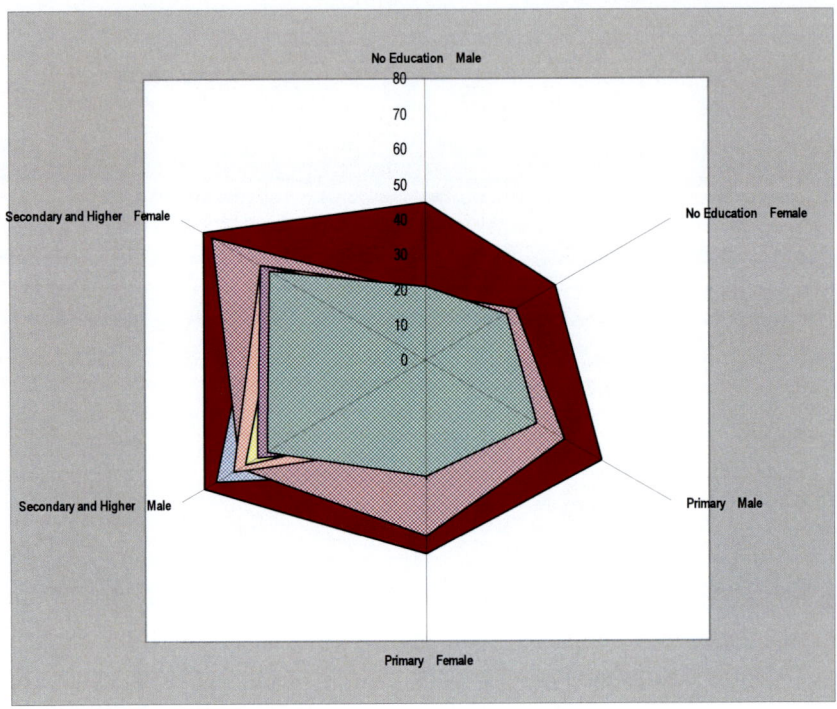

Figure 4: Relationship between comprehensive levels of HIV knowledge and education level for all men and women over the last 20 years in selected countries
Source: HIV and AIDS Survey Indicators Database. http://www.measuredhs.com/hivdata/, July 20 2008.
Notes to Figure 4: Detailed percentages can be found in Annex 1. Figure 4 shows, on a radial plot, how increased percentages of knowledge can be seen on the axes associated with "secondary and higher education – male" and "secondary and higher education – female" for all the countries plotted (n=77).

HIV-related knowledge and education levels

The evidence is overwhelmingly clear that more educated individuals have higher levels of comprehensive knowledge about HIV and AIDS[3]. Literate young women are three times more likely than illiterate women to know that a healthy-looking person can have AIDS and four times more likely to know the main ways to avoid HIV, according to a 32-country UN

---

3 'Comprehensive knowledge' is defined as an individual being able to correctly identify3 ways in which HIV is transmitted and reject 2 misconceptions about how HIV cannot be transmitted.

study (Vandemoortele, Delamonica, 2000). An analysis the Demographic and Health Surveys (DHSs) carried out over the past 20 years clearly show the correlation between education level and HIV knowledge for both men and women of all ages (figure 4) and young men and women aged 15 to 24 (figure 5).

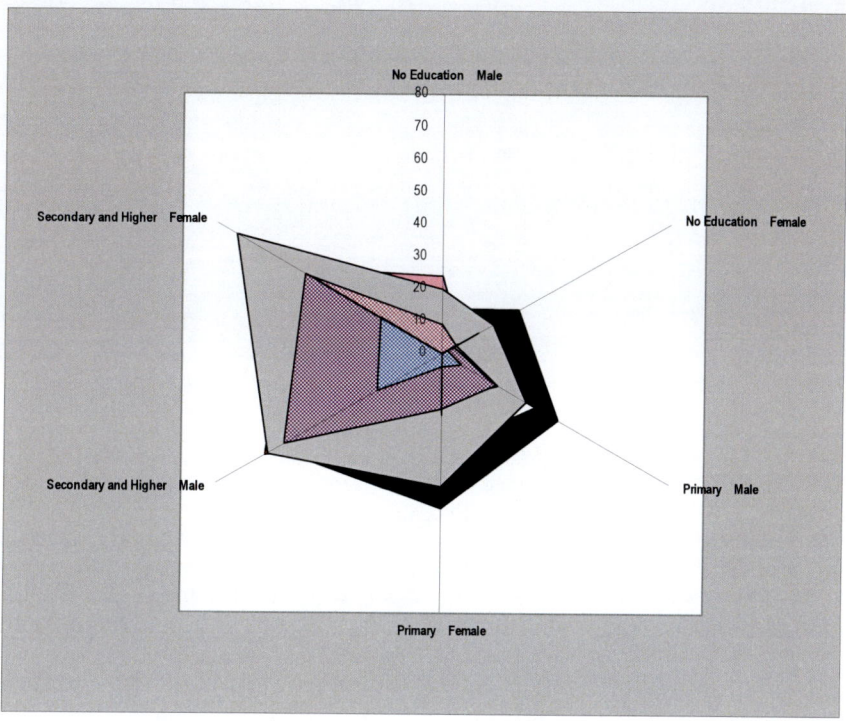

Figure 5. Relationship between comprehensive levels of HIV knowledge and education level for young men and women aged 15 to 24 over the last 20 years in selected countries
Source: HIV and AIDS Survey Indicators Database. http://www.measuredhs.com/hivdata/, July 20 2008.

However, the path from knowledge to action is not a straightforward one: Airhihenbuwa argues that the simple, linear relationship between individual knowledge and action does not take into account the variation among the political, socio-economic and cultural contexts that prevail. He suggests that sexual activity is not a rational straight-line undertaking, noting that emotions cause many deviations. George Bernard Shaw accurately described as 'brute sanity' the way in which we inflate our expectations by showing others the rational way and then expect them to follow it, without allowing for the predictable complication of all sorts of emotional sidetracks and detours. We would add the complex vertical and horizontal communications context in which young people exist, and note that this will be conditioned by the political, socio-economic and, particularly, cultural influences that both Airhihenbuwa and Shaw describe.

If the relationship between HIV knowledge and HIV infection risk was linear, then countries with high levels of comprehensive knowledge of HIV should have low HIV incidence. This has not, however, proven to be the case, thereby supporting the notion that the relationship is not as simple and straightforward as initially assumed. Fraser et al. (2008, forthcoming) plotted HIV incidence and comprehensive knowledge, and could not find a statistically-significant correlation – see figure 6.

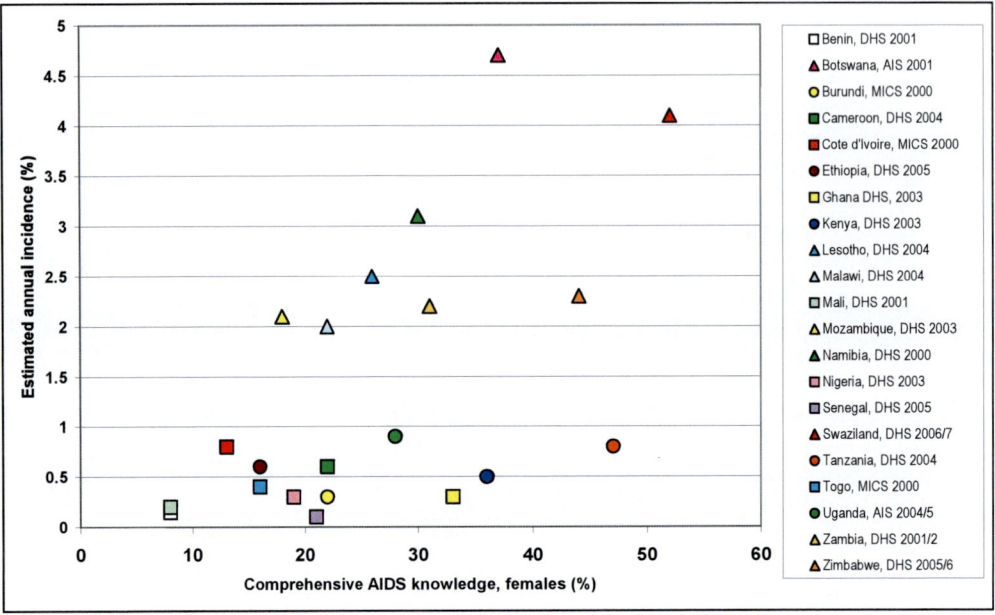

Figure 6. Comprehensive AIDS knowledge among females and estimated HIV incidence (same year of assessment) in selected African countries
(Legend: East Africa: ○, Southern Africa: Δ, West Africa: □)
Source: Fraser, Gorgens-Albino, Whitson, Gelmon and Wilson (forthcoming publication in AIDS, September 2008)

HIV-RELATED SEXUAL BEHAVIOUR AND EDUCATION LEVELS

Data about HIV-related behaviours and participation in selected HIV prevention programmes (for which data are available) that address the sexual transmission of HIV are presented here. Factors associated with the sexual transmission of HIV were chosen because these are the types of education programmes that are most likely to be found in schools, as opposed to, for example, PMTCT education programmes for pregnant women or education programmes for injecting drug users.

What is clear from the analytical results presented here is that secondary education, in particular, is a strong predictor of a number of positive and negative HIV-related behaviours, attitudes and practices. Although those with higher education levels are more likely to engage in premarital and high-risk sex, they are also more likely to use condoms.

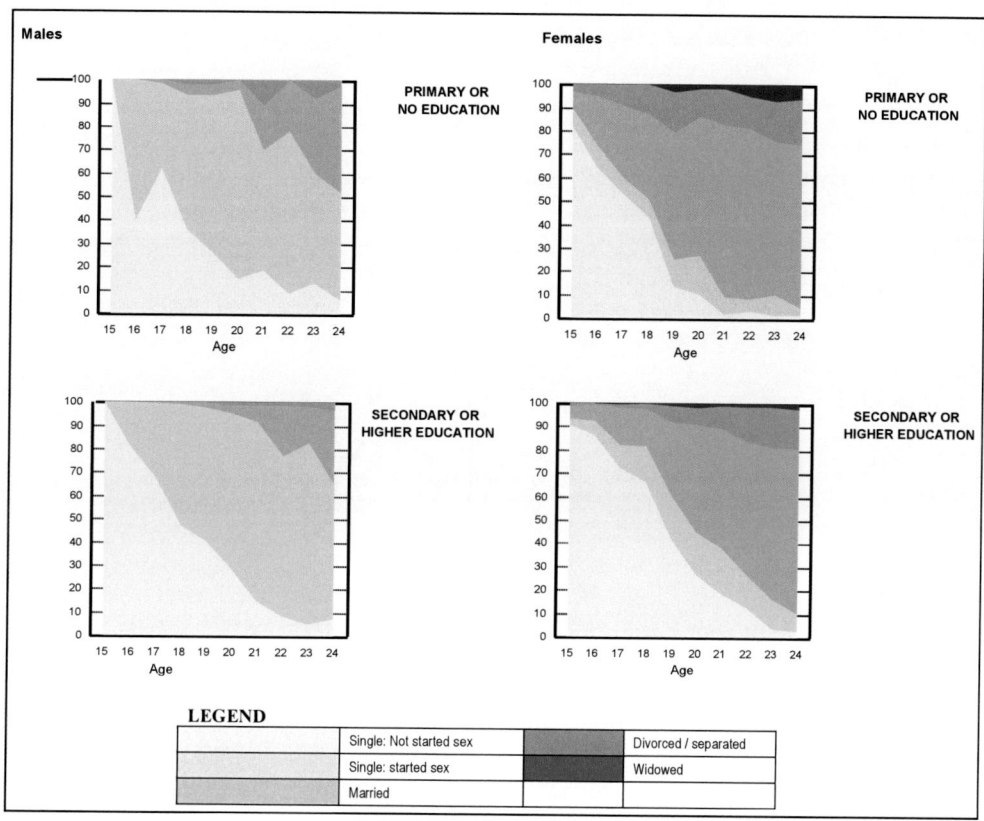

Figure 7. Sexual activity and marital status of 2,142 men and 2,274 women aged 15-24 years in rural areas of Zimbabwe, 1998-2000.
Source: Gregson et al., 2001

Age of sexual debut and education level

Evidence about the importance of the age of sexual debut is mixed. Although age of sexual debut was positively associated with reduced HIV prevalence in Uganda (Asiimwe-Okiror et al., 1997), a multivariate analysis carried out later by Hallett et al (2007) showed that the population-level effect of the age of sexual onset is small if women delay the age of marriage (i.e. if women start sex later, but also get married later, the number of years of sexual activity with multiple partners may remain the same).

Available data shows that men and women with higher education levels are most likely to have delayed the age of sexual debut (figure 7).

As the different grey-shaded areas of figure 7 shows, men and women with secondary education are more likely to have delayed sexual debut at young ages, and are also less likely to be married.

High-risk sex in the last 12 months

There is overwhelming evidence that having sex with more than one person – either consecutively or as a long-term concurrent partnership – significantly increases the risk of HIV transmission (Chen et al., 2007; Potts et al., 2008; Wilson and Halperin, 2008). Conversely, reducing such partnerships will reduce the number of new HIV infections (Asiimwe-Okiror et al., 1997). The evidence about high-risk sex and education levels is mixed and not always positive, as figures 8, 9 and 10 shows.

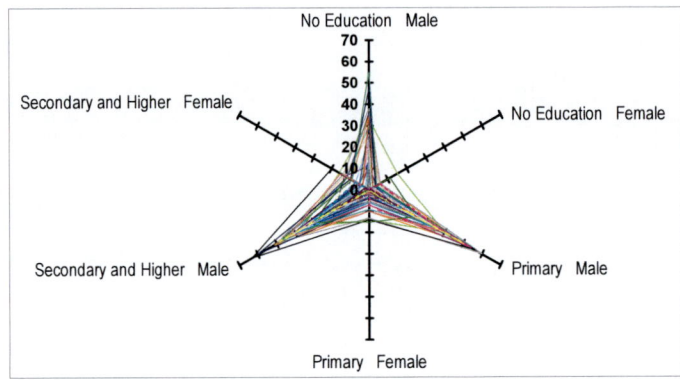

Figure 8. Young people in selected countries with multiple partners, by education level.
Source: HIV and AIDS Survey Indicators Database. http://www.measuredhs.com/hivdata/, July 20 2008.

Figure 8 makes it clear that more men than women of all education levels have multiple partners; whilst figure 9 shows that a lack of education may be a predictor for lack of premarital sex.

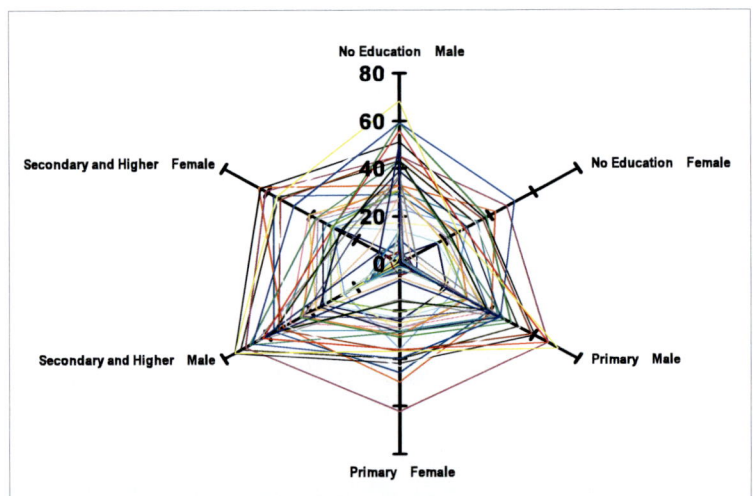

Figure 9. Young people in selected countries having premarital sex, by education level
Source: HIV and AIDS Survey Indicators Database. http://www.measuredhs.com/hivdata/, July 20 2008.

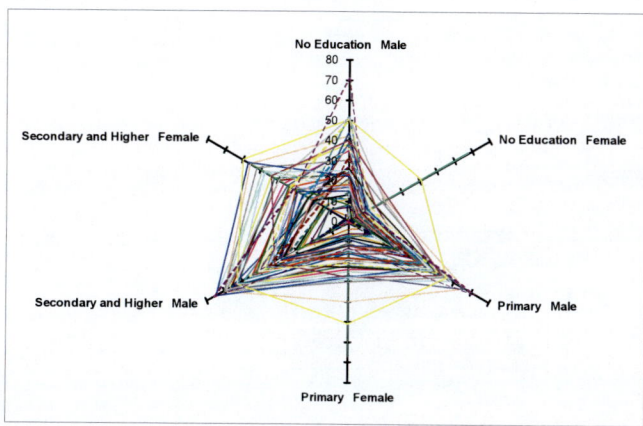

Figure 10. Men and women of all ages in selected countries who have had higher risk sex in the last 12 months, by education level
Source: HIV and AIDS Survey Indicators Database. http://www.measuredhs.com/hivdata/, July 20 2008.

The relationship between education levels and high-risk sex makes logical sense: More educated individuals change partners more rapidly, in part because they are more mobile and because they have greater control over their own sexual behaviour, greater leisure time and more disposable income (Jukes et al., 2008).

Condom use

A 2001 US government panel on "Scientific Evidence on Condom Effectiveness for Sexually Transmitted Disease (STD) Prevention" concluded that "based on a meta-analysis of published studies "always" users of the male condom significantly reduced the risk of HIV infection in men and women" (NIH, 2001: ii). However, the effectiveness of condoms radically decreases if condoms are not used consistently, as is often the case with marital and longer-term partners (Foss et al., 2007; Potts et al. 2008). Getting young people to use condoms, even after they are aware of them and their correct use, is also not always guaranteed. Hill and Abraham (2008), for example, found that a school-based condom promotion program increased discussions about condom use and carrying condoms, but not their use, whereas Schuster et al (1997) found that only 54% of school students who obtained condoms at school used them for sexual purposes. Nevertheless, condoms work well in countries where the epidemic is primarily driven by commercial sex workers (Foss et al., 2007); by contrast, it is difficult to maintain condom use in countries where the epidemic is primarily transmitted in multiple, longer-term relationships (Potts et al., 2008).

This statement is also supported by evidence from 17 African and 4 Latin American countries, which show better educated young women, delay their sexual debuts and are more likely to require their partners to use condoms (UNAIDS, 2000).

Our DHS analysis found that accepting attitudes towards condom education in schools, knowledge of where to source a condom, and condom use by adults and young people were all significantly associated with increased education levels, as figures 11 to 14 show.

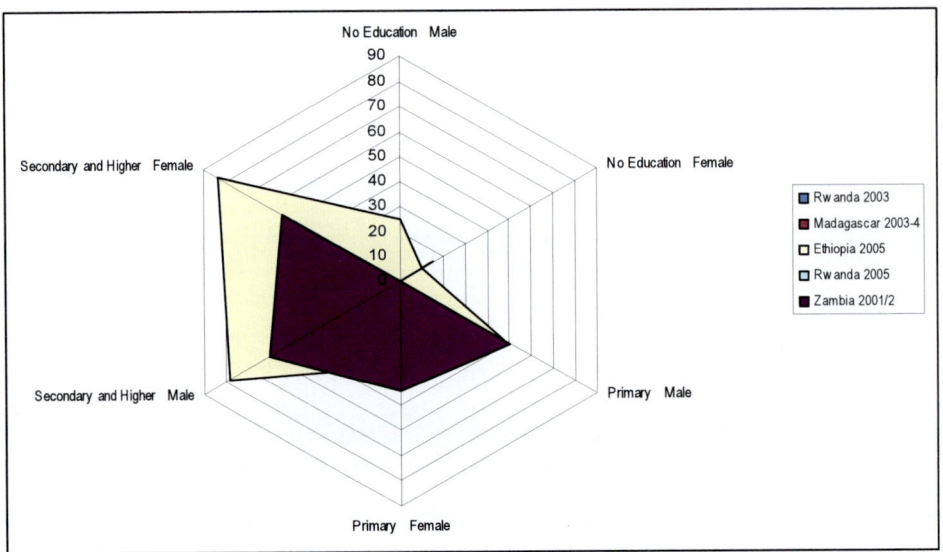

Figure 11: Young people who know where to source a condom
Source: HIV and AIDS Survey Indicators Database. http://www.measuredhs.com/hivdata/, July 20 2008.

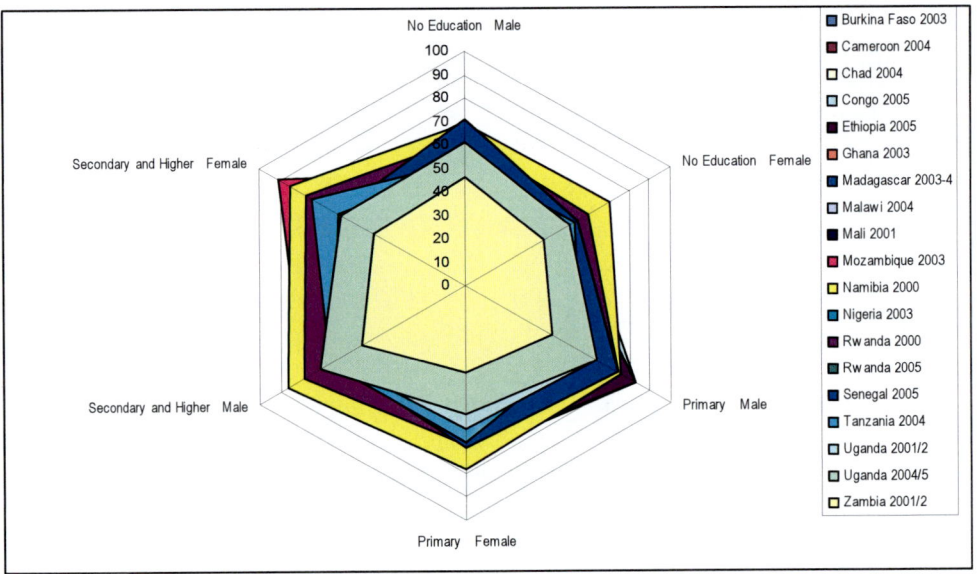

Figure 12. Adult support for condoms
Source: HIV and AIDS Survey Indicators Database. http://www.measuredhs.com/hivdata/, July 20 2008.

The Global Campaign for Education supported these findings: They found that young women with some schooling are nearly five-times as likely as their uneducated peers to have used a condom the last time they had sex – see figure 13.

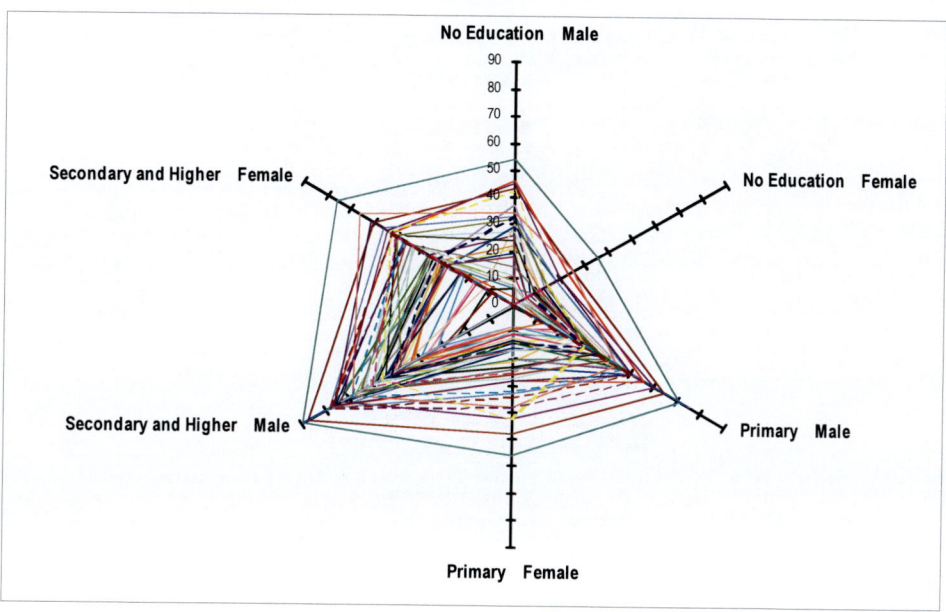

Figure 13. Condom use during high-risk sex amongst men of all ages in selected countries world wide
Source: HIV and AIDS Survey Indicators Database. http://www.measuredhs.com/hivdata/, July 20 2008.

(a)

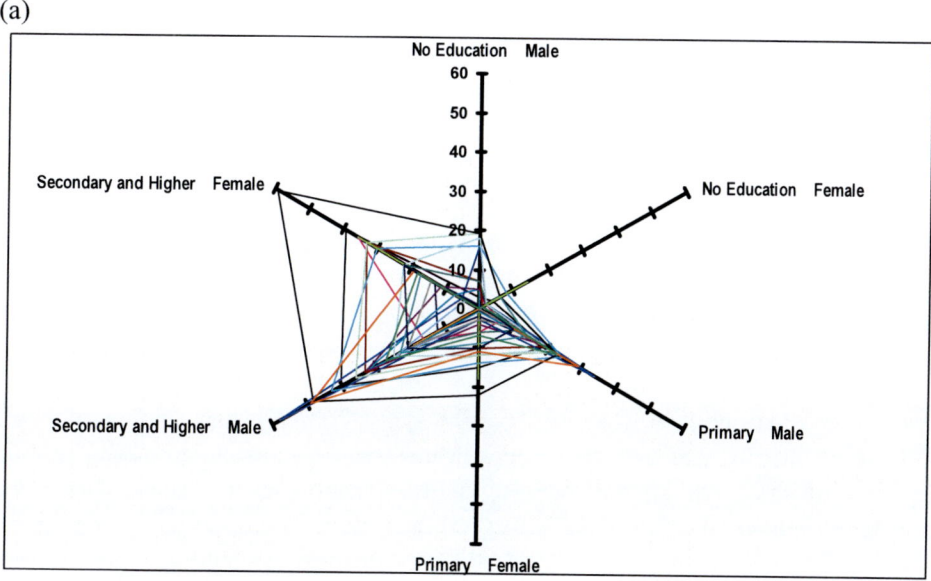

Figure 14. (Continued on the next page)

(b)

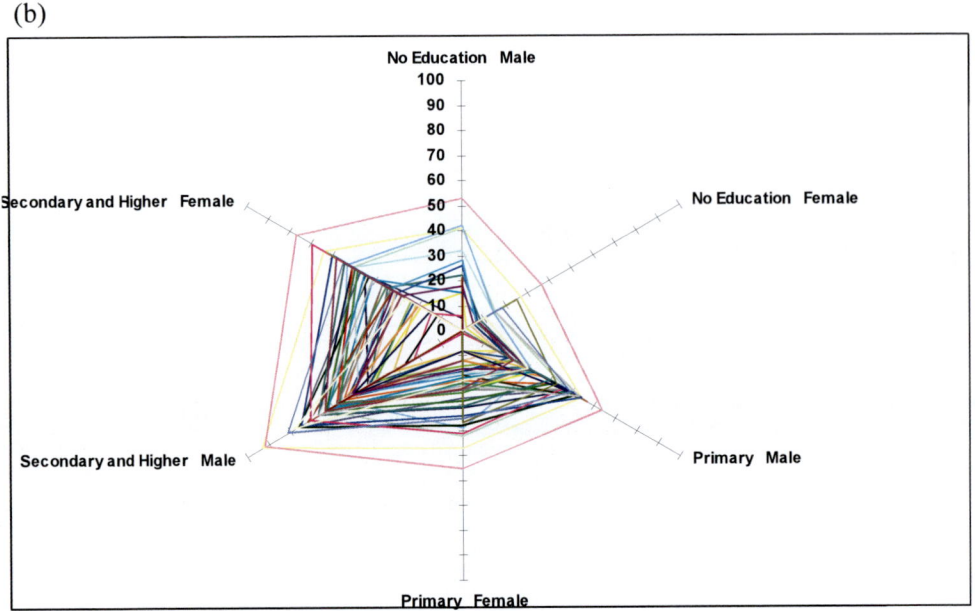

Figure 14. (a) Condom use at first sex and (b) condom use at last high-risk sex amongst young people in selected countries world wide, by education level
Source: HIV and AIDS Survey Indicators Database. http://www.measuredhs.com/hivdata/, July 20 2008.

Age-disparate sex

Leclerc-Madlala (2008) argues that age-disparate sex has contributed to HIV 'moving between generations' (Leclerc-Madlala, 2008:1), and that in societies where it is the accepted norm, it is often seen as meaningful on a social, psychological, as well as economic and symbolic level. Based on their modelling, Hallett et al (2007) have postulated that such age-disparate sex does not have a population level effect on HIV prevalence, but it is nevertheless an important factor to consider in countries where age-disparate sex is the norm and older men form a core transmitter group to younger women.

Data on age-disparate sex by education level is not comprehensive for many countries. However, in countries where data are collected, there is a somewhat surprising finding that the frequency of age-disparate sex increases with education level – suggesting that more education females have, the more likely they are to engage in age-disparate sex (see figure 15).

Commercial sex

Chen et al., (2007) found that "multi-partner sex, paid sex, STIs and HSV-2 infection are as important to HIV transmission in advanced as in early HIV epidemics. Even in high prevalence settings, prevention among people with high rates of partner change, such as female sex workers and their male clients, is likely to reduce transmission overall". As such, the rate of commercial sex use and its association with education levels (for men only, data not available for women) is also presented here in figure 16: It shows that commercial sex work is slightly more prominent amongst educated men than amongst those with no education.

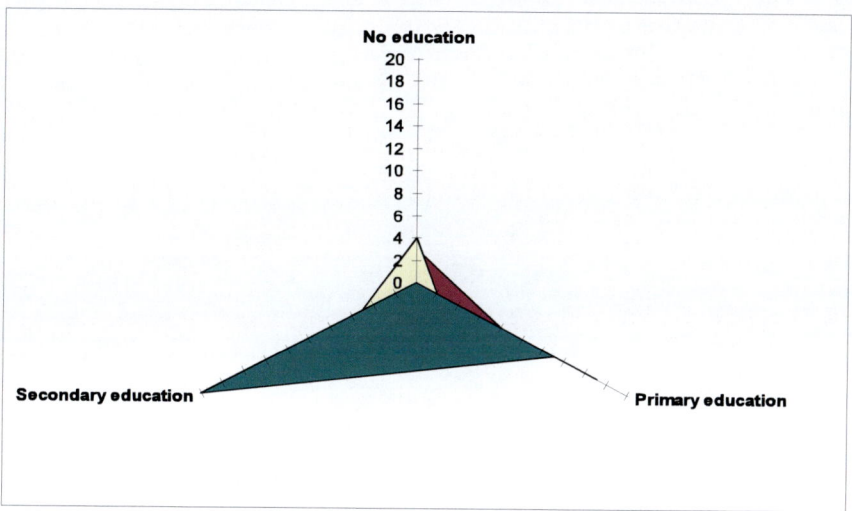

Figure 15: Age mixing by young females (with men 5 or more years older than them) in selected countries, by level of education
Source: HIV and AIDS Survey Indicators Database. http://www.measuredhs.com/hivdata/, July 20 2008.

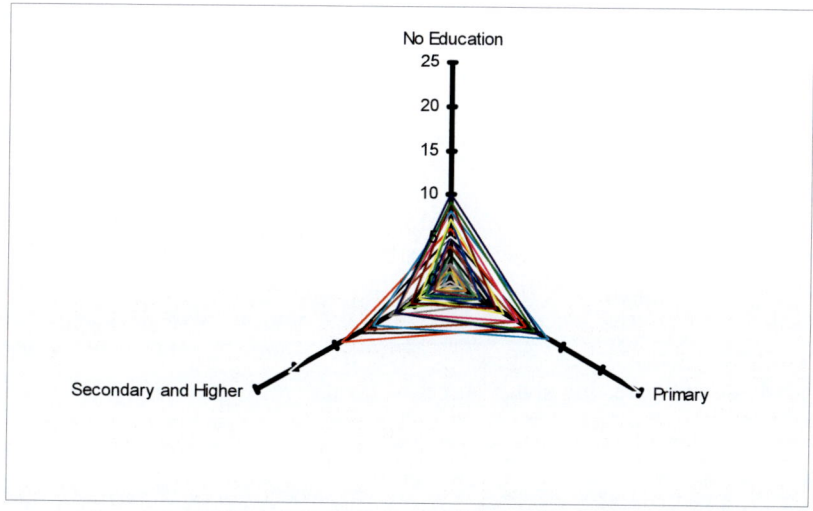

Figure 16. Commercial sex in the last 12 months by men in selected countries worldwide
Source: HIV and AIDS Survey Indicators Database. http://www.measuredhs.com/hivdata/, July 20 2008.

Accepting Attitudes towards PLHIV

At the community level (see figure 3), stigma and discrimination is said to be a driver of HIV in the sense that it limits access to HIV care and support, and inhibits discussions about condom use. The DHS analysis we conducted showed that men and women with higher education levels are more accepting of people living with HIV and AIDS – figure 17 shows the details.

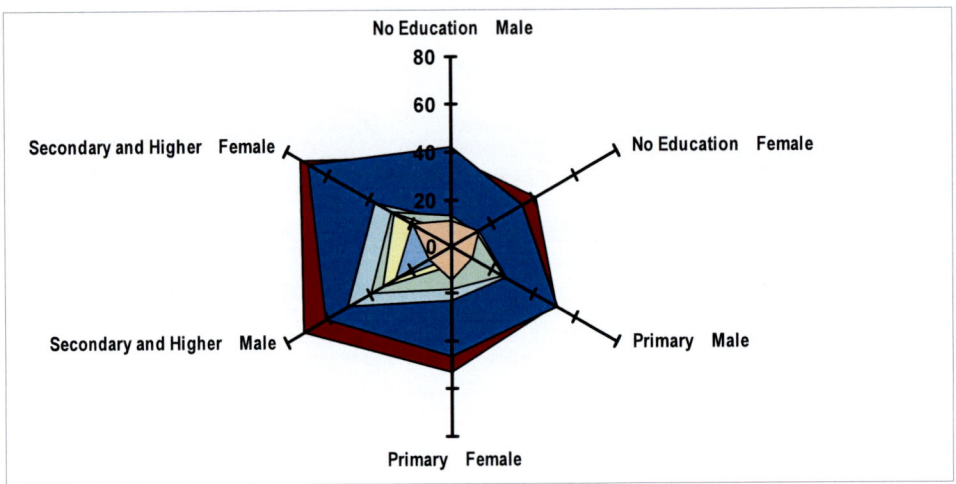

Figure 17: Men and women of all ages in selected countries around the world with accepting attitudes of PLHIVs
Source: HIV and AIDS Survey Indicators Database. http://www.measuredhs.com/hivdata/, July 20 2008.

Other evidence not considered

Given the recent research results around the lack of effectiveness of STI syndromic management to reduce HIV transmission risk (Potts et al., 2008), and the evidence that VCT is not effective as an HIV prevention intervention (Epstein, 2007; Pisani, 2008; Wilson and Halperin, 2008), these two factors and their association with HIV education was not considered for this paper. Drawing a radial graph did, however, show a strong positive correlation between HIV testing status and education.

HIV PREVALENCE AND EDUCATION LEVELS

In this section, we consider the evidence about HIV prevalence levels and education levels in a country by reviewing the latest available research. This section will show that although there is some conflicting evidence about HIV prevalence and education, recent evidence seems to point to a plausible explanation – that education levels are significantly associated with levels of development in a country and that development facilitates more extensive early spread (Jukes and Desai, 2004), but that it also facilitates more rapid control of new HIV infections.

At the individual level

Qualitative research and evaluations point to the benefits of education for individuals (Kelly, 2000; Vandemoortele and Delamonica, 2000; Gregson et al., 2001; WFP, 2006; Jukes et al., 2008). WFP concluded, after an extensive literature review, that more educated individuals have an "increased ability to understand HIV prevention information, better access to health services, reduced social and economic vulnerability that exposes women to risky activities and a higher likelihood of participation in community groups that foster protection against AIDS" (WFP, 2006:2)

The impact of education on HIV prevalence should, however, also be seen within the context of other community-level risk factors (such as the nature of the community, proximity to a trading post or major access road). When controlling for community-level risk factors, Bloom et al (2002) found that the statistical significance of individual levels of education attenuated.

At the population level

The Global Campaign for Education (GCE) has estimated that some 7 million cases of HIV and AIDS could be avoided by the achievement of Education for All[4]. What is the association between HIV and education, and has this changed in the past few years?

In the past, the relationship between education and HIV prevalence correlated positively: More educated individuals were more likely to be HIV positive (Gregson et al., 2001; Jukes and Desai, 2004; WFP 2006; Jukes et al., 2008). Out of 27 studies reviewed by Hargreaves et al (2002), only one by Fontanet (Fontanet et al, 2000), among sugar estate workers in Ethiopia, reported a significantly negative association between HIV infection and education – also see figures 18 and 19, for the latest correlation of HIV positive status and education, as per the latest DHS data.

The GCE report (2004) confirmed that 36% of young adults in low-income countries are without a complete primary education yet are likely to experience 55% of new HIV cases for that age group.

In Malawi, for example, the 2003 ANC data shows *increased* HIV-prevalence with increased educational attainment: Rates rose from 19.2% for those with no education and 19.1% for those with primary level education, to 23.2% for those with secondary education and 27.9% for those with post-secondary education.

Data in Figures 18 and 19 should be interpreted keeping in mind that Gregson et al (2001) and Jukes and Desai (2004) have both criticised the extent to which it is possible to compare education status to the HIV prevalence levels between countries in different epidemic phases.

---

[4] The World Bank. 2008. HIV and AIDS and Education. Accessed on 17 July 2008 at http://go.worldbank.org U583AZLIY0

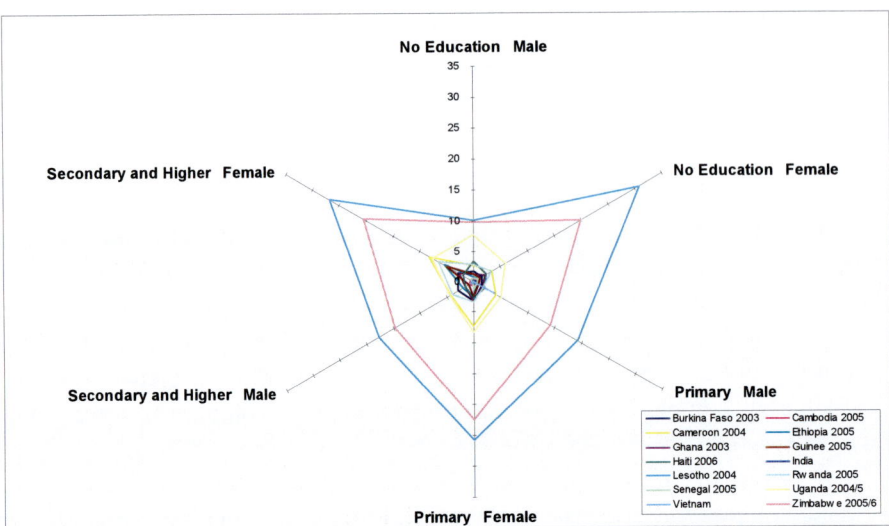

Figure 18: HIV prevalence of all persons in selected countries world wide by education level
Source: HIV and AIDS Survey Indicators Database. http://www.measuredhs.com/hivdata/, July 20 2008.

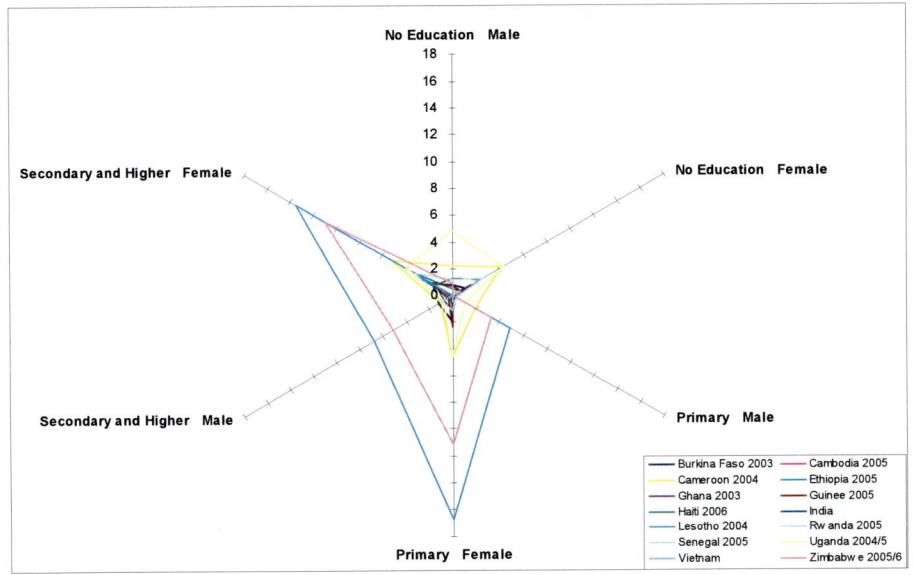

Figure 19: HIV prevalence in young people by education level in selected countries in the world by educational level
Source: HIV and AIDS Survey Indicators Database. http://www.measuredhs.com/hivdata/, July 20 2008.

Multivariate analysis confirmed this early finding of a positive correlation between education status and HIV prevalence: Drain et al (2004) found that HIV prevalence was inversely correlated with literacy rates (also refer back to figure 1, which points to the same possibility – that more literate countries have higher HIV prevalence). Forston (2008) found a robust link between education levels and HIV infection status, using 2003 data from Kenya, Tanzania, Burkina Faso, Ghana and Tanzania.

CHANGES TO THE RELATIONSHIP BETWEEN HIV PREVALENCE AND EDUCATION OVER TIME

Changes at the individual level

Gregson et al (2001) have noted that there is evidence at the individual level of a changing correlation between HIV and education at the micro (individual) level, in that there is an almost universal shift towards reduced relative risk of HIV infection in those with secondary education. Jukes et al (2008) carried out a substantial literature review and concluded the same – that HIV education poses risks but can also be protective against HIV transmission. In particular, two recent studies – a randomised control trial by Duflo et al (2006) and a longitudinal study by Barnighausen et al (2007) show that education protected individuals against HIV infection; for example, in the longitudinal study, individuals were 7% less likely to become HIV positive for every year of education that they attained. The RCT showed that keeping girls in school reduced unprotected sex (as it decreased the prevalence of teenage pregnancies in the intervention group) (Jukes et al., 2008).

Changes at the population level

There are some data that education levels are becoming negatively associated with education levels at the population level, especially as epidemics mature. De Walque (2004), in studying HIV prevalence by education category in rural Uganda 1990-2001 (see figure 20), shows that while there were some similarities between education level and HIV prevalence in the early 1990s, there is now clear evidence of reducing prevalence associated with both primary and secondary education in rural Uganda.

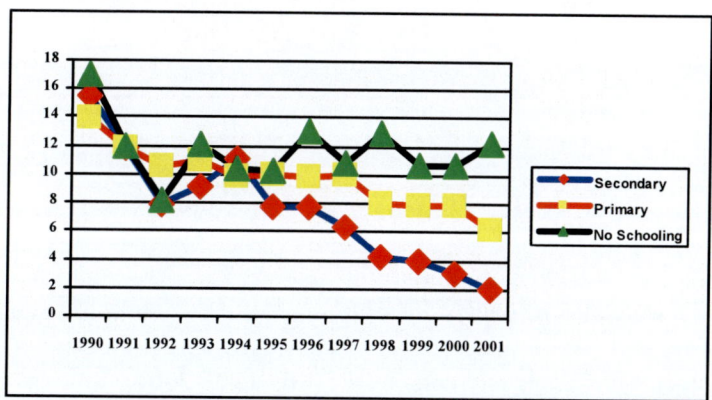

Figure 20. HIV Prevalence (%) by Education Category, Medical Research Council General Population Cohort, Rural Uganda, 1990—2001 (Individuals aged 18-29)
Source: De Walque (2004)

Glynn et al. (2004) found, using data from the well-known 'four city study' that the association between educational attainment and risk of HIV infection varies over time and between populations, and that in each city there was evidence of reduced high-risk behaviour associated with increased educational levels.

CONCLUSION: EDUCATION LEVELS AND HIV

Given the data presented over time, an increasingly cogent picture begins to emerge: Education (as a proxy for development) facilitates more extensive spread of HIV in early epidemics, and in mature epidemics, education offers protection as educated individuals change their behaviour faster and have more access to health care (Gregson et al., 2001).

The evidence presented here confirms that in cross-sectional studies, there has been a positive correlation between HIV infection, certain risk behaviours and education. Data from other, more recent studies have, however, started to show that at least at the individual level, education offers protection against HIV transmission in mature epidemics. Evidence of this changing relationship at the population level is not yet confirmed, although evidence from two countries with mature, hyper-endemic epidemics (Lesotho and Swaziland) shows an inverse relationship between educational attainment and HIV: HIV prevalence decreased with education status (figures 21 and 22).

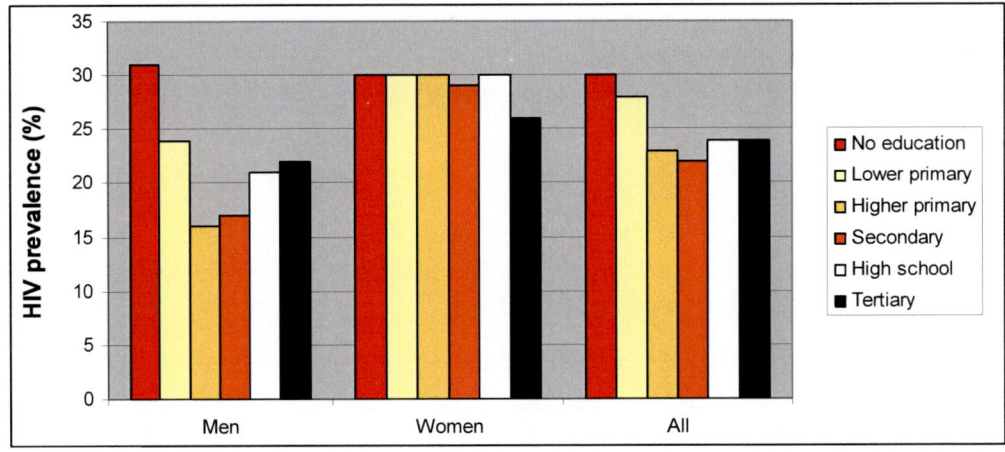

Figure 21: HIV prevalence and education status in Swaziland (2007).(Percent HIV positive in each category of education status)
Source: Swaziland DHS, 2006/07 (Table 14.5)

ANC data from Swaziland corroborate the relationship between HIV prevalence and education status for women: The data of the 10th sentinel survey of ANC clients concur with the SDHS – it showed the lowest HIV prevalence in those women with the highest educational attainment (higher/tertiary completed) (MOHSW, 2007).

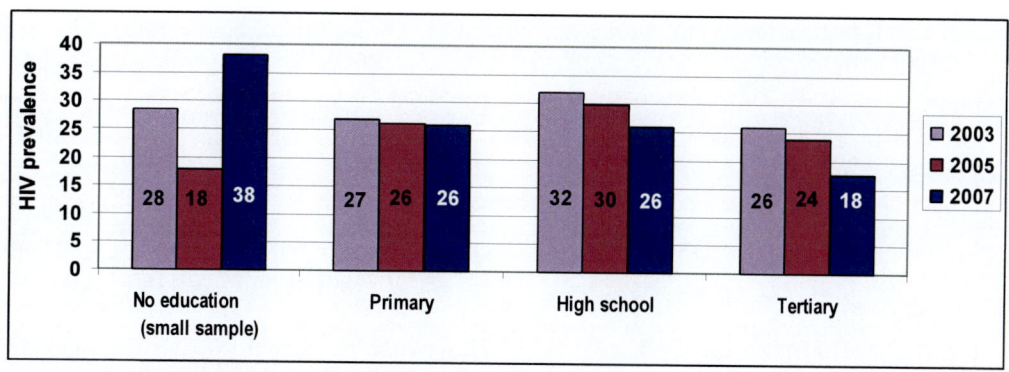

Figure 22: HIV prevalence in ANC clients, by education status in Lesotho (2003 - 2007)
Source: ANC sentinel reports various years for Lesotho

IMPACTS OF HIV EDUCATION ON BEHAVIOUR CHANGE

The next section is designed to facilitate a better understanding of the evidence on the impact of HIV education on HIV-related behaviour change. In this section, we will present evidence that the link between HIV education and HIV knowledge is well established, and that while the link between behaviour change and HIV education is also established, there has not as yet been a study that could link HIV-related education positively to changes in HIV incidence.

In this section, we take a broad view of HIV education and include in it both in-school and out-of-school interventions.

HIV EDUCATION AND KNOWLEDGE LEVELS ABOUT HIV

Over the past two decades, very many millions of dollars have been invested in behavioural interventions providing information, education and communication to motivate behaviour change amongst young people. We note that all programmes on which evidence could be found, have positively impacted on knowledge and awareness about HIV (Wassif, et al., 1993; Klepp et al. 1994; Applasca et al., 1995; Mellanby et al., 1995; Klepp et al., 1997; Sankaranarayan et al., 1999; Saleh, 1999; Noo et al. 2005; Al-Mazrou, et al., 2005; James et al., 2006; Kirby, 2006; Jodati et al., 2007)

HIV EDUCATION AND HIV-RELATED BEHAVIOUR CHANGE

But have these programmes led to positive behaviour change at the individual and population levels?

The relationship between HIV education and behaviour change has been studied from a variety of points of view, using different study methodologies. A GCE study (2004) found, for example, that school-based interventions had a clearer impact on age at first sex and the number of sexual partners than any other measure, and had an equally strong impact on condom use as peer counselling, workplace education and voluntary counselling and testing. A survey of 15 to 24 year olds in South Africa by the Reproductive Health Research Unit, University of the Witwatersrand (Pettifor et al., 2004) found that 32% of young people in that country said that they changed their behaviour as a result of what they heard about HIV education at school.

Overall, however, the evidence is mixed: Kirby et al (2006) found, using a meta-analysis of 22 studies which analyzed significantly improved sexual behaviour (i.e. positive outcomes), that only one study reported an increase in the level of reported sexual intercourse (i.e. a negative outcome).

In the rest of this section, we have conducted our own meta-analysis of available studies on the impact of HIV education on behaviour change. In selecting the studies to be included in this meta-analysis, we support Van de Ven and Aggleton's argument that not only purely quantitative studies, but also evidence gleaned through a variety of methods, should be considered in such meta-analyses. With this in mind, we considered 13 experimental and observational studies from different parts of the world (Margetts, Vorster and Venter, 2002), including:

a) **Experimental studies**, such as field trials, clinical trials, randomized control trials (RCTs); and
b) **Observational studies,** such as cross-sectional studies (prevalence studies), case-control studies, cohort studies (longitudinal studies)

The main difference between these is that in observational studies, neither the participants nor the intervention are manipulated in any way. In an experimental study, the intervention is 'applied' to a selection of participants (trial group) and outcomes are then measured in the trial group as compared to a control group.

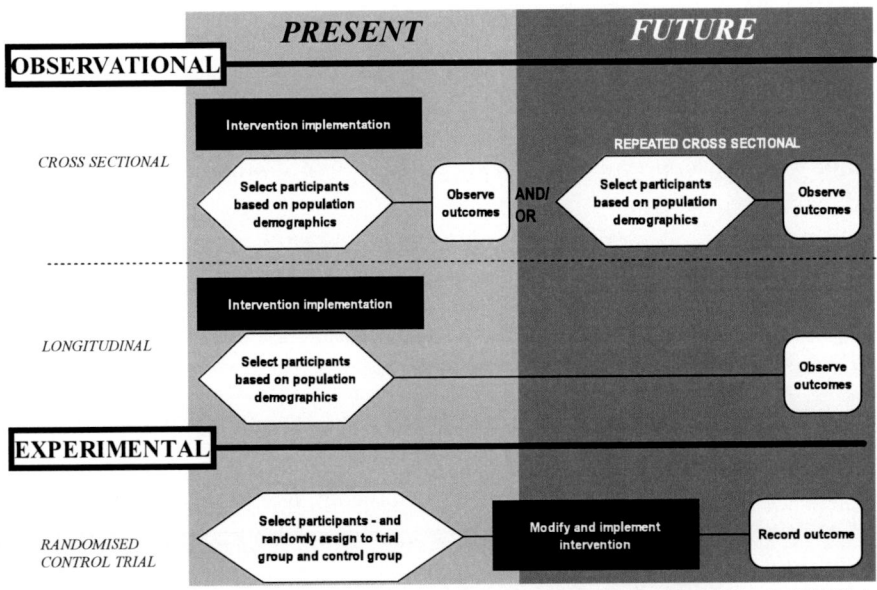

Figure 23: Sampling and intervention time order for the main types of study designs

Limitations of the meta-analysis centred mainly on the lack of standardisation of terminology and study design, which is not unique to HIV research: NRSMG[5] state in their draft set of Guidelines that there are many study designs and the terminology is not standardised. Major textbooks often have their own favourite recommendations and not even words as simple as 'retrospective' and 'prospective' are unambiguous'.[6]

Range of evidence for behaviour change: The scattergram in Figure 24 depicts, by the evaluation study design type (experimental/observational) the extent of behaviour change that the study reported.

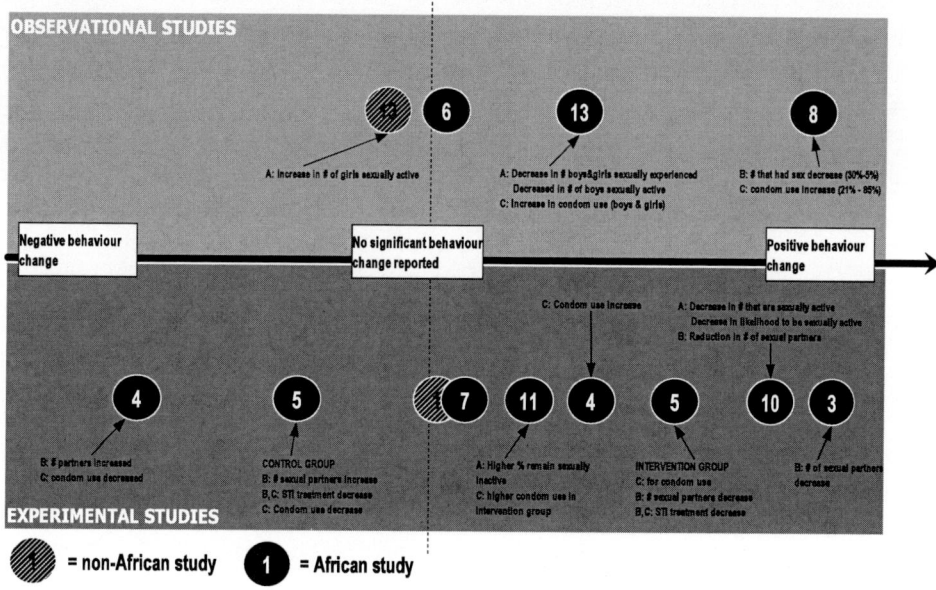

Figure 24: Scattergram noting type of study design and type of behaviour change reported, for all studies where behaviour change was measured
Key:
Aplasca et al. (1992), School-based AIDS prevention program; Philippines
Caceres et al. (1990), Short STD/AIDS program on knowledge, attitudes, and intended behaviour, Peru
Fawole et al. (1996), School-based education program, Nigeria
Fitzgerald et al. (1996), Face-to-face sex education, Namibia
Harvey et al. (1993/94), Drama-based programmes/education, South Africa
Kinsman (1996/98), AIDS education program, Uganda
Klepp et al. (1992/93), School-based education, Tanzania
Makelele et al. (10/97;11/98;12/99), IE&C, Zambia
Re et al. (1995), Sexual education, Argentina
Shuey et al. (1994/96), primary school health and peer education program, Uganda
Stanton et al. (1996/97), School-based education, Namibia
Watts et al. (1999), Costing of school interventions on STI/HIV, Cameroon
Wedderburn et al. (1994 & 96), School-based education program, Jamaica

---

5 The Cochrane Non-randomised Studies Methods Group (NRSMG) was set up to make recommendations and write a set of guidelines about when and how to include non-randomised studies in systematic reviews of health care interventions
6 From: http://www.cochrane.dk/nrsmg/docs/chap3.rtf

CONCLUSIONS RELATING TO HIV EDUCATION AND HIV-RELATED BEHAVIOUR CHANGE

Several points arise from the scattergram analysis of the 13 behaviour change studies:

a) All 13 studies were grouped under the category of Behaviour Change and the sub-category of School Based Studies;
b) 10 of the 13 studies were African, while one (Peru,2) was focused on the cost analysis of an educational program manual for teachers and students, and does not warrant inclusion;
c) Of the 3 observational studies, the Zambian study (8) showed significant positive behaviour change with reduced numbers having sex and increased condom use. The Ugandan study (6) showed no significant behaviour change, while the Jamaican study (13) was confusingly split: It showed an increase in the number of sexually active girls (negative behaviour change) but a decrease in the number of sexually active boys and girls, and an increase in condom use (positive behaviour change). This is a good example of a small study that may confuse more than inform;
d) Of the experimental studies, 2 of these were firmly located in negative behaviour change territory: The worst of these, from Namibia (4), showed gratifying increases in knowledge but alarming increases in the number of sexual partners and a decrease in condom use; it provides evidence of increased negative behaviour in the intervention group compared to the control group. While this is a small study of 262 and 253 secondary school students respectively, it provides ammunition for those who have concerns about such interventions. In the second study, from South Africa (5), a drama intervention in 10 secondary schools, the control group and intervention groups split, with the former showing an increase in the reported number of sexual partners and decrease in condom use, while there was an encouraging decrease in the treatment of STIs;
e) 6 experimental studies were grouped on the positive behaviour side of the scattergram, plus intervention group from the South African study (5) who showed a decrease in the number of sexual partners, and increase in condom use and a decline in STI treatment. There was little difference between the intervention and control groups in the percentage of students who had initiated sexual activity before and after the interventions in this South African study however. The Philippine study (1) hovers on the cusp of no significant behaviour change: After implementation of the AIDS prevention program, statistically significant effects favouring the intervention group were observed in knowledge and attitudes toward people with AIDS, but there was no statistically significant overall effect on intended preventive behaviour (although the program appeared to delay the students' intended onset of sexual activity).
f) Of the other 5, three - the Tanzanian (7) and two Namibian (11 & 4) studies - showed marginal to fair positive behaviour change. In Tanzania, the difference between intervention and comparison sites was not statistically significant; in the first Namibian study (11) the number of students in the intervention group who remained sexually inactive after one year was more than double that of the control group and

condom use was up. In the second Namibian study (4) there was an increase in condom use from 7% to 22% and a decrease in HIV seroconversion rates;

g) The two final and most positive studies were those from Uganda (10) and Nigeria (3). In the former, there was a decrease in the number likely to be sexually active and were actually sexually active as well as a reduction in the number of sexual partners overall. And in Nigeria, the mean number of reported sexual partners among the experimental students decreased significantly while increasing among the controls; and a higher proportion of students in the experimental than in the control group reported that they used condoms during their last sexual exposure.

While the dissimilarity of the studies militates against any clear analytical outcome and the evidence is mixed, on balance they confirm that there are quite strong and demonstrable links between education (in the widest sense) and positive behaviour change. It should be remembered that these studies - some of them quite small in scale - were carried out in the mid- to late-1990s and, as we have noted above, are somewhat 'dated' in respect of the evolving dynamics of the pandemic and the education response to it.

Yet, it is clear from the meta-analysis that many of the studies have yielded positive behaviour change at the individual level: The real challenge lies in how to enable these changes to filter through to the population level, where it will impact on HIV incidence rates.

TYPES OF COMMUNICATION CHANNELS AND TYPES OF MESSAGES

The final part of this chapter considers the types of communication channels and the types of messages that need to be in place for changes in HIV incidence to take place.

Low-Beer and Stoneburner (2000) classify channels of communication for the acquisition of HIV and AIDS knowledge into three groups:

- Mass – Radio, TV, newspapers, pamphlets etc;
- Institutional – Religious, school, health clinic etc;
- Personal – Friend/relative, community, workplace etc.

In a 2000 study of six high prevalence countries in East and Southern Africa, including Uganda, Kenya, Zambia, Malawi, Tanzania and Zimbabwe, Low-Beer and Stoneburner found that despite different HIV and behavioural trends, measures or awareness of AIDS were consistently high - over 90% - in all these countries. In order to establish the source of knowledge by communication channel, they classified these as vertical sources (media and institutional) and horizontal sources (social networks of friends and family). They found considerable differences by country in their analysis of communication channel effectiveness, but interestingly found that social networks of friends and family dominated in Uganda, in contrast to all the other countries studied, in which media and institutional sources dominated. Whether Uganda's dramatically declining prevalence rates are coincidental is a moot point, but it is interesting that the percentage of Ugandans (91.5% of men and 86.4% of women) who know someone with AIDS or who has died of AIDS is *substantially* higher than equivalent percentages in the other countries studied. We thus argue that behaviour change may require a trigger, perhaps a traumatic or life-changing experience, in order to 'operationalize' the latent messages absorbed through a variety of sources; in Uganda for example, the same study shows 19.7% of men 15 to 24 who knew someone with AIDS started using condoms, compared to 4.9% of condom-using men in the same age group who did not know someone with AIDS.

Low-Beer and Stoneburner (2002) state that there has been a distinctive behavioural response and decline in HIV prevalence in Uganda in the 1990s compared to other countries in Sub-Saharan Africa, but add that this coincides with a significant shift from mass and institutional to personal channels for AIDS communication – not seen to the same extent in other countries.

In terms of the sources of these comparatively high levels of awareness and knowledge, there is limited evidence that this emanates primarily from formal education in the classroom, although several studies cited the wider school community (including teachers and peers) as an important source of information. Chapter 6 of the South African National Survey of 15 to 24 year olds (Pettitfor, et al 2004) cites 18% of respondents talking to teachers and classmates in the 'classroom' about HIV and AIDS, while 32% said they had learned the most about HIV and AIDS from these sources. In fact, the research suggests unsurprisingly that knowledge and risk-reducing skills are acquired from a complex network of formal and informal sources, including but not limited to the education system. What does appear to hold true is that the cognitive and literacy skills required to make informed choices in respect of HIV and AIDS risk and behaviour change, are substantively based on levels of education and literacy. Thus the inherent value of formal education in this context is to enhance skills required to process the HIV and AIDS education on offer, and make sense of the proliferation of related messages from a variety of media sources. This suggests that access to, and retention in, the school system is indeed the uniquely important 'social vaccine' so often referred to by Kelly, Stoneburner and Low-Beer (2000, 2001).

But if education, and the education system, is only one of many influences on behaviour, what then are the others?

As the HIV and sexual behaviour study of young South Africans shows, the messages come from all angles and ricochet in the conscious and subconscious minds of everyone who sees and hears them. Absorption may be tempered by AIDS information 'fatigue' or indifferent messaging, but it is clear that the net effect is the very high levels of awareness reported in virtually every study available. Which bit worked may remain a mystery; since the 'market' for these messages comprises millions of individuals of variable age, whose receptivity and sensitivity to the content of the information may literally change from day to day.

The comparative importance of key information sources also varies considerably by country, as Bennell, Hyde and Swainson (2002) show; among secondary school students in Botswana, Malawi and Uganda, radio was the most widely-cited source in all three countries. Interestingly, teachers ranked second in both Botswana and Malawi for both genders, yet teachers only managed fifth-place among male students in Uganda and second among female students there, reinforcing the view that HIV and AIDS education in schools is not necessarily the principal reason for that country's declining prevalence. If we divide these sources into the mass, institutional and personal channels described above, we find that the mass channel is roughly twice as important as institutional channels and three to five times as important as personal channels. However, personal channels in Uganda are very much more important than those in Botswana and Malawi, confirming Low-Beer and Stoneburner's

(2001) findings on the comparative importance of these social networks in Uganda. The influence of churches and faith-based organizations as an information source is low, with the exception of Malawi, emphasizing again the importance of local context and influence.

Table 1: Key Information Sources on HIV and AIDS among Secondary Students in Botswana, Malawi and Uganda

Information source	Botswana		Malawi		Uganda	
	Female	Male	Female	Male	Female	Male
Radio	75	70	73	87	48	68
Print media	43	39	21	23	47	34
Posters	7	3	8	9	1	2
TV	26	37	9	11	34	29
Parents	27	24	20	18	44	29
Medical personnel	42	47	3	0	27	40
Friends	8	12	19	10	29	21
Teachers	46	48	50	50	33	45
Relatives	1	6	8	4	6	3
Church	9	5	24	14	8	11
Other	0	0	0	0	1	2

Source: Bennell, Hyde and Swainson (2002). Synthesis of the Findings and Recommendations of Three Country Studies

Can we deconstruct this complex equation and say that media and institutional sources influence behaviour change more than social networks and formative experiences, or that HIV and AIDS education in schools works in isolation from information gleaned from newspapers or roadside billboards? Certainly not; but we can say with surety that all these channels converge and contribute to the internal decision support system upon which every young person must ultimately rely. After all, as the South African survey of the sexual behaviour of almost 12 000 young people shows (Pettifor et al., 2004), the most commonly cited source of HIV and AIDS knowledge was school (32% of respondents). The caveat is that in this case 'school' was defined as a source including teachers, classmates, the classroom and the school – in other words, a vertical and horizontal mix of institutional and personal channels.

But can we say that schools have a *unique* role in HIV and AIDS education?

The answer, we would argue, is almost certainly yes, inasmuch as it is the school, assuming some acceptable degree of access, retention and quality, which will provide the cognitive and processing skills to facilitate the use of the information available, from whatever source.

Given the complexity of the media, what of the message? As much as we would like to report the success of curricular design and cite best practice, there is little information available to provide this level of detail. A three-country comparative study on Botswana, Malawi and Uganda (Bennell, Hyde and Swainson, 2002) notes that the formal curriculum on HIV and AIDS has a number of common weaknesses: While the primary curriculum in Botswana with respect to HIV and AIDS is adequate, there are still important concepts or facts missing. These include the active promotion of abstinence (or delay of sexual initiation) and the life skills that will help children to avoid sex if they want to. There is also relatively little systematic coverage of the emotional changes that occur during puberty and adolescence, for example. In Malawi, the study found that HIV and AIDS are infused into carrier subjects, such as Health and Science Education, while in secondary schools the main carrier subject is biology, and HIV and AIDS topics are only covered under the topic 'sexually transmitted diseases'.

However the study notes that in 1997, the Ministry of Education, Science and Technology (MoEST) in Malawi also began to develop Life Skills Education (LSE) as part of youth reproductive health, although this was only introduced into primary schools in early 2000. LSE was designed as a stand-alone subject for one hour a week but was initially only offered in Standard 4, with teaching and learning materials for Standards 5 to 8 in development for introduction from 2002. And while there has been a long-standing life skills project in Uganda, life skills *per se* have not yet been fully integrated into primary education. A new primary education curriculum was introduced during 2000 in which Integrated Science has been organised into eight themes, three of which (Human Health, the Human Body, Community-Population and Family Life) are relevant to HIV and AIDS education. However, the coverage of HIV and AIDS is surprisingly sparse; it is first mentioned under the Human Health theme in the second term of Primary 7 (P7) – in other words, shortly before the student leaves primary school.

This last statement is intriguing in that it appears to suggest that whatever may have motivated behaviour change in Uganda – and there is firm evidence of significant changes in sexual behaviour, especially among young people (Asiimwe-Okiror et al, 1997) – it may not be directly attributable to education in school as the comparative three-country table below suggests. However, we need to underscore two important contextualizing facts: First, the populations showing such change as there was, school attendance during years when education quality was very poor (as it still is, in many cases) and, second, this school attendance occurred at a time when there was almost no HIV education whatsoever, either in principle or in practice. We contend that these facts in combination confirm the positive impact of education and the educative process within a school system.

Table 2: Teaching of HIV and AIDS topics at secondary schools: percentage in agreement

Country	STUDENTS Topics on HIV and AIDS are well taught			TEACHERS - Teachers are confident teaching about HIV and AIDS topics		
	Female	Male	All	Female	Male	All
Botswana	42	46	44	30	29	29
Malawi	41	30	35	33	9	17
Uganda	23	24	24	14	28	22

Source: Bennell, Hyde and Swainson (2002)

CONCLUSIONS

On balance, this body of evidence confirms that clear links exist between HIV and AIDS education, and levels of awareness and knowledge about HIV and AIDS and associated high-risk behaviour. We believe it also shows that the inherent value of formal education in this context is to enhance skills required to process the HIV and AIDS education on offer, and make sense of the proliferation of related messages from a variety of media sources. In other words, it strongly suggests that the cognitive and literacy skills required to make informed choices in respect of HIV and AIDS risk and behaviour change, are substantively based on levels of education and literacy.

In this regard, the review of available evidence confirms the contention, as the Global Campaign for Education puts it, that the general cognitive and social gains from a basic education are the most important factor in protecting adolescents and young adults from infection. This reinforces the importance of the EFA and MDG goals, confirming that education lays the substratum that allows the internalisation of other messages about HIV and AIDS; as we note: *It is not what one learns that is important, but that one has learned.*

The second conclusion is that there may well be a watershed between the evidence of the 1990s and that of the new century: Many of the earlier studies are ambivalent about the reported outcomes, while the limited scale of much of the research before 2000 may limit its reliability. Indeed, one or two of these early studies show positive correlation between levels of education and HIV prevalence, and may have fostered some misapprehension about HIV and AIDS interventions in quarters that might wish these away.

By contrast, a large and fairly recent (2004) South African survey of 904 15, 11 to 24 year-olds (Pettifor et al., 2004) shows indisputable evidence of related behaviour change, a finding supported by the de Walque study from rural Uganda and the Global Campaign for Education report – all published in late 2003 and early 2004. This suggests, as we have already postulated, that this trend towards more evidence of increased knowledge – functional AIDS literacy – and linked behaviour change, is directly related to the improvement in the quality of education generally and HIV and AIDS education in particular over the last 10 years or so. In other words, the learning environment and the quality of the education, educators and messages have radically transformed in many cases, relative to the conditions that obtained when those sampled by earlier research were in school. Directly linked to this, the proliferation of media support – inside and outside the classroom – as well as the quality and consistency of messaging and the extent of its reach, have created an entirely different socio-educational environment from that of the last decade.

However, before making the assumption that these improvements will continue to grow exponentially, it would be wise to note an important and complicating change in the media environment: HIV and AIDS are inexorably slipping from the headlines everywhere, in the face of 'AIDS fatigue' and rapidly emerging and competitive issues and needs. Three examples impacting on the lives of people everywhere will make the point: Food insecurity, the energy crisis and global warming have captured the attention of populations around the world, and will make it harder still to focus attention on the impact of HIV and AIDS. This context will doubtless intrude into the education environment and will be exacerbated by another twenty-first century phenomenon: In many of the high HIV-prevalence countries under discussion in this chapter, ART has been rolled out to the point that personal experience of AIDS mortality may be reducing in and around the classroom. Taken together with the widely reported 'exaggeration' of AIDS mortality statistics by UNAIDS, these background issues may have the effect of reducing concern and awareness amongst young people, and may even reverse the behaviour-change dividends now in increasing evidence.

The third conclusion is that, even if there is still ambivalence in some quarters about the links between education and behaviour change (notwithstanding the increasing weight of evidence), we cannot postpone the use of education as a channel for raising awareness while we indulge ourselves in the need to demonstrate more clearly defined causal links than presently exist. We would argue that the evidence already to hand puts its value beyond question and we should get on with both increased support for education and its role, *and* improving the quality of the research that confirms this.

Fourth is the conclusion that studies of this type are problematic in the way in which they rely on *reported* behaviour change. We have no indication of what controls have been built in to monitor truthfulness or consistency of response and note the issue of response bias, in which the respondent may provide answers that they think the researcher would like or which show them in a better (less reprehensible?) light. We recognize that such issues complicate any self-reporting methodology, but note that it may be a greater problem in this research area than in others. In noting that the only sure way of finding out whether the programmes have had a beneficial impact is to test for HIV, we point to the success of the South African study which tested *all* respondents, with interesting results.

The fifth and linked conclusion is that studies that attempt to establish levels of behaviour change based on a single snapshot of attitude and activity are bound to provide limited results and insights. While we acknowledge that longitudinal and other studies designed to benchmark and track the sustainability of change over time are complex and expensive, we will continue to have a superficial understanding of response to education and other influences until we can resolve this. Again the South African study can be commended for its commitment to this research process and determination to find a reliable way to move forward from its benchmark – linking with similar studies, past and planned, in the same country.

In this regard, we suggest that it is imperative to establish a prioritized international research agenda to target issues of this kind, and so reduce the credibility gaps inherent in much of the research available. We have already noted the difficulties of the non-standardised way in which behaviour change has been measured (where it has been measured) in many of the studies, for example. We have noted too that in the literature that was studied, there are neither definitive guidelines for classification and definition, nor precise guidelines on how to measure behaviour change for school-based programmes. These issues point to the need to underpin what is now quite staggering international expenditure in the HIV and AIDS field, with research guidelines capable of ensuring a reliable and sustained research output competent to facilitate measurement and monitoring in this dynamic field. This suggests the need for an agenda or framework within which researchers can minimize expensive duplication and focus on the key issues in a comprehensive and comprehensible way.

Finally, it will be clear that HIV knowledge is an essential HIV prevention mechanism, but that its success depends on *who* we communicate to; *what* kind of message we use; *who* does the communicating; and *what* the education levels are of the person receiving the communication.

ANNEX 1. DETAILED PERCENTAGES THAT SHOWS INCREASES IN HIV KNOWLEDGE FOR HIGHER EDUCATED MEN AND WOMEN AROUND THE WORLD

		No Education		Primary		Secondary and Higher	
		% Male	% Female	% Male	% Female	% Male	% Female
3	Albania 2000	-	-	-	-	-	0
4	Armenia 2000	-	-	-	-	11	7
5	Azerbaijan 2000	-	-	-	1	-	3
6	Benin 2001	5	3	8	8	23	28
7	Bolivia 2000	-	12	-	6	-	33
8	Bolivia 2003	1	1	5	4	26	25
9	Botswana 2001	-	-	-	-	-	-
10	Burkina Faso 2003	16	6	29	21	59	59
11	Burundi 2000	-	16	-	23	-	41
12	Cambodia 2000	-	23	-	35	-	61
13	Cambodia 2005	17	22	31	39	58	72
14	Cameroon 2000	-	1	-	9	-	29
15	Cameroon 2004	9	5	16	13	47	42
16	Chad 2004	20	5	9	9	33	24
17	Congo 2005	10	12	20	16	46	35
18	Cote d'Ivoire 2000	-	6	-	15	-	32
19	Dominican Republic 1996	5	7	14	14	37	33
20	Dominican Republic 2000	-	6	-	21	-	42
21	Egypt 2005	-	1	-	3	-	10
22	Eritrea 2002	-	11	-	38	-	62
23	Ethiopia 2005	17	7	28	21	56	53
24	Gambia 2000	-	11	-	22	-	31
25	Ghana 2003	18	22	25	24	53	43
26	Guinea-Bissau 2000	-	3	-	12	-	31
27	Guyana 2000	-	10	-	21	-	35
28	Haiti 2000	6	7	17	12	43	34
29	Honduras 2006	-	13	-	23	-	46
30	Indonesia 2002/3	0	0	0	0	2	2
31	Jordan 2002	-	0	-	1	-	7
32	Kenya 2000	-	17	-	22	-	38
33	Kenya 2003	14	9	43	32	70	56
34	Lesotho 2000	-	9	-	14	-	28
35	Madagascar 2003/4	1	1	7	11	44	44
36	Malawi 2000	22	27	36	33	55	53
37	Malawi 2004	25	14	35	22	53	36
38	Mali 2001	6	5	13	13	34	34

		No Education		Primary		Secondary and Higher	
		% Male	% Female	% Male	% Female	% Male	% Female
39	Morocco 2003/4	-	2	-	8	-	23
40	Moldova 2000	-	-	-	14	-	20
41	Moldova 2005	-	-	-	-	-	-
42	Mongolia 2000	-	14	-	22	-	33
43	Mozambique 2003	19	9	28	20	58	54
44	Namibia 2000	10	10	25	20	50	39
45	Nepal 2006	9	6	19	16	53	48
46	Nicaragua 2001	-	7	-	14	-	38
47	Niger 2000	-	2	-	7	-	33
48	Nigeria 2003	10	13	16	14	35	27
49	Philippines 2003	2	2	11	10	22	16
50	Rwanda 2000	13	16	23	26	53	54
51	Rwanda 2005	45	42	57	55	73	73
52	Sao Tome 2000	-	4	-	6	-	16
53	Senegal 2000	-	7	-	18	-	40
54	Senegal 2005	12	11	21	24	53	56
55	Sierra Leone 2000	-	11	-	16	-	28
56	South Africa 1998	-	8	-	11	-	26
57	Tajikistan 2000	-	-	-	0	-	2
58	Tanzania 1996	9	11	28	28	54	57
59	Tanzania 1999	14	11	35	32	69	54
60	Tanzania 2004	19	29	45	50	61	70
61	Togo 2000	-	11	-	15	-	32
62	Trinidad & Tobago 2000	-	-	-	34	-	36
63	Turkmenistan 2000	-	0	-	7	-	5
64	Uganda 2000/1	20	12	30	24	63	54
65	Uganda 2004/5	15	12	29	26	54	51
66	Uzbekistan 2000	-	-	-	5	-	5
67	Uzbekistan 2002	6	3	8	6	20	20
68	Vietnam 2000	-	3	-	12	-	32
69	Vietnam 2004	9	4	23	18	59	47
70	Zambia 2000	-	-	-	-	-	-
71	Zambia 2001/2	17	13	22	23	55	54
72	Zambia 2003	-	-	-	-	-	-
73	Zimbabwe 2005/6	21	26	36	33	52	51

Chapter 4

AN ANALYSIS OF POPULATION INFORMATION EDUCATION AND COMMUNICATION (IEC) PROJECTS IN ANGLOPHONE AFRICA

Waithira Gikonyo and Isaac Obeng-Quaidoo*

This chapter is organized into three main sections. The first section deals with the theoretical thought and the inter-relationships between and among communication, population and development. Section two uses some basic data gathered from UNFPA Information, Education and Communication (IEC) project officers and managers to illustrate how population communication is utilized or under-utilized to aid and facilitate sustainable development. The third section provides extensive conclusion, discussion and specific recommendations for the appropriate use of population communication projects to support behavioural change and development.

Keywords: population communication, sustainable development, IE&C, Africa

INTRODUCTION

Communication, in the form of interpersonal, group, mass media, and machine-mediated exchange is often called upon to support and facilitate developments in social, cultural, economic and technical fields. Since the fields of development endeavours and approaches are numerous and varied, communication's facilitating functions also tend to be numerous, albeit quite similar generally. For instance, in the use of communication to support the "introduction" of a new drought resistance hybrid seedling or new female condom, the general approach would be informing people about the new seedling and condom and working with specific segmented communities to find out whether this new agricultural innovation or condom device is part of their long term farming or family planning needs. Working with a segmented group in a community (through the mass media, interpersonal communication, group discussions, drama or folklore, etc) to determine their own needs for or about a particular innovation in their own context is quite different from the old diffusion innovation paradigm which perceived people as passive recipients of innovation, but did not bring much behavioural change (Rogers, 1962, Servaes and Malikhao, 1994).

POPULATION COMMUNICATION AND DEVELOPMENT

Some population programmes and projects have either failed or been discontinued after the initial donors have left because implementers did not initially involve the beneficiaries; they did not listen to the community, respect their local ideas and opinions and mutual trust was not built from the start. Lack of genuine involvement of target groups lead to blurred objective setting for projects, fuzzy strategies, inconsequential project activities and lack of evaluation in impact terms. Projects with dismal performances should not be blamed on "communication" but the project's document formulators and the implementers who manage the projects. For, the assertion that communication can be a facilitating factor in sustainable development is no longer an assumption or a hypothesis to be tested since numerous data exist to attest to the applied use of the discipline for development. The application of development support communication (DSC) in the "Masagana 99" campaign during 1973 turned the Philippines (over a period of three years) "from a net rice importer to meet domestic requirements to becoming an exporter of its excess harvest" (Gary Coldevin and Teresa H. Stuart, 1993). UNICEFs information, education, communication (IEC) intervention in its GOBI strategy (growth monitoring, oral rehydration, breastfeeding and immunization) and the WHO'S EPI (expanded programme on immunization) have brought about significant reductions in levels of childhood mortality through immunization against six of the major infectious diseases prevalent in developing countries (Koenig, Fauveau, Wojtyniak, 1991).

In delineating the above interventions, we are essentially dealing with activities which bring about the inter-relationship between population and socio-economic and cultural development; population information which supports mother and child health and family planning (MCH/FP); and population information, education and communication (IEC) which support population and family awareness creation, motivation, attitude and behavioural changes in society.

PARTICIPATORY COMMUNICATION

The participatory communication approach/model of development is in tune with the current thinking in IEC where audiences are no longer perceived as amorphous, and ready to be injected with any kind of messages. Rather, they should be segmented; their opinions sought, planned with and allowed to be participants in all facets of a project if the audiences are going to be useful beneficiaries. The participatory model stresses certain basic points (Servaes and Malikhao, 1994:18).

1. The participatory model views ordinary people as the key agents of change, and for this reason it focuses on their aspirations and strengths. Local cultures are respected. Development is intended to liberate people and, in so doing, enable them to meet their basic needs.

2. The participatory model entails lifting up the spirits of a local community to take pride in its own culture, intellect and environment. Participatory development also aims to educate and stimulate people to be active in self and communal improvements, while maintaining a balanced ecology [for future generations]. Due to their local concentration, participatory programmes are, in fact, not easily implemented, nor are they neither highly predictable nor readily controlled.
3. In essence, participatory development involves the strengthening of democratic processes and institutions at the community level and the redistribution of power. For these reasons, it often threatens those whose position and/or very existence depends upon control over others. Reactions to such threats are sometimes overt, but most often are manifested as less visible, yet steady and continuous resistance to change in the status quo.

Four main kinds of participation have been identified (Uphoff, 1989). These are:

1. Participation in *decision-making* where individuals or communities take part in identifying problems, formulating alternatives and planning activities.
2. Participation in *implementation,* where individuals or groups partake in carrying out activities, for example, volunteering as Community Based Distributors (CBD) of contraceptives, etc, or managing and operating programmes with assistance from project officers and experts.
3. Participation in *benefits;* individually or as groups from their previous activities, they enjoy what thy have brought about in the community.
4. Participation in *evaluation;* finding out the effects or the impact of their ongoing activities and also at the end of their own activities.

Many project implementers do not consider these four interactive processes on their projects since project beneficiaries do not assume central role in their projects. Sometimes the lack of centrality of beneficiaries in partaking in all aspect of projects emanates as a result of foggy long and short term objectives, inappropriate strategies, Utopian and universal work plans, and especially, lack of audience analysis and segmentation of beneficiaries.

SECTION A: INTER-RELATIONSHIPS BETWEEN POPULATION AND SUSTAINABLE DEVELOPMENT

The fact that population and development variables are highly inter-related is no longer in question. "Such inter-relationships derive from the fact that the focus of development is on people, that development is by people and for people, and that demographic factors are both determinants and consequences of development" (Morah, 1990). For instance, demographic measures such as infant and child mortality rates, crude death rates, life expectancy, total fertility rate, etc., are treated as integral components of the indicators of development. Specifically, however, we perceive *economic and social development* as "a process of achieving sustainable increases in health, education, material consumption, and environmental protection—in short, improving standards of living over the long term" (The World Bank, 1994). The World Bank document also explains that development depends also on good governance, appropriate infrastructure and institutions, and better-trained people. Since we have outlined the inter-relationships between population and development and situated communication as performing a facilitating function to enable these two variables to operate, it is necessary to emphasize the sustainability of the whole interactive process.

Sustainable development "is typically taken to mean that the; well-being of the current generation should not be advanced at the expense of future generations. Within a generation, sustainability also implies particular concern for the most disadvantaged in society" (Tutu, 1994). The author follows Barbier *et al's* argument that the economic interpretation of sustainability should follow the following sequence:

a. In order to ensure that future generations are not disadvantaged by the present generation, actual compensation to future generations by the present generation is required
b. The form which this compensation must take is through transfer of capital assets
c. This capital compensation requires that no less than the current capital stock in terms of its value, be passed on to future generations (Maler, 1989; Warford and Pearce, 1980 as cited by K. Tutu, 1994).

The capital compensation consists of all man-made capital assets as well as environmental assets such as soil, minerals, biomass, etc. If a resource is going to be depleted, then the profits should be re-invested in other forms of capital (machinery, roads, research, development of democratic institutions and new hybrid seedlings, etc) so as to compensate for the decline in natural resources and safeguard future generations. If this is not done, then the particular development is not sustainable. If we take Ghana as an example of the sustainability issues we have discussed above, we see that there has been fair increases in the production and export of resources like timber, cocoa and gold due to the Structural Adjustment Programme (SAP). However, first, we observe that most of these commodities are exported without any processing, thus giving less employment to Ghanaians. Second, the "relative low earnings we are achieving compared to past years show that we are not taking care of the future generation as we did many years ago" (Tutu, 1994). Tutu concludes that "....Ghana is not over-exploiting its resources in a sustainable way. Part of the increased resources is done at the expense of the environment while both current and future generations are not getting the investment which could compensate for the depletion and mismanagement of the natural resources." A follow-up argument to the above theoretical arguments is that when population project implementers are not aware of the linkages between and among communication, population and sustainable development, then IEC support for development becomes haphazard, unfocused and eventually leads to project failure.

SECTION B: MICRO-LEVEL DATA AND SUSTAINABLE DEVELOPMENT

The first section has examined the inter-relationships between communication and sustainable development at a macro-level. This section looks at micro-level data and issues related to the implementation of population IEC projects and programmes in Anglophone Africa and examines their inter-face with sustainable development.

The Data

To this end, a short questionnaire was administered to participants attending a population IEC course mounted by the UNFPA regional training programme in Nairobi. The instrument consisted of questions related to project document formulation, audience research, materials development and dissemination and project evaluation. A few questions dealt with respondents perceptions of the sustainability of their projects and their understanding of various development concepts. The respondents consisted of 12 women and 17 men from sixteen countries of Anglophone Africa. The respondents were made up of programme managers, directors and project personnel in on-going IEC projects. In terms of educational background, nine respondents had a Masters degree, eleven had a first degree and the rest had diplomas in various social science fields.

The data collected represent over 29 population IEC projects in the Anglophone Africa region which are slightly less than ten percent of the IEC projects under implementation in the region. Therefore, while the number may appear small, it is fairly representative of the projects in the field.

Framework for the Analysis

While these data were collected from individuals, the unit of analysis is the project. One major problem in analysing project level data is the development of a framework that will allow for sufficient comparison without losing information. For the purpose of this paper, the Development Support Communication Process Model developed by Coldevin (1987) has been adopted. The model has been tested and found valuable in the formulation of development communication projects and programmes (Coldevin 1990; Coldevin and Stuart, 1993). The model has eleven steps. The first three steps, named "front end analysis," consist of needs assessments, development of project objectives and situation analysis. The three steps under this process are where the project idea originates. This involves an analysis of the community needs and the prioritization of needs as well as identification of how the problem can be addressed. The remaining eight steps, which they call support communication process, are the major focus for this paper. These are: target audience analysis, setting DSC objectives, message design and channel strategy, and production of materials including pre-testing, monitoring and impact evaluation. These steps relate to the core IEC process.

DATA ANALYSIS

Most projects come about via a project document which is subsequently used as a blueprint in the implementation. The respondents were asked who were involved in the drafting of their project documents. It is notable from the pie chart that project beneficiaries were involved in only 7.2 percent of the cases in the formulation of the project document.

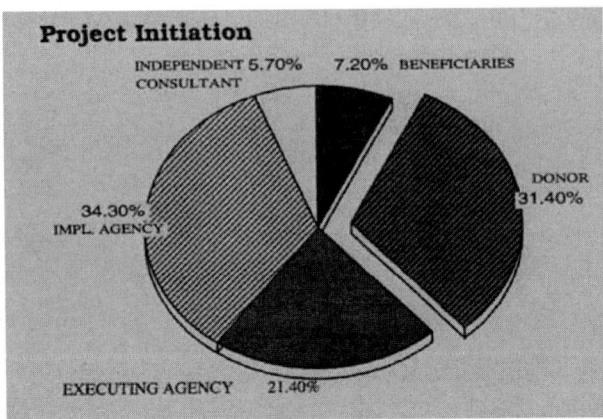

This clearly shows that while in theory the concept of participatory development has been endorsed, it is not happening in practice. The IEC projects remain by and large donor driven with the initiation of projects solely lying in the hands of the donor, executing and implementing agencies.

Project Beneficiaries

A major premise in this paper is that communication intervention will seldom be effective if directed to a mass audience. There is a wealth of research data that suggest that interventions are most effective when designed for carefully selected segments of the population (Grunig, 1989).

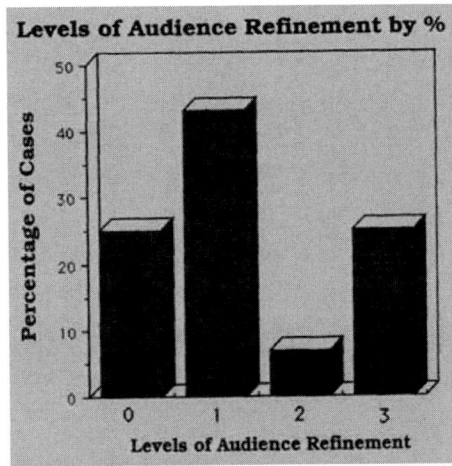

In this case, we asked the respondents to identify the beneficiaries of their projects. One way to analyze target audience segmentation is to look at the steps in the refinement of target audiences. For this purpose, a scale ranging from 0 (no segmentation) to 4 (well defined segment) was created and the stated project beneficiaries were graded accordingly.

The accompanying bar chart presents the findings. One quarter (25 percent) of the project dealt with general unrefined mass type audience, for example "citizens of country 'x' generally and the rural communities in general." Another relatively large number (42 percent) dealt with a one-step refined mass audience, for example "men and women of reproductive age." Only four projects had a two step level of segmentation, for example "women in the reproductive age." Another 25 percent had a three-step level of segmentation. An example of this is "youth in schools." None of the projects had reached a four-step level of segmentation.

Some examples of general, unrefined mass audiences are quoted below:

"Family members, including children, youth, parents, elderly, handicapped"
"All workers"
"The sick persons"
"Adults in rural communities"

Therefore, despite some attempts in audience segmentation, the beneficiaries remained large and unrefined for most of the projects. To further complicate the situation, some projects represented in this analysis had a multiple of these amorphous audiences as their target. Lack of proper targeting and segmentation works against sustainability of projects in two major ways; For one, the involvement of beneficiaries in project implementation becomes an elusive ideal and one that is not likely to be pursued. Secondly, while there are fewer research costs if an intervention is directed at a mass, the overall project costs become much greater. It is also the case, if we consider the personnel size within these projects, that the target audience is beyond the absorptive capacity of the projects, to implement any activities in any meaningful and effective way.

Sustainable development emphasizes the recognition and incorporation of the less disadvantaged in the society. The term "disadvantaged" is normally understood in material and economic terms. However, from an IEC perspective, there are segments in the society which are disadvantaged in terms of information and education and whose needs ought to be addressed. Among these are youth and men. In analyzing the data, we looked at the extent to which these groups are considered as beneficiaries. In the projects under analysis, only *one* project had men as a *discrete* target audience. The youth represent only 30 percent of the beneficiaries mentioned. None of the projects had youth as a discrete target audience but rather the youth tended to be subsumed as "part beneficiaries" out of a whole array of target groups.

Audience Analysis

Respondents were asked to indicate whether or not audience research has been undertaken in their projects and whether the research was undertaken at the inception of the projects. Only 34.5 percent of the projects had undertaken audience research, with 31 percent of them having undertaken the research at the inception of the project. The obvious conclusion is that about two thirds of the IEC projects in this analysis are implementing activities without much knowledge of the audience they hope to reach. For those who had undertaken some audience analysis, we also wanted to find out how the data from the audience research was utilized. The most surprising finding was the vagueness of the responses to this question.

The data from the 13 who responded to this question are presented below:

Table 1. Utilization of Research Data

Use of Research Data	No. of mentions
To formulate strategies	3
To develop materials	5
To implement intervention programs	4
Audience segmentation	1
Total	**13**

Some respondents attempted to qualify their answers and notable among them were: "Results do not seem to have been fedback into the project." "The data was found to be too academic, and we tried to do our own interviews to bridge the gap." While the above statements appear to be isolated, these are common phenomena in population IEC projects. Worthy of note is the limited use of research data. There are some major omissions in data use, for example, in monitoring evaluation and as feedback for modifying project strategies and activities. Considering the cost of research, the cost-effectiveness of poorly utilised research data is in question.

Materials Development

The respondents were asked whether their projects had developed IEC materials and whether these materials were pre-tested. In both instances they were asked whether the beneficiaries were involved.

Sixty nine percent of the projects under analysis had developed some IEC materials and 75 percent said the materials had been pre-tested. On the involvement of beneficiaries, only 40 percent of the projects had involved the project beneficiaries in the development of the materials. Of those who pre-tested the materials, 15 percent did not involve the beneficiaries in the process. What the data are unable to clearly reveal is the nature of the involvement. Not that the question was not asked, but the nature of the responses defy any logical analysis. A few examples will suffice to illustrate this:

"There has been a gap in this area"
"FGD/Seminars/Workshops"
"There is a committee called Inter-ministerial Technical Committee which discusses these issues"
"The materials were developed with some community opinion leaders" (Youth Project)
"The women were told that the Ministry is planning to develop IEC materials"

It appears reasonable to conclude that there has been no meaningful involvement of the beneficiaries in the process of message and materials development.

Dissemination Strategies

The respondents were asked to rank (with 1 being the most common) the media commonly used by their projects in disseminating information/messages. The table below presents the results:

Table 2. Rank Order of Communication Channel Use

Communication Channels	Rank			
	1	2	3	4
Radio	12	5	2	-
TV/Film	4	9	2	4
Print	4	7	10	5
Interpersonal	6	1	3	2
Drama/Folk media	-	1	1	1
Audio cassettes	-	-	1	-
Workshops	-	-	-	1
No response	3	6	10	16
	29	**29**	**29**	**29**

The results show a clear preference for mass media channels of communication. This faith and reliance upon mass media and the non-use of interpersonal channels might explain why in many countries there are high levels of awareness and low levels of practice of fertility management. It has been demonstrated that the mass media (as they are currently utilized) are effective in awareness creation while interpersonal and group media are more effective in changing behaviour. Notable and unused are the traditional communication channels. In trying to match the identified beneficiaries (unsegmented as they are) one has to wonder about the extent to which the selected media can be effective in reaching them.

In using mass media, the opportunities are limited, for the mass media are commonly urban based and spread while populations remain mostly dispersed and rural. It is also the case that the mass media are less "participatory friendly" in terms of desirable beneficiary involvement in both message development and dissemination.

Monitoring and Evaluation

The respondents were asked a series of questions related to the evaluation and assessment of their projects. These included project objectives, existence of a benchmark study and the inclusion of an impact assessment as a project activity. While the more logical point to start the analysis would be with project objectives, we leave that to the end as there is more to say which brings the point we are trying to make clearer and more emphatic.

Over half (59%) of the projects under analysis claim to possess a monitoring system mainly in the form of periodic progress reports and mid-term reviews. However, only one project reported to have a formative evaluation system in place. Some 15 percent of the respondents said they did not know whether their projects have a monitoring and evaluation system. Only 24 percent of the projects had undertaken a benchmark study. The timing of these so called "bench-mark" surveys are interesting. Only 4 projects (13 percent) undertook the study prior to the implementation. The others were undertaken at dubious times along the implementation phase:

"Mid-term"
"End of First Phase/Pilot Phase"
"Evaluation stage of the 2nd phase of project expansion"

The absurdity of the situation is that 38 percent of these projects have, as part of their projects' activities, an impact assessment exercise. How that can be accomplished in the absence of a bench-mark study is anybody's guess. However, the paradox is incomplete without a review of project objectives as stated by the respondents. In analysing the project objectives, the "SMART Criteria" were used. (SMART is an acronym for *specific, measurable, attainable, realistic and time-bound*) The main emphasis in the analysis was the specificity and measurability of the objectives.

None of the projects under analysis had a specific and measurable objective. In fact, none of the projects had a population IEC objective, that is, an objective related to a specific population variable. In short, given all the best intentions, the projects cannot be evaluated in impact terms. A few examples to illustrate the point:

'To provide information, education and counselling on adolescent reproductive health"
'To reduce the incidence of STD/AIDS among rural households"
"To motivate men towards accepting FP concepts"
'To bridge the gap between awareness and use"
'To create and sustain aggressive enlightenment for the rural communities on Pop/Family Life issues"
'To increase the welfare of rural populations"

Notable among the findings about "objectives" are:

a) The misplaced emphasis in terms of expected change. Over 50 percent of these "objectives" were to create awareness. It is clear from KAP studies that most countries in Anglophone Africa have awareness levels of 60 percent and over while few have attained a practice level of 20 percent. It would therefore appear reasonable that IEC activities should be geared towards motivating beneficiaries to practise rather than mere continued awareness creation.

b) The discrepancy in relationship between stated "objectives" and project beneficiaries. In over 75 percent of the cases, the project "objectives" were not related to the project beneficiaries. For example, a project with youth as beneficiaries might have a project objective - "to train 300 community educators."

c) The inadequate framing of objectives, for example: "to improve the KAP of farm household in Population and FLE" "to reduce the incidence of teenage pregnancy and sexual activity among youth 12-19 years"

d) The substitution of activities for objectives, for example: "to organize workshops" "to train staff in IEC/service delivery."

Perceptions of Sustainability of Projects

The respondents were asked whether they thought their projects would be sustainable in the absence of donor funds. A majority (87 percent) said their projects could not continue without donor funds. Only *two* projects were perceived as sustainable. This is an expected finding given that most of the projects are both donor-driven and do not involve the beneficiaries in crucial matters in the formulation and implementation.

CONCEPT COGNITION

(i) Participation

The respondents were further asked what they understood by the term "participation." Most respondents understood the concept of "participation" as *involvement of* project beneficiaries" (73 percent); a few did not appear to have any rudimentary idea about participation. One said, "Personally and physically engaged in any activity undertaken" while others defined it in more limited terms, "all project staff should have the participation in developing a project." Given that many of them relate the term to the involvement of the beneficiaries, then the question is why is this not happening in the projects as shown by the data.

(ii) Sustainable Development

The respondents were asked to explain what they understand by the term "sustainable development." The responses were as varied as the number of respondents. Thirty eight percent of the respondents related the concept to the sustainability of a project/programme. The following quotation captures this meaning: "It means that with the departure of the donor, the programme can be maintained by local people." Twenty seven percent of the respondents related the concept to the "here-and-now" situation as illustrated by this quotation: "Development based on utilization of available resources that continues to grow to certain levels and be maintained." Only one respondent defined the concept as is generally accepted: "Development that ensures that its resources are continually replenished and replaces and regenerates what it has expended.

(iii) Development that balances consumption and growth

The rest of the respondents did not appear to understand the concept as indicated by the following two responses: "Progress without failure," "Process which does not stop at a point, but continuing for the improvement of the beneficiaries." It is encouraging to note that most of the project implementers have an understanding of the concepts of participation and sustainability. The question then becomes, why are the projects designed without consideration of sustainability and implemented without reference to the beneficiaries?

SECTION C: DISCUSSION AND CONCLUSION

As the saying goes, if one goes out looking for problems, one rarely gets disappointed. However, this paper is based on a premise of lesson learning and the following discussion, although not entirely new, is one that needs a revisit. It is quite clear from this paper that there are problems at the macro and micro level in the implementation of sustainable development.

At the macro-level there is a need to better understand the relationship between populations, economic planning and the role communication needs to play. This paper recommends frequent and on-going dialogue between government, the media and the people, to ensure that present and future generations are taken care of. Recognition that sustainable development is not attainable without the participation of all is an important first step. A second step is the understanding that there are limitations to the problems that are solvable by communication, but that structural modifications can go a long way in further enhancing the role of communication in sustainable development.

At the micro-level, all is not well with the formulation and implementation of population IEC programmes and projects as the data so clearly indicate. For too long now, there has been a glaring gap between what is known in theory and what is practised, what is known to work and what is done. The data presented in this paper imply negligible involvement of beneficiaries of population IEC projects despite the demonstrated evidence that such involvement is indispensable if any meaningful impact is to be achieved and sustained. Looking at the data, the model that has been consistently applied to population IEC programming in the region is a "top-down", "we/they" model.

This paper recommends the application of the four main kinds of participation as outlined earlier, that is, in decision making, implementation, benefits and evaluation. This requires a major shift in processes involved in project formulation, implementation and evaluation. While participatory approaches have been endorsed by donor agencies and governments for almost two decades, the will has not been forthcoming and the way is still illusive in any demonstrable and practical form.

The failure of IEC projects is normally attributed to the project implementers, and particularly their lack of knowledge and skills. This paper argues that the project staff is only part of the "problem" and indeed all the actors (with an exception of the beneficiaries) have a share in the blame. What is also strange is that the project implementers have little responsibility in taking decisions on project strategies and activities yet they carry the blame for failure. Emphasis should not be placed on apportioning blame but instead on looking closely at the whole process of project formulation and implementation with a view to providing a remedy.

Participatory approaches call for "a learning process approach" to project formulation in which tentative plans are made and reviewed and feasibility studies and arrangements revised in light of situational experience, based on the assumption that neither ends nor means can be fully known in advance. This process implies team work among the donors, implementers and beneficiaries, as they are all stake-holders in the process. One major advantage of this approach is that it creates difficulties for any attempt to ignore the beneficiaries. In addition, it provides information on *what* works and just as important, *why*. This is one aspect of population IEC programming where little data exists.

The common practice in project document formulation does not allow the participation of the beneficiaries. All too often, any understanding of the audience, in the form of audience analysis, is provided for as part of project implementation rather than as a pre-project activity that would lead to viable strategies and activities with the beneficiaries themselves. To further compound the problem, project documents are perceived as blueprints (cannot be easily modified) by the donors and the implementers. It is therefore not surprising that data from audience analysis is often not utilized and are seen to be of limited value. An example from one participant to the training programme is worth noting and well illustrates this difficulty. In this case, the project document called for audience analysis at the initial stage of the project, but the document contained pre-conceived strategies and activities with their corresponding budget. The audience analysis data indicated the need for different strategies, activities and, accordingly, a change in budget. The project was put on "hold" for some time awaiting the usual mid-term review.

While initial audience research is now commonplace as a means of concretizing or changing the many possibilities outlined in a project document, allowance for the input of the data into the implementation of the project is often not made and lessons learned are often lost. In addition, audience research is static, in that when it is undertaken, it is done once. Most projects do not have formative research as a continuous learning activity. It is not unusual to find project strategies that are based on stale data. The irony of the situation is that it is the people who are in the business of facilitating change who fail to acknowledge that circumstances do indeed change.

This paper recommends the need for a long pre-project phase in which audience analysis can be undertaken and activities piloted. It also recommends project documents that are flexible, with a stepwise development of activities in a progressive manner, and which would allow input of lessons learned. This would further require continuous assessments of all activities undertaken, and a recognition that strategies and activities adopted by a project document are but a few possibilities among a myriad of other (and changing) possibilities in problem solution.

The approach would also require the empowerment of project implementers to modify project strategies and activities. The assumption here is that the project personnel possesses the necessary knowledge and skills to do so. While much needs to be done in training of project staff, there now exists in some countries and projects a core of trained people who can immediately be so empowered. The trained staffs need an encouraging and nurturing environment in which to put their knowledge and skills into practice.

There are some implications for training, both at institutions of higher learning or as an in-service activity. Much of the communication training at African universities tends to be academic and theoretical. There are no real attempts to train in day-to-day application of theories into practice, as is required to effectively implement an IEC programme or project. There is need, therefore, to orient the curriculum so as to produce graduates who not only know, but can also do. Conversely, IEC project personnel need to know the theories so that they understand what should be done and how it should be done. Such an approach in capacity building for IEC operations would be a beginning in the courtship between theory and practice.

In: Contemporary Discourses on IE & C Theory and Practice ISBN: 978-1-60962-360-3
Editor: Theophilus K. Gokah © 2009 Nova Science Publishers, Inc.

Chapter 5

THEORY AND PRACTICE OF IE & C: A CASE OF THE MEDIA AND HIV/AIDS

Alex Buertey Puplampu

In this chapter, the author argues that the notion of the media priding itself as frequently providing information about health issues is not a universal truth. What is needed is an action oriented media that can facilitate sustainable information and education of people on the HIV/AIDS scourge aimed at reducing infection rates or eliminating it altogether through behaviour change. In a mass society, our whole lives are mediated. The mass media have supported dominant ideologies including the ways in which healthcare systems, meanings and healthcare work are organized. The mass media have given some degree of attention to discourses surrounding the HIV/AIDS crisis. This analysis examines how the media uses Information and Communications to educate the public about HIV/AIDS pandemic through the medium of radio. On the basis of a Ghanaian commercial radio prime time news bulletins, it discusses: (a) the extent of HIV/AIDS representation, (b) the dynamics of representing HIV/AIDS issues across time and (c) the agenda of issues that are produced as a result of expansions in programmes to accommodate more closely the dynamics of the disease.

Keywords: HIV/AIDS, Sociology of News, News Bulletin, News Framing, Radio, Ghana

INTRODUCTION

The media have been key players in promoting the fight against HIV/AIDS. Many media organisations have risen to the challenge of promoting awareness of the disease by educating their viewers, readers and listeners about the facts of HIV/AIDS and how to curb it. No doubt the media is viewed by some as the most important social institution which influence people's knowledge, perceptions and actions (Sandberg, 2005). It provides information to people which define and warn them for instance, about risk (ibid). This being said, it is the main source of scientific and medical information for lay people and the general public. The 21st Century could be said to have become 'mediated' whereby the media arguably have become a major player in HIV/AIDS information dissemination irrespective of geographical location; in deed, it plays an important role in the social construction of HIV/AIDS in the world. In the views of Airhihenbuwa & Obregon, (2000), the HIV/AIDS problem needs to be understood as a cultural phenomenon constructed largely by the media possibly because of its influence and reach. The mass media is said to have shown dominant support to ideologies including the ways in which healthcare systems, meanings and health care work are organized (see for instance, Altheide, 2002 and Cheek, 1997). Altheide (2002) in fact suggests that our whole lives are mediated in a mass society. What this means is that the media has the capability to inform and educate us in what I call our 'knowledge-ability base' about social or health issues which HIV/AIDS is a typical example, because of its trickle down effects.

Parallel to the above thinking is Cottle's (2003: 3) view that the field of journalism 'occupies a pivotal site in the communication of conflicts and in relation to the surrounding voices that vie and contend for media influence, representation and participation'. Cottle is however not alone in this thinking. For instance, Schudson (2000: 175) describes journalism as an 'important constitutive element of public life'. In relation to Schudson's description, Singhal & Rogers, (1999) and Singhal, Cody, Rogers & Sabido (2004) indicate that over the last two decades, mass media-based entertainment-education campaigns have been used effectively to influence awareness, knowledge, attitudes, and practices regarding various public health issues. The mass media could be described as having become central in the life of citizens. For instance, as citizen's knowledge of health keeps growing, it's imperative to make the public more knowledgeable about health issues of which HIV/AIDS is one. In this regards, the news media are vital in mediating between specialised forums for the dissemination of medical and public health research and policy to the public. What this means is that, it is through the news media that specialised knowledge such as messages about HIV/AIDS can be brought to the awareness of the public and made accessible to them. Ryfe (2006: 69) supports this position by asserting that 'a major goal of news is to inform readers'. It is therefore, not surprising that for instance, mass media messages about HIV/AIDS prevention have been associated with correct conceptions about the mode of HIV transmission (Vaughan et al., 2000). An evaluation of a South African television drama series Tsha-Tsha indicates that exposure to the first 26 episodes of the series had a positive impact on audience members attitudes toward people living with HIV/AIDS, and on their adoption of HIV-prevention behaviours (CADRE, 2005).

It should be acknowledged that the mass media have been the main source of disseminating HIV/AIDS messages since the first clinical evidence of the disease was reported in 1981. Myhre and Flora (2000: 29) observed that 'the mass media have been the primary method for disseminating human immuno-deficiency virus (HIV) and acquired immune deficiency syndrome (AIDS) prevention messages worldwide'. Ryfe (2006: 60) says 'journalism serves as a model ''of'' reality by expressing the structure of public life in another medium; the news'. Similarly, Patterson's (2000) contention that journalism encompasses the provision of information about public affairs through its watch-dog role is worth considering. However, due to complexities involved in the selection of news stories based on ideology, news values, media organisational structures and events, certain 'issues' or stories are under represented. The media therefore, set negligible agenda on those issues or stories which could not lead to adequate education and sustained awareness creation. Issues about risk of which HIV/AIDS is an example, are rarely put on the news agenda possibly because of the perceived 'event-oriented' nature of news rather than being 'issue-oriented' (see Tuchman, 1978; Traquina, 2004) - an argument which is contestable and which we will return to later. In situations where HIV/AIDS issues are put in the public sphere, media frames are used to construct the HIV/AIDS news (see Souza, 2007). Health communications is adopted as a strategy to increase and provide knowledge and understanding on health-related issues in order to improve the health status of an intended audience within a geographical location where there might be barriers in communicating about health issues. What this statement presupposes is that there are difficulties with regards to disseminating certain information concerning health issues through the media. Hence, health communications is adapted as a specific strategy [by the media/health promoters] to communicate or comment on issues regarding health of which HIV/AIDS is a case in point. It is now imperative perhaps to elaborate on some aspects of the sociological perspective of news which could assist us assess IE&C practices through the media.

CONTEXT

Ideas about broadcasting for national development and the potential role of the media in social transformation f Ghana started as far back in 1935. The Empire Service, as it was then called, and later changed to station ZOY was established by the then British Colonial Government under Governor Sir Arnold Hodson (Alhassan, 2005). There are ample studies pointing to the role of radio in the development process of Ghana (see for example Alhassan, 2005; Abbey-Mensah, 2001; Kugblenu, 1974). From table 1, it is acknowledge that there are about 141 radio stations throughout the country, hence, other private radio stations news bulletins could have be used for this study. Arguably, they were not selected because they did not fit the selection criteria of this study which is 'independence' and coverage. JoyFM was thus chosen as a case. This station was purposively selected because it enables us to select a specific commercial radio station [first commercial radio station] that cuts across the country through its flagship mid-day news bulletins. Its mid-day (12 noon) news bulletins was chosen for this study because (a) it is the flagship of the station (b) it is one of the 'most popular' established private/commercial radio stations in Ghana with a 'nationwide' broadcast through its mid-day news which is hooked on by its sister stations across the country. The reason is to establish the percentage of stories which were broadcast about HIV/AIDS to ascertain whether it is enough to enhance effective IE&C towards HIV/AIDS curtailment and possible prevention, a process which can partly be understood within sociology of news.

The sociology of news is about social interactions and activities that consciously or unconsciously impacts on journalists in writing news stories for wider public dissemination. News production involves more than writing. It is about social hierarchical structures that have been institutionalised or normalised and which inform the production of news by journalists or media practitioners. According to Zelizer (2004: 47) the 'reigning function of sociological inquiry has been to provide a wide-ranging research setting that targets people and the interactions among them, the organisations and the institutions in which they reside, and the structures by which their lives proceed'. Sociological inquiry emerged as a significant means for the study of journalism around the world.

Table 1. Regional Distribution of Radio Stations in Ghana

Region	Number of FM stations	
	FM licences issued	On air
Greater Accra	26	20
Ashanti	32	14
Western	22	9
Central	11	8
Eastern	12	8
Brong Ahafo	16	14
Upper West	4	3
Upper East	2	2
Volta	6	1
Northern	10	5
	141	84

According to Zelizer (2004: 51) sociology offers 'a valuable way of tracking journalist simultaneous existence in occupations, organisations, professional communities, and institutional settings, revealing how they are constrained and empowered by their interactions with others'. She continues to explain that early sociological inquiry of journalism provided a broad framework through which journalism is considered as a set of interactions and patterned behaviours (ibid). Hence, there is the need to consider both journalists and social responses about what they write or broadcast. This will enables us to understand the extent of HIV/AIDS representation, explore the dynamics of representing HIV/AIDS across time and space and explore the agenda of HIV/AIDS issues produced by radio. Three main concepts revolving around the sociology of news are discussed below beginning with *media framing*, *news access and sources* as well as the *ideology of journalism*.

MEDIA FRAMING

Framing occurs when journalists:

'selects some aspects of perceived reality and make [it] more salient in a communicating text, in such a way as to promote a particular problem definition, casual interpretation, moral evaluation, and/or treatment recommendation for the item described'.(Entman, 1993: 52)

What this means is that, the entire aspect of an issue is never made nor deemed important than a fraction of it which arguably leads to misunderstanding and representation. A Media frame is a concept that communication scholars and sociologists often engage with when talking about the media construction of reality (Souza, 2007: 258). Media frames emerge within specific cultural contexts (ibid). As a result, for instance to make stories intelligible, journalists draw on pre-existing cultural frames to construct their narratives (Iyengar, 1991). Giltin (1980: 9) is of the view that media frames are 'largely unspoken and unacknowledged, organise the world both for journalists who report it and, some important degree, for us who rely on their reports'. Frames often compete with each other for legitimacy, marginalising certain viewpoints in their process (Souza, 2007: 258). Adding to this debate, Gamson, Croteau, Hoynes, & Sasson, (1992) assert that the news media in particular are an arena in which symbolic contests are carried out over the construction of reality and the public's understanding of problems are often shaped by politics. The competition does not occur only among broad issues but also among viewpoints on any single issue (Hilgartner & Bosk, 1998). This is because different ways of framing the issues vie to be accepted as authoritative, hence, journalists and policymakers decide not only on which problems will occupy their respective agendas, but how to define those problems (see Souza, 2007). It is therefore important to acknowledge and explore media frames in a health context i.e. HIV/AIDS because the incomplete coverage of certain health topics and the misrepresentation of reporting the prevalence of health threats can have negative implications for health beliefs and behaviours (Kline, 2003). Journalistic framing happens in the media production phase and conceived as the process in which journalists work under the influence of cultural principles and cognitive schemata to endow meaning to events they cover as news (D'Angelo, 2002; Wicks, 2005). In editorial terms, framing includes the 'angle' that journalists adopt in their approach to writing stories about emerging broad issues. These include the particular perspective of the issue that is selected and highlighted for broadcast or publication. I acknowledge that Gamson and Modigliani's (1989) definition of frames as the internal structure in media discourses and the central organising idea for making sense of events is relevant here. This is because it assists us to explore and explain the reasons behind the over or under representation of HIV/AIDS stories in news bulletins through IE&C.

NEWS ACCESS AND SOURCES

Research in journalism has shown that not all events receive similar coverage. Events and individuals have to compete for a limited space in the media; and those that do not get covered, are filtered through editorial gatekeepers. This is because personality or source of event, arguably positively and negatively, affects the level of coverage given to a particular event. My experience as a broadcast reporter on the beat revealed that, some events receive massive publicity because of the personalities who are invited to grace the occasion. Schlesinger (1978) similarly mentions that sources are not equal and their access to journalists is not distributed equally. What this means is that sources are prioritised according to who the media organisation deems as powerful in terms of providing credible information. Fishman (1980: 51) in his study at a California newspaper discovered that journalists are used to bureaucratic organisations of government and that 'the world is bureaucratically organised for journalists'. He explains that the bureaucracy enables journalists to continuously detect events. The question then is how do editors determine the propensity of HIV/AIDS events and consequently assign reporters to give coverage to those events? Also, what criteria do they adapt to in deciding who gets on the news, and who speaks first?

In one discourse on the relationship between journalists and their sources, Traquina (2004: 102) (also Sigal, 1973) confirms that official sources are the dominant sources in the production of news. That study revealed that American and foreign government officials accounted for 75 percent of all news sources and 60 percent of news stories originated through routine, source-controlled channels. Media practitioner's dependence on elite or powerful sources has been an enduring theme of the sociology-of-news making studies (Tuchman, 1978). Cottle observes that:

> 'Questions of media source involvement raise fundamental concerns about who is delegated to speak or pronounce on social affairs and wider conflicts, of how exactly this communicative entitlement is conducted, and by whom it has been authorised' (Cottle, 2003: 5).

What this means is that there are fundamental concerns as to who should be given the voice to speak or make pronouncement on any particular issue. To digress a little, one will have thought that the media will eschew this 'undemocratic tendency' in their work by not proclaiming to know everything and therefore give access to those authorities who claim to know and thereby the media effectively becomes a mouthpiece of others. As far as the issue of HIV/AIDS is concerned, this 'bureaucratic bias' will not lead to the fight against the HIV/AIDS pandemic in the world because the 'true people afflicted' with the disease are seldom given a voice to speak. I believe it is important to give the opportunity to the people who are afflicted and affected to tell their own stories so that listeners, viewers and readers will realise the danger and magnitude of the disease.

In their analysis of the dominance of official sources in news production, Hall et al (1978: 58) note that the daily struggle to negotiate the professional demands of news-making produces a 'systematically structured over-accessing to the media of those in powerful and privileged institutional positions'. Hall and his colleagues therefore indicate that the news media reproduce the voices of the powerful who become the 'primary definers' of events. News coverage of stories or issues therefore privilege the interpretations of the powerful, particularly those that are articulating the interest of capital (Manning 2001: 138). Manning claims the situation or circumstances are not through conspiracy theory or conscious design. This scholar, however, explains is because the hierarchy of credibility perceived by journalists reflects the structure of power in society. What is Manning alluding to? Journalists are supposed to serve the interest of everyone in a society because of the nature of their work. This I believe should be executed through the provision of Information, Education and Communications (IE&C) about a particular or peculiar issue to all and sundry. Therefore, if they decide to give privilege to people that they deemed to be more credible to make pronouncement or speak on issues which they are not well vest in, they will not be doing the society in which they operate any good. Communicating about health of which, HIV/AIDS is a case in point should go beyond this narrow perception if the fight against HIV/AIDS is to be achieved. This is because the high level of the representation of HIV/AIDS stories through IE&C will have a tremendous effect on the curtailment and probably the fight against the disease. Thus, the more HIV/AIDS issues are represented by the media through IE&C, the more people will be aware about the disease and invariably have a behavioural change.

Traquina's (2004: 111) study on *Theory consolidation in the study of journalism* also affirms that one of the major findings of the sociology of journalism is the dominant role of official sources. That study was based on comparative analysis of news coverage of HIV/AIDS issue in four countries (Portugal, United States of America, Spain and Brazil). It revealed that nearly half of the news coverage in all newspapers sampled for the study featured official sources. Traquina (2004) drawing inspiration from Cook (1991) contends that 'only when authoritative sources- most often government officials and established scientists- created a news event that served as news peg for reporters would the epidemic become newsworthy'. We tested these claims by examining how HIV/AIDS news is prioritised by the media in Ghana in terms of 'who is news' in the coverage of HIV/AIDS and the news angles which are adopted by media practitioners.

JOURNALISM IDEOLOGY

A set of beliefs, values, and opinions shape the way journalists think, act, and understands their profession. In line with this, journalists are classified as discharging their duties within a cultural setting in the newsroom and influenced only by the norms and the political economy governing their news organisations. According to Deuze (2005: 444) the 20th century history of (the professionalisation of) journalism can be typified by the consolidation of a consensual occupational ideology among journalists in the world. Deuze explains that conceptualising journalism as an ideology (rather than, e.g. other options offered in the literature such as a profession, an industry, a literary genre, a culture or a complex social system) primarily means understanding journalism in a manner in which journalists give meaning to their news work. Schudson (2001) is of the view that occupational ideology of journalism is culture that constitutes news judgment rooted deeply in the communicator's consciousness. In other words what this means is that there are cultural knowledge that judge and influences what should be regarded and considered by journalists or communicators as news. As a result of this, what kind of knowledge and influence enhances the selection of HIV/AIDS news stories? Schudson is not the only one with this perception. Stevenson (1995) and Van Ginneken (1997) also share Schudson's opinion. Journalists in the discharge of their work feel they have values that legitimise and give them credibility in constructing news. Journalists idealise themselves when disseminating messages to citizens in terms of 'doing it for the public' (Deuze 2005).

So far, we have attempted to discuss the notion of sociology of news by deliberating on, *media framing, news access and sources* as well as the *ideology of journalism*. It should be noted that journalists through the use of various forms of mass communications channels are affecting the society in which they live credibly with the information that they disseminate to their intended audience within their geographical areas. Therefore, the media has become the platform through which interactions between the sender/encoder (journalists) and receiver/decoder (citizens/publics) takes place on issues of concern. Much as the media have served or are serving as a platform for the provision of information which invariably is meant to enhance education and further becomes an issue to be deliberated upon or communicated about within the public sphere, there is still a lot to be done with regards to the HIV/AIDS menace.

RESEARCHES INTO HIV/AIDS

AIDS is arguably the most studied epidemic in history (Cochrane, 2000: 205). There have been numerous narratives about the history of the disease (Fee & Fox, 1988). Some of these studies include epidemiological and sociological analyses (Rushing, 1995), specialised biomedical texts (Schoub, 1994), and global projections of the impact of the disease (Mann and Tarantola, 1996). Other aspects of the disease which have been explored are the ideological content of prevention and education discourse as well as the cultural ramification of the disease (see Patton, 1985, 1990, 1994; Bersani, 1988; and Weeks, 1991). There have also been studies conducted about the disease with regards to the mass media. My study focuses on this aspect of HIV/AIDS exploration and is interested in finding out how the media quantitatively and qualitatively represents HIV/AIDS stories in radio news bulletins in Ghana. I am aware of some existing studies which have already been carried out in relation to the HIV/AIDS and the mass media. Clarke's (2006) studies which examined the portrayal of HIV/AIDS in high circulating mass print media magazines during 1991, 1996 and 2001 with regards to the presence of heterosexist and homophobic discourses is one of such studies. Hoffman-Goetz et al (2005) also undertook a study which described the portrayal of HIV/AIDS risk factors and the perceptions of risk as framed in the Canadian Aboriginal newspapers relative to the established risk factors for the disease. Souza (2007) similarly explored media frames adopted/used by Indian newspapers to make sense of the HIV/AIDS problem. In addition, Sood et al (2006) investigated the impact of a mass media entertainment-education campaign on HIV/AIDS in three low HIV-prevalence states in north India. Within the Ghanaian context, Benefo (2004) examined the relationship between mass media exposure and knowledge of HIV/AIDS prevention and behavioural response. Benefo's (2004: 13) study discovered that:

> HIV/AIDS information in the mass media has done a great deal to teach Ghanaians about the disease. It has raised the awareness of the importance of condom use, partner fidelity and avoiding parental threats and made fidelity in sexual relations and condom use come to be seen as feasible and likely behavioural responses to the epidemic. Exposure to multiple mass media channels reinforces messages about safe sex and HIV/AIDS. However, the information has failed to raise awareness of the importance of abstinence and avoiding commercial sex as protective strategies and has had only limited impact on raising interest in avoiding commercial sexual activities, abstaining or delaying sexual activities.

According to Benefo, out of the three mass media considered for the study, radio was the most 'commonly mentioned as a major source of information'. He said it was 'a more significant source of accurate information about HIV/AIDS and a more powerful source of behaviour transformation than information propagated through television and print media' (ibid). Benefo (2004: 13) declares that:

> HIV/AIDS information conveyed through radio media reach as many people as information conveyed through interpersonal networks and are very effective in providing them with accurate knowledge of HIV/AIDS disease and instilling in them ideas about appropriate behavioural responses.

Even though it can clearly be deduced from Benefo's findings about the effectiveness of the media (radio) in providing information about the HIV/AIDS epidemic for public awareness and behavioural change, there are limitations in his studies about the media's dissemination of useful information as reported in his study. Benefo himself acknowledged that information conveyed through the medium of radio has not been effective in 'warning against the importance of avoiding prostitution and persuading Ghanaians about the role of abstinence and delayed sex as ways of preventing infection'.

Benefo's study did not inform us about the extent of HIV/AIDS representation as far as the medium of radio is concern. It also explicitly did not inform us about the dynamics of representing HIV/AIDS issues across time. We therefore, attempt to bridge the gaps in Benefo's study and contribute to the existing knowledge on HIV/AIDS and media representations by looking at how the media employ IE&C strategies in providing information about the HIV/AIDS disease. The mass media has indeed, been a major source of information about the HIV/AIDS epidemic. According to Muturi (2005: 78) in HIV/AIDS prevention for example, effective communication is an integral part of service delivery programmes. Muturi explains that effective communications in rural communities for instance, involves more than simply disseminating health messages using popular media. Indeed, communications empowers people with knowledge and understanding about particular health problems and in some cases arguably, spells out measures that are needed to be taken concerning the health problem. As a result, without education and communications, there will not be dissemination of information on an issue which will lead to the generation of knowledge and understanding about that particular issue [for example HIV/AIDS].

It is therefore appropriate that MacDonald (1998) indicate that communication is seen to be a central premise in health promotions. MacDonald however, does not explain what he means by the central premise in health promotion. This scholar deduces and proposes that MacDonald was referring to 'knowlegeability' on the subject or a particular health issue at stake. Therefore, the person who is communicating about any health related issue must have adequate knowledge about the topic. It is important to note that health communications scholars have been attempting to understand how individuals process information in relation to factors that contribute to appropriate behaviour change.

As a means of communicating to vast majority of people irrespective of their geographical location, the mass media i.e. television, radio, newspapers, internet among others offer an enormous potential to promote health (Whitehead, 2000: 812). This is because of the power to reach out to mass audiences. It is therefore commendable, arguably, that the mass media is seen within the new millennium as an appropriate means of influencing health-related behaviours.

The mass media frequently cover health related topics and are the leading source of information about important health issues like HIV/AIDS since its discovery hence, they are targeted by all and sundry whose objective is to influence the behaviour of the populace e.g. professional workers. What is more, everything around us is heavily influenced by mass media messages that are intended to 'inform, instruct, persuade, coerce, shock or delight'. According to Nandy and Nandy (1997) the mass media serve to update the public constantly on matters of health and health risk. They play an important role in individual and public health, disease prevention and environmental movements. Consequently, the media influence our lives and the way we live as well as serve as a major resource for promoting health. In their study on designing health communication, Byrne and Curtis (2000: 190) contest that research which focus on the impact of communication modality on the effectiveness of health warning or risk communication emerged in the 1990s. They explain that many health-related warnings involved the communication of new and complex facts, for example communicating details of newly discovered contagious disease of which HIV/AIDS is a case in point. We are aware that communication can indeed be used for the purpose of development. In health promotion for instance, communication is used to 'inform, educate, and persuade behaviour change while promoting healthy behaviours and lifestyles as in the case of HIV/AIDS' (Muturi 2005: 82). Muturi (2005) gave an example that in Kenya, reproductive health programs have used the mass media and other communication interventions to inform and educate the public about healthy sexual practices.

Lupton (1995) for her part claims that health promotion has mostly enjoyed a 'love/hate' relationship with the media. This claim brings two different variables to light. One being that the media makes health promotions their priority, thereby given it adequate coverage. The other could mean that the media do not see the need to cover health issues; therefore less priority is accorded to health issues at the expense of others for instance, political and economic stories. These variables are crucial and necessary because it enables us to understand the way HIV/AIDS issues are reported and represented in our chosen case. Perhaps, we need to justify the reason for choosing radio as a mass communication tool for HIV/AIDS awareness creation through IE&C.

THE MEDIUM OF RADIO

Radio continues to be one of the most popular mediums through which information is transmitted to catch the attention of people throughout the world. For instance, governments, HIV/AIDS pressure groups among others have employed radio as a 'powerful tool to achieve a broad range of goals'. According to Coll-Seck (1999):

> 'HIV/AIDS continues to be a subject of serious misconception, misunderstanding, ignorance and fear. There is an urgent and ongoing need to present facts about HIV clearly, unambiguously, to reduce the fear, stigma and discrimination associated with HIV, and to provide practical advice on how to minimise the risk of being infected and how to provide care and support to infected and affected people. Radio has a vital role to play in this educational and life-saving challenge'.

Radio is the first modern mass medium which created national crazes across America by teaching Americans new ways to talk and think as well as sold products that they never knew they needed (Lewis, 2004). According to Trautschold the world of radio broadcasting is an 'institution whose means and power of transmission of information has penetrated national frontiers...' (Trautschold, 2004). He indicated that, in Ghana, and particularly Africa in general, sound broadcasting offers one of the best means of educating, informing and entertaining people as well as activating them to national development (ibid, p.1). In IE&C activities, radio could be used to inform people and create awareness about an issue, motivate people and give additional credibility to 'multi-media communications HIV/AIDS campaigns on the ground'. It could also help to create a demand for services. The use of radio is therefore appropriate to provide information and raise awareness about the HIV/AIDS issues which will invariably bring about positive changes in behaviour and attitudes.

The next section presents a brief overview about the HIV/AIDS epidemic since it is the main variable adopted to assess IE&C practices through the media.

THE HIV/AIDS EPIDEMIC

It is a relatively new disease first diagnosed in the early 1980's when five young homosexual men were reported to the Atlanta Center for Disease Control to have been diagnosed with pneumocystic carinii (PCP) (Clarke, 2004). Because of its link to homosexual men, it was called the gay disease or the Gay Plague (Altman, 1986). The disease was further discovered among intravenous drug users, Haitian men and then haemophiliacs (Clarke, 2006: 317). It was also discovered in black women and children, particularly in Harlem (ibid). Now, the disease is prevalent among people around the globe whether heterosexual or homosexual. It should be noted that currently, the spread of the disease is faster among intravenous drug users and heterosexuals. More women are being diagnosed with the disease and in the developing countries for instance, the gender ratio of infection is 1:1 and it is mostly a disease transmitted through heterosexual relations (Clarke, 2002). It can therefore be contracted through unprotected heterosexual or homosexual intercourse; sharing of needles or syringes for drug injection; contaminated blood transfusions or blood products; and vertical transmission from mother to baby during pregnancy, delivery, or breast feeding. The HIV virus now runs rampant through the heterosexual populations of many sub-Saharan nations. Africa is reported to be the most affected continent accounting for the highest prevalence rate of the disease. According to World Focus (2005), AIDS is a major problem in Sub-Saharan Africa accounting for 70 per cent of the total number of infections in the world. Approximately 3.1 million new infections are reported to have occurred in 2004 with AIDS related diseases claiming the lives of an estimated 2.3 million people in the region in the past year (AVERT, 2005).

At the end of 2002, Africa had 28.1 million of the world's estimated 42 million people living with HIV (Anarfi and Appiah, 2004). The HIV/AIDS pandemic is one of the greatest challenges facing developing countries. It is a disease that threatens to reverse decades of hard-won development gains. The disease is having a disastrous impact on the social and economic development of countries highly affected by the epidemic and described by the UN as the 'biggest single obstacle for reaching the Millennium Summit development goals' (UN, 2001) [On-line]. Drimie (2003) confirms that HIV/AIDS is the major development issue facing sub-Saharan Africa, since the epidemic will increasingly devastate people's lives – particularly in the poorer areas of the continent. The AIDS Epidemic Update of December 2006 by the Joint United Nations Programme on HIV/AIDS and the World Health Organization estimate that 40 million people worldwide were living with HIV, with an estimated 21.8 to 27.7 million in Sub-Saharan Africa. The number of individuals newly infected with the disease in 2006 was estimated at between 2.4 and 3.2 million whilst the number of estimated adults and children deaths was calculated to be between 1.8 and 2.4 million. For instance in Angola, the UNAIDS (2006) indicates that the adult prevalence rate is 3.9 percent. At the end of 2003, two hundred and forty thousand adults and children were living with AIDS with estimated deaths at 21 thousand (OCHA, 2008) [On-line]. According to a UNAID report on *The Media and HIV/AIDS* (2004), 8,000 people will lose their lives to HIV/AIDS every day. The HIV pandemic continues to evolve in both magnitude and diversity. Sub-Sahara Africa still remains the worst-affected region in the world with one in five adults across southern Africa now HIV-infected. Several countries in West Africa for instance have a high prevalence of HIV/AIDS-infected people. Cote d'Ivoire is seven [7%], Nigeria four [4%], but estimates remain relatively low in Guinea [1.5 %], Mali [1.7%], Niger [0.5%], and Senegal [0.9%] (UNAIDS, 2006).

HIV/AIDS IN THE GHANAIAN CONTEXT

The HIV prevalence rate in Ghana has increased from 2.7 % to 3.2 % reverting prevalence to the 2004 levels. According to the HSS report (2007: 7):

> The highest prevalence was recorded in the 25-29 year group (4.2%). Age group prevalence showed two peaks, the first among the 25 to 29 year age group and the second in the 40 to 44 year age group (3.3%). The least level of infection (1.4%) was found in the 15 to 19 year age group. Prevalence among the youth 15 to 24 years which is used as a marker for new infections is 2.5%.

Ghana was among the first countries in West Africa which recognised the danger posed by HIV/AIDS and took a decisive step to control its spread. In Ghana, the first official case of HIV/AIDS was recorded in 1986. Sero-surveillance data have established that heterosexual activities involving commercial sex workers and young people are contributing to the spread of the disease. I acknowledge that, Ghana's HIV prevalence status is a generalised epidemic (epidemic in which HIV prevalence among antenatal clinic attendees consistently exceeds 1%). Hence, the HIV/AIDS prevalence is monitored mainly among the antenatal clinic population as a means of measuring the HIV/AIDS epidemic in Ghana. I am aware that although the use of antenatal attendees tends to overestimate HIV prevalence in Ghana, it is believed to be closed to actual prevalence in the general population as it samples sexually active individuals who have been exposed to unprotected sex (HSS report, 2007: 43). The HIV prevalence is highest among both women and men in the middle class (Ghana Statistical Service et al., 2004). According to Anarfi and Appiah (2004) by December 2002, the Ministry of Health recorded 64,316 AIDS cases. This means that on average, the country records about 3,783 AIDS cases annually since 1986. Currently, the Ministry of Health (MOH) and the National STDs/AIDS Control Programme (NACP) estimates that about six hundred thousand of the Ghanaian population are infected with HIV. Over 200 persons are estimated to be infected every single day. The present rate might escalate astronomically if measures are not instituted to curb the spread of the disease. Projections have therefore been made to the effect that 1.36 million people will be infected with HIV/AIDS if the present rate continues. By the year 2009 and 2014 respectively, 380 and 510 persons will be infected daily with HIV/AIDS. Beyond this, one million persons in Ghana will have died from AIDS related diseases in 2014. In the next section we discuss the methodological tool employed to gather data to write this chapter.

RESEARCH DESIGN

For the purpose of this paper quantitative research was the preferred approach. Content analysis was used as a strategy to generate data for analysis. There is awareness that several debates have been held in social research literature about the usage of either qualitative or quantitative research approaches in any research work as well as whether the two approaches can be combined. Some schools of thought e.g. Richie (2003: 38), argue that qualitative and quantitative research methods have different philosophical and methodological origins hence they cannot be effectively blended. This is reminiscent of the on-going debate within academia. In other words, the consideration of methods in conducting any research has been an age-old struggle. It is however evident that qualitative or quantitative approach can be used in any research work (see for example Gokah, 2006). Scholars contend that researchers are adopting mixed methods in order to expand the scope of their studies and improve on the analytical power of their research work. Snape and Spencer (2003: 15) cautions that qualitative and quantitative research methods should not be seen as opposed approaches to research. They noted that qualitative and quantitative methods can and should be part of the social researcher's toolkit. This implies that, both methodological considerations can be used in any kind or type of research depending on the objectives and purpose of any research work. There is force in Deacon et al. (1999: 114) advice that whichever analytical method a researcher adopts in the study of written media texts, one must 'avoid the trap of regarding his/her own approach as mutually incompatible with others'. Quoting Williams et al. (1988: 47), they noted that the use of more than one analytical method is advantageous. In particular, a mixed approach enabled this researcher to triangulate data (Denzin, 1994) and to establish validity in my study (Hansen et al., 1998).

Data collected for this study were divided into secondary and primary. Secondary data are data obtained from other sources concerning an aspect of an issue which have been investigated already. Secondary data and information are very important sources for comparing primary data and information generated during research fieldworks. As a result, the secondary data used in this study helped to substantiate the findings in this research. The secondary data used for this study was drawn from books, journals, academic papers and published as well as unpublished thesis. Indeed, secondary information brought some distinctive advantages in this work. For instance, it enabled this researcher to learn and find out about the particular subject area in terms of what is already known or done about that particular subject in order not to duplicate other studies.

On the other hand, primary data are generated first hand directly during field work. As indicated earlier in this chapter, content analysis was adopted as a strategy to generate the primary data.

CONTENT ANALYSIS

Content analysis was the preferred technique to analyse prime-time news bulletins (12 mid-day news stories) of JoyFM because it is one of the most commonly used research methods by scholars writing on media and communication (see for example Berger, 2000: 173). The term content analysis is about 60 years old and has been used to analyse the content of media and communications documents, i.e. newspapers, transcripts and visuals among others (Kippzendorff 2004). According to Wimmer and Dominick (2003: 140), its history dates back to the Second World War when Allied intelligence units monitored the number and types of popular songs played on European radio stations. They noted that by comparing music played on German stations with others in occupied Europe, the allies were able to measure the changes in troop concentrations on the continent. Various definitions have been given to this method of scientific enquiry. On the other hand, Kippzendorff (1980: 21) reminds us that it is a research technique for making replicable and valid inferences from data to their context. Similarly, Bryman (2001: 177) sees the technique as an approach to the analysis of documents and texts (which may be printed or visual) that seek to quantify content in terms of predetermined categories in a systematic and replicable manner. Hsia (1988: 318) asserts that content analysis is simply the analysis of what is said, printed, broadcast or written, however, it does not only examine content but infers underlying intent, motivation, orientation and effects, either implicit or manifest. The use of content analysis enabled us to gain more information on the topic and other relevant issues (Berger 2000: 174). I acknowledge that there are other methods which could be used to explore this topic such as discourse analysis, in-depth interviews and semi-structured interviews. Like all research methods, it should be noted that this research technique is not without flaws. For instance, this method is not well suited for studying deep questions about textual and discursive forms, aesthetic or rhetorical nuances within texts as noted by Deacon et al (1999: 117).

SAMPLE

All HIV/AIDS issues in the selected news bulletins were purposively sampled for analysis because those issues were the bench mark for the study in unearthing the representation of HIV/AIDS stories. The sample was over a two year (2002 and 2003). This time frame was chosen because it was believed to provide and establish a trend of representing HIV/AIDS issues. Stories emanating from World HIV/AIDS Day (which is commemorated on December 1st every year) were used as special emphasise to explain how journalists adhere to the elements of news in their reportage. The unit of analysis therefore, was mainly stories about HIV/AIDS issues. The coding procedure adopted was first to classify the content of the HIV/AIDS stories into 'HIV/AIDS Issues' and 'Non HIV/AIDS Issues' in order to make a clear distinction between the HIV/AIDS stories which were contained in the bulletins and other stories. This helped to establish the frequency of HIV/AIDS stories broadcast/represented for categorisation and analysis. The 'HIV/AIDS Issues' were categorised into five major topics relating to the HIV/AIDS stories broadcast for effective investigation and analysis. These categorisations were generated based on the five 'ws' and the one 'h' structure of news. In the light of this, the classifications for gathering information for analysis were:

a) What is the frequency of HIV/AIDS stories contained in the news bulletins broadcast during the sampling time frame?
b) Who were the stories referenced to in the news bulletins?
c) How was the HIV/AIDS story portrayed in the bulletins?

d) What did the stories refer to?
e) Who were highlighted in the news bulletin?

DATA ANALYSIS

Data used in this study was analysed using the Statistical Package for Social Sciences (SPSS) (Silverman, 2001, 2003). This method of analysing data was chosen to enable the researcher to safely calculate and display the data gathered accurately (Puplampu, 2004: 44). Data was coded numerically so that variables can simultaneously be analysed in order to examine the relationship between two variables i.e. HIV/AIDS and News Stories (Bryman 2001: 227).

FINDINGS

During my sample time frame, there was only one (1) news story about HIV/AIDS in 2002 news bulletin. On the other hand there were thirteen (13) HIV/AIDS stories contained in the news bulletin in 2003. In total there were 14 news items analysed. Majority of the HIV/AIDS stories were referenced to Non Governmental Organization (NGOs) (50%) biased towards the HIV/AIDS phenomenon. 42.9% were attributed to government officials. Interestingly, 7.1% of the stories were referenced to an HIV/AIDS infected person. The stories to some extent were based on the causes, prevention and portrayal of the HIV/AIDS epidemic. As far as the causes of the disease were concern, 78.6% of the stories fell within the variable 'other' adopted by this researcher. Some of the issues which emerged under this variable were behavioural change, human rights abuse of women as well as rape of girls and women. The rest of the variables adopted such as having sex without condom, having anal sex with a woman and oral sex respectively received 7.1% coverage. The variable 'other' in the category for preventive measures of the disease highlighted by the news bulletins recorded 57.1% of coverage. The variable 'testing' and 'drugs' recorded 14.3% respectively whilst 'abstinence' and 'drugs' recoded 7.1% each (see the graph below in figure 1.1).

Here, the news stories about the disease encouraged behavioural change, avoidance of stigmatisation and provision of funds. 50% of the stories portrayed the disease as human suffering whilst 42.9% was about the variable 'other'. 7.1% of the stories portrayed the disease as an economic/development problem. More so, 50% of the stories about the disease were not headlined. 42.9% of the stories were however headlined whilst 7.1% of stories were introduced immediately after advert break. Government officials to whom stories were referenced to in the news bulletins recorded more (3) headlines. NGOs received two (2) headline stories whilst infected persons had one (1) headline story.

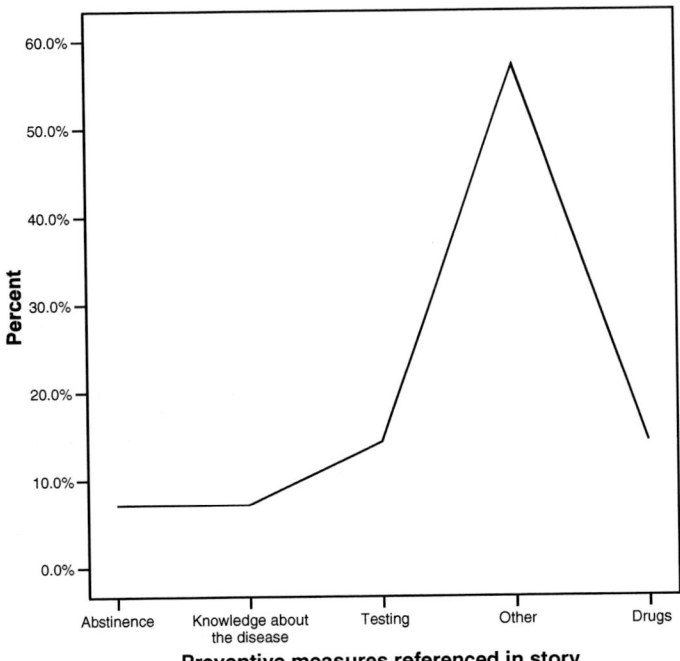

Figure 1.1

DISCUSSIONS

It can be glean from the above deliberations that the media does play a role in disseminating information about health issues .i.e. HIV/ADS but the extent of that role may vary in terms of the quantum of information, education and communication that the media gives to its publics. Behaviour change, among other factors, is reliant on sustained public education and information. Although the number of times (14 times) a media decides to inform and educate the public on say HIV/AIDS is relative, it is doubtful if the reported number of times within a two year timeframe will make any impact. This is contrary to what the literature says about the influence of media on behaviour change. Perhaps other strategies are needed to complement mass media efforts in addressing HIV/AIDS infections.

Majority of public education campaigns about HIV/AIDS tend to assume that people are capable of making choices about safe sex and drug use (Vass, 1987). Hence, when adequate information is made available by the media on a continuous basis about the HIV/AIDS phenomenon, people will in turn be much more aware of the disease as well as it dangers. This is one reason why it is imperative that now that there is no cure or prevention of the HIV/AIDS disease, the media will continually put HIV/AIDS phenomenon on their news agenda. In situations and circumstances whereby the issue [HIV/AIDS] is put on the media agenda, adequate time should be dedicated to the stories. Comparatively, even though the 2003 news bulletin is much better than that of 2002, the HIV/AIDS stories broadcast during these periods were not enough. Since good health information, education and communication are recognised as essential to human well-being, the media should make information about the HIV/AIDS pandemic accessible to people in a more intense way as other countries like Uganda have done. In deed, the media to some extent has used their medium to educate their listeners about the HIV/AIDS crisis. However, there is a lot more education to be done. In the first instance, one could argue that the media have failed in their education of their audience about the HIV/AIDS crisis. This is because education is supposed to be a continuous phenomenon. Thus, it should be an on-going exercise to be executed. But inferred from the above data the media [JoyFM] have shown inconsistency in the education of their listeners about the disease because of the limited/negligible coverage/information provided/broadcast about the disease. This implies that contrary to the notion that the media frequently covers health related topics is not universal truth. This study further refutes suggestions by Benefo (2004) that the media have done a great deal to teach Ghanaians about the disease.

Indeed, radio is the major source of information and should be consistent source of information about pressing issues or challenges. It should not merely be acclaimed to have proven information about the disease. It is evident from the news bulletins analysed that, the media rarely covers health [HIV/AIDS] related stories despite their ability to provide information about these issues which leads to education to bring about attitudinal as well as behavioural changes.

CONCLUSION

The intention in this chapter to critically analyse how the media uses information and communication to educate its listeners about the HIV/AIDS crisis; the sociology of news served as a pivot to explore the extent of HIV/AIDS representation and the dynamics of issues concerning HIV/AIDS which are represented. In my opinion, such representations are not helpful to generalise the effectiveness of the media providing information about HIV/AIDS. That the notion of media priding itself as frequently providing information about health issues is not universal truth; What is needed henceforth is an action oriented media like those discussed by Warren Parker that can facilitate sustainable information and education of people on the HIV/AIDS scourge aimed at reducing infection rates or eliminating it altogether through behaviour change. One way by which this can be achieved is to consider mixing approaches to compensate for gaps that may be created in this monolithic regime.

Chapter 6

Knowledge Management for Public Health Subspecialties Using Diffusion of Innovations Theory and Information and Communication Technology

Theresa C. Norton

As the public health field evolves, new subspecialties emerge—such as HIV/AIDS and family planning integration—some of which comprise hybrids of existing knowledge areas. Professionals working in these new subspecialties require a body of scientific literature, evidence-based information, and communication mechanisms tailored to their needs in order to advance the field. The evolution of a public health subspecialty poses a particular knowledge management challenge in that, in the early stages, important information may yet to have made it to formal scientific publications. For this reason, much tacit information sharing takes place in the form of presentations and conversations at professional conferences and meetings and in unpublished (grey) literature, such as project reports. This type of information sharing has significant access restrictions (geographic) and poses a problem to advancement of a field that needs innovative global solutions, often with a critical time consideration, such as halting mortality due to HIV/AIDS. Considering *Diffusion of Innovations*, Everett Rogers' book (1995) on the ways in which new ideas spread, knowledge management strategists can address Rogers' elements of diffusion, particularly the time element, and encourage innovation through effective use of Information and Communication Technology.

Introduction

As the public health field addresses a wide range of issues posing a threat to community health, new subspecialties develop to address emerging concerns. Identification of a subspecialty may stem from changes in demographics—such as an aging population and demand for services from that subgroup leading to, for example, a subspecialty of geriatric dentistry (Hebling 2007). Evolution of infectious diseases can lead to new specialized avenues of public health research and thus subspecialties, such as with HIV/AIDS, Avian Influenza, and Severe Acute Respiratory Syndrome (SARS). But perhaps the most challenging emerging type of subspecialty—from the perspective of knowledge management to bring about innovation—comes from a hybrid of two existing public health specialty areas, such as with HIV/AIDS and Family Planning Integration. In the case of an emerging subspecialty with a rapidly escalating global health threat—as is the case with HIV/AIDS—professionals seeking to address health problems within the subspecialty need to use systematic approaches to developing the field for maximum effectiveness. These approaches need to incorporate proven knowledge management strategies, aided by information and communication technology where appropriate, and be guided by diffusion of innovations theory to speed the timeline of adoption of innovations. This chapter steps through the key concepts of diffusion of innovations as they apply to a public health subspecialty, and presents a model of knowledge management incorporating judicious use of information and communication technology. It then presents a case study demonstrating use of knowledge management and diffusion of innovations principles with an emerging subspecialty.

DIFFUSION OF INNOVATIONS CONCEPTS AS THEY APPLY TO PUBLIC HEALTH

Examples abound of innovations in medicine that have been eagerly embraced, such as rapid government approval of Salk's polio vaccine after clinical trials (Maybury Okonek 2008). But there are also cases of innovation not so readily adopted for betterment of health. In Everett Rodgers book, *Diffusion of Innovations* (1995), he presents the memorable example of the innovation of citrus fruit use to combat scurvy, which took over 100 years for the British merchant marines to adopt. The rate at which an innovation—an idea perceived as new by members of a social system—is adopted relates to the way in which it is diffused throughout a group of potential adopters. Rogers (1995) defines diffusion as "the process by which (1) an innovation; (2) is communicated through certain channels; (3) over time; (4) among members of a social system."

Diffusion of innovations theory suggests that key factors predict the rate of adoption or diffusion of an innovation. One may match these key factors with illustrative public health considerations, as shown in Table 1.

By examining the public health considerations related to diffusion factors, those seeking to advance a public health subspecialty can design strategies that aid diffusion. The following case example illustrates how the key factors of diffusion have posed challenges to adoption of an innovation in a particular subspecialty.

Table 1.

Key Factors in Diffusion of innovations	Related Illustrative Public Health Considerations
Attributes of the innovation For example: --relative advantage, --compatibility, --complexity, --trialability, --observability	--Will the mortality rate drop more rapidly using the innovation than with other approaches? (advantage) --Can it be offered within existing health care facilities? (compatibility) --Can behavior change information be easily explained to the public? (complexity) --Can a pilot program be implemented to test the innovation? (trialability) --Can policy makers be convinced to incorporate indicators into health care service delivery guidelines so that impact of the innovation can be measured? (observability)
Attributes of the audience For example: --exposure to media and interpersonal channels --information seeking behavior, --innovator vs. laggard, education, literacy, --social mobility, size and connectedness of networks, --attitude toward change, --tolerance for ambiguity and risk	--Is the innovation being mentioned at professional meetings and conferences that the audience attends? (exposure) --Does the health professional read scientific journals? Participate in on-line discussions? (information seeking) --Is the innovation appropriate for the health care cadres involved? (education, literacy) --Is the innovation perceived as a possible health risk? (risk)
Environmental Constraints/facilitators For example: --access to information and means of communication, --access to the innovation, --access to education, --normative pressure,	--Does the health professional have access to the Internet? Access to distance learning options? (access to information) --Does the innovation involve medical supplies such as new vaccines not available everywhere? (access to innovation) --Does the health professional have disincentives not to innovate (national service delivery guidelines)? (normative pressure)
Characteristics of the communication system For example: --homophily (similarity of people communicating about innovation) --heterophily (dissimilarity of people communicating about innovation)	--Do the health program managers who are communicating tend to develop similar programs with similar environmental attributes, with similar barriers to innovation? --Is communication of innovation occurring between different health care service delivery cadres, which may pose a social barrier? (heterophily)

Diffusion Factors and a Public Health Innovation: Male Circumcision and HIV

In public health, a field characterized by focus on the health outcomes of groups of individuals, the social implications of an innovation can play a key role in its adoption. One example of social considerations in public health innovation adoption concerns a public health subspecialty that has evolved, which is referred to as HIV/AIDS and Sexual and Reproductive Health (SRH) Integration. This subspecialty concerns the benefits to both HIV prevention, care, and treatment outcomes, and sexual and reproductive health of individuals when health care services are offered together at a facility (or with client-friendly referral systems). One HIV/SRH integration innovation that has gained much attention in the public health community is male circumcision for HIV prevention. Since about 2000, there has been growing advocacy for male circumcision to help HIV prevention. This advocacy escalated in 2006, when the U.S. National Institutes of Health announced that two trials studying the impact of male circumcision on HIV risk would be stopped because the interim data clearly pointed to a strong protective effect of the intervention. Trials in Kenya and Uganda revealed at least a 53% and 51% reduction in risk of acquiring HIV infection, respectively (NIAID 2006). This followed results from a 2005 study in South Africa that demonstrated at least a 60% reduction in HIV infection among circumcised men. Yet despite these impressive results, much debate surrounds potential adoption of this innovation. Why the resistance? As one journal article asks, wouldn't a similar announcement of an HIV vaccine that reduced risk by at least 60% been met with a massive surge of excitement (Klausner et al 2008)?

The reasons for a relatively slow adoption of this public health strategy, in the light of the HIV crisis, can be seen by examining the key factors of diffusion involved.

Attributes of the innovation

Supporters of male circumcision for HIV prevention point to its relative advantage—an approximately 60% risk reduction according to clinical trials, while others question the relative advantage if requirements are not met: if the surgery is not done in a sterile environment, men do not wait for the wound to heal before resuming intercourse, or risk behavior increases. Scaling up circumcision services by trained providers in a sterile environment poses a compatibility challenge: capacity of health care systems need to be increased. The caveats to male circumcision protective benefits make the intervention complex: men and their partners need clear communication that explains the health risks of circumcision in an unsterile environment, not waiting for healing, or increased risk behavior (such as multiple concurrent partners). The trialability and observablility of male circumcision—in the form of clinical trials—poses potential ethical issues, as do many clinical trials, and relates also to complexity—researchers must strive to ensure informed consent by trial participants, who must understand the risks.

Attributes of the audience

This is a particularly important factor in adoption of male circumcision for HIV prevention, as the innovation has sparked heated debate due to its social implications. Throughout history, male circumcision has been done as a rite of passage for men, as part of religious ceremonies, to mark hierarchy and social difference, and as part of political and power struggles (Aggleton 2007). While HIV researchers may eagerly embrace the protective benefits of male circumcision—serving as early adopters—change agents must appeal to other audiences in a "culturally appropriate, rights-based and gender sensitive way" (Aggleton 2007). Communication channels for male circumcision information have expanded since 2000, and have included surveys of potential circumcision clients to determine acceptability (Westercamp 2007), scientific journal articles, blogs, e-mail lists, bulletins from the World Health Organization, community meetings, and more. Both risk and relative advantage have been presented in these communication channels, effectively slowing down the rate of adoption. And as this is a relatively new posed benefit for male circumcision—following negated ones through history—information seeking behavior is by and large coming from the scientific community (highly educated, early adopters) rather than the ultimate beneficiaries of the innovation.

Environmental constraints/facilitators

As mentioned under Attributes of the Innovation, scaling up health care systems to offer safe male circumcision services presents a significant environmental constraint for adoption, as providers need to be trained (education factor) and health care facilities prepared (access factor). And, unlike a potential vaccine or substance, there is no pharmaceutical company to speedily champion adoption of the innovation with the lure of future profits (Klausner 2008). A facilitator to innovation, however, came in two steps, when (1) the World Health Organization—clearly an opinion leader in public health—recommended male circumcision as an important HIV risk reduction approach, followed by (2) the U.S President's Emergency Plan for AIDS Relief announcing support (i.e., funding) for safe male circumcision services when included in a country's HIV prevention strategy.

Characteristics of the communication system

Communication about male circumcision for HIV prevention has occurred within and between similar and dissimilar social systems. Scientific researchers, a similar group, have clearly shared research results. However, behavior change communication between public health experts and men in communities where circumcision is not already practiced clearly is an example of communication among dissimilar members of a channel. In addition, communications from social activists who have protested male circumcision from a human rights standpoint have muddied the waters of debate.

KNOWLEDGE MANAGEMENT IN PUBLIC HEALTH

The confounding effects of mixed factors in getting a public health innovation diffused and adopted, as described with the male circumcision example, can be mitigated with effective use of knowledge management. Knowledge management (KM) refers to the process of systematically creating, gathering, organizing, sharing, adapting, and using knowledge to achieve goals and objectives (Kols 2004). As a public health subspecialty emerges, those seeking to advance the field face three main knowledge challenges (Kols 2004):

- Sharing knowledge: Public health professionals conducting research and implementing innovating programs need to share their findings and experiences.
- Learning from experience: Program managers need to use proven practices and lessons learned to design public health programs and make decisions.
- Coping with either too much or too little information: In the case of a new hybrid subspecialty, professionals may be overwhelmed with information related to the separate fields, but not easily identifiable as relating to the hybrid field (e.g., HIV/AIDS and Family Planning Integration). In addition, with global health issues, a professional may be located in a remote region geographically separated from access to information via personal exchange or the Internet with others sharing his interest.

KM tools and approaches can help overcome these challenges and accelerate the timeline for adoption of innovation in a subspecialty.

LEVERAGING KM AND ICT TO ADVANCE INNOVATION

Information and Communication Technology (ICT)—encompassing electronic devices such as telephones, computers, and the Internet—increasingly plays a part in knowledge management and diffusion of innovations on a global scale because of growing capabilities. According to a United Nations report (2006), developing countries accounted for more than 60 per cent of the world's telephone lines in 2005, most of the growth coming from mobile telephones, which outnumber fixed ones. In addition, worldwide Internet use more than quadrupled between 2000 and 2005 (United Nations 2006).

ICT makes a likely support tool for diffusion of innovations because of its nature, which involves an interrelationship between technology and the social environment: information systems require interaction with people (Berg 2003). Similarly, Rogers (1995) stresses the critical part that interpersonal networks play in diffusion of innovations. Taking the similarities one step further, the nature of health care as a field involves a social system of clients and providers, matching problems and solutions, through interaction of members of the system (Berg 2003). When the social aspects of knowledge management are considered (e.g., personal sharing of tacit—undocumented—knowledge), one can envision a model of KM using ICT that addresses the social contact aspect of diffusion. For example, for each of the KM challenges described previously, using tools and approaches that also address factors in diffusion of innovations while making use of ICT to speed the timeline can be particularly effective. Table 2 lists KM approaches and tools used in public health (Kols 2004) with their related diffusion factors and ICT aids.

Table 2.

KM Approach or Tool	Diffusion of Innovations Factor	ICT Aids
Challenge: Share Knowledge		
Build social networks: --hold meetings and conferences --establish teams --form communities of practice (COPs)(i.e., network of people with a common interest sharing knowledge and support in-person or on-line)	--Access to information and means of communication --Connectedness of networks --homophily and heterophily (e.g., COPs bring together people similar in interest, but different in ways such as job titles, organizations, and geographic location)	--On-line collaboration tools --On-line forums and listservs (e-mail discussion lists) --Videoconferences --Webcasts (presentations over the Internet) --Teleconferences --Short message service (text messages over cell phones)
Help people locate key sources of knowledge: --Knowledge maps (identifies where all knowledge exists on a given topic, it be with people, documents, etc.)	---Opinion leaders need organized information from which to base a decision to adopt or reject an innovation	--Web site maps --Canned search queries of database for popular topics --On-line information indexed by terminology commonly used in the subspecialty
Preserve institutional memory: --knowledge harvesting through interviewing of experts --Storytelling	--Sharing of recommendations from opinion leaders or change agents throughout a social system	--Audio and video recordings of interviews with experts, digitized and offered on the Web or CD-ROM
Challenge: Learn from Experience		
Collect lessons learned and best practices: --Evaluation tools and results --Adapt proven approaches to local context (more efficient than starting brand new)	--Help perceive reduced risk of innovation --improve attitude toward change by viewing positive results of others	--Electronic data entry and analysis tools for evaluation results --Searchable on-line repositories of evaluation results
Exchange tacit knowledge of best practices	--High identification with source of knowledge if viewed as similar to recipient (homophily) --Interpersonal contact aids diffusion	--Listservs --Blogs (Web-based journals) --On-line forums

Table 2. (Continued)

KM Approach or Tool	Diffusion of Innovations Factor	ICT Aids
Challenge: Coping with too much or too little information		
Find trustworthy sources to filter, prioritize, and validate knowledge and information: --Use content experts --Author publications --Create systems to share knowledge among workers at isolated locations	--Receiving information from trusted content expert reduces perceived risk of innovation --Decreasing time to awareness of innovation may also shorten entire timeline to decision to adopt	--Electronic publications --E-mail alerts --RSS feeds (Real Simple Syndication—news aggregators from multiple sources displayed in one software program) --Distance education

Teaming of KM approaches and ICT can result in unexpected complications, though. While technology-based outreach approaches can be useful in developing subspecialties in regions where there is a lack of specialists and dedicated departments (Pradeep 2007), the social implications may not be readily apparent. For example, participants around the world of a videoconference may not know the power struggles behind the scenes that determined which content experts were selected to make presentations. In addition, global knowledge sharing facilitated by the Internet (e.g., on-line forums) may still entail language barriers and cultural biases (e.g., reluctance to offer insights and lessons learned in the virtual presence of a perceived "expert").

The following case example illustrates an approach to using the intersection of innovation theory, good practices in knowledge management, and information and communication technology to advance a public health subspecialty.

BRINGING TOGETHER INNOVATION THEORY, KM, AND ICT: CASE OF THE FAMILY PLANNING AND HIV/AIDS INTEGRATION WORKING GROUP

According to the United Nations Population Fund (UNFPA) and the World Health Organization (WHO) (2006), there are clear interactions between reproductive health and HIV/AIDS, most HIV infections being sexually transmitted or associated with pregnancy, childbirth, and breastfeeding. In addition, as people living with HIV experience a better quality of life with effective use of antiretrovirals, the need for family planning or fertility services rises among this group. There is emerging evidence of important synergies between reproductive health (RH) and HIV prevention, care and treatment interventions. Both expert organizations have stated that public health will benefit from linkages between reproductive health and HIV service delivery. The relative advantage of Integration innovation is clear—at least to many public health experts—and a subspecialty of public health has emerged specifically addressing these linkages.

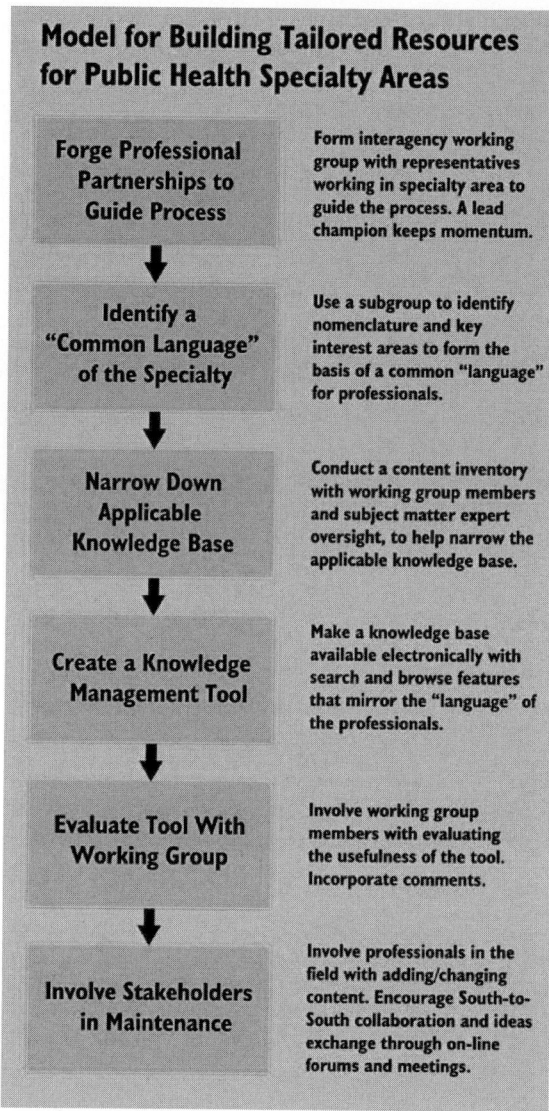

But adoption of Integration innovations in health systems must be funded and effectively sustained, posing equally clear environment challenges. Donors say "show me the evidence" that Integration innovation benefits—before releasing funds. And further among the communication channels, program planners and providers say "show me the best practices"—to help them implement integrated service programs. So a critical need to advance the field of HIV and RH Integration is knowledge management.

Forming a Knowledge Sharing Network

To address challenges in moving Integration forward, in 2004, the U.S. Agency for International Development (USAID) established a working group—the Family Planning and HIV/AIDS Integration Partners Working Group—with representatives from over 30 organizations, including private foundations, USAID and its partners and contractors, United Nations Population Fund, International Planned Parenthood Federation, U.S. Centers for Disease Control, and other key organizations involved in family planning and HIV/AIDS programming and research sought to explore ways to promote integration of family planning and HIV/AIDS services. The group initially met twice a year and early in discussions began identifying knowledge management needs, particularly regarding sharing information on key research and programming gaps. In 2005, the group tasked the Johns Hopkins Bloomberg School of Public Health Center for Communication Programs (CCP) with developing a knowledge management solution for the international development organizations that participated in the USAID working group. The first knowledge management tool developed was an on-line database and portal Web site: Resources for HIV/AIDS and Sexual and Reproductive Health Integration (http://www.hivandsrh.org). This initial tool was later supplemented by on-line collaboration tools, on-line forums, videoconferences, and an e-newsletter.

Helping People Locate Key Sources of Knowledge

As mentioned in an earlier section, KM approaches seek to facilitate sharing knowledge. Forming the FP/HIV Integration Working Group provided a social network and valuable source for knowledge sharing. CCP then needed a way to capture both tacit and explicit knowledge of group members and make that knowledge easy to locate.

Once the working group decided on a need for a knowledge management solution, a development process began in which a subcommittee of the working group screened Integration content and advised on the information architecture for the database tool, while CCP leveraged its existing resources including over 350,000 citations in six databases that included scientific articles, communication materials, programmatic documents, photographs, and news items. A champion from the funder, USAID, was instrumental in keeping momentum in the process.

To jumpstart the effort to identify content, the working group members agreed to contribute to an inventory of known Integration resources that could be candidates for the tool. Most of the resources came from the working group member organizations. This process tapped into the tacit knowledge of group members, many of whom knew of Integration programs being conducted in the field, but about which information would be difficult to find because the programs were in early stages and had yet to be documented in scientific journals. In fact, early on, the group agreed to include program documents in the inventory as well as research articles to reflect the state of Integration and document institutional knowledge. As the subcommittee reviewed and organized the inventory, familiarity with the body of knowledge grew, adding to the sense of commonality of the social network.

Mapping Knowledge

Creating a uniquely useable tool for the specialty area of Integration involved identifying the nomenclature that health professionals used when thinking about and discussing Integration. The subgroup members, USAID champion, and CCP jointly identified the Integration nomenclature. This terminology—consisting of a list of key topics, client groups, interest areas, and keywords—became part of the resources tool as one-click searches or browse features of the database. For example, clicking on the key topic, "Contraception for HIV-Positive Women," automatically searches the resources by a string of terms including

HIV-positive, Persons living with HIV/AIDS, contraception, family planning, girl, women, and female.

Avoiding Too Much Information

CCP worked with an information technology partner to create a custom search interface for the tool—termed an "integrated user experience" because the tool needed to be more than just a search engine. The tool needed to give the user ways to filter through resources in a broad range of ways, such as by resource subtypes (e.g., communication materials, scientific articles), regions, keywords, and availability of full-text for downloading. By tying the database to CCP's existing large-scale document delivery service, developing country users would also have the option to order free hard copy or electronic copy of many documents.

Helping Members Learn from Experience

An important avenue for diffusion of innovations is sharing of recommendations from opinion leaders or change agents throughout a social system. With this in mind, CCP facilitated multiple ways for network members to gain access to the views of opinion leaders. In an emerging public health subspecialty, the first important information may surface in professional presentations at meetings and conferences. CCP actively sought to archive and index presentations from significant conferences and meetings and make them searchable in the database tool. Further, CCP hosted multiple videoconferences and Webcasts, in which participants could view presentations by experts—thus addressing the geographic challenges in diffusion. These videoconferences were followed by on-line forums to discuss issues raised during the videoconferences. CCP also developed conference web pages with links to resources recommended by the experts. An on-line collaboration site allowed other members of the working group to upload documents to share, and a submission form on the website allowed members to submit documents for inclusion in the database. Finally, CCP interviewed program managers from successful Integration programs about their best practices and lessons learned, and posted the interview transcripts on the website in a "Voices from the Field" section, to give the sense of interpersonal communication with an expert.

HOW HAS THE KNOWLEDGE MANAGEMENT TOOL BEEN USED?

In approximately two years, the on-line tool showed evidence of much information seeking behavior: it received over 64,000 visits from over 44,000 visitors in over 170 countries. Of the 1000 organization accessing the site, the World Health Organization and USAID—opinion leaders in Integration—feature in the top forty active organizations (where the other 37 were unidentified organizations, Internet Service Providers, and one university in Germany). From 2007-2008, over 22,000 searches were performed on the database, with three search phrases appearing high on the list: "youth" (1899), "PMTCT" and "counselling" (1052), and "VCT" and "counselling" (454). These top search phrases correspond with high interest areas of innovation in Integration:

- Offering integrated services to youth, who are at the forefront of the HIV epidemic;
- Preventing mother-to-child transmission of HIV by counselling pregnant and postpartum women on family planning; and
- Incorporating family planning counselling in HIV voluntary counselling and testing services.

CCP conducted a voluntary on-line survey to solicit feedback from users of the Integration site. The survey was launched in May 2007 and completed by a total of 137 users from 42 countries.

Overall, 74% of respondents reported that the Integration site positively influenced their daily work. Repeatedly, respondents indicated that the site was a great resource because it provided them with convenient access to the latest information and tools selected by subject matter experts, and it saved them considerable time in researching relevant and evidence-based resources on the Internet.

In addition, survey respondents indicated that they incorporated the information they obtained from the Integration site and database into policy, programs, research practice as well as training or education efforts. Specific examples are presented below.

Policy: Respondents whose primary job responsibility is in the area of policymaking and advocacy reported that they used the Integration resources to develop or improve policy or national service delivery guidelines.

> "UNFPA Country Office is developing guidelines on HIV/AIDS and SRH Integration in Pakistan. We reviewed various resource documents." – *Program Officer working for UNFPA in Pakistan*
>
> "We have used the information in the design of HIV/AIDS and SRH Integration guidelines." – *Policymaker working for USAID in Nigeria*

Program: Respondents whose primary job responsibility is in the area of program development and management reported that they used the Integration resources to design or improve projects or programs.

> "It has been very useful in the implementation of two HIV/AIDS projects that I am currently coordinating, particularly in the training of nurses and midwives on PMTCT activities." – *Educator/program manager working for an academic institution in Ghana*
>
> "I am writing a position paper on integration of HIV and SRH services in our country program and information from integration website has been very the key to make our paper strong, professional and evidence informed." – *Program manager working for an NGO in Myanmar*
>
> "We have used the research studies as the basis of public awareness campaigns on sexual health issues." – *Health service provider working for an NGO in Australia*

Research: Respondents whose primary job responsibility is in the area of research and evaluation reported that they used the Integration resources to guide research agenda or methods, and to put research findings into practice.

> "We are conducting a review of the evidence that exists for HIV-SRH linkages at the service delivery and policy levels. The review is meant to summarize experiences to date, identify promising practices and potential for scale-up and identify research gaps." – *Researcher working for an academic institution in the U.S.A.*
>
> "Our organization produce different research on areas of SRH, we use to refer to the HIV/SRH integration web-site for this." – *Program director working for an NGO in Ethiopia*

Training: Respondents whose primary job responsibility is in the area of teaching and training reported that they used the Integration resources to develop training programs or workshops, and to assist in designing educational materials.

> "I am currently using it for training of church leaders to create an enabling environment for increased uptake of reproductive health services among Presbyterian Church of Nigeria members." – *Program manager/trainer working in a religious/faith-based organization in Nigeria*
>
> "The information available was used in the training programs organized for various stakeholders. This also helped to our staff for updating their knowledge and skills." – *Program manager/trainer working for an NGO in India*
>
> "The information was used in developing a training program known as PEER EDUCATOR for rural areas in Abia State, Nigeria. Some of the materials used in the training were taken directly from the web site." – *Educator working for an NGO in Nigeria*

Case Summary

Along the process of working with the FP/HIV Integration Working Group, CCP conceived of knowledge management approaches using information technology to foster innovation in Integration. These approaches related to factors in innovation adoption as follows (JHU/CCP 2006):

- Demonstrate the benefits of certain approaches to Integration by highlighting best practices and evaluation results of pilot programs (relative advantage),
- Relate emerging Integration policy, program and research practices to current HIV/AIDS and family planning practice (compatibility),
- Provide clear steps for application through sample program documents, job aids, and training materials (complexity),

- Provide examples and exchange among policy makers, program managers, and researchers of the experience with different approaches to Integration through on-line forums, videoconferences, and documented interviews (observability), and
- Suggest easy ways to try these methods through descriptions of pilot programs (trialability).

By addressing some of these key predictors of adoption and diffusion of innovations, the project increased the use (adoption) of Integration information by key decision-makers, thus informing and enhancing policy, programs, and research. In turn, the Integration resource contributed to better, integrated healthcare programs through which HIV-positive and – negative clients can efficiently access needed sexual and reproductive health and HIV services and make informed choices about their health care.

In addition, by systematically finding sound innovations and pulling content on Integration from non-USAID and Southern (e.g., Africa) partners and disseminating that information through the website, on-line forums, and e-newsletter, CCP provided greater access to innovations through a variety of means of communication, one of the environmental factors stated previously.

CONCLUSION

Emerging public health subspecialties are often characterized by lack of a readily identifiable and useable body of knowledge. Innovative ideas may be diffused slowly through interpersonal contact or unpublished literature until traditional means of scientific communication catch up, such as scientific publishing and conferences. Accelerating diffusion of innovations within an emerging public health subspecialty can be aided by using approaches that leverage the intersections of diffusion of innovations theory, knowledge management principles, and information and communication technology.

Chapter 7

UTILIZATION OF EFFECTIVE COMMUNICATION CHANNELS FOR TUBERCULOSIS CONTROL: EMERGING SCENARIO IN SOUTH INDIA

Rajeswari Ramachandran* and M. Muniyandi

The Revised National TB Control Programme (RNTCP) of India based on global Directly Observed Treatment Short-course (DOTS) strategy has achieved 100 percent geographical coverage of the country under DOTS in March 2006 and has also consistently achieved the global target of treatment success rate of over 85 percent and the case detection rate close to the global target of 70 percent. India's RNTCP has been recognised internationally for the fastest expansion in the history of DOTS implementation. The RNTCP has put mechanisms in place to make services accessible, acceptable and affordable through partnership with the community based organizations and greater community participation and empowerment.

There is a need to plan and implement suitable information, education and communication (IEC) strategies/interventions focusing on the community / patients behaviour (from the time of diagnosis till patients complete the treatment) that needs to be modified to achieve the objectives of the programme. This is so because TB control programme is a felt need oriented programme expecting patients to seek relief of symptoms on their own. There is a need to improve awareness of chest symptoms suggestive of TB among the community. Also, the community to be informed regarding the availability of free diagnostic and treatment services to achieve effective TB control. Since default of patients started on treatment lead to poor treatment outcomes of patients registered under RNTCP, it is also necessary those patients are made to understand the importance of regular treatment.

This communication describes various strategies tried by Tuberculosis Research Centre (TRC), over two decades to identify effective channels of communication and its merits in rural communities to improve case holding and case finding of the programme.

In eighties, health massages have been communicated through the health personnel on a one-to-one basis and the use of mass media for spreading health messages were minimal. In early nineties in a study done in Madurai by our centre, the health messages were communicated through various channels like radio, mike announcement, street play and wall posters and it was observed that wall posters played a key role (54 percent of chest symptomatics) in sensitizing the community. Over the years, the picture of communication modes have changed and the main source of communication observed in the year 2006 was television (100 percent) followed by wall posters (55%); publicity through panchayat office meetings (53 percent) and dandora (43 percent). Year 2007 had seen paradigm shift in communication modes with the wide availability of mobile phones both in rural and urban areas. More than 90 percent of our TB patients were accessible through mobile phones and this has been extensively used for tracking defaulters, patient management, for collecting follow-up sputum specimens and organizing drug logistics. In the urban areas among the literates yet another popular mode of communication has been the wide availability of internet providing access to facts on TB and TB programme. Studies are needed for adopting the newer communication channels for better management of TB patients in a manner that suits patients from rural and urban areas. Well planned IEC strategies utilizing modern tools will facilitate greater appreciation of RNTCP by stakeholders, will promote de-stigmatization, make TB services available to marginalized communities, will ensure completion of treatment and make DOTS a familiar name associated with cure.

Keywords: Communication channels, IEC, Tuberculosis, Mobile phone, India

INTRODUCTION

TB is the world's biggest single infectious cause of death among adults. India accounts for one-fourth of the global TB incidence and is estimated to have the highest number if active TB cases amongst the countries of the world. Nearly 1.8 million new cases occur each year [Central TB Division 2008]. TB has killed more people than any other infectious disease in India. The National Tuberculosis Control Programme (NTCP), established in 1962, created an infrastructure for TB-control throughout the country and was integrated with the general health services. The programme provides free service to the community. The Government of India (GoI) evolved a Revised National Tuberculosis Control Programme (RNTCP) in the year 1993 on the basis of the strategy of directly observed treatment, short course(DOTS) recommended by the World Health Organization (WHO). Objectives of RNTCP included achieving a 70 percent case detection rate and a treatment success rate of 85 percent of new smear-positive cases [Central TB Division 2002]. The RNTCP has put mechanisms in place to make services accessible, acceptable and affordable through the Information, Education and Communication (IEC) strategies, partnership with the community based organizations and through greater community participation and empowerment.

The IEC strategy for RNTCP aims at awareness generation about symptoms, curability, and free availability of high quality diagnostic and treatment services for TB in a patient-friendly environment. The major target groups for IEC are patients, including families and the community, health providers and opinion makers. IEC can be defined as 'a public health approach aiming at changing or reinforcing health-related behaviours in a target audience, concerning a specific problem and within a pre-defined period of time, through communication methods and principles' (WHO).

Large-scale adoption of health practices by the people, resulting in lower TB morbidity and mortality rates, requires appropriate behaviour change tools and techniques throughout the planning, design and implementation of communication activities. A necessary pre-condition is to learn the most appropriate ways to communicate desirable behavioural change and convert this information into effective health messages for Inter Personal Communication (IPC), broadcast media and print materials to provide skills-based training and implement programmes to support health practices over time. This process pre-supposes a thorough understanding of RNTCP and of working with stakeholders in applying an appropriate health communication methodology.

This paper describes I) communication channels used in India to propagate health messages II) various studies done at Tuberculosis Research Centre (TRC), over two decades to identify effective channels of communication and its merits and III) health communication strategies adopted by RNTCP in India.

COMMUNICATION CHANNELS USED IN INDIA TO PROPAGATE HEALTH MESSAGES

Introduction

For many years, in India health communication has focused on the methods of delivering messages about good practice and policy to a wide variety of audiences including health workers, patients, community members, opinion shapers, and policy-makers. From 1950-70 health massages have been communicated through the health personnel on a one-to-one basis and the use of mass media for spreading health messages were minimal. To educate patients flip charts and posters were used. It was felt that no single approach is likely to achieve the goals of any health communication project, programme or activity. The use of the most appropriate approaches, methods and communication tools to stimulate and support a sustainable communication process needs to be identified. Determining which will work in a given situation requires skill, patience and sufficient time to understand the situation, and the health and communication needs of the people involved.

EXPERIENCES IN THE FIELD OF FAMILY PLANNING

India's Family Planning Programme was initiated in 1951 in an effort to regulate the growth of the country's population and in this programme a number of health communication methods were used. Also few studies were done to assess the impact of the strategies used in communication in this programme. Earlier studies done in India and neighbouring countries had shown that both channels of communication namely mass media and interpersonal media were significant predictors of use and future intention to use contraception. Mass media was more effective in case of India, whereas, interpersonal communication had greater impact in case of Bangladesh [Dwivedi et al 2006 & Manoj KR 2006]. It was observed that in case of those who were less motivated interpersonal media should be employed, while in case of relatively higher motivated ones, mass media could suffice. Media exposure seemed to help reduce misconceptions, fears and apprehensions regarding birth control methods. In India this was the first programme that had used multiple channels in health communication.

TUBERCULOSIS RESEARCH CENTRE (TRC) EXPERIENCE IN IDENTIFYING EFFECTIVE CHANNELS OF COMMUNICATION AND ITS MERITS

Tuberculosis Research Centre (TRC), Indian Council of Medical Research (ICMR), Chennai, has been conducting randomized controlled clinical trails in the treatment of pulmonary and extra pulmonary forms of tuberculosis in the past five decades. During the first two decades, the centre focused all its attention on chemotherapy of tuberculosis and mycobacteriology that resulted in extraordinary results that shaped the management of tuberculosis in the world. In the third decade TRC's participation in ICMR's Bacillus Calmette Guerin (BCG) trial helped the Government of India shaping its policy on BCG vaccination in the country. The attention of TRC in the fourth decade was on establishing the ground rules for management of extra-pulmonary tuberculosis. In the fifth decade TRC joined hands with central TB division of Ministry of Health, Government of India, in strengthening Revised National Tuberculosis Control Programme in the country. In the last few years TRC strengthened the infrastructure for basic research, initiated HIV-TB related studies, established HIV vaccine trial center and NIH center for excellence in research. TRC has always addressed issues in research that has direct implication in benefiting the TB community. In addition to the basic research towards developing newer drugs, diagnostics and vaccines, TRC is conducting Operational Research studies on key aspects of TB control programme. Under operational research studies, the following studies were done by TRC to identify effective channels of communication and its merits: (a) Utilising village *DAIS* and student volunteers from colleges who are enrolled in National Service Scheme (NSS) and other propaganda measures to improve tuberculosis case finding and (b) Identifying effective communication channels in a rural community [Tuberculosis Research Centre 1997].

UTILISING VILLAGE DAIS AND STUDENT VOLUNTEERS FROM COLLEGES WHO ARE ENROLLED IN NATIONAL SERVICE SCHEME (NSS) AND OTHER PROPAGANDA MEASURES TO IMPROVE TUBERCULOSIS CASE FINDING

Introduction: In 90's our centre tried out various strategies to improve case finding in Tuberculosis programme in rural and urban areas. The National Tuberculosis Programme adopted a positive case finding policy, i.e., cases are to be detected from among the chest symptomatics attending the various Government health facilities for medical advice. The efficiency of case finding in programme was estimated to be around 30 percent. In order to improve case finding Tuberculosis Research Centre has undertaken two different studies one in a rural area by utilising village *DAIS* and another in an urban area utilising student volunteers from colleges who are enrolled in National Service Scheme (NSS) and other propaganda measures. *DAIS* (Mid Wife) are traditional birth attendants and their services are well accepted in the community.

Study area and population: The *DAIS* study was undertaken in 63 villages in Sriperumbadur taluk, covering a population of 18320 of whom 11808 were above the age of 15 years. Village *DAIS* were mobilized for case finding in this area. The NSS study was undertaken at Madurai and for this study the population covered was 50,000 and of whom 35,000 were above 15 years of age. Student volunteers from 4 city colleges who are enrolled in the National Service Scheme were utilized in this study.

Training methodology: The identified personnel were trained by TRC staff. Staff members briefed them about TB in general and taught them to identify chest symptomatics in the community. Lectures with flash-cards, slides, exhibitions, group discussions and film shows were conducted for both *DAIS* and students. Since the *DAIS* were mostly illiterate role plays were enacted for them. In addition they were given practical training in the field, in making home visits, identification of chest symptomatics and sputum collection. Booklets and hand bills were distributed to the student volunteers.

Community Health Education Methods: Another important aspect of these two studies was education of the community on TB. The methods used in the rural area included exhibition, door to door visits, periodic meetings, role play and film shows. In the urban area the methods used were exhibitions, street plays and villupattu (folk songs) at important street corners and junctions, mike and All India Radio announcements, posters and film shows.

Outcome of utilization of student volunteers and propaganda measures: In Madurai City, in the selected area, 3 camps were held over a period of 10 months. Among the 35,000 population aged above 15 years, following the student motivation and other propaganda measures 1561 chest symptomatics attended the corporation dispensaries and 72 were smear positive. Estimated smear positive from this population is 91.

Case finding by **DAIS**: *DAIS* did active case finding by doing door to door home visits and identifying chest symtomatics and collecting sputum in a population of 11808, a total of 276 chest symptomatics have been identified by the *DAIS* and sputum collected by them. 41 were found to be sputum positive either by smear and or by culture. As many as 41 were sputum positive as against the expected 47 as per the national prevalence survey. *DAIS* have been able to identify about 85 percent of the existing pulmonary tuberculosis patients in the community.

Conclusion: These two studies showed that with proper training, existing forces in the community can be effectively mobilised for case finding. It is encouraging to note that using these task forces it has been possible to identify about 80 percent of the sputum positive patients existing in the community. NSS volunteers and *DAIS* are potential taskforces available throughout the country and it was felt that their services can be utilised for case finding in TB programme.

IDENTIFYING EFFECTIVE COMMUNICATION CHANNELS IN A RURAL COMMUNITY

Introduction: Poor awareness on all aspects of TB including symptoms suggestive of TB, availability of free diagnosis and treatment in the community might adversely affect the programme performance. Earlier studies have shown that TB awareness was not up to expectations due to poor literacy rate or lack of availability of effective communication channels resulting in improper health seeking behaviour and the treatment compliance [Rajeswari et al 1995; Singh at al 2002 ; Geetakrishnan et al 1988; Neeta et al 1998]. TRC initiated a study in Thiruvallur district a predominantly rural area. The main objective of this study is to try and identify communication channels that are available in a rural community and also the channels that are utilised to get the information by different segment of the population [Rajeswari et al 2006].

Study area and population: The study was undertaken during 2004, in one of the randomly selected Ellapuram panchayat union (block) of Velliyur tuberculosis unit, Tiruvallur district, Tamilnadu, south India. The study block included 39255 populations in 51 villages. Key informants from each village were selected. One key informant from each village who will be able to give the information about available communication channels selected by the villagers formed the study population. They were either panchayat leader or village teacher or post master or any other community leader identified by the villagers.

Data collection: All the key informants were interviewed in the villages by a medical social worker. Semi-structured pre-coded interview schedule was used to collect the information. The following information were collected: major occupation of the villagers, availability of transport, education, health facilities, electricity and other services like Mill, Societies, Market, Rations shop, Social groups and place of worship. In addition we also collected detailed information on the communication facilities available in the villages, such as announcements by Dandora /mike, modern communication facilities such as television, radio, newspaper etc. All the informants were specifically asked which communication channel was utilized maximum by them for collecting new information.

Outcome of the study: The study block included 51 villages, 9893 households and 39255 populations. Electricity was available in all the villages. Main occupation was agriculture in (86%) of villages and the remaining included weaving, self employment etc. In all villages the main source of any information was through television. Other available sources were: wall posters in 28 (55%); publicity by panchayat (village administration) office meetings in 27 (53%); dandora in 22 (43%); friends and relatives in 11 (22%); announcement by loud speakers in 9 (18%); television with cable connection in 8 (16%); radio in 5 (10%) and through health workers like VHN/ICDS workers in 4 (8%).

This study highlights availability of many associations like cine stars association, mahila mandal (women organization) etc in these villages. All matters including health programmes are discussed in these associations. Earlier studies also had shown that a variety of community members including students, village leaders, school teachers, community health workers, religious leaders, trade unions and women's organizations were used to raise awareness of the signs and symptoms of a number of health programmes through verbal communication (leprosy, diarrhea, malaria) [Rajeswari et al 1997]. Therefore a good programme like RNTCP should aim to tap all these resources in creating awareness on TB especially in the rural community.

This study also highlights the existence of multiple communication channels including television facility in the rural villages of Tamilnadu. The most important channels that are being commonly used to get day to day information are mass media /television, wall posters, meetings at panchayat office and through dandora. These channels can be utilised for spreading any health messages effectively. In addition most of the villages have local associations and place of worship where the community meet and exchange information. Policy makers and programme managers should tap all these resources to educate the community especially the rural community.

Conclusion: Main communication channels commonly used to get any information were television and wall posters. More than 50 percent of villages had local associations which can be used for effective communication. This information is vital for disseminating important information on public health programmes and educating the rural community. More studies are needed for adopting the newer communication channels for better management of TB patients in a manner that suits patients from rural and urban areas. Well planned IEC strategies utilizing modern tools will facilitate greater appreciation of RNTCP by stakeholders, will promote de-stigmatization, make TB services available to marginalized communities, will ensure completion of treatment and make DOTS a familiar name associated with cure.

Current scenario: Year 2007 had seen paradigm shift in communication modes with the wide availability of touch screen information booth and mobile phones both in rural and urban areas. More than 90 percent of our TB patients were accessible through mobile phones and this has been extensively used for tracking defaulters, patient management, for collecting follow-up sputum specimens and organizing drug logistics. In the urban areas among the literates yet another popular mode of communication has been the wide availability of internet providing access to facts on TB and TB control programme.

HEALTH COMMUNICATION STRATEGIES ADOPTED BY RNTCP IN INDIA

Introduction

IEC activities under the RNTCP aim to promote a better understanding of TB and its cure among the masses, improve the quality of care provided to TB patients, and to reduce stigma [Central TB Division 2005; 2007). Communication is a vital element in any development activity. It prepares people for change, provides information on key areas and helps in decision-making. Getting individuals to adopt new kinds of behaviour has been the chief aim of the health sector for a number of decades. It has also been the primary focus of numerous health education campaigns. IEC is an important component of all public health programmes. The role of IEC is to assist the RNTCP in achieving its overall objective of curing significant numbers of TB patients so that TB ceases to be a major public health problem in India. IEC is playing a distinct role in creating awareness about the disease, its curability and the availability of free high quality anti-TB drugs in health centres. IEC activities at the national and state levels are complimentary. While mass media activities are planned at the national level, state-level activities are more specific and need-based, with emphasis on sensitization of the health provider, production of state-specific IEC material, dissemination of this material to local levels and optimum use of folk media at the district levels. Effective, regular and consistent IEC activities are expected to enhance the performance of the RNTCP [Agarwal et al 2005].

STRATEGIC FRAMEWORK FOR IEC IN RNTCP

The aim of developing a strategic framework for IEC is to identify the communication need (objectives), communication players/audience (target groups) and communication tools (channels, activities and materials) [Central TB Division 2005]. The framework has six components: objectives, target groups, messages, channels, activities/materials and research, and monitoring. These are applied to each of the three objectives or IEC components. All IEC sub-components will be analysed qualitatively to assess the needs, correct and refine the programme as it evolves and help in gauging programme success in real time. The core strategic framework has been developed for use across the programme to ensure a clear and unified strategic direction for IEC throughout RNTCP. The communication approach is people-centred and client-friendly. This means understanding the audience, their context, their perceptions and their beliefs, and that too from *their* perspective, by learning from them, listening to them and working with them.

Target audience

The target audience includes two groups namely primary target group (TB patients/potential TB patients and families/ neighbours/ general public) and secondary target group (Doctors/RMPs/clinic operators/medical students, DOT providers, Local leaders, ANMs/AWWs, SHGs/CBOs and NGOs).

BARRIERS

Having defined the primary and secondary target audiences and the communication objectives, the next step is to use the available knowledge and/or findings of the needs assessment to identify barriers and means to overcome them. The possible barriers that could emerge in such an exercise are identified and listed as follows:

Target Group	Possible Barriers
Primary target group	
TB patients / potential TB patients:	Low risk perception
	Misconception about cure and treatment
	Fear of TB
	Stigma and discrimination
	Accessibility to services
	Cost of services and treatment
	Attitude of service providers
	Treatment process and time taken
	Low awareness of TB
Families / neighbours/ general public:	Low risk perception
	Misconception about cure and treatment
	Fear of TB stigma and discrimination
	Accessibility to services
	Cost of services and treatment
Secondary target group	
Doctors/DOT providers/local Leaders/ANMs/AWWs/SHGs	Inability to communicate effectively
	Lack of relevant information
	Lack of counselling skills

COMMUNICATION CHANNELS USED UNDER RNTCP

A number of channels have been used effectively to disseminate health communication messages. These are: 1. Folk media, 2. *Melas* /festivals, 3. Interpersonal communication, 4. Trialogue approach, 5. Sensitisation meetings for PRIs, 6. Print media, 7. Electronic media, 8. Broadcast media, 9. Workshops and seminars, 10. Health camps and 11. Other innovative channels. Using an appropriate multimedia mix enhances the reach and impact of health communication messages. The point of contact for interaction with patients at the health facility or the directly observed treatment short-course centre can be effectively used for patient education and information. However, this calls for skills in interpersonal communication. Supportive supervision as part of monitoring can be used to address misinformation and misunderstandings concerning TB. Other channels that can be used are exhibitions, camps, radio, television shows, public service announcements, panel discussions, print advertisements, workshops and seminars.

Communication activities proposed throughout the year [Central TB Division 2005]

Fortnightly
- Patient-provider interaction meetings

Monthly
- (Re)orientation training of ICDS officers and supervisors (different blocks)
- Orientation of Panjayat Raj Institution (PRI) members (different blocks)
- Interactive stalls in weekly markets
- Interaction meetings with Self-help Groups (SHGs) and women's groups

Quarterly
- (Re)orientation training for Non-government Organizations (NGOs) and Community Based Organisations (CBOs)
- (Re)orientation of tribal link workers (in tribal districts/blocks)
- (Re)orientation of traditional healers, Traditional Birth Attendants (TBAs), Village Health guides (VHGs)

Half-yearly
- Workshop for media personnel (All India Radio, Doordarshan [Indian national television network], field publicity officers)
- (Re)orientation of NSS volunteers
- (Re)training of cured former TB patients as DOT providers
- (Re)orientation of industrial workers, union leaders and representatives
- (Re)orientation of members of Nehru Yuva Kendra (NYK)
- (Re)orientation of SHG groups at district and block level
- Workshop to develop posters and other printed materials
- Workshop on the role of media for increasing visibility of RNTCP at state, district and block-levels
- Street theatre technique and script writing workshop

Yearly
- CME programmes at medical colleges and nursing institutions
- (Re)orientation of NGOs at district-and state-level
- Audio-visual material development with tribal and other un reached communities
- (Re)orientation of PRI members at block-level
- Trialogue approach with patient group; interaction with people at Peripheral Health Institution (PHI) level
- Workshop on script writing of TB related dramas for professional writers (usually conducted at state-level)
- Patient group meeting at PHI level
- (Re)orientation of jail inmates and employees

Special IEC Activities
- Leading up to and on World TB Day, 24th March
- Health Communication Activities Throughout the Year

CONCLUSION

Government of India has realised the importance of communication to reach the vast number of people in a nation characterised by tremendous diversity. But, given the diversity and uneven development of the country in terms of infrastructure and socioeconomic indicators, this will be a challenging task.

Chapter 8

BETWEEN KNOWLEDGE, THEORY AND PRACTICE: HOW HEALTH-PROMOTING SCHOOLS "HAPPENED" IN CHINA

Carmen Aldinger, Cheryl Vince Whitman, Zhang Xin-Wei and Jack T. Jones

In this chapter, we examine the extent to which processes and factors we think are important are consistent with the processes and factors expressed in a successful effort to scale up the development of Health-Promoting Schools in Zhejiang Province, China. In doing so, we: (1) Review theoretical frameworks associated with the planning, implementation and success of school health programs, including the *Health-Promoting School (HPS)* framework put forth by the World Health Organization (WHO); *Key Factors in Changing Policy and Practice*, a framework developed by Cheryl Vince Whitman of Health and Human Development Programs at Education Development Center, Inc., Newton, Massachusetts, U.S.A. and a framework of success factors for health education programs from WHO's publication, *Skills for Health*. (2) Present new research, based on grounded theory analyses, designed to discover and describe how Health-Promoting Schools "happened" in schools in Zhejiang Province, China. Qualitative data gathered in interviews with and written responses from school administrators, teachers, students, and parents are presented to illustrate key processes through which schools became Health-Promoting Schools, including processes to engage participants; promote conceptual understanding; plan, implement and evaluate overall program activities; conduct interventions at the classroom, school and community-levels; and overcome challenges. Self-reported changes in individual lives, including knowledge, attitudes and behaviours are also presented. (3) Identify and discuss consistencies and differences between the processes and factors cited in the theoretical frameworks and those found through the grounded theory analyses of the Zhejiang effort. (4) Conclude by suggesting how the findings of consistencies and differences can be useful to persons striving to strengthen theoretical frameworks and those striving to implement Health-Promoting Schools. This includes the identification of processes and factors cited in theoretical frameworks that are validated or supported by processes and factors discovered through the grounded theory analyses; and the identification of processes and factors discovered through the grounded theory analyses that are not cited in the theoretical frameworks and should be considered in the further development of theoretical frameworks.

INTRODUCTION

Knowledge is the foundation of *theory* constructed to make sense of what we "know". We promote theory as a well informed framework for thought, planning and action. We qualify *practice* that is based on theory as "best practice". But knowledge is not truth, and invariably differences occur *between* a program's theory-based plan and its practice—sometimes to the program's benefit, sometimes to its detriment. By analyzing statements about how a program *happened,* as described by persons directly involved we may be able to discover ways to strengthen knowledge, theory and practice, as well as improve program outcomes. This is what we strive to do here.

In this chapter, we review three theoretical frameworks offering processes and factors thought to be important in planning and implementing successful comprehensive school health programs. We present new research, based on grounded theory analyses, designed to discover and describe how Health-Promoting Schools "happened" in schools in Zhejiang Province, China. We discuss the consistencies and differences between the processes/factors cited in the frameworks and those found through the grounded theory analyses. We conclude by suggesting how the findings of consistencies and differences can be useful to persons striving to strengthen theoretical frameworks and those striving to implement Health-Promoting Schools.

WHAT WE THINK WE KNOW ABOUT IMPLEMENTING EFFECTIVE SCHOOL HEALTH PROGRAMS

Three frameworks, used internationally to promote the development of effective school health programs, are reviewed in depth below. The first framework, *The Concept of the Health-Promoting School* (WHO, 2006) (Figure 1) was framed by the World Health Organization (WHO). This framework guided the planning and implementation of school health programs in Zhejiang Province, China. The second framework, *Key Factors in Changing Policy and Practice* (Whitman, 2005) (Figure 2) was developed by one of this chapter's authors, Cheryl Vince Whitman of Health and Human Development Programs (HHD), Education Development Center, Inc. (EDC). This framework describes factors that systemic changes experts believe are necessary to diffuse new concepts and implement changes in policies, systems and everyday practices. The third framework, *Critical Success Factors in School-based Approaches to Health Education* (Figure 3) was developed by another of this chapter's authors, Carmen Aldinger of HHD/EDC (WHO, 2003). This framework is a compilation of success factors derived from school health-related research and experience in less developed as well as more developed countries. Theory, research and consensus underpinning and/or complementing these frameworks are also cited.

The Framework of the Health-Promoting School (HPS)

Many schools, worldwide, strive to influence health by using a comprehensive model that includes health education, a healthy environment, health services, and other factors. Major global and national initiatives foster this "comprehensive" approach to school health. This model is not new, but it gained substantial definition and momentum through actions taken globally and nationally in the mid-1980s.

At the global level, the concept of the Health-Promoting School (HPS) is based on public health theory that builds on the Ottawa Charter of Health Promotion (WHO, 1986). The Ottawa Charter calls for five health promotion "actions" that should be adapted to the local needs and possibilities of individual countries. These are: building healthy public policy, creating supportive environments, strengthening community action, developing personal skills, and reorienting health services. Adapting the Ottawa Charter for use in school environments calls for: school health policy, healthy school environments, school-community partnerships, life skills education, and school health services.

What is a Health-Promoting School?

A Health-Promoting School is one that constantly strengthens its capacity as a healthy setting for living, learning, and working.

A Health-Promoting School:
- Fosters health and learning with all the measures at its disposal.
- Engages health and education officials, teachers, teachers' unions, students, parents, health providers, and community leaders in efforts to make the school a healthy place.
- Strives to provide (1) a healthy environment, (2) school health education, and (3) school health services along with (4) school/community projects and outreach, (5) health promotion programs for staff, (6) nutrition and food safety programs, (7) opportunities for physical education and recreation, and (8) programs for counselling, social support, and mental health promotion.
- Implements policies and practices that respect an individual's well being and dignity, provides multiple opportunities for success, and acknowledges good efforts and intentions as well as personal achievements.

Strives to improve the health of school personnel, families, and community members as well as pupils; and works with community leaders to help them understand how the community contributes to, or undermines, health and education.

Figure 25. Concept of the Health-Promoting School by the World Health Organization
Adapted from: http://www.who.int/school_youth_health/gshi/hps/en/index.html (retrieved April 8, 2008)

At the national level, in 1987, Allensworth and Kolbe in the United States proposed a model with eight components that could have complementary, if not synergistic, effects. This model included school health services, school health education, school health environment, integrated school and community health promotion efforts, school physical education, school food service, school counselling, and school health-promotion programs for faculty and staff (Allensworth and Kolbe, 1987).

In 1995, WHO launched its Global School Health Initiative (GSHI) that drew on the Ottawa Charter and the eight-component model by Allensworth and Kolbe. The goal of this initiative is to support schools to become Health-Promoting Schools. WHO's concept of a Health-Promoting School (HPS) is shown in Figure 1.

In 2000, at the World Education Forum in Dakar, Senegal, WHO, the United Nations Educational, Scientific and Cultural Organization (UNESCO), the United Nations Children's Fund (UNICEF), and the World Bank - recognizing the education sector's need to play a greater role in improving *health for all* to achieve its own goal of *education for all* - came together to create a *joint* initiative for school health. They titled the joint initiative *Focusing Resources on Effective School Health (FRESH)* (UNESCO, UNICEF, WHO, & World Bank, 2000)

FRESH draws on and complements the HPS concept. As an act of consensus, the initiating partners, and other agencies that have since joined the initiative, call upon schools worldwide to implement a core framework for action that includes health-related school policies, the provision of safe water and sanitation as the essential first steps towards a healthy learning environment, skills-based health education and school-based health and nutrition services. They also call for schools to support such action through strategies that include partnerships between teachers and health workers, effective community partnerships and pupil awareness and participation.

WHO supports FRESH and encourages health and education agencies to act on its calls. To facilitate action, WHO develops and publishes manuals and other documents, in collaboration with FRESH partners, to help health and education officials and practitioners understand the HPS concept and assist schools to become HPS. However, despite the consensus for FRESH and despite the joint and complementary actions of WHO and other international partners, a recent systematic review of the HPS approach found that none of the schools in 12 controlled before and after studies had implemented all of the components of this approach (Stewart-Brown, 2006). These findings are consistent with earlier studies of HPS programs that found that none incorporated all 5 components of the HPS concept (Lynagh et al, 1997).

Calls for action and technical guidance from major international organizations foster attention and interest in HPS and offer some technical guidance, but changes in national, community and school-level policies and practices are needed to substantially diffuse the implementation of HPS and similar comprehensive school health programs. The following framework provides a set of factors that are thought to be important in facilitating change in policies and practices.

KEY FACTORS IN CHANGING POLICY AND PRACTICE

Diffusion, according to Everett Rogers, whose name has become virtually synonymous with the study of diffusion of innovations, "is the process through which an *innovation*, defined as an idea perceived as new, spreads via certain *communication channels* over time among the members of a *social system*" (Rogers, 2004). One can view Health-Promoting Schools (HPS) as an "innovation", its "communication channels" policies, practices and programs; its "social system" education and health agencies from the national-level to the school/community-level; and its "members", policymakers, practitioners and individuals. To implement HPS—or to facilitate the adoption of any other new concept—systemic change experts believe that certain critical factors are necessary.

Key Factors in Changing Policy and Practice (Figure 2) was developed to help ministries and schools identify factors that can be addressed to create changes at the policymaker, practitioner and individual-levels and facilitate necessary changes in policies, systems and everyday practices. It is thought that the more program planners can address these factors, the greater the likelihood they will gain the capacity to transform research findings into policies and practices that help schools develop effective school health programs (Whitman, 1999& 2005).

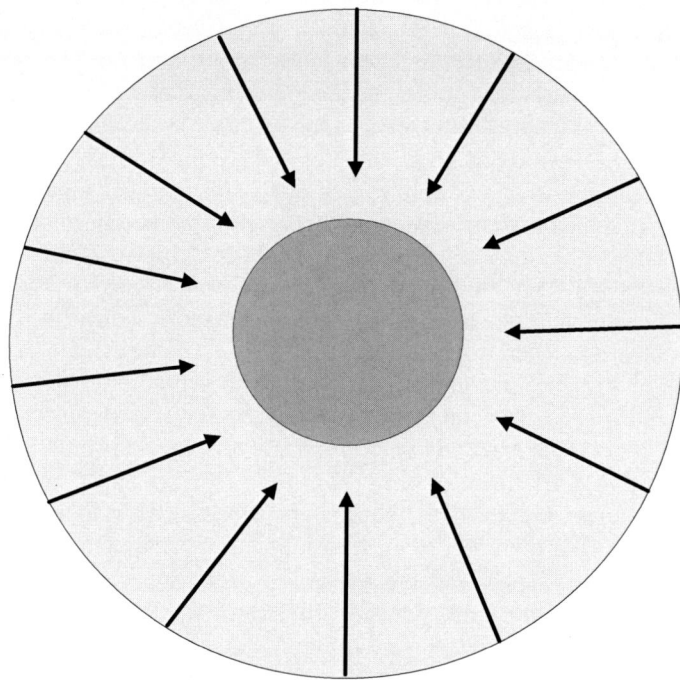

Figure 2.
Adapted from Vince Whitman, C. (2005). Implementing research-based health promotion programmes in schools: Strategies for capacity building. In B. B. Jensen (Ed.), *The health promoting school: International advances in theory, evaluation and practice* (pp. 107-135). Copenhagen: Danish University of Education Press.

Each of the factors identified in Figure 2 are thought to be important for the process of developing and implementing a sustainable HPS program (Whitman, 2005).

- **Vision and concept**: One of the first key factors in the process of changing policy and practice is to have a <u>clear vision or big idea</u> to guide outcomes. A clear vision can be instrumental in leading educators to adopt new and more effective practices. The HPS concept, which combines policy, instruction, a healthy school environment and services, is a broad vision in comparison with the narrower traditional view of school health as classroom instruction. Implementation of the HPS concept requires a large change. Some critics, particularly from the education sector, may reject international calls to create HPS because they feel education systems are already overburdened. However, research shows that more often than not, change occurs as a result of outside influences and ideas requiring large changes are more likely to be embraced than ideas involving small, incremental ones (Berman and McLaughlin, 1975).

- **International and national guidelines**: National and international guidelines, such as the regulation for quality education in China and the WHO concept of Health-Promoting Schools, are often theory- and research based. Such guidelines are an attempt to improve policy and practice based on what has been studied and found to be effective. Research shows that among school districts informed of principles related to the effectiveness of school health-related policies, many school districts reported that they applied the principles and selected research-based curriculum (Hallfors and Godette, 2002). There is little doubt that the presence of national or international policies and guidelines from ministries of education and health or international organizations often sparks the efforts of schools.
- **Champions and leaders at all levels**: Leadership provides the inspiration and ability to galvanize and motivate people to achieve a mission and a goal. Research shows that good outcomes are associated with principal or headmaster support. Without principal support, it is sometimes not possible to achieve intended outcomes (Kam, Greenberg and Walls, 2003) and a leader's commitment, dedication, support and ability to articulate the vision and inspire others is a key factor in determining outcomes (Kotter, 1988). According to Rogers, "Change agent effort, whether [by] the leader or [by] her designee, is known to be a predictor in the rate of diffusion (Rogers, 1995). To implement complex ideas, such as Health-Promoting Schools, leadership talent must exist and be applied at every level, not just at senior level.
- **Administrative and management support**: Human and financial capacities are necessary to plan and manage the change process. This includes clarifying roles, responsibilities, maintaining clear communication channels, and making sure that tasks proceed on time and within budget.
- **Data-driven planning and decision-making**: Data can help program planners identify problems that are important to the nation and/or community and set priorities for addressing needs. Data can provide evidence to help policy-and decision-makers justify increased support for school health programs. Data are needed by program administrators and practitioners to understand health, academic and behavioural patterns that underlie risk and protective factors, to analyze demographics for how interventions fit the target population, to assess the financial, human and other resources that can be obtained for program implementation, and to assess the organizational properties that affect the school or district's readiness to implement the program. Tracking progress also requires data, as well as mechanisms to supply the data to planners for course correction and to document the impact of the program.
- **Team training and ongoing coaching/learning community**: Training and coaching are important ways to develop capacity within institutions to implement new concepts. Administrators and teachers first need to be familiar with a new concept before they can implement it. Research shows that technical assistance can build capacities for change by nurturing, enhancing and employing the skills and talents of people and institutions at all levels (Yates, 2000).
- **Critical mass and supportive norms**: "A critical mass of people who share supportive norms is necessary for creating new thinking and practices within and

across systems. People in groups tend to move toward normative actions ... Until and unless enough staff are trained and committed to implementing research-based practices, it is unrealistic to expect a single teacher or administrator returning home from off-site training to be able to effect change" (Whitman, 2005). For this reason, any training provided should involve at least three or four people from the same school or ministry, who can become the critical mass that influences the norms.

- **Dedicated time and resources**: A core team must be dedicated adequate time--and willing to use that time--to implement new programs. A common reason for failure of new projects is that managers underestimate how much time it will take and overestimate the readiness of their staff and systems to take on the project. It is important to assess realistically how much time an institution will need to move in a new direction and to determine the staff readiness and willingness to engage in the effort.
- **Attention to external forces**: "More often than not, change occurs as a result of outside influences" (Whitman, 2005). These influences might include national or international guidelines or movements.
- **Adaptation to local concerns**: Programs might move to settings that are not identical to the original. The cultural diversity of students, the type and setting of school system, and the income level of families might vary from the program's original context. It is, therefore, important to consider how much change a program can undergo without failing to produce the original results. Research shows that attention to fidelity is critical for successful outcomes (Backer, 2001).
- **Mechanism for cross-sector collaboration**: Collaboration between various sectors is essential, especially between the health and education sectors. Sometimes this involves a (national) coordinator and/or a Memorandum of Understanding.
- **Stage of readiness**: A country might be at either of the following stages of readiness: Pre-contemplation (a country or school has not seriously thought about taking action in this area), Contemplation (a country or school has thought about taking action, but has not developed plans), Preparation (a country or school has thought about taking action and is developing plans), Action (a country or school has taken action and continues to take action), or Maintenance (a country or school has been taking action for several years and has developed a plan of action for sustaining it)
- **Stakeholder ownership & participation**: Ownership and participation of ministries, schools, communities, and students are important for successful implementation.

All of these factors are considered important for the process of developing and implementing a sustainable HPS program. They are also consistent with protocols and guidelines for Health-Promoting Schools published by St. Leger (2005). The next framework offers program planners and practitioners a set of factors thought to be particularly important for success.

CRITICAL SUCCESS FACTORS IN SCHOOL-BASED APPROACHES TO HEALTH EDUCATION

School health education, often referred to as "skills-based health education", is a core component of the HPS concept and the FRESH initiative. Nine factors are thought to be critical to the success of school-based approaches to health education, and these factors are likely to be important to the success of other components of the HPS concept. The nine factors are derived from research and experience in less developed as well as more developed nations. They serve as a framework for improving school health education and other components of comprehensive school health programs (WHO, 2003).

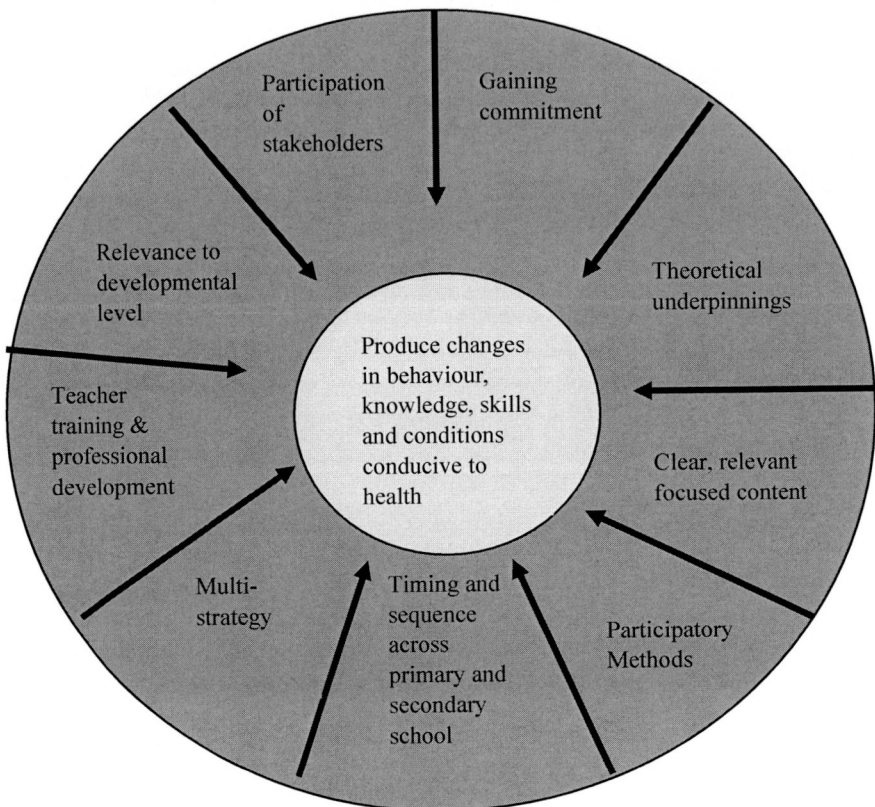

Figure 3. Success Factors in School-based Approaches to Health Education
(Original design for a new figure)

- **Gaining commitment**: Intense advocacy is required from the earliest planning stages to influence key national leaders; to mobilize the community to place skills-based health education on its agenda; and to hold the community accountable for implementing national and international agreements. Advocating with accurate and timely data can convince national leaders and communities that prevention from an early age is important. It can also help ensure that programs focus on the actual health needs, experience, motivation, and strengths of the target population, rather than on problems as perceived by others (UNICEF, 2000; Webb & Elliott, 2000). Communicating the evidence, listening and responding to community concerns, and valuing community opinions can help garner commitment, while effective resource mobilization will underscore the success of such efforts (UNESCO & UNFPA, 2001; South Africa Ministry of Health and Ministry of Education, 1998). At the school level, effective skills-based health education programs rely on the larger vision of health promotion, which incorporates health into education reform. They also rely on the extent to which the school itself makes a priority of promoting health, that is, whether it links its own health policies and services to skills-based health education and provides a healthy psychosocial and physical school environment.

- **Theoretical underpinnings**: Effective programs are based upon theoretical approaches that have been demonstrated to be effective in influencing health-related risk behaviours. Common elements exist across these theories, including the importance of personalizing information and probability of risks, increasing motivation and readiness for change/action, understanding and influencing peers and social norms, enhancing personal skills and attitudes and ability to take action, and developing enabling environments through supportive policies and service delivery (UNICEF, 2000). Social learning theories suggest that performing a behaviour will be affected by an understanding of what needs to be done (knowledge), a belief in the anticipated benefit (motivation), a belief that particular skills will be effective (outcome expectancy), and a belief that one can effectively use these skills (self-efficacy) (Kirby, 2001). Other theories that frequently serve to underpin health education include the health belief model, social cognitive theory, theory of planned behaviour, self-efficacy theory of behaviour change, child and adolescent development theories, problem behaviour theory, social influence theory, cognitive problem solving, multiple intelligences and resilience theory.
- **Clear, relevant focused content**: The information, attitudes, and skills that comprise the program content should be selected for their relevance to specific health-related risk and protective behaviours. For example, resisting peer pressure to smoke or use drugs, delaying the initiation of intercourse or using contraception, or identifying a trusted adult for support during depression. Programs that address a balance of knowledge, attitudes, and skills — such as communication, negotiation, and refusal skills — have been most successful in affecting behaviour. Programs with heavy emphasis on (biological) information have had more limited impact on enhancing attitudes and skills and reducing risk behaviours (Wilson, Mparadzi, & Lavelle, 1992). Effective programs focus narrowly on a small number of specific behavioural goals and give a clear health content message by continually reinforcing a positive and health-promoting stance on these behaviours (Kirby, 2001). General programs and those that have attempted to cover a broad array of topics, values, and skills without linking them are generally not recommended where *prevention* of specific risk behaviour is the goal (Kann et al, 1995).
- **Participatory Methods**: Effective programs utilize a variety of participatory teaching methods, address social pressures and modelling of skills, and provide basic, accurate information. Effective participatory teaching methods, such as debate, discussion, and plays actively involve the students and target particular health issues (Kirby, 2001). Programs with a heavy emphasis on information can improve knowledge, but are generally not effective in enhancing attitudes, skills, or actual behaviour (Wilson, Mparadzi & Lavelle 1992). However, effective programs do need to provide some basic, accurate information that students can use to assess risks and avoid risky behaviours (Kirby, 2001).
- **Timing and sequence across primary and secondary school**: Effective education programs are intensive and begin prior to the onset of risk behaviours. As a guide, at least 8 hours of intensive training or at least 15 hours of classroom sessions per year will be required to provide adequate exposure and practice for students to acquire skills. Subsequent booster sessions are needed to sustain outcomes (Jemmott et al., 1992; Kirby & DiClemente, 1994; Wilson, Mparadzi & Lavelle, 1992; Botvin, 2001). A planned and sequenced curriculum across the primary and secondary school years is recommended. The age and stage of the learner need to be considered. Concepts should progress from simple to complex, with later lessons reinforcing and building on earlier learning. Education and other prevention efforts need to be

constant over time to ensure that successive cohorts of children and young people are protected.

- **Multi-strategy**: Programs need to be coordinated and consistent with other strategies, such as policies, health and community services, community development, and media approaches. Coordination within and among donor agencies and between regional and national programs is also important. Because the determinants of behaviour are varied and complex, and the reach of any one program (e.g., in schools) will be limited, a narrow focus is unlikely to yield sustained impact on behaviour in the long term. Only coordinated multi-strategy approaches can achieve the intensity of efforts that yields sustained behaviour change in the long term (UNESCO, UNFPA, 2001; South Africa Ministry of Health and Ministry of Education, 1998).

- **Teacher training and professional development**: Teachers or peer leaders of effective programs believe in the program and receive adequate training. Training needs to give teachers and peers information about the program as well as practice in using the teaching strategies in the curricula (Kirby, 2001). Research shows that teacher training for the implementation of a comprehensive secondary school health education curriculum positively affects teachers' preparedness for teaching skills-based health education and has positive effects both on curriculum implementation and on student outcomes (Kann et al, 1995; Ross et al, 1991).

- **Relevance to developmental level**: Programs must be relevant to the reality and developmental levels of young people and must address risks that have the potential to cause the most harm to individuals and society. Issues that attract media attention and public concern may not be the most prevalent or harmful. Reinforcing clear values against risk behaviour and strengthening individual values and group norms need to be central to prevention programs. The program goals, teaching methods, and materials need to be appropriate to the age, experience, and culture of children and young people and the communities they live in, and need to recognize what the learner already knows, feels, and can do (Kirby, 2001).

- **Participation of stakeholders**: A collaborative approach to program development can reinforce desired behaviour through providing a supportive environment for school programs. The participation of learners, parents, community workers, peer educators, and others in the design and implementation of school health programs can help ensure that the needs and concerns of all these constituencies are met in culturally and socially appropriate ways. Participants whose concerns are addressed are more likely to demonstrate commitment to and ownership of the program, which in turn enhances sustainability and effectiveness (UNICEF, 2001: Jemmott, Jemmott & Fong, 1998).

The three frameworks above express what we think we know about the factors and processes associated with the implementation of effective school health programs. In the next section, we will describe our findings about how such programs were implemented in Zhejiang, China, based on the reported experiences of the people involved.

How Effective School Health Programs "Happened" in Zhejiang Province, China, According to the People Involved

In 2003, when officials of Zhejiang Province, China decided to systematically expand their effort to promote the development of HPS throughout their province, WHO agreed to provide partial financial and technical support for evaluation. The Zhejiang official's decision was based on the positive experiences of two HPS pilot projects previously conducted in the province (Ma et al, 2002; Xia et al, 2004) and a third project that used materials from UNICEF to address school-based injury prevention. WHO decided to assist the effort to fill gaps in the knowledge-base related to HPS. Researchers questioned the sufficiency of evidence to support the efficacy and feasibility of implementing a HPS approach (Lynagh, et al, 1999; St Leger, 2001) and the lack of consensus for how such efforts should be evaluated (Lynagh, Perkins & Schofield, 2002; St Leger & Nutbeam, 2000).

From the beginning of the effort, EDC, WHO, and Zhejiang officials worked together, and with national health and education experts, to investigate whether the complex framework of Health-Promoting Schools could be successfully implemented in a variety of schools that differed by levels of students, economic conditions and geographical settings; and whether it could positively affect the participants. As an integral part of the expansion effort, Zhejiang officials conducted a series of surveys to gather *quantitative data*: the Global School-based Student Health Survey (GSHS) for 13-to-15-year-olds which assessed risk and protective behaviours related to health; Evaluation Index for Health-Promoting Schools Bronze Awards (from WHO/WPRO), which assessed in detail the various aspects of HPS components that the schools implemented; WHO Psycho-Social Environment Profile (PSE), which assessed perceptions of the social and emotional school environment, and a content-related questionnaire from former pilot projects in China, which assessed knowledge, attitudes, and behaviours. The first three instruments were generated through WHO; the latter was developed by Chinese experts. Results show that participating schools were able to implement all of the components of a HPS and positive changes in knowledge, attitudes and behaviours occurred among the groups targeted (Zhang et al, 2008; Aldinger et al, 2008; Aldinger et al, 2008b; Whitman, et al, 2008).

As a complement to the *quantitative measure*, authors of this chapter developed *qualitative measures* that were applied during the HPS expansion to assess the processes and procedures of implementing HPS and the participants' experience with the project. The "Qualitative Study", described below, was designed to obtain data to answer *four questions, from the perspective of the people directly involved in the processes*:

- What were the key processes through which schools in Zhejiang Province became Health-Promoting Schools?
- What intervention activities did schools in Zhejiang Province implement to become Health-Promoting Schools?
- What were the major challenges that schools in Zhejiang Province have to overcome to become Health-Promoting Schools?
- What changes were reported in the participants' lives as evidence that their schools were successfully promoting health?

The resulting data provide a unique account of what "happened" from the perspective of the people involved.

The Qualitative Study - Theoretical Basis

The qualitative study of the Zhejiang HPS expansion falls into what Smith (2002) calls institutional ethnography, a process in which *interviewing* is part of an approach to investigate organizational and institutional processes. An institution, in this case, does not refer to a particular type of organization, but to coordinated and intersecting work processes involved in developing a HPS. The purpose of this type of study is to discover and describe "how it happens" based on putting together an integrated view from the otherwise truncated accounts of each informant (DeVault & McCoy, 2002).

Grounded theory served as the basis for analyzing the data obtained through the interviews. This means that "theory must emerge or be developed from the data and not from predetermined hypotheses or formulation" (Chamberlain, 1999). This approach provided an opportunity to gain new insights by looking at the factors and processes of HPS development "with fresh eyes" and not by simply superimposing the three theoretical frameworks cited above (HPS, Change and Success). It should, however, be noted that the HPS model influenced the work in Zhejiang Province. We used the HPS framework as a planning model for the effort. Nevertheless, the Grounded Theory methodology provided an opportunity to generate theory that is grounded in data (Strauss & Corbin, 1998). Thus, the data were first analyzed by original coding and, only in the second phase of the analysis, by going back to the theoretical frameworks described above. In this study we will compare the analyses.

The Qualitative Study - Selection of schools and interviewees

The Health Education Institute of Zhejiang Province chose the participating schools, based on guidance from the research team: For the first round of data collection, one former pilot school and two schools that joined the project in the first scaling-up phase—one from a poorly resourced environment and one from an adequately resourced environment—were included. The following two rounds of data collection included only schools from the scaling-up phase. At least one school from a poorly resourced environment was investigated in each round. The rationale for this choice was to examine if and how HPS could be implemented in both adequately and poorly resourced environments.

Schools chose the interviewees, based on guidance in the research protocol that called for: 1–2 school administrators (e.g., principal, vice principal), 4–6 teachers (from different subject areas) and/or other implementers (such as school doctor), 4–6 students (from different grade levels), 4–6 parents (from different socio-economic backgrounds), representing a mixture of males and females for each group.

Nine schools with a total population of about 15,200 students participated in the study. The sample of 191 interview participants for this qualitative study included: 26 school administrators (19 male, 7 female), 56 teachers and school staff (21 male, 35 female), 64 students (25 male, 34 female, 5 genders not recorded by research team), and 45 parents (14 male, 31 female). Gender balance was not always possible for practical reasons such as more males than females being in the school's administrative positions. This sample represented two elementary schools, two middle schools, two junior high schools, one high school, and two vocational schools.

The Qualitative Study – Interview questions

School administrators, teachers and other implementers, students, and parents were interviewed in three separate rounds of interviews, each in different schools. For each round of data gathering, a questionnaire with structured, open ended questions, developed by the research team, had a different focus. The first round of data gathering focused on *program planning*, the second round focused on *program implementation*, and the third round focused on *program assessment*. In the second and third round participants were asked to provide written answers during the first part of the interview which was then collected at the end of the interview. The study protocol and questions were reviewed by EDC's Institutional Review Board (IRB) which found that they met the criteria for exemption from expedited or full IRB review because the research was a normal educational practice conducted in an established educational setting. The questions were translated from English into Chinese prior to the interviews for use by the interpreter and some of the interviewees.

The Qualitative Study - Data gathering

Data collection took place during three separate visits to Zhejiang Province at approximately 7, 14 and 24 months after the start of operations. Each round of data collection included four group interviews in each of three schools. Each group interview with one of the target groups (school administrators, teachers, students, parents, respectively) lasted approximately one hour. The interpreter asked the questions in Chinese and translated the responses into English. One member of the research team was Chinese. He assisted with translations or clarifications, as needed. In the first round of interviews, all data was gathered by interview. In the second and third rounds, interviewees were given the opportunity to read over the questions in their own language and to make notes in preparation for the interview. The notes were collected after the interview to serve as additional data for which there may not have been sufficient time to obtain during the interview. The research team also reviewed files with documents and pictures at the schools and toured all but one school (one school was not toured for lack of time) to make observations in an effort to triangulate the data from the interviews.

Prior to the interviews, the interpreter received some background on the project, HPS documents, and the protocol and instructions for the interviews. At the beginning of each interview, and as part of the protocol, the interpreter mentioned that the interviews were to gather the participants' experiences and opinions in order to strengthen the implementation of the HPS project. The interpreter stressed that each participant's opinion was important, that there were no right or wrong answers, that participants should feel comfortable expressing their ideas about the topics discussed, and that their answers would be reported anonymously to ensure confidentiality. Interviewees agreed to have the interviews tape-recorded.

The Qualitative Study - Data analysis

After transcribing notes from the group interviews and obtaining translations of the respondents' written comments, Atlas.ti software was used for the systematic process of qualitative data analysis and coding. Indexing codes were created for the types of respondents (administrators, teachers, students, parents), number and types of schools (elementary, middle, high, vocational school), and round of interviews. Free codes were created for the first part of the analysis, based on the data. Most codes started with the prefix of a broad concept, such as "Organization," "Activities," or "Challenges" followed by the various aspects of each concept that emerged from the data, such as: "Activities: health ambassadors," or "Organization: HPS planning committee." Codes were created for: different types of activities; different types of attitude change, behaviour change, and knowledge change; different types of challenges; different processes of decision-making (e.g., selection entry point and class activities); different aspects of the school environment; different mechanisms of organization; and different types of teaching methods and training. The final list of codes included 178 codes. These codes emerged from the content of the data and were unguided by any framework. For the second level of analysis, data were coded according to the components of the three theoretical frameworks cited above (HPS. Change, Success). For each framework, sub-codes were created for the components of the framework, such as HPS: health education, Change: adaptation to local concerns, Success: gaining commitment.

The Qualitative Study – Results

The results of the qualitative study are the synthesis of what school administrators, teachers, students and parents told us about what "happened" as they undertook the challenge of creating a HPS. The *processes* that emerged from their descriptions are organized by the study's *research questions* and by school and/or respondent. Their descriptions express *processes* in terms of what was attempted, how it was done, who was involved and/or to what extent the process was perceived to be important or challenging. We have sought to present much of their original (translated) descriptions because putting participants' responses in "our" terms is an interpretation that might not always be correct and "their" words sometimes convey a sense of intensity, satisfaction or importance that may be lost without the original phrasing.

1. RESEARCH QUESTION: WHAT WERE THE KEY PROCESSES THROUGH WHICH SCHOOLS IN ZHEJIANG PROVINCE BECAME HEALTH-PROMOTING SCHOOLS?

Participants reported:

- **Pre-implementation processes**
- **Implementation processes**
- **Evaluation processes and perceived achievements**

Pre-implementation processes - Several pre-implementation activities emerged as important processes in preparations for the implementation of the HPS project. They are:

- gaining leadership support
- motivating willingness to take part
- learning the HPS concept
- choosing an entry point
- setting up a special HPS committee
- developing a work plan
- setting up policies and systems of operation

Gaining leadership support – The effort to expand the development of Health-Promoting Schools started with *gaining leadership support,* especially from the education and health bureaus at the provincial, city, and municipal levels. Leadership support included getting leaders to *pay attention, give priority to the project and provide technical and /or financial assistance.* The following examples demonstrate the importance with which the *process of gaining leadership support* was perceived and explain who, how and what this entailed.

- In an urban middle school, one of the school administrators' responsibilities was to communicate with the government and win their support. The report of the school stated, "We fought for the support strongly of the city Bureau of Education and [our town's] government actively. Only in 2003, [our] town threw in 3,400,000 Yuan to set up a dormitory building for teachers and students of an apartment type. The Bureau of Education invested more than 100,000 Yuan for auxiliary facility in the dormitory building and the acquiring of more than 10 classrooms multimedia equipments." An administrator acknowledged that the school "has treated this project as the key work to do and governments at the provincial, city, and town level paid enough attention to us and support us." The administrators considered support from the government very helpful for implementing the HPS program.
- In a rural elementary school, one of the administrators wrote, "We gained the support from the supervising department, especially the financial support." Most of the teachers also mentioned the importance of attention from leaders and government support and told us that officials at all levels "tried their hardest to make all resources they could find available to support the implementation of this project." Teachers and students also paid a lot of attention to this project. A student mentioned that conditions changed, "owing to the attention of leaders."
- In an urban junior high school, administrators answered that it was helpful to get "support from leaders at different levels of the municipal public health departments" and that "the concern from WHO" was also helpful. Three of the parents also responded that receiving more attention from leaders was helpful.

Being motivated – Motivation to take part in developing a HPS stemmed from several factors. They included *anticipating awards, fame and honour, supporting government mandated quality education for students' all around education, and hopes of moving the society forward.* The following examples demonstrate the importance of motivational factors and explain who, how and what this entailed.

- An urban elementary was part of the pilot project and had already received the Health-Promoting Schools Bronze Medal. Now the school was striving to obtain the Health-Promoting Schools Silver Medal. The participants reported *being motivated* by the reputation their school had acquired. They indicated that the HPS program made their school famous; there were reports about their school in the daily newspaper and many teachers from other schools visited this school.
- In an urban middle school, an administrator mentioned "fame" and "honour" as a motivating factor. He said they "won good response from the society [and the] school's fame was spread more widely across the society." The school received honours such as "Middle School to be the Health-Promoting Schools". Participants also seemed to be motivated by the government's encouragement of "quality education" which they the felt was supported by the HPS program. They also seemed motivated by their perception that the program was "well designed" and described their level of support as "everyone was very devoted to it".
- In a rural vocational school, a high sense of priority seemed to serve as a motivational factor. Administrators applied the ISO-9000 international standard for quality management to ensure that this project got high priority. Furthermore, parents seemed motivated by the benefits that they perceived for their children, their society and themselves. They noted that children are the adults of tomorrow and thus "very important for the deep progress of society." "If we want to push the society [to] keep on moving, we have to educate our kids." As parents, they had "no such opportunity to take their formal education. So when…children have a chance to know more about health…the parents can learn from their children."

Learning about the Health-Promoting Schools concept – One of the first steps taken in the project was to involve participants in learning about the HPS concept. This was done by school administrators and teachers learning from the CDC and former pilot schools through workshops, training sessions, site visits and materials; by students learning from headmasters and teachers; and by parents learning from teachers and students. The following examples demonstrate who, how and what was involved in *learning about the HPS concept* and the types of responses it evoked.

- In a suburban middle school, administrators read about the HPS concept in the newspaper, but they were not really sure what it was. They contacted the CDC and Ministry of Education to explain it. They thought it was "significant" and sent representatives to the initial HPS training session in Hangzhou. The English teacher was put in charge of the school's project. He got "a general idea of HPS concept…what to do and how to do it." He learned more by studying the WHO documents, visiting a former pilot school, and searching on the Internet for relevant information. Other teachers were oriented to the HPS concept at their school's training. They thought it was a good idea. Students said they heard about HPS from the headmaster and from teachers. They thought it is "a good thing, of course" and can help "to get knowledge about good health and improve skills for health."
- In a sub-urban high school, the principal heard about the HPS concept and felt it was already "deeply rooted in his mind and in this school." The school published an article about the concept in its newsletter and made a clear case why it was needed. The newsletter read, in part:

Efforts to improve school health education have made great progress. However, health education is still limited, and there is still an emphasis on standard academic education and on increasing the proportion of students passing into higher levels of the education system. For these reasons, school health education has never been able to achieve the expected goals. The occurrence of common health conditions among students, such as poor nutrition, vision problems and cavities, remains high and has not decreased. Among students, such problems as psychological illness, accidental injury and cardiovascular diseases appear to be increasing. Therefore, taking effective measures to increase the quality of students' mental and physical health is an issue that must be addressed immediately. Moreover, to solve this problem, we must develop "health promoting schools." Only in this way can we ensure that students grow up healthy and promote the health of all community members, including school staff and parents. School will not only be a place to obtain knowledge but also a place to obtain health.

In a suburban vocational school, administrators said that, at first, the community and the parents did not understand health promotion. However, after half a year, the parents and the community "gradually realized and accepted the concept." Parents received information about Health-Promoting Schools from the materials that their children shared with them. Their comments revealed their growing understanding of the broadness of the HPS concept. A mother said that health was not just related to the school and students, but should be aimed at every community and every family. A student said that health included many aspects including good behaviour.

Choosing an entry point - Schools used a variety of mechanisms to choose their "entry point"— i.e. health topic to address *first* in the HPS program. They considered advice from health officials, their own experience and perception of a health issue's importance, surveys and observations conducted by school personnel, reports of health problems in local media, their satisfaction with progress made in dealing with other health issues, and the potential impact of a health issue on societal or personal levels, and the level of support among teachers, students and parents for addressing the issue. The following examples demonstrate who, how and what was involved in *choosing an entry point* and how that choice was perceived by participants.
- In an urban elementary school, the principal attached "great importance to nutrition." She noted that, "even though this is an advanced city, people do not realize the importance of nutrition and do not balance how they eat …With the advance of life here, people automatically realize that health is the most important. Even old people are aware that health is important, saying: if you don't have good health, wealth equals zero." When asked if they used data in choosing the entry point, the principal said that the newspaper reported data and they used it in class. The government made a survey and the "disappointing results" were that people from this city "did not enjoy good health, and nutrition was not satisfying." The school, "after full consideration" decided to have a Health-Promoting School with nutrition as the entry point. Teachers noted that many children suffered from obesity [and] …students' immunization systems were not strong. They thought students had "irregularities" because they did not have "scientific diet," therefore, a "proper diet would be useful…"
- In a suburban high school, which chose psychological health as its entry point, the principal said they related the decision to the school's needs. Students in this elite school were under pressure. Participants reported that the school had a "good foundation" and already had a psychological consultant with a master degree. Teachers, students and parents

all noted that because their school was a key school, society expected a lot and loaded a great burden on them. Students were expected to make great contributions to provincial development. Teachers also had stress and pressure. Therefore, all involved agreed it was very important for the school to pay attention to psychological well-being and produce a good environment to study and work.

- An urban middle school chose tobacco control as its entry point. School administrators gave three reasons for their choice. First, their city had a heavy consumption of cigarettes. Second, previously no students were smokers, but now some students had started. Third, smoking greatly affected both physical health and economics. One administrator wrote, "Smoking is harmful to health and it is a tendency that people start to smoke from younger ages…it is important to prevent more youth from smoking and reduce the number of adults who smoke." Teachers thought that tobacco prevention is "very, very important and meaningful." A parent said that the topic of tobacco prevention is "very clear, and accepted by almost everyone."
- A suburban vocational school chose nutrition as its entry point. School administrators mentioned two points related to choosing the entry point. First, nutrition was very important based on "the puberty state and the development of the body for the students." They noted some students, especially female students, tried to lose weight, although they were actually not overweight. Second, as a vocational school, they had a cooking department and thus nutrition was particularly relevant. Representatives of the students, teachers and school leadership decided together to choose nutrition as their entry point.

Setting up a special Health-Promoting Schools committee - Virtually all schools set up special HPS planning committees and one school setting up a "HPS office". Setting up the committees included designating a leader in charge of the committee; designating school staff according to their regular area of work; including students; parents and community members; holding meetings; creating a common understanding of what was to be done; making rules and regulations; and designating authority, time and tasks to committee members to ensure project implementation. The following examples demonstrate the importance with which the *process of setting up a HPS committee* was perceived and explain who, how and what this entailed.

- In a rural middle school, school leaders chose committee members according to the duties they held, so as to attach the project to their regular work. The committee consisted of eight people. Three people—the headmaster, the deputy headmaster who was also cafeteria manager, and the deputy headmaster in charge of teaching—shared leadership responsibility. Other committee members included the person in charge of morality who headed the office in charge of this project, the secretary of the League of the Communist Party, the person in charge of teaching, and the person in charge of instruction for girl students and psychological consultation. The head of the committee organized the work for the people. Students had no role in the committee.
- In an urban junior high school, a special committee was set up to make sure the school could carry out the project successfully. In this committee, the principal was the general leader, responsible for planning and supervision; the vice-principal and the director of the county's health center were vice group leaders; and the director of the political work group, who was in charge of training students in good behaviour, habits, and virtue, was the chief

leader responsible for organizing and implementing the project. Other members in this leading group included the school physician, psychological health instructor, and representatives of teachers, parents, students and the community. This group met regularly. The leading group considered their primary task to reach a common understanding. They held working conferences before the school implemented the project. Everybody "studied relevant HPS documents conscientiously, comprehended the real meaning of health promotion at the meeting, reached a common understanding and deepened the understanding." Their common understanding of the importance of health laid a solid foundation for further work including the development of "Health Promoting Implementation Regulations" for their school.

- An urban junior high school set up a special organization committee, led by the principal, with staff as members. This committee took responsibility in project implementation. The school selected a special person to be in charge of this project and designated special health teachers. Parents and community representatives also served on the committee. The school invited teachers to join with the principal for the daily management of the school, using a democratic process. Participants said that with the launch of the HPS project, health became the whole school's responsibility.

Developing a work plan - Schools developed a work plan each semester. The plan integrated HPS into the school's "regular work" and its development involved consulting with teachers, students, and parents as well as health and education officials; reviewing existing regulations; requesting proposals for actions; informing students and parents of planned actions; and designating responsibilities for carrying out planned activities and time bound tasks. The following examples demonstrate who, how and what the process of *developing a HPS work plan* entailed.

- In an urban elementary school, the committee developed a work plan for nutrition education during the school year. The headmaster and the committee led the development of the work plan, basing it on "regular work." They consulted with teachers in making the plan. In a staff meeting, they asked all teachers to give a proposal. The committee member in charge of this project then wrote the plan. The plan contained three components: carefully studying school regulations for hygiene and health—this is the largest component, organizing teachers to take part in psychological health education, and emphasizing safety education. There was a separate plan for activities to achieve the WHO Silver Medal for Health-Promoting Schools that focused on nutrition, health and hygiene education; the development of school's nutrition/health-based curriculum and related research. It included a detailed outline of the proposed curriculum.
- In an urban junior high school, the leading group of the committee prepared the work plan and the committee received it. This plan spelled out, for a 15-month period, several activities for each month and who, or which committee, was responsible for carrying out the activities. The plan was influenced by what had been learned from other schools, including different phases of evaluation and outlined HPS activities. School administrators based the content of the work plan on a baseline investigation, their own experience and meetings with the parents.
- School 7 made a semester plan that included HPS regulations each semester. The basic principle of the school was to adopt this project by "taking the practical situation into consideration." Thus, the HPS effort became part of an overall school responsibility, not a

separate one. The deputy headmaster said the school incorporated the HPS project as a part of the whole school working plan.

Setting up policies and systems of operation - One of the first steps in implementing the work plan was setting up policies and operating systems. This involved establishing or improving rules and regulations; informing the school of them; altering materials based on the conditions of the school; reporting and gaining affirmation of regulations and plans from health authorities; and creating clearly defined targets, expectations and systems for appraisal. The following examples demonstrate the importance with which the *process of setting up policies and systems of operation* was perceived and explain who, how and what this entailed.

- In a rural middle school, HPS project leaders told us that after the initial training, they altered the materials they had received, based on their own conditions, and set up their own rules and regulations for the work. After they wrote the HPS regulations, they organized people to print them on a wall of the school. The rules applied to the units involved, including the HPS authority committee, morality department, logistics department, and teaching department. There were also rules for health campaigns, reporting of health work, and the canteen. Also they posted rules for nutrition, non-smoking, regular health check-ups, preventing common diseases, infectious disease control, and preventing food poisoning. Their plan was affirmed by the local CDC.
- An urban middle school listed some of the specific systems of operation to be carried out:

   a. We run relevant certificates of staff members, we accomplish to abide by the laws and we act in accordance with the regulations.
   b. We combined school reality, made dining room hygiene detailed rules and regulations, working system of the staff members of the dining room. We handle affairs according to the rule strictly, require staff members to carry on the physical examination of the hygiene every year, hold the card on duty.
   c. We set up strict management system, implement differentiated control, set up successive check, and responsibility is fulfilled concretely down to everyone. We guaranteed that the food source is rested assured to be qualified, stop the accidental event happening.

- Students in this school reported that the school also had its health policy publicly posted on many nicely designed wallboards.
- A rural vocational school set up HPS policies and issued handbooks which were reviewed with students at the beginning of each semester. They included specific rules about students' behaviour, such as "forbidding smoking, drinking, and gambling." Previous guidelines for daily behaviour were general, but the new guidelines were more specific and quantifiable. The vice headmaster said that before the HPS project, the activities were not systematic, nor "realized certain targets." Teachers said that there was careful planning, step by step, with an emphasis on real implementation and effects. A teacher wrote, "This is a system project, which includes clear target, good planning, serious implementation and appraisal…" A student wrote, "The school included the work of 'Health-Promoting Schools' into the whole plan this term. School adjusted the timetable into a more reasonable way."

- In a rural elementary school, HPS project leaders made modifications to the school policy. In particular, they made "many changes in the management concept. For example, for the managing staff, they made "more specific labour divisions." They made guidelines for teachers' behaviour and for "teacher inspection of students' activities." The vice headmaster wrote, "the regulations and rules are more reasonable, different people take clear responsibility for their own jobs and increase their working efficiency greatly." Teachers said that "all the regulations and rules in the school are better arranged." A parent wrote that there is a "better policy system in the school."

Implementation processes – The following processes or factors were commonly described as being part of, and/or important to, the implementation of Health-Promoting Schools. These are described, as described to us, below:

- prioritizing health
- being guided by rules and obedience
- holding a start-up or mobilization meeting
- popularizing the HPS concept
- cooperating with governmental departments
- ensuring community cooperation and participation
- obtaining input from students, parents, and teachers
- being a role model
- choosing interventions
- providing training
- conducting study visits
- utilizing the Internet
- choosing class topics
- using new teaching and learning methods
- teaching social skills and life skills
- adapting new textbooks and materials.

Prioritizing health - Schools placed clear, visible priority on health. This involved statements from school leaders and attention to health in all school activities. The following examples demonstrate the importance with which *prioritizing health* was perceived and explain who, how and what this entailed.

- The leading group of an urban junior high school promised publicly that the school would emphasize the concept *"health is first"* in running the school. The concept ran through all its activities so that "eventually consciousness for health should be automatic." As the principal said, "the most important thing is [for] both the school and parents to set goals that *"health is first."* Based on publicity, education and a series of activities, the concept of *"health is first"* was accepted by teachers and students. Teachers put the concept into the ordinary teaching process so they could "greatly let the students know this concept." Several teachers said they considered setting up and promoting the concept as one of the most important aspects that worked well, and that they would recommend to other schools.
- In an urban junior high school, the principal put "health is a priority" as a schooling principle, noting that the school combined health education "into daily education work" and treated it as a "priority in their daily work." An administrator who was responsible for this

project noted that health was very important, not only for the health of students, but also for the development of the school. The core idea of this project was to focus on the healthy development of students and teachers in order to promote the future development of the school. School administrators wrote, "Since the Health Promotion School was launched in our school, the school started to change their concept on how to run school. Now they put health as the priority, and put 'training healthy talents' as their goal. Now all the work will be extended from this basic point." A teacher said that since the HPS project began, the school treated health as a priority of the education of the children, instead of only focusing on their academic study, and some political study. Teachers stated, "School persuaded teachers and students to realize that health is the most important by consultancy, symposiums, and questionnaire investigations. So teachers and students can take an active part in all the events which would help improve the health condition," "The key is: both teachers and students thought that health is the most important," and "the school treat the health as a priority. Based on this idea, they will promote the long-term development of the school itself."

Being guided by rules and obedience - Participants were guided by rules and an expectation for obedience. The following examples demonstrate the importance with which *being guided by rules and obedience* were perceived and explain who, how and what this entailed.
- In an urban middle school, a parent stated, "All the students should strictly obey the rules of Health-Promoting Schools…According to school's rules, I encouraged my child to obey school's rules…According to school's rules, parents should be good examples for their kids…In order to cooperate with the school, I start to quit smoking." One parent recalled that there was a "class meeting about creating a no-smoking school and encouraged students to sign their names to stick to the rules."
- In a suburban vocational school, one of the students wrote about how students were helping their school to become a Health-Promoting School: "(1) Obey the rules made by the school and I should do it by myself first. (2) I should start to follow the rules from trivial things. (3) Not only obeying the rules made by the school, at the same time, I will try to improve my comprehensive quality as well."
- In a rural vocational school, the vice headmaster wrote, "From the students' management point, we asked our students to follow a series of rules… [We then provided]… praise and punishment based on students' behaviour. Students have been improved based on this."
- In an urban junior high school, teachers and students seemed to express much love and "caring" in their responses to calls of compassion for disadvantaged students and poor people. Administrators told us that there were similar cases before the project, but they observed, "…now they become active activities, not just a response for the requirements of the school."

Holding a start-up or mobilization meeting - Most of the schools reported having start-up or mobilization meetings to launch the HPS project. The following examples describe who, how and what *holding a start-up or mobilization meeting* entailed.
- In a rural middle school, students participated in the "opening evening". Short speeches were given by representatives of the Ministries of Health and Education and others. The program included dances, songs, body building, music play, sketches, play, chorus, folk songs, and gong fu by the participating schools. The sketches performed at this opening event

were all produced by students. Each class had its own project and put on a show applied to health. It ended with students swearing that they would support the HPS program.
- Participants from a rural elementary school and an urban junior high school reported that their schools held a start-up or mobilization meeting for the HPS project. In addition, parents in the junior high school said that school authorities organized a study conference to call more people to join in.

Popularizing the Health-Promoting Schools concept– Outreach and communication processes played key roles in popularizing the HPS concept among teachers, students, and communities. The following examples show who, how and what *popularizing the HPS concept* entailed.
- An urban elementary school reportedly used over 10,000 materials / brochures to popularize the HPS concept. Teachers took students to the community to publicize the project. Students organized special programs for publicity and made "posters for propaganda to let people know about the importance of this project."
- A rural middle school contacted the community and "reported about the project in hope they [would] support it, and they replied that they would like to cooperate." The administration "let students know" about the project by telling them in several meetings what they were going to do and issued some materials about the project. Teachers advocated for students to take part in the project by encouraging students to follow regulations set by the school and committee; and by asking all classes to publicize the new idea on classroom blackboards, the school's blackboard, and the publicity window in schoolyard. Students were asked to contribute one issue related to the subject of nutrition to put into the window.
- A suburban vocational school publicized the concept about health. A teacher drew a small diagram about implementing effective school health programs: "(schools) students <-- > parents <-- > society. Based on [this] relationship, all the involved people will affect each other so that the knowledge and skills about the nutrition and health will be popularized." One student wrote, "We help our school to be a Health-Promoting School by popularizing knowledge and changing our own habits."
- An urban junior high school held various kinds of activities to "popularize" the concept of health. When asked what was helpful in getting the desired attention to the concept, one teacher answered, "communication, communication and more communication; study, study and more study," and a parent responded, "Publicity about the Health Promotion School project and attention from the government."

Cooperating with governmental departments - Cooperating with governmental departments such as traffic, fire, environmental protection and public security was helpful in linking efforts and gaining partners that could help work toward HPS goals. The following examples show the importance with which the *process of cooperating with government departments* was perceived and explain who, how and what this entailed.
- An urban junior high school cooperated with the Department of Industry and Commerce, Environmental Protection, Public Security and others "to purify the surrounding environment of the campus". This cooperation made sure that vendors did not "disturb students" and helped establish conditions that enabled students to cross the road safely.

- In a suburban vocational school, a teacher stated that cooperation between the school and a local security bureau had helped the school improve safety for students. "It…recommended setting up the Security Guard System [in]…relationship with the local public security bureau and making sure that students can go home safely."
- In a rural vocational school, administrators acknowledged that the most important aspect to implement this project was to work together: "You can't accomplish it by your own part. You have to ask other parts to co-work. With joint efforts, you can make accomplishments."
- In a rural elementary school, the principal mentioned that many departments were involved in implementing interventions and providing financial support. The vice headmaster mentioned that the police team, fire prevention team, sanitary and disease prevention department, and traffic department had provided help.

Ensuring community cooperation and participation – The cooperation and participation of the community was helpful in supporting the development and goals of HPS. It made the development effort a co-responsibility of the school, family, community and government. The following examples show the importance with which e*nsuring community cooperation and participation* was perceived and explains who, how and what this entailed.
- Actions to ensure community cooperation and participation were built into the work plan of a suburban high school:
- Families and community members should participate in the activities of the 'Health-Promoting Schools' program. The school and the community should have an intimate relationship. The city Health Education Office and individual schools will jointly appeal to each work unit and each individual member of the community to encourage them to show concern for and participate in activities related to the program of Health-Promoting Schools.
- In an urban middle school, students said that one of the helpful aspects of the HPS project was that "school and family…cooperate together."
- In an urban junior high school, the principal wrote, "… the school, parents and community can work together organically in harmony." The school leadership "realized that parents and [the] community are great helpers for us to carry on the work," so they paid close attention to this factor and encouraged widespread participation of students, staff, and community members. Parents and community members were involved in planning and implementing the project, and helped improve the surrounding environment of the school.
- In a rural elementary school, a mother mentioned that she used to think that if she gave the child to the school, then it was the teacher's responsibility to take care of her child. Since the project, however, she came to realize that it is a co-responsibility of teachers and parents. A teacher said one of the helpful aspects was "the joint effort by all the members in the community, where is the source of the social power."

Obtaining input from students, parents, and teachers – As the HPS concept was being implemented in schools, teachers, students and parents were given opportunities to provide input about what to do, how to do it and how to improve upon what was being done. The following examples demonstrate who, how and what *obtaining input from students, parents and teachers* entailed.
- In an urban elementary school, students offered to have a theme class meeting on a special topic and "to bring back home the idea to educate parents to pay attention to nutrition

education." The students suggested that before they ventured forth into the community, they should know the information for themselves and practice what they know. Students suggested that the school ask parents to "put on a menu every day and let children know what they eat; to find out what elements it contains, and if elements are missing, to buy food to make up the deficiency."

- In a rural middle school, the vice headmaster consulted students for advice. Students suggested correcting problems in the canteen. Consequently, the vice headmaster talked to canteen staff and they improved the situation so that all could see the change. Students also complained that they did not have instructions for eye exercises, and the vice headmaster responded very quickly. This showed the students that the school respected students' suggestions.
- In an urban middle school, teachers suggested "paying more attention to the indirect effect from environment and good samples from people; exchanging study experiences with students, and "get[ting] …experience" especially from parents during the parents' school.
- In an urban junior high school, parents reported that they suggested that courses include more psychological health content. They wanted to work with the school to address the psychological changes during the "growing up process" of students. They suggested that health promotion should be implemented at the school and in the family at the same time.

Being a role model – The willingness to be a role model was commonly reported by participants. Headmasters served as healthy role models for their staff, and teachers and parents served as role models by setting good examples for their children to follow. The following examples show who, how and what some participants did in *being a role model* for others.

- In a rural middle school 2, the headmaster acted as a role model by stopping smoking in public when the school started the HPS project.
- In an urban school, a parent wrote, "I cooperated with all the work from the school and I…try to be the good example for my child."
- A student in School 5 responded, "of course, everybody should try to be a good example for other people so that more students can be healthy and civilized students."
- In an urban junior high school, teachers said they should become "students' good examples" since physical and psychological health is their life goal as well. One teacher wrote, "I thought: healthy teachers can teach well healthy students." A teacher summarized that it was good to promote health and to be a healthy teacher because only in this way can they teach health to students.
- In an urban junior high school, the headmaster set an example of increasing physical activity by walking home from school 20 minutes each day. A teacher noted "I should try to realize my personal physical and psychological health target. Then I can teach my students to become healthier in physical, psychological and social conditions."

Choosing interventions - Interventions were chosen in a variety of ways. Some were chosen by following the requirements and plan of the project and others by considering what is helpful for students' development. The following examples demonstrate the importance with which the *process of choosing interventions* was perceived and explain who, how and what this entailed.

- An urban middle school reported choosing interventions based on five reasons: "requirement, expected result, feasibility, daily work condition, and matching the features of the school. The administrator explained that, since this was a junior middle school, fewer students smoked, so their interventions were chosen to "publicize and affect the community."
- In an urban junior high school, interventions were chosen because they were "helpful for students' development and social development and based on the administrators' experience." The principal wrote, "The purpose is to guarantee the health development of all the teachers and students based on the practical situation of the school."
- In a suburban vocational school, school administrators said that interventions were chosen and implemented in two ways: publicity and participation."
- In a rural vocational school, administrators told us that they chose psychological consulting because of the background of the students. Most of the students of this school experienced failure in high school. Therefore, they thought it was necessary for them to do some "psychological supporting work." They had a course of career development because some students "lacked confidence in their future." They considered this very important in the HPS project.

Providing training - Training was commonly reported as an important and highly desired component in the process of implementing the HPS concept. The following examples show the importance with which *providing training* was perceived and explain who, how and what this entailed.

- All participating schools sent people in charge of the HPS program to a training workshop in Hangzhou to become oriented to the concept and the overall plan of the HPS project. This 4-day workshop, organized by the Health Education Institute of Zhejiang Province in collaboration with the Education Commission, featured national and international experts who introduced the HPS concept and its components, and provided opportunities for discussions about how to apply the concepts to their schools. HPS guidelines, materials and assessment tools were also provided.
- In suburban high school, following this initial training workshop, the psychologist, who was responsible for implementing the project, planned a training course for all teachers so that they could participate in the project. The training course was designed to "allow all teachers and school staff to master the basic health knowledge central to project, including its goals, standards, strategies, and steps for implementation." The school also planned ongoing technical support and training by health authorities.
- In an urban junior high school, teachers received special training about health promotion, organized by CDC and the Health Promotion Institute. Local level health and educational institutions also provided assistance. The school invited some experts and leaders of the municipal CDC, a middle school in their prefecture, and the City Teaching and Research Center for seminars. The province and the city offered psychological training and special lectures by mental experts. Five teachers obtained certificates.
- In an urban junior high school, administrators said they did "a lot of training …and invited other professionals to do the lectures." By doing these activities, more and more teachers realized "that health included three aspects, namely: physical, psychological, and social skills." With guidance from the municipal health bureau and the CDC, they set up additional training. For the training of teachers, they ordered psychological health textbooks and asked

teachers to take training. They noted that in China, one can study by him or herself and get a certificate, and the school paid the cost for self-study and examination. Students informed us that many of their teachers had taken psychological education training and examinations. A student noted, "Teachers...have to take...examinations about psychological education to check whether they're qualified, or not. By taking those examinations, more and more teachers can do a better job. For instance, try to make friends with their students."

Conducting study visits - Study visits to other HPS were conducted by the schools participating in the HPS expansion. Schools that had reached the first level of becoming a HPS were encouraged by the HPA award system to host study visits for the schools that had just started their projects. The following examples show who, how and what *conducting study visits* entailed.
- An urban elementary school, which had reached the first level of becoming a HPS, hosted study visits for personnel from other participating schools. Staff noted, "Very many teachers from other schools visited and the school was busy meeting guests."
- A rural middle school sent people in charge to pay visits to Health-Promoting Schools and to bring back materials from the schools.
- An urban junior high school sent teachers to investigate and study at a middle school and primary school where they had already implemented the project. Then, they relayed the information obtained through the visits at teachers' meetings.
- In an urban junior high school, teachers informed us that they took visits to schools in other cities of Zhejiang Province. Administrators thought that "many samples around us were helpful." A vice headmaster wrote, "We went to other schools to learn from their experiences."

Utilizing the Internet - The Internet was used as a source of information for teachers and students. The following examples show who, how and what this entailed.
- In an urban elementary school 1, each office had a computer with easy access to the Internet and teachers were free to go online and get information about nutrition education.
- In an urban middle school, a teacher reported about providing information, both from the Internet and from the newspaper, about the health consequences of smoking. A teacher indicated that it was helpful to "share the experience and measures" from the HPS project through the Internet. Students also benefited from access to the Internet. A student reported that one of the differences since the project began was the ability to check information on the Internet.
- In an urban junior high school, teachers and students worked together to collect information about infectious diseases, their symptoms, and their pathology from various media sources, including the Internet.
- *Choosing class topics* – Although most schools started the HPS project with a single health topic (entry point), schools branched out to other health topics as they implemented the HPS concept. At the class level, multiple topics were commonly chosen and addressed based on conditions in their cities, students' input, students' developmental needs and "practical considerations." The following examples show who, how and what *choosing class topics* entailed.

- In an urban middle school, a teacher reported, "I discussed with our students about this topic. We had chosen the topic of Environment Protection. However, many students suggested that we discuss how to control the smoking population—we should suggest our family members to reduce the smoking amount and to purify our environment! So, we finally decided to choose the topic of smoking control."
- In an urban junior high school, teachers chose the topic on how to communicate with students for the reason that many students would like to talk instead of listen to others. Teachers encouraged students to speak their opinions and often adopted their suggestions for health topics. They chose the topics including how to prevent and treat SARS and chicken flu because these diseases threatened their country and other countries. Other topics included patience, nutrition and sanitation, based on the "practical condition of students." One teacher said she addressed psychological health problems, self-protection and nutrition for students because students were "in the physical development period and they will have psychological changes so that it is important to provide specific education related to certain problems."
- In a suburban vocational school, teachers said that the topics that had been chosen for them to teach were banning smoking and nutrition. They said these topics were chosen for the following reasons: (1) The age when people started to smoke is getting younger and younger and. (2) To encourage students to pay more attention to setting up a scientific diet. Teachers chose additional topics to address, including education about adolescence, oral hygiene, and safety.

Using new teaching and learning methods - Teachers used new teaching and learning methods that involved less lecturing and more participatory, interactive, and democratic methods. The increased use of participatory methods was considered one of the "greatest achievements" of the project. The following examples demonstrate the importance with which *using new teaching and learning methods* was perceived and explain who, how and what this entailed.
- In an urban elementary school, teachers said that primary school senior students had "great creativity" for plays, did it independently, and were "more creative than teachers." Students applied what they learned about non-smoking by trying to persuade their parents not to smoke and by teaching their parents the dangers of second-hand smoke.
- In a rural middle school, a student said that classes were held "very vividly." Students were encouraged to talk about their own experiences. The students thought the new styles of teaching and learning was very successful.
- In an urban junior high school, teachers used participatory methods such as "elicitation, communication, questions, cooperation" as well as group discussion, group activities, and student led lessons and appraisals. Teachers tried to communicate more in class meetings and students were encouraged to talk and express their opinions. As one teacher reported, "educating people is more important than giving the contents [of] the book. So when we finish every lesson, we would like to encourage students to freely express their opinion. From the point of view about health, students would talk about…their feeling after the lessons and their future target."
- A suburban vocational school provided courses that encouraged students to participate. As teachers told us, "Before, usually the teachers were involved in projects, and the students just followed. Now, the students are actively involved in this project." The physical activities

teacher implemented student-centered activities. He also developed some "good interpersonal relationships" among the students, and he "let the students be independent, active, and creative." An administrator noted that participatory activities had worked well so far.

- In a rural vocational school, many of those we interviewed told us that teaching methods had changed. We were told that while inspecting classes, school administrators had noted that some students were asleep. Students told them the atmosphere in classrooms was boring. Consequently, as they implemented the HPS project, the school required teachers to pay more attention to teaching methods, to be less talkative, and to engage students in fun and interactive methods such as case studies, imitation, and classroom discussion. Feedback from students showed much more satisfaction with the teachers using the new methods and lecturing less. Students mentioned that classes were not boring anymore and that they were encouraged to learn from each other and help each other to increase the team spirit.
- In a rural elementary school, the principal made changes in teaching methods to make classes more fun. This included students' speeches, students' drawings on the wall, various contests, and other interactive methods. The principal reported that students felt more involved and learned more. Administrators noted that they used positive and negative examples to help students develop for themselves a sense of staying healthy. Students wrote songs and poems about daily behaviour, and what they should do and not do, such as to encourage people to stop buying unqualified things to eat.
- In an urban junior high school, teachers mentioned a change in the education concept: from simple target to comprehensive target including knowledge and "real skills." As for the teaching method, a teacher explained that the teaching concept was about adopting more democratic and more equal ways to negotiate and communicate with her students. They would do various activities, organized by monitoring teachers that would "educate students…through activities." A teacher thought that the greatest achievement of this project was about the teaching concept, because the teacher used to focus on academic teaching, but since they implemented this project, they had started to care more about their students, in all aspects. Teachers treated their students as individuals, to see what they really thought about, to learn about their likes and dislikes, and to find out their future plans.
- In an urban junior high school, teachers told us that there were changes in appraising students and in teaching styles. "The conclusion is more active cooperation and participation by students…Before, students were passive when they had questions. But now, they will find out questions actively and explore how to solve them." Teachers made classes more fun and interesting instead of just having students listen to their lectures. One teacher stated, "We nurtured the atmosphere for students to raise questions. In terms of their study, students will be problem students if they doesn't have questions...[We] praise students who raised questions... [We] encourage students to find questions which teachers can't answer." A student said it was helpful to "incorporate the education with the entertainment activities—incorporate some serious topics with the lively and interesting activities, which [leave] deeper impression on students."

Teaching social skills and life skills – Schools focused on skills-building in their application of new teaching and learning methods. This included skills such as gaining confidence for job hunting, communication and health self management. The following examples demonstrate the importance with which *teaching social skills and a life skill were* perceived and explain who, how and what this entailed.

- A rural vocational school helped students to gain confidence and prepared them for career development. They taught students to set goals, make a record of every day life and to compare their goals to their daily behaviour. The school also helped students learn skills related to finding and interviewing for jobs. They practiced job hunting skills in an "imitated employment fair" with practice sessions in which both interviewer and interviewee were students. A student said they had made a lot of improvements in expression, negotiation skills, and social skills, by participating in those activities. In addition, students told us that "the school… makes[s] students participate in lots of activities to make them more confident and more active and more communicative, more sociable." A student indicated that if a teacher found that a student was "not so open"; he would make some changes and make more sociable students to sit next to him.
- In the dormitories of an urban junior high school, a teacher was responsible for each floor and could help students cultivate social skills and hygiene. Another teacher explained that in the past, when something wrong happened in class, she used to just teach a lesson. After the project, however, she changed her teaching methods. First, she tried to put herself in the other person's shoes and tried to think from the other person's point. "How do they think? Why did this happen?" After thinking of these factors, she would do an "equal discussion" with the students. She thought this could make for better communication.

Adapting textbooks and materials - Some of the schools used new text books or adapted textbooks and materials to better address their needs in becoming a HPS. The following examples demonstrate who, how and what was involved in *adapting textbooks and materials* for use in the HPS project.

- In an urban elementary school, teachers had lots of textbooks from which to select. A provincially issued textbook included nutrition, therefore, they selected this. The school added to the textbook and developed additional materials themselves, depending on each teacher. They reportedly did an excellent job, so the education bureau did not ask the school to buy or use the bureau's nutrition reading materials. Students themselves compiled a song book regarding health, sports, health care.
- An urban middle school developed a health education textbook. It covered topics of personal hygiene; hand washing; daily physical activity; diet and nutrition; psychological health; smoking and health. They also developed another little book on the various national or worldwide events: China Student Nutrition Day, World No Tobacco Day, World Environmental Day, and HIV/AIDS Day. Furthermore, they had an environmental education book that the school had helped develop that included a chapter on Health-Promoting Schools and information on smoking. Teachers used these books to integrate health content into their lessons.
- An urban junior high school used newly-published textbooks that included psychological issues and new teaching standards. The textbook was published by the Department of Education. They adapted some of the contents according to their school's needs.
- A rural vocational school developed handbooks about health that were given to students at the beginning of each semester. Students used these books to spread knowledge to their parents. They also prepared a brochure for parents about safety and made a textbook about

career development that many schools in China adopted. The school documented its experiences in these materials to help other schools.
- An urban junior high school did a subject reform about psychological health. As there was no subject about psychological health, they made changes and ordered psychological health textbooks and asked teachers to take training in this subject.
- The processes and factors above were reported by the people who were directly involved in implementing the HPS concept in schools. The next section describes processes and factors they reported in evaluating the project, and their perceived results.
- Evaluation processes and perceived results - Evaluation was built into the HPS expansion project from its very beginning. Schools were asked to use WHO recommended evaluation measures as well as measures developed by Chinese experts. Interviews with administrators, teachers, students and parents revealed that schools also had their own distinct monitoring and evaluation processes that helped them perceive problems and achievements. This section primarily focuses on the evaluation processes discovered through the qualitative data analysis. They include:

- carrying out process evaluations
- conducting baseline, mid-term, and final evaluation
- changing standards of evaluation.

Carrying out process evaluations - Process evaluation was undertaken to determine if the project was being implemented as expected. Some of the schools had extensive processes involving filing, documenting activities through pictures and collecting teaching materials. Schools also used international quality control systems and conducted regular compliance checks of the school and students to standards or rules. The following examples demonstrate who, how and what *carrying out process evaluations* entailed.
- An urban elementary school used an extensive file system that documented far-reaching processes. Part of the final report for this school states:
- The files work is conscious and norm...Every activities have plan, record and summary; the document of picture, video and words are complete. At present, all of them have been filed and have totalled 80 files.
- An urban middle school, according to the mid-term report, had a system "responsible for...the arrangement and compilation of materials, such as planning, summarizing experience, etc, in health education." School authorities launched a daily activity to examine students from five respects: attendance, hygiene, discipline, sleeping, and having dinner. Results were summarized every week and month. Scientific and normal checks were attributed to making the campus living environment orderly, neat and hygienic. The checks were considered a process of training students to have good habits and they were perceived to advance the activities for health promotion. Some activities were carried out by members from Students' Union.
- In another urban junior high school, observation showed that this school, like others, had large numbers of folders as part of extensive record-keeping systems for process evaluation. For example, teachers were asked to hand in their teaching materials on specific health topics for record-keeping. The principal's report noted, "we check and feedback the situation of implementation that every department works regularly... After the project was implemented,

we still have carried on an overall assessment on the safety… and also the value for the health promoting project." There was also a "class teachers' assessing system" and 'special students' helping monitoring system."

- An urban junior high school monitored the whole process of this project according to the requirements of ISO9000 Quality Monitoring System. Administrators thought that these efforts should be convenient for supervising and solving problems in the implementation. The school also had a process of internal auditing of the school's own standards such as its four standards to monitor the food and environmental quality in the dinning room. These included monitoring of raw materials, bowls and plates, cooking processes, and personal sanitary habits.
- A rural vocational school regularly evaluated and rated students' behaviour. In the past, guidelines for daily behaviour were general, but since they implemented the HPS project, the guidelines were much more specific and quantifiable. Behaviour was addressed systematically to ensure it conformed to guidelines. Students competed to become model students, and those who did so were recognized in a Red Flag Class Winner Competition. One teacher reported, "As a teacher in charge of a class, according to the school's arrangement, I am responsible for checking whether students follow the behaviour standards set by the school, announce the results of the checking, draw monthly conclusions…and select the Good Example students. So far, more and more students could be selected [as Good Example students] according to the results of behaviour standard appraisal." This school also evaluated changes that took place after they changed the teaching methods and found that students' satisfaction with the teachers increased greatly. Teachers also had opportunities to appraise themselves. As one teacher reported, "In the Appraisal for Teachers, all the teachers passed. It meant that teachers were changing their teaching ways, which attracted students." There were also self-appraisals for students. As one student reported, "I took [part] in the social practice activities that were arranged by the school…I could appraise myself through these activities. Meanwhile, I also could appraise myself by comparing with the Target Management Booklet. I felt that the project of Health Promotion School is effective."
- In a rural elementary school, school administrators used a questionnaire to get feedback from students about their impression of their teachers. The students had a chance to make comments about the behaviour of teachers, their teaching content, and their teaching methods. They also conducted a survey among the parents to gather their opinions about the school to find out which activities they thought were the best, and which did not work. The principal took comments from the teachers, so the teachers had a chance to offer suggestions about the principal's work. According to the feedback from these surveys, they made modifications and corrections in their daily work.
- An urban junior high school organized students into a team to investigate the campus environment. They then organized teachers and students to listen to the feedback and provide comments. The school accepted suggestions from teachers and students to further improve "the working style… knowledge scale… and…materials." A teacher informed us that the "school conducted [a study to learn] how to solve the worried condition of students before tests, relieve the confused mood in juvenile students, and improve communication between students and their parents. After that, big changes took place in the school. Students

improved their ability in becoming independent, respect other people, [be considerate] to other people and [use]...problem solving skills."

Conducting baseline, mid-term, and final evaluations - Schools participated in the evaluations that were recommended by WHO and Chinese officials. Most schools with students ages 13 to 15 conducted the Global School-based Student Health Survey (GSHS). Almost all participating schools completed WHO's Psycho-Social Environment (PSE) profile, and students from all schools were asked to fill out a Chinese-developed survey related to the entry points of their school. Schools also added their own surveys and obtained information in other ways to assess their school' pre- and/or post-project conditions and to document aspects in which the HPS project had made a difference. The following examples show who, how and what was involved in *conducting baseline, mid-term and final evaluations* and what was *perceived to have changed or been achieved* by administrators, teachers, students, and parents as a result of the project.

- In a rural vocational school, teachers visited students' homes to assess how they lived and to get a sense of their health and health behaviour. They filled out WHO's PSE profile and reviewed the results. They made a statistical record of injuries. Asked about the situation before the school became a Health-Promoting School, school administrators informed us that, "Before this project, we...extended some activities. However, those activities were not systematical, nor realized certain targets. Students lack[ed]...consciousness about health." They also noted that students knew little about how to avoid injuries, lacked good sanitary habits, and did not have a good psychological quality. Teachers informed us that before the HPS project, "Students' behaviour didn't follow the standards; their understanding about health was only about physical health." Students stated that before the HPS project it was "of course not as good as right now. The atmosphere in the class was not very active, and the environment was worse than present." Parents reported that before the school became a Health-Promoting School they did not pay much attention that their son "was not so mature and considerate," and their daughter "was not very healthy, lack[ed]...confidence and didn't want to study." At the final evaluation of this school, virtually all of those we talked to gave as their assessment that the HPS project at their school "was necessary and successful". A school administrator remarked, "The intervention measures showed that Health Promotion Project is necessary...General impression: this project is effective and successful. Because of the change, some graduates [were]welcomed into...companies, which is the biggest happiness to me." Students responded, "From the experiences...I took part in...I thought that this project is a must for our school to implement and the result is obvious, which helped students a lot," "After this project, we regained our confidence in our life and we are more optimistic about our future. Moreover, we grasped more knowledge about health. So I thought that this project is very necessary." A parent responded, "Very good impression. They provided complete health knowledge. My daughter improved herself in many sides, which also promoted the development of us." Teachers summed up the experience by noting, "physical and psychological health is improved" and "everything is getting better and better."
- In a rural elementary school, the principal used existing survey information and information gathered by teachers in home visits to better understand students and their home conditions. They found that 34.7% of parents did not stay in the village but went out for work. The survey discovered that students were sometimes late for school, played on the way back home, seldom finished homework, and did not like studying. Students lacked healthy

living habits and lacked self-control in daily life. They paid "no attention to hygiene" and had "untidy nails." Students also lacked self-confidence. School administrators told us that because many young parents went out of the province for their job, they left their children at home to live with their grandparents. So students lost the "existence of parents." Asked about the school situation before this school became a Health-Promoting School, a school administrator described it as "not satisfying." Teachers portrayed it as "Many potential security problems; lack of enough security [and sanitation] consciousness among teachers and students; and the school environment was bad." Parents depicted the pre-project school situation as "dirty, messy and bad" and "My kid was not very happy before." During the final evaluation, virtually all the responses expressed a very good impression with the project. Two school administrators stated in writing that they had witnessed big changes. One of the administrators gave four examples of these changes: "(1) construction of the campus, (2) spirit conditions, (3) the relationship between students' parents and the school, and (4) supervisors pay more attention." Another school administrator stated, "Very effective. The 'hardware' [physical environment] and 'software' [psycho-social environment] of the school are improved greatly." A teacher responded, "This project is important to family, school, and society. Only when the next generation of youth grows up healthily, will our country have a brighter future." Another teacher gave specific examples, "The general impression is good. Since we launched this project, the outlook of our school is changing every day. The first is that the campus is more beautiful; the second is that students have better security guarantee. Students younger than age 12 are no longer allowed to ride bikes to school, instead of that, school provides the shuttle bus service and students will be escorted by teachers to walk out of the campus. Now the injury incident cases happened less than before." A parent stated that the implementation of this project not only pushed the development of the school, but it also made the parents more relaxed when they were working outside the city or province. Another parent expressed that "substantial changes have taken place in all the places of the school. With the joint efforts from the school leaders and all the teachers and students, I believe that school will have brighter future."

- In an urban junior high school, administrators told us that survey questionnaires and discussions helped them find out that some teachers felt high pressure and psychological stress because they felt pressure from students and parents. Parents had high expectations of their child because they had only one child. Before the project started, the school knew there were some problems in families but they did nothing about them as they felt it was not their responsibility. With the change to the HPS concept, they realized that they could care so much more and could help children in many aspects, not only in academic studies. Administrators informed us that since they implemented this project, they did a lot of surveys, questionnaires, and training. This included the PSE and the GSHS. Asked about the situation before the HPS project started, responses from administrators and teachers included: "Teachers only cared about their teaching work," "Lack of the consciousness about health and...in changing their behaviour," "Because our school is very big, many students are afraid of facing teachers and school leaders," "School organized some health education activities, but teachers and students didn't pay enough attention to the health and the activities were limited in styles and numbers," and "The understanding about health was too simple and narrowed minded." Some students responded, "Students might only think that study was the most important and neglected the psychological health issues and some potential problems," and "the campus was not so nice and no complete psychological service measures." Some parents also said that the school paid attention only to academic education, and one said, "Before it was not bad. But now it is much better." Asked about their overall impression of the HPS project after more than 1year, two administrators wrote that they could see improvements in teachers' and students' health condition and that teachers and students were physically and psychologically healthy. A person working in the school clinic stated that the disease outbreak rate was dropping, and a teacher stated, "Students and teachers are healthy physically and psychologically, active in their daily life, and harmonious people relationship." Administrators also responded that teachers, students, and their family members had a deeper understanding about health; and the relationship between teachers and students was harmonious. They noted that they put health as the priority, put "training healthy talents" as their goal, and paid more attention to trivial things. Teachers mentioned that the clear target of the HPS project realized development in multi-directions and that the project was well planned and organized and would make teachers and students happier. Students paid more attention to themselves, and they better realized their own strengths. One teacher thought that the most important change was the improvement in the physical and psychological condition of teachers and students. After the project, students could better express their problems to teachers, and teachers could better cooperate with each other and exchange their teaching experiences. Students responded that the project brought true benefits to them for their whole life. It was very meaningful and encouraged them to pay more attention to health. One student thought the project was very necessary for them since they were living in such a competitive age and knew only to study hard. He noted that teachers and school administrators told them that they should realize healthy and complete development to lay a solid foundation for their future. Parents also had a very good general impression and responded that the project matched the general principle of quality education in China; and the school was experiencing many big changes, including concept change, behaviour change, environment change, and school style change. They noted the target had changed from only focusing on academic study to focusing on quality education. The school changed its style from a school that only focused on how to achieve good results in different exams to a school that focused on training healthy students.

Changing standards of evaluation - In some of the schools, we learned that the evaluation standards changed as understanding of the link between health and education advanced. The following examples show who, how and what the *changing standards of evaluation* entailed.
- In a rural elementary school, the principal thought the biggest change that happened was the "teaching aim." In other cities, and before he came to this school, he only focused on one thing that he thought was very important: the teaching quality. So he did a lot of surveys, but mainly about the academic results. When he made a judgment about a teacher, it was only by the scores of the students. After the HPS project, he treated health education as a priority. He focused on physical exercise, other class activities, social activities, the leisure time of teachers and students, whether students were tall or short, and their eyesight. So health was listed as one part of the overall goal of education. School administrators further informed us that a change happened in the teaching idea of teachers. The teachers used to focus only on the scores of the students, whether they could get high marks in examinations. After the project, they also took health into consideration, thus the health situation of a student was also one of the standards of the assessment of students. A parent described the current situation as

"Pay much attention not only to the development of student's academic results, but also to students' physical and psychological health."

- An urban junior high school used to focus only on academic studies, but after the project, the school developed a broader focus and strove to help children develop in all aspects of life: physical, emotional, and social. A parent expressed that the school changed its definition of a good student: in the past they thought a student was good when he or she studied well, now they thought if students did not do so well in academic study, he or she could do other things. "Now school pays attention not only to the academic study, but also study about other field, for example, starting from quality education to develop students' all round ability training."
- The next section focuses on what we learned about the interventions that were implemented to help schools become Health-Promoting Schools.

2. RESEARCH QUESTION: WHAT INTERVENTION ACTIVITIES DID SCHOOLS IN ZHEJIANG PROVINCE IMPLEMENT TO BECOME HEALTH-PROMOTING SCHOOLS?

Participants reported implementing:

- **classroom-based activities**
- **school-wide activities**
- **outreach activities**
- **activities to change the school environment.**

Classroom-based activities - Classroom-based activities included:

- integrating health into regular teaching
- holding class meetings
- providing individualized instruction and care.

Integrating health into regular teaching - Each school integrated teaching about health into regular teaching in various ways by purposely putting health into their class design and relating the HPS project to their particular teaching subject.

- In an urban elementary school, every teacher participated in the project and emphasized the importance of nutrition. Teachers had to make a schedule for each year in which they purposely put nutrition education into the plan, and they "handed the plan to the school authority." Depending upon the subject matter, teachers used several methods to share nutrition information with students. The math teacher assigned health-related problems for students to solve. The English teacher used pictures or fresh fruits to introduce fruits and made statements that they were healthy foods—this was considered "vivid." In Chinese writing class, the teacher asked students to write poems about nutrition.

Holding health-specific class meetings - Class meetings served for the dissemination of knowledge about health topics and sometimes included interactive activities, videos, and lectures from experts outside the school.

- In an urban elementary school, we had the opportunity to observe a class meeting in "moral education." It focused on the love of parents for their children and included many interactive and technology-facilitated activities, such as children sharing pictures and stories of how their parents cared for them, a mother sharing a story, short videos and cartoons, and children writing on a heart-shaped paper a note to their parents.
- In a rural middle school, a female student said they had several class meetings about this project. Classes were held "very vividly." Students were encouraged to talk about their own experiences. The student thought this was very successful.

Providing individualized instruction and care -Teachers and even students gave individual attention to help students pursue a healthy lifestyle.
- In an urban junior high school, after their classes, teachers would try to help those students "who lacked in the classroom." Students also helped each other begin to demonstrate a sense of caring. A father of a student told us about a daughter in the neighbourhood who did very well in academic study but never shared her study experience with others. After the HPS project, he observed that many schoolmates visited the young girl's home to ask for her help with solving academic problems and the girl also began to actively offer her help to those who struggled.
- In the same school, another teacher explained that in organizing an athletic team, one student she approached was reluctant to join because his family was not very rich. When the student agreed to join the team, the parents were worried that if their child did more physical exercise, he would expend a lot of energy and needed more food. They were also concerned that he would spend less time on his academic studies, with which he was already struggling. To respond to the parents' worries, the physical education teachers bought milk for the child and took responsibility to help him in their spare time. At the time of our visit, the child had developed very well. The teacher told us that the student would attend a municipal sports match on behalf of the school. He was doing well in his studies and his parents had expressed support.

School-wide activities - School-wide activities included:

- adding extracurricular activities
- creating wallboards and bulletins
- holding competitions
- sponsoring signature activities
- launching arts days and other festivals
- providing psychological consultation and care
- offering physical examinations and health services
- checking students' appearance
- encouraging physical exercise
- broadcasting through school radio stations
- providing nutritious food
- instituting safety measures
- forming unique student support groups

Adding extracurricular activities - Extracurricular activities supplemented class room activities.
- In a suburban high school, the "Strategy and Steps for the Program" stated that:

> There should be a plan for extracurricular health activities that will consolidate the knowledge learned in the classroom. This will ensure that students master skills for dealing with common health conditions (in themselves and others) and that they will learn how to maintain their psychological health.

- An urban junior high school had a policy that every day, before the students were dismissed, they spent 15 minutes to talk. During this time, the teacher would have a deep discussion with her students about psychological health: what had happened that day, and why, and how to solve any problems.

Creating wallboards and bulletins - Schools utilized wallboards and bulletins to disseminate knowledge about health through postings that were made available for all to see.
- In an urban elementary school, teachers organized activities to encourage students to turn in pictures related to nutrition. They also held blackboard competitions. Every classroom had a blackboard in the back and students took turns to design the blackboard.
- An urban junior high school issued documents about health and posted articles in the school bulletin to popularize health knowledge. Wall newspapers or wallboards disseminated knowledge about health promotion on topics such as "hygiene and health" and the "health is first" concept. School administrators appointed several teachers to maintain this work regularly. They frequently changed the contents of the wallboards to give students more information.

Holding competitions – All schools held special writing, calligraphy, drawing and knowledge competitions about health topics.
- An urban junior high school encouraged students to write articles about "life, health and development." The winning pieces were compiled into a book for all the students to read. The school organized a health poster painting exhibition and held a unique competition to choose students as "health ambassadors," which many of the people we talked to recommended to be shared with other schools. The competition included a series of tests including what students thought about their health, both physical and psychological, and self introductions during which teachers assessed the students' comfort level of public speaking. The school then chose 10 health ambassadors who were "key persons" for the HPS project. Health ambassadors were models for other students, distributed "knowledge about health," and did special tasks. Since it was an honour to be chosen as a health ambassador, one of the students told us he tried to behave himself to keep the reputation of the school.

Sponsoring signature activities - At least three schools in this study held signature activities to show commitment.
- An urban middle school held a signature activity in which students committed through their signature "not to smoke". Students were encouraged to sign their names as a commitment to stick to the rules. A teacher reported, the "signature ceremony was held jointly with all the teachers and students."

Launching arts days and other festivals - Some schools had an arts day or other special festivals that let students and teachers display their talents.
- A rural vocational school had an arts festival where the students got a chance to give a performance, such as "singing together and doing things together." Participants thought that through these performances, they could learn more about how to communicate, negotiate, and cooperate with other students. The school also launched a physical education festival.
- An urban junior high school had a students' evening party in which 80% of the teachers participated during their leisure time. Administrators showed us a picture in which the principal and some teachers did a performance to "cultivate values."

Providing psychological consultation and care - Some schools offered psychological consultation by specifically trained staff.
- An urban junior high school provided psychological consultation in a special room set aside for this. The school held consultations with students or parents when a student failed an exam and offered consultations about communications between the students and the teachers. Specially-trained teachers provided these services. They also opened a hotline for psychological consultation. Its name meant, "Know your heart, know ... each other." This was a channel for students to talk freely. Since the beginning of the HPS project, the school had an intimate "Close to Your Heart" mailbox for students. Into this mailbox, students could write their "secrets" which they might not want to share with their parents. The school considered this especially important during this "special time of adolescence" where issues such as the relationship between female and male students were very sensitive.
- In a suburban vocational school, the principal reported that they had psychological assistance stations called "know each other." They offered specialized assistance, regular psychological consultation to solve psychological problems, and dissemination of psychological knowledge. A mother found this assistance quite important, because students were at a "very special stage." She thought this assistance would "greatly help students to fully develop full health in the future."

Offering physical examinations and health services - Schools arranged or offered annual health check-ups and prevention and treatment services for students and teachers.
- In an urban elementary school, teachers arranged medical check-ups for students at the local hospital. The school had students' blood tested once each year. The examinations covered teeth, eyes, allergies/sneezing, and other conditions, including "heart disease." After the check-ups, the school distributed the results to the family and the head teacher and kept an office copy. In the report to the family, the school reminded parents of the importance of "the state of their child" and gave specific instructions to address identified problems. The head teacher paid home visits to parents to "watch what they do." They also did a class activity to educate students about the exams and their health.
- A suburban vocational school offered regular annual physical exams for every student and provided physical exams every 2 years for staff. They established health files for students and teachers, and they gave feedback to parents in a timely fashion and provided suggestions regarding treatment. They also had an independent medical station with two staff with certificates as primary care providers and two nutrition advisors. Two school doctors were on

duty 24 hours a day and could escort students to a hospital for treatment. They also took measures to prevent infectious disease and vaccinated students.

Checking students' appearance - Some schools checked students' appearance, such as fingernails and personal hygiene, and daily behaviour.
- In an urban middle school, the mid-term report stated:

We heightened students' healthy life's awareness by checking students' appearance, students' daily behaviour. For example, every week we check appearance of all the students. Now students have good personal hygiene consciousness, they wear neat and natural clothes; they do not have phenomena such as long hair, having hair dyed and wearing long nails, etc.

Encouraging physical exercise - Schools offered a variety of physical activities, military training (concentrated physical activity that requires discipline), outdoor sports and matches of various kinds.
- A suburban vocational school, as a special feature of the HPS project, established morning exercises which "let students get up early" and ensured enough time for breakfast and cleaning their rooms. All the groups we talked to—school administrators, teachers, students, and parents—mentioned these morning exercises. A student said that the morning exercises were not only to increase their physical activity, but also to encourage other students to participate in exercises. The morning exercises could also help form good habits about "early wake up and early get up." Teachers said that they also promoted competitions and matches to try to develop the students' physical health.
- In a rural vocational school, every morning, all students had to run to help them improve their health. The year before we visited the school, administrators had invested 100,000 RMB for sports facilities to ensure 1 hour of physical activity every day for each student. All younger students had to take physical exercise, in addition to PE. Students told us, "Every year in school, there is a sports match, participated by students, and also there are regulations that all students have to run in the early morning… because in China, there is a saying that the physical health is the most important points."

Broadcasting through school radio stations - Some schools had a radio station that broadcast health messages or programs at specific times.
- In an urban junior high school, many participants told us that the school had a radio station, called "voice of schoolfellow," that addressed topics of life and health. It provided psychological programs from 8:00 to 8:30 on Monday and Wednesday, every week. Students chose articles or got knowledge from the Internet and broadcasted it throughout the campus.

Providing nutritious food – Some schools provided nutritious food and balanced meals under strict hygiene controls.
- In a suburban middle school, administrators got a nutritionist to give advice how to make a nutritious menu for junior and middle school students. A parent reported that the school decided to have a special balanced diet for each grade. Students were encouraged to check with the canteen staff to find out if they were taking a balanced diet. A male student thought it was very good that the school allowed students to choose how much rice they wanted to eat. This helped to prevent waste and also helped poor students.

- An urban middle school started to provide fixed meals so they could make sure students could get a balanced diet. Each day, the dining room offered a different, balanced, colourful meal. As a student told us, this nutritious food "is warmly welcomed by students and teachers." In the dining room, we saw that each table had posted notes with reminders about the responsibilities of each student who sat at the table, and oranges were set out on the tables, presumably for dessert. In the kitchen, cooks were using fresh ingredients to prepare the food.
- An urban junior high school paid attention to providing nutritious food and strict hygiene control in the dining hall. The school offered balanced meals and encouraged kitchen staff to have training. A chef responded by earning a certificate.

Instituting safety measures - Several schools addressed safety and prevention of injury.
- A suburban vocational school asked policemen to come in front of the school to direct traffic when students left the school for the weekend, because the streets in front of the school were big and could have traffic problems. After the project, the school had a security office that worked 24 hours a day, and also had video monitoring to ensure the safety of the students, as well as the property of the school.
- A rural elementary school did not allow students younger than age 12 to ride bicycles to school. Instead, the school opened a shuttle bus service for children who lived more than 3 miles away. It ran four times a day, and the cost for students was 1 RMB per day. The local government supported other expenses. Without the bus, students would have paid 3 to 6 RMB per trip in non-school shuttles. Every day, a teacher was responsible for the bus transportation. Teachers also escorted students as they walked home. A policy required the school to arrange for one teacher, each morning, to be the first to arrive at the school, to stand at the gate, and to welcome students. The teachers were responsible for safeguarding the students, and they could not leave until the students arrived safely. The school also gave each student a yellow safety cap that they wore when they went to school and when they left the school. When all the students wore such a cap, it made them feel very honoured. One of the parents said that the achievement of the HPS project that she cherished most was the yellow safety cap because when the students wore such caps when they crossed the road, it could arouse attention of the drivers. She felt that the caps decreased students' risk of injury from traffic on the road.

Forming unique student groups - Some schools formed unique student groups to help students support and care for each other.
- In an urban junior high school, a four-student group was encouraged by the former principal, including advanced students, normal students, and slower students. The students taught each other, communicated and cooperated with each other and supported each other. When one student got behind, they helped him or her along. As one parent said, "the four-student group is worth to be developed and expanded, because the four-students can take care of each other. So the four-student group is not [personal centered]. It is team-centered. This is encouragement of the teamwork." With the help of the four-student groups, even slower students won awards at the end of the semester.
- A suburban vocational school implemented a similar feature, called "companion health education association," which many participants talked about. Students created this activity,

and it was related to students' caring for and educating themselves, including educating each other about AIDS/HIV, puberty, adolescence, and mental health. Before students formed the association, education was just one-way, from teacher to student. In forming the association, they created an interface between the students so the students could communicate via this association.

Outreach activities - Outreach activities included:

- disseminating information to parents
- disseminating information to communities
- conducting social research
- engaging in social practice.

Disseminating information to parents - Schools distributed information to parents in the form of printed guidance, letters, meetings and "parents' schools."

- In an urban elementary school, the principal reported that they distributed thousands of materials to students' families. The school gave families printed suggestions for a balanced menu for dinner and breakfast, and the school "let parents know" the importance of a special menu for obese children. A mother mentioned that the school issued: a 6-page letter the first year, a 2-page letter the next year, and a 2-page letter the third year. The letters classified food in seven elements of nutrition, informed parents of Nutrition Day, and included information about the importance of washing hands before a meal. The mother said she thought these letters were really "significant and beneficial to her family." Parents also attended lectures the school provided for them. The school also had a special class to educate parents and families, as well as students.
- In an urban junior high school, a teacher said that even though families had only one child, the communication between parents and children had "decreased". This school communicated with families through home visits, telephone calls, letters, and chatting through the Internet. During the HPS project, the contacts between school and family became more frequent. Teachers made home visits and telephone calls to get information about students' families. In the past, they used to do this without informing the students, but, after the project, they talked with students before they made a home visit. Teachers felt this could avoid quarrels in the family. Also, by talking with them before visiting their parents, the teacher would understand what the children really wanted them to share, and that made the child feel more comfortable. They also had conferences between teachers and parents to work jointly, and they offered guidelines to help the parents in their daily lives.
- An urban junior high school provided a lot of "explanations and publicizing works," and organized a lot of parents' meetings, trying to make more parents understand what is meant by health, and to let them know that the school was going to adopt the HPS project. In the parents' meetings, the teachers would emphasize how important psychological health was, and they tried to persuade parents to communicate more with their children. Some children did not listen to their parents, in "such a sensitive age" (puberty and adolescence). Thus, the school tried to persuade the parents to be more active. Teachers told parents that they could initiate communication instead of waiting for their children to come to them and many parents followed their advice. Administrators also invited experts to offer workshops on health at "parents' school". This school also shared studying materials with parents, so they could

"learn some knowledge by themselves." Whenever the school found some good materials about family education, they collated the articles as a textbook and sent it to the parents. In doing this, the school wanted to help parents and "make them know more, and understand more about their children." This school also implemented "some experience works" that helped students understand their parents by experiencing the "real-life" world. Farm visits provided an opportunity for children to experience what many of their parents had experienced.

Disseminating information to communities- Schools "disseminated knowledge" about health promotion to the nearby communities through their students.
- An urban middle school's mid-term report stated that:

> The healthy education is in daily pursuit of the school, it also has gone deep into students' families, the street communities and other schools....Supported by communities and street residents committees, we often organize students to go to the residential blocks to propagate health knowledge, grant the propaganda materials of the health education, these activities have improved health consciousness and technical ability of residents of communities of residential district effectively.

- One of the parents mentioned that a great difference after the health promotion project was that "before the project, something changed just within the school. Now the project has extended to the societies outside the campus."

Conducting social research - Schools conducted surveys and research among the community.
- An urban elementary school gave parents questionnaires to fill in as part of a "social survey." School administrators told us that it covered many topics including "how to protect eye sight, teeth, attitude toward non-smoking, and attitude toward school project." The school developed the survey to obtain responses from parents, children, and the community. One question asked parents what they thought should be done about the obesity problem. The school asked children to make suggestions to their parents and shared children's responses with parents.
- In an urban junior high school, teachers told us that students did "social investigations" by themselves. This included conducting surveys in the community and in companies about feelings among family members or about the environment and water protection.
- An urban junior high school adopted a policy to encourage teachers to combine the idea of health with their own research, which was different from the subjects they taught. One female teacher researched how to raise the awareness of students to ask more questions in the classroom. UNESCO had recently pointed out that in the twenty-first century, people should learn how to survive and how to learn. One of these ideas included that one should learn how to ask questions.

Engaging in social practice – Schools engaged students in social practices to better understand the world and others, especially their parents.
- In an urban junior high school, school administrators asked students to do "social work." Participants thought this helped students understand parents, teachers, and interpersonal

relationships better, as well as engaging them in serving society. Social work included going to visit senior citizens, helping them and gathering food for senior citizens and for orphans. This gave students a chance to understand those living in poverty. During the previous autumn holiday, they invited poor students to a gathering. They created a "parent day" when students would do things for their parents as an expression of love from their son or daughter. This school also asked students to sell goods in shops in one of the biggest shopping malls in town. Administrators told us that after one day of hard work, the students felt very, very tired, but they gained insight into how hard the adults have to work.

- Activities to change the school environment - The schools paid a lot of attention to setting up good physical ("hardware") and psycho-social ("software") surroundings. Activities included:

  - improving facilities
  - enhancing cleanliness and beautification
  - assuring a harmonious psycho-social school environment
  - maintaining a caring atmosphere

Improving facilities - Schools sought to improve and upgrade their dining rooms, dormitories, teaching, sports and sanitary facilities and playgrounds during the HPS project. For example:

- In a rural vocational school, many people told us that the school environment was improved. The school invested a lot of money in rebuilding the dining room and upgrading the facilities of the school and the dormitories. One of the students responded, "The most important outcome [of the HPS project] is the environment is getting better and better. Students and teachers can have better life here." The vice principal informed us that the school improved its sports facilities and added a toilet for each dormitory room with eight students; before, there was only one toilet per floor.
- In a rural elementary school, administrators told us that they tried "all the ways" to protect children, and they created a sound environment so students could study well and live well. A frequently mentioned improvement was the school playground. School administrators thought this was the greatest achievement of this project because the playground used to be a land fill—not very convenient or comfortable. On sunny days, when the wind came, the earth blew up. On rainy days, it was very muddy, and the classrooms became covered with mud. After the project, and since the playground had been rebuilt, it was better for the students and for people from the village to do physical exercises. They also added a gate to the schoolyard with a little office for the safety guard. Since 2004, the school also had student paintings on the topic "Prevention of injury Health-Promoting School" on a school wall.

Enhancing cleanliness and beautification - Schools enhanced their cleanliness and sanitary conditions and had beautification projects.
- A rural middle school held a dormitory beautification competition including attention to health and hygiene. The majority of students were active in this competition. During the competition, students were encouraged to bring in plants and fishbowls, etc. A teacher noted that students cleaned the floor carefully and paid more attention to hygiene after the dormitory beautification competition. From this activity, the school believed that they

developed a good habit. Overall, there was a clean atmosphere that helped them to improve good habits, including washing hands before eating.
- An urban junior high school established a cleaner and more beautiful environment by keeping classrooms clean, checking garbage bins every day, conducting investigations about water protection, and offering free clean water to students. According to the principal's report, the sanitary condition was improved and "all the classes and the teacher's offices have been equipped with a water purifying system." Furthermore, the school banned smoking and was designated a smoke-free school.
- In a rural elementary school, several participants said that the campus became "cleaner and more beautiful." Students mentioned that there were regular clean up activities. A mother thought that the greatest achievement of the HPS project was the change in the environment. In the past, it used to be not very tidy and clean. After the project, it changed, "totally."

Assuring a harmonious psycho-social environment - Schools improved their psycho-social environments.
- In an urban elementary school, a mother, who talked excitedly, said the school had done very well in psychological education and in maintaining good relationships between teachers and students. Students and teachers were "like friends." The school took students out for camping, BBQ, and outdoor activities. During that time, students felt close to teachers and had the desire to "let go what was on their mind." The mother felt this could relax students.
- In a rural middle school, students mentioned that the authority of the school was special, which was different from other schools. The headmasters were very respectful, approachable, friendly, and easygoing with students. When the vice headmaster saw students eat instant noodles, he told them about malnutrition, not by scolding but by giving instruction. Students said that this kind approach moved them.
- In a suburban high school, the "Strategy and Steps for the Program" in the newsletter stated, "among students and teachers there should be an environment of mutual concern, honesty and warmth. This should include guidelines for helping less advanced students, respecting the customs of different ethnic groups and encouraging polite behaviour." Two mothers told us how the school put this strategy into practice. One of the daughters entered the school as a top student but then felt not so confident. The teacher discussed the problem with the girl's parents in a timely manner and communicated with the girl to strengthen her self-confidence. During her first year on campus, the daughter gained self-confidence and was now the class monitor. The other mother's daughter ranked in the middle when she entered the school, received encouragement and praise from her teacher in class and the school contacted her parents regularly. Now the daughter was going to a prestigious school in Beijing, without an entrance exam.
- In rural vocational school, students said "The most important positive change is that my study and living environment is changed. Study atmosphere is better than before and good living habits have been formed." In terms of the relationship between teachers and students, before [the HPS project] only teachers would come to us and talk with us. And students would never go to teachers and ask for help. But now, we always go to teachers and discuss with them about our problems and try to find out the solutions. Now teachers are not only our teachers, but also our friends." Parents also told us that no discrimination existed in the school between students and between students and teachers.

- In an urban junior high school, the person in charge of the HPS program told us that they tried to create harmonious working surroundings so teachers and students had a "good mood" to work and study better. Teachers described their school's activities as a Health-Promoting School as: "the change of the atmosphere—more respect from teacher for student and more concern by teachers about their own health condition." "[A] friendly, encouraging and supportive atmosphere is forming. It happens between teachers and students, supervisors and teachers, students and students, and teachers and teachers."

Maintaining a caring atmosphere - Schools fostered "equal relationships between students and teachers" and an atmosphere where teachers, students and parents truly cared about each others well-being. For example:
- In a suburban high school, a mother told us that her daughter had an accident the previous year and twisted her leg. The doctor said she had to stay home for one month. Since this was a vital period in the semester for a Senior III student, she was very worried. After the accident, all her teachers, not only the head teacher gave her calls to encourage her. After one week at home, during which the head teacher sent all class exercises to her, the daughter went back to school. The teacher arranged students to help her. All classmates took turns helping her up and down the steps during the whole month so the daughter did not miss class. She was very grateful to the school for this.
- An urban junior high school taught children to love their parents and to help each other. The school also fostered equal treatment among students and between teachers and students. Students told us that teachers treated all students equally regardless of their academic record, and whether they were advanced or not advanced. Students said there was "a very, very good relationship between teachers and students," and that they were often more comfortable talking to their teachers than to their parents. One of the teachers wrote that the establishment of equal relationships between students and teachers was one of the most helpful aspects of this project.
- In a rural elementary school, to meet parents' concerns, the school tried to give students equal opportunities. One parent explained that there were many students in one class. Some were very outstanding and could arouse more attention from teachers. Other students were not so outstanding, and got fewer opportunities to participate in joint activities. This gave a deep impression to the teachers that a child in class was just one of many, while in the family; it was the whole life of the parents. This reminded the teachers to show respect and pay attention to each child and to encourage him or her to participate in all kinds of activities.
- The interventions described above are described as they were reported to us by the people directly involved in the HPS project. The next section describes the challenges of becoming a Health-Promoting School as reported by the people involved.

3. RESEARCH QUESTION: WHAT WERE THE MAJOR CHALLENGES THAT SCHOOLS IN ZHEJIANG PROVINCE HAD TO OVERCOME TO BECOME HEALTH-PROMOTING SCHOOLS?

Participants reported challenges relating to:

- understanding and integrating the HPS concept
- lacking professional development and support
- encountering no challenges

Understanding and integrating the HPS concept - Reported challenges included:

- balancing academic studies and health interventions
- coping with an increased workload for administrators and teachers
- understanding the concept of a Health-Promoting School
- needing motivation and courage to participate
- requiring time to change habits
- resisting project rules
- addressing health and environmental problems
- improving relationships between schools and parents
- strengthening communication between teachers and students
- extending health promotion to the community and families
- sustaining and expanding health promotion efforts

Balancing academic studies and health interventions - There was a concern among administrators, teachers, students and especially parents that addressing health interventions would distract students from focusing on their academic studies.

- In a suburban high school, a physical education teacher said that many parents would not agree with what the school was going to do. Parents hoped children would study hard to achieve well in their studies, and they did not want children to pay attention to other things. Parents thought this way because of the pressure from living in a competitive society. One of the students said very passionately that "The competition is fierce. [Students have to] focus their time and energy on study rather than on other things. If students do not enter a better university, parents and society would regard it as not having a good opportunity for their career." Another student said that "[implementing the HPS concept] would be a great challenge to the teachers in this competitive state. Some teachers found it difficult to adjust to the new concept, and they continued to focus on students' achievements in studying".
- In an urban middle school, all four groups that we spoke to—school administrators, teachers, students, and parents—mentioned that parents were concerned that the project would have a negative impact on the students' academic education, and it was difficult to get the support of parents. Indeed, parents did express concerns about health promotion because they thought too many activities would distract some of the students "away from education." One student wrote, "Some parents didn't allow us to publicize this campaign to communities because they are afraid that this activity will affect our study."
- In an urban junior high school, students mentioned that the new focus on health was a bit difficult to apply to daily life because it was new and they were used to studying.

Coping with an increased workload – Participants indicated that this project added an extra workload for persons involved.

- In a rural middle school, a teacher recognized that the HPS project would add extra work and it would be difficult to carry out all items, but it would be worthwhile doing it. A mother elaborated that this project would add to the workload of teachers, families, parents, and

students, but it would be beneficial. She said the headmaster and other teachers were very busy with the project. According to the mother, the headmaster devoted himself totally and had no time for personal things. The English teacher of this school spent the 6-day holiday looking on the Internet for relevant information. Parents were moved by what the school was doing.
- In an urban junior high school, the woman who was mainly responsible for this project told us that she had to learn for herself first before she could do this job. She worked very hard, and she sometimes felt a little tired. But she still thought that it was worthwhile, and she said that it was very interesting to learn more about the concept of health.

Understanding the concept of a Health-Promoting School - Participants found it initially challenging to understand the HPS concept.
- In a suburban high school, the psychologist said it was difficult for all staff and students to accept the concept. Once they understood the concept and accepted it, they could implement it smoothly. It was very hard for people to accept new ideas. Students said they totally agreed that the school should participate in this project, but it was hard to encourage their parents and society to accept this concept.
- In an urban middle school, one of the parents told us that, "society didn't totally understand the 'health'."
- In a suburban vocational school, teachers asked for "education [about the] updated health concept" as Health-Promoting Schools was quite a new concept for them. Parents told us that this was the first time they learned about Health-Promoting Schools, and they were quite unfamiliar with that concept. A mother said that they had a "confused concept" about nutrition and safe sex and physical activities and psychological issues. She asked for more explanation about these issues.
- In a rural vocational school, an administrator told us that it was not a big challenge for him to understand the broad concept of health, because he had a lot of experience in education. He noted that he met a lot of challenges during the "practical promoting" because it was not very easy for students to change their minds. "It's very difficult to make more people understand the definition of health made by the WHO. And it is hardworking, painstaking working."

Needing motivation and courage to participate - Participants indicated the need for motivation and courage, especially for students, to see the benefits of the project.
- In a suburban high school, a teacher thought publicity was not enough. Some kind of activity was needed "to let students see the benefits and to let them see that their school's project out wins the other schools."
- In an urban junior high school, a teacher thought it was a challenge to win trust. Students who needed help were embarrassed to ask for help. The person in charge of the HPS project explained that 43 students came for help in the first month after they opened the consulting room. But since the beginning of the semester, no student asked for help. A student acknowledged that some students needed help, but were afraid to go and accept help because there was a possibility that other students would laugh at them. If he was that student, that would make him feel very embarrassed.

Requiring time to change habits - Many participants said that health promotion and changing habits takes time.
- In a rural middle school, administrators mentioned that it was likely to take a long time to get rid of bad eating habits. "To say is one thing, to do is another."
- In an urban middle school, some of the students found it very hard to change habits. One teacher mentioned that quitting smoking, for example, was a long-term effort and a specific system should be established "to guarantee the continuous effort."
- In an urban junior high school, students felt that health promotion was a long-term project. They pointed to the old Chinese saying, "Habit is very, very hard changed. So you must take some time to form good habits." Teachers also felt the project needed more time to develop and "have an accumulated process."
- In a suburban vocational school, school administrators said that health promotion was "large and complicated work and is a long-term goal." An administrator wrote, "It is a big project to take part in the health promotion activity. It can't be realized in one or two days. We must make out a feasible plan and then take measures to realize it step by step."
- In an urban junior high school, administrators said that it was challenging "how to encourage teachers to arrange their time reasonably." And a student wrote, "Maybe teachers can't be changed in short period. Maybe teachers have their own pressure as well. But they are working hard."

Resisting project rules – Participants indicated that some students were passive and others were rebellious and did not obey the rules of the project.
- In a rural middle school, students mentioned that some students did not want to obey the regulations and were rebellious. Students who were rebellious did not want to participate in any activity. Students suggested that the school hold practical activities to get them interested in the project, such as a creative activity.
- In suburban vocational school, students told us that some of the students were not positively involved in the project, but only passively. This meant passive students would do nothing or avoid discussion of sensitive issues, such as sex.
- In an urban junior high school, students made the following statements about challenges: "Some students couldn't take an active part in the events and had some worries," "Some students threw away garbage everywhere and didn't want to obey schools' rules," and "Students were not devoted into this project."

Addressing health and environmental problems – Participants recognized physical, mental, and environmental health problems as challenges.
- In an urban middle school, parents told us that children were "very fragile" and could not express frustration.
- In a suburban vocational school, a teacher said that McDonalds and Kentucky Fried Chicken shops sold "garbage food," but the children liked it.
- In a rural elementary school, the principal reported that those who were disadvantaged with "weak power" (not confident) suffered discrimination. There were also problems with drinking water and drainage systems.

Improving relationships between schools and parents – Participants identified relationships between parents and schools as a challenge, especially when there was a lack of communication.
- In an urban middle school, a parent wrote, "Family and school should have more communication, which is important in the whole campaign and worth popularizing." But students also said that parents ignored them when they talked about the health promotion project.
- In a rural elementary school, a parent mentioned communication between families and the school as a challenge. One parent wrote, "In the school, teachers told me that my kid became mature and considerate. But sometimes, he was not so nice to us."

Strengthening communication between teachers and students - Communication between teachers and students was mentioned as a challenge.
- In an urban junior high school, despite the many positive comments about the good relationships between teachers and students, some people felt that there was room for improvement in this area. A student wrote "I thought that the biggest problem is that the communication between students and teachers is not enough. Teachers and students can't talk freely. I think that we can try together because I believe that everything can be done better if we pay enough attention and effort."

Extending health promotion to the community and families – Participants indicated that extending health promotion to the community and family is a challenge.
- In an urban elementary school, students said when they "got knowledge," they wanted to pass it on, but people did not want to "accept advice." They had to talk a lot without results.
- In an urban middle school, an administrator identified as a key problem "how to get support from the society, especially family members who smoke." A parent wrote, "There are not too many community members who took part in this campaign. More communication needs to be done between the school and community." Another parent wrote, "Some people thought that it is not necessary to do those things because they didn't realize those problems yet. We should educate them."
- In an urban junior high school, school administrators acknowledged problems with "implanting and implementing the health promotion idea in the community." This was particularly true for communities with low educational levels.
- In a suburban vocational school, promoting the HPS project to communities and families was a challenge because of the location of the school and the location of the hometowns of the students.

Sustaining and expanding health promotion efforts - Schools identified a need for further expansion and continued efforts.
- In a suburban high school, a teacher mentioned that only one school participating was not enough. "All the society" should take part to improve all citizens' quality of life. A mother said that this project was important not only to her family, but also "to the nation and the world."
- In an urban middle school, administrators told us that other schools in the neighbourhood showed strong interest in participating in this project. A teacher also expressed a hope for

more Health-Promoting Schools to "promote the development with the other schools in the same area together."
- In an urban junior high school, one of the parents mentioned that since China had a large population, if the HPS project could be done successfully here, then it should be expanded to other places, since it would be very meaningful and significant for the whole world.
- Lacking professional development and support - Participants identified a range of challenges related to professional development including:

  - needing to expand knowledge, skills, and experience about health promotion
  - requiring technical support
  - addressing shortages of qualified staff
  - needing governmental support
  - lacking funds and facilities

Needing to expand knowledge, skills, and experience about health promotion - Participants mentioned a lack of knowledge, skills, methods, theoretical guidance, and experience of health promotion many times.
- In an urban elementary school, teachers first thought their nutrition knowledge was enough, but when the project gained in intensity, they felt a need for more professional instruction and hoped for more expert talks, though they also acknowledged that "knowledge is not enough" and that some students knew better than teachers. They had invited students with rich knowledge to be the instructors.
- In a rural middle school, there was a need for more information and guidance on nutrition and skills (e.g., how to carry out nutrition education). The person in charge of the HPS project felt short on materials, especially related to skills for nutrition.
- In an urban middle school, a teacher said that one of their challenges was their lack of experience because they were just beginning their project. They had "no idea" how they could reach their goals and objectives. They would have liked to have more opportunities to visit other Health-Promoting Schools to obtain more experience.
- In an urban junior high school, teachers felt a lack of skills and methods to deal with students' psychological problems. Teachers also reported a "lack of health promotion theory" and an inadequate understanding of the "health" concept. One teacher expressed, "During the implementation, we don't have enough ways and skills to realise our target. We wish that we can pay visit to other places and invite experts to our school so that we can make our work better." Another teacher added, "Sometimes, we have no idea where to start."
- In a sub-urban vocational school, an administrator said since this was the very beginning of the project and although they had some experience, he thought it was immature and not worth being shared with other schools. He believed that, when the school's health promotion efforts became "very, very mature and fully developed," they would have more experience and would like to share with other people. A teacher proposed more information exchange among the Health-Promoting Schools, "Because we have, in every city, different schools with different entry points, and different interventions of different experiences and resources…"
- In a rural vocational school, an administrator mentioned that they made efforts previously on changing the concept of health to a more comprehensive one. "However, owing to the lack of correct understanding and enough theoretical directions, we didn't make it well."

Requiring technical support - Many participants called for more technical support, especially since they were still in the early phases of the project and still learning.
- In an urban elementary school, teachers thought they did not do their job well and asked for guidance.
- In a rural middle school, teachers hoped for more instructions and more information on the project Website. They also asked if WHO had a Website or information available in Chinese.
- In a suburban high school, the principal hoped WHO would provide good examples of international HPS achievements.
- In an urban junior high school, administrators specified that technical support was needed to diagnose psychological problems. Since the school was located on an island and thus a bit removed, teachers felt they were away from "advanced information" and asked for experts to provide technical assistance, direction in skills, and knowledge about health promotion. A teacher wrote, "now the key difficulties…are: lack of skills and sometimes we don't know how to do it better. The key measure to solve this problem is to strengthen the training and study in this regard."
- In a sub-urban vocational school, one of the administrators wrote, "Now it is the first phase and we don't have enough experience…we wish that officials from WHO and …officials from departments concerned can give us directions often." Teachers acknowledged that Health-Promoting Schools, or health promotion, was quite a new concept for them, so they needed more guidance from experts about health promotion.
- In a rural elementary school, administrators hoped that WHO could provide training of teachers and more technical support.
- In an urban junior high school, a teacher asked for more professional support because even if teachers took some courses or studied by themselves, they still lacked sufficient knowledge. So they needed more help from experts and professionals.

Addressing shortages of qualified staff - Some schools lacked qualified staff for health promotion.
- In an urban elementary school, the school nurse was the only one who had psychological training. Other teachers did not have this professional knowledge. Since many students had psychological issues, they needed more teachers with this knowledge.
- In an urban junior high school, one of the challenges was a lack of qualified staff, especially for psychological assistance since children were at a "very special stage" during adolescence.
- In a rural elementary school, an administrator suggested to "Pay more attention to schools in the countryside in… teacher supply and training support." Parents thought the teachers needed more training, especially in psychological education.

Needing governmental support - Some schools expressed a need for additional governmental support.
- In a rural middle school, a school administrator said that he hoped WHO would encourage the Departments of Health and Education to carry out the project smoothly. Practical policies needed to be set up and support from the upper level was needed, such as a leader from the government.

- In an urban middle school, administrators indicated that policies were a challenge. They were pleased that the Department of Public Health paid high attention to this project and strived to gain similar attention from other provincial and local bureaus. They clearly recognized that attention and visits from leaders at different levels can have a useful and direct effect on their work.
- In a rural elementary school, a teacher stated, "We wish that our supervising departments and leaders could show more concern to the schools in those undeveloped areas." And a parent hoped that officials at higher levels could offer more help and more support to those rural schools that were less developed.
- In an urban junior high school, one of the challenges mentioned by teachers was a need for "support and directions from supervising departments."

Lacking funds and facilities - Schools identified a lack of funds, and, in some cases, a lack of facilities.
- In an urban elementary school, administrators planned to have nutritious snacks between the two morning classes. However, it was hard to get a supply of this food. Furthermore, they needed funds for the extensive filing system (for HPS process evaluation), and blood tests cost a lot, too. They wanted to buy more facilities to expand school size and teacher training. They appealed to the city authority to give support in money and policy to expand the campus and they hoped for money from W.H.O as well.
- In a rural middle school, there were monetary restrictions to providing a balanced nutritious diet. The school had to ask students for money and minority families were poor.
- In an urban middle school, administrators and teachers mentioned a lack of funds as one of the challenges. Teachers said, "Health-Promoting Schools is a developing project which needs the strong financial support from the society," and "Lack of funds: need joint efforts from the town government and education bureau."
- In an urban junior high school, one teacher pointed to a lack of facilities for students such as physical activities facilities and reading rooms. Another teacher pointed to a need for more funds "to prepare facilities compatible with the advanced concepts."
- In a suburban vocational school, school administrators mentioned that for health promotion, they needed a large amount of funds and personnel to be invested into the project. Administrators mentioned a lack of funds for teaching resources, the process of publicity and implementation, and publicity materials.
- In a rural elementary school, all four administrators who provided written answers mentioned funds as a challenge. In addition, a teacher stated, "I thought that the biggest challenge is lack of funds and the joint efforts by people from all the walks."
- In an urban junior high school, one parent hoped that WHO could offer more sufficient financial support, besides other things.

(Note: Even though this program was being implemented with support from the WHO, that support did not include financial support for activities undertaken by the schools. The WHO's financial support was provided only to hold an initial training meeting of participating school leaders, to convene a summing up conference at the end of the project, and to augment the provincial leader's evaluation efforts. All financial support for the school-based efforts came from the province, local communities, and schools.)

- Encountering no challenges to implementation - Some participants mentioned that they faced no challenges in implementing the HPS project.
- In an urban elementary school, some students and some parents saw no challenges.
- In an urban middle school, parents initially said they had no problems, and then said there was a difficulty, but they could solve it.
- In an urban junior high school, at least one of the students acknowledged no challenges.
- In a sub-urban vocational school, one of the mothers saw "no problem at all."

In a rural vocational school, one of the administrators expressed that for him, personally, the project did not present a very big challenge because he had a lot of experience in the education field.

4. RESEARCH QUESTION: WHAT CHANGES IN THE PARTICIPANTS' LIVES WERE REPORTED AS EVIDENCE THAT THEIR SCHOOLS WERE PROMOTING HEALTH?

Participants reported:

- **Attitude changes**
- **Knowledge and concept changes**
- **Behaviour changes**

The changes described below are not presented by school. They are summarized to express the kind of changes that were perceived by the persons involved. Changes that were broadly perceived by many people are attributed to "participants". Where changes were most strongly, frequently or uniquely noted by a particular group, that group is identified. Additional information about these changes and the strategies involved are published elsewhere (Zhang, et al, [forthcoming]; Aldinger, 2008; Aldinger, 2008b; Whitman, 2008).

Attitude changes – Attitude changes for many participants included *paying more attention to health*. For example, people realized a stronger sense of importance for nutrition and healthy surroundings, the danger of smoking, hygiene and safety. They also reported developing a stronger sense of *health consciousness*, such as for psychological health. Students (and staff) reported *attaining better psychological quality and confidence*. This included feeling that they could handle difficulties, be more communicative, and be more in control of their emotions and self. They recognized that these positive attitudes contributed to richer lives, increased motivation to study, and offered more enjoyment. School administrators indicated they began to "put themselves in others' shoes" to better understand others' behaviour. Some participants reported growing *friendships between teachers and students*. Students reported feeling they could turn to teachers for help if they had problems, and they felt they could treat teachers "like friends." Teachers reported feeling valued, like a "big brother," and experiencing more satisfaction with their work. Parents began to feel *more relaxed* because they gained confidence that the school was taking good care of their children, that the school was providing safe and harmonious surroundings, and that their child was improving his or her self-control and psychological quality.

Knowledge and concept changes – Participants reported that they gained increased knowledge about nutrition, hygiene, safety and security, the harm of tobacco, how to avoid injuries, and psychological knowledge, such as how to relieve anxiety and what is normal and abnormal. Parents reported acquiring knowledge from children. Administrators, teachers, students and parents reported developing a *broader concept of health* that included not only physical health, but also psychological and social health. Many participants reported that they developed an *understanding of the HPS concept* over time. This included gaining knowledge and understanding of different components among different participants. Actively involved school administrators reported knowledge gains that showed the most complex understanding of the HPS concept, followed by teachers, and students and parents whose comments demonstrated less complex understanding.

Behaviour changes - Participants' reported behaviour changes including more *active participation* in the project. Students and parents actively participated in activities such as publicising health knowledge to neighbours and friends, and taking part in school events. Some participants *increased their physical activity*, by doing more physical exercise, such as utilising the school playground or walking to school rather than taking the bus. Students reported *improving sanitary habits,* such as not throwing litter on the ground, and paying attention to personal hygiene such as brushing teeth twice a day, washing hands before and after dinner and after using the toilet, cutting their nails regularly, and washing their clothes. Many teachers and parents reported *reducing or quitting smoking.* Some children successfully persuaded their fathers and grandfathers to reduce or quit smoking. Administrators and staff reported that they quit smoking or did not smoke on school grounds, especially if the school established no-smoking rules. Participants also reported *changing bad habits* and developing good habits. This included not using bad words, keeping good sanitary habits, paying attention to personal health issues, displaying civilized behaviours, improving living habits, making self-adjustments and maintaining adaptability. Students persuaded their classmates and friends to change their unhealthy habits. Participants also reported they began to *eat more nutritiously,* such as not eating fried food, intentionally buying healthy food, and balancing their diets rather than over-eating special food preferences. Vendors who sold unqualified foods outside the school moved away because students and teachers stopped buying from them. Reports of *increased safety behaviours* included students wearing yellow safety hats and walking together, not taking vehicles that were uncertified, wearing safety helmets, and obeying traffic rules when riding a bike. Consequently, accidental *injuries decreased* significantly in some schools. *Parent-child communication* was also reported to have improved. Parents indicated they had more communication with their child and shared their own growing up experiences. Children also reported getting more attention from their parents after they had opportunities to express their talents at school in different ways other than academically.

The next section compares what "happened" in Zhejiang Province to what we think we know, as manifested by the components, factors and processes cited in the theoretical frameworks described above.

How Well Does What We Think We Know Fit With What "Happened" In Zhejiang, Province, China?

In this section, we return to the three theoretical frameworks presented earlier, listing our assumptions about the components of a Health-Promoting School (HPS) and the processes and/or factors that we think help schools to make needed changes and become successful as a HPS. We rate each assumption according to how strongly we think what "happened" confirms the assumption, and we present our reasoning and other relevant information to support our rating. We also identify factors not found in the frameworks that may be helpful if considered in future efforts to implement HPS.

Components of Health-Promoting Schools (HPS and FRESH Frameworks)

- **School health policy**
- **Physical school environment**
- **Psycho-social school environment**
- **Health education**
- **Health services**
- **Nutrition services**
- **Counselling/mental health**
- **Physical exercise**
- **Health promotion for staff**
- **Outreach to families and communities**

This study shows that schools participating in the Zhejiang HPS expansion project implemented, to varying degrees, all of the components of a Health-Promoting School as well as similar components reflected in the Ottawa Charter for Health Promotion and the FRESH Framework. This finding is unlike the studies of HPS where no schools were found to have incorporated all such components (Lynagh, Schofield & Sanson-Fisher, 1997; Stewart-Brown, 2006). This study shows that schools with few resources as well as those with adequate resources, and schools in rural as well as urban areas implemented school health policies that helped improve health promoting processes, behaviours and conditions. Results, published elsewhere, show that positive changes in health, behaviour, knowledge and attitudes occurred between the beginning and end of the project (Zhang et al, 2008; Aldinger, 2008).

Assumption: *School health policy* is a feasible and effective means of addressing health issues and improving health through schools.

What happened: This assumption was **strongly** confirmed.

All schools established and/or improved health policies in the form of rules, regulations and guidelines for a variety of health promoting processes and conditions. The policies served as feasible and effective means of promoting and improving health, as the non-tobacco use rules and sanitary improvements demonstrated.

Assumption: *The physical school environment* is a feasible and important means of addressing health issues and improving health through schools.

What happened: This assumption was **strongly** confirmed.

All schools altered and improved their physical environment to serve as feasible and effective means of promoting and improving health, as demonstrated by improved facilities such as dormitories and sports facilities, enhanced cleanliness and beautification projects.

Assumption: ***The psycho-social school environment*** is a feasible and important means of addressing health issues and improving health through schools.

What happened: This assumption was **strongly** confirmed.

All schools altered and improved their psycho-social environment to serve as feasible and effective means of promoting and improving health, as demonstrated by the establishment of harmonious and caring school and classroom atmospheres, good relationships between teachers and students and increased attention to providing equal treatment.

Assumption: ***Health education*** is a feasible and important means of addressing health issues and improving health through schools.

What happened: This assumption was **strongly** confirmed.

All schools altered and improved their health education efforts to serve as feasible and effective means of promoting and improving health, as demonstrated by the integration of health topics into regular teaching, increased use of new teaching and learning methods, special health classes and meetings, extracurricular activities and outreach activities.

Assumption: ***Health services*** are feasible and important means of addressing health issues and improving health through schools.

What happened: This assumption was **strongly** confirmed.

Many schools altered and improved school health services to serve as feasible and effective means of promoting and improving health, as demonstrated by the improvement or re-establishment of health check-ups for students and staff members, increased communication and follow-up related to student health check-ups by school staff, prevention and treatment of common diseases, and increased availability of doctors or nurses.

Assumption: ***Nutrition services*** are feasible and important means of addressing health issues and improving health through schools.

What happened: This assumption was **strongly** confirmed.

Many schools altered and improved nutrition-related services to serve as feasible and effective means of promoting and improving health, as demonstrated by increase in nutritious and balanced meals, increases in food variety, prohibitions against street food vendors and training of kitchen staff.

Assumption: ***Counselling and metal health*** are a feasible and important means of addressing health issues and improving health through schools.

What happened: This assumption was **strongly** confirmed.

Schools offered psychological consultation to serve as feasible and effective means of promoting and improving health, as demonstrated by provision of specially trained teachers, hotlines, special mailboxes and special consultation rooms.

Assumption: ***Physical exercise*** is a feasible and important means of addressing health issues and improving health through schools.

What happened: This assumption was **strongly** confirmed.

Schools required and promoted regular physical exercise to serve as a feasible and effective means of promoting and improving health, as demonstrated by required morning exercises, sports days and competitions, and improvements to sports facilities and exercise opportunities.

Assumption: **Health promotion for staff** is a feasible and important means of addressing health issues and improving health through schools.

What happened: This assumption was **moderately** confirmed.

Some schools implemented health promotion for staff to serve as a feasible and effective means of promoting and improving health, as demonstrated by tobacco cessation promotions, "exercise more" promotions and psychological consulting for teachers. Although much of the overall HPS effort also benefited teachers and other school personnel, health promotion efforts aimed directly at staff were reported less frequently than other components of the HPS.

Assumption: **Outreach to families and communities** are feasible and important means of addressing health issues and improving health through schools.

What happened: This assumption was **strongly** confirmed.

Schools conducted outreach efforts to serve as a feasible and effective means of promoting and improving health, as the distribution of health materials to the community, letters and calls to parents and parents' schools demonstrated. Students found outreach efforts effective a fun way to learn by doing.

The next section focuses on how well the activities undertaken in Zhejiang's HPS project were consistent with processes and factors that we think are important in making changes that will help schools become HPS.

KEY FACTORS IN CHANGING POLICY AND PRACTICE (CHANGE FRAMEWORK) INCLUDE:

- **Attention to external forces**
- **Vision or big ideas**
- **National guidelines and movement**
- **Leadership skills**
- **Administrative and management support**
- **Data-driven planning and decision-making**
- **Team training**
- **Critical mass and supportive norms**
- **Dedicated time and resources**
- **Adaptation to local concerns**

<u>Assumption</u>: *Attention to external forces* is important in making changes that will help a school to become a HPS.

<u>What happened</u>: This assumption was **strongly** confirmed.

Qualitative data showed that health and education officials, school leaders, teachers, students and parents adopted changes in response to external forces. These forces included effects of China's one-child policy, actions by the political system, reform in the education system, and health issues.

One-child policy - China's one-child policy, introduced in 1979 and underpinned by a system of rewards and penalties, allows one child for urban residents and, with some restrictions, two children for rural residents (Hesketh, Li & Zhu, 2005). The effects of this policy played a role in implementing the HPS project in two aspects. First, because the government permits parents to have only one child, parents have an intense desire for that child to succeed and prosper. Because parents recognise that access to higher education is an important path to success and prosperity, they often have very high academic expectations for their child. Parents' high expectations often result in a lot of pressure for children to do very well in school, and such pressures are not supportive of social and emotional well-being. Data from the GSHS complemented these perceptions. An indication of this pressure is likely the fact that, on average, 19.6% of those age 16 or older in the participating project schools in Zhejiang Province responded in the GSHS that they seriously considered attempting suicide during the past 12 months. The highest rate reported in one of the schools in this study was 22.3% (Whitman et al, 2008).

Furthermore, the pressure extends beyond the children to their teachers, as families, principals and the teachers themselves expected teachers to enable students to succeed. School administrators, teachers, students, and parents in this study agreed that there is often too much pressure to succeed in school and this agreement served as an impetus for change. Also, as school principals, teachers, students and parents began to respond to the pressures stemming from the one-child policy they seemed to gain relief and satisfaction in changing to a broader concept of development and focusing on a variety of abilities rather than solely academic achievement.

Second, schools also were attentive to an opportunity that stemmed from the one-child policy. That is, that the child exerted quite a lot of influence on parents and grandparents. By ceasing this opportunity, schools were able to affect some of the changes they intended. Teachers, parents, and students repeatedly noted that parents and grandparents were likely to follow the suggestions and advice from their child and grandchild. Indeed, parents seemed to make behaviour changes, especially reducing or quitting smoking (mostly fathers or grandfathers) and changing dietary habits (mostly mothers) after children shared new knowledge and expectations.

Thus, the results of the study indicate that by paying attention to the affects of the one-child policy, people involved in the project were able to make changes that contributed to improved well-being and health.

Political system - Schools made changes needed to become a HPS partially as a result of paying attention to the opportunities afforded by their political system.

Strong efforts were mounted by health and education officials, and school leaders, to gain support from political leaders. Support was gained in the form of attention and sometimes financial assistance. Leaders from municipal governments gave priority to this project and sometimes attended HPS-related meetings. The translator during one of our interviews mentioned that the socialist/communist system might help this kind of project because if the party or government requires something, it has to be done. The essence of this remark is confirmed by Wang in his book *Education in China since 1976* where he explains, "The Central Committee of the Communist Party of China is responsible for directing the whole country's educational development and for guiding the reforms of the educational system" (Wang, 2003: 284).

In implementing the HPS project, most schools established HPS committees led by principals and vice principals. The vice principal was frequently a person from the Communist Party who was responsible for "moral" education and leadership. This leadership committee, which also included school staff from all important departments of the school, served to disseminate the HPS concept and interventions systematically throughout the school. Thus, the results of the study indicate that schools sought the attention to the political system, and that their attention and support contributed to the changes schools strived to make.

Educational system - It was apparent throughout the interviews that school leaders, teachers, students and parents paid close attention to factors of the educational system, especially the reforms.

School leaders paid close attention to the reform of "quality education" and its purpose of educating students in an all-round way. Through this reform, the education system showed concern about undue competition between schools and students, students working individually and not supporting each other, and the teaching methods, such as rote learning, that were not suited to all-round development. School leaders promoted the HPS project as a means to support quality education. Teachers implemented participatory activities and students enjoyed activities in which they were actively involved, working with and supporting each other. Teachers started to evaluate students not only according to their academic achievements but also according to physical, emotional, and social health and development. Thus, the results of this study indicate that the participants responded to factors and reforms of the education system and this contributed to the changes needed to become HPS.

Health issues - Since the HPS concept, by its name, focuses on health issues, it is no surprise that school leaders, teachers, students and parents paid attention to health issues and indicators in efforts to affect changes that would help their schools become HPS.

School leaders paid close attention to important national and local health issues. A major study of causes of death and modifiable risk factors in China suggested that smoking cessation, increased physical activity, and improved nutrition should be important strategies for reducing the burden of premature death and risks in China (He et al, 2005). Of the nine schools in this study, three had nutrition and one had tobacco prevention as their entry point. However, in at least six schools, participants reported they or their family members reduced or stopped smoking, and in at least five schools, participants reported that they made changes to their dietary habits. Virtually all schools promoted increased physical activity. Accidents are also a pressing health concern in China, where "injuries have become a major public health problem, especially in the working-age population" (Lee, 2004). Injuries were more prevalent in rural areas. Two of the three rural schools addressed injury prevention. Furthermore, "issues of ill mental health are increasingly apparent in China..." (Lee, 2004). Three of the schools addressed psychological or mental health as their entry points, but participants from at least six schools said that their schools offered psychological support.

At virtually every school, school leaders, teachers, students and parents were increasing efforts to address important public health issues and thus making changes that helped their schools to become HPS.

Assumption: **Having a big vision** is important for making changes that will help a school become a HPS.

What happened: This assumption was **strongly** confirmed.

Having a big vision was clearly evident among the leaders promoting the HPS project. The WHO at the global level, the Chinese CDC at the national and provincial levels, and principals at the school level pursued the vision of establishing *Health-Promoting Schools*. Schools translated this vision into a notion described as "health is first", which meant that schools kept health as a priority running through all the day's activities and integrated health content into daily education work. In some schools, it was initially challenging to get participants to understand the full scope of HPS concept, but this was well resolved as evidenced by the number of participants that described their notion of health as much broader than before the project. Furthermore, the HPS effort was closely tied to another big vision, "quality education", and together these two show a clear direction to improved education and health.

Building on the vision of the HPS concept and the vision of education reform through quality education, all 9 schools participating in the qualitative study and 41 of the 42 other schools participating in the expansion project were able to make the changes needed to receive the Bronze Medal for becoming a HPS.

Assumption: National guidelines and movements are important for making changes that will help a school become a HPS.

What happened: This assumption was **moderately** confirmed.

In China, the central government is responsible for setting up guiding principles and macro planning for primary and secondary education. The Ministry of Education has recognized the heavy study load on students in primary and secondary education in the name of high exam marks. In 2000, an investigation by the Municipal Education Commission in Zhejiang Province revealed that students stayed in their schools for more than 12 hours every day. The Ministry of Education issued "several documents aimed at reducing student workloads and increasing the quality of education" (Wang, 2003). Parents told us that the HPS concept fit exactly with the government mandated *quality education*. Furthermore, the notion that the HPS concept was an international movement, promoted by WHO and other international organisations, that it was a national effort to assess the feasibility for implementing HPS throughout China, and that it was a provincial effort to expand the HPS concept to all parts of the province, presented as sense of "movement" that helped schools foster participation and acquire local attention and even monetary support.

However, in some locations, despite governmental guidelines, regulations, proclamations and promotions, and despite the excitement generated by international, national and provincial movements, some schools were not able generate adequate monetary support to implement the project as they wanted. Perhaps governmental regulations and movements without complementary means to achieve adequate monetary support are not as helpful or important as ones with such means.

Assumption: *Leadership skills* are important for making changes that will help a school to become a HPS.

What happened: This assumption was **strongly** confirmed.

In addition to the support from the municipal government, and especially in cases where strong support from the municipal government was lacking, the strong leadership of the *school principal* and administrators was crucial. Some principals became role models for healthy behaviour by stopping smoking or walking to school. Teachers often followed suit. School principals or designated teachers led the special HPS committees, giving the effort a sense of priority within the work of the school. Some of the school administrators communicated with government departments and won moral as well as financial support. Some schools had a team of administrators who considered themselves "co-workers" on this project. Teachers, students and parents frequently cited the principal and other school leaders and providing the sense of priority and purpose that helped make the project work. Thus, the study shows that principals, administrators and other school personnel provided leadership that helped others to pursue the vision and enable their school to become a HPS.

Assumption: ***Administrative and management support*** is important for making changes that will help a school to become a HPS.

What happened: This assumption was **strongly** confirmed.

Schools set up special *HPS planning committees*. Principals and/or vice-principals led or co-led these committees, and committee members included administrators and teachers with authority from various areas throughout the school. Schools selected committee members according to the positions and roles they already held, and in some cases, students, parents, and/or community members also served on this committee. The committees discussed the kind of policy to carry out, made a work plan and discussed details and assignments of tasks and strategies to carry out the plan. They set up various systems in the school to monitor operations, made modifications to the school policy, and took responsibility for project implementation. They integrated HPS interventions, making them part of the overall school responsibility.

Study results indicate that schools provided administrative and management support through special HPS committees that ensured the HPS concept and interventions could be implemented efficiently and effectively throughout the school and the community.

Assumption: ***Data-driven planning and decision-making*** are important for making changes that will help a school to become a HPS.

What happened: This assumption was **not** confirmed.

Schools utilized different mechanisms for choosing their entry points (first health issue on which to focus). They considered issues based on advice from authorities and their own experience and perception. In some cases they collected their own information from visits to households or from discussions with teachers, students and parents. They sometimes used information they found in newspapers and other media to make a case for their choices. Several of the schools seemed to consider the developmental level and "sensitive age" of their students when choosing the entry point.

Schools, as requested, conducted the surveys recommended by the WHO -- the GSHS for 13- to 15-year-olds and the PSE profile at pre- and post-test, and implemented provincially recommend, locally developed surveys according to each entry point. However, few, if any participants used the WHO recommended survey data in a substantial or meaningful way during their planning processes. Some, may have used it for decision-making after project implementation, but few, if any participants, reported WHO survey data or even the locally developed surveys of entry point issues as being important to their planning or decision-making processes. This lack of use might have been due to the time delay in getting these surveys' data analyzed and receiving instructions from the HEI on how to use the results. It also might have been due to a different level of thinking in which advice from authorities and their own experience and perception were considered sufficient bases for project planning and decision-making.

Furthermore, participants simply may not have had a need for representative and statistically accurate data about risks or health levels to define a risk or health issue as a problem worthy of attention. Given the consistency with which their planning and decisions conformed to nationally identified health problems, the bases used by the participants were appropriate for HPS planning and decision-making. Thus, the study shows that schools did not practice "data-based" driven planning and decision-making in making changes that helped their school become a HPS school.

Assumption: **Team training** is important for making changes that will help a school to become a HPS.
What happened: This assumption was **strongly** confirmed.

As a team, delegates from each school participated in an initial orientation and training workshop with CDC, national, and international experts. Part of the training also included site visits to other Health-Promoting Schools in the province by principals and teachers from newly participating schools. Each school organized meetings in which those who had participated in the site visits passed on their observations to others in their school. Administrators and teachers who were designated to lead the project commonly held training meetings for groups of teacher and other school personnel. WHO-issued HPS documents were often used in trainings. Schools also organized additional *trainings by CDC staff and/or other experts*. We saw pictures in which the whole schoolyard was filled with participants for training by CDC staff. Thus, training was conducted in groups or teams as an important way of preparing participants to take part in the HPS project. This was vitally important because administrators and especially teachers admitted a lack of knowledge, skills, methods, theoretical guidance, and experience in health promotion many times during the interviews both early and late in the projects' implementation.

Thus, team training was important for making changes that helped the schools to become a HPS, and further training, guidance, and sharing of experiences was desired by those involved.

Assumption: **Critical mass and supportive norms** are important for making changes that will help a school to become a HPS.
What happened: This assumption was **strongly** confirmed.

It was clearly important to inspire a critical mass of people to support the HPS effort. The HPS concept was new, relatively unheard of. Furthermore, most school personnel and parents were passionate that nothing should interfere with academic pursuit and achievement. All schools held *start-up or mobilization meetings* as initial advocacy events for gaining commitment for the HPS project among the entire school population. Schools held some of the start-up meetings for students only, and some of the meetings involved families. In some cases, individuals were instrumental in moving the concept forward but much of the critical mass of support was generated through the establishment or improvement of health-related rules, regulations and policy, a commitment by school leaders to them, and a willingness of school personnel, students and parents to support them. These actions fostered supportive norms underpinning a growing critical mass of support. Our first round of data gathering showed that not all faculty members supported the HPS plan. Our third and last round showed that schools were viewing the HPS project as a co-responsibility of the school, parents, community, and government and participants were calling for the project to continue its efforts and expand to other schools. Thus, the study shows schools mobilized a critical mass of support and generated supportive norms that were very important to making changes that helped schools to become HPS.

Assumption: **Dedicated time and resources** is important for making changes that will help a school to become a HPS.

What happened: This assumption was **strongly** confirmed.

The *special HPS committees* set up by all schools were a dedication of time and resources and served as the organizational mode for the project's implementation. Committee members all played a role in planning and implementing the project. Integrating their HPS project responsibilities into their regular work seemed to make it more sustainable. Participants reported that they needed time to mobilize sometimes substantial amounts of financial support to make health related improvements to school facilities. Participants also noted that it required time to change habits that might have been established over a long time, and that health promotion was a long-term goal. In some cases, a lack of funds or facilities was a challenge. This study shows that schools dedicated time and resources for making changes that helped them to become HPS, and that there is a need to continue to dedicate time and resources to sustain and build on achievements.

Assumption: **Adaptation to local concerns** is important for making changes that will help a school to become a HPS.

What happened: This assumption was **strongly** confirmed.

Schools aimed to support the overall HPS concept, but they also adapted it to local situations. Each school developed a *work plan* for implementing the HPS concept and related it to their school's condition. The basic principle was to develop the work plan taking the "practical situation" of each school into consideration. The vocational school with students who previously experienced failure focused its efforts on helping its students develop confidence. Rural schools, where students and families had low basic educational levels and frequently suffered injury, focused their plans to help students and families learn about safety and injury prevention. Urban schools, where students experienced a lot of pressure to achieve high academic scores, focused their plans to enable students to benefit from psychological consultation. This study shows that schools adapted their work plans to local concerns for making changes that helped the school to become a HPS.

The next section focuses on how well the activities undertaken in Zhejiang's HPS project were consistent with processes and factors that we think are important in creating successful school health programs.

Success Factors of School Health Programs (Success Factors)

- Gaining commitment
- Theoretical underpinning
- Content (relevant)
- Time and sequence
- Multi-strategies
- Teacher training
- Relevance
- Variety of teaching/learning methods, especially participatory methods
- Participation

Assumption: **Commitment** is important for achieving desirable results relating to the implementation and effectiveness of school health programs.

What happened: This assumption was **strongly** confirmed.

Commitment was important at the school level, from the principal, and at the governmental level, from the education and health bureau. Six schools in this study reported that they received strong support and financial support from the municipal government. In some instances, administrators worked hard and finally won support from the government. In many cases, it was challenging to gain the commitment of parents as they feared the programs could deter academic success.

Assumption: ***Theoretical underpinnings*** are important for achieving desirable results relating to the implementation and effectiveness of school health programs.

What happened: This assumption was **strongly** confirmed.

The interventions were based on the *theoretical underpinnings* of the HPS framework (introduced earlier in this chapter). This required that participants first became familiar with the HPS concept through workshops, studying WHO and CDC HPS-related materials, and visiting Health-Promoting Schools. This provided a common vision and served to underpin a willingness to participate.

The participating schools addressed virtually all HPS components and understanding of the concept of health and Health-Promoting Schools was broad by the last round of school interviews. The theoretical framework also may have enabled participants to quickly identify their needs for more professional development and technical support as they strived to improve their efforts.

Assumption: ***The content of programs*** is important for achieving desirable results relating to the implementation and effectiveness of school health programs.

What happened: This assumption was **strongly** confirmed.

The *content of HPS programs* was chosen for various reasons such as the advice of authorities, experience and perceptions of school leaders and interest among teachers, students and parents. Although the entry points were often chosen by the school principal or leader, schools quickly took on additional health issues, as expected, in their effort to become a HPS. The initial entry points and additional topics offered content relevant to the participants and gave them reason to participate. Furthermore, in diffusing content about the topics, schools used new and participatory learning methods in which students were more actively involved and outreach methods that engaged parents and community members. The content served as an important means of generating a willingness to implement the HPS concept and take part in the opportunities it afforded. It was surely one of the reasons the program participants viewed it as important, useful and worth expanding to other schools.

Assumption: ***Time and sequence*** are important for achieving desirable results relating to the implementation and effectiveness of school health programs.

What happened: This assumption was **moderately** confirmed.

Schools developed work plans in which they specified the *timing and sequence* of major activities. Schools had special activities for health promotion, and they integrated health topics into regular teaching in many class subjects. However, we did not see a plan with a range of activities over the full set of school years, such as a plan based on students' developmental levels and in a sequence that would build upon the learning experiences previously provided. Such plans may or may not have existed.

Assumption: ***Use of multi-strategies for maximum outcomes*** is important for achieving desirable results relating to the implementation and effectiveness of school health programs.

What happened: This assumption was **strongly** confirmed.

Schools implemented a wide variety of activities related to virtually all components of the HPS model and Ottawa Charter. These activities were coordinated to address the chosen health topics. The large number of activities generated within each of the HPS components, engaging a wide variety of participants both within and outside of the school provided *a multi-strategic approach* that probably contributed significantly to maximizing the project's implementation and effectiveness.

Assumption: ***Teacher training and professional development*** are important for achieving desirable results relating to the implementation and effectiveness of school health programs.

What happened: This assumption was **strongly** confirmed.

Teacher training and professional development started with learning the HPS concept. Additional training included principals' orientation and training meetings, training through experts, study visits to other Health-Promoting Schools, and brainstorming among teachers. These training efforts were critical to the projects implementation and success. Furthermore, as experience was gained, teachers recognized that they would need further training to increase their knowledge and skills and build on their experience. They also recognized the need for and value of ongoing technical support from qualified staff to improve their efforts and build on their success.

Assumption: ***Relevance*** is important for achieving desirable results relating to the implementation and effectiveness of school health programs.

What happened: This assumption was **strongly** confirmed.

Schools chose interventions based on various factors such as the requirements of the project, expected result, feasibility, daily work conditions, students' development, and administrators' experience. Schools also selected class topics for a variety of other reasons including economic development (e.g., the city being a cigarette manufacturing city, more economic development necessitating the need for environmental protection, mental health being important for the future development of the whole society); health condition (e.g., age of smokers getting younger, nutrition affecting students' physical condition, family members smoking, SARS and chicken flu spreading in the country); and development and actual situation of students (e.g., students' preferring to talk rather than to listen, students going through physical and psychological development, and wanting to encourage students to participate). Like the factor of *content*, addressed above, the project's *relevance* served as an important means of generating a willingness to implement the HPS concept and take part in the opportunities it afforded. It was surely one of the reasons the program participants viewed it as important, useful and worth expanding to other schools.

Assumption: ***Using a variety of teaching/learning methods, especially participatory methods***, is important for achieving desirable results relating to the implementation and effectiveness of school health programs.

What happened: This assumption was **strongly** confirmed.

It is clear that a wide variety of teaching/learning methods were used by all schools participating in the project, as evidenced by the inclusion of health-related learning opportunities in a variety of subject areas, communication about health policy and related rules, extracurricular activities and school/community outreach and collaboration. In implementing these methods, teachers used new teaching and learning methods that significantly involved participatory processes, such as elicitation, communication, questions, cooperation, group discussion, group activities, and student led lessons and appraisals.

Teachers tried to communicate more in class meetings and students were encouraged to talk and express their opinions. School principals, teachers and students noted that *the increased use of participatory methods was considered one of the greatest achievements of the project.*

Assumption: **Participation** is important for achieving desirable results relating to the implementation and effectiveness of school health programs.

What happened: This assumption was **strongly** confirmed.

Participants acknowledged that *participation* was one of the most important factors to the project's successful implementation. It was also perceived to have contributed significantly to the project's success. Participants acknowledged that the participation of the WHO, CDC, HEI, and other government experts and agencies brought wide attention to the project and honour to the schools. School principals recognized that there would need to be wide participation of staff and students if the project was to be implemented successfully and dedicated time and resources to ensure such participation. Students and teachers took active parts in the project. Students passed out health information to parents and community members, actively participated in the health promotion activities of their school, and formed good habits doing so. Participation is an inherent part of becoming a Health-Promoting School, and it is impossible to be one, without it. The substantial support of and participation in health promotion generated by persons involved in the HPS project is an important demonstration of its success.

IMPROVING KNOWLEDGE, THEORY AND PRACTICE BY CONSIDERING "WHAT HAPPENED" IN THE ZHEJIANG PROVINCE HPS PROJECT

What can be said about the framework of the Health-Promoting School?

The findings of this study reveal that the comprehensive school health programs that were successfully implemented and found to be effective in Zhejiang Province consisted of all the components promoted by WHO's framework of the Health-Promoting School, as well as the similar components called for by the Ottawa Charter for Health Promotion and the international initiative to Focus Resources on Effective School Health (FRESH). These findings confirm the value and importance of each of the HPS components and their synergistic nature in promoting health. Thus, the authors of this study recommend that practitioners wishing to implement effective school health programs should be guided by the theoretical framework of the HPS, and *implement all of the components together, in partnership and participation with health and education officials, school leaders, teachers, students, parents and the community.* Furthermore, practitioners in schools that had become HPS provided a significant impetus to this project by serving as models for principals, administrators and teachers from other schools wishing to become HPS. Thus, health and education officials should follow the lead of the Zhejiang health and education officials, who fostered collaboration between experienced and inexperienced schools. Such actions reinforce the commitment of schools that have become HPS, give such schools a sense of "honour" for what they have achieved, and enable new schools to learn from their experience. This is a successful strategy for scaling up the development of HPS.

What can be said about the Key Factors in Changing Policy and Practice framework?

The findings of this study reveal that the comprehensive school health programs that were successfully implemented and found to be effective in Zhejiang Province were implemented using almost all of the processes and factors that are described in the Change Framework. The one exception was *data driven planning and decision-making.* Perhaps data may not be as initially important to school personnel because school leaders, teachers, students and parents feel confident moving ahead based on advice from authorities and /or their own experience and perceptions. Planning from these bases may even be preferable because such plans hold the dimension of *relevance* from the perspective of the persons involved. The plans and decisions made at the start-up of each school project in Zhejiang Province focused on important national and local health issues, and therefore fail to confirm the assumption that data, such as that recommended to be collected through the WHO's school-based student health survey, are important for initial planning and decision-making. Thus, the authors of this study recommend that practitioners wishing to implement effective school health programs *should be guided by the factors and processes for change as cited in the Change Framework and give strong consideration to the perceived relevance of health issues of the people involved, along with the conditions of the school, its students and community, as primary driving forces for planning and decision-making. This recommendation should not be misconstrued to diminish the value of data driven planning and decision-making as a project evolves and as planners and decision-makers must demonstrate what has been accomplished to sustain or improve school health programs.*

What can be said about the Success Factors in School-based Approaches to Health Education framework?

The findings of this study reveal that the comprehensive school health programs that were successfully implemented and found to be effective in Zhejiang Province were implemented using almost all of the processes and factors that are described in the success framework. Although the study found only moderate attention to time and sequence factors in health education plans in Zhejiang projects, there was sufficient attention to them in the planning of other activities and interventions to consider this a factor that contributes to program success. Thus, the authors of this study recommend that practitioners wishing to implement effective school health programs *should be guided by the factors and processes for success as cited in the Change Framework and give strong consideration to training and professional development as ongoing processes to meet the needs of administrators and teachers as program experience is gained and additional needs arise.*

What can be said about processes and factors relevant to the Zhejiang Project that were not substantially addressed in the theoretical frameworks.

Regarding the framework for HPS: Orientation to the HPS concept and on-going training and professional development should be added as a basic component of a HPS.

The findings of this study reveal that substantial efforts were undertaken in virtually all schools in the Zhejiang project to orient staff to the HPS concept. Orientation to the concept was an essential first step in gaining school leaders' attention and commitment to participate. The participants' understanding of the concept grew as school leaders oriented school staff, as teachers oriented students and as students participated in orientations for parents and the community. Substantial efforts were also undertaken to provide training and opportunities for professional development. These efforts led to improvements in health-related practices such as safety and hygiene, major changes in the way teachers taught and students learned through the increased use of participatory teaching and learning experiences, and a broadening of their concept of health to include psycho-social as well as physical health, and holistic development in addition to academic achievement. As administrators and teachers began to see changes from their new ways of teaching and thinking, they also recognized the need for further training and professional development to enable them to improve their efforts. Although the component "Health Promotion for Staff" might be construed as including orientation, training and professional development, it is generally viewed as a call for health interventions for school personnel, as well as students, *thus, the authors of this chapter recommend that orientation and on-going training and professional development opportunities should explicitly be added as one of the basic factors supporting a Health-Promoting School.*

Regarding the Change Framework: Monitoring and evaluation, in terms of process and outcome, and reports of change, should be added as a key factor of the Change Framework.

The findings of this study reveal that substantial efforts were undertaken in virtually all schools in the Zhejiang project to define the changes desired. The changes were clearly defined in rules, regulations, guidelines or standards of conduct, as well as in work plans. Systems were devised to monitor compliance with the rules and progress in implementing work plans. Periodic reports of progress were often shared with the whole school and achievements were often celebrated. Although these processes might overlap with processes that might be described under "Administrative and Management Support" and /or "Data driven planning and decision-making" the Change Framework does not explicitly call for desired changes to be clearly defined, monitored and reported. *Thus, the authors of this chapter recommend that monitoring and evaluation, in terms of process and outcome, and reports of change, be added to the Key Factors for Changing Policy and Practice framework.*

Regarding the Success Framework: Fostering connectedness between the school, students and teachers should be added as a factor of the Success Framework.

The findings of this study reveal that schools made substantial efforts to help students feel more connected to the school. They focused on improving relationships between school principals, teachers and students. Many participants reported that the relationship between students and teachers became more like friends with teachers showing more personal concern for students and students feeling they could talk more openly with teachers. This strong sense of connectedness between students and teachers was frequently cited as evidence of making the school's psycho-social environment more conducive to health. These findings are consistent with a comprehensive school-based study of health-related behaviours of adolescents in the United States of America which found that "when students feel they are part of a school…and feel close to people at school, they are healthier and more likely to succeed"(Blum, McNeely & Rinehart, 2002). *Thus, the author's of this chapter recommend that connectedness between the school, students and teachers be added to the framework of Success Factors in School-based Approaches to Health Education.*

What can be said to help practitioners further the development of HPS?

CONCLUSIONS

The processes and factors that were used to help schools become Health-Promoting schools in Zhejiang Province, China confirmed almost all of the components currently recommended for inclusion in an effective school health program, the processes and factors associated with affecting changes in policy and practice, and the factors associated with the success of school health programs. School health program planners and practitioners should give strong consideration to the three frameworks discussed in this chapter as they strive to improve health through schools. Furthermore, by discovering "what happened" in the Zhejiang Project, from the perspective of those persons involved, we have identified components, processes and factors that can be added to the frameworks and are likely to strengthen them.

As we have moved back and forth between knowledge, theory and practice, we have been able to add confirmations to many of our assumptions and discover new elements that can be added to our theoretical frameworks. Thus, if we continue to move back and forth in this manner, we may get lucky and actually move ahead. We wish you all the best in your health promoting endeavours.

SECTION II:
IE & C PRACTICE FOR SOCIAL AND BEHAVIOUR CHANGE

Chapter 9

WHAT WORKS IN IE&C PRACTICE: AN INTRODUCTION

Theophilus K. Gokah

IE&C programme activity is the subject of discussion in this section. These initiatives increasingly take place within communities some of which begin with traditional consultation processes. What is interesting in IE&C procedure is that community participation is common practice. This is because it is people around who all programmes and activities evolve. Participatory methods are born out of the recognition of uniqueness of an individual as an entity who is capable of making unique contributions to decision making (Tlamelo and Gerard, 2000).

Participation is not only about 'right of involvement'; it is also about learning and capacity building. Unfortunately, not everyone within the community learns neither do learning occur in all development agencies (Solomon, Mushtaque and Chowdhury, 2002). The common excuse for some organisations or programmes not learning has often been blamed on a lack of donor support and by inference lack of financial resources. Solomon, Mushtaque and Chowdhury (2002) think that this is a lame excuse. They attribute the failure to organisations inability 'to see the importance of learning. Organisations (and individuals) are so embroiled in demands for action that they cease to value learning'. There is more to it than meets Solomon, Mushtaque and Chowdhury's thinking; I hold a shared view with Hailey and James (2002) that ability to learn is dependent on many factors and in particular the development of an internal culture of learning. Sight should not be lost of the fact that without learning, action is doomed to ineffectiveness. This is why, for example, learning and knowledge management are crucial capacities for social change.

Put in context, Brehony (2000) sees the involvement of communities in planning their own projects as a new direction. Much of this involvement, Brehony argues, is in the form of verbal communication whereby village dwellers, for example, can inform development workers of their problems and how they propose to solve them. A close review of the various text presented in this book, reveals that a community's practice, beliefs, and knowledge has a firmer foundation on which to build a project. Notwithstanding, organisations have to work hard to avoid being 'merely academic'. They require constant evaluation to see if their campaigns are having an impact. In fact, IE&C programmes that do not engage in periodic, if not constant, evaluation and monitoring of their programmes are a sheer waste of resources. Particular interest in this thought is shared by John Durant. This demand enable recipients and in some cases donor organisations to consider more closely what is going on than what has been orchestrated and said in official forums (Fox, 2003).

WHAT WORKS IN IE&C PRACTICE?

To reiterate an earlier point, research is central to IE&C based on a number of approaches and practices (Bradbury and Reason, 2003). The ethos of IE&C involves action and reflection in participation with targeted audience with the intention to seek practical solutions to issues of concern to people or communities. IE&C is thus a tool used in turning the process from theory to practice. This becomes a point of reference in improving participants' lives.

IE&C lends itself to reflexive culture which can only be attained through consultation and systematic study of the people to who behaviour or social change is necessary. This approach is an overlap between critical social constructivism and critical realism which seeks to empower beneficiaries for change to happen. Change becomes sustainable in this way because ownership of change resides with its beneficiaries other than 'foreign' imposed (Lincoln, 2001).

Artistic representations of behaviour that do not represent authentic cultural expression will be rejected. As an ethnographic subject IE&C practitioners ought to assume the role of reflexive anthropologist seeking to understand the inside-out of a particular society. It is important for the IE&C practitioner to work with skilled people whose professional acumen will seek to capture true images and representations in the targeted community. Interviews and observations are research tools needed in data gathering to construct concepts for IE&C material. This means that public service adverts (PSAs) or TV clip targeting behaviour, for instance, will also have to be based on evidence. IE&C data, depending on *how* and *what* it is gathered for should not be generalised. Unless the evidence can be said to reflect the general population, any attempt to translate data from one cultural setting to another (without relevance) into an IE&C material will be misplaced. There is evidence from Kothari's (1999) work to show that Third World countries are experiencing a process whereby development decision making is shifting from the hands of communities to national governments and to private entrepreneurs or trans-national corporations. Ironically, it is trans-national corporations (TNCs) that decide the direction of national economies to the disadvantage of poor nations (Cavangah and Barnet, 1994; see also Korten, 1995). There is likelihood of communities seeing through foreign concepts that are refracted in IE&C material and will almost certainly reject them.

In one such practice in a suburb of Nairobi, Kenya where reproductive health of young people in a less endowed community was targeted, we engaged the services of a local artist to make an artist impression of some identified social and cultural practices (based on observation) that in our view harm the community. The piece of art work was based on a written script. We then conducted another research in the community to test whether the community was familiar with the images and what they represented. The community disassociated themselves from some of the drawings because it did not reflect their culture and social norm. This is what Gill Karamjit refers to in his paper as cultural Holon. Here, Gills's advice to 'mind the cultural gap' is very relevant in practices that aim at promoting social change.

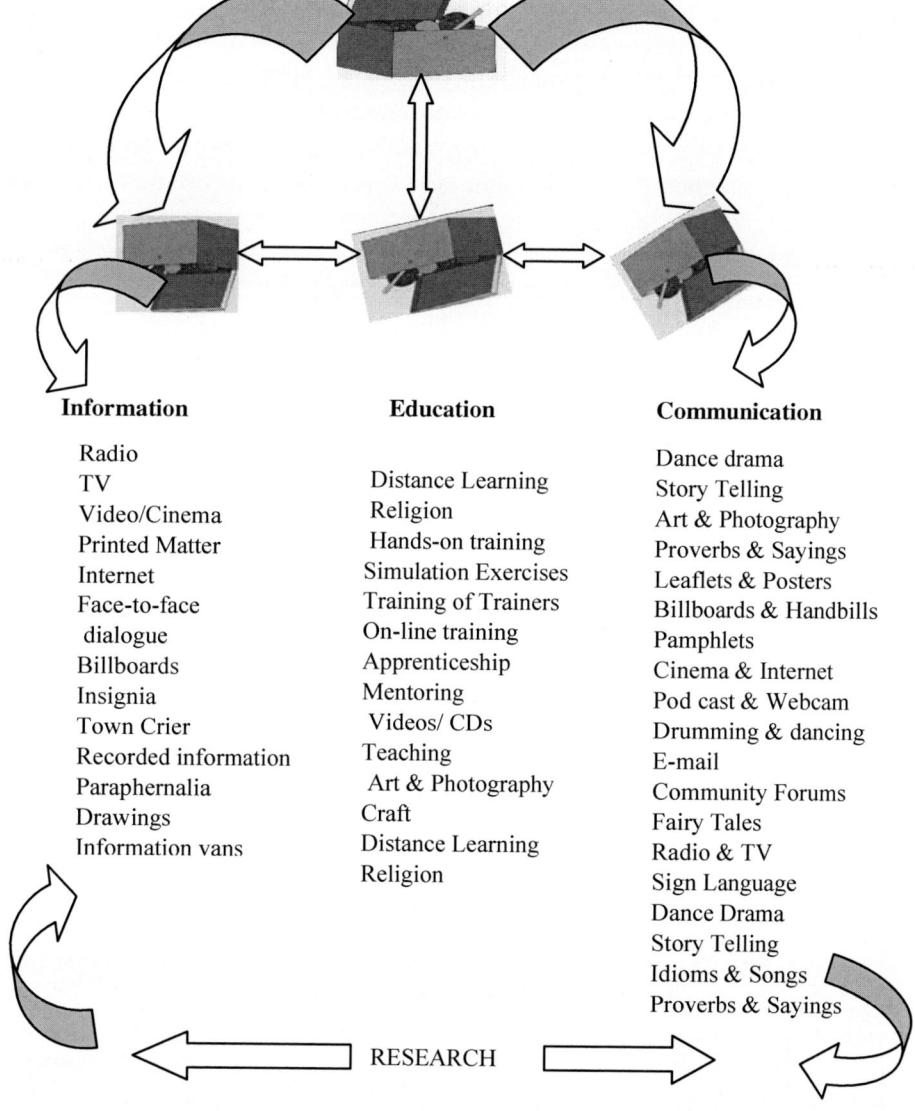

Figure 1. IE&C Systems Tools Box ™

We can liken the above scenario to Demian's (2006) reflection on loss in Papua New Guinea in which she views the relationship between reflexivity and 'culture loss' as one between method and subject that may hinder anthropologists from considering the possibility that their positions can be reversed according to the particularity of an ethnographic setting. In certain respects these observations are not new among ethnographic researchers and anthropologist but somehow seem to be missing in IE&C practice. There is no doubt that this type of 'member-checking' as it is called in Social Science phenomenology is particularly devoid of criticisms levelled against the method in social research practice (Shaw, 1999). The practice of checking for accurate representation can be done at community level or among targeted audience. Gokah's paper (in this section) reflects this representation. Apart from it being democratic, its participatory nature ensures that people are not unduly marginalised in the community and in decision making processes. Buhl's (2005) argument that 'visual culture as a strategic approach focuses on conditions surrounding viewing rather than on the substance of aesthetic objects' is interesting; this is because the challenge of visual culture, be it art and media, traditional versus contemporary forms of representation is also an issue for IE&C. Similarly, Media, be they traditional or contemporary, are useful vehicles for IE&C programme implementation. Understanding how the various media operates is necessary not only for smooth implementation of programmes and projects but how they are understood within the broad canvas of IE&C practice. This construction opens up an anecdote for selecting appropriate IE&C tools. A tools box, in the opinion of this author, is relevant. It is a resource from which both skilled and unskilled practitioners can easily draw upon. In other words, it is a ready reference point for practice.

The illustration in figure 1 depicts a typical IE&C systems tools box. There are three component parts of the systems box (three – in – one system box). Each component is unique with a set of tools. It is important that component boxes are unpacked to know and acquaint with its contents and possibly how each tool functions. Each tool is designed to function in a particular way in order to achieve a particular objective. In other words, the way the tool works is epitomised by channels through which we could use the tool for successful result. Incidentally, some tools are inter-related and are a function of each other but are not the same. Similarly, some media channels may cross-cut in a way that is beneficial for reaching intended targets across fields. Unlike channels that are designed as fit-for-all-purpose, others might not be. For instance, channels that are appealing to certain categories of young people may not work for older generations; the same principle will apply when dealing with literate and non-literate populations. An omnibus approach will be as good as putting 'square pegs in round holes'.

The reason for unpacking key tools i.e. information tools, education tools and communication tools, is to facilitate the best use within their proper context. The selection of tools must be explicit and done within the appropriate socio-cultural framework in mind. This requires systematic approach (and where possible strategic choices) based on informed reasoning about what works. Implied in this thinking are notions of innovation, deliberate IE&C policy directions and changes that need to be made in contested areas.

The use of combined tools increases the analytic power and understanding of the approach being used and offers potential benefits of yielding maximum result. It also provides opportunities for both programme implementers and beneficiaries to choose from a wide range of options available. Baseline surveys (Covey, 2001) or pre-testing (Dimiter and Phillip, 2003) of tools offers windows of opportunities to know which tool(s) are more appropriate to reach target groups. This pattern follows the basic tenets of social research ethos.

The argument here is that, the extent to which strategic choices and debates are informed and the role of purposeful intervention for progressive social change must inform all IE&C practitioners (Eyben, Kidder; Rowlands and Bronstein, 2008). Among the gamut of implementation strategies are contemporary visual representations such as video, mass-media productions and advertorials deployed to educate, inform and communicate messages to audiences. Here, it is important that practitioners develop and or build upon existing IE&C systems tools box from which they can select tools that are appropriate within their particular social context.

IE&C is not about 'racing against time'. It is a systematic process that can be tested against any rigorous methodology. I have known in some social and organisational context which holds a contrary view to the above position. Their central argument is that 'the job is about saving lives and deplorable conditions and not expending time and resources on IE&C'. This position should not be dismissed without giving it a further thought because it is fraught with ignorance and many inaccuracies. IE&C has currency if properly planned and executed. It dispels the notion of knee-jerk approaches to programme action. In deed, cost is an essential part of its implementation and for this reason a cost-benefit analysis of its methodology has to be properly considered. To a large extent we are not running against time but against scarce resources which defines what is done and that which must be done. Many countries operate indirectly or directly on beggar-my-neighbour policy; they bemoan lack of resources whilst huge funds are cast into the drain by negotiating dangerous and fruitless shortcuts. To reiterate; information, education and communication are essential parts of social change. In other words, it is the social economics around which we must balance people's needs and that of our environment and human development. A lack of information leaves people groping in darkness; similarly 'people perish for lack of knowledge' and in a society where communication is scarce or non-existent progress is stifled.

The discourses in this section, though practical, are grounded in empirical understanding. This marriage between empiricism and practice makes the whole idea of IE&C a valuable tool for social change. Not all projects or programmes start on that note but it is important that lessons are learnt in order to rectify any mistakes before retributions mars the programme at the end or in some cases make the programme unsustainable.

In this respect, chapter ten reminds us to "mind the cultural gaps" that might exist in any programme implementation including IE&C programmes.

Harmful practices such as female genital mutilation occupies a centre stage in chapter eleven. It expresses the need for urgent action, from government to local communities, to stamp out the practice. One way of doing this, it argues, is through IE&C.

Chapter twelve deals with what the author calls "action media". This is a methodology for the development of media products that integrates the interests of both the communicator and representatives of target audiences within a health promotion context.

Chapter thirteen demonstrates how different media and channels of communication are woven together in an interlocking spur to inform, educate and communicate health and environment issues within a particular social context.

Dina DuBois' paper in chapter fourteen explains how different organisations used a variety of strategies to educate women of reproductive age, adolescents, and sexually active men with the objective of increasing the use of modern contraceptives in their designated districts.

In Chapter fifteen Utpal Sharma breaks the *health reliance* mode of IE&C and takes up the issue of experimenting for sustainable Human Habitat and their policy responses. What makes its discourse special is not just the role of IE&C in the whole process but the idea of 'Planning and Design framework of a settlement looked upon as a 'model' of balanced settlement design in Indian context comprising mostly poor people and yet create a sense of identity and coherent image. The effect here is a pattern of framework for community formation and people's participation in housing design and construction processes to help create an informal character associated with a traditional settlement.

Finally, in chapter sixteen, John Durant's paper takes a retrospective view of programme evaluation and the lessons that can be learnt from them. The basis of his paper puts project evaluation at the heart of any successful and effective IE&C programme if the objective is not to simply promote change but maximise scare resources to its effective use; hence the question, Evaluation - the what, the wherefore and the how? The instructive and illustrative nature of this paper is beneficial for equipping reader's knowledge and understanding of a hitherto complex subject. In other words, it is a must for all to read.

In: Contemporary Discourses on IE & C Theory and Practice
Editor: Theophilus K. Gokah

ISBN: 978-1-60962-360-3
© 2009 Nova Science Publishers, Inc.

Chapter 10

MIND THE CROSS-CULTURAL GAP

Karamjit S. Gill

When we move beyond the linear gaze worldview, and explore our interactions within cross-cultural spaces, we encounter both the reality and actuality of interactions. In these inter-cultural encounters, it is not just how we see others but also how others see us. These encounters go beyond the functionality of the 'here and now' interaction to that of an encompassing interaction encapsulating the reality within the reality-actuality whole. When we envision these interactions as a developmental process, we begin to see development from an interdependent perspective, which goes beyond the "utility" aspects of interactions and includes multiplicity of social and cultural rules, norms and values underlying these encounters. These interactions also draw upon the vast pool of collective basic knowledge accumulated by societies and cultures in their long process of evolution.

The development process can be seen in terms of identifying knowledge and communication gaps that hinder development, and locating potential of interlocking interactions that facilitate it. To understand the dynamic nature of the development process, we need to understand the interactive relations between knowledge, culture and society, and explore cultural architectures, which facilitate them. Developing cross-cultural interfaces is then not just about coping with the interaction space of reality but also of the overarching spaces of reality and actuality, as well as, with the 'in-between' space of actuality-reality gaps. In this paper, we explore how the concept of the 'Holon' enables understanding of cultural architectures, and designing interfaces. It also explores how the concept of 'symbiosis' provides a tool for interdependence and mutuality of relationships of reality and actuality, and thus the core concept of interfacing and collaboration, how the concept of the 'culture of the artificial' enables the sharing and pooling of experiences, how the concept of 'valorisation' enables to find a coherence (commonality) between diverse interactions, and how the concept of 'cultural Holon' can be used to conceptualise the network architecture for cross-cultural interactions. The discussion briefly reviews the limitations of the linear gaze view of development, provides glimpses of inter-cultural encounters, and explores knowledge networking as a tool for mediating an interconnected vision of development.

Keywords: Linear economic gaze; development; knowledge networking; cross-cultural innovation; inter-cultural encounters; cultural architecture; actuality and reality; symbiosis; Holon; culture of the artificial, valorization

BEYOND THE LINEAR GAZE

How do we move beyond seeing development from a linear economic gaze and towards a Holonic vision? This vision is at the heart of the exploration of some of the key issues of cross cultural interaction and collaboration, which lifts the idea of 'development', from the level of a purely functional reality to that of an interdependence of the reality and actuality within the 'Holonic' whole. Linear gaze here refers to a reductionist view of development, a view of utilitarian economy. The term 'reality' refers to the 'here and now' state of the world (the observed present), and the term 'actuality' refers to the interconnected state of the world (being experienced in unity drawing on the past, present, and future expectations). 'Holon' represents the interconnectedness of relationships between and among human systems, between the unit and whole – an interdependent model of the uni-verse, where whole is not sum of parts but inter-connectedness of parts. It is this Holonic perspective, which drives the inclusive vision of development, transcending the linear utilitarian view. Some of the key concepts, which guide this vision, are the Symbiosis, Kyosei, Ying and Yang, Swikriti, and Valorisation:

Symbiosis

The concept of symbiosis in the European human-centred tradition refers to a dialectical relationship between the objective and the tacit, exemplified by the idea of human-machine symbiosis, meaning making the best of the combined potential of human capability and machine capacity (Cooley 1991, Gill 1996). Symbiosis in this paper refers to seeking unity and coherence between diversities, and interdependence and mutuality of relationships of reality and actuality.

Kyosei

Kyosei in Japanese conception of the notion of symbiosis signifies the mode of living together with the sense of equality and mutuality, transforming one another mutually while acknowledging one another's difference, opposition and diversity. It has come to obtain a new positive significance in the field of thought and social sciences in Japan. It was originally conceived as an ecological concept that pointed to the cohabitation of different living creatures in the ecological context of physiological and life-maintaining activities (Satofuka 2007).

Yin and Yang

The concept of yin and yang (or earth and heaven) describes two opposing and, at the same time, complementary (completing) aspects of any one phenomenon (object or process) or comparison of any two phenomena. In this paper, Yin-Yang refers to a process of seeking balance between knowledge, technology, economy and society, and emphasises that it is this balance that transforms quantitative change to qualitative change in the development process (Zhouying 2002).

Swikriti

The idea of *Swikriti* in the sense of acceptance of the other invokes the principle of 'equity of toleration' and is seen to be rooted in the idea of plurality of existence. *Swikriti* is thus a momentous issue in its own right. But, separated from other objectives and priorities, it does little to guarantee – or advance – the cultural or social equality or distributive justice (Sen 2005: 35)

Valorisation

Valorisation is a French word which means 'to make useful, to use, to exploit'. In this paper the concept of valorisation is used to mean making the most of cultural diversities while seeking coherence of cultural differences. In this paper, the concept of valorisation provides a conceptual tool for inter-connected development, creating cross-cultural collaboration, understanding the dynamics intercultural interaction, and building connections of diversities and harnessing differences as a resource for development (Gill 2007).

These concepts facilitate our understanding of the pluralistic and overlapping nature and scope of inter-cultural interactions. The discussion on knowledge networking as a developmental process, accepts the significance of these concepts as rich tools for cultivating and enriching cross-cultural dialogues, discourses and collaborations.

Sen (2001) promotes the idea of inclusive development as freedom, which goes beyond the linear gaze of economic progress and emphasises inter-connections between different kinds of freedoms, social, cultural, political. He emphasises that an inclusive development approach "allows us to acknowledge the role of social values and prevailing mores, which can influence the freedoms that people enjoy and reason to treasure..... The exercise of freedom is mediated by values, but the values in turn are influenced by public discussions and social interactions, which are themselves influenced by participatory freedoms. Each of these connections deserves careful scrutiny" (ibid: 9). He further notes that "the gap between the two perspectives (that is, between an exclusive concentration on economic wealth and a broader focus on the lives we can lead) is a major issue in conceptualizing development. An adequate conception of development must go much beyond the accumulation of wealth and the growth of gross national product and other income related variables. Without ignoring the importance of economic growth, we must look well beyond it" (ibid: 14).

Hofstede and Hofstede (2005) provide an insight into the permeation of the notion of economic wealth, as a driving force and market as tool for the pursuit of development. They point out that the root of this philosophy lies in the choice between individualism and collectivism at the level of society, and this has considerable implications for economic theories. Based on this individualistic idea, the discipline of Economics has remained an individualistic science, promoted and consolidated by contributors form strongly individualistic nations such as Britain and the United States. However, because of indivualistic assumptions on which they are based, economic theories developed in the West are unlikely to apply in societies in which group interests prevail. For Hofstede and Hofstede, this has profound consequences on development assistance to poor countries and for economic globalisations (ibid: 107). Following their argument, it is suggested that there is an urgent need for an alternative vision of development, which builds upon the inter-dependence between the individualistic and collective perspectives, and is additionally situated in cross-cultural settings, taking into account the cultural diffrences.

Looking beyond the economic gaze is to understand the current driving forces of development. Influenced by dynamics of technology, world economy is developing rapidly towards the direction of globalization and knowledge-based. This is rapidly changing the nature of development from the traditional capital and technology transfer models to knowledge transfer models. The impacts of technology dynamics are so influential that knowledge and technology are seen interchanging factors of development. While technology acts as a dominant factor in international economic competitions, it has also brought about many social, environmental and ecological problems. To understand the changing nature of development we need to understand deeply the interactive relations between knowledge, technology and society, and explore cultural architecture structures, which facilitate them.

Jin Zhouying (2002) provides a way forward to shape cross-cultural collaboration, by creating the Yin-Yang (symbiotic) relationship between the diversity and aspiration of common cultural space. She sees Yin-Yang process in terms of the balance between knowledge, technology, economy and society, and argues that it is this balance that transforms quantitative change to qualitative change. While technology is the medium for knowledge transfer, it is the cultural diversity that facilitates its further transfer into a qualitative resource for creative and innovative applications. It may be that this role of cultural diversity is not visible to the deterministic mind, but it exists in the living form of the tacit knowledge. Rather than being seen as a constraint, it can be shaped as a driving force for sustainability by constraining the move towards technology-centred development. Zhouying emphasises that the errors and defects arising form the technological solutions of complex social and economic problems cannot be solved through technology itself. The purposeful solutions lie in the balances and coordination of the various factors of the human dimension. These can be achieved by creating a 'yin-yang' environment, which seeks a balance between hard technology (machine-centred) and soft technology (human-centred).

It is important to emphasise that communication and media infrastructures (hard technology) cannot in themselves be either determinants or mediators of cross-cultural collaboration; they are just one of many social and technological determinants which vary from society to society and culture to culture. The technological infrastructure may be global but its applications and impacts can only be determined by the local human condition. It is this perspective of the local-global nexus, which provides a stimulant to seeing development in terms of multiplicity roles of communication, interaction and collaboration in local, community, regional and local-global contexts.

The Road to the Linear Gaze

It is perhaps worth reflecting on what led to the dominance of the linear economic gaze as the guiding hand of development. Max-Neef in his incisive article on "The Forgotten Map" (2008) gives an insight into the historical roots of this gaze. The roots of the current permeation of a feeling of uneasiness and anxieties in our lives in the world today are seen to lie in the 'Machiavellian path of competition and fear', which had shaped the construction of social, political and economic conceptions in Europe. Following this path, Descartes' conception of absolute truth and certainty witnessed the triumph of mechanism and reductionism. This mechanistic path, bypassing the 'Franciscan way of compassion and love' and 'Pico della Mirandola's way of multiple truths and reconciliation', followed to the age of reason. Galileo and Newton gave us mathematics as the language of nature and science as the supreme manifestation of reason, and reason as the supreme attribute of the human being. Max-Neef says that we are still under the spell of Galileo and Newton, and we have chosen not to navigate the route of Goethean science which seeks harmony between the spiritual and the physical worlds. Feeling, intuition, consciousness and spirituality are still banished from the realm of science. This reductionist view of science is well illustrated by the linear gaze view of economics, which in its "value free" conception has become an instrument of measurement and control, thereby becoming "totally divorced from reality". Our attention is further drawn to the historical evolution of the reductionist conception of knowledge, technology and economics. In our pursuit of the path of reason, the mechanistic conception of knowledge has become increasingly detached from the actuality of the world we live in. He notes that this historical evolution is also shaped by the language of that period. For example, the dominance of the teleological language during the first three centuries of the second millennium of Western civilisation made possible the construction of the great cathedrals and monasteries. The language dominating the 19th century was basically that of the consolidation of the nation-state. The language dominating the 20th century was that of economics, especially the emergence of Keynesian economics, which reflected and interpreted the crisis of the late twenties and early thirties, the time of the so-called Great Depression. This was followed by the emergence of optimistic language of development, reflecting and interpreting the desire to promote true development and overcome world poverty in the fifties and sixties. Max-Neef describes the emergence and domination of the neo-liberal discourse over the last three decades of the 20th century. He notes the devastating consequences of this language on the developing countries: the dramatic increase in global poverty; crippling of national economies of many poor countries arising from the debt burden; over-exploitation of both people and natural resources; the destruction of ecosystems and bio-diversity; and the "obscene" accumulation of financial wealth in ever fewer hands. He says that "The disastrous effects of this language, absolutely incoherent with its historical challenges, can be clearly seen by anyone, although decision makers and holders of power prefer to look in the opposite direction."

Max-Neef sends a timely message when he says "We are perhaps beginning to realise that knowledge without understanding is hollow, and that understanding without knowledge is incomplete. We therefore need to undertake, at last, the navigation we have so far postponed. But in order to do so we must face the great challenge of a language shift."

This challenge of language shift requires deep understanding of the changing nature of cross-cultural communication and inter-cultural discourse, reflecting and interpreting the globalisation process of development. Revisiting Sen's conception of development, we can envision development as interconnected relationships between knowledge, society and economy, where interconnections between knowledge, culture and communication are becoming the main driving force of development. Knowledge networking in this context can be seen as the facilitating tool for understanding the engagement of these interconnections.

GLIMPSES OF INTER-CULTURAL ENCOUNTERS

Although knowledge as power still remains a powerful tool for competitive development, dynamics of knowledge networking have already been shifting to inter-disciplinary and cross-cultural perspectives. This shift raises the issue of not only of sustainability of inter-relationships of knowledge, culture and communication, but also the dynamics of these relationships. While new media and Internet technologies facilitate globalisation of language and culture, the challenge is how to sustain the dynamics of relationships of local and global cultures. While the globalising world may transcend the traditional linear and homogenising view of discourse, in actuality the local cultural identities strongly influence our patterns of conversational behaviours and our interpretation of such behaviours of others by establishing norms and values. The challenge is how we can find commonality and coherence in our cross-cultural encounters while recognising our cultural identities. We need to find a way of using inter-cultural encounters as a resource for bridging the cross-cultural interaction and local-global knowledge gaps. Here we present a glimpse of inter-cultural encounters to illustrate how they shape our worldview, as how we see others and as how others see us.

Borderline culture and 'in-between'

Bhabha (1994) gives an insight into cross-cultural encounters and cross-cross-cultural communication. He argues that the borderline work of culture demands an encounter with 'newness' that is not part of the continuum of past and present. It creates a sense of newness as an insurgent act of cultural translation. Such act does not merely recall the past as social cause or aesthetic precedent; it renews the past, configuring it as a contingent 'in-between' space, that innovates and interrupts the performance of the present. The 'past-present' becomes part of necessity, not the nostalgia, of living (ibid: 7).

Commenting on cross-cultural discourse, he suggests that this discourse takes place at the crossroads of what is known and what is permissible and that, which through known must be concealed; a discourse uttered between the lines and as both against the rules and within them. On the 'doubleness' (being both the insider and outsider) of such a discourse, we can be tempted to note that cross-cultural encounters "disperse the homogeneous" view of 'horizontal' society, and thereby question the homogeneous and horizontal view associated with the contemporary cross-cultural communities.

On cross-cultural interaction, Bhabha gives us a further insight into the inter-disciplinary nature of emerging cultural forms and the need for overcoming the limitations of the cross-cultural experiences. He notes that, "To enter into interdisciplinarity of cultural texts means that we cannot contextualise the emergent cultural form by locating it in terms of some pre-given discursive causality or origin. We must always keep open a supplementary space for the articulation of cultural knowledges that are adjacent and adjunct but not necessarily accumulative, teleological or dialectical. The 'difference' of cultural knowledge that 'adds to' but does not 'add up' is the enemy of the implicit generalisation of knowledge or the implicit homogenization of experience" (ibid: 163). Bhabha warns us of the tendency of locating cultures in 'universal' terms in this cross-cultural era of globalisation, when he quotes (Said, 1978, p.273) on Enlightenment: 'For Enlightenment itself, to assert its sovereignty as the universal ideal, needs its Other; if it could ever actualise itself in the real world as truly universal, it would in fact destroy itself'

Cultural differences

Trompenaars in his book, *Riding the Waves of Culture* (1993), provides an insightful overview of inter-cultural interactions impacted by cultural perceptions and cultural differences. He identifies cultural differences arising from how human beings deal with each other, our attitude to time, and how we relate to the environment. Trompenaars relates the Walkman story of Mr. Morita, Chairman of Sony. To Morita, Walkman was a way of listening to classical music on his way to work without disturbing fellow commuters. The Walkman was a way of not imposing on the outside world; but a way of being in harmony with it. Contrast this view with most Walkman users in other cultures; say in the West, who would like to listen to the music without being disturbed by other commuters (ibid: 10-11). Here we interpret Morita seeing the world around him in terms of the interdependence of 'actuality' (past experiences, present situation and future directions) and reality, while the 'other' user seeing the world in terms of the 'here and now' reality in narrow individualistic terms.

His discussion on Universalist versus particularist cultures and on groups versus individualism sheds further light on the notions of particularism and individualism. Trompenaars notes the dominance of Universalist focus of American research into culture (organisational, business) leading to the view that "universalism is a feature of modernisation per se. of more complex and developed societies". In this view, Particularism is seen as a "feature of smaller, largely rural communities in which everyone knows everyone personally. The implication is that universalism and sophisticated business practice go together and all nations might be better off for more nearly resembling America" (ibid: 33).

Commenting on Groups vs. Individualism, Trompenaars notes that, "The individual society, with its respect for individual opinions, will frequently ask for a vote to get all noses pointing in the same direction. The drawback to this is that within a short time they are likely to have reverted to their original orientation. The collectivist society will intuitively refrain from voting because this will not show respect to the individuals who are against the majority decision. It prefers to deliberate until consensus is reached. The final result takes longer to achieve; but will be much more stable." (Ibid: 58).

However, it is also the case that in almost all cultures, many individuals with their personal motivations and commitments stimulate and lead innovative developments, while contributing to the cultivation of a culture of collaboration and collective innovation at the societal level. Whilst contrast between individualistic and collective opinions is essential to our understanding of the cultural differences, we need also to study the underlying social and cultural dynamics of the individual and group interactions to understand cross-cultural interactions and collaborations.

Intercultural communication

Trompenaars discusses the difficulties of cross-cultural communication arising from the differences between affective and neutral cultures. He notes that, "overly neutral or affective (expressive) cultures have problems in doing business with each other. The neutral person is easily accused of being ice-cold with no heart; the affective person is seen out of control and inconsistence. When such cultures meet the first essential is to recognise the differences, and refrain from making any judgements, based on emotions or lack of them" (ibid: 70).

He notes subtle cultural differences during verbal and non-verbal communication. For example speakers from Anglo-Saxon culture would consider it impolite to interrupt a speaker during the discussion; while more verbal Latins may frequently interrupt each other to show how interested they are in what the other is saying. However, the silence in oriental communication would generally disturb the Western participants in the discussion. Commenting on the tone of voice, he notes that "in most Latin societies, an 'exaggerated' way of communicating shows that you have your heart in the matter. Oriental societies tend to have a much more monotonous style; self-controlled, it shows respect. Frequently the higher the position of a person hold, the lower and the flatter their voice" (ibid: 68). Trompenaars notes that 75% of all communication is non-verbal. Through a tale of his colleague, Leonard Brug, he illustrates how 'eye contact' signifies cultural differences. Brug was "brought up in both Curacao and Surinam. As a boy he would try to avoid eye contact, where upon his Curacao grandmother would slap him in the face (in some cultures body talk is very effective) and say "Look me in the face". Respecting an elder involves eye contact. Leonard learned fast, and when in Surinam looked his other grandmother straight in the face to show respect. She slapped him too; respectful kids in Surinam do not make eye-contact" (ibid: 70).

This example illustrates how the same reality (eye contact) can be seen by different people from different perspectives in different cultures (i.e. grand mothers). It also gives a hint for the cultivation of a cross-cultural dialogue (between the grand mothers) that bridges the intercultural gaps, bringing into play the past experiences, present happenings and future expectations of cultural encounters.

Inter-cultural Encounters

Hofstede and Hofstede (opcit: 365) note that successful intercultural encounters presuppose that the partners believe in their own values. If not, they have become alienated persons, lacking a sense of identity. A sense of identity provides the feeling of security from which one can encounter other cultures with an open mind (ibid: 365). Intercultural encounters raise the question: if we think, feel, and act differently, how can we manage one world together? An increased consciousness of the constraints of our mental programs versus those of others is essential for our common survival. A consciousness can be developed and that while we should not expect to become all alike, we can at least aspire to become more cosmopolitan in our thinking (ibid: 264).

They provide a deep insight into intercultural differences, and how these differences affect our lives as individuals, members of our communities, citizens, and members of organizations and institutions. They argue that main cultural differences between nations lie in values, about power and inequality, with regard to the relationship between the individual and the group, with regard to the emotional and social roles expected from men and women, with respect to ways of dealing with the uncertainties in life, and with respect to whether one is mainly preoccupied with the future or with the past and present. Our view of the self, values and motivation, are rooted and shaped by different social and cultural traditions (ibid: 364). Drawing our attention to identity and values, they argue that contrary to identity differences, value differences do form the core of cultures. Identities are visible, values are invisible. Cultural values affect the consequences of identity differences (ibid: 322). Culture as collective programming influences our motivation, our behaviours and our explanations we give for our behaviours. For example, an American expert may take an individualistic stance and argue for market forces as driving force of development, an Indian may take a socially oriented stance, a French may take a stance relating to national honour, a Chinese may emphasise mutual obligation, and a Dane may focus on collegiality. In other words an understanding of our behaviour in the globalising world should be validated by taking into account the cultural environments which constrain it.

Following their argument on cultural impact on organizations, it is noted that not only management and organisation are value laden, but theories, models and practices are also culturally specific. Thus, their transfer across cultures is problematic without regard for the values context in which they were developed and values context in which they are received. Unfortunately the silent assumption of universal validity of culturally restricted organizational models is quite common. The basic skill of surviving in a multicultural world, Hofstede and Hofstede emphasise, is understanding first one's own cultural values (and that is why one needs a cultural identity of one's own) and next the understanding of cultural values of the others with whom one has to cooperate (ibid: 367).

The Organizational Culture

We get a glimpse of the perpetuation of the value laden organizational cultures and business models in a lunch interview of Theodore Zeldin by John Thornhill (Financial Times, 9 February 2008), in which Zeldin dismisses much of what is taught at business schools by lecturers who have a vested interest in perpetuating their traditional specialisms. He suggests that the hierarchical century-old US-style Corporation has outlived its time. Many professions – medical, legal, architectural – are in crisis. The world of work must be revolutionised to put people – rather than things – at the centre of all endeavours. Zeldin recalls, "I remember talking to some CEOs in London. One of them said: 'We can no longer select people, they select us.' If we want the best people and we want to attract them, we have to say: 'What do you want in your job?'" Zeldin further recalls a visit to an Indian factory making electrical equipment, where he saw "rows and rows of Indian women fiddling around with bits and pieces". The manager said he wanted to turn these employees into entrepreneurs. After talking to the women, Zeldin suggested that it would be impossible if they spent eight hours a day performing boring tasks. The manager accepted this observation and saw the need to mechanise some of the routine functions of the factory and devote two hours a day to educating his workers. "That's the kind of revolution that interests me," Zeldin remarks. "You need to make a profit to survive. But business today has to be a cultural and educational institution." This example gives a glimpse of the changing nature of business as a cultural and learning enterprise in the globalising world.

These brief glimpses of inter-cultural encounters gives an insight into how we see reality (as we observe it) through our cultural prisms and how our understanding of cultural differences and values help us to see actuality as it appears from the perspective of others in diverse contexts. Cultural differences permeate between and among individualistic and pluralistic cultures, between disciplines, professions and organisations, and these differences play their part in defining our cultural identities and values. How do we then valorise these differences and envision development in terms of inter-cultural dialogue and knowledge networking process?

ENVISIONING THE CULTURAL ARCHITECTURE

When we interact with others within our own cultural space, our interactions are bounded by the social and cultural architectures, in which we live and act. However, when we interact with others from other cultures, our interactions are not just bounded by architectures of both cultures but also by the gaps of these cultural architectures (e.g. Irish and Japanese cultures). But where these cultural architectures are seen to overlap (e.g. British and Irish cultures), our interactions may also overlap, sharing many common experiences and learning from differences. If we extend this cross-cultural interaction to more than two cultures, we begin to visualise interactions taking place at various levels, at times overlapping and intersecting. We call this overlapping and intersecting architecture, a Holonic cultural architecture. Here the term 'architecture' is used to represent the structure (e.g. individualistic, collective) and the term 'Holonic' is used to reflect the connectedness of the architecture. Depending upon the complexity of a culture, a cultural node may itself represent a subculture within the cultural network architecture. Thus the complexity of inter-cultural or cross-cultural interactions depends upon the levels of hierarchy of the cultural architecture, and the complexity of interactions within a culture depends upon the levels of hierarchy of the architecture of its culture.

The idea of the Holon (Koestler, 1989), combining the Greek word *holos* (whole), and the word *on* as in prot*on* or neutr*on*, gives us a holistic concept - connectedness of parts and wholes, where the whole is not sum of parts but is an inter-connectedness of parts. In the Holonic architecture, hierarchies or wholes exist only in relations to sub-hierarchies or sub-wholes - they are inter-connected. The members of the hierarchy, like the Roman God Janus, all have two faces looking in opposite directions: the face turned towards the subordinate levels is that of a self-contained whole; the face turned towards the apex, is that of a dependent part. One is the face of the master, the other the face of the servant. This Janus effect is a fundamental characteristic of sub-whole in all types of hierarchies. The notion of Holon of interest in this paper is the interconnectedness of relationships between and among human systems, between the unit and whole – an interdependent model of the uni-verse, where whole is not sum of parts but inter-connectedness of parts. We can view this concept in terms of interconnectedness of commonalities and of differences, a world in which diversities are valorised.

To illustrate the nature and complexity of the cross-cultural interaction, we consider an exemplar model of cultural Holons (Fig.1), ranging from the one-one interaction in a Linear Holon; dialogical interaction in the 'Trinity' Holon, and to interlocution in the 'Dragon' Holon. In this architecture, each node represents a 'cultural space' and the link between two nodes represents interaction space. Borrowing from the notion of 'Holon', we introduce here the concept of 'cultural Holon', representing a cultural architecture and the concept of 'Holonic node', representing a cultural space. The idea of the 'cultural Holon' is that it represents the dynamic nature of culture as it is observed from within and from outside. Similarly, Holonic node represents the dynamic nature of a cultural space (or cultural identity). We use the term 'cultural space' rather than the static term 'node' to emphasise the dynamic nature of culture in interaction. In our case, we can say that the cross-cultural network architecture is a Holonic cultural architecture, in which cross-cultural interaction takes place between different cultural Holons. Here cultural Holon is seen as one of the many possible ways of modelling and representing cultural architectures. For example, the 'linear' Holon represents the linear architecture, which can be said to exist in highly, individualised cultural architectures; but of course linear architectures can be found to exist or created in almost all cultures. The 'trinity' Holon representing interaction between three nodes allows for mediation by the third node in case of disagreement or conflict between any two nodes within the cultural Holon. It can be regarded as the minimal interaction model of a democratic dialogue in a collective culture. For example, to reach a democratic agreement or consensus within the Trinity Holon, an agreement or a consensus must be reached at each level of interaction, both at the hierarchical and horizontal levels of interaction between the nodes of the Holon. The 'panchtantra' Holon representing interaction between five nodes represents the next level of complexity of interaction. This Holon can be seen to consist of two interconnected Trinity Holons. In this case, we begin to see interaction between nodes at both the vertical and horizontal levels, thereby representing a much more robust model of democratic dialogue. For example to reach a democratic agreement in this cultural Holon, the process takes place at two levels. At the first level, agreement takes place within each of the two interconnected trinity Holons, and at the second level, the agreement takes place between the representatives of these Trinity Holons. The next two cultural Holons, the 'samurai' and the 'dragon' represent further levels complexity of cultural architectures. We see that as the complexity of cultural architecture increases, we need to build more and more complex interaction architectures in order to deal with the diversity of interaction.

To illustrate the problematics of interaction between diverse cultural Holons, let us consider interaction between the Linear Holon (individualistic) and the Trinity Holon (Collegial). Let us say that the linear Holon represents a dominant architecture, steeped in the culture of individualistic and direct interaction, whilst the Trinity Holon represents an organisation which inhabits a collective and consensus culture. It is also assumed that the dominant organisation dictates its individualistic nature of interaction. One possible way for the dominant culture to have its way is for the Trinity (collegial) Holon to transform itself into the culture of the Linear Holon. This may imply deconstructing the Trinity Holon into three linear components, each linear component acting as it were a Linear Holon, thus creating three levels of interaction between the Linear Holon and three linear components of the

Trinity Holon. This implies that interaction between the nodes of each linear component is independent of the structural links and contextual relationships with other nodes and other components of the Trinity Holon. This is to say that the only way to construct interaction between the Linear Holon and the Trinity Holon (and for that matter with other more complex Holon) is to reduce the complex structure of the Trinity Holon to the level of the Linear Holon. If we follow this reductionist logic to its own logical conclusion, then what we are implying is that interaction between different cultures can take place only if we either reduce the more complex cultural architectures to map onto the more linear architectures, or we reduce both the cultural architectures to a common denominator, amenable to dominant architecture. This reductionist logic so inherent in the mechanistic paradigm reduces cultural architecture to a technical construct, thereby reducing cross-cultural interaction to a technical interface. It is therefore hardly surprising that the dominant presence of the techno-centric model of interaction rooted in the rationality of the 'one best way', leads to a belief in technological solutions of complex societal problems. If we continue to pursue this techno-centric path, the whole socio-economic and cultural development may not be an exception to this technological logic.

Consider the implication of reducing complex interaction architectures (e.g. panchtantra, samurai and dragon) to a linear Holonic architecture. If this model of interaction, promoting direct interaction at the individual levels (e.g. internet, virtual reality), becomes a dominant interface, then the issue is how sustainable this interaction architecture is? We note that the interaction in the linear Holon can only be sustained if both the nodes are always actively engaged in interaction and there is no breakdown in communication between the nodes. Although the linear architecture may be regarded as the most cost effective architecture at a direct interactional level and most explicit form of individual interaction, it remains in danger of instability and breakdown without being continuously serviced at all costs. Since this architecture has no structural mechanism for third party mediation or intervention in case of uncertainty or conflict, it therefore lacks any room for coherence necessary for even functional interaction, let alone complex forms of social, cultural or cross-cultural interactions. We already are beginning to witness the social and cultural vulnerability inherent in the linear interactive network communication structures (e.g. internet) promoting direct communication between individuals without social filtering or cultural mediating structures. For example in the UK, the dominating mantra of electronic democracy is propagating the individual interaction with various facets of governance, under the guise of equal opportunity and individual responsibility. This linear model of governance is already beginning to impoverish and ultimately dismantle the very traditional social (e.g. family, voluntary and community groups) filters, which in the past facilitated social cohesion in the form of social mediation, pastoral care, social mentoring. The consequence is that already disadvantaged groups in society are being directed to interact with governance structures using internet, excluding and alienating further those who are already being excluded from the mainstream society without the support of social filtering. There thus lies an ethical dilemma of 'governance' of using technological architectures as they impact societies and cultures.

REALITY AND ACTUALITY OF INTERACTION

How do we conceptualise a cross-cultural interface to facilitate interaction between different cultures, or between cultural Holons in our case (Fig. 1)? When we consider interaction between different cultures, we mean here interaction between different cultural Holons. Within the same cultural Holon, interaction takes place between 'Holonic nodes' (cultural spaces). The notion of cultural space here reflects the dynamic nature of culture, in the sense that just as space can be created, shaped and recreated, cultural identity dynamically evolves to reflect the changing nature of social and cultural contexts. Just as the observations of one reality may vary depending upon the observer and the observer context, so the observed reality of a culture may vary as the observer moves from one context (or culture) to another context (or culture). It is also the case that two observers from the same culture may observe the same culture differently in different contexts or two observers from different cultures may observe the culture same way within the same context. Furthermore, in a cross-cultural context, a participant may observe the culture as it is experienced (reality); but the culture itself evolves out of long historical events and shaped by interconnected experiences the past, present and future predictions (actuality). In our case, we say that reality refers to culture as objectively experienced by the observer, and actuality refers to culture as being experienced as a whole. In summary the concepts of reality and actuality enable us to conceptualise cultural identity as a dynamic process in an interconnected cultural architecture.

The notion of actuality draws upon Uchiyama's work on "The Theory and Practice of Actuality" (Uchiyama 2003). In understanding the concept of actuality, Uchiyama notes that when we play and hear music being played, we not only hear what is being played but also use our past experiences of music and sounds as well as sounds we expect to create in future to hear the music as a 'whole'. In other words we hear music as a whole, in a sort of 'time, in which the 'past' and the future are always present (and absent) in the very "now" of notes which are being played. It is this notion of the music as 'whole', which according to Uchiyama, resides 'between' real notes and us, in *actuality*. In clarifying the distinction between reality and actuality, Uchiyama draws upon the work of the eminent Japanese psychiatrist, Bin Kimura. Uchiyama notes that Kimura claimed that self exists in a duality of the real self and of the actual self. The 'real self' is a *neomatic* or 'experienced self' and the 'actual self' is *neotic* 'experiencing self'. In a healthy person, the real and the actual self progress in an interdependent way, draw upon each other. It is this notion of the interdependence between the reality and the actuality, which is at the heart of the process of the cross-cultural interaction in this paper.

The discussion above suggests that any conceptualisation of the cross-cultural interaction and therefore conceptualisation of the interface should be shaped by both the realities and actualities of the interacting cultures. This conception encompasses the commonality of cultures (overlapping space of actuality and reality), as well as, the difference of cultures (between-ness space of actuality and reality). What interests us from a developmental perspective is how to build cross-cultural alliances for collaboration whilst seeking coherence between different realities and actualities. That is to say that in a development process, how we pool our shared cultural experiences (also share our pooled experiences) while valorising gaps in actuality and reality of collaborating cultures. The challenge of development then is also to valorise cultural differences and use them as catalysts and resources rather than treating them as noise and constraints of development.

Here we introduce the concept of the 'culture of the artificial' (Negrotti 1999) to seek coherence between diverse cultures. This concept enables individuals (or groups) from two different cultural spaces to create a third artificial cultural space (culture of the artificial) in which to meet and share and pool their common cultural experiences for a common purpose, while accepting their cultural differences as a further resource for cross-cultural learning. We call this process, 'valorising' of cultures, which says that we make best use of our common cultural experiences while seeking coherence in cultural differences for cross-cultural collaboration. In other words, the concept of valorisation' enables us to find coherence between cultural diversities, thereby facilitating cross-cultural interaction. For example, in the culture of the artificial architecture (Fig.2), we envision a scenario in which users from two different interaction spaces (Reality A and Reality B) come together by creating a new 'third' reality C, the space of the artificial, or culture of the artificial'. This can be seen as finding a symbiosis of two realities (cultures), providing a common communication space for common purpose and mutual understanding. This 'third' culture, an artificially created cultural space, initially created for bringing two cultures together in a harmonious relationship, slowly takes the shape of a new 'third' cultural space, where conflicts can be shared and resolved, while respecting the diverse identities and divergences of two cultures, thereby enriching both the artificial (may also be called 'virtual') cultural space and the cultural spaces (realities) of the users. In this scenario, cultural realities can be seen to be valorised through shared interaction and collaboration. The 'third' reality (space of the artificial) may also be called as the 'valorised reality'. The notion of valorisation emphasises making 'the best' of the differences during the process of reaching an agreement, a common purpose, or finding a common ground. Valorisation thus enables the processes of seeking cohesion of diversities (e.g. social, economic, and cultural) while recognising and respecting differences. For example, in collaborating situations, participants from diverse cultures may create a new different cultural space (cultural of the artificial space) in which they engage in dialogue and interlocution in finding a common ground of their differences, while at the same time retaining their unresolved difference (identities) to themselves (i.e. located in their own cultural spaces). This process of 'valorisation' allows for continuous enhancing of cross-cultural collaborating (or engagement) spaces while at the same enriching their own cultural horizons of participants. It is suggested that the valorisation process can also be used as a tool for conflict resolution in complex societal situations.

It is worth noting that in seeking coherence between diversities, valorisation also enables learning from actuality-reality gaps (e.g. cultural differences). In this sense diversity becomes a tool for cross-cultural understanding and learning. The implication of this articulation of learning is that any interfacing design process dealing with actuality-reality gaps (e.g. cross-cultural) should be seen as a learning process, involving both the users and designers in the process of design.

CONCEPTUALISING THE CULTURAL INTERFACE

Uchiyama sheds further light on notions of reality and actuality from a cultural perspective. He draws a distinction between the way Western and Japanese participants comprehend situations. While the Western participant 'sees' the situation and relates to it as an objective observer, the Japanese participant "hears" the situation, and relates to it by feeling to be "in the situation". In the first case, the interaction between the observer and the situation is through information, and in the second case the interaction is through language. In the human-centred tradition (Cooley, op.cit), we call the 'information'-oriented perspective of comprehension as the 'techno-centred' paradigm of interaction design and the 'language'-oriented perspective as the 'human-centred' paradigm of interaction design. In the techno-centric paradigm, the situation is modelled as an explicit representation of the observed reality, and this model of simulated reality is used to design interfacing technologies. This design implies that actuality of the situation becomes engulfed by the reality self, leading to the narrowness of the interface to cater for the interaction of the 'between-ness' spaces of reality-actuality (e.g. inter-cultural interaction), and ultimately leading to breakdown of the cross-cultural interaction. Also, the interface based only on the observed reality does not attend to the gaps between reality and actuality of the situation; hence there is not much scope of learning from difference, which is essential for any cross-cultural collaboration.

In articulating the case for interface design for cross-cultural interaction, we turn to the notion of symbiosis, which refers to a dialectical relationship between the objective and the tacit in the human-centred tradition. Drawing upon work on dialogical modelling and the definition of knowledge in terms of the objective, personal and experiential (Gill, 1995), the 'tacit' is seen here as the inter-relationship between the 'personal' (feeling/experiencing) and 'experiential' (collective experience/practice). The tacit provides a conceptual handle to articulate interdependent (symbiotic) relationships between the 'personal', the 'experiential' and the objective. It can be argued that part of the 'personal' knowledge can become part of the 'experiential' dimension over time during the process of participation in a group, and that part of the 'experiential' knowledge can become absorbed into the 'objective' dimension over time through the process of collaboration. Following the similar argument, it is proposed that part of the 'objective' knowledge can also be transferred to the 'experiential' domain, and part of the 'experiential' knowledge to the 'personal' domain. It is further proposed that this idea of transference between 'personal' 'experiential' and the 'objective' provides an insightful framework for designing interfacing architectures for 'in-between' interactions. It is this symbiotic notion of transference and 'between-ness', which provides for interdependent and mutuality of relationships of reality and actuality, and thus the core concept of interfacing and collaboration. In summary, the essence of the argument here is that in seeking interdependence between the reality and actuality, the 'symbiosis' provides a conceptual tool to find coherence between diversities, ambiguities and uncertainties of the cross-cultural situations.

THE LIMIT OF THE OBSERVED REALITY

What are the limits of observed reality in the conception of the cross-cultural interface? By focusing on observed reality, we limit our interaction to only one component of the observation space (reality), thereby excluding the interconnected component, residing in actuality. Moreover, the observation may be further limited by our own limits of reality as observers. This implies that our conceptualisation of the interaction space and therefore the conception of interface are bounded by the objectified reality. Here, we see this separation of reality and actuality as synonymous with the separation of the objective and the tacit dimensions of knowledge. Cooley in his book, Architect or Bee (1991), illustrates the conceptual distance between calculation and judgement, thus drawing our attention to gaps between data, information, knowledge, wisdom and action. If we conceptualise interaction tools based on data, they can only deal with first order interactions (based on observed data) and are too limited to deal with the second order interactions (information) arising from the impact of the first order interactions, and consequently with third order interactions (knowledge) arising from the cumulative impact of first and second order interactions, and in some cases with fourth order interactions (wisdom) arising from the cumulative impact of the preceding interactions, leading to fifth order interactions (action) arising from the cumulative impact of the preceding four interactions. We thus see the increasing impoverishment and brittleness of data and information based interfacing tool to deal with the complexity of interactions involving the knowledge, wisdom and action chain, the essential parameters of cross-cultural interaction.

To illustrate the complexity of interfacing from a complex socio-cultural setting, consider an example of the national health care system in the UK, where a patient interacts with the hospital consultant, with the family doctor, with the primary/public health care, voluntary/community health carers, and family and friends in different roles and in different contexts (Fig.3). In its simplest form of interaction, the consultant may see the patient with an propositional eye (e.g. patient data and diagnostic rules); the family doctor with both the objective eye (e.g. patient observations, medical records) and from a experiential perspective (e.g. personal observations); the primary/public health carers from functional (e.g. rules and regulations) and experiential (similar professional contacts) perspectives; voluntary/community cares from experiential and social perspectives; and family and friends from the personal, social, cultural perspectives. Considering culture in its broader scope (e.g. including institutional culture), we can term this interaction space between the patient and providers and facilitators of health care, as a form of 'cultural Holon'. We see that even in this simple interaction space, interaction takes place at different levels in diverse contexts. If the interface between the patient and others in this space is conceived only in terms of the objectified reality (e.g. patient records, diagnostic rules), then we exclude the personal, social, cultural knowledge and experiences of the interaction space. This perception of the interaction space thus leads to design of interfaces which can only cope with propositional knowledge, thereby leaving a accumulation of gaps between what the patient interaction needs are what the data handling requirements of the health care system are. This type of propositional (technical) interface leads gives rise to a first order gap of rationality (conceptual gap) between what is termed 'actuality' (the experiencing that draws on past, present, and expectations of future) and 'reality' (the observed present). The second order gap of rationality arises from the design competency - gap between the conception and design of the interface model. The third order gap of rationality of design is technical competency, the application gap. The cumulative affect of these interface gaps arising from the gaps between the propositional, objective, experiential and personal knowledges is that it can lead to the severe breakdown and disruptions of interaction.

The tragedy of this breakdown is that the designers of the technical interface may not even be aware of the existence of such interfacing gaps, and thereby fail to recognize the limitations of the propositional knowledge of the observed reality. The consequence of this conceptualisation is that it leads to designing systems and tools in the 'one best way' method, rooted in the scientific rationality of 'cause and effect'. We can say that this conception neither sees nor hears the actuality of interaction spaces of the users of health care services (e.g. the patient and those interacting with the patient). In other words by limiting the interface to observed reality, the designer fails to see the user from the holistic use context situated in the unity of reality and actuality.

To overcome the limitations of this 'one best way' model of the interface, there is a need to cultivate a cultural vision of the interface, which is rooted in the notion of interdependence and mutuality of reality and the actuality. A possible way forward towards the design of cross-cultural interfaces to deal with interaction in the evolving globalising world, is to examine their conceptualisation in various cultural visions, for example the European notion of the symbiosis, the Chinese notion of Ying and Yang, the Japanese notion of Kyosei, the Indian notion Swikriti. The notion of 'valorisation' could provide an overarching concept to seek coherence among the diversities of these cultural visions.

KNOWLEDGE NETWORKING- A TOOL FOR DEVELOPMENT

Knowledge networking in this vision is seen in terms of a tool for seeking possibilities and opportunities of development, finding what exists and what is possible. As a facilitator of development, it provides a tool for bridging knowledge gaps, not just how to but what can be done, recognising the reality and actuality of interaction gaps, and mediating an alternative vision of development. This vision emphasises the interconnection and networking of knowledge resources to bridge these gaps. This in turn requires the development of interaction tools to communicate, transfer, and exchange knowledge across social, cultural and national boundaries. To develop such tools we need to understand the potential of cultural differences and cross-cultural interactions. Knowledge networking as a resource for bridging cross-cultural gaps thus requires breaking the mould and finding an alternative paradigm of development.

KNOWLEDGE NETWORKING – DEVELOPMENT AS INNOVATION

We present here a EU-India cross-cultural innovation network (Gill 2003), as an exemplar of the dynamic interactions between the universities and entrepreneurs, and through them interactions with social actors, governing institutions and funding bodies. This network project was formed to explore how the overlaying interactions between the university, enterprise and institutional relations stimulate process of cross-cultural innovation. This unique collaboration (Brandt 2003, Smith and Kochhar 2003) nucleated an innovation network between European and Indian universities and research institutes, focusing on the value added applications of university research into the areas of social and economic change, regional models of innovation and entrepreneurship, and their transferability between regions and cultures. Cultural in this context emphasises the social, economic and communication environments in which technology is designed and applied to solve problems. The Cross-cultural dimension emphasises the diversity of entrepreneurial cultures both within India and the EU. Innovation refers to sustainable development of cultural, social and economic worlds. At the heart of this project is the creation of proactive and cross-disciplinary activities to facilitate the flow of innovative knowledge. It is based on the hypothesis that knowledge drives economic and entrepreneurial innovations, which in turn drive innovations in new forms of socio-economic and technological innovations.

The diversity and the complexity of the network is illustrated by its regional and institutional diversities both within India and the EU, as well as, across EU and India. The EU-India innovation network, consisting of 9 partners, 5 from the EU and 4 from India, is itself seen as innovation in creating a complex web of cross-cultural and cross-regional linkages. The EU partners represent five countries and diverse regions: Aachen (Germany); Lyngby (Denmark), Bologna (Italy), Brighton (UK) and UWCN (Wales). The Indian partners, PAU (Punjab), GLS (Gujarat), DU (Delhi) and NISTADS (Delhi), represent three diverse regions: Punjab, the home of 'Green Revolution', Gujarat, the 'entrepreneurial hub', and Delhi, the 'connecting hub' of India.

From its inception, the EU-India network focused on the development of an integrated framework for cross-cultural collaboration, pooling knowledge and expertise from both India and Europe, linking the network to regional knowledge centres, local and regional entrepreneurs, local communities and social actors. The collaboration among partners has involved interaction at the individual (researchers), group (e.g. research team), local community (e.g. village cooperative) organisational (university), regional (e.g. Bologna, Aachen, Punjab, Gujarat), national (e.g. Indian Ministry of Information Technology), and International (e.g. European Union) levels, both between and across European and Indian cultures, as well as, regional entrepreneurial cultures. Thus, at the functional level, the user (network partners) can be seen to play the roles of an individual researcher, an integral node of the institution, an actor and facilitator of the bilateral interactions with other institutions both within Europe and India, and facilitator and mediator for cross-cultural interaction between and across Europe and India. In addition to these functional interactions, the network was enriched by complementary interactions at social and cultural levels both within the network community as well as with the local and regional communities and entrepreneurs. For example at the institutional level the project partners have successfully created a network framework for research into the applications and impact of ICT and multimedia in socio-economic development (rural areas) and entrepreneurial (small and micro-enterprise, artisanal) sectors. At the bilateral institutional level, the partners have formed collaborations in the development of action research models in the dairy sector, and cluster models of innovation. In the field education, postgraduate courses in IT and ICT, multimedia tools for entrepreneurial training, and IT supported self-learning tools for collaborative learning have been implemented.

What this project has achieved is that at the institutional level the project partners have successfully created a network framework for research into the applications and impact of ICT and multimedia in socio-economic (rural development) and entrepreneurial (small and micro-enterprise, artisanal) sectors. At the bilateral institutional level, the partners have formed collaborations in action research models in the dairy sector, cluster models of innovation, postgraduate courses in IT and ICT, Multimedia tools for entrepreneurial training, and IT supported self-learning tools for collaborative learning. At the individual level, the project has opened up new opportunities for network researchers to work in cross-cultural and trans-disciplinary environments. At the EU-India cooperation level, the project has made a major contribution to the understanding of the richness of cultural traditions of research, entrepreneurship and innovation. This network framework has opened up new and sometimes unexpected possibilities of working across cultural and regional boundaries, breaking away from the traditional mono-cultural, mono-disciplinary and techno-centric model of research.

Our experiences of creating, evolving and sustaining this complex network, have given us valuable insights into the working and functioning of cross-cultural collaborative environments. Some of key lessons which could be beneficial for future collaborations in cross-cultural settings are: the need to build upon the knowledge, expertise and experiences of individual researchers/practitioners; to build experience of inter-institutional, inter-regional collaborations; to create spaces for articulating cross-cultural experiences in research writing; to emphasise the cross-cultural and trans-disciplinary nature of collaborations; and find a symbiotic relationship between the formal structures and the need for informal interactions. In summary the collaborative networks should be built on both the individual interests, group (community) purposes, and institutional contexts, cultivating both big and little pictures, but defining network activities in terms of achievable objectives; recognising the need to evolve mechanism for professional recognition, being aware of institutional value of effective publicity, and the need for the coordinator to act as catalyst for sustained innovation.

OUR APPROACH

Evolving an action-oriented participatory approach has been central to the success of our project. The key activities of the project, especially R&D, ICT innovations, postgraduate training, publicity and dissemination, and virtual knowledge networking, were seen as an interconnected set of common actions both on functional and time scales. Senior researchers through the mechanism of exchange visits established university links by means of seminars, lectures, student supervisions and joint publication activities. This led to the extension of partner collaboration in the development of IT and multimedia training tools for entrepreneurs and stakeholders in rural development. The network coordinator acted as an **animateur** *and catalyst for progression and sustained innovation. The future sustainability of the project has been assured by creating long-term networking links and bilateral collaboration between partner universities, networking of individual researchers, and extending these links to a wider community of researchers, entrepreneurs and stake holders through the 'Virtual Innovation Network.'*

This networking example provides an insight into an action-oriented policy and research into knowledge systems and human development, building on the vast reservoir of tacit dimension of knowledge and grass root innovation reflecting the cultural richness of experiential knowledge of people and societies. Knowledge networking in the cross-cultural context focuses on promoting a culture of shared communication, values and knowledge, seeking cooperation through valorisation of diversity. The process is seen here in terms of creating new alliances of creators, users, mediators and facilitators of knowledge.

At the global level, knowledge networking is seen as a symbiotic relationship between local and global knowledge resources. This focus is informed by the human centred vision of Information Society, which seeks a symbiotic relationship between knowledge, technology and society. It explores the nature of the knowledge in transition, raising issues of technology and knowledge transfer in the local-global context. The notions of human-machine symbiosis, and diversity and coherence provide a handle to explore the role of technology for sustainable development.

The notion of knowledge networking for sustainable development here refers to the interdependence between local and global socio-economic systems, and is informed by two human centred notions, subsidiarity and 'valorisation' of diversity The notion of subsidiarity refers to bringing science and scientific knowledge nearer to people with the hope of fostering inter-dependence between the local and the global. The notion of 'valorisation' here refers to common/global knowledge networks, which build upon the commonalties of local knowledge bases while sustaining local diversities.

These notions are rooted in the idea of the symbiosis between human and the machine; between technology and knowledge, and in this particular case a symbiosis between the 'objective' knowledge and the 'tacit' dimension of knowledge. This symbiosis recognises the essential contribution of the 'objective' knowledge as a global resource for knowledge transfer and development. However, it emphasises that sustainable development depends upon the local capacity for acquiring and interpreting new knowledge and then absorbing the transferred knowledge for practical use within new application contexts. This in turn depends on the level of interdependence between the local knowledge and global knowledge. The notion of the 'symbiosis' is intertwined with the dialectical notions of the 'cause and purpose' and that of the 'diversity and coherence'.

Knowledge networking here reflects a belief in the need for much wider diffusion of knowledge, expertise and experience in society. The discussion accepts the argument that whereas the notion of technology transfer has been central to the development of industrial society, knowledge transfer in the wider sense has become a cornerstone of innovation in the information society. Knowledge networking is thus not just about increasing the quantity of information, the speed of its transmission and 'user friendly' interaction, it is also rather about the quality, appropriateness and situatedness of information, and the processes of conversion of information into knowledge. Knowledge networking is seen as a way of life, sharing knowledge and cultures, building basic trust, democratisation of dialogue, as a process of action, development of coalitions. Networking as an activity is not just about knowledge transfer but also about knowledge gaining. While systems and models of innovation may be transferable, cultural models of innovation may not be transferable, for example, Gujarat model of innovation, rooted in its rich family, social and cultural networking traditions, may not be transferable outside Gujarat, where these traditions are either weak or marginal. To transfer a cultural model to a new context, it should either be included as integral part of the transferred culture or a similar cultural context may need to be generated for its effective transfer to the new place. New economic sectors are becoming tacit knowledge intensive rooted in the informal sector; however, old economic sectors have traditionally been objective knowledge intensive rooted in the formal sector. The challenge is how to synchronise the parallel knowledge networks representing the new and economic sectors?

KEY OUTCOMES OF THE PROJECT

The central focus of the networking project (Brandt, Gill, Smith & Kochhar, ibid.) has been the development of an integrated framework of cross-cultural collaboration and integrated models of research and postgraduate training. In developing these models, we have integrated research and training activities into the networking activities, particularly project workshops, exchange visits of senior researchers, visibility events of the project, and the coordination and monitoring activities.

This integrative approach is embedded in the articulation of the following project outcomes:

- A Cross-cultural Model of Collaborative Research and Entrepreneurial Innovation
- A Network Model of Action Research in the Cross-Cultural Setting
- A Network Model of Post Graduate Training
- A Framework for Interactions of Researchers
- A Framework for Multidisciplinary Research and Teaching

CHALLENGES OF CROSS-CULTURAL COLLABORATION

One of the key challenges of this cross-cultural collaboration was to develop future sustainability through the creation of long-term links between universities, entrepreneurs and the civic society. We propose a set of principles of sustainability for future cross-cultural collaborations: Network Approach for multiplier effect; Commitment to Human Centred Systems; Valorisation of diversity; Principle of movement - from looseness to connectedness; Principle of institutional change process; Capacity Building; Process of monitoring as catalyst for sustained innovation; Principle of equality and distributed involvement; Coordination as principle of distributed equality; Principle of visibility for wider participation.

Some of the specific aspects of European developments with significant implications on economic development excited Indian partners were:

- Combining artistic and cultural activities with Information and Communication Technology to create 'cultural industry' (Wales).
- Creating an enterprise network of distributed production systems by a systematic approach to participation of stakeholders and using the University system as an important change agent in this area (Denmark, Aachen and Italy).

- Extending Information and Communication Technology teaching and research in the Universities beyond the technical aspects of computer programming and technology to incorporate learning issues at the interface of human-machine interaction (Brighton & Aachen).
- In general, the term 'entrepreneur' commonly understood in India to mean a person engaged in organised business or industry is also applicable to artisans and small farmers.
-

Some of the specific aspects of Indian developments with significant implications on research development excited European partners were:

- Cooperative models of entrepreneurial innovation embedded in the Indian society especially the cooperative models of dairy enterprise in Punjab and Gujarat,
- 'Rich pool of tacit knowledge' inherent in the artisanal traditions and grassroots innovation movements of India, and which are not accessible in Europe.
- The diversity of models of entrepreneurship in Indian regions, for example the individualistic entrepreneurial model of Punjab region and the cooperative family model of entrepreneurship of the Gujarat region
- 'Kisan Mela' model of networking of Punjabi farmers and the Punjab Agricultural University (PAU), as a model of community based participation and the catalyst of 'Green Revolution' in India
- The unfamiliar juxtaposition of emphasis on individual achievement in the academic learning environment in India with a strong tradition of mutual cooperation and support.

These factors presented considerable challenges to develop collaborative research and teaching programmes.

LESSONS OF CROSS-CULTURAL COLLABORATION- A SYNTHESIS

Network partners have gone through a stimulating learning experience of new dimensions of collaboration in the complex cross-cultural environment of this project. Our experiences of creating, evolving and sustaining this complex network, have given us valuable insights into the working and functioning of cross-cultural collaborative environments. Some of key lessons which could be beneficial for future collaborations in cross-cultural settings are articulated here.

Need for partners to own the project at early stages of its implementation

The network should ensure that project partners start owning the project and its activities from the early stages of implementation. In this complex EU-India project of regional and cultural diversities, as well as, interdisciplinary diversity, it took almost a year for partners to realise the potential and possibilities of long term collaborations. However, once the project had created a mutual understanding of cross-cultural collaboration, Indian partners became enthusiastic about the process and outcomes and got actively engaged in the ownership, For example, Delhi University in the development of Master in ICT course: PAU in the design and implementation of Postgraduate in IT course, and in the IT applications for rural development; GLS in the establishment of an Entrepreneur Innovation Centre, and NISTADS in the application of multimedia tools for artisans training (Bankura project). In the case of EU partners, the focus mainly remained on individual ownership and general sensibility of cross-cultural collaboration within the established institutional research traditions. This enabled EU researchers to initiate new directions of research in their own institutions and to stimulate new collaborative research within Europe and also between India and Europe, Examples include collaboration between Brighton and PAU (IT training); between Lyngby and PAU (organic farming) and between UWCN (Wales) and NISTADS (Delhi) in multimedia and artisans. From our collaboration over the life of this project, it has become clear to us that the structure and organisational culture of Indian universities do not allow innovation at the individual levels and this inhibits their engagement in innovative activity. What is so impressive, however, is that a large minority of Indian researchers are still willing to initiate innovatory actions, despite being aware of the difficulties imposed by the Indian university structures. Our conclusion is that it is by networking of individual researchers we facilitate institutionalisation of innovation, and thereby the creation of environments for sustainable collaboration.

Need to build experience of inter-institutional, inter-regional collaboration among Indian universities

Our experience of collaboration is that although Indian partners were successful in creating new postgraduate courses and new directions of research within their own institutions, inter-institutional collaboration among Indian partners was very limited. On the other hand, collaboration between European partners took place both at individual and institutional levels, because of their experience of working together over an extended period, while Indian partner rarely worked together in the past and in fact did not know each other before joining this cross-cultural project. Our conclusion is that European collaboration has evolved over a span of 10 - 15 years of working together under the aegis of strategic collaborative programmes supported by the European Commission. Indian researchers and Indian institutions may have to go through a similar process of sponsored collaboration experience before it would be possible to sustain effective cross-cultural cooperation and Inter-institutional and inter-regional collaboration in India.

Need to create spaces for articulating cross-cultural experiences in research writing

At the individual level, the experience of participation has been very positive and has led to a valuable reflection. It is important to define project objectives in such a way that there are spaces for sharing and reflecting on personal experiences as well as formal reporting. It was felt that the impact or contribution of Indian experiences is not adequately reflected or articulated in the writings or project reports of European partners. This apparent separation of cross-cultural experiences may be explained in terms of the way in which project tasks were approached by European and Indian partners. Although European partners responded personally to Indian experiences and their impact on formulating future research and collaborations, they saw cross-cultural collaboration in terms of transfer of European educational experiences and research methods, thereby separating their own Indian subjective experiences from their formal report writings. Perhaps the lesson for coordinators is to create an expectation that project partners will create spaces for articulating and responding to cultural experiences in their writings.

Need to avoid too rigid a definition of cross-cultural and trans-disciplinary projects

There is a need in projects such as this one to negotiate shared meaning. It is therefore important to provide space and time for this negotiation by delaying formal definition of project parameters. Our experience of collaboration has shown that by starting with the conceptual and rather overarching description of the project, enough space and time is available to individuals to get to know each other personally, to build a network of like minded people with a common purpose, and to create a facilitating environment for sustainable partnerships and institutional impact. It also enables the network coordinator to identify interests, expertise and competencies of individuals and partner institutions relevant to project activities and research themes, thereby leading to the effective concrete definition of various phases of the project and its products.

Need to be aware of the formal limitations imposed by the rigidity of funding structures

Funds should be directed to project activities rather than allocated to individual institutions. Where as the EU partners have had considerable experience of the complexity and rigidity of European funding rules, this was a new cultural experience for Indian partners. In cross-cultural collaborations the project coordinators and partners should be aware of the potential negative synergy between the very rigid financial/accountability system of Indian institutions and the EU funding structure. There is a very real risk that these will work together to make flexible adaptation to changing circumstance almost impossible to make. Funding should be managed in a central pool rather than allocated to individual institutions; and should be used to support activities rather than the personnel. The coordinators have to recognise the asymmetry between the Indian institutional norms and funding terminology used by the EU. We should also be aware that the notion of the equality of funding advocated by the EU might become a hindrance. We found that project partners, especially Indian partners saw funding as the only yard stick of equality, separated from the technical equality as the funding was seen as the only criteria for evaluation, rather than focusing on the technical contribution as the evaluation criteria it should have been.

Need to build the project on both the individual interests and institutional contexts

The strength of this project is that it started and remained mainly as a network of individuals, and this facilitated very effective collaborations at the personal levels. Because of this personal development, it maximised institutional impact. It is our experience that in India, bottom up innovations are very difficult and top down developments are rather slow. Engaging the interest of the committed individuals and supporting the development of their profiles within their institutions proved to be an effective strategy.

Need to cultivate both big and little pictures, but project activities should have limited objectives to achieve

Our experience is that proverbial advice "to think global and act local" is as valid here as anywhere else. It is necessary while keeping the overall picture in mind that specific activities need to be very effectively targeted. We made the mistake on some occasions of attempting to satisfy too many objectives at the same event, and consequently sometimes seemed to lose specific focus. For example, some workshops and exchange visits were loaded with too many objectives during the same activity. A workshop could be simultaneously the forum for students (second level) participation, entrepreneurial networking, visibility events, R&D presentations, and course developments in addition to extension of the network. This was generally managed without problems, but could still be rather confusing.

Need to evolve mechanism for professional recognition

There is a need to recognise that the contributions of individual researchers are understood within the contexts of both the project and within their Institutions. In cross-disciplinary projects of this kind, it is important to cultivate a working environment in which the professional development of the individual is not prejudiced by working outside the conventional disciplinary boundaries. This is essentially a personal development issue and requires the constant cultivation of senior academics and policy makers to ensure their understanding of the project for personal development and institutional status.

Need to be aware institutional value of effective publicity

The network coordinators should never lose sight of the positive impact of the visibility of the project on the commitment of participating institutions. This project has been very effective in maintaining a very high profile for the project and collaborating institutions, as well as, that of the EU-India Cross-Cultural Cooperation Programme.

Need for the Coordination Centre to act as a catalyst for sustained innovation

The role of the coordinator should be to act as an *animateur* and catalyst for sustained innovation and a sense of progression. The financial management should be separated from technical management. There is need to define and evolve the project sufficiently flexibly to allow the coordinator room to manoeuvre. This allows the coordinator to be effective in strengthening network collaboration and the continuous development of the project.

COMMENT

What the EU-India Innovation Network project has highlighted is that networking partnerships of universities across cultures, regions and nations can play a key role in mediating an interdependent vision of development in the globalising world. Through their partnerships with local communities, enterprises and entrepreneurs, these partnerships act as catalysts of cross-cultural collaborations at the local-global levels. As mediators of cross-cultural knowledge and interlocutors of inter-cultural encounters, they play an active role in cultivating and enriching cross-cultural dialogues, discourses and collaborations, thereby breaking the linear economic gaze mould and promoting an alternative Holonic paradigm of development.

CONCLUDING REMARKS

Seeing development as dynamic interconnections of knowledge, culture and communication, enables us to seek commonalities while valorising diversities that impact upon cross-cultural discourses and inter-cultural interactions. This idea of development requires identifying and recognising cross-cultural gaps, and finding ways to bridge these gaps through cross-cultural and cross-disciplinary networking. Some of the conceptual tools, which can facilitate the crossing of these gaps and building of common interaction spaces, are the notions of the actuality, symbiosis, ying and yang, keyosei, swikriti, culture of the artificial, and valorisation; by mapping these interactions to local-global interaction architectures, leads first to understand the nature of these interactions and then to design interfacing tools.

The concept valorisation promotes the harmonisation of the immense untapped potential of cultural resources for enriching the cross-cultural vision of development. In the globalising world, this also means rethinking about the role of information and communication technologies (ICTs) as the new driving forces of intercultural cooperation and development. It is undeniable that new media and communication technologies, such as digital television, e-mail, internet, and mobile telephones, are new form of tools, enabling people across the globe to interact with each other. However to extrapolate further that these tools will bring people around the world together in a global village where cultural difference cease to matter, is a mistaken illusion. As Hofstede and Hofstede (opcit) point out that, " The software of the machines may be globalised, but the software of the mind that use them is not." Although ICTs enormously increases the amount of information accessible to its users, it does not, however, increase their capacity to absorbe this information, nor does it change their value systems. As users we selectively process information according to contexts and our values.

Although, communication technologies increase our consciousness of differences between and within countries, they will not by themselves reduce the need for intercultural interaction.

The cultural architecture proposed in this paper provides a model for exploring cross-cultural interactions at various levels of complexity. This architecture can be used to build further complex architectures to deal with cross-cultural interactions in more complex societal systems. The concept of cultural Holon is introduced to conceptualise cross-cultural interactions within complex cultural architectures. The concept of symbiosis is used to conceptualise interactions within the overlapping interaction architectures. The concept of culture of the artificial enables cross-cultural collaboration while resolving differences. The concept of 'valorisation' enables us to seek coherence of cross-cultural interactions in both overlapping and intersecting interaction architectures. The concept of actuality enables seeing the world through a holistic prism, promotes the building of cross-cultural alliances which seek coherence of diverse realities and actualities.

A Holonic cultural architecture for cross-cultural interaction

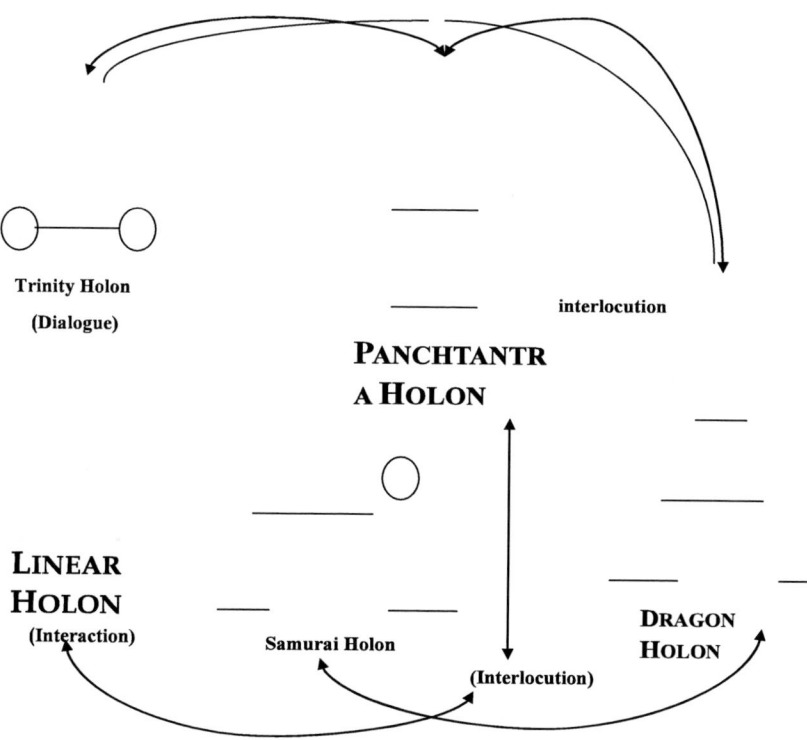

Figure 1. Holonic Cultural Architecture for cross-cultural interaction illustrating interaction and communication modes between cultural Holons, each cultural Holon as a simplified representation of the observed reality of interaction within a cultural structure of communication

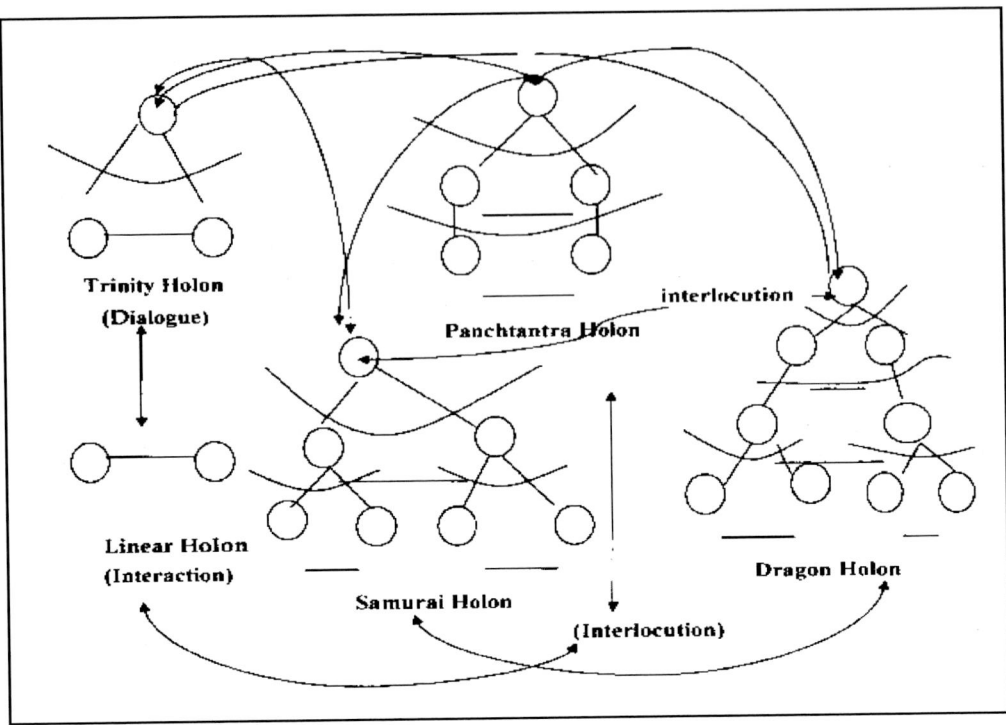

Figure 2: Culture of the artificial- users from two different interaction (cultural) spaces (Reality A and Reality B) collaborate by valorising their difference by creating a new 'third' reality C (culture of the artificial).

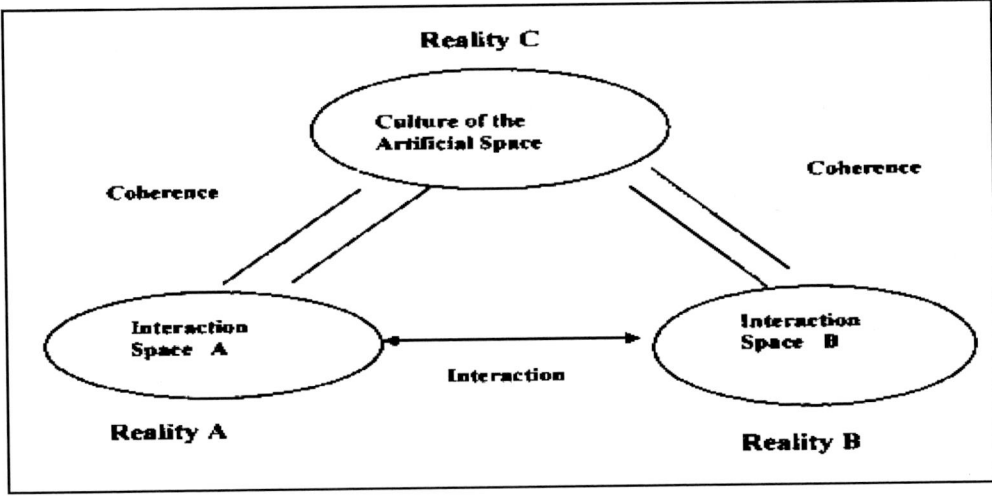

Figure 3 shows communication and knowledge gaps between various levels of health care system; illustrating knowledge gaps arising from the gaps between the objective, empirical, experiential, functional, personal and subsidiary knowledge, as well as gaps arising from interaction at clinical, professional, public, community, social, personal and cultural levels.

Cross-cultural interaction viewed from a narrow functional perspective, often gets translated from transformational interaction into transactional interaction. This perspective then promotes the given orthodoxy of the 'horizontal gaze', 'one best way', and the culture of the 'exact language', thereby raising the spectre of seeing development as imposing universal values rather than seeing valorisation (making the best of differences) as resource for sustainable development. Knowledge networking as a facilitating tool for development overcomes these orthodoxies, crossing the horizontal economic gaze of development and finding ways to bridge knowledge and interaction gaps across disciplines and cultures. EU-India Cross-Cultural Innovation Network project, as an exemplar of a complex of cross-cultural collaboration, reflects a belief in the need for much wider diffusion of knowledge, expertise and experience in society. It recognises the pluralistic and overlapping nature and scope of inter-cultural interactions, arising from the interdependence between local and global social, cultural and economic systems.

In: Contemporary Discourses on IE & C Theory and Practice ISBN: 978-1-60962-360-3
Editor: Theophilus K. Gokah © 2009 Nova Science Publishers, Inc.

Chapter 11

CHANGING A HARMFUL SOCIAL CONVENTION: FEMALE GENITAL MUTILATION/CUTTING[*]

Innocenti Digest, UNICEF and IRC

This discussion examines the social dynamics of FGM/C. In communities where it is practiced, FGM/C is an important part of girls' and women's cultural gender identity. The procedure imparts a sense of pride, of coming of age and a feeling of community membership. Moreover, not conforming to the practice stigmatizes and isolates girls and their families, resulting in the loss of their social status. This deeply entrenched social convention is so powerful that parents are willing to have their daughters cut because they want the best for their children and because of social pressure within their community. The social expectations surrounding FGM/C represent a major obstacle to families who might otherwise wish to abandon the practice. Taking this as its point of departure, the discussion presents some of the most promising strategies to support communities to abandon FGM/C. These approaches recognize that the decision to abandon the practice must come from communities themselves, and must reflect a collective choice, reinforced publicly and grounded on a firm human rights foundation. Greater understanding of human rights provides communities with the tools to direct their own social transformation. The explicitly collective dimension empowers individual families, while liberating them from having to make the difficult choice of breaking with tradition.

INTRODUCTION

There are an estimated 130 million girls and women alive today whose human rights have been violated by female genital mutilation/cutting (FGM/C). This harmful practice not only affects girls and women in Africa and the Middle East, where it has been traditionally carried out, but also touches the lives of girls and women living in migrant communities in industrialized countries. Although concerted advocacy work over recent decades has

---

[*] Text reproduced with kind permission of the Innocenti Research Centre.

generated widespread commitment to end this practice, success in eliminating FGM/C has been limited – with some significant exceptions.

In the context of human rights, it integrates concrete field experience with academic theory to provide the global community with a greater understanding of why FGM/C persists. This harmful practice is a deeply entrenched social convention: when it is practiced, girls and their families acquire social status and respect. Failure to perform FGM/C brings shame and exclusion. Understanding how and why FGM/C persists is crucial for developing strategies that are most likely to lead to the abandonment of the practice. This discussion is intended to serve as a practical tool to bring about positive change for girls and women. It:

- analyses the most current data to illustrate the geographic distribution of FGM/C and outlines key trends;
- identifies the principal ways in which FGM/C violates a girl's or woman's human rights, including the serious physical, psychological and social implications of this harmful practice;
- examines the factors that contribute to perpetuating FGM/C; and
- outlines effective and complementary action at the community, national and international levels to support the abandonment of FGM/C

On the basis of analysis conducted, there is good reason to be optimistic that, with the appropriate support, FGM/C can be ended in many practicing communities within a single generation.

WHAT IS FGM/C?

Female genital mutilation/cutting includes "a range of practices involving the complete or partial removal or alteration of the external genitalia for nonmedical reasons[1]". This procedure may involve the use of unsterilised, makeshift or rudimentary tools. The terminology applied to this procedure has undergone a number of important evolutions. When the practice first came to be known beyond the societies in which it was traditionally carried out, it was generally referred to as "female circumcision". This term, however, draws a direct parallel with male circumcision and, as a result, creates confusion between these two distinct practices. In the case of girls and women, the phenomenon is a manifestation of deep-rooted gender inequality that assigns them an inferior position in society and has profound physical and social consequences.[2] This is not the case for male circumcision, which may help to prevent the transmission of HIV/AIDS.[3]

The expression "female genital mutilation" (FGM) gained growing support in the late 1970s. The word "mutilation" not only establishes a clear linguistic distinction with male circumcision, but also, due to its strong negative connotations, emphasizes the gravity of the act. In 1990, this term was adopted at the third conference of the Inter African Committee on Traditional Practices Affecting the Health of Women and Children (IAC) in Addis Ababa.[4] In 1991, WHO recommended that the United Nations adopt this terminology and subsequently, it has been widely used in UN documents.

The use of the word "mutilation" reinforces the idea that this practice is a violation of girls' and women's human rights, and thereby helps promote national and international advocacy towards its abandonment. At the community level, however, the term can be problematic. Local languages generally use the less judgmental "cutting" to describe the practice; parents understandably resent the suggestion that they are "mutilating" their daughters. In this spirit, in 1999, the UN Special Rapporteur on Traditional Practices called for tact and patience regarding activities in this area and drew attention to the risk of "demonizing" certain cultures, religions and communities[5]. As a result, the term "cutting" has increasingly come to be used to avoid alienating communities. To capture the significance of the term "mutilation" at the policy level and, at the same time, in recognition of the importance of employing non-judgemental terminology with practicing communities, the expression "female genital mutilation/cutting" (FGM/C) is used throughout this chapter.

MAGNITUDE, ASSESSMENT AND MEASUREMENT

According to a WHO estimate, between 100 and 140 million women and girls in the world have undergone some form of FGM/C[6]. Although overall figures are difficult to estimate, they do indicate the massive scale of this human rights violation. FGM/C affects far more women than previously thought. Recent analysis reveals that some three million girls and women are cut each year on the African continent (Sub-Saharan Africa, Egypt and Sudan)[7]. Of these, nearly half are from two countries: Egypt and Ethiopia. Although this figure is significantly higher than the previous estimate of two million, this new figure does not reflect increased incidence, but is a more accurate estimate drawn from a greater availability of data. Effective efforts to end this practice require a more detailed picture of this situation.

WHERE IS FGM/C PRACTICED?

The majority of girls and women at risk of undergoing FGM/C live in some 28 countries in Africa and the Middle East. In Africa, these countries form a broad band from Senegal in the west to Somalia in the east. Some communities on the Red Sea coast of Yemen are also known to practice FGM/C, and there are reports, but no clear evidence, of a limited incidence in Jordan, Oman, the Occupied Palestinian Territories (Gaza) and in certain Kurdish communities in Iraq. The practice has also been reported among certain populations in India, Indonesia, and Malaysia[8].

The most reliable and extensive data on prevalence and nature of FGM/C are provided by Demographic and Health Surveys (DHS) and Multiple Indicator Cluster Surveys (MICS). Prevalence is defined as the percentage of women aged 15 to 4[9] who have undergone some form of FGM/C. Obtaining data on FGM/C prevalence among girls under 15 years of age poses a number of methodological challenges, not least of which include ascertaining if and how the procedure was carried out. Currently DHS and MICS data on FGM/C prevalence are available for 18 countries. The most current data from these sources indicate that the prevalence of FGM/C varies significantly from one country to another – from as low as 5 per cent in Niger to as much as 99 per cent in Guinea9. Countries in which FGM/C is practiced but for which there are not, as yet, DHS or MICS data are Cameroon[10], the Democratic Republic of Congo, Djibouti, Gambia, Guinea Bissau, Liberia, Senegal, Sierra Leone, Somalia, Togo, and Uganda. The latter countries also demonstrate a wide range of prevalence: the Democratic Republic of Congo is thought to have less than 5 per cent prevalence, while both Djibouti and Somalia are estimated to have prevalence around or above 90 per cent.

Patterns of FGM/C prevalence emerge when countries are grouped by region. For example, in the countries of northeast Africa (Egypt, Eritrea, Ethiopia, and Sudan), it ranges from 80 to 97 per cent, while in East Africa (Kenya and Tanzania) it is markedly lower and ranges from 18 to 32 per cent[11]. Care is required, however, when interpreting these figures, since they represent national averages and do not reflect the often marked variation in prevalence in different parts of a given country. In Nigeria, for example, national prevalence is 19 per cent; prevalence in the southern regions reaches almost 60 per cent, while in the north it is between zero and 2 per cent.

The practice of FGM/C is no longer restricted to countries in which it has been traditionally practiced. Migration from Africa to industrialized countries has been an enduring characteristic of the post World War II period, and many of the migrants come from countries that practice FGM/C. Beyond economic factors, migratory patterns have frequently reflected links established in the colonial past. For instance, citizens from Benin, Chad, Guinea, Mali, Niger and Senegal have often chosen France as their destination, while many Kenyan, Nigerian and Ugandan citizens have migrated to the United Kingdom.

In the 1970s, war, civil unrest and drought in a number of African states, including Eritrea, Ethiopia and Somalia, resulted in an influx of refugees to Western Europe, where some countries, such as Norway and Sweden, had been relatively unaffected by migration up to that point. Beyond Western Europe, Canada and the USA in North America, and Australia and New Zealand in Australasia also host women and children who have been subjected to FGM/C, and are home to others who are at risk of undergoing this procedure.

Data on the prevalence and characteristics of FGM/C in industrialized countries are rare and extrapolations are sometimes used to gain insights on the extent of the practice. By combining data from the office of migration with data on prevalence from countries of origin, the Swiss National Committee for UNICEF estimated that, in Switzerland, some 6,700 girls and women have either undergone FGM/C, or are at risk of undergoing the procedure. Of these, more than one third are of Somali origin. This number does not include women and girls holding a Swiss passport.

DISAGGREGATED DATA[12]

Both DHS and MICS permit national level data to be disaggregated by age group, urban-rural residence and region or province. Many surveys also show differences in prevalence by ethnicity and religion. The possibility of analysing disaggregated data on prevalence is of crucial importance since national averages can disguise significant in-country variations. This is less the case in countries where the prevalence of FGM/C is very high, such as Egypt, Guinea and Sudan, with prevalence rates of 90 per cent or over. However, in countries where a significant proportion of the population does not pursue the practice, disaggregation can significantly enhance understanding of the phenomenon and inform programmatic interventions to support its abandonment.

The value of disaggregation by region or province is illustrated by the case of the Central African Republic, where data from MICS2 indicate that, at the national level, 36 per cent of women aged 15 to 49 have undergone FGM/C. Looking at the situation from a sub-national perspective reveals significant geographic variations. In five prefectures in the west of the country and two in the east, FGM/C prevalence is between 0 and 19.9 per cent, while in three prefectures in the north of the country, the prevalence is between 85 and 100 per cent[13].

The variation is largely explained by the presence of diverse ethnic communities with differing attitudes and practices regarding FGM/C. In the Central African Republic, countrywide FGM/C prevalence ranges from 5 per cent among the Mboum and Zande-N'zakara to 75 per cent among the Banda, one of the largest ethnic groups in the country. Among the Gbaya, the largest ethnic group, the prevalence rate is 24 per cent. DHS analysts point out that data vary far more by ethnicity than by any other social or demographic variable. In other words, ethnic identity and the practice of FGM/C are closely linked. Some groups rarely or never practice FGM/C, while in others; virtually all women have been cut.

Data on ethnicity are available for only a limited number of countries, and when analysing them, at least three important issues need to be considered. First, ethnic groupings rarely correspond to clearly define national administrative divisions, and groups that practice FGM/C may be present in a number of provinces or districts. Second, even in a relatively detailed survey, the ethnic groups listed may in fact be an ethnic category consisting of many subgroups with differing practices. Finally, while the disaggregation of FGM/C prevalence by ethnicity is useful for informing programmatic action, these data should be interpreted with care to avoid stigmatization.

Urban development has been considered as a possible factor influencing prevalence, although the link between urbanization and prevalence is not unequivocal. Of the 18 countries covered by DHS or MICS, 12 demonstrate a higher prevalence of FGM/C in rural areas than in urban areas; although in certain cases the difference is very small. In two cases (Ethiopia and Guinea), urban and rural rates were both found to be identical or near identical, while in four cases (Burkina Faso, Nigeria, Sudan and Yemen), prevalence in urban areas is higher than in rural parts of the country, a phenomenon most likely explained by the confounding effect of ethnicity.

Education, especially of women, can play an important role in safeguarding the human rights of both women themselves, and those of their children. Overall, daughters of mothers who are more highly educated are less likely to have undergone FGM/C than daughters of mothers with little or no education[14]. Only in Guinea does no relationship appear between the FGM/C status of daughters and a mother's level of education, a finding which can largely be explained by the very small proportion of women in this country with secondary schooling or above. Although there is a statistical difference between women with secondary education and those with no education, FGM/C is still practiced by women with higher education. In other words, women's education may contribute to a reduction of the practice, but alone it is not sufficient to lead to its abandonment.

THE CIRCUMSTANCES SURROUNDING FGM/C

DHS and MICS provide valuable information regarding the circumstances surrounding the act of FGM/C, including the age at which a girl or woman is subjected to the practice, the type of cutting involved and the practitioner who carried it out. These surveys reveal notable variations in both the form and meaning of FGM/C – variations which largely occur between different groups rather than within groups.

The age at which large proportions of girls are cut varies greatly from one country to another. About 90 per cent of girls in Egypt are cut between the ages of 5 and 14 years[15], while in Ethiopia, Mali and Mauritania, 60 per cent or more of girls surveyed underwent the procedure before their fifth birthday[16]. In Yemen, the Demographic and Health Survey carried out in 1997 found that as many as 76 per cent of girls underwent FGM/C in their first two weeks of life. In-country variations are also apparent, often reflecting the distribution of ethnic groups. In Sudan, a cohort study in 2004 found that at least 75 per cent of girls had undergone FGM/C by the age of 9 to 10 in South Darfur, a state which has a predominantly Fur and Arab population, while in Kassala, which has a predominantly Beja population, 75 per cent of girls had already been cut by the age of 4 to 5[17].

Information regarding the type of FGM/C performed is useful in helping to anticipate the extent of the physical consequences of the practice. There are, however, certain challenges in obtaining these data, including ascertaining whether survey respondents understood what was meant when asked about which type of FGM/C they had undergone. In the majority of countries where DHS or MICS included a question regarding type of FGM/C, the "lightest" form[18] was found to be most common. Only in Burkina Faso was the more extensive procedure, involving excision of the labia minora, most frequently carried out (accounting for 56 per cent of all cutting[19]).

Infibulation – cutting followed by stitching or narrowing – was found to affect large proportions of women in two countries: Sudan, where the MICS2 survey in 2000 estimated that as many as 74 per cent of women who had been cut had undergone this procedure; and Eritrea, where the DHS survey in 2002 estimated that 39 per cent had been subjected to infibulations. This procedure is also known to be widely practiced in Djibouti and Somalia. The large majority of girls and women are cut by a traditional practitioner, a category which includes local specialists (cutters or *exciseuses*), traditional birth attendants and, generally, older members of the community, usually women. This is true for over 80 percent of the girls who undergo the practice in Benin, Burkina Faso, Côte d'Ivoire, Eritrea, Ethiopia, Guinea, Mali, Niger, Tanzania and Yemen. In most countries, medical personnel, including doctors, nurses and certified midwives, are not widely involved in the practice. Egypt offers a clear exception: in 2000, it was estimated that in 61 per cent of cases, FGM/C had been carried out by medical personnel. The share of FGM/C carried out by medical personnel has also been found to be relatively high in Sudan[20] (36 per cent) and Kenya (34 per cent).

FGM/C AND CHANGES OVER TIME

FGM/C is an evolving practice, and its characteristics and distribution have changed over time. In Yemen, for instance, the practice only emerged in the course of the 20th century as a result of contacts with practicing communities in the Horn of Africa. Evidence of changes in the prevalence of FGM/C can be obtained by comparing the experiences of women in different age groups in a given country. Using this method, 9 of the sixteen countries in which DHS has collected data demonstrate a marked decrease in prevalence in the younger age groups (15 to 25 years of age): Benin, Burkina Faso, Central African Republic, Eritrea, Ethiopia, Kenya, Nigeria, Tanzania and Yemen. In the remaining seven countries (Côte d'Ivoire, Egypt, Guinea, Mali, Mauritania, Niger and Sudan[21]) prevalence is at roughly the same level for all age groups, suggesting that rates of FGM/C in these cases have remained relatively stable over recent decades. Of the four countries that demonstrate the highest rates of prevalence (Egypt, Guinea, Mali and Sudan[22]) – none have shown any evidence of change in prevalence over time.

Changes in prevalence can also be assessed in a number of countries where two surveys have been carried out, thus enabling a comparison of results at different points in time. Data indicates that of the seven countries where this type of comparison is currently possible, there has been a clear decrease in overall prevalence in Eritrea, Kenya and Nigeria.

The data provide grounds for cautious optimism. Asked if they think that FGM/C should continue, younger women are generally less likely to agree than older women. This difference was highest for the DHS survey in Eritrea in 2002, which found that 63 per cent of women between 45 and 49 years of age supported FGM/C compared to only 36 per cent of women between 15 and 19 years of age. While these findings are encouraging, attitudes may shift with age. Moreover, field experience indicates that a lack of support for FGM/C (i.e. a change of attitude towards the practice) is not always translated into a change in behaviour. In addition to changes in prevalence, there are three significant trends which are emerging in a number of countries where FGM/C is practiced[23].

• *The average age at which a girl is subjected to cutting is decreasing in some countries.* Of the 16 countries surveyed by DHS, the median age at the time FGM/C was performed has dropped substantially in Burkina Faso, Côte d'Ivoire, Egypt, Kenya and Mali. Reasons for this may include the effect of national legislation to prohibit FGM/C, which has encouraged the practice to be carried out at an early age when it can be more easily hidden from the authorities. It is also possible that the trend is influenced by a desire on the part of those who support or perform the practice to minimise the resistance of the girls themselves.

• *The "medicalization" of FGM/C, whereby girls are cut by trained personnel rather than by traditional practitioners, is on the rise.* This trend may reflect the impact of campaigns that emphasise the health risks associated with the practice, but fail to address the underlying motivations for its perpetuation. Analysing survey data by age group reveals that in Egypt, Guinea and Mali, the medicalization of FGM/C has increased dramatically in recent years.

• *The importance of the ceremonial aspects associated with FGM/C is declining in many communities.*

This trend may also be related, in part, to the existence of legislation to prohibit FGM/C that discourages public manifestations of the practice.

STANDARDIZING INDICATORS FOR SITUATION ANALYSIS AND MONITORING PROGRESS

The information contained in this section represents only a brief introduction to the data on FGM/C available from DHS and MICS. The questions posed in these surveys enable a range of inter- and intra-country comparisons to be carried out. The potential for comparison is further enhanced as these surveys move towards a set of standardised indicators for situation analysis and monitoring progress towards ending FGM/C. In November 2003, international agreement was reached on appropriate indicators for these purposes at a UNICEF Global Consultation on Indicators[24]. At this consultation; five standard indicators for situation analysis were established.

1. *Prevalence of FGM/C by age cohorts 15-49.* This is the most important indicator. Age cohorts are 15-19, 20-24, 25-29, 30-34, 35-39, 40-44 and 45- 49.
2. *FGM/C status of all daughters.* This indicator refers to FGM/C prevalence for all daughters of mothers aged 15 to 49 years. It is recommended to collect data on the current age of daughters as well as on the age at which they were cut.
3. *Percentage of "closed" FGM/C (infibulation, sealing) and "open" FGM/C (excision).* This simplified category is introduced to help overcome the difficulty of identifying the specific type of FGM/C a woman or her daughter has undergone.
4. *Performer of FGM/C.*
   Support of, or opposition to FGM/C by women and men age 15-49.

The Global Consultation also sought to extend the collection of data on prevalence to girls aged 5 to 14. It may be possible to obtain these data through local surveys, although these do not yield prevalence data at national levels. To assess the effectiveness of programmes promoting the abandonment of FGM/C, three indicators were agreed upon.

• *Public declaration of intent.* The questions should capture the stated intent of individuals, communities and villages to abandon FGM/C. Forms of public declarations may vary from one community to another.

• *Community-based monitoring mechanisms to follow up on girls at risk of FGM/C.* Information should be gathered from the community through the health and school systems and from youth groups, along with other community-selected monitoring mechanisms. Information might include the number of girls who have or have not been cut, the age at which the practice is carried out (and any changes in this age), the number of men who would marry women who have not undergone FGM/C, and the dissemination of messages by community members and former practitioners.

• *Drop in prevalence.* This is the ultimate quantitative measure that demonstrates progress towards the abandonment of FGM/C and hence the effectiveness of programmes in place. It can be obtained though household surveys organized with international support (MICS or DHS) or locally. Data measuring these indicators can be derived from smaller community studies and programme monitoring and evaluation. Communities should be involved throughout any evaluation process in order to identify indicators and information that reflect their own perception of progress.

THE SOCIAL DYNAMICS OF FGM/C

In every society in which it is practiced, FGM/C is a manifestation of gender inequality that is deeply entrenched in social, economic and political structures. In practice, however, this dimension is not explicitly addressed and may not even be recognised by those who support and perpetuate FGM/C.

Researchers seeking to understand how and why the practice of FGM/C persists are confronted with what appears to be a paradox: in many cases, parents and other family members are perpetuating a tradition that they know can bring harm, both physical and psychological, to their daughters. The explanation lies in the social dynamics among individuals in communities that practice FGM/C. Mothers organize the cutting of their daughters because they consider that this is part of what they must do to raise a girl properly[25] and to prepare her for adulthood and marriage. In discussions about FGM/C, Maninka women in central Guinea explained that parents have a threefold obligation to their daughters: to educate them properly, cut them, and find them a husband[26]. This obligation can be understood as a social convention to which parents conform, even if the practice inflicts harm. From this perspective, not conforming would bring greater harm, since it would lead to shame and social exclusion.

Social convention is so powerful that girls themselves may desire to be cut, as a result of the social pressure from peers and because of fear – not without reason – of stigmatisation and rejection by their own communities if they do not follow the tradition[27]. FGM/C is an important part of girls' and women's cultural gender identity and the procedure may also impart a sense of pride, of coming of age and a feeling of community membership. Girls who undergo the procedure are provided with rewards, including celebrations, public recognition and gifts. Moreover, in communities where FGM/C is almost universally practiced, not conforming to the practice can result in stigmatization, social isolation and difficulty in finding a husband. Girls and women living in immigrant communities may also value the procedure because it can play a role in reinforcing their cultural identity in a foreign context.

Understanding FGM/C as a social convention provide insight as to why women who have themselves been cut and suffer the health consequences favour its continuation[28]. They resist initiatives to end FGM/C, not because they are unaware of its harmful aspects, but because its abandonment is perceived to entail loss of status and protection. This also helps to explain why individual families that voice a desire to abandon the practice nonetheless submit their daughters to the procedure. The convention can only be changed if a significant number of families within a community make a collective and coordinated choice to abandon the practice so that no single girl or family is disadvantaged by the decision[29].

MECHANISMS THAT REINFORCE THE SOCIAL CONVENTION

The justifications offered for the practice of FGM/C are numerous and, in their specific context, compelling. While these justifications may vary among communities, they follow a number of common themes: FGM/C ensures a girl's or woman's status, marriageability, chastity, health, beauty and family honour. In some cases they are presented positively to emphasise the advantages of undergoing FGM/C, while in others they point to the consequences of not undergoing the procedure.7 "Why do you think people here in the village support the practice?"

> "It is a norm that has to be fulfilled. The girl must be circumcised to protect her honour and the family's honour, especially that now girls go to universities outside the village and may be exposed to lots of intimidating situations."

Interview with woman from Abu Hashem village, Upper Egypt[30]. Among groups that practice FGM/C, cutting constitutes a social, ethnic and physical mark of distinction[31]. FGM/C assigns status and value both to the girl or woman herself and to her family.

Among the Chagga of Arusha in Tanzania, the link between FGM/C and the value of girls is explicit: the bride price for a girl who has undergone the practice is much higher than that for one who has not[32]. FGM/C is also practiced on the grounds that it preserves a girl's virginity, making the procedure a prerequisite for marriage. In part of Nigeria, for instance, FGM/C serves the purpose of allowing the future mother-in-law to verify the virginity of the bride[33]. Similarly, FGM/C is often justified on the grounds that it protects girls from excessive sexual emotions and therefore, helps to preserve their morality, chastity and fidelity. FGM/C may additionally be associated with bodily cleanliness and beauty. For instance, in Somalia and Sudan, infibulation is carried out with the express purpose of making girls physically "clean". Religious justifications are also given for the practice. Often communities that cite a religious motivation consider the practice a requirement to make a girl spiritually pure. Among the Bambara in Mali, for example, excision is called Seli ji, meaning ablution or ceremonial washing[34].

FGM/C is not prescribed by any religion. This is not, however, the general perception, especially regarding Islam. Although there is a theological branch of Islam that supports FGM/C of the sunna type, the Koran contains no text that requires the cutting of the female external genitalia and it is widely accepted that the practice was current in Sudanese or Nubian populations before Islam[35]. Moreover, the majority of Muslims around the world do not practice FGM/C. There is no evidence of the practice in Saudi Arabia and it is not found in several North African Muslim countries, including Algeria, Libya, Morocco and Tunisia.

Whether they are religious, aesthetic, hygienic or moral, the justifications given for FGM/C are all mechanisms that maintain the social convention of cutting girls and women and contribute to the perpetuation of the practice. Information regarding the validity of these justifications helps to change attitudes towards FGM/C, but real and lasting change in behaviour is most likely to result from transforming the social convention itself.

CHANGING THE SOCIAL CONVENTION: TOWARDS THE ABANDONMENT OF FGM/C

As with any self-enforcing social convention, the choice of an individual – in the case of FGM/C, a single family's choice of whether or not to cut its daughter or daughters – is conditioned by the choice of others. This social pressure tends to perpetuate the practice. It can also be the key to promote rapid collective abandonment. The practice of Footbinding in

China, for example, which lasted some 1000 years, was abandoned in little more than a generation.

To understand how a social convention might be transformed, it is helpful to use a simple metaphor. A group has a convention whereby audiences (at the cinema, at plays, at recitals) stand up rather than sit down. An outsider comes along and explains that elsewhere audiences sit. After the shock of surprise wears off, some people begin to think that sitting might be better. If only one person sits, that person can't see anything on the stage. However, if a critical mass of people in the audience can be organized to sit, even a group of people who are less than the majority, they realize that they can sit comfortably and have a clear view of the stage[36].

Similarly, in communities where cutting is a prerequisite for marriage, if only one family abandons FGM/C, its daughter doesn't get married. A critical mass is needed to bring about change. Once enough individuals are willing to abandon FGM/C, they will work to convince others to follow suit because this will reduce the social stigma associated with not cutting.

The critical mass need not be a majority, but simply a sufficient number of individuals to demonstrate to others the relative benefits of *not* practicing FGM/C. Individuals within the group who have opted to abandon the practice will still face social pressure to cut their daughters, as illustrated by the challenges faced by a mother in Sudan. For this pressure to disappear, the number of people who have expressed their intention to abandon the practice must reach a "tipping point". At this point, those who still consider following the practice recognise that the status and honour it brings to a girl and her family no longer outweigh the risks involved.

Once the new convention of valuing a girl's physical integrity is established, it becomes, like the old convention, self-enforcing. For those who have abandoned FGM/C, there is no incentive to revert to the practice, while the few individuals who continue to support FGM/C will face the disapproval of the community.

ABANDONING FGM/C: SIX KEY ELEMENTS FOR CHANGE

Concrete field experience, together with insights from academic theory and lessons learned from the experience of Footbinding in China suggest that six key elements can contribute to transforming the social convention of cutting girls and encourage the rapid and mass abandonment of the practice.

1. *A non-coercive and non-judgmental approach whose primary focus is the fulfilment of human rights and the empowerment of girls and women.* Communities tend to raise the issue of FGM/C when they increase their awareness and understanding of human rights and make progress toward the realisation of those they consider to be of immediate concern, such as health and education. Despite taboos regarding the discussion of FGM/C, the issue emerges because group members are aware that the practice causes harm. Community discussion and debate contribute to a new understanding that girls would be better off if everyone abandoned the practice.

2. *An awareness on the part of a community of the harm caused by the practice.* Through non-judgmental, non-directive public discussion and reflection, the costs of FGM/C tend to

become more evident as women – and men – share their experiences and those of their daughters.

3. *The decision to abandon the practice as a collective choice of a group that intramarries or is closely connected in other ways.* FGM/C is a community practice and, consequently, is most effectively given up by the community acting together rather than by individuals acting on their own. Successful transformation of the social convention ultimately rests with the ability of members of the group to organize and take collective action.

4. *An explicit, public affirmation on the part of communities of their collective commitment to abandon FGM/C.* It is necessary, but not sufficient, that most members of a community favour abandonment. A successful shift requires that they manifest – as a community – the will to abandon. This may take various forms, including a joint public declaration in a large public gathering or an authoritative written statement of the collective commitment to abandon.

5. *A process of organized diffusion to ensure that the decision to abandon FGM/C spreads rapidly from one community to another and is sustained.* Communities must engage neighbouring villages so that the decision to abandon FGM/C can be spread and sustained. It is particularly important to engage those communities that exercise a strong influence. When the decision to abandon becomes sufficiently diffused, the social dynamics that originally perpetuated the practice can serve to accelerate and sustain its abandonment. Where previously there was social pressure to perform FGM/C, there will be social pressure to abandon the practice. When the process of abandonment reaches this point, the social convention of not cutting becomes self-enforcing and abandonment continues swiftly and spontaneously.

6. *An environment that enables and supports change.* Success in promoting the abandonment of FGM/C also depends on the commitment of government, at all levels, to introduce appropriate social measures and legislation, complemented by effective advocacy and awareness efforts. Civil society forms an integral part of this enabling environment. In particular, the media have a key role in facilitating the diffusion process.

FGM/C AND HUMAN RIGHTS

As a harmful "customary" or "traditional" practice, FGM/C is addressed under two important legally binding international human rights instruments: the 1979 Convention on the Elimination of All Forms of Discrimination against Women (CEDAW) and the 1989 Convention on the Rights of the Child (CRC). CEDAW addresses FGM/C and other cultural practices in the context of unequal gender relations and calls upon States Parties to (article 5):

> [...] take all appropriate measures: [...] To modify the social and cultural patterns of conduct of men and women, with a view to achieving the elimination of prejudices and customary and all other practices which are based on the idea of the inferiority or the superiority of either of the sexes or on stereotyped roles for men and women.

The Convention on the Rights of the Child, ratified by 192 countries[37], makes explicit reference to "harmful traditional practices" in the context of the child's right to the highest attainable standard of health. This broad category includes, among others, FGM/C, early marriage (See *Innocenti Digest* No. 7) and preferential care of male children[38]. In addition, Article 19 of the Convention calls upon States Parties to "take all appropriate […] measures to protect the child from all forms of physical or mental violence, injury or abuse […] while in the care of parent(s), legal guardian(s) or any other person who has the care of the child."

International human rights instruments promote the right of an individual to participate in cultural life, but they do not uphold traditional practices that violate individual rights. Therefore, social and cultural claims cannot be evoked to justify FGM/C. In deciding to abandon FGM/C, a community is not rejecting their cultural values, but rather a practice that causes harm to girls and women and reinforces gender inequalities.

FGM/C AND THE RIGHTS OF THE CHILD

The impact of all types of FGM/C on girls and women is wide-ranging, and the practice compromises the enjoyment of human rights including the right to life, the right to physical integrity, the right to the highest attainable standard of health (including, with maturity, reproductive and sexual health), as well as the right to freedom from physical or mental violence, injury or abuse. The practice is also a violation of the rights of the child to development, protection and participation. FGM/C has often been raised as a matter of concern by the Committee on the Rights of the Child, which, in the light of the CRC, has called upon States Parties to "take all effective and appropriate measures" with a view to abolishing such practices.

BEST INTERESTS OF THE CHILD AND THE RIGHT OF THE CHILD TO RESPECT FOR HIS OR HER VIEWS

One of the guiding principles of the CRC is the "best interests of the child". It is recognised in Article 3, which calls for the best interests of the child to be taken as a primary consideration "in all actions concerning children". This principle is of decisive relevance within the family context. Indeed, "[…] Parents or, as the case may be, legal guardians, have the primary responsibility for the upbringing and development of the child. The best interests of the child will be their basic concern[39]" (article 18 CRC). Parents who take the decision to submit their daughter to FGM/C perceive this procedure to be in the child's best interests. In fulfilling a social and cultural expectation that girls should be cut, parents are promoting the status and acceptance of their daughters in the community. Although they – and especially mothers and other female relatives – may be aware of the potentially serious physical and psychological implications of FGM/C, there is the perception that the benefits to be gained from the procedure outweigh the risks involved. These perceptions should not in any case justify the violation of girls' and women's rights[40]. As discussed in other sections of this digest, there are effective ways to resolve this tension and to work with parents, families and communities to promote an approach that is consistent with human rights and promotes the abandonment of FGM/C.

As in many other situations, in the context of FGM/C, the consideration of the child's views has particular relevance. As stressed by the CRC (article 12), "States Parties shall assure to the child who is capable of forming his or her own views the right to express those views freely in all matters affecting the child, the views of the child being given due weight in accordance with the age and maturity of the child." In the majority of cases, FGM/C is performed on a girl against her will. In cases where a girl is in apparent agreement, it is hard to argue that her consent is truly informed and meaningful. In reality, it is strongly subject to tradition and culture, community expectations and peer pressure – including songs and poems that deride girls who have not been cut[41] – and conditioned by the girl's own aspirations to be accepted as a full member of her community. All of these dimensions are compelling motivations for a girl or woman to submit to the procedure [42].

THE RIGHTS TO LIFE AND TO THE HIGHEST ATTAINABLE STANDARD OF HEALTH

FGM/C irreversibly compromise a girl or woman's physical integrity. The damage caused by this procedure can pose a serious risk to her health and wellbeing[43]. In extreme cases, FGM/C can also violate a girl or woman's right to life. Fatalities are often due to severe and uncontrolled bleeding or to infection after the procedure[44]. Moreover, FGM/C may be a contributory or causal factor in maternal death[45]. The mortality rate of girls and women undergoing FGM/C is not known, since few records are kept and deaths due to FGM/C are rarely reported as such[46]. Medical records are also of limited use in determining morbidity due to FGM/C because complications resulting from the practice, including subsequent difficulties in childbirth, are often not recognised or reported as such and may be attributed to other causes. In some cases, these assigned causes may be medical in nature, but in others, they may reflect traditional beliefs or be attributed to supernatural causes. As a result, many girls who experience complications are treated with traditional medicines or cures and are not referred to health centres.

Until recently, information on the physical complications associated with FGM/C has tended to be based on case history reports from hospitals. Moreover, there have been few comparisons with uncut women to establish the relative frequency of these complications[47]. In recognition of the need for better data, WHO has now developed research protocols on FGM/C with a network of collaborating research institutions as well as biomedical and social science researchers with linkages to communities concerned[48].

The specific impact of FGM/C on the health of a girl or woman depends on a number of factors, including the extent and type of the cutting, the skill of the operator, the cleanliness of the tools and of the environment, and the physical condition of the girl or woman[49]. Severe pain and bleeding are the most common immediate consequences of all forms of FGM/C. As the great majority of procedures are carried out without anaesthetic, the pain and trauma experienced can leave a girl in a state of medical shock. In some cases, bleeding can be protracted and girls may be left with long-term anaemia.

Infection is another common consequence, particularly when the procedure is carried out in unhygienic conditions or using unsterilised instruments. The type and degree of infections vary widely and include potentially fatal septicaemia and tetanus. Sometimes the risk of infection is increased by traditional practices, such as binding of the legs after infibulation or applying traditional medicines to the wound. Urine retention is another frequent complication, especially when skin is stitched over the urethra. All these elements may contribute to the wound failing to heal quickly, as may other factors affecting a girl's general health, including anaemia and malnutrition[50].

FGM/C can result in long-term physical effects. Slow or incomplete healing leaves abscesses, painful cysts and thick, raised scars called keloids. These in turn can cause problems in later stages, including in pregnancy and childbirth. Deinfibulation - the procedure to re-open the orifice after it has been stitched or narrowed - and reinfibulation - to re-stitch the vagina - may be performed at each birth. Both procedures seriously compromise the health of women.

FGM/C also jeopardises the health and survival of the children of women who have undergone the procedure. A recently completed WHO study investigated the effects of FGM/C on a range of maternal and infant outcomes during and immediately following delivery. These include caesarean section, length of labour, postpartum haemorrhage, perineal injury, low birth weight, low Agpar score[51] and perinatal death. Initial analysis of the data from some 28,000 women in Burkina Faso, Ghana, Kenya, Nigeria, Senegal and Sudan indicates a relationship between some maternal and infant outcomes and FGM/C, especially in its more severe forms.

Concern has been raised at the possible link between FGM/C and HIV transmission. To date, no concrete evidence for this link exists, and rates of HIV infection in Africa are generally lower in the 28 countries where FGM/C is practiced. This may, however, be due to factors that prevail over the additional risk factor of FGM/C, including cultural and religious attitudes to sexual life. A community-based study in rural Gambia in 1999 identified a significantly higher prevalence of herpes simplex virus II among women who had been subjected to FGM/C, a finding which suggests that these women may also be at increased risk of HIV infection[52].

Some of the early advocacy efforts aimed at stopping FGM/C placed a very strong emphasis on the health consequences of this practice. While these initiatives have been important in raising public awareness of the health risks involved, an overemphasis on the health implications of FGM/C outside the context of a holistic human rights approach, has inadvertently contributed to the phenomena of "medicalization" and "symbolic interventions". Partly as a result of campaigns that have focussed exclusively on the health risks associated with FGM/C, a growing number of parents have preferred to have the operation performed on their daughters in hygienic conditions where pain is minimised and the risk to the girl's health is reduced. Medicalization is also partially supported by those health workers for whom FGM/C represents a source of income[53].

FREEDOM FROM PHYSICAL OR MENTAL VIOLENCE, INJURY OR ABUSE

For many girls and women, FGM/C is an acutely traumatic experience that leaves a lasting psychological mark and may adversely affect their full emotional development. Here too, scientific research is limited, but the anecdotal evidence from girls and women who have undergone the practice is testament to the impact it has had on their lives. Girls are generally conscious when the operation is performed, and for many, it is a shocking experience marked not only by acute pain, but also by fear and confusion. In cases where there has been some preparation for the operation, girls are often expected to suppress such feelings and collaborate in the proceedings. The experience of FGM/C has also been related to a range of psychological and psychosomatic disorders such as disturbances in eating and sleeping habits, moods and cognition. Symptoms of these include sleeplessness, recurring nightmares, loss of appetite, weight loss or excessive weight gain, as well as panic attacks, difficulties in concentrating and learning, and other symptoms of post-traumatic stress[54].

The physical damage resulting from FGM/C, together with the psychological trauma and pain associated with it, can compromise an adult woman's normal sexual life. Moreover, women who have been infibulated may be deinfibulated upon marriage, a process that is a source of both pain and, potentially, further psychological trauma[55]. Marital problems can arise and eventually lead to divorce[56] which, in turn, may jeopardise women's social and economic status and that of their children.

In many cases, women and girls who have been traumatized by FGM/C remain silent about their experience. In some cultures they have no socially acceptable means of expressing their feelings of psychological unease or distress. In cases where they cannot or will not speak openly about a psychosocial difficulty, individual women or girls may present it in terms of a physical complaint. Some evidence of the psychological effects of FGM/C is also emerging among immigrant communities in Europe, America, Australia and New Zealand. Migrant women who have undergone FGM/C often face an additional psychological burden, since both the values associated with FGM/C and its physical and psychological impact are poorly understood in their host country[57].

The practice of FGM/C can compromise other human rights, including the right to education. States Parties to the CRC are required to take measures to promote universal access to quality education, encourage regular attendance at schools and reduce drop-out rates, while promoting the child's development to reach his or her fullest potential. FGM/C is increasingly indicated as a factor in school drop-out rates for girls[58]. The health problems, pain and trauma experienced by girls concerned can lead to absenteeism, poor concentration, low performance and loss of interest. In certain parts of sub-Saharan Africa, such as Kenya and Tanzania, FGM/C is performed on the occasion of ceremonies and rites that require long preparations, making it difficult for girls to follow classes. Moreover, in many cultures girls who undergo the procedure are considered to have become adults ready for marriage and, as a consequence, they may be removed from school. This not only has a serious impact on a girl's personal development, but also on her community, since girls' education and informed participation in social life is a key to reducing discrimination and promoting development and social progress.

STATE OBLIGATIONS

Upon ratification of the CRC and other relevant human rights instruments, States Parties undertake legal obligations to prevent the practice of FGM/C among their citizens and others under their jurisdiction[59]. These measures are relevant and needed at the national and sub-national levels, and call for the involvement and mobilization of a wide range of partners, including community leaders and grassroot organizations; Article 24 (3) of the CRC calls upon States Parties to "take all effective and appropriate measures with a view to abolishing traditional practices prejudicial to the health of children." These measures include promoting awareness-raising and education campaigns, developing mechanisms to protect children from these practices, introducing legislation to prevent them and ensuring the provision of health care and health information[60]

The Committee on the Rights of the Child is mandated to monitor the implementation of the Convention and assess the progress made by States Parties to ensure the realization of children's rights. Upon the examination of States Parties' reports on the implementation of the CRC, the Committee has often expressed concern on FGM/C and issued recommendations to prevent its continuation. In 1995, the Committee held a general discussion about the girl child in the run-up to the Fourth World Conference on Women in Beijing. This discussion emphasised the importance of the promotion and protection of the rights of girls in breaking the cycle of harmful traditions and prejudices against women and drew attention to the importance of education for giving children the necessary confidence and skills to make free choices in their lives.

Like the Committee on the Rights of the Child, the Committee that monitors the 1979 Convention on the Elimination of All Forms of Discrimination Against Women (CEDAW) has made specific reference to the obligations of States Parties with respect to FGM/C. In its 1990 General Recommendation (no. 14), the Committee recommended that States Parties "take appropriate and effective measures with a view to eradicating the practice of female circumcision". The Recommendation also proposes that States Parties "include in their national health policies appropriate strategies aimed at eradicating female circumcision in public health care. Such strategies should include the special responsibility of health personnel, including traditional birth attendants to explain the harmful consequences of female circumcision[61]." More recently, the Committee has issued a General Recommendation on Woman and Health that calls upon States parties to ensure that laws are enacted and enforced to prohibit female genital mutilation.

The 2001 Resolution of the UN General Assembly on traditional or customary practices affecting the health of women and girls reaffirms the obligation of all States to promote and protect human rights and calls upon them *inter alia* to collect and disseminate data regarding FGM/C and other practices, adopt and implement legislation, provide support services for victims, address the training of health workers and other personnel, empower women and strengthen their economic independence, mobilize public opinion, address traditional practices in education curricula, promote men's understanding of their roles and responsibilities and work with communities to prevent the practice[62]

The breadth of the measures proposed in this Resolution indicates that the promotion and protection of human rights must be supported through the commitment of governments. It is their duty to adopt a wide range of measures, including an effective legal framework, as well as to promote awareness raising and education campaigns. The Resolution also indicates that action needs to be taken and sustained at the local level.

Many non-governmental actors have also adopted a human rights framework to address FGM/C. A recent major review of the methods used to sensitize communities to abandon the practice, carried out by the NGO RAINBO, confirms that the human rights approach is especially effective in empowering girls and women, transforming their status and building community consensus[63]. Providing opportunities for all members of local communities to learn about human rights and to participate in discussions on how these rights relate to their own situation is an essential element in the development of a protective environment for children[64] and a key factor in accelerating the societal transformation necessary for the abandonment of FGM/C.

COMMUNITY-BASED ACTIONS

Changing the social convention: from theory to practice

A number of programmes, working at the community level, are protecting girls from FGM/C. The most successful are participatory in nature and generally guide communities to define the problems and solutions themselves. They harness positive village traditions to encourage people to speak out and engage in discussion. They equip families with knowledge on human rights and responsibilities. They encourage communities who have made the decision to abandon the practice to spread their message to their neighbours. All these elements help to bring about the social change needed to protect girls and women from FGM/C.

In Senegal, Tostan, an international NGO specializing in non-formal education, has developed and refined an approach that is based on the promotion of human rights. It embodies key elements necessary to change a social convention at the community level, including collective action, public declaration and organized diffusion. Tostan's Community Empowerment Program is a participatory, non-formal, education programme that lasts 30 months. With the support of UNICEF and in collaboration with the government, it has been implemented in over 1,500 communities in 11 regions of the country.

At the outset of the programme, a community establishes a management committee to coordinate activities and ensure sustainability. This committee develops implements, manages, and evaluates small projects to address community-identified needs, oversees classroom activities and serves as a link between Tostan and the community.

Tostan's education programme typically establishes two classes in each community: one of 25 adults and another of 25 adolescents, mainly women and girls. Programme modules cover democracy and human rights, problem-solving, hygiene and health, literacy, math and management skills. These themes are reinforced using interactive literacy workbooks. The programme is carefully planned to ensure that sessions are inter-related and build upon previous learning. Classroom sessions actively engage participants with little or no formal schooling through a combination of approaches including sharing of personal experiences, the use of written and pictorial materials, theatre, poetry and song. The programme helps develop key skills and promote the reflection necessary for social change. Classes promote consensus and unity through activities that bring together diverse members of the community, including men and women, youth and elders and members of all ethnic groups.

Information and lessons learned are shared with family, friends, relatives, and other communities through a process of organized diffusion. Following a practice that is common in Wolof society, participants in the classes adopt a friend or family member with whom to share programme information. Villages reach out to neighbouring villages – an effort that engages surrounding communities in change at a larger scale.

Tostan's Community Empowerment Program has achieved notable results in the communities in which it has been implemented, including increased enrolment of girls in school, systematic birth registration, and a significant increase in vaccination rates. One of the most significant outcomes has been the grassroots movement for the abandonment of FGM/C, which is spreading across Senegal. The opportunity to understand human rights and explore their direct relevance in the village setting creates confidence, especially among girls and women. It also increases the capacity of the group to tackle more challenging issues and prepares the ground for community members to take the decision to abandon FGM/C. In turn, communities share this information and experience with other intra-marrying groups. Motivated communities host inter-village meetings to reach consensus on abandoning this practice that affects their common future. As of December 2004, these meetings have led to 18 public declarations by 1,527 communities, or approximately 30 per cent of the population estimated to practice FGM/C in Senegal in 1997[65].

Extensive media coverage of these public declarations helps to introduce the alternative of abandonment to communities that continue the practice. It also contributes to creating a supportive environment for change at the national level. Since 1977, the programme has reached some 700,000 people and continues to expand. An independent evaluation of the Tostan Community Empowerment Program, recently completed by the Population Council, compared the knowledge, attitudes and behaviour of women and men living in 20 villages in which Tostan had been active to 20 similar villages in which it had not. The evaluation found that the programme significantly increased women and men's awareness of human rights, gender-based violence, reproductive health and the consequences of FGM/C. There was also a notable decrease in approval of FGM/C among both women and men living in the intervention villages, although 16 per cent of the women who participated in the programme did not change their attitude. Of those women who voiced their disapproval of FGM/C, 85 per cent said that they had come to this position since participating in the Tostan programme. Immediately before the programme began, 7 out of 10 women stated that they wished to have their daughters cut. At the end of the programme, this proportion had fallen to approximately 1 in 10 among women who had participated in the programme, and 2 in 10 among women who had not participated directly, but lived in the same village[66]. MACRO International, the Population Council and UNICEF will support a further study of the social dynamics that lead to positive change in villages covered by the Tostan programme. The study will complement the DHS survey planned for 2005[67].

In Burkino Faso, the NGO Mwangaza Action has adapted and applied the Tostan Community Empowerment Program in 23 villages[68]. Efforts are also currently under way to adapt the approach in Guinea and Sudan. Prior to 2002, the Sudanese Programme for Accelerated Social Transformation (PFAST) had focused on providing information about the health consequences of FGM/C and on disassociating the practice from Islam. As it became apparent that this alone was insufficient to promote the abandonment of FGM/C, the programme began to shift its focus to the empowerment of women and the promotion and safeguard of human rights. There is evidence that this shift has initiated a process of change: reformers and resisters of FGM/C have appeared in the selected communities, suggesting that a social dynamic has been set in motion; traditional beliefs about honour, shame, virginity and marriageability are being debated; and there are indications that many community members, including leaders, are questioning their deeply-held convictions and exploring alternative behaviour. Operating primarily in the states of Kassala, West Kordofan, South Darfur and Al

Gadarif, PFAST covers some 120 selected communities, representing a population of approximately 6,000,000. It is creating a social environment in which people can respond to the messages about the consequences of FGM/C that they have received in recent years.

Activities carried out by the Coptic Evangelical Organization for Social Services (CEOSS) and the Centre for Education, Development and Population Activities (CEDPA) in Egypt also point to the effectiveness of a holistic, human rights-based approach that enables communities to discuss and subsequently abandon FGM/C.

CEOSS strategies – the result of more than 50 years of experience – place particular emphasis on improving the status of women and identifying patterns of effective partnerships with male and female community leaders; Village-level activities support a variety of development projects aimed at empowering communities and individuals in all aspects of life including education, health, income-generation, agriculture and environmental protection. Specific activities promoting the abandonment of FGM/C include: establishing local women's committees; raising awareness of harmful traditional practices; providing training to local community members, teachers, health workers and the media; making home visits to families with girls who are identified as being at risk of undergoing the practice; and supporting the establishment of local NGOs to ensure both relevancy and a sense of community ownership[69].

The experience in the village of Deir el Barsha, in the governorate of Minya in Upper Egypt, demonstrates that change is possible. An external evaluation conducted in 1997-8[70] found a clear change in both attitudes and behaviour towards FGM/C in the village, with the proportion of uncut girls reaching 50 per cent (DHS indicates that national prevalence in Egypt in 1995 was 97 per cent). According to the evaluation, a number of factors contributed to this result including: gender-based development activities carried out in the village over more than two decades; temporary male labour migration abroad that permitted women more decision-making power in the community[71]; and the role played by the clerical order in providing information on FGM/C and socializing people against the practice[72]. In 1991, after nearly a decade of CEOSS activity directed at FGM/C, traditional practitioners, including barbers and midwives, publicly signed a document in which they pledged to abandon the practice.

Also in Egypt, the experience of CEDPA points to the importance of providing support to those members of the community who have already chosen to abandon the practice of FGM/C. This support both reinforces their decision and enables them to initiate discussions on the issue with others. CEDPA has been engaged in promoting the abandonment of FGM/C since 1988, using the "Positive Deviance Approach". Its FGM Abandonment Program is based on participatory community mobilization, relies on local knowledge and aims to build on solutions that already exist within communities. It identifies community members who have chosen to oppose the practice of FGM/C and supports these individuals to recruit others to this position. Internal assessments have indicated that this is potentially an effective strategy and have encouraged CEDPA to undertake a systematic scaling-up of the programme[73]. However, the longer term impact of the approach in the promotion of behaviour change still needs to be evaluated.

In partnership with CEDPA, UNICEF supports nongovernmental organizations that have organized peer educators and advocates in four governorates of Upper Egypt (Assiut, Sohag, Quena and Minya) and who, with the assistance of religious leaders, lead discussion groups and make house-to-house visits to raise awareness within communities[74]. These peer educators, which include women and men of different backgrounds and ages, demonstrate a high level of commitment and also have extensive reach within the community. The potential of these individuals to engage their neighbours on the subject of FGM/C is enhanced by their deep understanding of the internal dynamics of their communities and the trust they enjoy among fellow villagers. As with other programmes that have demonstrated success, the approach adopted is both respectful and non-judgmental. When interviewed, peer educators emphasised the importance of offering information on FGM/C in a non-directive manner.

By providing support to those who have chosen to abandon FGM/C and promoting community-based discussions, CEOSS and CEDPA initiatives have contributed to changes in attitude and behaviour toward FGM/C. Replication of the approaches to additional villages, however, has been limited.

FACILITATING DIALOGUE AND NON-JUDGMENTAL DISCUSSION

Creating appropriate spaces and opportunities in the community for discussion – spaces in which individuals feel safe and confident to share their views – enables community members to be active agents who control their own development rather than passive recipients of communication messages. They also provide an opportunity to those who would normally be voiceless to express their opinions. In the case of FGM/C this is often women and girls themselves, but it may also include men who do not always have the opportunity to discuss this issue.

Through non-judgmental, non-directive public discussion and reflection, the previously hidden costs of FGM/C tend to emerge, as women and men share their own experiences and those of their daughters. At the same time, individuals wanting to end the practice join hands with others similarly committed, and spread the message to other members of the community.

The German Agency for Technical Cooperation (GTZ) has applied these principles to the issue of FGM/C in Guinea through its "listening and dialogue approach". The organizers of this project suggest that it turned out to be their most effective intervention. The opportunity to express views in a respectful and non-judgmental setting enabled women and men to share their ambivalences regarding the practice of FGM/C and introduced a new discourse and behavioural options for the community. This approach to communication is also sensitive to the use of images and messages that communities may perceive to be inappropriate and in some cases offensive. The experience of GTZ in the Kolda region of Senegal illustrates the importance of using a non judgmental and respectful approach that stimulates discussion and reflection.

ALTERNATIVE RITES OF PASSAGE

In contexts where the practice of FGM/C is associated with initiation rites or coming of age ceremonies that mark transition to adulthood, such as in certain communities in Gambia, Kenya, Tanzania and Uganda, action has often focused on developing alternative rites of passage. These alternative rites preserve the positive socio-cultural aspects of the ritual, but do not require girls to undergo FGM/C. The potential of this strategy is limited to communities that associate FGM/C with such rites or ceremonies. It is further limited by the trend among many of these communities towards cutting girls at a younger age and with less associated ritual[75].

Alternative rites have enjoyed varying degrees of success in promoting the abandonment of FGM/C. In isolation, they have limited impact since they do not address the underlying social values associated with FGM/C and therefore, provide little assurance that a girl will not be cut at a later date. However, as indicated by the experience of Maendeleo Ya Wanawake (MYWO), a Kenyan women's organisation, alternative ceremonies are well received and contribute to a reduction in the incidence of FGM/C when they are accompanied by community awareness and discussion[76]. MYWO, with technical assistance from the Program for Appropriate Technology in Health, has developed a programme that begins with community-level awareness raising activities to recruit participants, introduces family life education for girls, and culminates in a public event modelled on a community's traditional ceremony to mark the passage to adulthood. The education component builds on the traditional knowledge imparted to girls prior to these ceremonies, often during a period of seclusion, and is enhanced with additional information on sexual and reproductive health.

According to a study carried out by the Population Council in 2000[77], the work of MYWO had an impact on both attitudes and behaviour associated with FGM/C. It was found to be more effective, however, when other institutions and socio-cultural developments contributed to changing attitudes toward FGM/C and when the groundwork was laid through awareness-raising activities. It is too early to know whether this initial success can be sustained over time and what kinds of rituals work best[78]

ALTERNATIVE EMPLOYMENT OPPORTUNITIES FOR TRADITIONAL EXCISERS

In a number of countries, including Burkina Faso, Ethiopia, Gambia, Kenya, Mali, Sudan and, Uganda, there have been initiatives to educate those who perform FGM/C about the health risks associated with the practice and to provide them with opportunities for alternative income. Projects usually combine education on the harmful effects of FGM/C with the development of new skills and provision of loans or other incentives to find an alternative source of livelihood. In some cases, this training is followed by a public or private ceremony, which may involve the excisers denouncing the practice and symbolically surrendering their instruments or making an oath on the Koran to stop their activities. Although these initiatives have succeeded in supporting cutters in ending their involvement in the practice, they do not change the social convention that creates the demand for their services, and families continue to seek out individuals who are willing to perform the practice.16 Providing opportunities for alternative income for excisers may complement approaches that address demand for the practice, but alone it does not have the elements necessary to end FGM/C.

WORKING WITH MIGRANT COMMUNITIES IN INDUSTRIALISED COUNTRIES

The fact that many migrant communities continue to practice FGM/C in their new countries of residence is evidence of the strength of social convention. The key elements necessary to address the issue among migrant communities in countries where FGM/C is not traditionally practiced are essentially the same as those in countries with higher prevalence.

"Due to our migration and the passing of time, we have come to think differently, and we now see the harm caused by our tradition. However, our parents could not have acted otherwise and it is out of the question to suggest any kind of abuse. They wanted the best for us, their children. After all, we all looked forward to the day we were able to announce in the school playground that we had been circumcised too.

We are now able to express the sadness and pain in our history and that the genital mutilation of girls is no longer appropriate in this day and age. We want to give our daughters a happy future, a future in which they can fully develop emotionally, and a future in which they can be allowed to play and feel protected." Somali woman, Netherlands

The work of Pharos, an NGO active in the field of health care for refugees, and the Federation of Somali Associations in the Netherlands illustrates the importance of adopting a respectful and culturally sensitive approach, working with groups rather than individuals, facilitating discussion and raising awareness rather than imposing solutions, and investing the time necessary for communities to reach their own decisions regarding the practice.

FGM/C first became a major issue in the Netherlands during the 1990s with the arrival of women refugees from Somalia. Although the practice was prohibited under general criminal injury law in 1993, girls continue to be subjected to the procedure. In 2000, with funding from the Ministry of Health, Welfare and Sport, Pharos and the Federation of Somali Associations established a collaborative project with the aims of empowering the Somali community to discuss FGM/C and of promoting expertise in FGM/C in the health sector.

Recognizing that dialogue within a community on FGM/C must be lead by the community itself, project partners established tailored educational sessions, led by trained "educators" and "key figures" drawn from Somali communities. These are individuals who enjoy the trust and respect of their own communities, who can facilitate discussion, and who are familiar with Dutch institutions. Most of the sessions are held on weekends, when participants have free time. Sometimes men, women and youth meet separately: men may meet in mosques after Friday prayers, while women may meet in community centres or at their homes in the evening. One of the important achievements of the project to date, however, has been a series of meetings in which women and men have come together to discuss the issue. These sessions have served as a catalyst for more widespread discussion of FGM/C in the community. At the same time, the sessions have demonstrated that there are still many Somali parents who intend to have their daughters cut. The most recent assessment of the project emphasizes that awareness of the issue is increasing, but that continuity is necessary to achieve behavioural change[79].

Among migrant groups, the convention of cutting girls is often reinforced by the social and cultural link the practice establishes with their communities of origin. A recent development of the Tostan programme, discussed at the start of this section, has the potential to use these same links as a means to reach and influence practicing groups in industrialised countries. In May 2005, representatives from 44 villages in the Kolda region of Senegal gathered in the village of Marahkissa to make a public declaration of their communal decision to abandon the practices of FGM/C and child marriage. This decision had been reached after a period of meetings and discussions not only among participating villages, but also with wider kinship networks in the main cities of Senegal and, significantly, in the Gambia and USA. Delegations from these countries attended the declaration, the first to directly involve emigrant relatives in the decision to abandon FGM/C. The declaration was an opportunity for migrant members of Diola communities to affirm their rejection of FGM/C while reinforcing positive aspects of their culture:

> "It is a wonderful day for all of us Diolas living in the United States. We now can send our daughters home to the village during vacation so they can know their family and our positive Diola traditions without worrying that they will undergo this cutting practice."
> (Son of the Village Chief, Houston, USA)

REATING AN ENABLING ENVIRONMENT FOR CHANGE

Communities need support if they are to abandon FGM/C on a large scale. National governments must create a protective environment for women and children and support abandonment of the practice through social measures and appropriate legislation. Advocacy and awareness-raising activities, involving media and opinion leaders, also play an important role in increasing local, national and international level commitment.

NATIONAL LEGISLATION

Introducing national legislation that prohibits FGM/C can accelerate change most effectively when a process of societal change is already under way, and citizens are sensitized to the issue[80]. Legislation has at least three clear purposes: to make explicit a State's disapproval of FGM/C; to send out a clear message of support to those who have renounced, or would wish to renounce the practice; and to act as a deterrent to the practice. It is important that legislation introduce or be complemented by appropriate child protection measures, comprehensive social support mechanisms, and information and awareness-raising campaigns, which are dissuasive rather than punitive. Imposing sanctions alone runs the risk of driving the practice underground and having a very limited impact on behaviour change.

In Africa and the Middle East, a large number of countries have introduced specific legislation to address FGM/C, by statute or decree. These include Benin (2003), Burkina Faso (1996), Central African Republic (1966[81]), Côte d'Ivoire (1998), Djibouti (1995), Egypt (1996), Ghana (1994), Guinea (1965, updated 2002), Kenya (2001), Niger (2003), Senegal (1999), Tanzania (1998) and Togo (1998). In some cases, the practice is forbidden under the national Constitution. For example, in Ethiopia, the 1994 Constitution explicitly prohibits harmful traditional practices, including those that oppress women and cause them physical or mental harm. The Constitutions of Ghana, Guinea and Uganda contain similar prohibitions. In a number of other countries, including Chad, Mali and Niger, FGM/C is addressed as an injury, in the context of criminal law.

A study of national laws published in 2000 found that of the 28 countries of Africa and the Middle East where FGM/C is practiced, prosecutions had been brought in only four: Burkina Faso, Egypt, Ghana and Senegal[82]. In Burkina Faso, the first detention of an *exciseuse* followed soon after the introduction of legislation in 1996. The national law stipulates a prison sentence of six months to three years and/or a fine between the equivalent of $US300 and $US1850[83] for anyone found guilty of performing FGM/C. Higher penalties applies where the procedure results in death, and there are special measures against medical or paramedical staff who perform the operation. The law also introduces fines for anyone who, aware that FGM/C is taking place, fails to inform the authorities. In Burkina Faso, the law is one component of a broader approach that includes awareness raising initiatives and social support. The 1999 DHS survey of Burkina Faso provides evidence of positive attitudinal change. The survey found that only 23.8 per cent of circumcised women claimed that they wished FGM/C to continue, while 63.7 per cent wanted the practice to end. These responses may reflect a reluctance to give explicit support to an outlawed practice, rather than a personal conviction that FGM/C should end.

Laws prohibiting FGM/C have also been introduced in a number of countries where the issue has arisen among immigrant communities including Australia (various states 1994-6), Canada (1997), New Zealand (1995), USA (1996) and several countries in Western Europe. While acknowledging the significance of national legislation, it is also important to recognize its limitations. In some cases, loopholes may remain which can be exploited by those who seek to perpetuate FGM/C. In Egypt in 1996, the Ministry of Health issued a decree prohibiting FGM/C, except when it was required for medical purposes. Despite a subsequent ruling by the Egyptian High Court in 1997 confirming that the practice was prohibited, the exception regarding medical grounds remained. Effectively, this clause has provided a loophole which, together with strong advocacy messages on the potential health risks of FGM/C, has contributed to the rapid medicalization of the practice.

REGIONAL STANDARDS

Developing and adopting international legal instruments is also important for creating an enabling environment that can lead to support efforts and to the abandonment of the practice. The Protocol to the 1981 African Charter on Human and Peoples' Rights on the Rights of Women in Africa, known as the Maputo Protocol, is a legal document adopted by consensus in 2003 by Heads of States of the African Union. Article 5 of this Protocol explicitly prohibits and condemns FGM/C and other harmful practices. It calls upon States Parties to take measures to create public awareness of the issue, introduce legislation to prohibit and sanction the practice of FGM/C, provide support for victims of harmful practices and protect women who are at risk of these practices. For the Protocol to enter into force, it must be ratified by 15 Member States of the African Union. By April 2005, it had been ratified by 10 states[84].

In Europe, significant developments have also taken place and supported the process of change in countries concerned. Resolution 1247 of the Parliamentary Assembly of the Council of Europe (2001) on Female Genital Mutilation urges governments to take a range of actions, including the introduction of national legislation, the promotion of awareness raising, the prosecution of those who perpetrate FGM/C and the adoption of more flexible measures regarding the granting of asylum to mothers and their children who fear being subjected to FGM/C[85]. The European Parliament Resolution on Female Genital Mutilation, also dating from 2001, strongly condemns FGM/C as a violation of fundamental human rights and inter alia calls upon the European Commission to draw up a complete strategy to eliminate the practice of FGM/C in the European Union which should "establish both legal and administrative and also preventive, educational and social mechanisms to enable women who are or are likely to be victims to obtain real protection"[86].

Major international conferences have supported governments in their efforts to introduce appropriate national legislation and social mobilization initiatives on FGM/C. In June 2003, the Afro-Arab Expert Consultation on Legal Tools for the Prevention of Female Genital Mutilation served to define both legal content and strategies for more effective legislation to prevent FGM/C[87]. The resulting "Cairo Declaration" makes 17 concrete recommendations, including that government adopt specific legislation addressing FGM/C, and that these laws be one component of a multi-disciplinary approach to stopping the practice. The declaration also recommends that governments and NGOs work together to support an ongoing process of social change leading to the adoption of legislation against FGM/C.

In September 2004, the Government of Kenya hosted an international conference, which focused on developing a political, legal and social environment for the implementation of the Maputo Protocol. In February 2005, a sub-regional conference hosted by the Government of Djibouti, organized by the NGO *No Peace without Justice* and supported by UNICEF, provided a platform for Djibouti's official ratification of the Maputo Protocol. Further conferences around the Maputo Protocol are planned for 2005.

RAISING AWARENESS AND PROMOTING DIALOGUE

Legislative measures are most effective when complemented and even preceded by a range of broader policy measures, involving both general and focused awareness raising and the promotion of dialogue within and among different groups. If the introduction of a law is poorly timed (prior to a shift in social attitudes towards the practice, for example) or is not accompanied by complementary social support mechanisms, it may drive the practice of FGM/C underground or encourage cross-border movement. The threat of imprisonment or a fine may act as a deterrent, but alone it does little to change parents' perception that it is in the interest of their daughters to undergo this procedure.

The media can play an important role in "breaking the silence" around FGM/C and bringing the issue into the public realm. The experience of the Tanzanian Media Women Association (TAMWA) indicates that providing media with accurate, up-to-date information regarding FGM/C and strengthening media operators' skills to disseminate this information can contribute to the abandonment of the practice. This experience is consistent with the findings of a UNICEF-commissioned study in Egypt which noted that lack of knowledge of FGM/C is a major obstacle preventing many media professionals from discussing the issue.

The involvement of opinion leaders, including traditional leaders, political figures, religious chiefs and intellectuals has had an important role in raising awareness and stimulating public debate. In Senegal, parliamentarians have not only been instrumental in passing legislation to prevent harmful traditional practices, they have also actively promoted its application by visiting villages in the process of abandonment and explaining the legal situation during inter-village meetings. They regularly attend public declarations and have established a partnership with other West African parliamentarians to collaborate on promoting successful strategies. At the international level, the Inter-Parliamentary Union (IPU) decided in 2001 to develop an online database on FGM/C accessible from its own website14 and to establish a parliamentary think tank for the eradication of FGM/C. When this panel met for the first time in Marrakech, Morocco in 2002, it identified key strategies for ending FGM/C, including public awareness campaigns, the provision of economic support to campaigns, the development of campaigns in partnership with NGOs, the introduction of legislation, and mobilisation of the media[88]

In communities where there is a strong perception that the practice of FGM/C is required by Islam, the engagement of religious leaders in public discussion has proven to be an essential element in raising awareness of this practice, disassociating it from religious considerations and creating an enabling environment for change. The sub-regional conference on FGM/C, hosted by the Government of Djibouti in February 2005, was notable for the two-day debate among religious leaders from Djibouti and neighbouring countries on the theological dimensions of FGM/C. Following an important debate, the outcome document, the Djibouti Declaration, asserts that claims that the Koran requires FGM/C are baseless and reaffirms that all types of FGM/C are contrary to the religious precepts of Islam.

INTEGRATING THE ABANDONMENT OF FGM/C IN GOVERNMENT PROGRAMMES

Creating an enabling environment to support the abandonment of FGM/C requires a strong commitment and policy action on the part of governments to promote equal rights for girls and boys and for women and men. It also entails addressing FGM/C as a component of development programmes and projects that promote poverty eradication, income generation and education, as well as gender equality, girls' and women's participation in society and the labour force, girls' and women's health, safe motherhood, and HIV/AIDS prevention.

A variety of professional staff are in contact with girls and women who have undergone FGM/C. In Switzerland, for example, a survey undertaken by the Swiss National Committee for UNICEF in collaboration with the Institute of Social and Preventive Medicine of the University of Berne[89] showed that 61 per cent of gynaecologists[90], 38 per cent of midwives, 6.3 per cent of paediatricians, and 8 per cent of welfare centres surveyed were confronted with FGM/C victims. The survey also revealed a considerable need for information. All of the surveyed professions called for integrating the issue into their initial or continued training.

Health personnel constitute an important group for the management of FGM/C related complications as well as for the promotion of its abandonment. WHO, UNICEF and UNFPA have recognized the critical role of health workers and have identified their training in FGM/C related issues as a priority strategy[91]. The antenatal period in particular, constitutes a timely opportunity to provide information to women and other family members about the health consequences of the practice[92]. In Sweden, health care professionals are advised that discussions regarding FGM/C should start at the time a new baby considered to be at risk is enrolled with the health services. It is recommended that the issue be raised again at the standard check-up after the child turns five. Health care workers are expected to advise parents of the health risks of FGM/C and inform them that the practice is prohibited under Swedish law[93]. In many countries, including Canada, Denmark, Germany, Italy, Switzerland and the United Kingdom, medical associations have forbidden any involvement of doctors in the practice of FGM/C on the grounds that it is a violation of their code of conduct.

Teachers, in both formal and non-formal learning contexts, can be supported to recognize girls at risk and discuss FGM/C related issues in science, biology and hygiene lessons, as well as in lessons involving personal, social, gender or religious education. Nurses, midwives and doctors can facilitate and assist teachers in these activities[94]. At times, the first to move in this direction are NGOs. FAWE Senegal, a NGO working to improve girls' access to education, has developed reference manuals and guides on FGM/C for teachers and students of third and fourth grade and has also provided training on FGM/C to trainers and teachers[95]. To strengthen national capacities, the Italian N GO AIDOS, with financing from the World Bank, has developed a prototype training manual for integrating FGM/C in development projects[96]. This manual is intended for trainers working with government officials and NGO staff. Local versions of the manual will be produced to ensure its most effective use.

COORDINATING ACTIONS

A number of countries including Burkina Faso, Egypt, Norway, Senegal, Sudan and Tanzania, have established national plans of action to coordinate and support the efforts of both government and non-governmental organizations in promoting the abandonment of FGM/C. In Sudan, the National Plan of Action on FGM/C, endorsed by the Ministry of Health in 2001, has promoted the establishment of mechanisms at all levels to end FGM/C. At the federal level, a steering committee ensures coordination among government departments, networks of NGOs and civil society groups. At the state level, there are councils and steering committees for FGM/C, while at the community level, community-based organizations bring together women's groups, religious leaders, midwives, community leaders, as well as children and youth to promote behavioural change. Media campaigns are promoted at the federal and state levels, while at the community level, radio programmes featuring key community members are broadcast in local languages.

The development of specific governmental institutions or coordinating mechanisms charged with carrying out activities to promote the abandonment of FGM/C, including in the broader context of a holistic child rights agenda, can facilitate the task of translating plans into concerted action. In Egypt for instance, this role is fulfilled by the National Council for Childhood and Motherhood with the support of UNDP and UNICEF. The Council is the highest national body entrusted with childhood issues and establishes policy, drafts legislation and mainstreams childhood and motherhood development in the five year state plans. It supports action at community level, promotes a national dialogue on FGM/C, as well as legal and policy reform. In recent years, there has been significant progress at the global level towards achieving a common framework for action to promote the abandonment of FGM/C. The stronger sense of common purpose is driven in part by the shared challenge of working toward the Millennium Development Goals. The 2001 "Road Map towards the Implementation of the United Nations Millennium Declaration" makes specific reference to "harmful traditional practices, such as female genital mutilation" under the goal of combating all forms of violence against women[97]. At the same time, *A World Fit for Children*, the outcome document endorsed by the 2002 UN General Assembly Special Session on Children, specifically calls for an end to such practices. More broadly, both the Millennium Development Goals and *A World Fit for Children* aim to achieve universal primary education for girls and boys. Education is one of the best means to overcome discrimination, empower girls and women and build societies founded on human rights principles. Concretely, it is becoming apparent that girls who have received some level of education are less likely to have their own daughters cut than women with little or no education.

United Nations Agencies are also increasingly coordinating policies and actions with bilateral donors. Since 2001, the Donor's Working Group on Female Genital Cutting, comprised of UN Agencies, the World Bank, governments and foundations, has met regularly to share strategies and increase their effectiveness as donors[98].

The NGO community plays a central role in generating national and international commitment to end the practice of FGM/C. At a regional level, the Inter-African Committee on traditional practices affecting the health of women and children (IAC) is the oldest NGO network dedicated to the abandonment of FGM/C in Africa. It works through National Committees in all African countries where FGM/C is practiced and promotes awareness raising and advocacy, evaluation of relevant laws and programmes, training and capacity building. Beyond Africa, the European Network for the prevention of FGM (Euronet-FGM) aims to improve the health of female immigrants in Europe and prevent harmful traditional practices affecting the health of women and children, in particular FGM/C.

The STOP FGM Campaign builds and reinforces public opinion to abandon FGM/C in African as well as European countries and stimulates action at national and international levels. The Campaign, established in 2002, is coordinated by the Italian NGO AIDOS in collaboration with *No Peace without Justice* and various African NGOs. In recent years, momentum to end FGM/C has been growing, and new actors, including the Governments of Italy[99] and Japan[100], are providing strong support to advance this agenda. Given the greater understanding of FGM/C and the encouraging indications that positive results at community level are possible on a large scale, conditions are ripe for the accelerated abandonment of the practice.

CONCLUSION

Female genital mutilation/cutting has been perpetuated over generations by social dynamics that make it very difficult for individual families as well as individual girls and women to abandon the practice. Even when families are aware of the harm it can bring, they continue to have their daughters cut because it is deemed necessary by their community for bringing up a girl correctly, protecting her honour and maintaining the status of the entire family. Not conforming to the tradition brings shame and stigmatization upon the entire family and prevents girls from becoming full and recognised members of their community. This chapter demonstrates that change is possible. Societal attitudes do shift and communities are making the choice to abandon this harmful practice. The elements needed to transform communities have become increasingly clear.

The most successful approaches guide communities to define the problems and solutions themselves to ensure that they do not feel coerced or judged. They also encourage communities who have made the decision to abandon the practice to publicly declare their choice and spread their message to their neighbours. Approaches that are based on the principles of human rights have demonstrated the greatest potential for promoting the abandonment of FGM/C. Rather than addressing FGM/C in isolation, they focus on building the capacity of people, and especially of girls and women, to promote and safeguard their own human rights. Finally, communities need support if they are to abandon FGM/C on a large scale. They need the engagement of traditional and religious leaders, legislative and policy measures, fora for public debate, and accurate and culturally sensitive media messages.

The time is right to catalyze a global movement for positive and lasting change. CEDAW and the CRC represent important international standards to shape States' policies and programmes to address and promote the abandonment of FGM/C and other harmful traditional practices. Regional initiatives are building on a growing momentum to end the practice. In Africa, ratification of the Maputo Protocol to the African Charter on Human and Peoples' Rights reaffirm States' commitment to promoting and protecting the human rights of women and children. Ending FGM/C is an ever-growing reality. The basic knowledge of how best to support communities to end FGM/C exists today. It can be applied widely, within and across countries. With global support, it is conceivable that FGM/C can be abandoned in practicing communities within a single generation.

NOTES

1. Shell-Duncan, Bettina and Ylva Hernlund, Eds, (2000), *Female "Circumcision" in Africa: Culture, Controversy and Change*, Lynne Rienner Publisher, London. WHO also offers a definition of FGM/C, however this is under revision at the time of writing. See WHO/UNFPA/UNICEF (1997), *Female genital mutilation. A Joint WHO/UNICEF/UNFPA statement*, World Health Organization, Geneva

2. Yoder, P. Stanley, Noureddine Abderrahim and Arlinda Zhuzhuni, *Female Genital Cutting in the Demographic and Health Surveys: A Critical and Comparative Analysis*, DHS Comparative Reports No. 7, September 2004, ORC Macro.

3. Reynolds SJ, Sheperd ME, Risbud AR, Gangakhedkar RR, Brookmeyer RS, Divekar AD, Mehendale SM, Bollinger RC (2004) "Male circumcision and risk of HIV-1 and other sexually transmitted infections in India", *The Lancet*, Mar 27, 2004; 363(9414); 1039-40.

4. Shell-Duncan, Bettina and Ylva Hernlund, Eds, (2000), *Female "Circumcision" in Africa: Culture, Controversy and Change*, Lynne Rienner Publisher, London.

5. "Third report on the situation regarding the elimination of traditional practices affecting the health of women and the girl child, produced by Mrs. Halima Embarek Warzazi pursuant to Sub-Commission resolution 1998/16", Commission on Human Rights, Sub-Commission on Prevention of Discrimination and Protection of Minorities, E/CN.4/Sub.2/1999/14, 9 July 1999.

6. *Prevalence of FGM/C by age cohorts 15-49.* This is the most important indicator. Age cohorts are 15- 19, 20-24, 25-29, 30-34, 35-39, 40-44 and 45-49.
7. *FGM/C status of all daughters.* This indicator refers to FGM/C prevalence for all daughters of mothers aged 15 to 49 years. It is recommended to collect data on the current age of daughters as well as on the age at which they were cut.
8. *Percentage of "closed" FGM/C (infibulation, sealing) and "open" FGM/C (excision).* This simplified category is introduced to help overcome the difficulty of identifying the specific type of FGM/C a woman or her daughter has undergone.
9. See, for example, WHO (2000), *Female Genital Mutilation.* Fact sheet no. 241, World Health Organization, Geneva.
10. Demographic and Health Survey, Niger, 1998: Women aged 15-49, and Demographic and Health Survey, Guinea, 1999: Women aged 15-49.
11. Provisional 2004 DHS data indicates a prevalence of approximately 1% in Cameroon.
12. Yoder, P. Stanley, Noureddine Abderrahim and Arlinda Zhuzhuni, *Female Genital Cutting in the Demographic and Health Surveys: A Critical and Comparative Analysis,* *13 DHS Comparative Reports No. 7, September 2004, ORC Macro. See also UNICEF (2004), *The State of the World's Children 2005,* The United Nations Children's Fund, New York,
13. For a more detailed discussion of the issues introduced in this section, see Yoder, P. Stanley, Noureddine Abderrahim and Arlinda Zhuzhuni, *Female Genital Cutting in the Demographic and Health Surveys: a Critical and ComparativeAnalysis,* DHS Comparative Reports No. 7, September 2004, ORC Macro.
14. All data from Multiple Indicator Cluster Survey 2, Central African Republic, 2000.
15. Yoder, P. Stanley, Noureddine Abderrahim and Arlinda Zhuzhuni, *Female Genital Cutting in the Demographic and Health Surveys: A Critical and Comparative Analysis,* DHS Comparative Reports No. 7, September 2004, ORC Macro. Considering the education level of a woman who has been cut is not helpful, since cutting nearly always takes place before a girls' education is complete, and in some cases, even before it begins.
16. Demographic and Health Survey, Egypt, 1995 and 2000.
17. Demographic and Health Survey, Ethiopia, 2000; Mali, 2001; Mauritania, 2000-01.
18. Bayoumi, Ahmed (2003), *Baseline Survey on FGM Prevalence and Cohort Group Assembly in Three CFCI Focus States,* UNICEF Sudan Country Office, Khartoum.
19. Excision of the prepuce, with or without excision of part or all of the clitoris. This refers to the original WHO classification, currently under review.
20. Demographic and Health Survey, Burkina Faso, 1998-99.
21. Surveys were conducted in northern Sudan.
22. Surveys were conducted in northern Sudan.
23. Surveys were conducted in northern Sudan.
24. Yoder, P. Stanley, Noureddine Abderrahim and Arlinda Zhuzhuni, *Female Genital Cutting in the Demographic and Health Surveys: A Critical and Comparative Analysis,* DHS Comparative Reports No. 7, September 2004, ORC Macro.
25. UNICEF (2004), "UNICEF Global Consultation on Indicators, November 11 - 13, 2004, NYHQ. Child Protection Indicators Framework. Female Genital Mutilation and Cutting", New York, USA, 12 July, 2004 revision.

26 Gruenbaum, Ellen (2001), *The Female Circumcision Controversy: An anthropological perspective*, University of Pennsylvania Press, Philadelphia.

27 Yoder, P. Stanley, Papa Ousmane Camara, and Baba Soumaoro (1999), *Female genital cutting and coming of age in Guinea*, Macro International Inc., Calverton, MD.

28 A number of observers have noted the power of peer pressure on girls and young women as regards FGM/C. See chapters 7, 9, 12 and 14 of Shell-Duncan, Bettina and Ylva Hernlund, [Eds.] (2000), *Female "Circumcision" in Africa: Culture, Controversy and Change*, Lynne Rienner Publisher, London.

29 Carr, Dara (1997), *Female Genital Cutting: Findings form the Demographic and Health Surveys Program*, Macro International Inc, Calverton MD.

30 For more on the social convention of FGM/C, see Mackie, Gerry (1996), "Ending Footbinding and Infibulation: A Convention Account", *American Sociological Review*, vol. 61, no. 6, December 1996.

31 For example, the Taguana from Côte d'Ivoire are among a number of groups who believe that women who have not undergone the procedure are unable to have children, see Dorkenoo, Efua and Scilla Elworthy (1992), *Female genital mutilation: proposals for change*, London, Series: MRG report ; no. 92/3. In some communities it is said that a woman's external genitalia have the power to blind anyone attending her during childbirth or to cause the death of her newborn if the child's head touches the mother's clitoris during delivery. Others believe that a woman who has not been cut may become physically deformed/mad, or may cause the death of her husband. See WHO (2001), *FGM. Integrating the Prevention and Management of the Health Complications into the Curricula of Nursing and Midwifery. A Teacher's Guide*, World Health Organisation, Geneva.

32 Bradford, Quiana and Kimberly Mc Clure (2003), "Qualitative Analysis of the Role of Human Rights Language in Efforts to Stop Female Genital Mutilation (FGM) in Egypt", policy analysis exercise for the Population Council, Office of West Asia and North Africa, Cairo, Egypt and The Carr Center for Human Rights Policy, John F. Kennedy School of Government, Harvard University.

33 Gachiri, Ephigenia W. (2000), *Female Circumcision. With reference to the Agikuyo of Kenya*, Paulines Publication, Nairobi.

34 Information provided by Ananilea Nkya, director of the Tanzanian Media Women's Association, 21 June 2004.

35 Dorkenoo, Efua and Scilla Elworthy (1992), *Female genital mutilation: proposals for change*, London, Series: MRG report; no. 92/3.

36 Carla Pasquinelli (2004), "Anthropology of Female Genital Mutilation" in Legal Tools for the Prevention of Female Genital Mutilation, proceedings of the Afro-Arab expert consultation, Cairo, Egypt, 21-23 June 2003 Non c'è pace senza giustizia, special supplement to periodical 1/2004. For further discussion of FGM/C and Islamic theology see, for example, Johnsdotter, S. (2003), "Somali Woman in Western Exile: Reassessing Female Circumcision in the Light of Islamic Teachings", Journal of Muslim Minority Affairs, vol. 23, no. 2, October 2003.

37 Mackie, Gerry (2000), "Female Genital Cutting: the Beginning of the End" in Shell-Duncan, Bettina and Ylva Hernlund, [Eds.] (2000), *Female "Circumcision" in Africa: Culture, Controversy and Change*, Lynne Rienner Publisher, London.

38 Only two countries are not yet party to the CRC – Somalia and the United States of America.
39 In addition to the CRC and CEDAW, a range of other important human rights instruments contain articles relevant to FGM/C. International instruments include the 1948 Universal Declaration of Human Rights (articles 2 and 3), the 1966 International Covenant on Civil and Political Rights (articles 7 and 24) and the 1966 International Covenant on Economic, Social and Cultural Rights (article 12). The UN Committee on Economic, Social and Cultural Rights has stated in its general comments on the right to health (article 12) that it is important to undertake action to protect women and children from the impact of harmful traditional practices that affect their health.
40 The principle of the child's best interests is established under article 3 of the CRC.
41 See, for example, Wheeler, Patricia (2003), "Eliminating FGM: The role of the law", *The International Journal of Children's Rights*, 11, 2003, pp. 257-71.
42 WHO (1999) *Female genital mutilation - Programmes to date: What works and what doesn't - A review*, World Health Organization, Geneva.
43 For a fuller discussion of meaningful consent in the context of FGM/C, see Mackie, Gerry (2004), "Ending Harmful Conventions: Liberal Responses to Female Genital Cutting", prepared for Yale University Political Science Department.
44 For a fuller review of health complications deriving from FGM/C see: World Health Organization (2000), "A Systematic review of the Health complications of Female Genital Mutilation including Sequelae in Childbirth", WHO, Geneva.
45 WHO (2000), *Female Genital Mutilation*, Fact sheet no. 241, World Health Organization, Geneva.
46 WHO (2001), "Management of pregnancy, childbirth and the postpartum period in the presence of female genital mutilation", report of WHO Technical Consultation, Geneva, 15-17 October 1997.
47 WHO (1996), *Female Genital Mutilation: Information Pack*, World Health Organization, Geneva.
48 Obermeyer, C. (1999), "Female genital surgeries: The known, the unknown, and the unknowable", *Medical Anthropology Quarterly*, 13(1), cited in Jaldesa, Guyo W., Ian Askew, Carolyne Njue, Monica Wanjiru (2005), "Female Genital Cutting among the Somali of Kenya and Management of its Complications", USAID.
49 WHO (2000), *Female Genital Mutilation*. Fact sheet no. 241, World Health Organization, Geneva.
50 WHO (1995), "Female Genital Mutilation. Report of WHO Technical Working group, Geneva, 17-19 July", World Health Organization, Geneva.
51 See Jones, Heather, Nafissatou Diop, Ian Askew and Inoussa Kabore (1999), "Female genital cutting practices in Burkina Faso and Mali and their negative health outcomes", *Studies in Family Planning*, September 1999, 30(3) pp 219- 30.
52 Agpar is an acronym from the five indicators employed to derive the score: activity, grimace, pulse, appearance and respiration.
53 Morison, Linda, Caroline Sherf, Gloria Ekpo, Katie Paine, Beryl West, Rosalind Coleman and Gijs Walraven (2001), "The long-term reproductive health consequences of female genital cutting in rural Gambia: a community-based survey", *Tropical Medicine and International Health*, vol. 6, no. 8, August 2001, pp. 643-53.

54 WHO (1999), *Female genital mutilation - Programmes to date: What works and what doesn't - A review*, World Health Organization, Geneva.

55 Frontiers in Reproductive Health and Population Council (2002), *Using Operation Research to Strengthen Programs for Encouraging Abandonment of Female Genital Cutting*. Report of the Consultative Meeting on Methodological Issues for FGC Research, April 9 – 11, 2002, Nairobi, Kenya.

56 Stewart, Holley, Linda Morison and Richard White (2002), "Determinants of Coital Frequency among Married Women in Central African Republic: the Role of Female Genital Cutting", *Journal of Biosocial Science*, 34(4), pp. 525 - 39.

57 The link between FGM/C, marital problems and divorce emerged clearly during fieldwork and interviews carried out in September 2004 in the UNICEF-funded ACDA projects in Assiut, Egypt.

58 The conflictual feelings experienced by migrant women are described in Johnsdotter, Sara and Birgitta Essen (2004), "Sexual Health among Young Somali Women in Sweden: Living with conflicting culturally determined sexual ideologies", paper presented at the conference "Advancing Knowledge on Psychosexual Effects of FGM/C: assessing the evidence", Alexandria, Egypt, 10-12 October, 2004.

59 See, for example, "Basic Education and Female Genital Mutilation", GTZ Topics www2.gtz.de/fgm/downloads/eng_basic_education.pdf, accessed 4.5.2005.

60 See Wheeler, Patricia (2003), "Eliminating FGM: The role of the law", *The International Journal of Children's Rights*, 11, 2003, pp. 257-71.

61 For an extensive list of State obligations as regards traditional practices affecting the health of women and girls see UN General Assembly Resolution A/RES/54/133, 7 February 2000.

62 Committee on the Elimination of Discrimination against Women, General Recommendation 14, 1990, HRI/GEN/1/ Rev.5.

63 UN General Assembly Resolution A/RES/56/128, 7 December 2001.

64 Toubia, Nahid and Eiman Sharief (2003), "Female Genital Mutilation: have we made progress?" *International Journal of Gynaecology and Obstetrics*, 82 (2003), pp. 251-61. Based on this review RAINBO has developed the Women's Empowerment and Community Consensus model (WECC) for the improved design, evaluation and monitoring of FGM/C projects. The model has two principal dimensions. The first is the promotion of women's self-empowerment – including economic empowerment - through raising their awareness and increasing their decision making abilities. This allows women to redefine their identity and social status in terms that do not include FGM/C. The second dimension is the building of community consensus around the protection of women's and children's rights and the advancement of social change through the negotiation of support from the hierarchy of power holders such as men, religious and civic leaders, health professionals and others.

65 UNICEF identifies eight key elements in a protective environment for children: government recognition of child protection abuses and commitment to promote the protection of children; legislation to protect children and to sanction those who abuse or exploit them; attitudes, customs, behaviour and practices that support, value and protect children; open discussion on child protection issues, with the full participation of civil society and the media; the life skills, knowledge and participation of children themselves in issues affecting them; awareness in the community, complemented by the

66 UNICEF estimated that some 5000 villages practiced FGM/C in Senegal in 1997.
67 Diop, Nafissatou J., Modou Mbacke Faye, Amadou Moreau, Jacqueline Cabral, Hélène Benga, Fatou Cissé, Babacar Mané, Inge Baumgarten and Molly Melching (2004), The TOSTAN Program. Evaluation of a Community Based Education Program in Senegal, FRONTIERS Final Report, Population Council, Washington DC.
68 To date, neither a DHS nor a MICS survey has been undertaken to determine prevalence of FGM/C in Senegal. Preliminary results of the DHS survey are expected in July 2005.
69 For more information regarding the activity of Tostan in Burkina Faso see Ouoba, Djingri, Zakari Congo, Nafissatou J. Diop, Molly Melching, Baya Banza, Georges Guiella and Inge Baumgarten (2004), Experience from a Community Based Education Program in Burkina Faso. The Tostan Program, FRONTIERS Final Report, Population Council, Washington, DC
70 Members of the women's committee make visits to families in which girls are considered to be at risk of FGM/C or early marriage until the girls are considered to have passed this stage. In particular, their efforts are oriented toward mothers in order to raise their awareness of the harmful consequences of these practices. During the follow-up period, other committees, together with informal leaders and religious figures work to change the position of other family members, especially men. CEOSS (2003), Empowerment: From theory into practice, Ceopress, Cairo.
71 Hadi, Amal Abdel (1998), we are Decided. Struggle of an Egyptian village to eradicate female circumcision, Cairo Institute for Human Rights Studies, Cairo
72 The evaluation shows a lower percentage of FGM/C among the daughters of men who had migrated abroad than among daughters of men who had not migrated. In-depth interviews indicated that male migration abroad had an important influence on the status of women within the village of Deir el Barsha, giving them more responsibility and opportunity for decision making beyond traditional domains.
73 For more information on the impact of these different factors see Hadi, Amal Abdel (1998), *We are Decided*. Struggle of an Egyptian village to eradicate female circumcision, Cairo Institute for Human Rights Studies, Cairo
74 CEDPA (2004), "Female Genital Mutilation Abandonment Program- Implementation results June 2003-June 2004". The CEDPA abandonment programme consists of five sequential phases: 1. Orientation activities and identification of individuals termed "positive deviants"; 2. Community mobilization through awareness raising activities to increase knowledge, engagement of leaders and creation of community support for abandonment of the practice; 3. Training of a team to promote the abandonment of FGM/C in the community; 4. Direct family approach. Every two weeks the team visits families with a girl identified as being at imminent risk of FGM/C until each family publicly manifests its firm intention not to subject their daughters to FGM/C on their daughters; 5. Monitoring and evaluation activities. Less frequent home visits continue until a girl is married, at which time she is no longer considered at risk of undergoing FGM/C.
75 UNICEF Egypt, (2004), "Campaigning against Female Genital Mutilation/Cutting in Egypt", UNICEF Update, September 2004.

76 See Herlund, Ylva, "Cutting without Ritual and Ritual without Cutting: Female 'Circumcision' and the Re-ritualization of Initiation in the Gambia" in Shell-Duncan, Bettina and Ylva Hernlund, Eds, (2000), Female "Circumcision" in Africa: Culture, Controversy and Change, Lynne Rienner Publisher, London, and Dorkenoo, Efua (1994), Cutting the Rose. Female Genital Mutilation: the practice and its prevention, Minority Rights Group, London.

77 For more information about the approaches carried out to promote the abandonment of FGM/C by MYWO/Path see: PATH/ Maendeleo Ya Wanawake Organization (2002), Evaluating Efforts to Eliminate the Practice of Female Genital Mutilation. Raising Awareness and Changing Harmful Norms in Kenya, PATH, Washington DC.

78 Chege, Jane, Ian J Askew and Jennifer Liku (2001), "An assessment of the alternative rites approach for encouraging abandonment of FGC in Kenya", FRONTIERS Final Report, Population Council, Washington DC.

79 (2001), Addressing Female Genital Mutilation; Challenges and Perspectives for Health Programmes. Part 1: Select approaches, GTZ, Eschborn

80 "Female Genital Mutilation in the Netherlands. From policy to practice. September 2000-December 2002", Extracts from the project evaluation, Pharos - Utrecht, translated by UNICEF National Committee for the Netherlands, 2004.

81 Rahman, Anika and Nahid Toubia (2000) *Female Genital Mutilation: A guide to laws and policies worldwide*, Zed Books, London.

82 In this case, a presidential order. Wheeler, Patricia (2003), "Eliminating FGM: The role of the law", *The International Journal of Children's Rights*, 11, 2003, pp. 257-71.

83 Rahman, Anika and Nahid Toubia (2000) *Female Genital Mutilation: A guide to laws and policies worldwide*, Zed Books; London.

84 Comoros, Djibouti, Lesotho, Libya, Mauritius, Namibia, Nigeria, Rwanda Senegal, and South Africa.

85 Parliamentary Assembly of the Council of Europe, Resolution 1247 (2001), Female genital mutilation, Para. 11. Under this Resolution, the Parliamentary Assembly urges governments, *inter alia*: "i. to introduce specific legislation prohibiting genital mutilation and declaring genital mutilation to be a violation of human rights and bodily integrity; ii. To take steps to inform all people about the legislation banning the practice before they enter Council of Europe member states; iii. to adopt more flexible measures for granting the right of asylum to mothers and their children who fear being subjected to such practices; [...] v. to prosecute the perpetrators and their accomplices, including family members and health personnel, on criminal charges of violence leading to mutilation, including cases where such mutilation is committed abroad[...]."

86 European Parliament resolution on female genital mutilation (2001/2035(INI), Para. 7.

87 For more details see *Legal Tools for the Prevention of Female Genital Mutilation*, proceedings of the Afro-Arab expert consultation, Cairo, Egypt, 21-23 June 2003, Non c'è pace senza giustizia, special supplement to periodical 1/2004.

88 Together with UNICEF, the IPU has also developed a child protection handbook for parliamentarians which include basic information on FGM/C, the major international standards on the subject, and the main challenges and strategies identified by the IPU panel. See O'Donnell, Dan (2004), *Child Protection. A handbook for parliamentarians*, IPU/UNICEF, Switzerland.

89 Edited by the Swiss Committee for UNICEF, "Les Mutilations Génitales Féminines en Suisse. Enquête auprès des sagesfemmes, gynécologues, pédiatres et services sociaux suisses." Zurich 2004. The survey was supported by Professor Patrick Hohlfeld, former President of the Swiss Association for Gynaecology.

90 As far as the gynaecologists are concerned, this is an increase of 10 percent compared to the survey conducted by UNICEF Switzerland in 2001. Jäger, Fabienne, Sylvie Schulze and Patrick Hohlfeld (2002), "Female Genital Mutilation in Switzerland: a survey among gynaecologists," Swiss Medical Weekly, 132, 2002, pp 259-64.

91 WHO/UNFPA/UNICEF (1997), *Female genital mutilation. A Joint WHO/UNICEF/UNFPA Statement*, World Health Organization, Geneva.

92 WHO (2001), *FGM. Integrating the Prevention and Management of the Health Complications into the Curricula of Nursing and Midwifery. A Teacher's Guide*, World Health Organisation, Geneva.

93 Rahman, Anika and Nahid Toubia (2000) *Female Genital Mutilation: A guide to laws and policies worldwide*, Zed Books, London.

94 WHO (2001), "Management of pregnancy, childbirth and the postpartum period in the presence of female genital mutilation", report of WHO Technical Consultation, Geneva, 15-17 October 1997.

95 UNICEF (2004), "Rapport de la reunion inter-pays sur les mutilations genitales feminines et pratiques nefastes", Dakar, Senegal 22-24 Septembre 2004.

96 The manual, produced by AIDOS is entitled "Mainstreaming the Fight against FGM/C"

97 Secretary General of the United Nations, (2001) "Road map towards the implementation of the United Nations Millennium Declaration. Report of the Secretary-General", A/56/326, 6 December 2001, para. 209

98 As of March 2005, members include UNFPA, UNICEF (Coordination Secretariat), UNIFEM, WHO, the World Bank, USAID, GTZ, The Dutch Cooperation, The Ford Foundation, The Wallace Global Fund and The Public Welfare Foundation. Membership has grown yearly.

99 In June 2004, the Government of Italy made a 1.8 million Euro contribution to support the work of UNICEF and international and national NGOs toward abandonment of FGM/C in 8 African and Middle Eastern countries.

100 In August 2003, the Government of Japan joined with the Government of Sudan and UNICEF to hold a Regional Symposium on the Abolition of FGM to Ensure Safe Motherhood in Khartoum. The symposium deepened understanding of FGM/C among sectors of government and throughout civil society, and reinforced Sudan's political will to end the practice.

In: Contemporary Discourses on IE & C Theory and Practice ISBN: 978-1-60962-360-3
Editor: Theophilus K. Gokah © 2009 Nova Science Publishers, Inc.

Chapter 12

ACTION MEDIA: CONSULTATION, COLLABORATION AND EMPOWERMENT IN HEALTH PROMOTION

Warren Parker

Action media is a methodology for the development of media products that integrates the interests of both the communicator and representatives of target audiences within a health promotion context. The methodology has its roots in participatory action research (PAR) approaches and incorporates qualitative contextual research with a media development process. The methodology involves an approach to democratic communication practice that differs from top-down, expert-centric approaches to health promotion.

INTRODUCTION

Communication approaches to health promotion often rely on linear models of communication whereby communication content is seen as objective and where communication processes are viewed as the transition of messages from 'communicator' to 'receiver'. In such approaches, the communicator is seen as the primary agent for determining the nature of the communication content and the mechanisms for information flow with the receiver being expected to internalise and act on the information they receive.

Health promotion communication, particularly communication utilising mass media, typically incorporates expert-led message development processes with limited engagement with intended audiences who are often referred to as 'target audiences'. Where there is engagement, it is of a technical nature through systems of pre-testing that are designed to assess technical efficiency of the communication rather than addressing the fundamental aspects of the contextual relevance of the messages from audience perspectives.

Communication approaches drawing on semiotic theory work past linear communication assumptions and can be utilised to provide a culturally open method for understanding both the making and the interpretation of messages and exploration of different class, political, language and historical contexts (see Tomaselli 1996). To achieve such engagement however, it is necessary to consider mechanisms for engaging with audiences that include participatory and democratic processes.

This chapter offers a discussion of such an approach. I have named the approach 'action media' and it is presented as a methodology for the development of media products that integrates the perspectives of both the communicator and representatives of intended audiences with a view to addressing contemporary health issues.

The methodology has its roots in participatory action research approaches (PAR) and incorporates qualitative contextual research with a media development process. PAR involves the integration of knowledge systems in communication production through a research process (Reason, 1994)

The Action Media approach is described through examples of activities undertaken during the development of its methodology in South Africa in the mid-1990s. This period represents the early phase of the HIV/AIDS epidemic in South Africa where overall HIV prevalence was relatively low and understanding of the disease at public level was still in its infancy.

It is not intended that Action Media be assumed to be an exclusive and absolute means for the development of health promotion materials. Rather, it adds to the range of methodologies health promoters can apply in communication development, whilst also providing important insights into context-based activities that are consultative, collaborative and empowering.

COMMUNICATOR-MESSAGE-RECEIVER MODELS AND SEMIOTIC APPROACHES

Theories that focus on communication as a linear process are not entirely unified, but are typically represented as 'models' of communication. Examples include Shannon and Weaver's 'mathematical theory of communication', as well as the models of Gerbner, Lasswell, Westley and Maclean, and Newcomb (see Fiske, 1982). In general, these models see information flowing from a communicator to a receiver with the potential for distortion (noise) between the two – for example static on a telephone line, or the absence of a common language. In this sense it is technical factors that impede the communication process, with an absence of consideration of power relations embedded in communication content that may underlie the intended interaction.

These communicator-message-receiver models (CMR) have a common-sense appeal in that they endorse the notion that communication is about how effectively a communicator transfers a message to a receiver in a linear fashion. Further, they do not contest the centrality of the communicator in the process, or any aspect of the communication content. CMR models thus offer only mechanistic understanding without addressing communication contexts.

Semiotic approaches involve a radical inversion of CMR models, placing deeper import on communication contexts with emphasis on the receiver (or reader) and in particular, the interpretation of communication content. Semiotics allows for acknowledgment of the reader's subjective interpretations of messages and may include critical readings of the communicator's intent – including possible ideological connotations.

Semiotics is often referred to as the 'study of signs' and semioticians have tended to focus on the process of construction of meaning – thus, language is a sign system where words stand for tangible objects or ideational constructs. The word tree, for example, stands for a real world tree. Semiology – which is related to semiotics – provides for a similar approach, but focuses more closely on the internal systems and rules within language related to the process of making meaning. Both semiotics and semiology provide for an understanding of the ideological dimensions and power relations embedded in communication.

COMMUNICATION METHODOLOGIES

For the practice of a dialogical or shared communication to occur, practitioners need to balance the interests of communicator and those of receivers (readers).

Health promotion provides a useful analytic context for communication practice. The concept of 'health promotion' is not without ideological dimensions related to differences between those empowered to communicate and those to whom communication is addressed, but in general such communication works from the premise of promoting information that individuals are able to utilise about their health and available health resources, to make beneficial health choices.

Health promotion is seen as an integral part of primary health care systems where information and resources are integrated into a holistic health infrastructure and where particular emphasis is placed on making resources accessible and relevant. The Population Communication Services of Johns Hopkins University (1993) outline primary health care objectives and services as follows:

- analysis of community needs related to health (for example, prevalence of waterborne diseases, prevalence of unplanned pregnancies)
- health education and promotion (for example, HIV/AIDS awareness, lobbying against smoking)
- preventative services (for example, immunisation, provision of condoms, antenatal and post-natal care)
- curative services (for example, therapeutic treatment of illness, surgical management of trauma)
- rehabilitative services (for example, physiotherapy and counselling).

Typical methodologies for the development of health promotion communication are professionalised and tend to be based on CMR theories, with the addition of feedback and research elements to facilitate the refinement of communication messages. Activities include assessment of 'target' audiences and audience needs, development of materials by health and communications specialists, pre-testing of materials by professional researchers, refinement of products and distribution. For example, analysis of research data may show low levels of child immunisation. The initial communication requirement would be raising awareness of immunisation and promoting related services. Health and communications professionals would work together to assess potential target audiences, develop key messages and concepts, pre-test these with representatives of the target audience, and then go on to develop finalised media products.

There are a number of shortcomings to this approach. Health and communications professionals tend to occupy somewhat different socio-economic contexts to broader target audiences and communication development is often skewed by professional perceptions of how messages should be framed, what media and media products should be utilised and so on. The incorporation of message and product pre-testing helps to contextualise products. However, pre-testing is limited by an inherent assumption that communication is an objective process, and further, that products can be understood independently of contexts. Participants in pre-testing sessions are limited in terms of what they are offered as messages and products to comment upon and are usually not engaged deeply on their perceptions of community needs and the relevance of such products within the repertoire of needs.

Communication concepts that emerge through such development processes are unidirectional in terms of their messages and tend towards issuing of imperatives. Linney (1995) describes such materials as 'one way' and lists typical components as including the issuing of orders and instructions and being aimed at 'target' audiences without engaging audiences in processes of critical awareness.

Whilst there is some narrowness in such communication, this is not to say that communication utilising this approach is without value. Campaigns utilising such methodologies do achieve tangible results and in many ways are similar to models used in commercial advertising – they raise awareness and link people to services or products. There are however limitations in terms of audience/community involvement and opportunities for organic needs assessment and message development are lost.

ACTION MEDIA

The Action Media methodology has grown out of my work in contextual communication in South Africa and has focused on the development of materials for sexual and reproductive health. In this country, the rapid growth in HIV infection has provided added impetus to health promotion around sexual and reproductive health and has allowed for broader focus on sexually transmitted diseases, HIV/AIDS, and growing emphases on related areas such child abuse, rape and sexual abuse. Specifically, there has been a need to explore how audience perspectives and critical thinking can be integrated into communication development processes around these issues.

The Action Media approach allows for integration of perspectives of representatives of audiences through a process that allows for deep reflection around issues that affect their lives, whilst at the same time integrating linguistic and cultural perspectives. This allows message development to become an organic process. The methodology is such that it engenders action amongst the participants and this impetus can be harnessed in subsequent activities at the individual, group, or local community level.

The process has been developed and adopted in a range of health promotion contexts related to reproductive and sexual health with groups of adolescents and young adults.

The Action Media methodology has its roots in social theories (and practices) that include the work of Freire (1996), Whyte (1994), as well as the broad discipline of cultural and media studies (see Tomaselli, 1994; Hall 1997). These include understandings of communications processes, semiotics, culture, ideology, social change and participatory research.

In relation to participation, Shoepf et al (1988) describe a participatory process followed with commercial sex workers for health promotion in Zaire as follows: "Grounded in principles of group dynamics, experiential training begins with the principle that people already know a great deal about their situation. Group leaders assist people to develop a 'critical consciousness leading to co-operative social action and self-reliance'." As Freire describes it: '... the process in which people, not as recipients, but as knowing subjects, achieve a deepening awareness both of the socio-historical realty that shapes their lives and of their capacity to transform that reality' (Freire, 1970: 27).

Action media provides a framework for dealing with the divergent emphases of communication theory and brings together imperatives of the communicator, on the one hand, and readers on the other. At the same time the methodology allows for a number of tangential benefits in terms of critical awareness and action.

In overview, Action Media as it pertains to health promotion has the following elements:

- Identification of significant health challenges — for example, the prevention of HIV/AIDS, sexually transmitted diseases and unplanned pregnancy amongst adolescents and young adults;
- Identification of sufficiently homogenous groups within defined geographic areas — for example, college students, youth formations in communities;
- Collaboration with individuals within each context to co-facilitate workshops — for example, lecturers, teachers, youth group leaders, health workers;
- Recruitment of 15-20 participants on a voluntary basis for participation in a series of four hour workshops of three hours duration each.
- Workshops that incorporate educative focus group sessions that engender participation, critical thinking and reflection. Elements include activities such as games, role-plays, which, in combination with discussions, lead to the development of communication concepts and products.

The workshops flow through a sequence that includes the development of trust between communication researcher-practitioners and the research participants. Channels for dialogue are informal. Participants are encouraged to engage with community problems critically through participant led discussion groups – for example, a participant group of 20 might be organised into four groups of five participants each to discuss problems related to HIV prevention, followed by a report back to the group as a whole. Role plays and other participatory activities enhance thinking and reflection around exploring the relation between contextual factors and health-beneficial action.

As the series of workshops progresses, communication concepts are drawn out, extending to the point where actual message constructs and media products are conceived. The emergent communication concepts are then utilised to develop actual products through referral to professional producers – for example, artists and designers. These are then returned to the group for critical comment.

The media products that emerge reveal deep insights into perspectives of the target group, are immediately relevant to the participant's peer communities, and may be relevant nationally as health promotion products. For example, a poster focusing on HIV prevention that was produced with youth in Johannesburg during the transition to democracy in South

Africa included the image of a condom in the colours of the new national flag above the slogan 'Viva Condoms'. This illustrates shifting relations to state power and responsibility and accountability, whilst at the same time drawing on the transformative revolutionary language of the period. In the period following the image and slogan were widely used including being printed and disseminated by the post-apartheid national Department of Health.

At the outset however, it is intended that the products be integrated into existing infrastructure and be utilised as a cornerstone for other community-based activities. In the case of reproductive health, participants in the process became strongly committed to safer sexual behaviour and promotion of peer awareness. In the case of the 'Viva condoms' poster, it was used by college students as part of their college-based HIV prevention activities, whilst in Soweto it was used by a youth group as a rallying point for condom promotion, where participants noted that 'we are now free and condoms should be freely available'

The methodology illustrates the potentials for inverting producer-centric approaches in favour of seeing contexts of media utility as dynamic, and furthermore, setting out to generate media products that are supportive of action, rather than simply as vehicles for information.

DISCUSSION

The Action Media methodology requires a commitment to democratic communication development practice and practitioners require a combination of qualitative research skills and an understanding of communication. However, the logic of the approach is quite simple – rather than design health promotion products for 'target' audiences via often dislocated experts who 'pre-test' their emergent products, Action Media emphasises integrating intended audiences into production processes so that development and appraisal processes for communication products form a relatively seamless whole.

The Action Media methodology offers a number of benefits:

- Participants learn how to think critically and are considerably enriched in terms of critical awareness about serious health issues that affect their lives.
- Researcher / practitioners are able to extract qualitative data relevant to broader research and planning activities. Many qualitative researchers rely on short duration, single interactions with respondents in tightly controlled situations. The deeper, longer series of focus groups, which are part of the Action Media approach, elicit a body of information that is relevant both for understanding contextual issues and designing interventions.
- A core group of highly aware individuals is created to the benefit of the immediate peer group and community. Clearly the workshops generate considerable impetus and the energy amongst participants and this can be channeled into subsequent activities that contribute to peer awareness and can be integrated into transformative activities.
- The products that emerge are deeply contextualised in terms of imagery, language, and potential utility. Pre-testing is not required as the methodology incorporates extensive analysis of imagery and messaging into the communication development process. Audience perspectives are thus embedded in the emerging products.

- The products are directly applicable in the context of the group or community within which they emerge and can be directly applied within a health promotion context — particularly when they can be linked to tangible products, resources and service. Interestingly, many of the products developed using this methodology has been used beyond the immediate contexts within which they were developed.

Products that emerge through Action Media do not always fit into conventions of political correctness. Some emerging products – for example a series of radio scripts – revealed a lived environment of sexism, which was articulated and challenged within the emerging media products; the 'Viva Condoms' poster was viewed as denigrating the flag into an image of a condom.

Within the development of such products it is not the task of researcher /facilitators to 'censor' products, but rather to open debate around contentious issues and seek resolution within the group that can be applied to the media products.

Such communication development processes illustrate the need to move beyond the scientised CMR perceptions that see communication products as having singular meanings or as functioning in direct linear ways. The power of communication products lies not in the direct intention of their messaging but rather in the contexts within which they are viewed and used. If a communication product generates discussion and debate, its relevance within a societal context is multiplied several fold, and is far better than communication products that seek simply to transfer specific concepts from communicator to receiver in a way that narrow and 'closed'.

CONTENT AND CONTEXT

The Action Media methodology is positioned largely within the framework of semiotic analyses of communication and can be seen as a process of applied semiotics that allows for signs, messages, readers and contexts to interrelate. The media products that emerge have value when analysed within cultural and ideological frameworks that incorporate notions of a 'struggle for meaning'. Much of the developmental work around the methodology has focused on youths and has provided an important voice to young people in contexts where they are typically disempowered. The methodology is the antithesis of top down approaches, allowing instead for collaborative effort and empowerment in the creation of media products.

The ideological contexts of the participants cannot be ignored either, and products emerging through the Action Media methodology are often revealing of this context. As Tomaselli (1996) puts it: 'If ideology accounts for the 'lived' relations between people and their world, then we must accept that meaning is saturated with the ideological imperatives of society'.

Action Media describes an interesting tension between the two strands of communication theory. On the one hand Action Media describes a process of efficiently producing methodologically grounded media products by overcoming limitations inherent in the application of CMR approaches that utilise professionalised conceptualisation and pre-testing. When analysed within semiotic perspective however, it becomes clear that communication products do not have to be seen as narrow in meaning and may instead be viewed dynamically and that the subjectivity of readers should be taken into account. Media products function within contexts, and are read from diverse subjective perspectives. We cannot assume an objectivity within media products that makes meaning and interpretation absolute. As Tomaselli (1996) observes: 'Readers appropriate the meanings which best fit their imaginary solutions as interpreted by their individual, cultural and class experiences. These interpretants coincide most closely with their individual subjectivities.'

At best, media products provide a stimulus for a range of possible interpretations on the one hand, and a range of contextual applications on the other. In the case of 'mass' media products, it is impossible to assume uniform interpretations. Even at the level of the individual, subjective responses can be framed by contextual factors, and meaning and interpretation may shift over time.

Meaning and interpretation need to be seen as dynamic processes, even at the level of an individual. Assumptions underpinning processes of media development need to incorporate subjectivity, dynamism and diversity amongst intended audiences, no matter how homogenous they are assumed to be. Media products should also not be seen as "stand-alone" interventions — an assumption that is embedded in CMR perspectives. Instead, media products need to be continually applied, contextualised and nuanced.

Within the complex contexts of media development, the Action Media methodology provides insight into the potential for integration and empowerment of individuals and groups within target communities. It demonstrates a replicable process that provides for the development of deeply contextualised media products on the one hand, and qualitative understandings of community contexts on the other.

Finally, it is important that the Action Media methodology is perceived as malleable within the principles that frame it. Researchers, facilitators, resources and contexts frame the application of the methodology and colour the products that emerge. In essence, if communication and meaning are framed as dynamic and subjective, then processes that seek to generate meaning should be seen as dynamic too.

In: Contemporary Discourses on IE & C Theory and Practice ISBN: 978-1-60962-360-3
Editor: Theophilus K. Gokah © 2009 Nova Science Publishers, Inc.

Chapter 13

INTERLOCKING MEDIA FOR COMMUNITY EDUCATION AND TRAINING

Theophilus Kofi Gokah

Folk media has the capacity of being a useful method of data gathering because of its significant role as expressions of everyday life. It poses a great challenge to traditional methods of learning for the simple reason that it lacks the potential to change attitudes and behaviour. An added benefit of tradition media is that, it has no borders and finds its forms in existing cultural expression of the communities that create it and offers a means of creating an analysis of the cultural and social conditions in challenging settings which is the very ethos of social science. To demonstrate this happy marriage, ethnographic data is used to show how a combination of media can be a resource for IE&C practice in a deprived community. The result shows that the community was able to relate their learning experiences to their own traditional values and aspirations.

Keywords: IE&C, Community education and learning, folk media and ethnography,

CONTEXT

Whatever sense we have of how things stand with other people's lives, we gain it through their cultural expressions, representations and performances (Geertz, 1986)

If the views in Gokah (2007) that there is no single or individually approved method of training populations and that each method is dependent on training 'content' and 'context' is compelling, then the extent to which training programmes and activities have utilised traditional resources such as folk media remain valid across education and training discourses. Understandably, the practice of training itself involves informing people of new approaches and educating people to improve their life styles. Communication stands at the threshold to make all these happen (see for instance Fenn, 2003). There are, however, issues about choice of appropriate communication tools or channels in doing IE&C at community level or even at national level. The settlement for folk media which includes a gamut of frames – dance, drama, songs, poetry recitals, story telling, rhymes, provide a wide range of activities from which ethnographic researchers and anthropologists can choose from in developing appropriate methodologies for IE&C. In some settings drama or theatre has been used to communicate and inform communities but whether the choices were based on rational approach or empirical assumptions is less founded (Chinyowa, 2007). Notwithstanding, theatre has no borders and finds its forms in the existing cultural expression of the communities that create it. It offers the means of creating an analysis of the economic, cultural and social conditions, particularly in challenging settings.

Wusuta Borborbor Group ©tgokah

In some societies folk media do not play any significant role as expressions of everyday life despite the existence of large numbers of folk lore repertoire. The reason may be religious, social or historical. For instance, Abramson (2004) explains that restrictions against certain forms of representation, together with the small value Jewish religious authorities traditionally placed on theatre for its own sake, were crucial factors militating against the development of folk dramas. On the contrary; in applied studies critical theatre, described in the literature as theatre that is created for a specific need, has been used to study the social context of certain diseases (Stuttaford, et al, 2006). It usually takes place in non-theatre spaces that encourage social change. Such theatre happens in a wide variety of settings and communities, from formal institutions such as schools, prisons and hospitals to informal spaces such as urban centres and rural communities. In this wise the assumption that applied theatre has a growing place in a complex world where its power as a medium that offers clarification is unique is valid. Its scholarship in using a combination of spoken word, different choreographies and signed meaning through images of the physical theatre makes it unique. It has potential for transforming social understanding than with textual presentation (Gray et al., 2000). In this way it challenges the academic privileging of written text (Paget, 1990). By virtue of its potential, it brings insight into the lives of those who have become marginalised and disempowered in their environment. By so doing it fits the critical social science approach that research should empower participants to change the context in which they operate or the way they behave (Mienczakowski, 1997: 163).

Traditional methods of learning such as lectures, reading and discussions seems somewhat of a cliché because they lack the potential to change attitude or behaviour, since hearing or reading about something is very far from experiencing it (Ments, 1989). Central to this argument is interactive learning which Greenwood (2002: 325) describes as moving from a predominantly theoretical domain engage participants emotionally and intuitively as well as intellectually. Like Sogunro (2004: 355) there is agreement with this line of thinking because as societies become complex, it is direct experience of a learning activity that is key to bringing about real understanding and desired change in people. One way of achieving this goal is via community drama and role-plays as will soon be discussed. IE&C is not limited to community training and education. In business environments the method can be used in generating data aimed at confidence building at the work place, instilling professionalism in the organisational staff, leadership qualities, creativity, decision making skills and teamwork. In fact, the list is endless (Jackson, 1995). It is for this reason that Nicolaidis and Liotas (2006) think that theatre has been unjustifiably overlooked as a very effective medium for the development of managers' skills.

© *Northern Ewe traditional dance drama*

Community dramas and role-plays described in ethnographic terms as 'human symbolic interaction of a performing kind' (Ben-Amos and Goldstein, 1975) have also been used to meet more specific needs. For example, role-play scenarios have been introduced into the international relations classroom to present the complexities of 'peacekeeping' operations, focusing on the interactions between diplomats, military representatives and nongovernmental organisations (Shaw, 2004; Sanyal, 2000). This approach is also supported by Holtom *et al* (2003), who propose interactive drama exercises to introduce ethical dilemmas and show the complexities of decision making

That 'any conceptual framework that may be formulated for popular theatre has to consider not only the cultural dimension of the agenda but also the language by which such development is communicated' (Chinyowa, 2007) reflects the very ethos and character of any effective IE&C application. Every art form, be they cultural performance texts such as ritual, storytelling, music, song, dance, poetry and masquerade not only express how people orient themselves in terms of time, space, movement, gesture and facial expression but also provide the frames upon which social reality can be interpreted and understood. From the perspective of cultural anthropology stories are told, rituals are performed, dances are made, drums are beaten and poems are recited to show the purpose of life (Turner, 1982). It is these exigencies that IE&C seeks to exploit to bring back to people lost glories.

There is a degree of permissiveness between folklore and contemporary media, notably; radio, television and cinema which present an interesting arena for IE&C (see for example Henderson and Cowan, 2001). A description of this harmonisation is found in the works of Adgebe (2003) which encompasses theatre, dialogue and social discourse, in an attempt to bridge fiction and social reality. In order words, this permissiveness allows for example different genre in folklore to be replicated on electronic media and in some cases print media. Although this may have their own challenges, their capability of reaching intended (and non-intended) audiences can not be underestimated (Narva'ez and Laba, 1986). Since then analysis of the relationship between contemporary media and folk media has become increasingly studied (see Bown, 2001; Henderson and Cowan, 2001; Purkiss, 2001). What makes their utilisation a useful undertaking is the audience recognition of the need for active participation in shaping the way folk media mimics and shape their life experiences as a way of sharing and apprehending the world through an ancient, yet, relevant concept (Bird 2006: 347) and by extension moving away from what Paulo Freire (1972: 121) refers to as 'welfare programmes as instruments of manipulation which ultimately serve the end of conquest; acting as an anaesthetic, distracting the oppressed from the true causes of their problems and from the concrete solution to their problems.'

Depending on what we purpose to use electronic media to achieve, its usage will have to be weighed against other options. If development (whatever that means) involves changes in the awareness, motivation and behaviour of individuals and in the relations between individuals as well as between groups within society as Adgebe (2003) puts it and from Burkey's (1993: 48) perspective that development will not take place unless there is a consensus among the group attempting to carry out the transformation through dialogue and awareness is true, then electronic media is not a policy option in bringing the needed change. Change takes time and no development programme (be they in the South or the North) has longer life spans than *change*. For this reason, listening clubs described in Adgebe (2003) are not just unsustainable but an icing on the cake and short-term. Most of these programmes talk about their successes and not about what has happened to the projects when the agencies are long gone (see Ezra and Mchakulu, 2007). In deed, development projects in the south have been known to fissile out as donor budgets elapse (see for example Gokah, 2008).

Whereas academic discourses are still evolving around programme and policies sustainability (especially in the South) when donor funds dry up, it is worthy of note that media (traditional and orthodox) interventions rarely achieve behaviour change on their own without facilitation and supporting literature. It is imperative therefore that programmes follow procedures which generally include formative and Summative research, choosing the right channels of communication and feedback, and promoting discussion (participatory approach) with and within community audience. In addition, extra care is needed when dealing with deeply entrenched topics.

CASE SCENARIO: THE POPULATION COMMUNICATION PROJECT IN GHANA

Following the International Conference on Population and Development (ICPD) in 1994, the UNFPA in conjunction with UNESCO and Government of Ghana instituted the population communication project in Ghana under the project code GH/89/PO2. The project was managed by the Ghana Institute of Journalism. The programme was in response to ICPD CAIRO programme of action in population and reproductive health that countries agreed were essential to realising global development goals including ending extreme poverty and hunger, empowering women, reducing maternal mortality, preserving the environment and stemming the HIV/AIDS pandemic. Strategies to implement the programme include training journalist in population communication and identifying appropriate communication methods to inform, educate and communicate the above themes in rural communities. Pilot programmes were initiated in two rural communities - Wusuta and Postin in the Volta and Central Regions of Ghana. For purposes of reporting, this discussion focuses on Wusuta.

The choice of rural settings is justified (in academic discourse) by the fact that sixty-three percent of Ghana's population live in rural settings where fifty-five percent either work in agriculture, forestry or fishing industries (Fiadzo et al, 2001). Rural settings in Ghana and elsewhere are thus synonymous with poverty (Christiansen, Demery and Paternostro, 2003) and deprivation (Barbier, 2000; Cavendish, 2000; de Janvry and Sadoulet, 2000). This is not to say that urban poverty and deprivation do not pose challenges to populations and resources. The emphasis on rural settings is based on statistics which calls for a revisit of social policies that impact harshly on rural communities. In referring to rural communities inferences are made from Hulme's (2004) notion that health 'shocks' can impoverish families, and social exclusion, based on gender, age and disability and keep people living in that social context poor (Bhola, 2005; Thomas, 2000).

THE RESEARCH SETTING

Wusuta is famous for its traditional dance groups, the *Dumas Borborbor* dance group and *Akpene* dance group. There is little information on the origins of *Borborbor*. However, an internet account (Anonymous, 2006) claims that *Borborbor* is the most popular social music and dance of the Central and Northern Ewes of Ghana and Togo. This music and dance, also known as *Agbeyeye* [New Life], or *Akpese* [Music of Joy], emerged from a village called Kpando in the Volta Region of Ghana during the independence struggle between 1947 and 1957. *Borborbor* is derived from an older circular dance called *Konkoma*. Although this music was initially confined to a few towns and villages in central and Northern Eweland, it has now spread to all Ewe speaking territories in Ghana and Togo.

The Wusuta *Borborbor* group was noted for its role in political campaign activities of the Convention People's Party (CPP), Ghana's first post-independence ruling party, together with others like *Konyako* brass band in the Central region of Ghana serving as a rallying force for the ruling party; apart from being a popular traditional dance among populations in Northern Volta, it is an artistic movement for praise and criticism of social, economic and political issues. No doubt it featured prominently in national politics during the first and second republic.

Wusuta has a population of about a thousand people. It occupies the middle portion of the Kpando district bounded to the West by the Volta Lake with a low lying area to the East. The town is located at the foot of the Kpando Mountain ranges rising about 1500 feet in height with forest reserves lining the foot of the mountain ranges. The main source of water is the *Dayi* River which takes its source from the Eastern lowlands. Generally, economic activity is subsistence farming. The subsistence nature of the community means that standard of living is low. Despite its low economic activity (a concern expressed in community education video), social activities like drumming and dancing are major forms of entertainment. These art forms also serve as medium for communicating social, economic and political messages to its people (Rogers, 1998; Picart and Gergen, 2004).

This chapter acknowledges different conceptualisations of 'community,' and stands by Behrman's (2002) notion of community as social network of two or more members who share common activity. There are also on-going discourses about what community education is. For instance, Smith (2006) sees it as 'a process designed to enrich the lives of individuals and groups by engaging with people living within a geographical area, or sharing a common interest, to develop voluntarily a range of learning, action and reflection opportunities, determined by their personal, social, economic and political needs'. This definition fits the chosen case study, Wusuta.

Some commentators, for example Asante (1996), have argued that modern media, particularly radio, have been successful in tackling development problems in health, education and agriculture in Ghana. Contrary to this thinking Aborampah and Anokwa (1984) argue that the media – radio, television, cinema and print - have not brought any significant changes in the life of Ghanaians. Prior to their views, Schramm (1964) did agree that television is an appealing vehicle for literacy in health, education and other areas of rural development; but unlike in urban areas not many people in rural Ghana have access to radio, television or print media because of infrastructural problems and access issues (Boafo, 1988). Instead, in rural areas of Ghana folk media fills literacy and communication gaps created by a lack of modern forms of communication and can play both supplementary and substitution roles. Its choice is however dependent on careful selection and utilisation based on project objective(s).

Like Easterby-Smith (1997), the discussions in this chapter draw from existing body of knowledge on social learning theory to argue that community practice where members participate in an activity will induce learning. There is a plethora of academic evidence that links education and training to poverty reduction (Ruud van der and Preece, 2005; Arimah, 2004; Harber, 2002; Drèze and Murthi, 2001). Closely linked to this thinking is Durham's (1998) view that people construct realities of the world around them. As readers will soon see, participants in the reported study were capable of constructing and deconstructing the themes, enacted through traditional dance, drama, and recitals about poverty reduction, family planning and environmental degradation. Prior knowledge of Bohla's text that mitigating the social conditions of people through participatory approaches creates incremental gains in socio-economic life, a view earlier expressed by van den Hove (2000) and Puertas and Schlesser (2001), influenced the choice of methodology (a process later explored in the chapter).

THE METHODS DEPLOYED TO UNDERSTAND THE ROLE OF TRADITIONAL MEDIA IN RURAL COMMUNITY LEARNING

The methodological framework in the study is qualitative (Bryman, 2001). In other words the research strategy through which the study evolved, assumed a descriptive or exploratory character in order to obtain results that will usefully inform rural community education and training policy (Potter and Subrahmanian, 1998]. Discourses on choice of methodology in social scientific research are on-going (Sarantakos, 1998; Sandelwoski, 2000]. For instance, some researchers have attempted to mix-methods in order to expand the scope and improve the analytic power of their studies. Within this whole debate, this paper holds to Sandelwoski's thinking that, the choice of methodology is dependent on the nature of research being undertaken. This reasoning drove the choice of approach in the reported study. Having said that, it paper acknowledges the existence of other approaches like experimental design that could offer insights to this study but unfortunately has a different focus and tend to suffer from being narrow in the type of information produced which makes it unsuitable for the kind of study being undertaken here. Given the exploratory nature of this study, it became essential to select a design that will accommodate the issues under investigation hence the choice of method (Hakim, 1987).

METHOD

In order to understand the different analytic frameworks in the reported study, mixed methods and approaches i.e. ethnography, participatory observation and community forum – were employed to generate sufficient data and to improve its analytic power (Winchester, 1999; Silverman, 2003). If Derry (1999) and McMahon's (1997) views about optimal learning environment as one where a dynamic interaction between instructors, learners and tasks provide opportunities for learners to create their own truth due to their interaction with others is true, then achieving a proper understanding of social events such as the one under consideration requires a holistic approach. After all, Constructivist do emphasize the importance of 'culture' and 'context' in appreciating what is happening in communities (e.g. rural communities) and constructing knowledge around existing issues (Taylor, 1998; Bhaskar, 1998: Ardebili, 2001; Rottenburg, 2006; Potter, 1996; Payne, 2000).

Ethnographic approach helped in understanding existing social issues in the chosen community [Conrad-Phillip, 2005). Participant observation created a close intimate familiarity with the community, groups and individuals like the chief, youth leader, and other opinion leaders (Magzoub et al, 1998). Community forum as a strategy enabled the project to remove hurdles to participation (especially in a culturally dominant society). Through the community forum technique it made it possible for voices of people, whom hitherto would not have been heard (for whatever reason), to be recognised.

RESEARCH DESIGN

Data Gathering Strategy

The research used different strategies at different stages to gather data. For instance, conversations (including interview) with the village chief were video filmed. Initial meeting with both resident dance groups was not filmed. This meeting was an opportunity to explain to all potential stakeholders within Wusuta community the research mission and objective. Upon further deliberation the *Dumas Borborbor* dance group was the most preferred performing artistes. The group was presented with four themes (derived from interview data) - 'over population', family planning, sexual immorality and environmental health – to explore whether these have roots in traditional lyrics, dance drama, proverbs and sayings.

Community forum
(a)   Palace Meeting

Elder of Wusuta Community takes his turn to contribute at the palace forum ©

An initial community meeting at the chief's palace was held to discuss and ascertain the level of community's knowledge on the issues under investigation (Khamis, 2000). This formative assessment enabled researchers to identify knowledge gaps in the issues under consideration and to tailor the educational video appropriately.

(b)   Market Square Meeting

The project held its first open air meeting at the market square. The reason for this meeting was to show the first edited edition of video film on the entire project – individual perceptions, group perceptions and education material by the *Dumas Borborbor* dance group. The project provided an electric generating machine and audio visual equipment (O'Meara, et al 2002). Outcomes from that forum were revealing.

For instance, there were (a) situations where both genders blamed each other for family crisis (b) acknowledgment that promiscuity and youth deviance were real social problems and (c) misconceptions about family planning. The selected dance group was also observed rehearsing without being filmed (Lofland and Lofland, 1995). The group was reminded about some key issues emerging from the palace forum which they factored into their performances. Also, two focus group interviews were held with adolescent boys and girls separately (Krueger, 1988). The reason for the various approaches was to triangulate data. In other words involving multiple sources of data – opinion leaders, young people, adult men and women in the Wusuta community and drawing on secondary information. This helped to cross check material and emerging conceptualisations, a process referred to as triangulation (Denzin, 1990; Shaw, 1999).

© *Market square: Night forum at Wusuta, Ghana*

INTERVIEWS

The in-depth interview was conducted by one researcher whilst group interviews were facilitated by all three researchers. Interviews were recorded on VHS tape. In-depth interviews were held with (a) chief (b) young people (c) youth leader (d) opinion leaders (e) Older women. 4 focus group interviews were held with adolescents (boys and girls) who were also captured on video. Results of both interviews were synthesised and grouped in themes.

SAMPLING STRATEGY

The sampling strategy was purposive and mixed (Frankel and Devers, 2000). Community forums were based on open invitation. Data gathering technique consisted of video-taping, group interviews and in-depth interviews with village Chief, 3 social group leaders and 1 village youth leader ($n = 5$). There was two sets of focus group meetings with adolescent boys and girls ($n = 32$) (Fontana and Frey, 2000) and 2 community forums (one at the Chief's palace and the other at the market square) [n = 1000]. Interviewees were purposely recruited. For instance, the study chose to interview the chief because of his position as custodian of community norms, values and tradition (Owusu-Sarpong, 2003). Other chosen informants were also perceived as possessing insights from different vantage points about community values, traditions and well-being. Researchers' local knowledge about community structures and organisation helped in deciding who were likely to be respondents in the study. Research questions evolved around traditional perceptions about sexual promiscuity, family planning, deviance and environmental degradation; how these perceptions shape learning and behaviour among adults and young people.

COMMUNITY ENTRY AND EXIT STRATEGY

Formal entry into the community was preceded by an initial visit. This was a fact finding mission and to familiarise with the community, meet opinion leaders to seek their support and mandate to stay in the community.

Researcher exit from the community was in phases. The first exit was to allow the community time to deliberate on the proposals before them and to plan for the grand production. The second exit was to allow for analysis of interview data and to edit video data before the third visit. It is important to understand that in rural communities in Ghana, video denotes 'luxury' where such means of education and entertainment barely exist. It is also a participatory mechanism where people are motivated by seeing themselves actively playing a role in community development thereby indirectly empowering indigenous people to be in control of their own development; and this is exactly what happened in Wusuta. Expectations of researchers return were therefore high possibly because people wanted to see themselves in the video film. For example, researchers observed pockets of groups lingering and waving from various points along the road leading into the community during one such visit. This heralded the dissemination phase of the project.

The purpose of a third visit to the community was to watch the final version of dance drama and performance by the *Dumas Borborbor* group together with other members of the community. The rationale here was to produce a community educational video using folk media. The film captured the community, performers, sceneries and village infrastructure. Confidentiality was not an issue as members of the community were willing to appear in the video and purposefully positioned themselves to be filmed. This action is understood from the point of entertainment and prestige. The performances included existing rhetoric about norms, traditions and cultural values that evolved around key themes. Recitals and artistic performances were video taped, a process familiar to Barford and Weston (1997) as a useful teaching resource.

ETHICAL CONSIDERATIONS

As at the time of this study, the project was not aware of any formal organisation or institution responsible for research approval in Ghana. However, researcher knowledge about social research methodology and their cultural awareness provided a basis for ensuring that the project runs without hitches. For instance, researcher's fore knowledge on traditional rules which dictate that any 'official' visitor to the community should seek audience with community elders including the Chief was valuable (Olufemi, 2003). The Chief's courtier subsequently informed other opinion leaders in the community. The research team was officially introduced to the community at the palace forum. It was this rite(s) that earned the project the Chief's approval for it to be housed in his community.

As indicated above, choice of informants was subjective as far as selecting between performing dance groups was concerned. As it were, informant selection was not done from a distance. Selection began on the second day of its consultation with the community by which time the research team would have had a good idea about who the potential respondents were. There are arguments for and against researcher familiarity with the research environment (Nukunya, 1996 Zhang, 1996). The choice of *Dumas Borborbor* dance group over Akpene dance group infuriated the former leading to them shunning the project. This however did not threaten the project because the *Dumas* group was willing to participate. Perhaps, additional artiste would have enriched the data which could have aided comparison of information gathered.

CONTENT OF FINAL VIDEO PRODUCTION

The packaged production had four scenes of a total duration of 2½ half hours video footage. Scene one, opens with narratives on history, culture and the socio-economic life of the community and art forms as mediums for information, education and communication. Scene two depicts the links between community well-being and its environment by contrasting present and past environmental conditions through traditional lyrics, drama, proverbs and sayings. Scene three is in a family setting. Here, the effects of 'wrong'[7] family and societal values are highlighted with consequences for poverty, disease, HIV/AIDS, substance abuse, deviance; crime and disrespect for authority are highlighted. Scene four (the concluding scene) shows community reaction to the various plots in the film, their strengths and weaknesses as a tool for community education and learning.

VIDEO DISSEMINATION STRATEGY

Various steps were taken to disseminate the community educational video which was produced by indigenes of the rural study community in Ghana. In the video footage the indigenous community provided information on rural peoples' attitude, beliefs and perception about sexual promiscuity, deviance, reproductive health, family planning and environmental degradation.

There were three dissemination strategies:

a) Screening an edited version of community video footage at the chief's palace to gauge reactions of community leaders.
b) Open – air video screening at the market square for people to comment and react to lessons learnt from the film
c) Video taping of reactions and feedback to aid further editing where necessary.

There was researcher awareness that in editing video recordings a risk of subjective analysis of the recordings were likely. In other words, the research was faced with what to

---

[7] Community determines what is right or wrong based on its values, norms and traditions

edit and what not to. Thus, only obstructive images were edited for purposes of motion uniformity and stability (Wolf and Webster, 1997; Becker, 1993). The final video production was screened at the market square during researchers' fourth visit. The video play back session was also filmed to capture people's reaction to the video and issues discussed.

VALIDITY AND RELIABILITY OF THE STUDY METHOD

The study sought to achieve sufficient validity to allow some modest claim that the analysis has relevance beyond the immediate community in question. It tried to do this, firstly, by linking the data (from forums, interviews, and video footage and focus group discussions) to a more general abstract understanding of rural community learning through folk media. The research involved multiple stakeholders – village authorities, youths and adults (both sexes) and folk media performers. The study also drew on secondary sources to help interweave different kinds of data. By using different data sources, researchers could cross check emerging material and conceptualisations, a process referred to as triangulation (as mentioned earlier)

There is no doubt that validity is a subject of long established debate within both qualitative and quantitative traditions. Some see the debate as a 'methodological worry' (Hammersley, 1990). The debate essentially is about criteria for establishing 'truth' or 'credibility' (Lincoln and Guba, 1985). In order to establish validity in the method used, the research linked data (interview data and video data) to a more general abstract understanding of community learning theory and participation. If reader's understanding regarding the links between community health and its wellbeing are correct, then the analysis offered in this project may well be applicable to other rural communities, or at least provide a useful focus for further research.

RESULTS FROM INTERVIEWS

Cross-cutting themes were evident in the interviews. These were: culture, sexuality, deviance, prostitution, teenage pregnancy and crime. Emerging issues from the focus group meetings were: sexuality, prostitution, irresponsibility and deviance (Hubbard, 1998). Views from community forums were classified as: adult views, young peoples' views and views from village elder (Chief). The following key themes sums-up data from the community project – poverty, family crisis, promiscuity, culture, deviance and family planning. Selection of data was guided by the research objective thus eliminating threats of bias. Initial challenges to the project centred on definitions of community and the selection of respondents (Gokah, 2006).

In order to test the level of cultural sensitivity the study brought together boys and girls in one discussion. It was found that girls were not as open on matters of sex and sexuality as they were not on their own. Boys on the other hand were articulate in their expression and sometimes ridiculed their female counterparts. This situation is a natural tension (although a setback in research settings where groups are separated by gender) because in real life viewing of visual art / performance the audience are mixed. Lengua and Stormshak (2000) found similar patterns in their research on gender differences in the prediction of coping and psychological symptoms. They argued that significant gender differences exist in the relations among gender roles and personality. This relationship did not however threaten the study because female participants in the other forums were articulate and provided useful information.

Popular concerns from respondent community are presented. Thus, indigenous people in Wusuta were able to point out four key themes from the final community educational video production. These are: poverty, parental responsibility, deviance and need for action. Research audience in the community forum reiterated this view by recounting some difficulties they faced in rural communities:

> We no longer have farm lands, so we cannot farm... peasant farming is not profitable, we are poor (Adult Woman in the Community)

Poverty no doubt has many implications for individuals and rural economies. This can create and in deed has created social problems for the people of Wusuta where parents especially abandon their family responsibility as was depicted in the video clip:

> Fathers who abandon children on women bring burden to the family and society. I think that lesson is a good one (Youngman in the village)

There were also comments like:

> There were good lessons from the performances. For instance we saw many children coming to their parents in tatted clothes, some feeling sick without parental support. Others scrambled for food and some were excluded from school for non payment of fees and their parents were unable to support them (Village youth leader)

> If children are not taken care of they will be forced to look elsewhere for material things. This can bring about promiscuity (Adolescent female in Community)

There were also appeals for action. An example being:

> If doctors (turning to researchers) can help women to have fewer children this will go a long way (Old woman in the Community)

Others in the forum were of the view that the onus lay on men to be more responsible:

> If men produce many children they must help to bring up the children. Impregnating a woman goes with responsibility which our men need to understand (Woman in the Community)

Child rearing is a parental responsibility (including extended family) but its upbringing is a collective responsibility (comprising parents and wider society) in traditional societies such as Wusuta. A lack of this practice can lead to a situation where children become social liabilities with all the problems that are associated with the phenomenon. It is not surprising that those issues about deviance were of concern to the community:

> The lead-singer was smoking cannabis. This is bad for young people and not a good act to depict in the performance. Smoking cannabis causes madness; young people take valium and alcohol and destroy themselves. This leads to low productivity (Chief of Wusuta)

The above concern is also a public health issue. The fact that community elders raised the subject implies a desire to address a social burden (truancy) on the community. This possibly will require a concerted effort by the community, social workers and public health officials to address the issue.

DISCUSSION

There is evidence to suggest that rural1 poverty is a result of multiple factors. Wusuta is just one among several rural communities in Ghana with low economic index. This may be due to many factors. For instance, the community lacks portable drinking water, good access road, electricity and social amenities. It is for this reason that readers should not see themes emerging from interview result differently from those summed in the research. The differences are more of researcher semantics than community perception. Wusuta can be classified among those Fields (2000) refers to as living in poverty in sub-Saharan Africa. From participants account, a shift in focus from community action to expert–led action (Hubbard, 1998) position the community in a 'powerless' situation to tackle its own problems. In other words, the community like many others lacks the capacity and know-how to resolve environmental tensions despite the abundance of resources which could be utilised. Perceiving the research team as 'experts' with a magic wand was therefore not surprising (Morrow, 2000). Similar lessons exist from distant projects like the Health Action Fund in the United States. This is a grassroots health communications and social marketing program that targets community groups who are involved in health promotion activities developed by large agencies. Rather than taking the traditional approach to health promotion and prevention where program development and implementation is left to professionals, it encourages members of neighborhoods, community groups, or churches to identify a problem and then develop ways to address that problem for their group (Maurana and Clark, 2000). Through this approach the community takes ownership of the learning activity and ensures that it works.

An issue about parental responsibility which was much highlighted in the community forum has force in academic discourse (Willekens, 2004). As Willenkens notes, motherhood simply follows from the fact of giving birth to a child but paternity is ascribed on the basis of either a genetic tie with the child, the man's legal relation to the woman who has given birth to the child or a combination of the two. Once legal parenthood has been established, a right and responsibility of duties follow which seems to be lacking among some families in the Wusuta community. Indeed, parents have a duty among others to take care of the spiritual and physical well-being of the child (p. 355).

There is a privileged lesson from Apteker (1994) which partly explains deviance in children in the developing world which is linked to the fact that children no longer grow up in extended families with strong community support. Mufune (2000) expands this notion further by arguing that nuclear family forms are less efficient in providing for large numbers of youngsters and do not readily accommodate distant relatives. It is possible that some children in Wusuta might be victims of this order. This situation has given rise to young people who experience family crisis not to be accommodated by kinship structures. Modernisation, Mufune argues, seems also to have enormous impact on children who are not prepared to adhere to parental rules and discipline (p. 239), a thinking which is corroborated by Gokah.

CONCLUSION

From the above discussion, three themes reflect the essential thrust and key findings. These themes are as follows:

(a) The analytic framework in respect of community learning through video production and folk media facilitated learning and a useful resource in identifying ways in which people think and talk about the social worlds they occupy and how this affects (and is affected by) local norms and traditions, and the way values are interpreted (Koshal, and Ashok, 1998). There is evidence in academic literature to suggest that facilitated learning through video recordings of learners in action has been used in formal teaching and learning settings (Minardi and Ritter, 1998). Its use in the informal sector to train and facilitate learning in rural communities via folk media is, however, relatively new. It thus offers opportunities to influence rural well-being (Minardi and Riley, 997). Video recordings of the various stages in the study were an effective means of receiving feedback (Kagan, et al., 1986). Although some studies (Raymond, 1983) have talked about the negative effect of seeing oneself in video-tapings this was not the case in *Wusuta* project.

The potential threat was the video-footage being misconstrued as a source of entertainment (because such facilities are scarce in rural communities) over and above its educational value. Should this happen the essence of the production is likely to be missed (Chang and Hirsch, 1994). It is difficult, if not impossible, to restrain audience participation (which includes children) in the open video forums. However, responses from those forums (as discussed earlier) indicate that the video recordings were valuable.

© *A sombre member of the community takes to the stage- night forum*

(b) The community's participation in health and environment related learning activity was an opportunity for the people of Wusuta to 'think through' issues that work against their well-being. Through this mechanism they were able to develop their own coping mechanism and ideas about resolving environmental threats. It also increased the community's desire and skills for action (Schon, 1983). Community participation is a highly promoted approach by change agencies and development donors (Johnson and Mayoux, 1998; Chambers, 1995). In fact Chambers (1994) has described community participation as 'a growing family of approaches and methods to enable rural and urban people to express, enhance, share and analyse their knowledge of life and condition to plan and to act'. In other words, they will be able to make their own voices heard, increase their own awareness and understanding and have a role in 'policy development' aimed at improving their well-being. Given the link between community participation and community empowerment, it is important that the lessons from the *Wusuta* project is given careful attention or at least serve as a basis for further research (Narayan and Srinivasan, 1994).

(c) Community learning theory has proven (in this study) to be a useful conceptual tool to explore how rural communities can be informed, educated and trained in ways to enhance or promote their well-being without necessarily relying on contemporary media – radio, television and print. Such initiatives involve the use of tested ideas and approaches to achieve intended results (Judge and Bauld, 2000). In order to address the complexities and challenges posed by community learning, there is need for conceptual frameworks that will link activities, outcomes and context (Connell and Kubisch, 1998). In the *Wusuta* study this took the form of gaining clarity of what community learning is all about and strategies needed to achieve learning. In generating this framework, steps were taken to link 'problem' with 'context' which helped in making explicit connection between the different components in the study and how they work. For instance, researcher's initial and continuous dialogue with stakeholders in the *Wusuta* community provided the fuel that sustained the research (Macaskill, et al., 2000) and the type of information needed to establish the usefulness of folk media and self video recordings to educate rural communities. This no doubt required careful but flexible planning and adaptive approaches to rural community learning (Granger, 1998)

NOTES:

1. Follow IFAD (2001) definition of "rural"

In: Contemporary Discourses on IE & C Theory and Practice ISBN: 978-1-60962-360-3
Editor: Theophilus K. Gokah © 2009 Nova Science Publishers, Inc.

Chapter 14

UGANDA FAMILY PLANNING PROGRAMS: LESSONS FROM THE FIELD PARTNERING WITH COMMUNITIES AND DISTRICT HEALTH TEAMS

Diana DuBois

This case study focuses on the family planning (child spacing) efforts of two U.S. private voluntary organizations (PVOs), each of which doubled modern contraceptive use in rural areas of Uganda. Minnesota International Health Volunteers (MIHV) implemented family planning activities in Ssembabule District, a rural south western district in Uganda, during the second phase of a U.S. Agency for International Development (USAID)-funded Child Survival Project (1993–2000). The Adventist Development and Relief Agency's (ADRA) Bunya Integrated Health Project (BIHP) implemented activities in two predominantly Muslim sub-counties of Bunya County during a Danish International Development Agency-funded Child Survival Project, ongoing in the Iganga District in southeast Uganda (1998-2006).

Both the MIHV and ADRA projects addressed family planning within the larger context of reproductive and maternal health using a multi sectoral community/participatory approach. Both organizations used a variety of strategies to educate women of reproductive age, adolescents, and sexually active men with the objective of increasing the use of modern contraceptives in their designated districts. Working with a variety of stakeholders including communities, district health units, local officials, community volunteers, and at times medical and nursing students (in the case of MIHV), both organizations forged partnerships and used five principal strategies to increase family planning use and to lower rates of infant, child, and maternal mortality and morbidity. MIHV and ADRA:

1. Expanded service delivery by enabling a range of providers (public sector, private sector, community volunteers, and medical/nursing students) to deliver family planning information, referrals, and services.
2. Educated and mobilized communities to increase demand for, and use of, family planning services

3. Built the capacity of health unit staff to mobilize communities, supervise health workers, establish systems, create realistic budgets and plans, and (in the case of ADRA) assist with clinic rehabilitation and equipping.
4. Collaborated with other PVOs, agencies, and stakeholders to leverage resources and increase access to family planning services; and
5. Developed innovative information, education, and communication methods to deliver family planning messages to low literate populations and assisted with material support such as bicycles and provision of handbags.

As a result, mothers' knowledge of modern family planning increased significantly. For MIHV, project interventions contributed to the following changes, as noted by Knowledge, Practice and Coverage (KPC) Survey results between 1996 and 2000 for women of childbearing age with a child under 24 months, in Ssembabule District [sample size=300]:

- Modern contraceptive use among women of reproductive age increased from 6% to 14%.
- Use of any family planning method more than doubled, from 10% to 22%.
- Contraceptive use among women who did not want a child in the next two years doubled, from 24% to 47%.
- Reported pregnancies declined by more than one-third (from 16% to 10%).
- The number of non-pregnant women wanting a child within the next two years fell by 9%.
- Condom use by male partners increased from 0% to 11%.
   Similarly, project interventions by ADRA resulted in the following results, for a population of 100,000:
- Among women of childbearing age, awareness of family planning more than doubled, from 30% in 1999 to 73% in 2004.
- The contraceptive prevalence rate increased from 11% in 1999 to 23% in 2003;
- There was increased demand on the part of the community for outreach, parish health days, and health talks.
- Twice as many patients sought information about family planning at sub-county health units. As a result of direct community-based involvement using an integrated approach, each organization learned many important lessons. MIHV's lessons learned include:
- Project activities sparked positive social change, which in turn facilitated family planning uptake.
- The Catholic Church provided strong support for natural family planning methods.
- Natural family planning can offer an effective entry to other short-term and long-term family planning methods.
- There is a strong unmet demand for the female condom.
- Traditional birth attendants (TBAs) are an essential family planning resource.
- TBA performance in relation to family planning can be enhanced with strong support.
- TBAs can be trained to include family planning in postpartum care.
- Private outlets can be quickly mobilized to become major suppliers of condoms.

- Nursing and medical students can contribute to community health programs and to family planning activities in particular.
- Decentralisation offers both opportunities and constraints for community-based public health programming.
- A comprehensive, integrated approach can improve individual child survival interventions.

ADRA's lessons learned include:

- The public sector cannot meet the demand for contraceptives.
- *Per diems* can contribute to the cooperation of extension staff.
- Joint planning and budgeting between a PVO and local authorities can improve resource utilization.
- Community volunteers should be certified.
- Community groups can greatly aid project implementation.

This study presents strategies, approaches, activities, and lessons learned as a learning model for other PVOs, government entities, and community members as they work to develop successful family planning projects in similar resource-poor environments. The available methods of family planning in Ntusi are visible (condoms, pills), so women find it problematic to hide them from their husbands.

ACRONYMS

ADRA	Adventist Development and Relief Agency International
AIDS	Acquired Immune Deficiency Syndrome
AMREF	African Medical Research Foundation
BIHP	Bunya Integrated Health Project CBO community-based organization
CORE	Child Survival Collaborations and Resources Group DHS Demographic and Health Survey
DISH	Delivery of Improved Services for Health FP family planning
HIV	Human Immunodeficiency Virus
IEC	Information, education, and communication
IUD	Intra-uterine device
KPC	Knowledge, Practice and Coverage Survey
LAM	Lactational amenorrhea method
MIHV	Minnesota International Health Volunteers
MOH	Ministry of Health
NGO-	Non-governmental organization
PATH	Program for Appropriate Technology in Health
PVO	Private voluntary organization
TASO	The AIDS Support Organisation
TBA	Traditional birth attendant

UDHS	Uganda Demographic and Health Survey
USAID	U.S. Agency for International Development
UNICEF	United Nations Children's Fund

Both MIHV and ADRA mobilized rural communities to increase demand for, and use of, family planning services.

PROJECT CONTEXT: UGANDA

In Uganda, women have shown a high level of awareness regarding family planning options. In the 1995 Uganda Demographic and Health Survey (DHS), virtually all women (92%) could name at least one family planning method, and a large proportion (79%) reported that they approved of contraceptive use. More than two-thirds of women (69%) wanted to either space their next birth or end childbearing altogether. Despite this interest, only 15% of married women were using a contraceptive method, and only 8% used modern methods (as low as 5% in rural areas).

Periodic abstinence, the pill, and injectables were the most common modern methods used, with condom use at less than 1% in rural areas. In 1995, MIHV found that only 10% of women in Ssembabule District were using any contraceptive method, and only 6% were using modern methods. The most common methods in the district were the lactational amenorrhea method (LAM)1; injectables, and periodic abstinence. There was almost no reported condom use.

According to the 1995 DHS, Uganda's total fertility rate was 6.9 (7.2 in rural areas), and the desired number of children in rural areas was 5.5 for women and 5.8 for men. Frequent and closely spaced childbearing is associated in Uganda, as elsewhere, with increased mortality and morbidity for both mothers and their children, a circumstance compounded in Uganda by inadequate maternal care. In 1995, Uganda's maternal mortality rate was reported at 527 deaths per 100,000 live births. The 2000 UDHS lists under- 5 infant mortality rate of 152, an increase over the 1995 under-5 rate of 147.

Teenage girls and their children are at special risk of mortality and morbidity. Women in Uganda on average begin sexual activity by the age of 16, and 43% of women aged 15–19 are already mothers or are pregnant with their first child (45% in rural areas) (UDHS, 1995).

Given such statistics, family planning professionals often struggle to bring family planning services to rural women and couples who want to space or limit childbearing. There are numerous social, institutional, and logistical factors that inhibit women's access to and use of modern contraceptive methods including:

- Family planning is rarely at the top of a community's list of priority issues given economic realities and educational levels;
- Women, their partners, and other family members often have misconceptions about the safety and efficacy of modern methods2, 1. The 1995 UDHS did not ask women about LAM use.
- Those who wish to use a modern method may believe that family or community members would oppose contraceptive use;
- Those who decide to use family planning often find services difficult to access;
- Health centers are few and far between, and health professionals are overstretched and often unable to focus adequate effort on family planning;
- Logistics systems are underdeveloped, leading to frequent contraceptive shortages, and the private sector often has no incentive to invest in the provision of contraceptives;
- When women ask men to use condoms, the women are often viewed as promiscuous, or the men perceive that the women think they are "dirty" (from MIHV key informant interview); and
- Local women do not like to use foam or cervical caps as they are unaccustomed to inserting things inside themselves (tampon use is nonexistent) (from MIHV key informant interview).

When projects manage to increase contraceptive use in rural Uganda, it is essential that they document their efforts and disseminate both lessons learned and data-based results. This case study was commissioned by the CORE Group to provide such information.

2. It should be noted that the term "child spacing" was used by MIHV in Uganda rather than the term "family planning" since some community members interpret the term family planning to mean preventing the population from having children. In Uganda "Entegeka ya maka" literally translates as a plan for the home, which has a more positive connotation for rural Ugandans.

MIHV Project: Ssembabule District

Ssembabule is an underserved, rural district approximately 170 kilometers southwest of the capital city, Kampala. The district's 2,500 square kilometers are home to approximately 160,000 people (including 30,900 women of reproductive age) living in 270 villages. At the time of the MIHV project (1996-2000), the district had limited infrastructure, no telecommunications system, no electricity, poor roads, and poor water supply. Nomadic pastoralists inhabit the low-lying grasslands of Ssembabule's northwest, while agriculturalists dominate in the southeast. The languages most commonly spoken are Luganda and Runyankole. The literacy rate for women at the time was 57% (MIHV KPC, 1996).

Formerly a sub-district of Masaka District, Ssembabule became its own district in 1997, shortly after the second phase of MIHV's project began. Little capacity building had taken place to prepare Ssembabule, or its new district officials, for decentralization. Because of Ssembabule's remote location and undeveloped infrastructure, officials had great difficulty filling critical staff positions. This, in turn, adversely affected the district's ability to formulate plans, establish systems, provide services, and supervise workers.

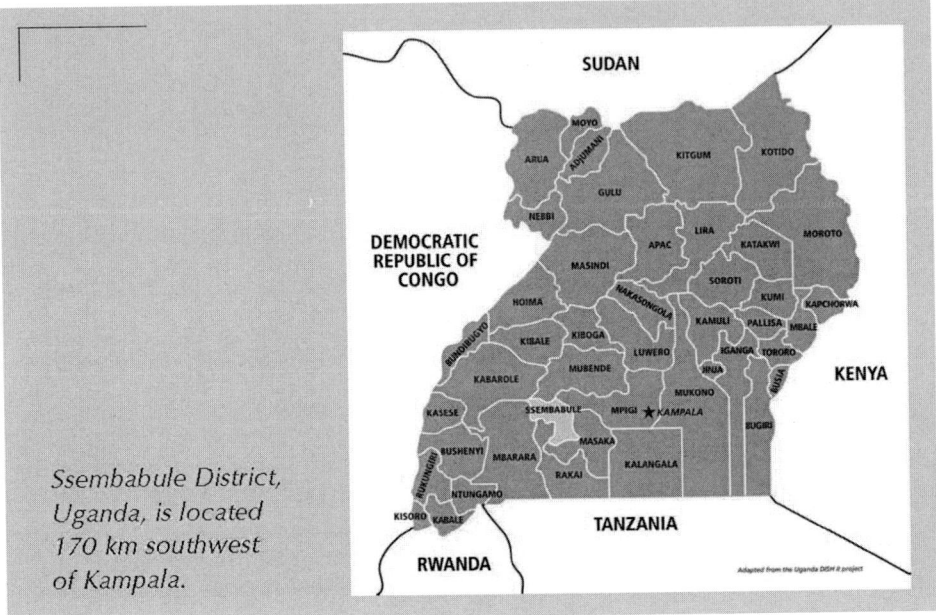

Ssembabule District, Uganda, is located 170 km southwest of Kampala.

The central government did not have sufficient funds to help the fledgling district build its capacity or develop its physical infrastructure. With decentralization, Ssembabule was expected to generate its own revenue, but the new district had little tax base.

In 1996, the health system, though progressing, needed much improvement in terms of service availability and quality of care. The population was served by one government health center staffed mainly by midwives and nurse aides; five sub dispensaries (including two nongovernmental facilities run by the Catholic Church); and numerous TBAs, traditional healers, community-based distributors, and drug vendors. Altogether, only 25 trained health care staff cared for approximately 160,000 people without the assistance of an emergency room or hospital. As noted above, family planning use in Ssembabule was low—lower even than in the country as a whole.

MIHV: APPROACHES

Expand Service Delivery

At the time of the family planning project, MIHV was the only international PVO in Ssembabule District. At the project's onset, public and private sector health workers were woefully overstretched since there was only one health center serving a population of approximately 160,000 people. The ratio of health care workers to district residents was estimated at 1:1,644. To increase client access to family planning information and services, it was necessary to upgrade health worker skills, and to train an additional group of volunteer community workers to provide family planning counselling, referral, and in some cases, methods.

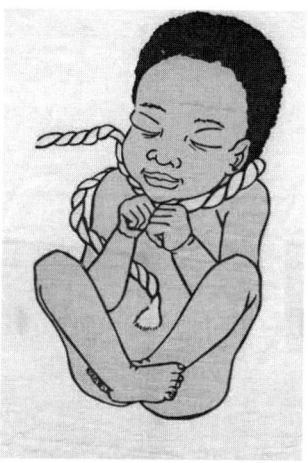

To accomplish this, MIHV created six Family Planning Implementation Teams (which consisted of a health unit staff member, MIHV's Maternal Health Coordinator, the MIHV Health Educator, and a community volunteer, such as a TBA). After receiving training from MIHV's Country Director and select family planning experts, the family planning teams were responsible for training, raising awareness, mobilizing communities, and imparting leadership skills.

Traditionally, men believe that if you have more children, you are considered an important person in the society.

The teams involved community leaders in all local advocacy activities. They used participatory rural appraisal methods to identify community health programs and to begin family planning program planning. The result of these advocacy efforts was a marked decline in opposition to modern family planning by religious and **political leaders. Table 1 lists the community health volunteers and health unit staff trained by MIHV project workers to address family planning issues in Ssembabule District.**

To improve both access to and quality of family planning services, it was important to build service capacity and develop systems to support the delivery of those services. Consequently, each training included a section on tracking referrals, recording supplies, basic recordkeeping, and reporting.

Educate and mobilize communities

MIHV involved communities in program design, implementation, and evaluation, always using a grassroots, rather than a top-down approach to ensure that communities "owned" family planning project objectives, processes, and outcomes. By involving the communities in all aspects of the projects (project needs assessments, planning, monitoring and evaluation, leadership sensitization, educational events, interpersonal communication and counselling), as well as through increased service availability and visibility, the project team raised community awareness of the importance of spacing children. In Bunya District, parish development committees shared information collected through village record books and on large hanging boards, so communities could use these data for decision-making in community meetings.

Build the capacity of health unit staff

MIHV focused on building capacity of health unit staff to mobilize communities, supervise health workers, establish systems, and create responsive budgets and plans. Activities included hands-on technical assistance and incorporating district health staff in family planning project trainings.

Because Ssembabule was unprepared for the redistricting that took place during the child survival project, MIHV was called upon to provide critical support beyond what otherwise might have been required. MIHV staff offered continuous technical assistance and support to the newly formed five-person District Health Management Team, which was never fully staffed during the project period.

The MIHV project team:

- provided technical assistance and training to district and clinic staff in health topics including primary health care and family planning, and in community mobilization and adult training methods
- linked district staff to communities, community providers, and nongovernmental health units (for example, arranging introductory visits to key community partners, bringing district staff to meet TBAs in their homes or drug vendors in their shops, including district staff in teams that supervised community volunteers, and bringing volunteers to visit clinics);
- provided essential logistical support for district management and health service provision such as the use of MIHV's vehicles for mobilization efforts; and
- contributed as members of the district planning team to the creation of District Health Plans and annual budgets, as well as to proposals submitted to the central ministry. In this final capacity, MIHV helped gather data, facilitated meetings, contributed expertise and its knowledge of community needs and priorities, and assisted in the production of plans and proposals.

MIHV collaborated with the Uganda National Family Planning Association4, the Ministry of Health (MOH), the African Medical Research Foundation (AMREF), UNICEF, the World Health Organization (WHO), the Ministry of Education, local government units, Lions Aid/Norway, Marie Stopes International, The AIDS Services Organization (TASO), and the USAID-funded DISH project. It also collaborated closely with all local groups including farmers, women's groups, TBAs, school and youth groups, and the Catholic Church. In addition, MIHV provided more than a dozen students field placements for Master's degree students from the United States.

Table 1. Community Health Volunteers and Health Unit Staff Trained by MIHV in Ssembabule District

Community volunteers trained through the project	Total trained
Traditional birth attendants: TBAs were trained by the project primarily on family planning, safe motherhood, nutrition, breastfeeding, immunization, STDs/HIV/AIDS, but also on malaria during pregnancy (risks and treatment).	200
Drug vendors: The project's training curriculum for drug vendors focused primarily on family planning methods and malaria, and provided stocks of condoms for these private sector providers.	167
Health unit staff: The project worked in close collaboration with government and non-governmental health unit staff to strengthen family planning services, providing yearly skill upgrades and involving health unit staff in supervision and monitoring of TBAs, drug vendors, and community-based distributors. Skill areas included modern methods, community mobilization, and condom negotiation.	25
Student doctors and nurses: The MIHV project was a field site for nursing students from the Comprehensive Nursing Training Center in Masaka and for young physicians from the University of Science and Technology in Mbarara. They obtained a practical introduction to village-level primary health care through the project. Nursing students joined family planning teams contributing their skills when possible. Medical students also provided their skills. Each medical student was assigned to work with a community to identify and address a major health problem.	200 nurses 75 doctors
Community-based distributors: The project identified and trained community members to distribute condoms to bar and lodge attendants as well as to set up kiosks in all major markets throughout the district. These kiosks sold condoms and could sell oral contraceptives provided by MIHV/DISH (Pilplan), if customer had already been seen by a clinical health provider.	90
Nun/Natural Family Planning Specialist: Worked with MIHV project staff and discussed natural family planning methods with interested community members and conducted referrals.	1 natural FP specialist
Peer educators: Volunteers based in primary and secondary schools counseled peers about family planning, and HIV/AIDS and sexually transmitted infection prevention through dramas, music and poetry. Peer educators were part of 95 school health clubs established by the project.	280
Members of women's groups: About 40 women's groups were formed and trained mainly on income generation activities (e.g., goat rearing, book keeping, management), but also on basic home health education.	400
Professional Associations: MIHV project staff nurtured the development of professional associations, one for TBAs and one for drug vendors.	2 CBO organizations

Collaborate with other PVOs, agencies, and stakeholders

One collaborative effort between MIHV and DISH II made high-quality condoms and pills more available in the district. DISH II did not have the resources to establish an office in Ssembabule, so did much of their work in the district through MIHV. DISH II used MIHV's office as a base and relied on MIHV's vehicles, logistical support, training site, and sometimes staff to conduct trainings or upgrade health units. MIHV served as a storage and distribution point for community-based distribution agents and drug vendors in the district, reporting to DISH II on commodities distributed.

Another major MIHV collaborative partner was the Catholic Church, which was highly influential in the district. At the time, the Church supported condom use for disease prevention but not for child spacing. MIHV had an excellent relationship with a nun well-trained in natural family planning, who advocated for project objectives, designed and taught a natural family planning component that was included in all family planning trainings, and referred clients, when appropriate, for modern methods.

Collaboration also occurred upon completion of the child survival project. MIHV raised additional funds from donors including the Government of Uganda, the World Bank, World Vision and the CORE Group (for polio eradication efforts), the Scandia Foundation, and PATH/Canada (for micronutrient education).

Develop innovative information, education, and communication methods

MIHV developed a number of communications strategies to deliver family planning messages to low literate populations. Community volunteers counselled clients on key messages including: (1) child spacing is important for the health of the mother and well-being of the family; (2) family planning decisions should be made by both partners together; (3) fewer children means more resources for the family; and (4) family planning methods are safe and effective.

MIHV family planning teams held special events (e.g. Child Health Days, World Health Days) in conjunction with local clinics. Events used games, dramas, songs, and contests to raise awareness. One drama featured a man whose wife spaced her children, explaining to the husband of a woman who did not space her children, how they had discovered the benefits of modern methods, how modern methods allowed them to choose when to have children, and how happy their family was as a result. Because caretakers were busy and often travelled great distances to attend, the project ensured that even "single-issue" events always provided information and services for other health issues, including family planning. As a result, these events were extremely popular.

MIHV helped establish 95 school health clubs to inform the community about family planning, HIV/AIDS, and sexually transmitted infections

The MIHV family planning team also utilized and adapted educational materials to increase awareness of family planning (e.g., calendars, posters, pamphlets, songs, dramas, and flipcharts). When appropriate, it also made use of materials developed by the MOH and other USAID-funded projects.

In developing materials, the project used traditional folklore and local knowledge to ensure relevant messages. One poster (adapted from existing educational materials) reminded farmers that to have a healthy banana plantation they needed to limit the number of sprouts; to have a healthy family, they needed to space their children. As virtually everyone grew bananas, the message was immediately understood and widely accepted. Referral information was printed on the bottom of the poster; and materials were distributed at events, to community volunteers, in drug shops, in clinics, and directly to clients.

MIHV: Results

Family planning activities were monitored and evaluated through baseline (1996) and end-of-project (2000) KPC surveys implemented with 300 women, service provider records, and clinic service statistics. Major family planning results included the following:

- The use of modern contraceptives (pills, injectables, IUDs) among women of reproductive age increased from 6% in 1996 to 14% in 2000[3]
- Use of any family planning method more than doubled, from 10% to 22%.
- Contraceptive use among women who did not want a child in the next two years doubled, from 24% to 47%.
- The increase in overall family planning method use could be entirely attributed to increased use of modern methods. The overall use of traditional and natural methods remained constant among women surveyed, while the use of a particularly ineffective method—periodic abstinence—decreased from 23% to 0% of all family planning users.

- Reported pregnancies declined by more than one-third (from 16% to 10%).
- The number of non-pregnant women wanting a child within the next two years fell by 9%.
- Condom use by male partners increased from 0% to 11%.

The most popular modern method was the injectables, in part because women could use it without their husbands' knowledge, followed by pills and condoms. Condom use may be underestimated; however, as women who used condoms for disease prevention may not have reported using them for family planning purposes. Still, more than half of those pregnant in 2000 had not planned their pregnancies. In citing reasons for not using family planning methods, one-third of women cited husband refusal, one-third said they "did not know" about family planning, and one-third cited "other" reasons. Religious belief was not a significant factor in non-use.

MIHV team members interviewed village mothers as part of the project's data collection efforts.

MIHV: Lessons Learned

Decentralization offers both opportunities and constraints.

Redistricting in Ssembabule happened quickly and without adequate training, staffing, or infrastructure development. In a very real sense and for a substantial period of time, the provision of basic health services was threatened. But decentralization also brought unexpected opportunities. Because MIHV was the first and only international PVO in the district, and had built trust during the four years of the project's first phase, communities were receptive to project messages and activities. Also, because the area was unaccustomed to the exercise of power, its emerging leaders, many with ties to the project, had not yet been jaded by it: they were often enthusiastic and idealistic. The project had an opportunity, therefore, to influence both communities and their leaders just as they were beginning to assume greater responsibilities.

A comprehensive, integrated approach can improve individual child survival interventions

To address Ssembabule's many needs, the project focused on multiple child survival interventions (maternal health/family planning, diarrhoea, immunization, breastfeeding, nutrition, malaria, and HIV/AIDS). This comprehensive approach allowed interventions to be linked in an efficient and responsive way. For example, a TBA trained in postpartum care could also discuss family planning and immunization with a new mother. Preparing community volunteers to respond to the broader health care needs of their communities improved the project's success with individual child survival interventions and may also have yielded greater openness to interventions seen as lower priority, such as family planning.

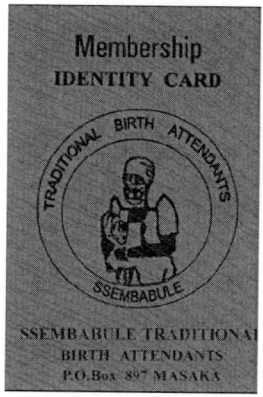

MIHV trained 200 traditional birth attendants in topics including family planning methods, nutrition, and immunization.

Project activities sparked positive social change which in turn facilitated family planning uptake

According to focus group discussions, project activities contributed to increased communication about sexuality between men and women. This type of dialogue was critical. As the DHS 1996 Negotiating Reproductive Outcomes study noted, only about one-third of men and women in 1995 reported having discussed family size or child spacing with their partners, even though more than 90% of rural respondents knew of at least one modern contraceptive method. DHS and MIHV researchers learned that both men and women assumed their partners wanted more children than they actually did. In a culture where large families are the norm and couples do not traditionally talk about such matters, lack of communication is an important family health problem. MIHV found that providing couples with a forum for discussing family size quickly dissipated this culture of silence. Conventionally excluded from the process, the men appreciated being part of the family planning conversation, learning how an entire family's well-being might improve with better spaced children, and discussing options with their wives.

Project activities also contributed to greater empowerment of women. Women joined project-supported women's groups, assumed leadership positions as project-trained community volunteers, contributed cash income to their families earned through project-supported garden and goat projects, and with their new prestige, ran successfully for political office. With this new confidence, financial independence, and access to resources, many women felt increasingly empowered to learn about family planning and spacing their children.

It is possible to gain support for natural family planning methods from the Catholic Church

The project gained credibility and responded to client needs by working with the Church at the district and local level. A nun specializing in natural family planning was heavily involved in family planning training and advocating for the project. Building this relationship took time, but as a result, the Church did not obstruct project activities, and clients in every parish had access to modern and more effective natural family planning methods.

Natural family planning can offer an effective entry to modern family planning

There is an unmet demand for natural family planning in the Ssembabule District as demonstrated by low modern family planning use, significant use of less effective traditional methods (e.g., periodic abstinence), negative attitudes toward family planning,6 and strong Church influence. To meet this unmet demand and to correspond with the guidelines on the rhythm method and LAM being issued by family planning and maternal/child health donors (e.g., the Uganda National Family Association, UNICEF, and USAID), MIHV included natural family planning in community volunteer and health worker trainings. Natural family planning education was provided by an expert representative of the Catholic Church. This program addition enabled couples with reservations about modern methods to still attempt to space their children, and the overall concept of child spacing became more acceptable.

One unexpected outcome of this activity was that men were competently educated by an unimpeachable source (the Church representative) on the complicated nature of natural family planning, as opposed to the perceived "easiness" of merely counting days. Stymied by the difficult and uncomfortable demands of natural family planning (e.g., intimate knowledge of woman's body, tracking menstrual cycle, postponing desire until a "safe" day) men attending training sessions would often instruct their wives to find a more convenient, less meddlesome modern method to use instead. Unexpectedly, the introduction of natural family planning often led project participants to embrace modern family planning methods.

TBAs are an essential family planning resource

Given proper training and support, TBAs greatly expand the accessibility of family planning information by providing referrals and services, and reinforce key family planning messages. To address the unmet need for family planning, TBAs provide antenatal care, perform deliveries, provide clinical postpartum care, and advise on natural family planning. Importantly, as trusted members of the communities, TBAs can efficiently carry out educational activities. MIHV discovered that both young and old TBAs were eager and able to learn new knowledge and skills.

TBA performance can be enhanced with strong support

The family planning team educated TBAs in family planning, maternal health, safe delivery, HIV/AIDS prevention, immunization, nutrition and breastfeeding, malaria and diarrhoeal disease control, the objectives of community-based health care, community mobilization, and how to make referrals. Further, the Maternal Health Coordinator created simple, flexible record-keeping tools. For example, to enable older, low-literate, innumerate TBAs to track the number of deliveries and unusual delivery conditions, the project taught various counting systems. One system used coloured stones, another hash marks on the wall, and another a simple pictograph-based tool. FP team members collected the data monthly.

The family planning team also fostered strong relationships between TBAs, clinic nurses, and clinic midwives. For example, MIHV involved clinic health unit staff in TBA training and quarterly supervision visits. TBAs visited clinics to check on referred clients and accompanied clients to clinics for follow-up care. Such 'two-way' feedback strengthened the referral system as TBAs continued to feel connected to and responsible for their clients.

Training TBAs in postpartum care can be an effective family planning intervention

Based on lessons learned working with TBAs for eight years, MIHV believes that the most important responsibilities of TBAs are to provide clients with education, antenatal and postpartum care, and referral. Postpartum care is particularly important. It is through postpartum care that TBAs can most easily and effectively promote care for new mothers, postpartum family planning, breastfeeding, children's immunization, nutrition, and appropriate care for childhood malaria and diarrhoea.

At the onset of MIHV's project, the few women who sought postpartum care sought it from trusted TBAs who lived close by. To utilize the current system, MIHV trained and supported TBAs to recognize danger signs in babies and postpartum mothers, to refer suspected problems, to promote immunization and optimal breastfeeding, and to counsel mothers about postpartum family planning options and child health. The project's strategy of training TBAs to provide postpartum care was successful as evidenced by the large number of women who reported, in the project's final survey, that they followed postpartum advice.

Private outlets can quickly be mobilized to become major suppliers of condoms

Between 1996 and 2000, private vendors (e.g., drugstores, kiosks, bars) replaced family planning clinics as the primary supplier of condoms. Specifically, use of clinics fell by one third to one half, while use of these private sector outlets more than tripled to 50%. This shift is attributable to several factors, including: condom shortages at clinics, increased availability of condoms through project-supplied community-based distributors and drug vendors, greater convenience of private sector sources, DISH II promotion of drug vendors, and reluctance by men to buy condoms at public clinics. This transition is presumed sustainable because private-sector providers are all trained, marketing efforts popularized the product, customers are satisfied with product quality, and private sector providers recognize the incentives associated with increased demand in continuing to stock the products.

Nursing and medical students can offer much to community health programs

The medical profession rarely emphasizes family planning or the development of skills in community health and outreach. Therefore, it is extremely valuable to involve nursing and medical students in community health programs while they are still learning and receptive to new ideas. The MIHV project site served as a practicum site for 200 future nurses and 75 future doctors. These young professionals benefited from designing their own community education interventions, and their involvement greatly extended the availability of medical expertise for the underserved population of Ssembabule. Due to shortages of doctors and hospitals, the approximately 15 student doctors in the district represented the district's greatest medical expertise. The project facilitated an environment where young medical professionals could develop skills to be used in future careers as rural public health physicians and nurses. Their presence revitalized health unit staff, raising spirits and reducing overwhelming workloads. MIHV also served as the practicum field site for more than a dozen Master's degree students from the United States.

There is a strong unmet demand for the female condom

During the last six months of the project, Marie Stopes International asked MIHV to pilot the female condom in Ssembabule. MIHV was chosen as a partner because of its collaboration with DISH II, its status as the only PVO working in Ssembabule, its family planning experience, its reach at the community level throughout the district, and its clear commitment to improving the health of women and families in the area.

The MIHV project site served as a practicum for 75 Ugandan medical students.

The MIHV team surveyed sexually active teenage girls in school about their needs and the potential acceptability of the female condom. Team members found surprisingly high interest and distributed approximately 2,000 female condoms. In a two-day training session, the family planning team introduced selected TBAs to the female condom and trained them in its cultural, physical, and financial aspects. The trained TBAs then distributed female condoms and educational materials (free of cost) to interested postpartum clients. Finally, the family planning team educated women leaders (e.g., women council members and members of Parliament) to advocate for the female condom. Through these activities, MIHV and Marie Stopes International discovered a strong interest in the female condom, as well as strong support for the condom among female leaders.

ADRA Project: Iganga District

In 1998, ADRA/Uganda partnered with the World Health Organization (WHO) and the Ministry of Health (MOH) to implement selective activities in Bunya County, Iganga District, in south eastern Uganda. The project, titled the Bunya Integrated Health Project (BIHP), targeted two sub-counties: Malongo and Kityerera. The target population included the total population in these two sub-counties, approximately 85,000 people. The project was planned in three phases over 8 years (1998 to 2001; 2001 to 2004; and 2004 to 2006) and is ongoing. The project area is predominantly Muslim, and 92% of the households are polygamous. A baseline survey revealed that the number of people using family planning methods was small (10.7% compared to the national figure of 15.2%). The survey also found that the average household size was eight people. Sexual debut was found to be early (at 6–10 years old) 8. Population growth was 3.5% (UDHS, 1995). Very few women (6%) who received antenatal care had their baby delivered by a health worker. As a result, morbidity and mortality both for women and children was very high.

Not unexpectedly, challenges in the district were numerous and included: a high level of poverty, long walking distances to the nearest health units, inadequately trained staff in the health centers, untrained TBAs delivering most of the babies in the villages (70% of all deliveries), ill-equipped health centers providing antenatal care services, and 90% of government health units housed in temporary and substandard premises contributing to poor service delivery. Much needed to be done to sensitize and strengthen community members through the existing local community systems such as Parish Development Committees, Health Unit Management Committees, Village Development Committees, and health unit staff.

In 2000, Bunya County became an independent district called Mayuge but retained the project area under its constituency. According to the 2002 population and housing census, Mayuge District has a population of 326,839, of whom 20% are children under five and 23% are women of childbearing age. The district's fertility rate is 7.2 as compared to the national figure of 6.9. The infant mortality rate is 125/1000 (national figure 97/1000) and the maternal mortality rate is 506/100,000. The under-five mortality rate is 208/1000 compared to the national figure of 147/1000 (Mayuge District Situational Analysis Report 2001)5.

ADRA: APPROACHES

Educate and mobilize communities

ADRA uses a multi-sectoral approach in Bunya County, integrating family planning activities into a variety of other programs (nutrition, literacy, income generation, and water/sanitation). The project has sensitized and trained a variety of community members, especially women of childbearing age (estimated at 27,000) about the importance of family planning through parish development committees, functional adult literacy classes, income generation activities, and other community groups. Manuals containing these messages are used as textbooks. Educational activities are integrated with establishing community contraceptive distribution systems through 29 trained community-based reproductive health workers. All community health workers are attached to the nearest health unit, through which BIHP channels all services.

BUILD THE CAPACITY OF HEALTH UNIT STAFF

ADRA works closely with health unit staff by funding training in basic family planning skills through the district and the MOH. Table 2 lists those staff trained by ADRA through BIHP's first two phases.

To improve support systems for family planning, ADRA trained personnel in support supervision and assisted the District Medical Office to establish a supervision system. The project team also linked community distributors with the nearest clinic for monitoring, supervision, contraceptive supply, referral, and reporting; and trained community workers and groups in monitoring and data collection. ADRA assisted health unit staff by rehabilitating and equipping eight health units for family planning service provision, and created eight bicycle stretchers or "bicycle ambulances" for transporting sick people to health units.

Table 2. Health Unit Staff Trained by ADRA Staff to Address Family Planning Issues

Health Unit Staff Trained	Total Trained
Midwives trained in basic family planning clinical skills for 30 days.*	8 midwives
Nursing Assistants educated as nurse-midwives for 2.5 years to improve the quality of service delivery in health units.*	8 nursing assistants trained as nurse midwives
Nursing Assistants trained in comprehensive nursing skills for three months to improve the quality of service delivery.*	6 nursing assistants
Community workers, district and sub county health officials, and health unit staff educated in participatory methods and community mobilization.**	29 reproductive health workers 38 TBAs 420 Parish Development Committee members 55 functional adult literacy instructors 13 sub-county trainers 21 sub-county Enterprise Management Committee Members 100 model farmers 20 sub-county officials 28 district health staff 56 health unit management committee members for eight health units
Community-based reproductive health workers educated to carry out community education, home visiting, counseling, distribution of contraceptives, and referral.	29 community-based reproductive health workers

*Training included: rationale for family planning, correct use of family planning methods, use of family planning/maternal health service delivery guidelines, client education, anatomy/physiology, integrating reproductive health services including antenatal and post-natal care, treatment of sexually transmitted infections, client counseling on informed choices, managing family planning side effects, client screening, and using a syndromic approach to manage sexually transmitted infections/HIV/AIDS.

** TBA training included: client history-taking, physical examination, mother screening and referral to health units for family planning services and maternal health, and use of the Lactation Amenorrhoea Method. Community-based health worker training included: rationale for family planning, client counseling on informed choices, client education, home visits and follow-up, client screening and referral to health units, and anatomy/physiology. Training sessions also addressed the benefits of family planning services in relation to general community development, family development, and economic growth.

ADRA and health unit staff also collaborated on monitoring and evaluation. The health unit staff and the BIHP family planning coordinator use a monthly family planning appointment card and a monthly monitoring family planning client card to collect information, then present monthly monitoring and evaluation reports to BIHP and ADRA-Uganda. Community reproductive health workers present monthly reports on the number of homes visited, the number of mothers referred for antenatal care, the number of family planning and information, education and communication sessions given, and materials requested by the community. In addition, BIHP, ADRA-Uganda and ADRA-Denmark review the project annually. This is followed by an impact assessment and evaluation every three years.

In terms of supervision, the district has given health unit staff responsibility to supervise community-based health workers and traditional midwives. They hold quarterly meetings to plan and review community activities. The district pays for transport to and lunch during these meetings. In turn, health unit staffs are supervised by the district and BIHP intervention coordinator.

Collaborate with other PVOs, agencies, and stakeholders

ADRA has collaborated with many community partners on its family planning initiative. These include the Government of Uganda (Ministries of Health, Gender, Labour and Social Development, and Uganda AIDS Commission), the district health office, local governments, Marie Stopes/ Uganda, the Family Life Education Project, the Program for Enhancing Adolescent Reproductive Health, local youth and women's groups, school and farmer groups, and faith-based groups. ADRA/Uganda also coordinated visits to its project site by other PVOs including Concern International, CARE Uganda, and Save the Children UK. In addition, they facilitated student placements from Busoga and Makerere Universities, as well as students from Sweden and Denmark.

ADRA collaborated with Marie Stopes International to improve the method mix available in project sub-counties. The district medical office provided pills, injectables, and condoms to area health units, but prior to ADRA's activities, health units could not provide longer-term and permanent methods. Together with communities and district health officials, the project was able to arrange for Marie Stopes International to conduct monthly outreach visits to each project sub-county, providing both Norplant and voluntary surgical contraception. Within a period of eight months, 52 clients had received Norplant inserts, 54 had received tubal ligations, and 1 had received a vasectomy.

Marie Stopes now offers two outreach sessions every month (one in each sub-county) providing permanent methods. Before Marie Stopes collaborated with the ADRA project, ADRA had transported couples interested in long-term surgical contraceptive services to Jinja Town, 80 kilometers away. This approach proved unsustainable with conflicting vehicle schedules and high transport costs.

Develop innovative information, education, and communication methods

ADRA has sensitized and mobilized the Bunya County community and conducted outreach sessions to raise awareness of family planning activities. The team has used educational dramas and videos, conducted project staff home visits, and used satisfied clients as family planning "witnesses." Parish Health Days provided family planning referrals, and dramas, presentations, and testimonials were also used. The project team also held multi-sectoral "model home" competitions, which integrated education regarding hygiene, energy-saving devices, agriculture, and family planning. Family planning messages were incorporated into literacy materials and income-generation training.

ADRA provided material support to reproductive health workers and other community actors (listed in chart, page 17), who were provided with more than 100 bicycles, more than 600 handbags, family planning client cards, referral forms, report forms, communication materials, brochures, and posters. These materials successfully increased both family planning awareness and client motivation to obtain family planning information.

ADRA: Results

- Among women of childbearing age, awareness of family planning more than doubled, from 30% in 1999 to 73% in 2004.
- The contraceptive prevalence rate increased from 11% in 1999 to 23% in 2003.
- The number of family planning counselling sessions in sub-county health units doubled, showing an increased demand (from 10% in 1999 to 24% in 2003) (BIHP Quarterly Summary Report).
- There was increased community demand for outreach, parish health days, and health talks.

ADRA: Lessons Learned

- The public sector could not meet demand for contraceptives. Even with ADRA's contraceptive contribution, the district did not have enough supply to meet rising demand for methods. This was due to underestimates by district staff, delay of distribution due to transport problems, and periodic shortages of supplies at national stores.
- Per diems contribute to extension staff cooperation. It was rather difficult to involve extension staff in the field without the provision of per diems. Such provision greatly increased cooperation.
- Joint planning and budgeting between a PVO and local authorities can improve resource utilization. This is especially true at the district and community levels. Since planning emphasizes community-defined needs, resources are focused on community priorities. Also, joint planning and budgeting eliminates duplication of services and allows for more rational government contributions to PVO efforts. Finally, joint planning and budgeting can familiarize local authorities with the efforts and value of community volunteers. When the PVO project phases out, governments may be more inclined to include volunteer support and incentives in their budgets.
- Community health volunteers should be certified. Since overburdening scarce trained health workers is a concern, PVOs should advocate for certification of community health volunteers, eventually lobbying that such workers be formally recognized by the government.
- Establishment of community-based organizations helps break down barriers and aid in project implementation. After training and dialogue, it is helpful to encourage communities to form associations (e.g., youth groups, income generation associations) that can register with the district to turn into community-based organization (CBOs). CBOs can (1) help maintain and consolidate project achievements; (2) be used by local governments to channel funding for community health activities; and (3) lobby with local authorities on behalf of their constituencies. These CBOs help maintain the achievements of the project after project completion and can be used by the local government as channels through which funds to run community health activities can be funnelled.

Table 3. MIHV and ADRA Projects: Results Summary

MIHV Project (1996–2000)	Result
Use of modern contraceptives, women of reproductive age	Increased from 6 % to 14 %
Use of any family planning method	Increased from 10% to 22%
Contraceptive use, women who did want children in next 2 years	Increased from 24% to 47%
Reported pregnancies	Declined from 16% to 10%
Condom use by male partners	Increased from 0% to 11%
ADRA Project (1999-2004)	**Result**
Awareness of family planning, women of childbearing age	Increased from 30% (1999) to 73% (2004)
Contraceptive prevalence rate	Increased from 11% (1999) to 23% (2003)

CONCLUSION

In many resource-scarce environments, fertility is high and contraceptive use is low. There are numerous social, institutional, and logistical factors that inhibit women's access to and use of modern contraceptive methods. Given this reality, it is often necessary to involve an array of partners and expand service delivery by training and motivating not only traditional health care providers but also community workers to deliver family planning information, referrals, and services.

Both MIHV and ADRA reached project objectives by educating and mobilizing communities to increase the demand for and use of family planning services. This was accomplished by involving communities in program design, implementation, and evaluation, and by using a grassroots rather than a top-down approach. Building the capacity of health unit staff and collaborating with multiple stakeholders led to successful outcomes.

Successful replication and/or scale up to the national level will require greater coordination and partnerships among NGOs and PVOs active in Uganda, as well as close collaboration with District Health Teams and the MOH. Both MIHV and ADRA played essential roles in the provision of family planning services by bridging the gap between communities and health units, sharing their reproductive health expertise while learning from their host country partners, transferring lessons learned from other projects, and modelling best practices in community health to raise awareness about family planning and decrease unintended pregnancies.

END NOTES

1. The 1995 UDHS did not ask women about LAM use.
The available methods of family planning in Ntusi are visible (condoms, pills), so women find it problematic to hide them from their husbands— *Ntusi Focus Group*

2. It should be noted that the term "child spacing" was used by MIHV in Uganda rather than the term "family planning" since some community members interpret the term family planning to mean preventing the population from having children. In Uganda "Entegeka ya maka" literally translates as a plan for the home, which has a more positive connotation for rural Ugandans.
3. Modern methods here include injectables, pills, condoms, tubal ligation, and the IUD. None of the women surveyed currently used vasectomy, diaphragm, female condom, or foam/gel to prevent pregnancy. LAM was not considered a modern method by the 1995 UDHS or by MIHV's KPC survey. MIHV later conducted a pilot project with the female condom.).
4. Traditionally, men believe that if you have more children, you are considered an important person in the society — *Lwebitakuli Focus Group*
5. The 1998 BIHP baseline survey found that age of sexual debut was 6-10 years among both boys and girls. Reasons for early debut included: 1) a community housing structure (i.e., no separation of parents' bedroom from that of the children) that exposes young children to sexual activity and leads to imitation of parents' behaviour; 2) regional cultural norms that encourage young boys to "explore and test their manhood"; and 3) high levels of school absenteeism among young girls, which contribute to vulnerability to coerced sex or sex with older boys for economic gain.
6. For example, many were initially afraid that modern contraceptives would make women sterile. Some men felt that access to pills or injectables would lead their wives to become promiscuous and the husbands (particularly pastoralist husbands) might never know. The idea that Western powers were promoting modern contraceptives in order to limit Africa's population was also not uncommon.
Men should also be trained on family planning, because they are the very people who are polygamous — Lwemiyaga Trading Center Focus Group
Women may get worried that if they controlled child birth, their men might get other women with whom to produce — *Lwebitakuli Focus Group*
7. The 1998 BIHP baseline survey found that age of sexual debut was 6-10 years among both boys and girls. Reasons for early debut included: 1) a community housing structure (i.e., no separation of parents' bedroom from that of the children) that exposes young children to sexual activity and leads to imitation of parents' behaviour; 2) regional cultural norms that encourage young boys to "explore and test their manhood"; and 3) high levels of school absenteeism among young girls, which contribute to vulnerability to coerced sex or sex with older boys for economic gain.

ACKNOWLEDGMENT

Diana DuBois, Executive Director, MIHV, was the lead author and researcher for this case study. Significant assistance was provided by Rachel Cantor and Paige Anderson, consultants to MIHV; Jolene Mullins, former Uganda Country Director, MIHV; and MIHV/Uganda staff including Kelley McTavish-Mungar, MIHV Uganda Country Director; Sister Mary Ssewamuwe, MIHV Maternal Health Coordinator and Deputy Director/Uganda; Mary Bukenya, Nutrition Manager, MIHV/Uganda; and Elijah Talemwa, MIHV Health

Educator. Information and assistance on the ADRA project was provided by Debbie Herold, ADRA Technical Advisor for Reproductive Health; Erin Anastasi, ADRA Technical Advisor for Family Planning/Population Leadership Program Fellow, and Israel Musoke Sebakigye, Project Manager, Bunya Integrated Health Project. Karen LeBan, Executive Director, CORE Group, and Julia Ross, Communications Manager, CORE Group, provided technical and editorial guidance. All photos courtesy of MIHV.

The activities described in this document were implemented with funding from USAID's Child Survival Program as well as from grants awarded by the Scandia Foundation, the Conservation Food & Health Foundation, Rotary International, and the Child Health Foundation. MIHV gratefully acknowledges their support.

This publication was made possible with support from the Flexible Fund, managed by the Office of Population and Reproductive Health, Bureau for Global Health, United States Agency for International Development (USAID) under Cooperative Agreement FAO-A-00-98-00030. This publication does not necessarily represent the views or opinion of USAID. It may be reproduced if credit is properly given.

Family Planning Case Study

Chapter 15

ARANYA TOWNSHIP, INDORE, INDIA: AN EXPERIMENT FOR SUSTAINABLE HUMAN HABITAT

Utpal Sharma

Rapid urbanization in India and South Asia has generated horrifying pictures of poverty in the form of slums & squatter settlements. This settlement form which has become an integral part of most of the growing urban centres in the country. Earlier, strategies adopted to deal with is problem by providing subsidised housing, low cost housing using innovative materials & construction technologies and slum clearance have not been able to provide any significant result. Subsequently a new approach of 'sites & services' was adopted. 'Aranya' project represents a new paradigm in urban planning to resolve this issue through a sites and services approach to provide housing for economically weaker sections of the urban population. What makes it special is – the idea of 'Planning and Design framework of the settlement, where serviced land is provided for people to build their own homes, incrementally over a period of time'. An attempt was made to address the issues of Identity and sense of community, using information, education and communication tools, which is often missing in conventional planning and design projects. While trying to create a cohesive settlement form, adequate & appropriate infrastructure planning also has been given due importance. Many of the conventional notions of economic infrastructure design were also formed to be not true. Aranya was provided with underground storm water and sewerage network instead of conventional open drainage which often results as a place for solid waste disposal. It was also possible to provide underground electricity cables than overhead network which eventually turned out to be cost efficient. The innovative layout plan helped optimizing the infrastructure cost without compromising on quality. In short, Aranya has been looked at as a 'model' of balanced settlement design in Indian context comprising mostly poor people and yet create a sense of identity & coherent image.

Keywords: Aranya, habitat, poverty, housing, planning and identity

ARANYA

INTRODUCTION

In most cities in India and South Asia, the poor live in appalling conditions. It is not just the poverty itself but the particularly degrading and dehumanizing patterns of urban poverty that have come into being. Obviously there is a mismatch between the way our cities have been built and the way people are compelled to use them. The Planner & Urban designer's role must necessarily encompass the needs of the poor in evolving the urban form sympathetic to their lifestyle.

Figure 1. Present state of housing of urban poor   Source: Mehta B., Feb. 2007

As a result of past experiences and the failure of approaches to ready built housing with heavy subsidies, a new outlook to housing has emerged and with that corresponding changes in policies have also occurred. In the programmes related to slum areas, the emphasis has shifted towards environmental improvement from just clearance and relocation. There is a growing realization that slum dwellings also constitute a part of the housing stock. While the public sector can provide road networks, water supply, sewerage, storm water drainage, electricity and other public amenities, the upgrading of houses can be done more conveniently and economically by the people themselves. Though accepted in principle, slum upgrading programs often fail, as most authorities shy away from granting security of tenure, which can induce the occupants to improve their housing conditions (Mehta, 1987: 72 -76).

In terms of planned efforts, slum improvement, site and services and core housing have emerged as alternate solutions to housing problems. All of these approaches accept a model of progressive house construction focusing on provision of secure tenure and a range of basic services.

The ancient texts on Town planning and Architecture have dealt at length with the design aspects of human habitat. Traditional settlements indicate efficient deployment of scarce resources suited to the culture and lifestyle of the people. Hence, changes in planning policy will have to engage all stakeholders in the proposed programme. It is important that beneficiaries of the programme are given sufficient information and education about the benefits of the programme. Communication therefore serves as a driving force in the intended programme. The symbiosis of activities and space in a hierarchical manner provides a spatial order that permits individuals and communities to adapt the spaces for multiple uses through soft edges or transitional spaces that fuse space at different areas and levels. Behind these concepts lie certain values, a close and enduring fit between action and form.

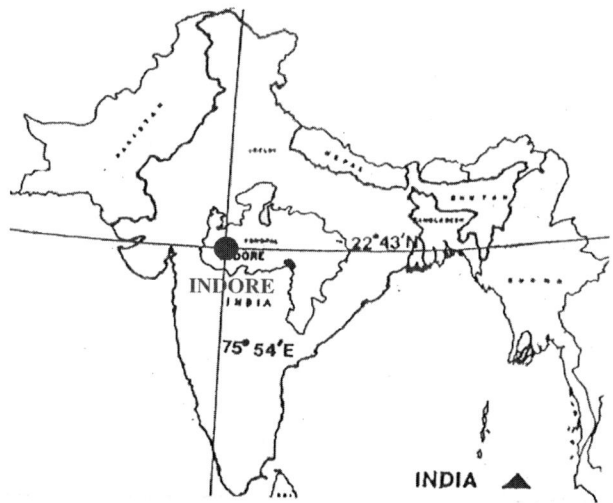

Figure 2. Geographical Location of Indore city. Source: Maps of India

The Aranya (meaning forest) Township is an innovative experiment of settlement planning and design supported by the Indore Development Authority (IDA)[1]. What makes it special is – the idea of 'Planning and Urban Design framework of the settlement where people build themselves'. The framework was evolved through understanding of needs of the people; an attempt was made to address the issues of Identity and sense of community, a process that reflect the ethos of IE&C practice but often missing in conventional planning & design projects.

---

[1] Conceived in 1981 and implementation started in 1986.

Various studies[2] were undertaken to understand traditional settlements in Indian context and evolve a planning and design framework to suit the prevailing social, economic and technological conditions. A study of 'how the other half builds' was done to understand the lifestyle, living environments and aspirations of the urban poor. Appropriate Planning & design principles along with norms for various facilities and public spaces were evolved. cultural, social and economic needs were taken into account to arrive at solutions sympathetic to the life style of the people.

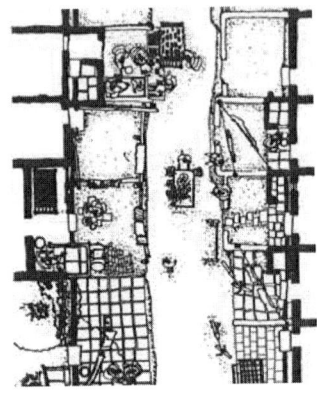

Figure 3. Nature of house extension
Source: VSF, March 1990

Figure 4. Small shops and workplaces
Source: VSF, March 1990

A study on the 'Code of Human Habitat' identified the qualitative parameters to be incorporated at various scales of planning and design, from the settlement to dwelling unit level. The study of neighbourhood streets showed that they were not merely corridors for movement but they also accommodated various social, economic and domestic activities. The relevant hierarchies and their desirable physical characteristics were identified. House extensions were identified as spaces in front of the house, and though located in the public realm, they acquired a private character through their use and physical modifications. These were seen not only as means to expand the small house, but in doing so; they enhanced the quality of the living environment. The study of various economic activities performed identified the nature of space requirements and showed how the design of streets and public spaces can accommodate these activities. These studies not only helped in evolving the framework but also helped in detailing out the design process.

Planning & Urban design framework of a well defined public domain incorporating various activities while accepting modifications and transformations of the private domain was the key to the concept plan. A transition zone of private use of public space along the edge of the building created a behaviour setting for various activities, were the basic tenets of the design.

---

[2] 'How the other half builds' - A study of the existing slum settlements in Indore provided an interesting insight into how the people build houses for themselves.
- 'Integrated Rural Development Plan for village Charodi' – The study investigated the nature of economic development, both formal and informal. As conventional housing project do not consider this vital need, such an investigation was considered significant.

Indented for 65,000 people, mostly from the economically weaker section (EWS) & lower income groups (LIG), Aranya represents in many ways a 'classic' approach to housing the urban poor. What is different, however, is that a "site and services" approach has been refined (while remaining flexible, attentive to individual resources and spontaneity) to include 'models' house-types, suggested materials & steps for implementation. This proposal searches a middle ground, between a house 'with no rooms' and a totally non participatory monotonous public housing schemes. In a site and services project, land and infrastructure are the principal cost components. Thus, efficient site planning was given due importance while keeping human aspects of urban form in strong focus. The infrastructure network (electricity, water supply, sewerage) were laid underground to provide a qualitative environment, toilets were located in the back of the plot to maintain privacy to the households. A fresh approach to infrastructure design was evolved to enhance economic viability and performance by using new materials, design methods and computer aided models. The use of infrastructure design principles while the master plan was being prepared created an innovative layout and affordable solution without compromising on quality of urban space.

It was felt necessary to set up training centres to teach industrial, constructional and other technical skills. Material banks were set up to feed the building activities in the early stages. Easy construction techniques and assembly methods were demonstrated through a cluster of demonstration housing. In essence, the self-help spirit was encouraged to boost the internal economy of the settlement. Particular care was taken to ensure that once the initial constructional activities are over, the workshops and the light industrial units can evolve to embrace a wider range of trades on a permanent basis. With this in mind, a full spectrum of spaces and built-forms were provided to accommodate these activities in Aranya Township.

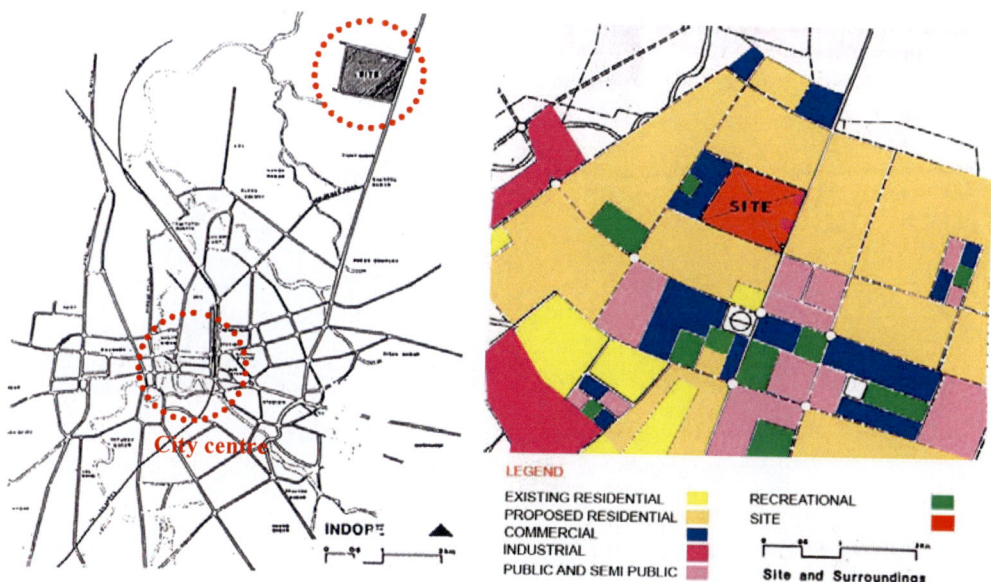

Figure 5. Location of Aranya in Indore
Source: TCPO Madhya Pradesh 1982

Figure 6. Site and Surroundings
Source: TCPO Madhya Pradesh 1982

The site, largely rectangular in plan, is located on the Mumbai – Agra highway, 6 km north of Indore city centre (Fig.5). Out of the net area of 88 ha, over 2.5 ha have been set aside to absorb the pockets of existing light industry. Around 6500 plots for individual houses are provided ranging in minimum size of 35 square meters for the EWS housing to 400 square meters for higher income groups. Of the total residential area, 65% of area was allocated to the EWS category.

Larger plots for upper income groups were also integrated into the scheme, to raise surplus capital to be used to cross-subsidise the EWS population to bring them with the loan repayment capacity. The residue was used in a revolving fund to assist the housing construction and to set up material banks.

At the dwelling unit level a fully serviced plot is allocated to each EWS household together with the basic building core (i.e. W.C., wash and one room) which can be extended by the occupants at a pace commensurate with their need and ability to generate resources. The concept of 'site and service' was emphasised as it helps to stretch the scarce resources of public agencies to the maximum as well as stimulate the 'self-help' element within the community.

THE CONTEXT

The Aranya Township is located in the city of Indore, which is the commercial centre of the state of Madhya Pradesh. According to the 1981 census, this city had a population of 8.27 lakhs Like most other cities in India, Indore was experiencing acute shortage of housing particularly for the lower income group, as well as, problems arising out of inadequate infrastructure. A survey carried out by the Indore Development Authority and the Madhya Pradesh Housing Board showed that about 60,000 families were living in slums and squatter settlements. The housing supply from both public and private agencies to the next four years was to the tune of 25,000 units, whereas there was an additional demand of 51000 units.

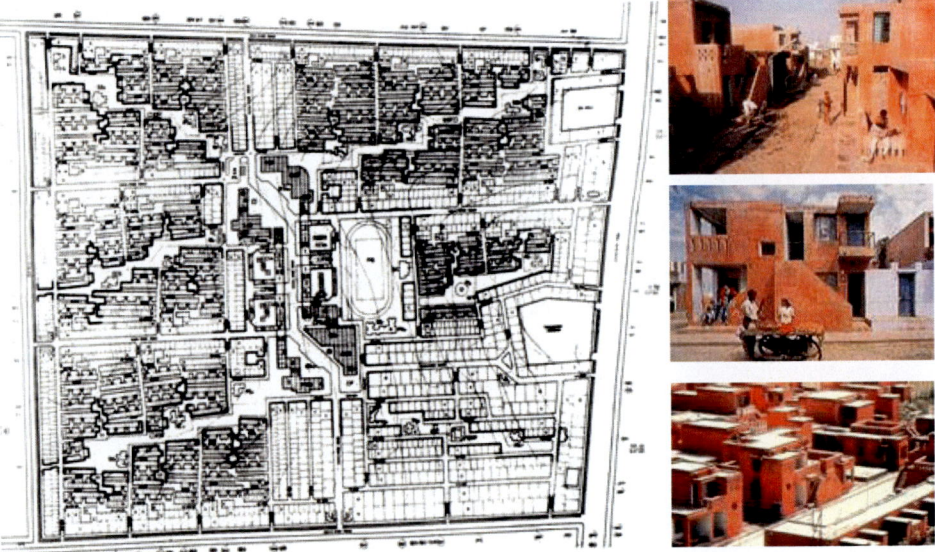

Figure 7. Master Plan with plot divisions
Source: Steele James, 1998

Figure 8. Demonstration houses.
Source: Steele James, 1998

The income distribution of Indore city showed that nearly 60% of the population belonged to the economically weaker section, with income less than five hundred rupees per month (at 1980 prices) and could not afford to spend more than 10% to 15% of their income on housing. Aranya Township was proposed by the Indore Development Authority to alleviate the housing shortage, particularly for the economically weaker section of the society.

Figure 9. Built form scenario
Source: Sharma U., 1995

Figure 10. Serviced plots
Source: Steele James, 1998

THE CONCEPT OF SITE AND SERVICES

'In the 'site and services' approach, each family is provided with a small plot which is serviced with a water tap, storm water drainage, a sewerage connection and a paved access with street lighting. The level of servicing varies with the beneficiary's ability to pay. Similarly, the plot may be supplemented with core housing, comprising of toilet and a water tap as a minimum, and a multi-purpose room, wash area and plinth as additional built-up area.' (VSF, March 1990)

The site and services approach has various advantages over conventional housing.

- Site and services projects cost less (as people manage and participate in the construction of houses) and hence cover more households with the same amount of resources.
- It can cover beneficiaries of very low income groups without heavy subsidies, thus reducing the financial burden on public agencies.
- It allows people to undertake incremental housing construction at a speed that matches their need and affordability.
- The houses are designed by people themselves to suit individual need and aspirations that create variety against the standard, repetitive housing unit provided to each household in ready built housing schemes.

However, the site and services concept has its limitations. These are not necessarily conceptual, but often arise due to weaknesses in the implementation process.

- The most important reason for the failure of the site and services projects is their location. The beneficiaries, primarily intended to be from the EWS, need to live close to their work place. The high cost and non-availability of land in prime locations results in many of these projects being located in peripheral areas of urban centres. These settlements often remain unoccupied.
- These projects are sometimes grossly subsidised by the public sector. This tempts the beneficiaries to resell the plots at a market price to higher income groups. Huge pockets of site and services projects reserved for EWS families can create undesirable residential segregation in a city. These projects should be developed as composite schemes integrating the rich and the poor.

Accepting site and services as a viable approach, there are three areas which show potential for technological innovation. First, infrastructure design can be made more effective. Secondly, though people are fairly innovative in house construction techniques, there is scope for improvement with little additional cost. Finally, in the planning of such projects, an efficient layout can save valuable land and infrastructure, thereby bringing down the costs. It is in this context that the planning & design of Aranya Township based on a site and services model, assumes special significance.

Basic Considerations

It has been observed that much of the present urban low-cost housing have generated unpleasant and unbalanced environments with complete disregard for the traditional lifestyle of people & uncomfortable and ill-thought out use of spaces, costly or inadequate infrastructure, poorly designed housing and the lack of community, recreational and commercial support. Aranya Township was thus an opportunity to address some of the issues. The following issues were considered in the project:

- *Indigenous character of built form suitable to the lifestyles of the poor*

    In traditional Indian towns and cities the level of public-ness and degree of privacy is maintained through spatial order. The clarity of spatial hierarchy enhances the Imageability of these traditional towns. The dense, low rise built form, comprising narrow streets and courtyards responds well to the hot - dry climate of Indore.

- *Site and services- an innovative approach*

    Being a site and services project, Aranya differs substantially from conventional housing. As only the basic building cores are provided on serviced plots, the built form can be extended by the occupants at a pace in tune with their capacity to mobilise resources. Thus, the emphasis was on providing building materials, technical know-how & finances.

- *Optimisation of land use*

    This can be achieved by taking suitable measures to increase the portion of marketable land and by increasing the areas allocated to residential plots. Hence the relevant optimisation process should focus on road network as well as public and community spaces. This can be done by considering multiple uses of public spaces. The present planning norms provide excessive areas for facilities and open spaces which is not affordable to the poor.

- *Marketing of land and the concept of cross- subsidy*

    Depending on zoning regulations and existing developments, a site provides opportunities for some non-residential development, which can enhance the marketability of a project. The design elements of the township will itself create potentials for various types of developments. Non-residential land uses, particularly commercial uses, should be organised around the major road network in order to generate more revenue. Similarly, bigger plots should be located on wider roads to get better prices and in turn be able to subsidise smaller plots for low income groups.

- *Economy of infrastructure and road network*

    Infrastructure, particularly roads, water supply and sanitation constitutes the largest cost component of land development and therefore becomes the prime target for efficient design. Hence, right from the layout planning to the detailed design of the service core, the emphasis was on judiciously reducing the cost of services without compromising the quality.

ACTIVITY STRUCTURE

The prime objective of the project was to create an integrated human habitat suited to the lifestyle and cultural background of the people following intensive education and communication of project plans to the people. Aranya was envisioned as a self contained town (living, working and recreational facilities within township), located outskirts of the city.

In Aranya, well defined communities and spatial organisation were incorporated in making the plan. At the township level, one perceives an entity with a distinct character and identity. Within that, functional groupings of populations of 8000 to 15000 support other needs such as commerce, public institutions, educational institutions and parks, and local commercial activities and play grounds. Communities of 500 to 1500 people satisfy the need for local level groups. The street or cluster level, with a population range of 30 to 100 people, strong social interaction was envisaged. The lowest in the hierarchy was the dwelling unit.

Various hierarchies of spatial organisation adopted were:

Table 1. Size of communities within settlement

Levels	Population range
Township	30000 to 60000
Sector	5000 to 15000
Community	500 to 1500
Cluster or Street	30 to 200
Dwelling unit	1 to 20

The land use within the Aranya Township was predominantly residential. A considerable institutional and commercial use has been provided. All basic community and institutional facilities were provided in the township, including social services like education, health, recreational areas, essential infrastructure and amenities like water supply, sewage, storm water drainage, roads, electricity and activities like commercial and other service establishments. Each activity system was analysed in terms of its population threshold and area requirements. To determine the total area requirements for various facilities and amenities, a population of 65000 formed the basis. Thus, growth and change in facilities over a period of time were given due consideration.

Table 2. Comparative Land Utilization

Particulars	Comparative Land-utilization			
	Initial IDA'S Proposal (Area in Hectares)	%	VSF'S Proposal (Area in Hectares)	%
Net Planning area	88.75	100.00	86.24	100.00
Residential Use	51.59	58.13	50.17	58.17
Roads	22.98	25.90	20.29	23.52
Open Spaces	7.42	8.36	7.03	8.15
Social Facilities	5.07	5.72	5.81	6.73
Commercial	1.68	1.89	2.80	3.26
Industrial Use	-	-	0.14	0.16
Total Marketable	58.34	65.74	58.92	68.16
Total Non-Marketable	30.40	34.26	27.32	31.84

Source: VSF, March 1990

Compared to IDA proposal and to enhance the employment activity, an increase in the commercial area was proposed. This resulted in a reduction of the number of plots to be provided in the township. In this process however, the proportion of plots for the EWS was not reduced and at the same time, the marketable area was increased.

Within Aranya, the road area of about 21% together with pedestrian walkways and public squares amounting to a further 1.5% of the net planning area compares very favourably with the norms set by the World Bank.

It was recognised that the EWS plot size was too small for living (though the World Bank and HUDCO had accepted EWS plot of 25 sq. mts) and it was increased from 33.45 sq. mts (IDA proposal) to 35.32 sq. mts, further it was increased to 44.65 sq. mts and estimated for Lower Income Group (LIG). The idea behind gradual increase in the plot sizes was to enable people (particularly of lower income strata) to choose from a wider range of options matching their affordability.

SETTLEMENT STRUCTURE

A detailed checklist of design principals for Aranya was organised into spatial hierarchies to assist in the settlement design process. Between the entire township and the individual dwelling, a variety of concepts had been used at different scales. Even though the hierarchy is principally determined by the underlying design concepts, it is nevertheless important for spatial organisation of the settlement. The design concepts determining hierarchy vary from intangible ones such as a sense of community, social interaction etc., to more tangible ones like the critical size of population or area that can support certain local facilities, or the formation of an environmental area free from thorough-traffic. Many of the physical and social bases of these hierarchies have overlapping boundaries and the success of the design depended largely on how they are integrated while retaining flexibility.

A clear preference was shown for smaller open spaces adjoining the homes, which would incorporate functions like access, play area, income-generating activities, etc. Besides accommodating these activities, these spaces would serve very important perceptual functions of giving identity to different areas by defining territories. The nature and amount of open spaces required at various levels was systematically identified and was then summed up in order to arrive at the total requirement. The area requirements for educational facilities proposed were much lower than those suggested by conventional planning norms. The reduction in area was achieved not by sacrificing the quality, but by envisaging multiple uses of spaces. Parks and playgrounds to be provided for the community could also be used for outdoor activities of the schools.

The township was divided into six identifiable sectors or neighbourhoods. The idea was to integrate different sectors by road and form a sense of community. The road network was designed in such a way that it defined entry points and discouraged thorough vehicular traffic to create an environmental area free from thorough traffic. Population compositions differed according to the location of each sector in the town structure. The sector on the south-east corner consisted larger share of higher income population, while the sectors on north-east and north-west corners comprised of mainly lower and middle income population. This pattern of spatial organisation took into account the marketability of land and built form relevant to the envisaged population. At the cluster and street level, the population composition was to be more homogeneous to create a behaviour setting for strong social interaction.

PLANNING AT TOWNSHIP LEVEL

Planning and Design principals considered at township level were to:

- Ensure that overall land use and marketable areas reflect economic planning in the Indian context.
- Adopt a self-financing approach through cross-subsidisation.
- Allow design population densities to accommodate future growth.
- Incorporate all the basic community and institutional facilities.
- Allow formation of environmental area by discouraging thorough traffic.
- Place the community facilities within easy reach.
- Provide a strong focus to the township to help create an independent identity in the larger context.
- Provide a well ordered hierarchy of open spaces, commercial activities & hierarchy of roads.
- Achieve an overall cohesion of different areas and activities.

The township had to blend within the urban fabric of Indore, but at the same time retain a unique and distinct identity of its own within which various social and economic activities could flourish. The planning and design principles adopted would in themselves generate a distinct character of the settlement. It was, however, decided to reinforce this identity in its built form. It was essential to provide a focus to the township. Various non-residential activities at the township level were grouped together to create this focus. The built form of this town-centre was raised above that of the other structures to accentuate its visual impact as a node.

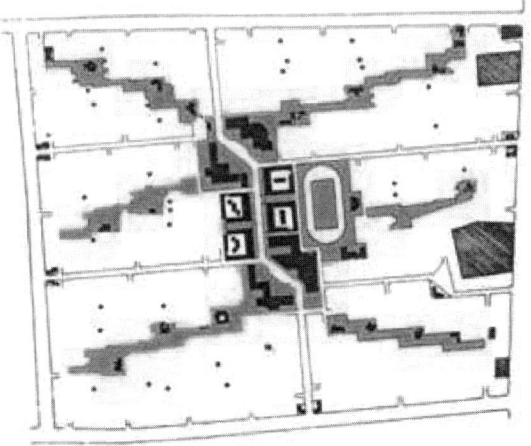

Figure 11. Open space network and Community facilities
Source: VSF, March 1990

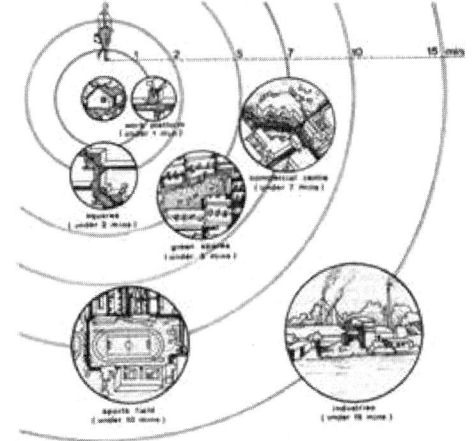

Figure 12. Level of Accessibility
Source: VSF, March 1990

Two potential locations for this town centre were considered, one at the south-west corner of the site which capitalised on the highway linkage, and the other, at the physical centre of the site. Although the south-west corner of the site is more accessible to various parts of the city, the corner location would have distorted the focus and the identity of the township. Therefore, a central location was decided as more appropriate. The centre thus created was within a 10 minute walking distance from the remotest part of the site. The linear form of the town-centre provided better accessibility. Thus, a linear town-centre in the tradition of an Indian bazaar was proposed.

The next important aspect was the linkages to the proposed town-centre. It was decided that the activity spine of the township should link the north and south boundaries of the site. This was to be done in such a way that the envisaged road network gave proper access to the town-centre and at the same time discouraged thorough traffic. Hence, this road was staggered at two places to break the continuity and thereby discourage fast and through traffic. The road network and the system of open spaces were organised so as to converge at the town-centre and highlight the concept of spatial organisation.

It was not enough to have only a town centre with facilities and amenities to act as a focus. The distribution of lower order facilities and amenities became another important aspect of the design concept. It was decided to have a fine grain distribution of lower order facilities, but organised in such a manner so as to maintain strong link with the town-centre.

The open spaces at the township level consisted of a formal playground and paved public spaces along the bazaar. Open spaces were conceptually organised in the middle of each neighbourhood as a continuous space, providing easy pedestrian access from each sector to the town centre. Various commercial activities, social amenities and utilities were to be located all along these continuous green, resulting in an even distribution of these facilities throughout the settlement. Thus, a coherent hierarchy of open spaces and other activities was achieved in the design.

The basic concept was to give due importance to pedestrians and cyclists. This required the integration of the environmental area by discouraging traffic through the township. The location and form of various activities, the system of road network, open spaces and the nature of the built form reflect this concept. Since accessibility in terms of walking distances from home to various activities was the prime measure of consideration at all levels, community and central facilities were placed within easy reach.

PLANNING AT SECTOR LEVEL

Planning and Design principals considered at sector level were:

- Provide a sense of boundary to each sector.
- Provide defined entry points and discourage thorough vehicular traffic.
- Provide local facilities within easy reach.
- Provide public information, education and channels of communication
- Foster a viable sub-community in each sector.
- Encourage interaction and integration amongst various groups.
- Provide well distributed open spaces.
- Promote multiple and overlapping land uses.
- Segregate pedestrian and vehicular movements.
- Optimise land use, roads and other infrastructure.
- Maintain contact with the land at all levels.

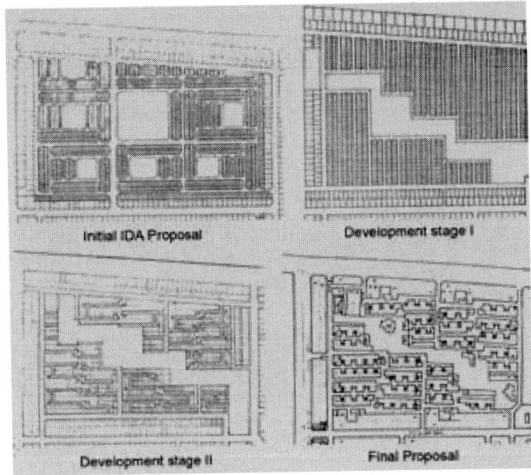

Figure13. Schematic development of a Sector
Source: VSF, March 1990

Figure 14. Sector built form scenario
Source: VSF, March 1990

The township was divided into six identifiable sectors or communities. Each of Aranya's six sectors contained a population range of 7000-12000. Although the basic reason behind the formation of this particular hierarchy was mainly functional in terms of providing easy access to various local facilities and amenities, it also helped to foster a sense of community and promote social interaction amongst the residents.

At the sector level, the pattern and distribution of open spaces was closely interlinked with the location of various facilities, amenities and the road network, so as to evolve a structure for the township and by locating social facilities in the open spaces, there was better chance of these spaces being used, maintained and self-policed against illegal encroachment. Community activities were combined with open spaces, thus promoting multiple uses.

PLANNING AT CLUSTER/ STREET LEVEL

Planning and Design principals considered at cluster/ street level were:

- Promote person to person contact through clusters of human scale.
- Define clearly each cluster's territory and the sense of entrance.
- Create well-designed space for information, education and communication
- Provide an individual character to each cluster.
- Have regards for pedestrians.
- Create a functionally sympathetic and aesthetically pleasing street environment.
- Optimize cluster patterns for economic infrastructure and easy access.
- Provide spaces for social and religious activities.
- Promote income generation at the cluster level.
- Provide all essential amenities and utilities to every cluster.

sharing of spaces for different activities at the dwelling unit level hence provision of outdoor spaces were promoted. The house form incorporated with elements like platforms, porches, courtyards and roof terraces. Various studies were made while evolving the house form. A veranda or house extension was the public face, which could be used for various work activities whilst the courtyard at the back could become the more private domain of the house. A living area followed by a kitchen and a toilet was sandwiched between the front extension and the courtyard at the back. Most of the houses were provided with an additional access at the back, which allowed them to keep animals and vehicles, and even rent a part of the house to augment income. It could also act as an access to the upper floor extension. Provision of an additional access to each plot was considered important, as was revealed through a study of plots in informal settlements. It has been observed that provision of access from the courtyard has limited people from encroaching on the open space.

While deciding on plot proportion and organisation of spaces within the house, various possibilities of expanding the house were taken into consideration. Possibilities of incorporating a staircase at the front or at the back were examined. The internal subdivision of each dwelling was kept simple so as to provide maximum efficiency with minimum circulation space. A minimal dwelling was designed so that it could be progressively upgraded and enlarged. At the initial stage, the dwelling consisted of a basic service core and a room. The basic core could be merged into the future ground floor extension. Space was provided for a staircase in the front porch or the rear courtyard to reach the roof terrace. This would eventually serve the first floor, built to cater to the growing needs of the family. The balcony and the roof terrace provided additional open spaces, useful for sleeping outside during summer nights.

Figure 18. House form evolution

Source: VSF, March 1990

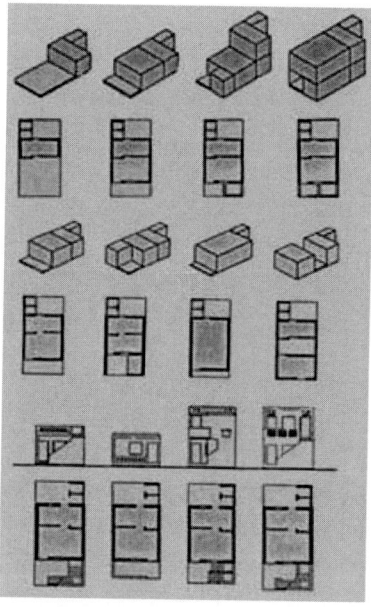

Figure 19. Incremental House within same plot and built form variation.
Source: Steele James, 1998

In India, house extensions not only help to expand a small house, but in the process, they also enhance the quality of public spaces. Such an important, but often neglected, aspect of habitat planning was given due recognition in the Aranya project. Changes in the conventional building and zoning regulations envisaged the creation of a transition zone of 0.5 mts width between the street and the house, where people would be allowed to build house extensions. The permissible house extensions were stoops, platforms, porches, balconies and open stairs, which created an interesting street character.

The degree of public-ness of various spaces of the house corresponded to a sequence which began with the entrance and the most public part, and led to the more private areas or domains. Ottas, platforms and porches were the transitional spaces between the street and the house. The degree of public-ness of these spaces was highest within the spatial arrangements of the house; these spaces could also be used as shops or work places. On the other hand, the courtyard at the rear was the most private space of the houses. The toilet core was justifiably located adjacent to the courtyard. Between the otta and the courtyard was the living area of the house, followed by the kitchen. The spaces were so arranged that the house became progressively private.

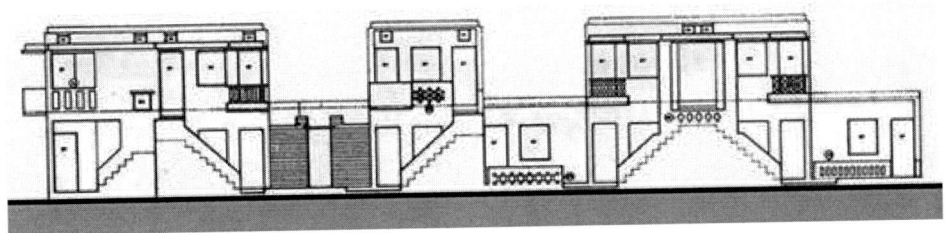

Figure 20. Variations in elements enhancing street elevation.

Source: VSF, March 1990

Variety of staircases, openings, projections, railings & parapets made each house unique and gave it an identity within the same plot area configuration. The demonstration housing cluster built demonstrated these variety and possible pattern of house extension.

INFRASTRUCTURE AND SERVICES

As discussed earlier, Sites-and services and slum upgrading emerged as the two viable options to tackle the problems of housing for the urban poor. In both options, provision of Infrastructure plays a crucial role as it constitute the major portion of the total project cost and hence become prime targets for efficient design. Thus, in Aranya, special emphasis was given on planning and designing the layout in relation to Infrastructure networks to arrive at optimal design solutions without compromising on the standards.

Infrastructure was designed in an integrated manner. It was realised that the design decisions for each component influenced the other components and hence, should not be considered in isolation. In order to achieve overall efficiency and economy, a particular component may turn out to be more expensive, but at the same time may result in substantial overall savings. For instance, additional cut and fill for the roads resulted in saving of manhole costs by reducing their depths. As most of the infrastructure follows the road, the layout of the road network with respect to the topography was given due consideration so that the roads are always on positive slopes which helped in achieving an efficient and cost effective infrastructure.

In Aranya, underground storm water drainage & electricity network was provided as against the conventional practice of open drains and overhead electricity cables, which generally results in the open drains getting choked due to solid waste disposal and in case of overhead cables resulting in a poor quality of environment. It is found to be economical to provide underground services as there is less maintenance; though the initial cost is higher but when a lifecycle costing was done, it turned out to be much more economical and efficient in comparison with conventional practices. To ensure efficiency, trade-offs in capital costs and subsequent maintenance costs were studied. It was realised that roads without curbs deteriorate faster and increase maintenance costs. Thus in Aranya, all roads were provided with appropriate curbs. Infrastructure was designed in accordance with topology to increase efficiency and reduce costs through computer-aided design.

The network design was kept flexible enough to accommodate changes in the nature of treatment and inflow of services. The network was decentralised but interconnected, so that the project could be divided into separate phases, each working independently and cohesively.

THE SERVICE CORE

It was decided to provide a basic service core consisting of toilet and a bathroom to every house. The planning of the service core had greater impact on the overall development cost. In addition, the location of the service core within the house was carefully considered in terms of user's socio-cultural preferences. The option of community toilets, though economical, was not considered, on grounds of health, hygiene and the quality of environment. While planning & designing the service core, following guidelines were considered:

- Consider the environmental impact of the sanitation core.
- Provide safe and adequate sanitation for all families.
- Make the sewage system adaptable to alternative treatment/disposal methods.
- Ensure full privacy to W.C. and wash areas.

In Indian cultural context, toilet and cleaning activities were considered private and should be separate from the entrance. Thus, in Aranya, the service core was located in the backyard. To integrate with the service lines, four conventional possibilities were studied:

1. Toilets at the front, facing the street, with the service lines in the street.
2. Toilets at the back, connected to the service lines in the street, with pipes running under the floor.
3. Toilets in the back, courtyards with common service lines running through the backyards of one of the rows of the back to back houses.

4. Community toilets with water taps.

While planning and designing the service core, the following criteria were taken into consideration:

- Link maximum service core to a single manhole to reduce cost.
- Remove minimum number if EWS plots to accommodate service access alleys.
- Combine four service cores on a single rectangular platform as often as possible to reduce cost of foundations especially in black cotton soil.
- Size of service areas should be such that it can be put to alternate use e.g. space for informal economic activities, play areas etc.
- Plan service alley so as to give maximum rear access to most of the plots.
- Space for service areas should fit the house plan module so that they can be altered or omitted at a later date without distributing the overall sartorial plans.
- Flexibility for alternative sewage treatment.

All four possibilities were found lacking in the location, cost or maintenance. Therefore a system was developed which avoided toilets at the front and at the same time saved on cost and performance. The service core was designed to extend into a full house at a later date with minimal change in the original core.

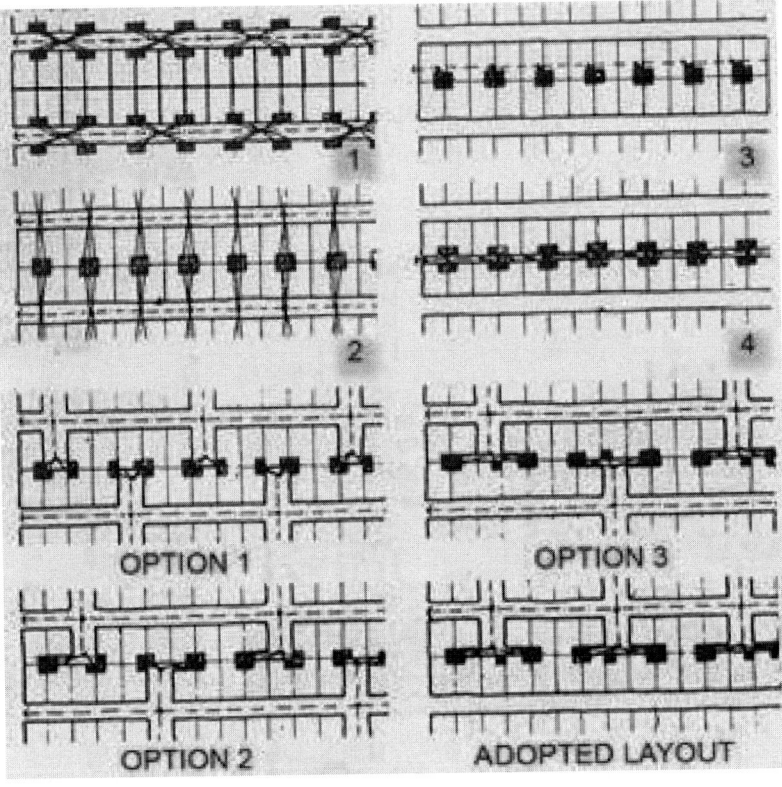

Figure 21. Study of service core network   Source: VSF, March 1990

Figure 22. Envisioned use of service core alcove
Source: VSF, March 1990

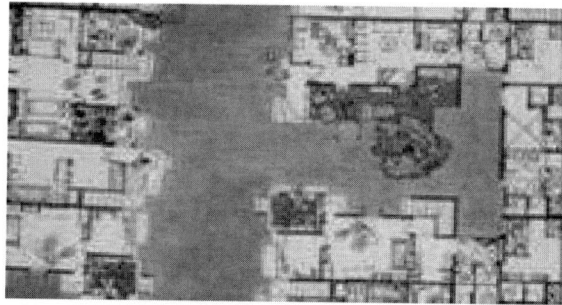

Figure 23. Present use of service core alcove
Source: Mehta B., April 2007

COST, REVENUE AND SURPLUS

A substantial surplus of 11.7 million rupees has been generated against the investment of 57.2 million rupees based on the 1982 prices. This has been achieved by judiciously locating the larger plots and the commercial activities which fetched maximum sale prices. The surplus created a seed capital for further EWS schemes in the future.

The EWS sale price is subsidised to the tune of about 35% on average, which was compensated within the project from the sale of upper income plots through the principle of cross subsidy. Thus it reduced the need for direct subsidy to housing poor from other sources.

SUMMARY

Aranya has demonstrated an innovative approach to the integrated development creating a holistic environment, rooted in socio-cultural and economic milieu of the place and being sympathetic to the way of life of the Urban Poor.

Aranya, since its inception and realisation, has created unprecedented awareness in the professional and the academic world. It has been a case study and inspiration to many similar projects. Generally, housing for the urban poor is planned in isolation from the city, but, in Aranya the realisation was that towns have to be a mosaic of culture where the rich & poor should live together. As the communities of Aranya grow socially, economically and culturally, the incremental composition and housing transformation process continues.

The idea of integrating different socio-economic groups worked well. The concept of cross subsidy became a good reference too for any integrated settlement planning.

It has been observed that the core houses built about 20 years ago have developed in their own way. The original idea of variation in house form (freedom to build by choice) by element like staircases, projections, openings, etc. was a complete success and it was observed that people built with more variety to create an identity of their own.

Aranya has also contested the argument that in such schemes the beneficiaries i.e. slum dwellers normally go back to their original site after selling the allocated plot. On the contrary, the post occupancy survey shows that almost 90% of EWS households lived and incrementally upgraded their houses.

However, there were limitations in terms of choosing the location of the house by the beneficiaries as the houses were allotted by lottery system. People could not choose their neighbours but eventually strong communities were formed on the basis of similar socio economic groups.

Though the houses were small but availability of open spaces with amenities to all occupants created a sense of equality. As Aranya was located outside the Municipal limits, initially the maintenance of streets and open spaces was an issue, but later the communities evolved their own system of maintenance and up keeping.

Figure 24. Residential Environment of Aranya. Source: Mehta B., April 2007

Underground Infrastructure with integrating topology became ideal example to other large scale development in Indore and Madhya Pradesh. In Aranya, landscaping was considered integral part of infrastructure, which is not the case with conventional housing schemes.

It was realized that additional urban design guidelines for larger part were required to create a coherent built form along the main streets.

This township model experiment by the Indore Development Authority has set a standard of balanced and harmonious environment which are now emulated by other organisations engaged in the field of low-cost housing. As the infrastructure constitutes the major component of the total cost, the methods developed for streaming the services assumed importance.

The study looked at the implementation process as a vital aspect in the housing project for the poor. It defines construction of the minimum, so as to allow people to add and develop the house as per their requirements and affordability in the future. This built into the project, the sense of belonging and identity, which is a strong social issue for the habitation of the poor.

Figure 25. Residential Environment of Aranya.   Source: Mehta B., April 2007

The efficient site planning, a fresh approach to infrastructure and the use of strong traditional urban design principles of the country with a hope to provide the most ideal environment for living to the poor has produced an example of great urban design in the context of rapid urbanisation. It has not only been accepted by the people but also serves as case study for further research in the field.

Figure 26. Cluster Open Space   Source: Mehta B., April 2007

Chapter 16

Evaluation - The What, the Wherefore and the How

John Durant

Acronyms

ADB	Asian Development Bank
MOV	means of verification
M&E	monitoring and evaluation
INGO	international non-governmental organisation
NGO	non-governmental organisation
OECD / DAC	Organisation for Economic Cooperation and Development / Development Assistance Committee
OVI	objectively verifiable indicators
PCM	project cycle management
SWAp	sector wide approach
SMART	specific / measurable / achievable / relevant / time bound – the criteria for setting evaluation indicators
TA	technical assistance
ToRs	terms of reference

<u>Multilateral-donors / agencies:</u>

IBRD	International Bank for Reconstruction and Development - The World Bank
EBRD	European Bank for Reconstruction and Development
IADB	Inter-American Development Bank
EC	European Commission
UNDP	United Nations Development Programme

<u>Bilateral donors / agencies include:</u>

DFID	Department for International Development - UK
DANIDA	Danish International Development Agency
CIDA	Canadian International Development Agency

DGIS	Royal Netherlands international development agency
JICA	Japanese International Cooperation Agency

WHAT IS EVALUATION AND WHY IS IT NEEDED?

How often have we asked:

"How was the meal? Did you have a good time at the...? Did you enjoy the play? Was it good for you? What did you enjoy the most? Did that make any difference? What did you learn from that experience? Did I do well? What did you do with your time in...?

All of these questions are asking you to **evaluate** something. They could be a judgment of our **performance** in an examination or the enjoyment of a play; they could be asking what **impact** or difference a change of a job routine has made; or they could have been asking you to be **accountable**. So, on an every day basis we make evaluations or judgments.

Evaluation in the development field is no different, evaluation is asking about impact on change in a community or an institution, about accountability to end-beneficiaries and to the donors, and, about performance of institutions and interventions such as projects and programmes. At the same time it is about **lessons learned** and from these lessons information should be, it is hoped, fed-back into the design of future interventions.

Evaluations ask what progress has been achieved in terms of reaching goals, reaching targets and objectives measured against baseline data gathered at the start of the interventions.

The measurement of attitudinal and behavioural change in development interventions is also part-and-parcel of evaluation in order to assess if the end-beneficiaries have developed their capabilities and abilities to be more self-sufficient. At the same time **participatory evaluation** which is increasingly being encouraged and used**,** will develop the skills and knowledge of end-beneficiaries and target populations through learning from their involvement in the evaluation process.

And it is to this broad definition that most donors work with possible occasional slight variations. DANIDA, the Danish bi-lateral donor agency, defines evaluation simply as:

... For retrospective studies of what has happened and why ...

In the context of project-cycle management – see below in "When to Evaluate" - donors evaluate to assess what and how much has changed; whether the interventions have been cost-effective and to feed-back into future interventions; and, to ensure accountability as well as to ascertain if a particular intervention is replicable or not.

> OECD / DAC have the following definition of **evaluation** to which most if not all donor agencies agree:
>
> *... an evaluation is an assessment, as systematic and objective as possible, of on-going or completed aid activities, their design, implementation and results. The aim is to determine the relevance and fulfilment of objectives, development efficiency, effectiveness, impact and sustainability...*
>
> OECD / DAC also define **outcome evaluation** thus:
>
> *An in-depth examination of a related set of programmes, projects and strategies intended to achieve a specific outcome, to gauge the extent of success in achieving outcomes; assess the underlying reasons for achievement or non-achievement; validate the contributions of a specific organisation to the outcome; and, identify key lessons learned and recommendations to improve performance.*
>
> **Source:** OECD / DAC Glossary of Key Terms in Evaluation and Results-based Management, 2002. (This definition is the one I prefer as it is more focused and accurate in its coverage.)

Evaluation is not an end-in-itself, its real value is in the use of the results, findings, conclusions and recommendations of an evaluation in order to inform, improve and contribute to the debate and decisions on future interventions of a similar nature, and, for political decision makers on future direction of development assistance.

IS THERE A DIFFERENCE BETWEEN MONITORING AND EVALUATION?

We regularly talk of **M&E** – monitoring and evaluation - and combine the two together, but is there a difference? Yes, there is and there have been, and there still is, considerable discussions between professionals on the difference, they are different but very much related. Certainly what they do have in common is the need for baseline data from which to measure change and upon which to base judgments. In my view the separation of monitoring and evaluation is important as these two activities are too often "lumped" together and confused, although they are very much part-and-parcel of the project cycle[1] and project cycle management (PCM) and do provide to decision makers and mangers different information and choices.

---

[1] The Project Cycle is defined by the EC as "... The Project Cycle follows the life of the project from the initial idea through to its completion. It provides a structure to ensure that stakeholders are consulted, and defines the key decisions, information requirements and responsibilities at each phase so that informed decisions can be made at each phase in the life of the project. **It draws on evaluation to build on lessons of experience into the design of future programmes and projects...**"

> " ... Evaluation is a much more in depth study of how the project has contributed to the Project Purpose and Overall Objectives (contained in the project log frame plan) *and analyses problems that have been experienced...*" It continues *"... Evaluation is carried out at a discrete point in time, usually upon completion or mid-term (sometimes referred to mid-term review) whereas **monitoring is an on-going process** which should be carried out at regular intervals throughout the duration of the project / programme..."*
>
> Source: EC, 2001, *Handbook for Monitors,* Brussels
>
> Performance monitoring is described by the OECD / DAC as:
> A **continuous** *process of collecting and analyzing data for performance indicators, to compare how well a development intervention, partnership or policy reform* **is being implemented** *against expected results ...*
>
> Source: OECD / DAC Glossary of Key Terms in Evaluation and Results-based Management, 2002.

Information gathered during on-going monitoring can, and should, be used in conducting final evaluations and decisions made from recommendations made from monitoring again should be looked at in an evaluation.

Monitoring uses the data and interpretation of those data and the knowledge gained, to correct and adjust on-going project implementation and management; at the same time this data is used to determine whether project objectives are being achieved, and to make whatever changes and adjustments are necessary to improve project performance and impact in order to achieve project results and outcomes.

Evaluation considers the results and effects (impact) of the project or intervention as well as the long-term effects of the project on the quality of life of the end-beneficiaries / target audience, or on improvements on the delivery of services by a local authority, or the planning capability of national authorities, or whether the project interventions will be sustainable and long lasting.

> *The evaluation plans should be incorporated in the initial project design... project evaluation is an assessment of project performance and results in light of the stated project objectives. And must include a participative approach...* is how the UNDP and EC describe evaluation in a staff operational manual.
>
> Source: EC / UNDP SGP PTF First Regional Operational Manual – Annexes.

WHEN TO EVALUATE?

Evaluations are most usually conducted at the completion of an intervention, thus at the end of a project or programme and are conducted at the end of the **projects cycle** – see the annexes for a simple project cycle diagram. The evaluation, in the case of donor funded projects, will be upon completion of the external aid funding to the project or intervention – a **final or end or outcome evaluation**, however, exactly when the process should be undertaken is open to debate. If done immediately, or very soon after the completion of the interventions, this may give some idea of the efficiency of delivery and to an extent the effectiveness of the interventions and will identify successes, short-comings and failures, but will provide little or no information on potential sustainability. The findings and recommendations from this type of evaluation can, and often are, used to assess whether any follow-up interventions are or will be required.

Ex-post or Summative evaluations are conducted some time after the completion of project interventions to measure both long-term impact and sustainability as the elapsed time from the end of the project or donor funded interventions will allow judgments to be made on whether the interventions will be sustainable and long-lasting.

Mid-term evaluations or **interim evaluations** are increasingly being conducted somewhere in the middle of the funding period, however, I prefer to call these, and increasingly so do the donors, **mid-term reviews**. These focus on the operational activities and provide a more detailed analysis of performance and direction that any on-going monitoring *may identify* and are most often conducted by outside professionals or agencies in order to preserve impartiality and "distance".

Ex-ante evaluation or **formative evaluation** is a needs assessment made during the project design stage in order to determine intervention needs that will enable a donor, or a government, to set policy and to gather data for project design. The studies at this stage of the project cycle are more often known as **feasibility studies** by most donors, where data is collected for a baseline survey which is used as a baseline from which to measure and evaluate progress and eventual impact of project interventions.

Most evaluations will be conducted by external evaluators to insure impartiality and "distance" that can only really be provided by an outside and impartial observer. Having these evaluations conducted by those involved with the implementation – be they end-beneficiaries, TA team, or the donor – would not eliminate bias and would be likely to reduce subjectivity.

WHAT TO EVALUATE?

The EC has quite a long history of evaluating its projects, but the major multi-lateral agency the IBRD or World Bank has an even longer history of monitoring and evaluating its project interventions. When I worked on an IBRD funded project in Nigeria, in the late seventies, there was an M&E technical assistance staff member attached to each project and the *Agriculture Projects Monitoring, Evaluation and Planning Unit* (APMEPU) unit in Kaduna provided overall monitoring of the numerous agricultural development projects that the Bank was funding in Nigeria at that time. The information gained from these monitoring activities certainly was used to monitor progress and assure that any redirection that may have been required was taken. I am uncertain whether this information was used to evaluate final end of project funding impact on agricultural productivity or the institutional development of the agricultural sector delivery agencies and whether or not this information was used to plan for future interventions in the sector. Nearly all donors, be they multi-lateral or bi-lateral now insist on both on-going monitoring of interventions and the final evaluation of their funding.

So what is it we are evaluating in an intervention, be it a project or a programme or even SWAp interventions? I like to think of it as a *"five finger exercise"* which includes the following evaluation criteria, which are accepted as the most significant by most donors:

1) ***Relevance and design of the interventions***:
Was the need correctly identified and relevant to the needs of the end-beneficiaries and did they address both local and national priorities; and, following that, was the intervention correctly designed?

2) ***Efficiency of implementation***:
The efficiency of the management of the interventions is judged to see if there was an *efficient use* of resources, be these human, physical or financial resources.

3) ***Effectiveness of implementation***:
Were the interventions effective in tackling the identified problem, did they do what was intended – was the objective achieved?

4) ***Impact of interventions***:
What was the impact of the interventions on the target group or the institution for which the interventions have been designed, what has changed and what is now different since the intervention?

5) ***Sustainability of project interventions***:
Will the benefits, accrued by the aid intervention, continue into the future? The sustainability of the interventions is rather difficult to judge as it is difficult to see into the future and thus should be judged more accurately in an **ex-post evaluation**. But the "crystal ball" of experience should, it is hoped, allow experienced practitioners to have a fairly accurate *"guestimate"* of the potential success, the long-term impact of the interventions and whether these will be sustained.

There are other **cross-cutting issues** such as environmental impact, gender equity and governance that should also be addressed in the final assessment of the performance. So technical impact, social impact, environmental impact, economic performance, institutional performance and improvements should all be looked at in the context of the interventions. Not all of these will be looked at in all evaluations; it will depend upon what types of interventions are being evaluated. The unintended consequences and the unforeseen factors will also be looked at so that lessons can be learned from those for future planning.

The **objectively verifiable indicators** (OVI) or indicators that are selected, at the project design stage, should comply with the five **SMART** principles, thus should be:

Specific – they must be specific to the project interventions, not just general indicators;

Measurable – they must be measurable, so that judgments can be made on the situation before the interventions and after the interventions;

Achievable and cost-effective – the indicators must be realistic and achievable in both the timeframe and within the budget– setting targets is never easy and in many cases can be counterproductive;[2]

Relevant – too often "bog-standard" indicators are used that provide no real indication of progress nor impact – so indicators must be relevant to the specific situation and intervention;

Time-bound – as stated above the indicators must be achievable within the timeframe of the "project" and once again setting these can be less-than-easy when there are so many imponderables in the planning of the interventions, particularly in a development context.

Performance evaluations assess the **performance** of individuals, groups and institutions; again I have a *"five finger"* exercise – thus resulting in two handfuls of measurables!! In the delivery of development interventions usually there are five players or partners. These include the following in no specific order:

- ✓ **the end-beneficiaries**[3] those who benefit directly from the interventions of the project or programme – these could be farmers benefiting from an agricultural project, or populations in a village or district benefiting from a new medical clinic or staff of a ministry or institution that have received training or new equipment or a reorganisation to their working practices;
- ✓ **the institution** in the recipient country that is responsible for the sector or for liaison with the donor group usually a government ministry or parastatal or a local or international NGO;
- ✓ **the donor head office** in that the credibility of their overall development policy direction is being evaluated as well as their correct identification of the need for the interventions followed by the design of the mode of the intervention;
- ✓ **the donors in-country office** and their relationships with local in-country partners in the provision of appropriate sectoral recommendations and project interventions suggestions to their head offices for final decisions for funding;
- ✓ **the technical assistance team** who have been contracted to implement the interventions.

Although there maybe others involved in this process these five main actors will contribute to the eventual successful, or less-than-successful, delivery of the interventions and their impact on the economy and the lives of the people for whom the interventions are intended.

WHO NEEDS AND USES THE RESULTS OF AN EVALUATION?

Who needs the information generated by an evaluation? All those involved in the development process and in the management of change. The hierarchy of importance of those

---

[2] I am ambivalent about setting quantifiable targets at the design stage of a project or set of interventions. It can be dangerous putting figures to an output, in that they can become the "be-all-and-end-all". Process and learning that should be a major part of an intervention can be sacrificed in the head-long dash to achieve quantifiable targets. Certainly if the intention is to build "x" kilometres of road, then fine, that is a target that was set within a realistic financial and time schedule. But to set "y" numbers of children who will be able to read or brought out of poverty, or set "z" numbers of cattle that will be vaccinated within a project timeframe can be dangerous. It does not matter if the exact figure is not achieved within the timeframe, what is important is that the intervention is setting-up sustainable systems and infrastructure that will be used long into the future for purposes for which they were designed.

[3] The institution, the people or groups who benefit directly from the programme or project interventions

who "need-to-know", is not important, but all those involved in the use of evaluation findings, if not in the process of the conduct of an evaluation, should have access to the findings.

The end-beneficiaries of a development intervention can benefit from information obtained from an evaluation exercise by using it to plan their future and to learn lessons on what "works-best-for-them" and in their approach to governments and donors in the future.

The politicians / political authorities require this type of information to assist them in decisions on national budgets, on development plans, on aid requests and directions and for overall pragmatic public finance management planning.

The donors who provide the funding for development interventions, so that they can assess performance and impact, in order that the planning of future interventions can learn from the lessons learned from the evaluation. They can also see where their financing is best focused to ensure the greatest and most appropriate impact and most cost-effective policies are put in place.

The planners should make use of the findings and recommendations of an evaluation so that the results of evaluation can be fed into the future planning of similar interventions. If these findings are not available then the purpose of evaluations is lost, lessons will not have been learned and used to plan and implement improved future interventions.

The managers of an intervention; be they a ministry, an NGO group or the technical assistance team implementing a project, so that they can improve their performance, become more effective and deliver cost-effective services. This should feed-into their planning, their allocation of staff, into planning of timeframes and to the eventual work-plans for a TA team.

LOGICAL FRAMEWORK ANALYSIS (LFA'S) AS A BASIS FOR PLANNING AND CONDUCTING EVALUATIONS

Many development agencies and donors use the *logical framework analysis* or **LFA** in the design of an intervention or project.

The OECD defines the **logical framework analysis** or log frame as follows:

A management **tool** used to improve the design of interventions, most often at the project level. It involves identifying strategic elements (inputs, outputs, outcomes and impact) and their causal relationships, indicators, and the assumptions and risks that may influence success and failure. It thus facilitates planning, execution and **evaluation** of a development intervention.

Source: OECD / DAC Glossary of Key Terms in Evaluation and Results-Based Management, 2002.

(The emboldening is mine, but notice also that it is called a tool *and tools take* practice to use well.)

Within the matrix of an LFA there are four columns:[4]

---

[4] See Annex A for a sample framework matrix used in log frame planning.

Column 1 – shows the **Intervention logic**[5] (sometimes called the **narrative summary**) – which briefly describes the **overall goal** of the intervention; the **purpose** of the intervention; showing the **outputs** (sometimes known as **results**) of the intervention that will achieve the purpose; and below these, the **activities** that will result in the outputs which then achieves the purpose.

Column 2 - incorporates indicators - **Objectively Verifiable Indicators or OVIs** - that can and should be used in both monitoring and evaluating the interventions. These should be indicators that show change or progress.[6]

Column 3 – shows **Means of Verification (MoVs)**. These are suggested ways of, and where to find, verification of the progress or impact of the project or intervention. The OVIs and the MoVs must be set at the design stage of the project or interventions if they are to provide a measurable basis upon which to make rational judgments of progress and impact.

Column 4 – shows the **Assumptions** that are made that may, or are likely to, impact on the implementation of the project and the achievement of the overall goal.

The LFA which is used in designing the interventions, and all projects should prepare something akin to the LFA at the design stage as maybe quite obvious, is a <u>starting point</u> for the monitoring and evaluation of a project or intervention as the definition shown above indicates. The LFA will provide a very quick and easy summary of what a project was designed to achieve, the measurable indicators that were planned for and where to find that information and the dangers or assumptions that were identified at the design stage. But once that overview has been obtained from the LFA the real work of an evaluation is then undertaken.

CONDUCTING AN EVALUATION

The processes of evaluation are continually being systematized (not my favourite word!) and so are evolving and hopefully becoming more responsive to the needs of planners, in order to introduce new designs and approaches to development interventions.

Participatory planning has been around since Robert Chambers recommended this approach in the sixties, but has really only becomes the norm within the evaluation process in recent years. The need for **participatory evaluation** has only been recognised more recently, in the last two decades or so and now forms, or should form, the basis of all evaluations. Participatory evaluation allows for active involvement of those who have a stake in the end-result of the interventions, be these the providers, the partners but most importantly the end-beneficiaries, those who will directly benefit from the results of the interventions. This participation should be at all stages of the evaluation process, from planning the evaluation exercise, to its conduct, to analysis, and, eventually the implementation of the recommendations that come from the evaluation. Having assisted in setting the indicators for

---

[5] The European Commission defines the **intervention logic** of a project or programme as ... *The strategy underlying the project. It is the narrative description of the project at each of the four levels of the "hierarchy of objectives" used in the log frame* – these are overall goal, purpose, outputs or results and the activities.

[6] **OVI**'s described by the EC as.... *measurable indicators that will show whether or not objectives have been achieved at the three highest levels of the log frame* – OVIs provide the basis for designing an appropriate monitoring system ... .

project measurement, the end-beneficiaries, by being involved in the evaluation of interventions alongside external evaluators, will also learn lessons and be able to articulate their needs more accurately in the future. Being involved at both ends of the project-cycle they will, it is hoped, have greater ownership of the project interventions and thus this will provide for greater sustainability of these interventions into the future.

Rapid rural appraisal – again another Chambers concept – has led to the use of rapid evaluation techniques, partly due to the need to reduce costs as more formal evaluations are costly in time and thus costly in monetary terms. Rapid evaluation techniques are quick with the delivery of their findings and the processes can be learned quickly for participating beneficiaries. However, drawbacks include limited reliability and validity, lack of quantitative data from which generalizations can be drawn, and possibly less credibility, given to the findings by the decision makers!! Thus this approach to evaluations can best be used when there is sufficient qualitative descriptive data available; motivation and attitudes affecting behaviour need to be better understood so that the "how and why" questions can be answered; quantitative data collected from on-going monitoring needs to be interpreted and understood; and, pragmatic recommendations are required for improving performance.

If a number of these "*quick-and-dirty*" evaluations have been conducted and it is required that there is a need for some "organising" of this data and that some form of consolidation and wider interpretation is needed, USAID, the American bilateral aid agency, recommends that an "evaluation synthesis" could be undertaken.

Data collection – evaluation needs data and reliable data at that. In most development contexts the availability and reliability of data can be a major problem. Too often the quality of available data is suspect, it is difficult to provide verification of that data, although **quantitative data** may be available in limited amounts, **qualitative data** maybe less reliable.

The need for baseline data – the data on what exists before the start of the project interventions and which should be collected with assistance and participation of the end-beneficiaries – is paramount but sadly not always readily available. This baseline data is used in order to measure progress, change and impact and will be used, at design stage, to construct the **indicators**.

Documentation - documentation from all phases of an intervention should be made available to the evaluators or collected by them – quarterly reports, annual reports, technical reports, occasional papers all written materials pertaining to the intervention. In an EC funded project the *Financing Agreement* between the recipient government and the Commission will state exactly what the agreement was and what the interventions were intended to provide – a good starting point for evaluation planning. Government records, NGO records, the records of local government as well as other partners and the financial records should be examined.

Surveys and the sample population - the selection of the sample of population or people who will be interviewed or who will complete questionnaires, should be representative and must assure that the validity of the population size and diversity will provide the requisite balance and broad spectrum of opinion. The **focus group discussions** that are arranged within the selected population should be well planned and the participants well briefed.

Interviews – can take up considerable time, but do provide most valuable information particularly feelings and expectations of the end-beneficiaries. They must be planned and conducted with care and sensitivity – the interviewers must be well prepared prior to the interviews or the validity of the responses could be brought into question. Who is best to provide qualitative information on the interventions, who are the "key informants" which is the best "focus group", what questions would best solicit the requisite information and should they be structured or informal interviews? However, the most important group of people to be interviewed will be the end beneficiaries, their opinions on the implementation and the success, or otherwise, of the interventions must be obtained. The donors will be interviewed for their interpretation of success of the interventions and how they feel the interventions have contributed towards improvements and whether they feel that they have obtained "value-for-money" from their development aid that they have provided. For capturing the qualitative and impressionistic findings / perceptions to supplement and complement the quantitative survey data, Focus Group Discussion sessions (FGDs) are worthwhile.

Questionnaires - the design, conduct and use of questionnaires is an art in itself. A good questionnaire should be specific in its topic and designed to solicit information as quickly as possible and with as little disruption to the lives of those being questioned. The enumerators who will receive training prior to conducting field surveys and administering questionnaires, must show clearly at the beginning of the interviews, the significance and purpose of the evaluation exercise and the questionnaire should seek only information that cannot be gained from elsewhere - if administered sensitively and designed with care, questionnaires can be particularly useful in gaining peoples understanding, perceptions and "feelings".

The analysis of data and survey findings - is the next stage. Collected data will be analysed for quantitative assessment of the performance, impact and acceptance of interventions. From these findings, conclusions on the impact of the interventions, the effectiveness of the project management and the sustainability of these interventions will be assessed. The use of qualitative data and the interpretation of the findings from questionnaire and interviews will be analysed, but this can be very often a subjective analysis, so care must be taken when bringing these analyses into the assessment of performance and impact of interventions. From these conclusions recommendation for future design will be incorporated into overall feed-back from an evaluation.

IN SUMMARY

A good evaluation:

- ✓ Adapts to meet changing circumstances;
- ✓ Is tailored to the project – no one-size fits all;
- ✓ Is part-and-parcel of good project design;
- ✓ Covers as wide a cross-section of the target group as possible;
- ✓ Covers a wide range of data sources;
- ✓ Ensure that lessons are learned for the future;
- ✓ Must be honest – admit to failures as well as successes – we can learn lessons from failure too;
- ✓ Should be reflective – also evaluate your evaluation ………..

All simple statements, all common sense and in a nutshell this is what evaluation should be doing and what should be the outcome of evaluations. Some tools, such as LFA and rapid appraisal / evaluation techniques for example, are helpful in the conduct of evaluations, but like all tools it is only with practice that they provide the outcomes of what we want. That, monitoring and evaluation, though different, are the twins that ensure that change and progress are measured, lessons are learned and design and implementation are undertaken most effectively and efficiently.

A FOOTNOTE

With regard to evaluation where do we stand now at the end of the first decade in the 21st century? After having evaluated many projects and monitored many more, I have found that there is little evidence that lessons-learned from evaluation studies have been incorporated into the designs of new interventions, with the same mistakes continuing to be made in both design and implementation. With considerable experience in both of these parts of the project cycle and over 20 years in the long-term implementation of projects, I have only ever been asked and been involved in one formulation and design mission – opportunities to bring that M&E experience to influence designs, sadly are thus lost.

A word of caution - evaluations are laden with judgements – not only judgments of the intervention being evaluated, judgements of the various actors but also judgments of the evaluators themselves. This means that the evaluators can be *"caught between the devil and the deep blue sea"* in that they can thus have their professionalism compromised if they do not deliver *"what is wanted to be heard"*. Their impartiality can be compromised when the donors want to hear about "success stories" where none exist, and if they do not hear what they want to hear, the future employment of the evaluator may be in jeopardy!! So a delicate path has to be negotiated between an honest assessment, between recommendations and criticisms if evaluations are to be used to the benefit of all the partners.

My hope is that the next generation of development professionals will look at evaluation reports and end-of project reports so that lessons are learned and incorporated into improved future designs, so that mistakes – and often costly ones – are not repeated. My optimism is that the development interventions for the people whom we are trying to serve, benefit from our knowledge and experience in order that the delivery of these interventions are responsive to identified needs, and thus hasten the improvements, that are both desired and deserved, to their lives.

ANNEXES

Log frame matrix

A sample layout

Narrative Summary or Interventions Logic	Objectively Verifiable Indicators	Means of Verification	Assumptions
Overall Goal			
Purpose			
Outputs or Results			
Activities			

The Project Cycle

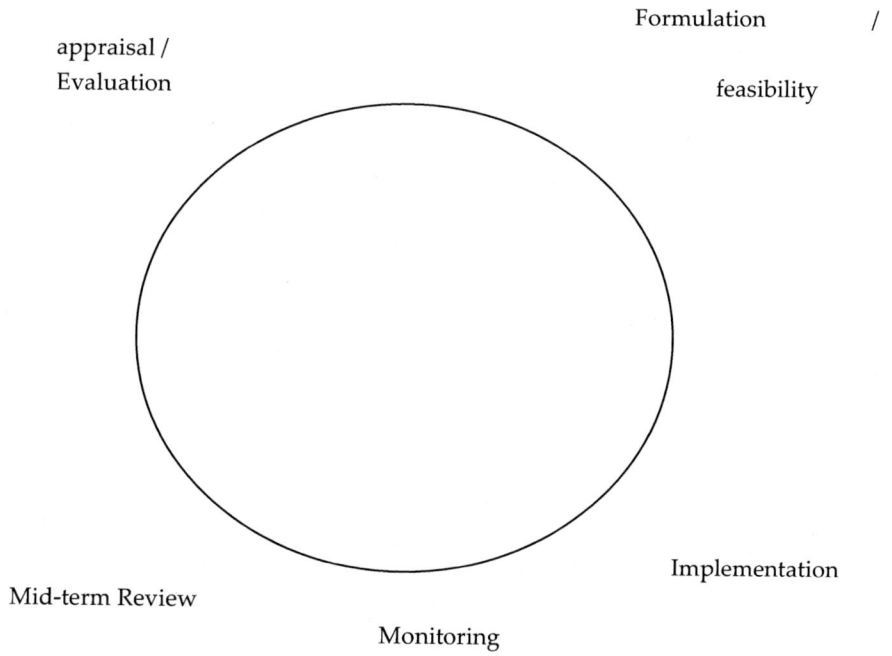

EPILOGUE

Throughout this book we have identified that information, education and communication acts as a catalyst to change by creating the right environment for it; the assumption is that the more informed people are, the less resistant they will be to change. This is subsumed in Wade's (2001) thinking about the importance of information as a primary determinant of learning.

Barzilai and Zohar (2008) have asked an important question and that is, is information acquisition still important in the information age? This kind of question has generated several debates in academic discourse (see for example, Karasavvidis 2002; Salomon, 2000; Land and Greene 2000; Slotta and Linn 2000; Breivik 1998). It is debates like these that prompt reflexive discussions and positions assumed by Theresa Norton's paper (chapter six) and future projections into ICT as sources of information, education and communication vis-à-vis knowledge, in Waheed Khan's 'forward' to this book. Nevertheless, it is important to situate the current debate in its appropriate context. Information, education and communication as sources of knowledge and learning may be hanging delicately on different points of the spectrum. For some, knowledge is better constructed through the use of artefacts, or cognitive tools, which personify their culture (Cole and Derry 2005). Similarly, ICT access and know-how may be an issue. For others, it may be the ability to build knowledge – defined here as networks of facts, ideas, and processes - may be an inhibiting factor (see Greeno et al. 1996; Eylon and Linn 1998; Linn et al. 2004.). What is important, as far as IE&C is concerned, is the ability of researchers and especially practitioners to learn from comparative cases some of which have been laid out in this book.

The early chapters (one to eight) provide readers with insightful theoretical understanding of IE&C. Theory not only provide a framework for us to interpret the meanings of observed patterns but they help us to determine when these patterns are meaningful and when they are not. It is important, therefore, for people who work or research IE&C be they clinicians; public health program planners and policy-makers to rely on well-tested models as a foundation for social change. This is because; their understanding promotes harmonious marriage between theory and practice of activities requiring change. After all, theory and research provide a basis for interventions that make a positive difference in community living and activities (Sarason, 2003: 209). There is equally useful knowledge in Wandersman (2003) which allude to the point that a major task of empirical data concerning the quality of life in communities is enhancing quality of practice. By extension, this should enable IE&C practitioners to 'effectively address, resolve or make progress toward resolving a whole host of problems at the community level'.

If interest affects discourse processing and learning as Wade et al (1993) would want us to believe then it follows that whatever IE&C practitioners do in the field would reflect that interest. This does not necessarily imply adding seductive details (Garner *et al.*, 1989) that are likely to threaten practice as illustrated in chapter nine. This is not to say that seductive details by rule of thumb should be avoided. In some instances we may find a rich humour from artistic representations that depict events in a community which require change. This can open an extensive debate about the consequences of the act. In that case seductive element would have worked positively. What is not clear is the extent to which such facets could be used? Here, Gill Karamjit's advice to mind the cultural gap (chapter ten) is useful in other not to loose the concreteness of the information or 'kill' people's interest altogether.

Cultural dispositions that are specific to individuals or even groups are associated with personal or group emotions. If used to their advantage, they can create currency, increased knowledge and motivation. In the eyes of Hidi and Harackiewicz (2000) this can lead to long-lasting personal interest which is a much needed resource for behaviour and social change. 'Right to information' is a cherished value in international and some national protocols; similarly, the right to remain in ignorance of information has also gained recognition in international legal instruments such as the European Bioethics Convention. Article 10 (2) of that Convention states:

> Everyone is entitled to know any information collected about his or her health. However, the wishes of individuals not to be so informed shall be observed

It is not clear how that law is interpreted in different social contexts. What is not also clear is how this thinking affects other facet of life such as informing and educating people on issues about the environment, climate change and waste management. In deed, these are contested areas because they fall under the "common good". If individuals do not want to know about their life threatening circumstance or behaviour, which is an individual decision and does not directly, affect the entire community; needless to say, it might still be a loss to the community but that interest can not be allowed to supersede the overall community interest. In fact, an information deficient society gropes in "darkness" and does not grow. Notwithstanding the power and influences of communication it is not easy to change people's attitudes that have evolved over a long period (Nyirenda, 1996).

That; Information, Education and Communication work together to affect behaviour change processes can no longer be contested. The five stages of behaviour change – pre-contemplation, contemplation, preparation, action stage and maintenance stage, referred to in the literature as "behaviour change spiral", requires the reinforcement of knowledge and awareness throughout each stage of development. The spiral (as shown) is vulnerable by itself and thus requires deliberate mechanisms to keep it from breaking. In other words, if attitude is not reinforced through IE&C mechanisms, there is the likelihood that a person seeking to change his or her behaviour may be discouraged and thus give up. Several social and environmental factors negate behaviour change. This may range from peer influence to stigmatisation (see Lopes, 2006; Gilbert, 2001; Goffman, 1963)

Notwithstanding the reactions involved in this Stages of Change model, individuals still have free-will regarding their ultimate actions toward change. Within that complex, education and information vis-à-vis the use of appropriate channels should be balanced harmoniously to make the required change to happen.

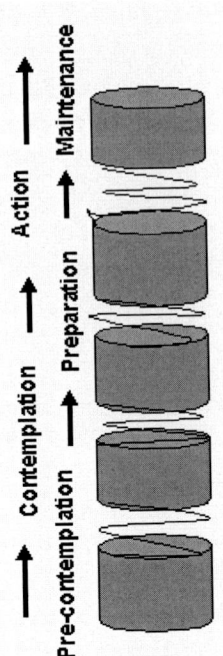

Source: FAO (1996)

LESSONS FROM COMPARATIVE STUDIES

There are ample lesson from Rose (2005: 41 - 54) that encourages practitioners to turn elsewhere for programme lessons. Learning from success stories is not an anathema nor a beggar-my-neighbour policy. Rather, its logic is gaining knowledge about how a specific programme operates and whether those lessons can be used as useful pegs in the other context. Here, chapter 7 to 8 and 13 to 15 have been significant in creating that comparative learning environment. In the process of transferring knowledge, details that are not symbolic to the particular social and cultural context are removed in other not to render the programme ineffective or not implementable. This is where programme evaluation (chapter sixteen) becomes a valuable tool in ensuring that project objectives are not only achieved but maximum use is made of scarce resources. In other words, programme evaluation, depending on its design, enables 'lessons to be drawn by learning what to leave out as well as what to include'.

It is probable that policy makers 'searching for IE&C programmes that works may look for competing alternatives; where to explore for such lessons are likely to be influenced by many factors including politics of north – south divide, technologically rich versus technologically poor and the like. Such introverted thinking, in Rose's (2005: 48) perception, is likely to be trapped in ignorance of innovations in many parts of the world. That, Africa or India is a textbook example of IE&C practice that has chalked successes in modifying behaviour in a given context should not create distinctive barriers to learning for reasons of cultural diversity, different values and systems. To reiterate an earlier point, what is needed is the *how* and *what* can be learnt from those contexts.

There is optimism that the various discussions in this book have generated or will create enough knowledge and understanding of IE&C theory and practice as an intervention mechanism in complex and non-complex social systems.

REFERENCES

Abbey-Mensah, S (2001). "Rural Broadcasting in Ghana" FAO: Rome. [Available:http://www.fao.org/documents/show_cdr.asp?url_file=/docrep/003/x6721e/x6721e12.htm] [Accessed: 18 – 4 – 2008]

Aborampah, M & Anokwa, K (1984). 'Communication and Agricultural Development: some theoretical and conceptual considerations'. *International Journal of Mass Communication Studies* 34 (2): 103 – 115

Adgebe, M. A (2003) 'Radio drama for development: ARDA and the Rainbow City experience'. *Journal of African Cultural Studies* 16 (1): 95 – 105

Agarwal, S.P., Saroj, D and Chauhan, L. S (2005). 'The role of IEC in the RNTCP. Chapter on Tuberculosis Control in India'. In: SP Agarwal, LS Chauhan. *Directorate of General Health Services Ministry of Health and Family Welfare*, New Delhi: Nirman Bhavan

Aggleton, P (2007). "Just a snip"? A social history of male circumcision. *Reproductive Health Matters* 15 (29): 15 – 21. May. http://dx.doi.org/ 10.1016/S0968-8080(07)29303-6

Airhenbuwa, C & Obregon, R (2000) *A critical assessment of theories/models used in health communication for HIV/AIDS. Journal of health Communication* 5: 5 - 15.

Airhihenbuwa, CO (1999) 'Of Culture and Multiverse: Renouncing "the Universal Truth in Health'. *Journal of Health Education*, 30(3): 298 - 304

Aldinger, C., Zhang, X.W., Liu, L.Q., Guo, J.X., Yu, S.H & Jones, J. (2008). Strategies for implementing Health-Promoting Schools in a province in China, *Promotion & Education* 15(1): 24 – 29

Aldinger, C., Zhang, X.W., Liu, L.Q., Pan, X.D., Yu, S.H., Jones, J., & Kass, J. (2008). Changes in attitudes, knowledge and behavior associated with implementing a comprehensive school health program in a province of China, *Health Education Research* 23(3): advance access published May 13, 2008.

Alexander C., et.al, (1977) *A Pattern Language*, Oxford: Oxford University Press

Alhassan, A (2005). 'Market valorisation in broadcasting policy in Ghana: abandoning the quest for media democratization'. *Media, Culture & Society* 27 (2): 211– 228

Allensworth, D. D & Kolbe, L. J. (1987). 'The comprehensive school health program: Exploring an expanded concept'. *Journal of School Health* 57 (10): 409 – 412

Al-Mazrou, Y.Y., Abouzeid, M.S., Al-Jeffrei, M.H. (2005). *Saudi Medicine Journal* 26 (11): 1788 – 95. November

Althede, D (2002) *Creating fear: News and the Construction of Crisis.* Hawthorne, NY: Aldine deGuyter.

Altman, D (1986) *AIDS in the Mind of America.* Garden City, NY: Anchor Press / Doubleday.

Anarfi, K. J. and Appiah, N. E (2004) 'mitigating the impact of HIV/AIDS in Ghana: The role of Education'. *Paper* Presented at the International Conference on Ghana at Half Century, ISSER and Cornell University. Ghana: Accra.

Andreason, A. R (1995). *Marketing social change: Changing behaviour to promote health, social development, and the environment.* San Francisco: Jossey-Bass.

Anonymous, (2006) 'Popular African Traditional Dances'. [Avalable: http://www.geocities.com/bamaaya/africandance1.html]. [Accessed: 13 – 2 –   2008]

Ansah, P (1985) *'Ghana Broadcasting Corporation Golden Jubilee Lectures'.* Ghana Publishing Corporation, Accra.

Aplasca, M.R., Siegel, D., Mandel, J.S., Santana-Arciage R.T., Paul J., Hudes, E.S., Monzon, O.T., Hearst, N (1995). Results of a model AIDS prevention program for high school students in the Phillipines. *AIDS* Pp S7-13. July Supplement.

Apteker, L. (1994) 'Street Children in the Developing World: a review of their conditions'. *Cross Cultural Research* 28 (3): 195 – 224

Ardebili, M. H. (2001) 'Unpublished Lecture Notes: Social Science 610, Philosophy of Social Science and Department of Economics & Social Science Consortium'. University of Missouri – Kansas City. Fall

Arimah, B. C. (2004) 'Poverty Reduction and Human Development in Africa'.   *Journal of Human Development* 5 (3): 399 – 415. November

Aro, M and Olkinuora, E (2007) 'Riding the information highway - towards a new kind of learning', *International Journal of Lifelong Education* 26: (4): 385 - 98

Asamoah-Odei E et al. (2004). HIV prevalence and trends in sub-Saharan Africa: no decline and large sub-regional differences. *Lancet* 364 (9428): 35 – 40

Asante, C. (1996) *The Press in Ghana: problems and prospects.* Maryland: University Press of America.

Asiimwe-Okiror; G., Opio, A.A., Musinguzi, J., Madraa, J., Tembo, G., Caraël, M. (1997). 'Change in sexual behaviour and decline in HIV infection among young pregnant women in urban Uganda'. *AIDS* 11 (14) November 15

AVERT (2005). 'How many people in Africa are infected with HIV'. [Available: http://www.avert.org/aafrica.htm]. [Accessed 16 January 2005]

Backer, T. (2001) *Finding the Balance: Program Fidelity and Adaptation in Substance Abuse Prevention.* Rockville, MD: National Center for Advancement of Prevention (NCAP).

Barbier, E. B. (2000). 'The economic linkages between rural poverty and land degradation: some evidence from Africa'. *Agriculture, Ecosystems & Environment* 82 (1-3): 355 – 70. December

Barford, J & Weston, C (1997) 'The use of video as a teaching resource in a new university'. *British Journal of Educational Technology* 28 (1): 40 – 50

Barnett, T. and Whiteside, A. (2002). *AIDS in the 21ST Century: disease and globalisation.* London: Palgrave McMillan

Basch, C.E. (1987). 'Focus Group Interview: An Underutilised Research Technique for Improving Theory and Practice in Health Education'. *Health Education Quarterly* 14 (4): 411 – 48

Bauni, E.K. and Jarabi, B.O (2000). 'Family Planning and sexual behavior in the era of HIV/AIDS: The case of Nakuru District, Kenya'. *Studies in Family Planning* 31 (1): 69-80. March

Barzilai, S and Zohar, A (2008). Is information acquisition still important in the information age? *Education Information Technology* 13: 35 – 53

Becker, H. (1993). 'Theory: the necessary evil'. In: Flinders, D and Mills, G (Eds.). *Theory and Concepts in Qualitative Research: perspectives from the field* [Pp. 218 – 229]. New York. Teachers College. Columbia University Press

Behrman, E.H. (2002) Community – based literacy learning. *Literacy – Oxford* 36 (1): 26 – 32

Ben-Amos, D & Goldstein, K. (1975). *Folklore: Performance and Communication.* The Hague: Mouton

Benefo, K. K (2004) 'The Mass Media and HIV/AIDS Prevention in Ghana'. *Journal of health and Population in Developing Countries.* Available: URL: http://www.jhpdc.unc.edu/

Berg, M., Aarts, J., & van der Lei, J (2003). ICT in health care: Sociotechnical Approaches. *Methods of Information in Medicine* 42: 297 – 301

Berger, A. A (2000) *Media and Communication Research Methods: An Introduction to Qualitative and Quantitative Approaches.* Sage Publications: London.

Berman, P. and McLaughlin, M. (1975). 'The findings in review' *Federal Programs Supporting Educational Change* IV. The RAND Corporation.

Bersani, L (1988) 'Is the rectum a grave'? In: Douglas Crimp (ed.), AIDS: Cultural Analysis, Cultural Activism [p. 243-64]. Cambridge, MA: The MIT Press.

Bessinger, R., Katenda, C., Lettenmeier, C (2000). Uganda Quality of Care Survey of Family Planning and Antenatal Care Services: Delivery of Improved Services for Health (DISH), Pathfinder International and Measure Evaluation Project. North Carolina, USA: Carolina Population Centre.

Bhabha, H K. (1994). *The location of culture,* London and New York. Routledge

Bhaskar, R. (1998) *The Possibility of Naturalism: a philosophical critique of the Contemporary Human Sciences* (3rd edition), New York and London: Routledge

Bhola, H.S. (2005). 'Potential of adult and lifelong education for poverty reduction: systems thinking for systemic change.' *International Journal of Lifelong Education* 24 (5): 405 – 17

Bird, S. E (2006). 'Cultural Studies as Confluence: The Convergence of Folklore and Media Studies.' In: Hinds, H.H., Motz, M. F & Nelson, Angela M.S [Eds.] *Popular Culture Theory and Methodology: A Basic Introduction.* pp 344 – 55 Madison, Wisc: University of Wisconsin Press.

Bloom, S.S., Urassa, M., Isingo, R., Ng'weshemi, J., Boerma, J.T. (2002) 'Community effects on the risk of HIV infection in rural Tanzania'. *Sexually Transmitted Infections* 78: 261 – 266

Blum, R. W., McNeely, C. A., & Rinehart, P. M. (2002). *Improving the odds: The untapped power of schools to improve the health of teens.* Minneapolis: Center for Adolescent Health and Development, University of Minnesota.

Boafo, S. (1988). 'Democratising Media Systems in African Societies: the case of Ghana'. *International Journal for Mass Communication Studies* 41 (1): 37 – 51

Botvin, G. J (2001). 'Life Skills Training: Fact Sheet'. Available from http://www.lifeskillstraining.com/facts.html

Bown, N (1996). 'There are Fairies at the Bottom of our Garden: Fairies Fantasy and Photography'. *Textual Practice* 10 (1): 57 – 82

Bradbury, H and Reason, P (2003). 'Action Research: An Opportunity for Revitalizing Research Purpose and Practices'. Qualitative Social Work 2 (2): 155 – 175

Brandt, D (Ed. 2003). *Navigating innovations: Indo-European cross-cultural experiences* Vols. I &II, New Delhi: India Research Press

Brehony, E (2000). 'Whose practice counts? Experiences in using indigenous health practices from Ethiopia and Uganda'. *Development in Practice* 10 (5): 650 – 661

Breivik, P. S (1998). Student learning in the information age. Phoenix: American Council on Education /Oryx Press.

Bryman, A. (2001). *Social Research Methods*. London. Oxford University Press

Buhl, M (2006). 'Visual culture as a strategic approach to art production in education' *International Journal of Education through Art* 1 (2): 103–14

Bumb, B.L., Teboh, J.F., Atta J.K. and Asenso-Okyere, W. K (1994) *Ghana Policy Environment and Fertilizer Sector Development.* Alabama, and ISSER, Legon Ghana: International Fertilizer Development Center.

Burnham, G and Stinson, W (1998). 'Assessing the Quality of the Supervision of Reproductive Health Surveys in Uganda'. *Quality Assurance Brief* 7(1):11 – 5. June

Buston, K., Wight, D., Hart, H., & Scott, S (2002). Implementation of a teacher-delivered sex education programme: Obstacles and facilitating factors. *Health Education Research, 17,* 59–72.

Byrne, M. & Curtis, R. (2000) *Designing health communication: Testing the explanations for the impact of communication medium on effectiveness. British Journal of Psychology* 5: 189 -199.

Calsyn, D.A., Saxon, A.J., Freeman, G., Whittaker, S. (1992). Ineffectiveness of AIDS Education and HIV Antibody Testing in Reducing High-Risk Behaviours among Injection Drug Users. *American Journal of Public Health.* 82 (4): 573 – 575

Campbell C (2003). 'Letting them die: why HIV and AIDS prevention programmes fail'. *African Issues.* Indiana: Indiana University Press.

Carr, W. & Kemmis, S. (1986). Becoming Critical: Education, Knowledge and Action Research. London: The Falmer Press.

Cavendish, W. (2000) 'Empirical Regularities in the Poverty - Environment Relationship of Rural Households: Evidence from Zimbabwe' *World Development* 28 (11): 1979 - 2003. November

Cavangah, J and Barnet, R. J (1994). *Global Dreams: imperial corporations and the new world order.* New York: Simon and Schuster

CBRI, India (1982) 'Building Digest' *Paper 13.* Delhi: Asia Press.

Central TB Division & DANTB (2005). 'A health communication strategy for RNTCP. Directorate of Health Services'. New Delhi, India: Ministry of Health and Family Welfare,

Central TB Division (2002). 'Managing the Revised National Tuberculosis Control Programme. Modules 1-4. Directorate of Health Services'. New Delhi, India: Ministry of Health and Family Welfare.

Central TB Division (2007). 'IEC–Baseline Document Central TB Division: Report compilation'. New Delhi, India: New Concept Information Systems..

Central TB Division (2008). 'TB India 2008 RNTCP Status Report. Directorate of Health Services'. New Delhi, India: Ministry of Health and Family Welfare.

Centre for AIDS Development, Research and Evaluation (CADRE) (2005). *Tsha, Tsha: Key findings of the evaluation of episodes 1 – 26.* Retrieved September 26, 2005, from http://www.cadre.org.za/publications.htm.

Centre for Minimum Cost Housing, McGill University (1984) *How the Other Half Builds. Volume 1: Space.* Montreal: Mimeo.

Centre for Minimum Cost Housing, McGill University, (1984) *How the Other Half Builds, Volume 2: Plots.* Montreal: Mimeo.

Chamberlain, K. (1999).'Using grounded theory in health psychology'. In: K. Chamberlain (Ed.), *Qualitative health psychology* (pp. 183-201). Thousand Oaks, CA: Sage.

Chambers, R. (1994) 'Participatory Rural Appraisal: analysing of Experience'. *World Development* 22 (9): 1253 – 68

Chambers, R. (1995) 'Paradigm Shifts and the Practice of Participatory Research and Development.' In: Nelson, N & Wright, S [Eds.] *Power and Participatory Development: theory and practice.* London: Intermediate Technology Publication.

Chang, B. L & Hirsch, M. (1994) 'Videotape intervention: producing videotapes for use in Nursing practice and education'. *Journal of Continuing Education in Nursing* 25 (6): 263 – 67

Cheek, J (1997) 'contextualizing toxic shock syndrome: Selected media representations of the emergence of a health phenomenon 1977 – 1995'. *Health* 1:183 – 203

Chen L, Jha P, Stirling B, Sgaier SK, Daid T, et al (2007). Sexual Risk Factors for HIV Infection in Early and Advanced HIV Epidemics in Sub-Saharan Africa: Systematic Overview of 68 Epidemiological Studies. *PLoS ONE* 2(10): e1001. doi:10.1371/journal.pone.0001001

Chinyowa, K. C (2007) 'Frames of metacommunication in African theatre for development'. *Studies in Theatre and Performance* 27 (1): 13 – 24

Christiansen, L., Demery, L & Paternostro, S. (2003) 'Macro and Micro Perspectives of Growth and Poverty in Africa'. *World Bank Economic Review* 17 (3): 317 – 47

Clarke, J. N (2002) *Epidemiology Fact Sheet of HIV/AIDS and Sexually Transmitted Infections, 2002 Update.* Joint United Nations Programme on HIV/AIDS (UNAIDS) (Geneva, UNAIDS/WHO).

Clarke, J. N (2004) *Health, Illness, and Medicine in Canada.* Toronto: Oxford University Press.

Clarke, J. N (2006) '*Homophobia out of the closet in the media portrayal of HIV/AIDS in 1991, 1996 and 2001: Celebrity heterosexism and the silent victims*', *Critical Public Health* 16 (4): 317 – 330.

Cochrane, M (2000). *The Politics of AIDS Surveillance. Professional Geographer* 52 (2): 205 – 218

Coggon D., Rose G., Barker D.J.P. (1997). *Epidemiology for the Uninitiated*, [4th Edition]. UK: BMJ Publishing Group.

Cole, M., & Derry, J. (2005). 'We have met technology and it is us'. In: R. J. Sternberg & D. D. Preiss (Eds.). *Intelligence and technology* (pp. 209 – 227). Mahwah: Lawrence Erlbaum Associates.

Coldevin, G. and Stuart, T.H (1993) "Initiatives in Development Support Communication for Agricultural Technology Transfer in the Philippines" *The Journal of Development Communication* 2 (4): 18 - 29. December

Coll–Seck, M. A (1999) 'Radio and HIV/AIDS: Making a Difference' Gordon Adam and Nicola Harford (Eds.). Scotland: Highland Printers, Inverness.

Connell, J.P. & Kubisch, A. C. (1998). 'Applying a theory of change approach to the evaluation of comprehensive community initiatives: progress, prospects, and problems'. In: Fulbright-Anderson et al (Eds.) *New Approaches to Evaluating* Community Initiatives, Theory, *Measurement and Analysis*. [Vol. 2] Washington, DC: Aspen Institute

Conrad-Phillip, K (2005) *Window on Humanity: a concise introduction to general anthropology*, (Pp. 2-3, 16-17, 34 - 44). McGraw Hill, New York

Cook, T. E (1991) *Notes for the Next Epidemic- Part One: Lessons from the News Coverage of AIDS*. Cambridge, MA: The Joan Shorenstein Barone Center.

Cooley, MJ (1991) *Architect or Bee?* : The Human Price of Technology", Chatto & Windus, London: Hogarth Press. 2nd Impression

Corbett, EL., Makamure, B., Cheung, Y B., Dauya, e., Matambo, R., Bandason, T., Munyati, SS., Mason, PR., Butterworth, A E., Hayes, RJ (2007). HIV incidence during a cluster randomised trial of two strategies providing voluntary counselling and testing at the workplace, Zimbabwe. *AIDS* 21: 483 – 498

Cottle, S (2003) *News*, 'Public Relations and Power: Mapping the Field'. In: Simon Cottle (ed.) *Media, Public Relations and Power*. London: Sage.

Covey, J. A (2001). 'People's preferences Safety Control: why does baseline risk matter?' *Risk Analysis* 21 (2): 331 – 40

Cullen, T (2006) `HIV/AIDS in Papua New Guinea: a reality check' *Pacific Journalism Review* 12(1): 153 – 164

D'Angelo, P (2002) *'News framing as multiparadigmatic research program: A response to Entman'*. Journal of Communication 52: 870 – 888.

DAI (2001). *Background Information – Evaluation and Field Based Data Collection Activities*, Washington Dc, USA. May

Damulira, E and Sebakigye, I. M (2003). 'Collaborating to Strengthen District Level Family Planning Programs through Partnership: The Case of ADRA-BIHP in Uganda'. *Abstract*, July

Danladi, M (1996). 'The Sleeping Dog Cannot Bark: media and mass disempowerment of civil society in Africa' *Africa Media Review* 10 (3): 79 -92

Danish Management A/S, February 2001, *Handbook for Monitors, External Monitoring System of EC Development Aid Programmes, European* Commission EuropeAid Unit 6,

de Janvry, A & Sadoulet, E. (2000). 'Rural poverty in Latin America: Determinants and exit paths'. *Food Policy* 25 (4): 389 – 409. August

De Walque D. (2004). 'How Does the Impact of an HIV and AIDS Information Campaign Vary with Educational Attainment: Evidence from Rural Uganda'? Washington DC. The World Bank, Development Research Group.

Deacon, D., Pickering, M., Golding, P. and Murdock, G (1999) 'Researching Communications: A practical guide to methods in media and cultural analysis'. Oxford University Press Inc: New York.

Demain, M (2006). 'Reflecting on Loss in Papua New Guinea'. *Ethnos Journal of Anthropology* 71 (4): 507 — 32

Denzin, K. N and Lincoln, S. Y (1994) 'Handbook of Qualitative Research'. Sage Publications: London.

Denzin, N. (1990) 'Strategies and Multiple Triangulations'. In: Denzin, N (Ed.). *The Research Act in Sociology: a theoretical introduction to sociological method* [Pp. 297-313]. New York: McGraw Hill

Derry, S. J. (1999) 'A Fish called peer learning: Searching for common themes'. In: A. M. O'Donnell & A. King (Eds.) *Cognitive perspectives on peer learning* (pp. 87-115). Mahwah, NJ: Lawrence Erlbaum

Deuze, M. (2005) 'What is Journalism? Professional identity and ideology of journalists reconsidered'. *Journalism* 6 (4): 442 – 64.

DeVault M, McCoy L (2002) 'Institutional Ethnography. Using interviews to investigate ruling relations'. In: Gubrium JF, Holstein JA, eds. *Handbook of interview research. Context and method.* [Pp. 751 -776]. Thousand Oaks, CA: Sage.

Development Demographic Health Survey (1997) 'Focus Groups Used for Study of Reproductive Decision making in Uganda'. *Macro System Institute Resource* 7 (2):1–2.

Dimiter, M. D and Phillip D. R, Jr. (2003). 'Pretest-posttest designs and measurement of change'. *Work - Journal of Preventive and Rehabilitation Assessment* 20: 159–165

Dodoo, A. N. O., Renner, L., van Grootheest, A. C., Labadie, J., Antwi-Agyei, K. O., Hayibor, S., Addison, J., Pappoe, V & Appiah-Danquah, A (2007) 'Safety Monitoring of a New Pentavalent Vaccine in the Expanded Programme on Immunisation in Ghana' *Drug Safety* 30 (4): 347 – 356

Domatob, J. K., Ausmus, W and Butler, J (1996). 'New communication technologies in tropical African development'. *Development in Practice* 6 (3): 228 – 239

Drèze, J & Murthi, M. (2001) 'Fertility, Education and Development: Evidence from India'. *Population and Development Review* 27 (1): 33 – 63. March

Drimie, S (2003) 'HIV/AIDS and land: case studies from Kenya, Lesotho and South Africa'. *Development Southern Africa* 20 (5): 647 – 58.

Durham, M. G. (1998) 'On the relevance of standpoint epistemology to the practice of journalism: the case of 'Strong Objectivity''. *Communication Theory* 8 (2) 117 – 40

Dutta, M J (2006) 'Theoretical Approaches to Entertainment Education Campaigns: A Subaltern Critique', *Health Communication* 20 (3): 221 – 231

Dwivedi L.K and Ram, F (2006). 'Change and Determinants of Contraceptive Use in Uttar Pradesh. In: Arvind Pandey (Ed), *Biostatistical Aspects of Health and Population.* India: Hindustan Publishing Corporation.

Easterby – Smith, M. (1997) 'Disciplines of Organisational Learning: contributions and critiques'. *Human Relations* 50 (9): 1085 – 113

EC / UNDP (undated), *SGP PTF First Regional Operational Manual* – Annexes.

Entman, R. M (1993). 'Framing: Toward clarification of a fractured paradigm'. *Journal of Communication* 43: 51 – 57

Epstein H. (2007). *The invisible cure: Africa, the West and the fight against AIDS* New York: Farrar Straus and Giroux.

Everett, S. A., and Colditz, G. A (1997). 'Skin Cancer Prevention: a time for Action'. *Journal of Community Health* 22 (3): 175 - 83 June

Eyben, R., Kidder; T., Rowlands, J and Bronstein, A (2008) 'Thinking about change for development practice'. *Development in Practice* 18 (2): 201 – 212

Eylon, B & Linn, M. C (1998). Learning and instruction: An examination of four research perspectives in science education. *Review of Educational Research* 58 (3): 251–301.

Ezra, J & Mchakulu, J (2007) 'Youth Participation in Radio Listening Clubs in Malawi'. *Journal of Southern African Studies* 33 (2): 251 – 65

Family Planning Association of Uganda (FPAU), (1992). Family Planning: We Cannot Use What We Do Not Understand! Qualitative Research on Family Planning in Uganda, Kampala, Uganda and Baltimore: FPAU and Johns Hopkins University/Population Communication Services.

Fawole, I.O., Asuzu, M.C., Oduntan, S.O., and Brieger, W.R. (1999). A school-based AIDS education programme for secondary school students in Nigeria: a review of effectiveness. *Health Education Research* 1999 14 (5): 675 – 83. Oct

Fee, E., & Fox, M. D (eds.) (1988) '*AIDS: The Burdens of History*'. Berkeley: University of California Press.

Feenan, D (2007) 'Understanding Disadvantaged Partly Through an Epistemology of Ignorance' *Social Legal Studies* 16: 509 – 531

Fenn, C. (2003). Arts in Health – research findings (draft). London: Arts Council England

Fiadzo, E., Houston, J. E & Godwin, D. D. (2001) 'Estimating Housing Quality for Poverty and Development Policy Analysis: CWIQ in Ghana.' *Social Indicators Research* 53 (2): 137 – 62

Fields, G. S. (2000). 'The Dynamics of Poverty, Inequality and Economic Well-being: African Economic Growth in Comparative Perspective'. *Journal of African Economics* 9 (1): 45 – 78

Finkle, J and McIntosh, C.A (eds.) (1994). *The New Politics of Population: Conflict and Consensus in Family Planning*. New York: The Population Council.

Fisher, L and Colditz, G A (1999). 'Tobacco industry advertising and adolescent smoking (United States). *Cancer Causes and Control* 10: 639 – 39

Fishman, M (1980) *Manufacturing the news*. Austin: University of Texas Press.

Fiske, J. (1982). *Introduction to Communication Studies*. London: Methuen

Foley, G (1999) *Learning in Social Action: A Contribution to Understanding Informal Education* (London: Zed Books).

Fontana, A & Frey, J. H. (2000) 'The Interview: From structured questions to negotiated text'. In: Denzin, N and Lincoln, Y.S (Eds.) *Handbook of Qualitative Research* (2nd Ed). [Pp. 645 – 72]. London: Sage Publications

Ford, N., Abimbola, W & Renshaw, M (2005) 'Communication Strategy for Implementing Community IMCI'. *Journal of Health Communication* 10 (5): 379 – 401

Fortson JG (2008). The gradient in Sub-Saharan Africa: Socioeconomic status and HIV and AIDS. *Demography* 45 (2):303 – 322.

Fox, J (2003). 'Advocacy research and the World Bank' *Development in Practice* 13 (5): 519 – 526

Frankel, R. M & Devers, K.J. (2000) 'Study Design in Qualitative Research'. *Education for Health: Change in Learning and Practice* 13 (2): 251 – 61. July

Fraser N., Gorgens-Albino, M., Whitson, D.T., Gelmon, L., and Wilson, D. (2008) "It takes a village": Theoretical considerations and practical suggestions for shifting the focus of HIV prevention in East and Southern Africa to what really works. AIDS [In press].

Freire, P (1970) *Pedagogy of the Oppressed*, trans. M. B. Ramos (New York: Herder & Herder).

Freire, P (1972). *Pedagogy of the Oppressed*. (Translated by Myra Bergman Ramos from the Portuguese). Harmondsworth: Penguin

Freire, P. (1970). *Pedagogy of the oppressed*. New York: Herder and Herder

Frosch, Caren A., Beaman, C. P & Mccloy, R (2007) 'A little learning is a dangerous thing: An experimental demonstration of ignorance-driven inference', *The Quarterly Journal of Experimental Psychology* 60 (10): 1329 – 1336

Gamson, W., & Modigliani, A (1989) 'Media discourse and public opinion on nuclear power: A constructionist approach'. *American Journal of Sociology* 95: 1 – 37.

Gamson, W., Croteau, D., Hoynes, W., & Sasson, T (1992) 'Media images and the social construction of reality'. *Annual Review of Sociology* 18: 373 – 93

Garner, R., Billingham, M and White, J (1989). 'Effects of "seductive details" on macroprocessing and microprocessing in adults and children'. *Cognitive Instruction* 6: 41–57

Geetakrishnan, K., Pappu, K.P and Roychowdhury, K (1988). 'A study on knowledge and attitude towards tuberculosis in a rural area of west Bengal. *Indian Journal of Tuberculosis* 35: 83 – 89.

George, N (1990). *The Dilemma of Appropriate Media Selection for Dissemination of Development Information. Communication Processes: Alternative Channels and Strategies for Development Support.* Canada: IDRC

Ghana Statistical Services, Noguchi Memorial Institute for Medical Research, & ORC Macro DHS (2004) *Ghana Demographic and Health Survey 2003*. Calverton, Maryland: GSS, NMIMR, ORC Macro.

Gikonyo, W and Quaidoo, I. O (*forthcoming*). 'An Analysis of Population Information Education & Communication (IEC) Projects in Anglophone Africa'. In: T. Gokah [Ed] Contemporary Discourses on IE&C Theory and Practice (forthcoming). New York: NOVA Science Publishers

Gilbert H (2001). 'Stigma and the Ethnographic Study of HIV: Problems and Prospects'. *AIDS and Behavior* 5 (2):141 – 49

Gill, K S (2003) Networking for cross-cultural collaboration, in Brandt, D (Ed.), *Navigating innovations: Indo-European cross-cultural experiences* Vol. I, India research Press, New Delhi

Gill, K S (2007). Rethinking the cross-cultural architecture, *A I & Society* 21 (4): 639-648

Gill, K S (ed. 1996) *Human machine symbiosis*, London: Springer

Gill, S P (1995) *Dialogue and tacit knowledge for knowledge transfer*, PhD Dissertation, University of Cambridge

Giltin, T. (1980) *The Whole World is Watching: Mass Media in the Making and Unmaking of the New Left*. Berkeley: University of California Press.

Ginsburg, M., Espinoza, O., Popa, S & Terano, M (2003) 'Privatisation, Domestic Marketisation and International Commercialisation of Higher Education: vulnerabilities and opportunities for Chile and Romania within the framework of WTO/GATS '. *Globalisation, Societies and Education* 1 (3): 413 – 45

Glenda Abramson (2004). 'Israeli Drama and the Bible: Kings on the Stage' *Association of Jewish Studies Review* 28 (1): 63 – 82

Global Campaign for Education (2004). Learning to survive: How education for all would save millions of young people from HIV and AIDS. Global Campaign for Education. Global Campaign for Education. www.campaignforeducation.org.

Glynn, J.R., Carael, M., Buve, A., Anagonou, S, Zekeng, L., Kahindo, M., Musonda, R. (2004). Does increased general schooling protect against HIV infection? A study in four African cities. *Tropical Medicine and International Health* 9 (1): 4 -14

Goffman, E (1963). Stigma: Notes on the Management of Spoiled Identity. Englewood Cliffs, NJ: Prentice-Hall.

Gokah, T (2006). 'The Naïve Researcher: Doing Social Research in Africa'. *International Journal of Social Research Methodology* 9 (1): 61 – 73.

Gokah, T (2006). *Children on the Boundaries of Time and Space in sub-Saharan Africa: policy achievement or aspiration*. Newcastle: Cambridge Scholars Press.

Gokah, T (2007). 'Health Education in Rural Settings in Ghana: a methodological approach' *Journal of Health Education Research* 22: 907 – 917

Gokah, T. (2008) 'Ghana's school feeding programme (GSFP) and the well-being of children: A critical appraisal'. *Journal of Social Development in Africa* 23 (1)

Granger, R.C. (1998) 'Establishing causality in evaluations of comprehensive community initiatives'. In: Fulbright-Anderson et al. (Eds.) *New Approaches to Evaluating Community Initiatives, Theory, Measurement, and Analysis.* Vol. 2: Washington, DC: Aspen Institute

Gray, R., Sinding, C., Ivonoffski, V & Fitch, M. (2000). 'The use of research-based theatre in a project related to metastatic breast cancer'. *Health Expectations* 3: 137 – 144

Greenwood, J. (2002), 'Marking the unmarked: using drama cross-culturally in teacher education in New Zealand', *Systems Research and Behavioural Science* 19 (4): 323 – 29

Greeno, J.G., Collins, A. M & Resnick, L. B. (1996). 'Cognition and learning'. In: D. C. Berliner & R. C. Calfee (Eds.). *Handbook of educational psychology* (pp. 15–46). New York: Macmillan.

Gregson, S., Waddell, H., and Chandiwana, S. (2001). School education and HIV control in Sub-Saharan Africa: from discord to harmony? *Journal of International Development* 13: 467 – 485 March

Grunig, James E. (1989) 'Publics, Audiences and Market Segments: Segmentation Principles for Campaigns.' In: Charles T. Salmon (ed.) *Information Campaigns: Balancing Social Values and Social Change: Sage Annual Reviews of Communication Research.* 18: 199 - 228.

Gupta, N., Katende, C., Bessinger, R (2003). 'Associations of Mass Media Exposure with Family Planning Attitudes and Practices in Uganda'. *Study Family Planning*, 34(1):19 – 31. March

Gutzwiller, F (2005). '"Social and Preventive Medicine" – past achievements and future challenges'. *International Journal of Public Health* 50 - 6 339 – 340

Hailey, J and James, R (2002) 'Learning leaders: the key to learning organisations' *Development in Practice* 12 (3/4): 398 – 408

Hakim, C. (1987) *Research Design: strategies and choices in the design of social research.* London: Allen and Unwin Publishers

Hall, S. (1997). *Representation: Cultural representations and signifying practices.* London: Sage.

Hall, S., Critcher, C., Jefferson, T., Clarke, J., & Roberts, B (1978) *Policing the Crisis: mugging, the state and law and order.* London: Macmillan.

Hallett, T.B., Garnett, G.P., Mupamberiyi, Z., and Gregson, S. 2008. Measuring effectiveness in community randomized trials of HIV prevention. *International Journal of Epidemiology* 37(1):77-87; doi:10.1093/ije/dym232

Hallett, T.B., Gregson, S., Lewis, J.J.C. Lopman, B.A., Garnett, G.P. (2007). Behaviour change in generalised HIV epidemics: impact of reducing cross-generational sex and delaying age at sexual debut. *Sexually Transmitted Infections* 83: i50-i54, doi:10.1136/sti.2006.023606

Hallfors, D. and Godette, D. (2002) 'Will the "Principles of Effectiveness" improve prevention practice? Early findings from a diffusion study' *Health Education Research* 17 (4): 461 – 70.

Hammersley, M. (1990). *What is wrong with ethnography?* London: Routledge.

Hansen, A., Cottle, S., Negrine, R. and Newbold, C (1998) Mass *Communication Research Methods.* Macmillan Press Limited: London.

Harber, C. (2002) 'Education, Democracy and Poverty Reduction in Africa'. *Comparative Education* 38 (3): 267 – 76

Hargrove, J. 2007. Migration, Mines and Mores: Inaugural lecture at University of Stellenbosch, South Africa.

Harvey, B., Stuart, J., Swan, T. 2000. Evaluation of a drama-in-education programme to increase AIDS awareness in Southern African high schools: a randomised community intervention trial. *International Journal of STDs and AIDS* 11 (2): 105 - 11. February

He, J., Gu, D., Wu, X., Reynolds, K., Duan, X., Yao, C., Wang, J., Chen, C.-S., Chen, J., Wildman, R. P., Klag, M. J., & Whelton, P. K. (2005). 'Major causes of death among men and women in China'. *New England Journal of Medicine* 353 (11): 1124 - 34

Hebling, E., Mugayar, L & Vendramini Dias, P (2007). 'Geriatric dentistry: a new specialty in Brazil'. *Gerodontology* 24(3): 177-180. (September)

Henderson, L & Cowan, E. J (2001) *Scottish Fairy Belief: A History.* East Linton: Tuckwell Press

Hesketh, T., Li, L., & Zhu, W. X. (2005). ,The effect of China's one-child family policy after 25 years'. *New England Journal of Medicine* 353 (11): 1171 – 176

Hidi, S and Harackiewicz, J. M (2000). 'Motivating the academically unmotivated: A critical issue for the 21st century'. *Review of Educational Research* 70 (2): 151–179.

Hilgartner, J & Bosk, C (1998). 'The rise and fall of social problems: A public arenas model'. *American Journal of Sociology* 94: 53 – 78

Hoffman-Goetz, L, Friedman, B. D. and Clarke, N. J (2005) 'HIV/AIDS Risk Factors as Portrayed in Mass Media Targeting First Nations, Metis, and Inuit Peoples of Canada' *Journal of health Communication* 10 (2): 145 – 62

Hofstede, G and Hofstede, G J (2005), *Cultures and Organisations: Software of the Mind,* McGraw-Hill, New York

Holtom, B.C., Mickel, A and Boggs, J.G. (2003), 'Using interactive drama to teach the complexities of decision making', *Decision Sciences Journal of Innovative Education* 1 (2): 295 – 301

Hornik, Robert C. (1990) 'Channel Effectiveness in Development Communication Programmes.' In: Ronald, E. Rice and Charles K Atkin (eds.) *Public Communication Campaigns.* [pp. 309 - 329]. Beverly Hills, CA: Sage Publications.

Housing and Environment Department, Madhya Pradesh, (1982) 'Madhya Pradesh Urban Development Project – *Aid Memoir* of the World Bank Appraisal Mission'. Bhopal: Mimeo

Hsia, H. J (1988) *'Mass Communication Research Methods: a step-by-step approach'*. Hillsdale, NJ: Lawrence Erlbaum.

Hubbard, P. (1998) 'Community action and the displacement of street prostitution: Evidence from British cities'. *Social Exclusion* 29 (3): 269 – 86

Hulme, D. (2004) 'Thinking small and the understanding of poverty: Maymana and Mofizul's Story'. *Journal of Human Development* 5 (2): 161 – 176

Indore Vikas Pradhikari, (1981) *Indore Development Plan*. Indore, India: Mimeo.

Innocenti Digest (2005). 'Changing a Harmful Social Convention: Female Genital Mutilation/Cutting'. Florence, Italy: UNICEF Innocenti Research Centre

Iyengar, S. (1991). *Is anyone responsible? How television frames political issues*. Chicago: The University of Chicago Press.

Jackson, P.J. (1995) 'Improvisation in training: freedom within corporate structures', *Journal of European Industrial Training* 19 (4): 25 – 28

James, S., Reddy, P., Ruiter, R.A., McCauley, A & Van den Borne, B (2006). The Impact of an HIV and AIDS Life Skills Program on Secondary School Students in KwaZulu-Natal, South Africa. *AIDS Education Preview* 18 (4): 281 - 94. August

Jemmott, J. B., Jemmott, L. S., & Fong, G. T (1992). Reductions in HIV risk-associated sexual behaviours among black male adolescents: Effects of an AIDS prevention intervention'. *American Journal of Public Health* 82 (3): 372 – 77

Jemmott, J., Jemmott, L & Fong, G. (1998). 'Abstinence and safer sex HIV risk-reduction interventions for African American Adolescents: A randomized controlled trial'. JAMA 279 (19): 1529 – 536. May

Jodati, A.R., Nourabadi, G.R., Hassanzadeh, S., Dastgiri, S., Sedaghat, K. (2007). International Journal of AIDS 18 (6): 407 - 9. June

Johns Hopkins Bloomberg School of Public Health Center for Communication Programs (1996). Expanding Resources for HIV/AIDS and Sexual and Reproductive Health Integration. *Unpublished work*. (March)

Johns Hopkins School of Public Health (1993). 'Reaching Young People', PCS Packet Series 5. Baltimore: Johns Hopkins University.

Johnson, H & Mayoux, L. (1998) 'Investigation as Empowerment: using participatory methods'. In: Thomas, A., Chataway, J and Wuyts, M [Eds.] *Investigation Skills for Policy and Development*. London: Sage Publications

Jonsson U (2008). A Conceptual Framework for the Understanding of HIV Infection of Young Women in Hyper-Endemic Countries in Southern Africa. Paper presented at the Technical Meeting on Young Women in HIV Hyper-Endemic Countries in Southern Africa. Glenburn Lodge, Gauteng, South Africa, UNAIDS and RHRU. 17-19 June, 2008.

Judge, K & Bauld, L. (2000) 'Strong theory, flexible methods: evaluating complex community-based initiatives'. *Critical Public Health* 11 (1): 19 – 38

Jukes, M & Desai, K. (2004). Education and HIV and AIDS. A report prepared for the UNESCO Global Monitoring Report 2005.

Jukes, M., Simmons, S & Bundy, D. (2008). How can education help protect young women and girls from HIV in Southern Africa? A paper prepared for the UNAIDS meeting

Johannesburg, June 17 to 19th 2008. To be published in AIDS (special supplement in September 2008, forthcoming)

Kagan, C., Evans, J & Kay, B. (1986) *A Manual of Interpersonal Skills for Nurses: an experiential approach*. London: Harper and Row

Kam, C., Greenberg, M.T. and Walls, C.T. (2003) 'Examining the role of implementation quality in school-based prevention using the PATHS curriculum' *Prevention Science* 4 (1): 55 – 63

Kanabahita, C (1993). 'A Lifetime as TBA in Uganda'. *Safe Mother* 12: 10. Jul– Oct

Kann, L., Collins J. L., Paterman, B. C., Small, M. L., Ross, J. G., & Kolbe, L. J. (1995). 'The School Health Policies and Programs Study (SHPPS): Rationale for a Nationwide Status Report on School Health'. *Journal of School Health*, 65, 291-294.

Kapiriri, L and Douglas K. M (2007). 'A Strategy to Improve Priority Setting in Developing Countries'. *Health Care Analysis* 15:159 – 167

Khamis, C. (2000) 'Establishing Community Forums that Make a Difference'. *Local Economy* 15 (3): 264 – 68. September

Kipp, W., Kabwa, P and Mwesigye, B (1992). 'Social Marketing in a Rural African District'. *AIDS Health Promotion Exchange* 4: 3 – 5.

Kiragu, K., Galiwango, M., Mulira, H and Sekatawa, E (1996). 'Promoting Reproductive Health in Uganda: Evaluation of a National IEC Program', *IEC Field Report* Number 7,

Kiragu, K., Nyonyintono, R., Sengenda, J and Lettenmaier, C (1993). 'Family Planning Needs in Uganda: Key Findings from a Baseline Survey of Selected Urban and Peri-Urban Areas, Kampala'. Uganda and Baltimore: FPAU and Johns Hopkins University/Population Communication Services.

Karasavvidis, I. (2002). Distributed cognition and educational practice. *Journal of Interactive Learning Research* 13(1): 11–29.

Kirby, D. & DiClemente, R. J. (1994). School-based interventions to prevent unprotected sex and HIV among adolescents.

Kirby, D. (2001). *Emerging Answers: Research Findings on Programs to Reduce Teen Pregnancy*. Washington, D.C.: National Campaign to Reduce Teen Pregnancy.

Kirby, D., Obasi, A., Laris, B.A. (2006). The effectiveness of sex education and HIV education interventions in schools in developing countries. World Health Organisation Technical Report Series 938: 103 - 50; discussion pp 317 – 41.

Klausner, J. D., Wamai, R.G., Bowa, K., Agot, K., Kagimba, J., & Halperin, D.T (2008). Is male circumcision as good as the HIV vaccine we've been waiting for? *Future HIV Therapy* 2(1):1-7. (January). http://www.future medicine. com/doi/full/10.2217/17469600.2.1.1?cookieSet=1

Klepp K.I., Ndeki, S.S., Melkizedeck T., Leshabari, T., Hannan, P, J and Lyimo, B.A. (1997). AIDS education in Tanzania: Promoting Risk Reduction among Primary School Children. *American Journal of Public Health* 87 (12): 1931 – 36. December

Klepp, K.I., Ndeki, S.S., Seha, A.M., Hannan, P., Kyimo, B.A., Msuya, M.H., Irema, M.N., and Schreiner, A. (1994). AIDS education for primary school children in Tanzania: an evaluation study. AIDS, August; 8(8): pp1157 – 62

Kline, K. N (2003). 'Popular media and health: Images, effects, and institutions'. In: T. Thompson, A. Dorsey, K. Miller, & R. Parrot (eds.) *Handbook of Health Communication* (p.557-581). Mahwah, NJ: Lawrence Erlbaum Associates, Inc.

Koenig, M.A., Fauveau, V and Wojtyniak, B (1991) 'Mortality Reductions from Health Interventions: The Case of Immunization in Bangladesh'. *Population and Development Review*.17 (1): 87 – 104

Koestler, A (1989). *The ghost in the machine*, London: Arkana Publishers

Kols, A (2004). Managing Knowledge to Improve Reproductive Health programs. MAQ Paper No. 5 (December).

Korten, D (1995). *When Corporations Rule the World*. West Hartford: Kumarian Press.

Koshal, M., Ashok K., Gupta, A. K and Koshal, R. (1998) 'Women in management: a Malaysian perspective'. *Women in Management Review* 13 (1): 11–18

Kothari, S (1999). *Inclusive, Just, Plural, Dynamic: building a civil society in the Third World*. Milton Keynes: Open University Press

Kotler, P and Zaltman, G (1971). 'Social Marketing: an approach to planned social change'. *Journal of Marketing* 35 (3): 3 – 12. July

Kotter, P. (1988). *The Leadership Factor*. Free Press, Macmillan.

Krippendoff, K (1980) *Content Analysis: An Introduction to its Methodology*. London: Sage Publication.

Krippendorff, K (2004) *Content Analysis: An Introduction to its Methodology*. Sage Publications: London. 2nd Edition

Krueger, R.A. (1988) *Focus Groups: A Practical Guide for Applied Research*. California and London: Sage Publications

Krystall, A and Johnston, T (1990). *An Alternative Model of Population IEC Organization and Management*. Monograph Series: 3. Nairobi: The Population IEC Operation in Eastern and Southern Africa, UNFPA

Kugblenu, J (1974). 'Ghana'. In: Head, Sydney W. *Broadcasting in Africa: A Continental Survey of Radio and Television* (pp. 89 – 95). Philadelphia: Temple University Press.

Land, S & Greene, B (2000). 'Project-based learning with the World Wide Web: A qualitative study of resource integration'. *Educational Technology Research and Development* 48 (1): 45 – 67.

Landry, D., Kaeser, L & Richards, C. L (1999). Abstinence promotion and the provision of information in public school district sexuality education policies. *Family Planning Perspectives*, *31*, 280–286.

Leclerc-Madlala, S. (2008). Intergenerational/age-disparate sex in Southern Africa: Moving HIV between generations. AIDS, (September 2008, special supplement), in press.

Lee, L. (2004). 'The current state of public health in China'. *Annual Review of Public Health* 25: 327 - 39.

Leeder, S (2007). 'The scope, mission and method of contemporary public health. Australian and New Zealand' *Journal of Public Health* 31(6):505 - 8. (December)

Lengua, L. J & Stormshak, E. A. (2000) 'Gender, Gender Roles, and Personality: Gender Differences in the Prediction of Coping and Psychological Symptoms'. *Sex Roles* 43 (11/12): 787 – 820

Lewis, T (2004) 'A Godlike presence: The impact of Radio on the 1920s and 1930s'. [Available: http://www.oah.og/pubs/magazine/communication/lewis.html] [Accessed 19 January, 2008].

Lincoln, Y & Guba, E. G. (1985) *Naturalistic Enquiry*. Berveley Hills, CA. Sage Publications

Lincoln, Y. (2001) 'Engaging Sympathies: Relationships between Action Research and Social Constructivism'. In: P. Reason and H. Bradbury (Eds.). *The Handbook of Action Research*, pp. 124 – 32. London/Thousand Oaks, CA: Sage

Linn, M. C., Eylon, B & Davis, E. A. (2004). The knowledge integration perspective on learning. In: M. C. Linn, E. A. Davis, & P. Bell (Eds.). *Internet environments for science education* (29–46). Mahwah: Lawrence Erlbaum Associates.

Linney, B. (1995). *Pictures, People and Power.* London: Macmillan.

Lofland, J & L.H. Lofland (1995) *Analyzing Social Settings: A Guide to Qualitative Observation and Analysis*, 3rd Ed. Belmont, CA: Wadsworth Publishing

Lopes, P (2006). 'Culture and Stigma: Popular Culture and the Case of Comic Books'. Sociological Forum 21(3): 387 – 414. September

Low-Beer Dand Stoneburner, R. (2002). 'Social communications and AIDS population behaviour changes in Uganda compared to other countries'. Johannesburg: Centre for AIDS Development, Research and Evaluation.

Lupton, D (1994) 'The Condom in the Age of AIDS: Newly respectable or still a dirty word? A discourse analysis'. *Qualitative Health Research* 4: (3): 304 – 20

Lupton, D (1995). *The Imperative of Health.* London: Sage Publications.

Lutalo, T and Kidugavu, M (2000). 'Trends and Determinants of Contraceptive Use in Rakai District, Uganda 1995–1998'. *Studies in Family Planning* 31 (3): 217 – 227.

Lynagh, M., Knight, J., Schofield, M.J and Paras, L (1999). 'Lessons learned from the Hunter Region health promoting schools project in New South Wales, Australia'. *Journal of School Health* 69 (6): 227 – 32

Lynagh, M., Perkins, J and Schofield, M (2002) 'An evidence-based approach to health promoting schools. *Journal of School Health* 72 (7): 300 – 302

Lynagh, M., Schofield, M. J & Sanson-Fisher, R. W. (1997). 'School health promotion programs over the past decade: A review of the smoking, alcohol and solar protection literature'. *Health Promotion International* 12 (1): 43 – 60

Lynch K. (1981) *Good City Form.* Cambridge, UK: MIT Press

Ma HL, Geng L., Xia, SC., Hou, JX., Xu, S.Y and Yu, W. P (2002) 'Development of Health-Promoting Schools with tobacco use prevention as entry point'. *Chinese Journal of Health Education* 18 (7): 414 - 17.

Macaskill, L., Dwyer, J.M., Uetrecht, C., Dombrow C., Crompton, R., Wilck, B. & Stone, J. (2000) 'An evaluability assessment to develop a restaurant health promotion program in Canada'. *Health Promotion International* 15 (1): 57– 67

MacAskill, S.G and Hastings, G.B (1991/2) 'Listen and You Will Be Heard: The Importance of the Consumer in the Development of Mass Media Material'. *HYGIE* 10(2): 28-31

MacDonald, T. H. (1998) *Rethinking Health Promotion: A Global Approach.* London: Routledge

Magzoub, M., Schmidt, H., Dolmans, D & Abdelhameed, A (1998) 'Assessing Students in Community Settings: The Role of Peer Evaluation' *Advances in Health Sciences Education* 3: 3 – 13

Makerere University (2003). *Improving Quality of Care for Family Planning Services in Uganda by the Regional Centre for Quality of Care.* Institute of Public Health, Makerere University. September.

Mann, J. & Tarantola, D (eds.) (1996) *AIDS in the World II: Global Dimensions, Social Roots, and Responses. The Global AIDS Policy Coalition.* New York: Oxford University Press.

Manning, P (2001) *News and News Sources: A Critical Introduction.* London: Sage.

Manoj, K.R (2006). 'Communication and contraceptive behaviour: insights and evidences from India and Bangladesh'. *Seminar Paper* Submitted in Partial Fulfilment of Master of Population Studies for the Academic Year 2005 - 2006. Mumbai, India: International Institute for Population Sciences (Deemed University).

Manyozo, L (2005) 'The practice of participation in broadcasting for development initiatives in post-independent Malawi'. *Journal of Social Development in Africa* 20 (1): 77 – 105

Mathews, J (1995), 'Holonic organisational architectures', in *Human Systems Management* Vol.15

Maurana C. A & Clark M. A. (2000) 'The Health Action Fund: A Community-Based Approach to Enhancing Health'. *Journal of Health Communication* 5 (3): 243 – 54. July

Max-Neef, M (2008), 'The Forgotten Map', In: Resurgence March/April No.247:7 - 9

Maybury Okonek, B.A. & Morganstein, L (Eds.) Access Excellence at the National Health Museum. Development of Polio Vaccines. http://www.accessexcellence.org/AE/AEC/CC/polio.html

Mayo, J. & Servaes J (Eds.) (1994), *Approaches to Development Communication Training and Orientation Kit.* Volumes 1 & 2. New York/Paris: UNFPA/UNESCO

Mbonye, A.K (2003). 'Delivering Family Planning Messages Through Prenatal Care Clinics in Kumi Uganda'. *The International Electronic Journal of Health Education* 6: 34 – 40

McCombs, M & Brewer, M (1996). 'Setting the Community Agenda.' *Journalism Quarterly* 73 (1): 7-16.

McKenzie, K. C., Burns, R. B., McCarthy, M. P and Freund, K. M (1998). 'Prevalence of Domestic Violence in an Inpatient Female Population'. *Journal of General Internal Medicine* 13:277–279

McMahon, M. (1997) 'Social Constructivism and the World Wide Web - A Paradigm for Learning'. *Paper* presented at the ASCILITE conference. Perth, Australia, December

Mehta, M (1987) 'Housing Policies: Retrospect and Prospect'. *Space and Society*, pp.72.76

Mellanby A.R., Phelps, F.A., Crichton, N.J. Tripp, J.H. (1995). 'School sex education: an experimental programme with educational and medical benefit'. *BMJ* 12 (7002): 414 – 7 Aug

Ments, M.V. (1989). *The Effective Use of Role-Play: a Handbook for Teachers and Trainers.* London: Kogan Page

Mienczakowski, J. (1997). 'Theatre of change'. *Research in Drama Education* 2 (2): 159 – 72.

MIHV Ssembabule Child Survival Project Uganda, Detailed Implementation Plan, April 1997.

MIHV Ssembabule Child Survival Project Uganda, Final Evaluation, August 2000.

Minardi, H. A & Riley, M. J. (1997) *Communication in Health Care: a skills-based approach.* Oxford: Butterworth Heinemann

Minardi, H. A & Ritter, S. (1998) 'Recording Skills Practice on Videotape Can Enhance Learning: a comparative study between nurse lecturers and nursing students'. *Journal of Advance Nursing* 29 (6): 1318 – 25

Ministry of Foreign Affairs - DANIDA, February 1999, *Evaluation Guidelines,* Copenhagen, Denmark

Ministry of Foreign Affairs (2003). *Evaluation Guidelines,* Evaluation Division, Economic Cooperation Bureau, Tokyo. March

MØller, V and Dictow, H (2002). 'The Role of Quality of Life Surveys in Managing Change in Democratic Transitions: the South African Case'. *Social Indicators Research* 58: 267 – 92

Morah, B.C (1990) 'Inter-relations between Population and Development'. In: *Population and Development: Proceedings of the Briefing Seminar and Workshop for Chief and Senior Executives of Mass Media Organizations.*

Morrow, A. L. (2000) 'Empowering communities to remove the pump handle: An emerging role in epidemiology'. *Annals of Epidemiology* 10 (7): 451 – 51

Mufune, P. (2000) 'Street Youth in Southern Africa'. *International Social Science Journal* 52 (164): 233 – 43

Murphy, B. K (2000). 'International NGOs and the challenge of modernity' *Development in Practice* 10 (3/4): 330 – 347

Muturi, W. N (2005) 'Communication for HIV/AIDS Prevention in Kenya: Social-Cultural Considerations'. *Journal of Health Communication* 10: 77 – 98

Myhre, L. S. & Flora, A. J (2000) 'HIV/AIDS Communication Campaigns: Progress and Prospects'. *Journal of Health Communication* 5: 29 – 45 (supplement)

Nandy, B.R. & Nandy, S (1997) 'Health education by virtue of its mission is centred around mass media and communications: implications for professional preparation'. *Journal of Health Education* 28: 238 – 44

Narayan, D & Srinivasan, L. (1994) *Participatory Development Toolkits: materials to facilitate community empowerment.* Washington: World Bank

Narváez, P & Laba, M [eds.] (1986) *Media Sense: The Folklore – Popular Culture Continuum.* Bowling Green, Ohio: Bowling Green State University Popular Press

National AIDS/STI Control Programme (2007). *HIV Sentinel Survey (HSS) Report 2006.* Ghana: Uneek Magazine publication.

National Institute of Allergy and Infectious Diseases (NIAID) (2006). Adult male circumcision significantly reduces risk of acquiring HIV: Trials in Kenya and Uganda stopped early. (December) http://www.nih.gov/news/pr/dec 2006/niaid-13.htm.

National Institute of Allergy and Infectious Diseases, National Institutes of Health, Department of Health and Human Services. (2001). Workshop Summary: Scientific Evidence on Condom Effectiveness for Sexually Transmitted Disease (STD) Prevention. June 12-13, 2000 Hyatt Dulles Airport Herndon, Virginia. Report date: July 20, 2001

Neeta, S., Sharma, P.P., Singla, R and Jain, R. C (1998). 'Survey of knowledge, attitude and practices for tuberculosis among general practitioners in Delhi, India'. *International Journal of Tuberculosis Lung Disease* 2 (5): 384 - 389.

Negrotti, M (1999), *The Theory of the artificial,* London: Intellect Books

Nicolaidis, C & Liotas, N (2006) 'A role for theatre in the education, training and thinking processes of managers'. *Industry & Higher Education* 20 (1): 19 – 24

Norr, K., Tlou, S., Moeti, M. (2004). 'Impact of peer group education on HIV prevention among women in Botswana'. *Health Care for Women International* 25 (3): 210 – 226. March

Ntozi, J.P., Kabera, J (1991). 'Family Planning in Rural: Uganda: Knowledge and use of modern and traditional methods in Ankole'. *Studies in Family Planning* 22 (2) 116–123. (Mar–April)

Nukunya, G. K. (1996) *Kingship and Marriage among the Anlo Ewe*. New York: Humanities Press

Nyirenda, J (1996). 'The relevance of Paulo Freire's contributions to education and development in present day Africa.' *Africa Media Review* 10 (1): 1 - 20.

O'Meara, P., Burley, M & Kelly, H. (2002) 'Rural Urgent Care Models: what are they made of?' *Australian Journal of Rural Health* 10: 45 – 50

Obeng-Quaidoo, I & Gikonyo, W (1995). 'Population communication and sustainable development: an analysis of population IE&C projects in Anglophone Africa' *Africa Media Review* 9 (1): 70 – 91

OCHA (2008). OCHA and HIV'. [Available: http://ochaonline.un.org] [Accessed: 18 – 4 - 2008]

OECD / DAC, 2002, *Glossary of Key Terms in Evaluation and Results-Based Management*, Paris: OECD

Okullo, J., Okello, Q., Birungi H., Askew, I., Janowitz, B., Cuthbertson, C and Ebanyat, F., (2003). 'Improving Quality of Care for Family Planning Services in Uganda, Delivery of Improved Services for Health (DISH II) Project'. Uganda.

Okwero, M., Ssempebwa, B., Okwero, P and Kipp, W (1994). 'The Realities of Unmet Need in Uganda'. *Plan Parent Challenge* 1: 17 – 9.

Olufemi, V. (2003) 'Chieftaincy, Politics and Communal Identity in Western Nigeria, 1893–1951'. *Journal of African History* 44: 283 – 302

Owusu-Sarpong, C. (2003) 'Setting the Ghanaian Context of Rural Local Government: Traditional Authority Values'. In: Ray, D. I & Reddy, P. S (Eds.) *Grass-Roots Governance: Chiefs in Africa and the Afro-Caribbean*. [Pp. 31 – 68]. Calgary: University of Calgary Press

Paget, M.A (1990). 'Performing the text'. *Journal of Contemporary Ethnography*, 19 (1): 136 – 55

Parker, W. (2003). Re-appraising youth prevention in South Africa: The case of loveLife. Retrieved from http://www.cadre.org.za/pdf/Youth%20prevention%20in%20SA.pdf]. Retrieved on 16/10/2003

Partnering with traditional healers and drug sellers in Uganda, MIHV. 'Integrated Management of Childhood Illness (IMCI) Conference', Baltimore, MD. January 16–19, 2001. *Paper* Presented by Jolene Mullins, MIHV Uganda Country Director.

Patterson, T (2000) *Doing Well and Doing Good: How Soft News and Critical Journalism Are Shrinking the News Audience and Weakening Democracy – And What News Outlets Can Do About It*. Cambridge, MA: President and Fellows of Harvard College.

Patton, C (1985) *Sex and Germs: The Politics AIDS*. Boston: South End Press.

Patton, C (1990) *Inventing AIDS*. London: Routledge, Chapman and Hall Incorporated.

Patton, C. (1994) *Last Served? Gendering the AIDS Epidemic*. London: Taylor& Francis, Ltd.

Payne, S. L. (2000) 'Challenges for Research Ethics and Moral Knowledge Construction in the Applied Social Sciences'. *Journal of Business Ethics* 26: 307–18

Pettifor A.E., Rees H.V., Steffenson A., Hlongwa-Madikizela L., MacPhail C., Vermaak K., Kleinschmidt I. (2004). *HIV and sexual behaviour among young South Africans: A national survey of 15-24 year olds*. Johannesburg: Reproductive Health Research Unit,

University of the Witwatersrand

Picart, C. J and Gergen, K. (2004) 'Dharma Dancing: Ballroom Dancing and the Relational Order'. *Qualitative Inquiry* 10 (6): 836 – 68

Pisani E (2008). *The wisdom of whores: bureaucrats, brothels, and the business of AIDS.* New York: W. W Norton.

Pool, R (1999). 'Acceptability of the Female Condom and Vaginal Spermicidal Protection'. *Sex Health Exchange* 1: 5 – 7.

Pool, R., Hart, G., Harrison, S., Nyanzi, S and Whitworth, J (2000). Men's Attitudes to Condoms and Female Controlled Means of Protection against HIV and STDs in South Western Uganda. *Culture Health & Sex* 2(2): 197 – 211. Apr– Jun

Potter, J. (1996) *Representing Reality: discourse, rhetoric and social construction.* London: Sage Publication

Potter, S & Subrahmanian, R. (1998) 'Conceptualising Policy-related Investigation'. In: Thomas, A., Chataway, and Wuyts, M (Eds.). *Finding Out Fast: investigative skills for policy and development.* Pp. 19 – 39. London: Sage.

Potts M., Halperin, D., Kirby, D., Swidler, A., Marseille, E., Klausner, J.D., Hearst, N., Wamai, R.G., Kahn, J.D., and Walsh J.D. (2008). 'Reassessing HIV prevention'. *Science* 320, 9 May.

Poundstone KE et al. (2004). The Social Epidemiology of Human Immunodeficiency Virus/Acquired Immunodeficiency Syndrome. Epidemiologic Reviews, 26:22-35.

Pradeep, P.V., Mishra, A., Mohanty, B.N., Mohapatra, K.C., Agarwal, G & Mishra, S.K (2007). Reinforcement of endocrine surgery training: Impact of telemedicine technology in a developing country context. *World Journal of Surgery* 31(8): 1665-71. (August)

Puertas, B & Schlesser, M. (2001) 'Assessing Community Health among Indigenous Populations in Ecuador with a Participatory Approach: implications for health reform'. *Journal of Community Health* 26 (2): 133 – 47

Puplampu, B. A (2004) 'Coverage of Election 2000 – A Study of Radio Ghana's December 0600 News Bulletins'. *Unpublished MA Thesis.* Wales: Cardiff University.

Purkiss, D (2001). *Troublesome Things: A history of Fairies and Fairy Stories.* London: Penguin

Quebral, N (2002). *Reflections on Development Communication (25Years after).* Los Baños: UPLB College of Development Communication.

Rajeswari, R., Diwakara, A.M., Sudha, G., Sudarsanam, N.M., Rajaram, K and Prabhakar, R (1995). 'Tuberculosis awareness among educated public in two cities in Tamilnadu'. *Lung India* 13 (3&4): 108 – 113

Rajeswari, R., Jaggarajamma, K., Muniyandi, M., and Balasubramanian, R (2006). 'Identifying effective communication channels in a rural community: a field report form south India'. Indian Journal of Tuberculosis 53:206 – 211

Raymond, D., Dorwick, P. W & Kleinke, C. L. (1983) 'Affective Responses to Seeing Oneself for the First time on Unedited Videotape'. *Counselling Psychology Quarterly* 6 (3): 193 – 200

Reason, P. (Ed.). (1994). Participation *in human inquiry.* London: Sage.

Research Councils UK (2005). *Evaluation: practical Guidelines,* Swindon, UK. March

Rice, R.E and Paisley W.J (1981) [Ed]. *Public Communication Campaigns,* Beverly Hills, California: Sage Publications

Richie, J and Lewis, J. (eds.) (2003) *Qualitative Research Practice: A Guide for Social Science Students and Researchers*. London: Sage Publications.

Richie, J. Lewis, J. and Elam, G (2003) 'Designing and Selecting Samples' In: Richie, J and Lewis, J. (eds.) '*Qualitative Research Practice: A Guide for Social Science Students and Researchers*' (pp. 77-108). London: Sage Publications

Rodgers, E.M in Saunders, L (1977). 'IE&C Strategies. *Their role in promoting behaviour change in family planning*'. Honolulu: East-West Communication Institute.

Rogers R. A. (1998). 'A Dialogics of Rhythm: Dance and the Performance of Cultural Conflict'. *Howard Journal of Communications* 9 (1): 5 – 27

Rogers, E. M. (2004). 'A prospective and retrospective look at the diffusion model'. *Journal of Health Communication, 9* (Supplement 1): 13-19.

Rogers, E.M (1962) *Diffusion of Innovations*. New York: Free Press.

Rogers, E.M. (1995) *Diffusion of Innovations*, 4th edition, Free Press.

Rosen, J (2002). Public journalism as a democratic art. Available: http://www.imdp.org/artman/publish/article_23.shtml. Last consulted 18 Jan 2008.

Rose, R (2005). *Learning from Comparative Public Policy*. London: Routledge

Ross, J. G., Luepker, R. V., Nelson, G. D., Saavedra, P., & Hubbard, B. M. (1991). 'Teenage Health Teaching Modules: Impact of Teacher Training on Implementation and Student Outcomes'. *Journal of School Health, 61*(1), 31-34.

Rottenburg, R. (2006) 'Social Constructivism and the Enigma of Strangers'. In: Rottenburg, R., Schnepel, B and Schimada, S [Eds.]. *The Making and Understanding Differences*. Pp 27 – 42. Oslo: Bielefeld

Rushing, W. A (1995). *The AIDS Epidemic: Social Dimensions of an Infectious Disease*. Boulder, CO: Westview Press.

Ruud van der, V & Preece, J. (2005) 'Poverty reduction and adult education: beyond basic education'. *International Journal of Lifelong Education* 24 (5): 381 – 91 (September - October)

Ryfe, M. D (2006) 'News, Culture and Public Life: A Study of 19th-century American Journalism'. *Journalism Studies* 7 (1): 60 – 77

Sager, T (2006). 'The Logic of Critical Communicative Planning: Transaction Cost Alteration'. *Planning Theory* 5 (3): 223 – 254

Saleh, M.A., al-Ghamdi, Y.S., al-Yadia, O.A., Shagran, T.M and Mosa, O.R. (1999). Impact of health education program on knowledge about AIDS and HIV transmission in students of secondary schools in Buraidah city, Saudi Arabia: an exploratory study. *East Mediterranean Health Journal* 5(5): 1068 -75. September

Salomon, G. (2000b). It's not just the tool, but the educational rationale that counts. Keynote address at the 2000 Ed-Media Meeting. Retrieved August 2 - 2008: http://www.aace.org/conf/edmedia/00/salomonkeynote.htm

Sandberg, H. (2005) *Information and Communication in Society*. Taylor and Francis Group Limited. Acta Paediatrica 94 (suppl 448): 38 – 39

Sandelwoski, M. (2000) 'Combining Qualitative and Quantitative Sampling, Data Collection and Analysis Techniques in Mix Method Studies'. *Researching in Nursing and Health* 23 (3): 246 – 55

Sankaranarayan, S., Naik, E, Reddy, P.S., Gurunani, G., Ganesh, K., Gandewar, K., Singh, K.P., Vermund, S.H. (1996). Impact of school-based HIV and AIDS education for adolescents in Bombay, India. *Southeast Asian Journal of Tropical Medicine and Public*

Health. 27 (4): 692 – 5

Sanyal, R. (2000), 'An experiential approach to teaching ethics in international businesses. *Teaching Business Ethics* 4: 137 – 49

Sarantakos, S. (1998) *Social Research.* London: Macmillan

Sarason, S. B. (2003). 'The obligations of the moral scientific stance'. *American Journal of Community Psychology* 31(3, 4): 208 – 212.

Satofuka, F (2007) Reflections on the social meaning of "Kyosei", *A I & Society* 21 (4): 633-638

Schaalma, H.P., Abraham, C., Gillmore, M R & Kok, G (2004) 'Sex Education as Health Promotion: What Does It Take?' *Archives of Sexual Behaviour* 33 (3): 259 –269. June

Schlesinger, P (1978) *Putting 'Reality' Together.* London: Methuen.

Schoepf, B.G. et al (1988). *Action Research on AIDS with Women in Central Africa.* Mimeo.

Schon, D.A. (1983) *The Reflective Practitioner: How Professionals Think in Action.* London: Temple Smith.

Schoub, B. D (1994) *AIDS and HIV in Perspective: A Guide to Understanding the Virus and its Consequences.* Cambridge: Cambridge University Press.

Schramm, W. (1964) *Mass Media and National Development.* Stanford, California: Stanford University Press

Schudson, M. (2000). 'The Sociology of News Production Revisited (Again)'. In: James Curran and Micheal Gurevitch (Eds.) *Mass Media and Society* [pp. 141-159]. Arnold: London.

Schuster, M.A., Bell, R.M., Berry, S.H., Kanouse, D.E. (1998). Students' acquisition and use of school condoms in a high school condom availability program. *Paediatrics* 100 (4): 689 – 94 October

Sekatawa, E (1993). 'Uganda Women Shy Away From the Pill'. *African Women Health* 1: 27 – 30. Apr – Jun

Sen, A. (2001). *Development as Freedom*, Oxford: Oxford University Press.

Sen, A. (2005). *The argumentative Indian*, London: Penguin Books

Servaes, J (2007). 'Harnessing the UN System into a Common Approach on Communication for Development.' *The International Communication Gazette* 69 (6): 483 – 507

Servaes, J. (2007) (Ed.) *New Approaches to Communication for Development and Social Change.* London-New Delhi: Sage.

Servaes, J. and Malikhao, P (1994) 'Concepts: The Theoretical Underpinnings of the Approaches to Development Communication'. In: John Mayo and Jan Servaes (eds.) *Approaches to Development Communication: An Orientation and Resource Kit,* Paris and New York: UNESCO/UNFPA.

Shaw, C.M. (2004), 'Using role-play scenarios in the IR classroom: an examination of exercises on peacekeeping operations and foreign policy decision making', *International Studies Perspectives* 5: 1 – 22.

Shaw, I (1999). *Qualitative Evaluation.* London: Sage Publications

Sigal, L. V (1973) *Reporters and Officials: The Organization and Politics of News –making.* Lexington, MA: D. C. Heath.

Silverman, D. (2003) *Interpreting Qualitative Data: methods for analysing talk text and interaction.* London: Sage Publications, 2nd Edition.

Silverman, D. (2003). '*Interpreting Qualitative Data: methods for analysing talk, text and interaction*'. London: Sage Publications. 2nd Edition.

Singh, M.M., Bano, T., Pagare, D., Sharma, N., Devi, R., Mehra, M (2002). 'Knowledge and attitude towards tuberculosis in a slum community of Delhi'. *Journal of Communicable Disease* 34 (3): 203 -14

Singhal, A. & Rogers, E. M (1999) *Entertainment-education: A communication strategy for social change*. Mahwah, NJ: Lawrence Earlbaum Associates.

Singhal, A., & Rogers, E. M. (2002). 'A theoretical agenda for entertainment-education'. *Communication Theory* 12: 117–135

Singhal, A., Cody, M., Rogers, E. M., & Sabido, M. (Eds.) (2004) *Entertainment-education and social change: History, research, and practice*. Mahwah, NJ: Lawrence Earlbaum Associates.

Slotta, J. D & Linn, M. C (2000). The Knowledge integration environment: Helping students use the internet effectively. In: M. L. Jacobson, R. B. Kozma (Eds.) *Innovations in science and mathematics education: Advance designs for technologies of learning* (pp. 193–226). Mahwah: Lawrence Erlbaum Associates.

Smith D and Kochhar, R (2003), 'The Dhokra Artisans of Bukura and Daripur, West Bengal: A case study in knowledge archive of technological change in progress'. In: Brandt, D (Ed.). *Navigating innovations: Indo-European cross-cultural experiences* Vol. I, India research Press, New Delhi

Smith, D. E. (2002). 'Institutional Ethnography'. In: Tim May (Ed.), Qualitative research in action: An international guide to issues in practice (Pp. 150-161). London: Sage.

Smith, M. K. (2006) Community development, the encyclopaedia of informal education. [Available: www.infed.org/community/b-comdv.htm [Accessed: 24 - 2 – 2008]

Smith, W. A (2006). 'Social marketing: an overview of approach and effect' *Injury Prevention* 12 (Suppl I): 38 – 43

Snape, D. and Spencer, L (2003) 'The foundation of qualitative research' In: Richie, J and Lewis, J. (eds.) *Qualitative Research Practice: a Guide for Social Science Students and Researchers* [pp. 1 – 23]. London: Sage Publications

Snell, C and Bailey, L (2005). 'Operation Storefront: Observations of Tobacco Retailer Advertising and Compliance with Tobacco Laws'. *Youth Violence and Juvenile Justice* 3: 78 – 90

Sogunro, O.A. (2004) 'Efficacy of role-playing pedagogy in training leaders: some reflections'. Journal of Management Development 23 (4): 355 – 71

Solomon, M. J., Mushtaque, A and Chowdhury, R (2002). 'Knowledge to action: evaluation for learning in a multi-organisational global partnership'. *Development in Practice* 12 (3/4): 346 – 354

Sood, S., Shefner-Rogers, L & Sengupta, M (2006). 'The Impact of a Mass Media Campaign on HIV/AIDS Knowledge and Behavior Change in North India: Results from a Longitudinal Study'. *Asian Journal of Communication* 16 (3): 231 – 50

South Africa Ministry of Health and Ministry of Education. (1998). *Life Skills Program Project Report 1997/98.*

South Africa Ministry of Health and Ministry of Education. (1998). *Life Skills Program Project Report 1997/98*

Souza, d. R (2007). 'The Construction of HIV/AIDS in Indian Newspapers: A Frame Analysis'. *Health Communication* 21 (3): 257 – 66

St Leger, L (2001) 'School, health literacy and public health: Possibilities and challenges'. *Health Promotion International* 16 (2): 197 – 205

St Leger, L and Nutbeam, D (2000). 'Research into health promoting schools'. *Journal of School Health* 70 (6): 257 – 58

St Leger, L. (2005). 'Protocols and guidelines for health promoting schools'. *Promotion & Education, XII* (3-4): 145 – 147

Steele, J (1998). *The Complete Architecture of Balkrishna Doshi: Rethinking Modernism for the Developing World*, Thames & Hudson Ltd.

Stevenson, N (1995) *Understanding Media Cultures: Social Theory and Mass Communication*. London: Sage.

Stewart-Brown, S. (2006). *What is the evidence on school health promotion in improving health or preventing disease and, specifically, what is the effectiveness of the health promoting schools approach?* Copenhagen: World Health Organization Regional Office for Europe.

Strauss, A., & Corbin, J. (1998). *Basics of qualitative research: Techniques and procedures for developing grounded theory* (2nd ed.). Thousand Oaks, CA: Sage.

Strengthening Midwifery (1993). 'Safe Mother'. *Strengthening Midwifery* 10: 8 – 9. Feb

Stuttaford, M., Bryanston, C., Hundt, G. L., Connor, M., Thorogood, M & Tollman, S (2006) 'Use of applied theatre in health research dissemination and data validation: a pilot study from South Africa' *Health: An Interdisciplinary Journal for the Social Study of Health, Illness and Medicine* 10 (1): 31–45

Tallis, V (2002) 'Gender and HIV' Overview Report. BRIDGE, Institute of Development Studies: Brighton.

Tarc, A. M (2006). 'In a Dimension of Height: Ethics in the Education of Others' *Educational Theory* 56 (3): 287 – 306

Taylor, P. (1998) 'Constructivism: Value added'. In: B. Fraser & K. Tobin (Eds.), *The International handbook of science education* (pp. 111 – 123). Dordrecht, the Netherlands: Kluwer Academic

The 1995 Uganda Demographic and Health Survey (UDHS); carried out by the Department of Statistics of the Ministry of Finance and Economic Planning of Uganda.

The Johns Hopkins School of Public Health, Center for Communication Programs, Baltimore, Dec 1996.

Thomas, A. (2000) 'Poverty and the End of Development'. In: Allen, T and Thomas, A (Eds.) Poverty and Development into the 21st Century. Pp. 3 – 22. Milton Keynes: OU Press / Oxford University Press

Tlamelo, M and Gerard, P (2000) 'Ethnicity and participatory development methods in Botswana: some participants are to be seen and not heard', *Development in Practice* 10 (5): 625 – 637

Tomaselli, K. (1994). *Appropriating Images: the Semiotics of Visual Representation*. Hojberg: Intervention Press.

Tomaselli, K. et al (1988). 'Community and Class Struggle: Problems in Methodology'. *Journal of Communication Enquiry* 12: 11 – 25.

Town and Country Planning Department, Madhya Pradesh (1982) *Urban Development Report for Indore*. Bhopal, India: Mimeo

Traquina, N (2004). 'Theory consolidation in the study of journalism: A comparative analysis of the news coverage of HIV/AIDS issues in four countries'. *Journalism* 5 (1): 97-116.

Trautschold, J (Undated) This is Radio Ghana [Available: http://donmoore.tripod.com/genbroad/stations/ghana.htm] [Accessed: 23/02/2008].

Trompenaars, F (1993). *Riding the Waves of Culture*, London: Nicholas Brealey Publishing

Tuberculosis Research Centre (ICMR), Chennai 1997. A study on feasibility of involving male student volunteers in case holding in urban tuberculosis programme. (Unpublished-1997)

Tuchman, G (1978). *Making News: A Study in the Construction of Reality*. NY: The Free Press.

Tutu, K (1994) "Environmental Impact of Ghana's Structural Adjustment" *Mimeo*, Legon: University of Ghana.

Uchiyama, K (2003). *The theory and practice of actuality*, Institute of Business research, Daito Bunka University, 1-91- Takashimadaira Itabashi Tokyo Japan 175-8571

Uganda Bureau of Statistics (2001). 'The Uganda Demographic and Health Survey'. Entebbe, Uganda: Uganda Bureau of Statistics,

Uganda Bureau of Statistics (2001). 'The Uganda Demographic and Health Survey 2000–2001'. Entebbe, Uganda: Uganda Bureau of Statistics.

Uganda Bureau of Statistics (2002). Uganda Demographic Population and Housing Census, Preliminary Results. Entebbe, Uganda: Uganda Bureau of Statistics.

Uganda Demographic and Health Survey, Entebbe, Uganda and Calverton, Maryland: Uganda Ministry of Finance and Marco International, 1996.

Uganda DISH (2002). Delivery of Improved Services for Health. USAID. www.ugandadish.org

Uganda Ministry of Finance and Economic Planning and Macro International. (1995).

UNAIDS (2006) '*AIDS Epidemic Update*', {Available: www.usaid.gov/our work/global _health/aids/countries/africa/angola] [. Accessed: 18 - 4 – 2008]

UNAIDS/ WHO (2000). Second-generation surveillance for HIV: The next decade. UNAIDS, Geneva

UNAIDS/WHO (2000). Report on the Global HIV and AIDS Epidemic. UNAIDS. Geneva

UNDP (1998). UNDP *Poverty Report: Overcoming Human Poverty*. New York: Oxford University Press

UNECA (1991) *Manual for the Integration of Population Variables into Development Plans in African Countries*. Addis Ababa: United Nations Economic Commission for Africa

UNESCO, PROAP Regional Clearinghouse on Population Education and Communication, UNFPA. (2001). *Communication and Advocacy Strategies: Adolescent Reproductive and Sexual Health: Booklet 3, Lessons Learned and Guidelines*. Bangkok, Thailand: UNESCO, UNFPA.

UNESCO, UNICEF, WHO, & World Bank (2000). *Focusing Resources on Effective School Health: A FRESH start to enhancing the quality and equity of education*. Dakar, Senegal: World Education Forum 2000.

UNFPA (1993) *Population Policies and Programmes*. New York: United Nations

UNICEF (2000). *Involving People, Evolving Behaviour*. Edited by McKee, N., Manoncourt, E., Saik Yoon, C., & Carnegie, R. New York: UNICEF

UNICEF (2001). The Participation Rights of Adolescents: A Strategic Approach. Prepared by R. Rajani. New York: UNICEF

United Nations (2006). Fourth annual report of the Information and Communication Technologies Task Force. Geneva: United Nations. (5 May).http://www.unicttaskforce.org/perl/documents.pl?do=download;id=9 68

United Nations Population Fund & World Health Organization (2006). Glion Consultation on Strengthening the Linkages between Reproductive Health and HIV/AIDS: Family Planning and HIV/AIDS in Women and Children. Geneva: World Health Organization.

United Nations Programme on HIV/AIDS (2007) 'UNAIDS Terminology Guidelines' UNAIDS: Geneva.

United States President's Emergency Plan for AIDS Relief (undated). The World Health organization and UNAIDS announce recommendations from expert consultation on male circumcision for HIV prevention. http://www.pepfar.gov/press/82311.htm

University of Wolverhampton (2005). *An Introduction to Multi-Agency Planning Using the Logical Framework Approach,* Wolverhampton, UK

Uphoff, N (1989) *Approaches to Community Participation in Agricultural and Rural Development.* Washington, D. C: The World Bank

USAID Cooperative Agreement Number FAO-0500-A-00-6025-00 September 1, 1996– August 31, 2000.

van den Hove, S. (2000) 'Participatory approaches to environmental policy- making: the European Commission Climate Policy Process as a case study'. *Ecological Economics* 33 (3): 457 – 72. June

van Der Veen, R (2003) 'Community development as citizen education'. *International Journal of Lifelong Education* 22 (6): 580 – 96

Van Ginneken, J (1997) U*nderstanding Global News: A Critical Introduction.* London: Sage.

Van Rooy, A (2000) 'Good News! You may be out of job reflections on the past and future 50: years for Northern NGOs'. *Development in Practice* 10 (3/4): 300 – 318

Vandemoortele J., Delamonica E. (2000). Education 'Vaccine' against HIV and AIDS. Current Issues in Comparative Education 3(1).

Vastu-Shilpa Foundation (1979) *Integrated Rural Development Plan for Village Chharodi.* India: Mimeo, Ahmedabad.

Vastu-Shilpa Foundation (1979) *Tribal Training Centre for Surat Panjarapole Project.* India: Mimeo, Ahmedabad.

Vastu-Shilpa Foundation (1985) *Urban Open Spaces: A Behavioural Analysis.* India: Mimeo, Ahmedabad

Vastu-Shilpa Foundation (1990) *Aranya: An approach to settlement design; planning and design of low cost housing project at Indore.* India: Mimeo, Ahmedabad.

Vaughan P.W., Rogers, E.M., Singhal, A., Swalehe, R.M (1999). Entertainment-Education and HIV and AIDS Prevention: a Field Experiment in Tanzania. *Journal of Health Communication* 20. Supplement, pp 81 – 100

Vaughan, P. W., Rogers, E., Singhal, A & Swalehe, R. (2000) 'Entertainment-education and HIV/AIDS prevention: A field experiment in Tanzania'. *Journal of Health Communication* 5: 81 – 100.

Vince Whitman, C (2005). Implementing research-based health promotion programmes in schools: Strategies for capacity building. In: B. B. Jensen (Ed.). *The health promoting school: International advances in theory, evaluation and practice* (pp. 107-135). Copenhagen: Danish University of Education Press.

Vince Whitman, C. (1999). 'Health and Human Development Programs at Education Development Center, Inc'. In: I. Birdthistle (Ed.), *Improving health through schools: national and international strategies* (pp. 27-33). Geneva: World Health Organization.

Vince Whitman, C., Aldinger, C., Zhang, XW, & Magner, E. (2008, in press). Strategies to Address Mental Health through Schools with Examples from China, *International Review of Psychiatry.*

Vorster, M.B.H., Venter, C.S. (2002). Evidence-based nutrition – review of nutritional epidemiological studies. *SAJCN* 15 (3) South Africa. November

Wade, S. E., Schraw, G., Buxton, W and Hayes, M (1993). Seduction of the strategic reader: Effects of interest on strategies and recall. *Reading Research Questions* 28: 93 – 114.

Wade, Suzanne E (2001). 'Research on Importance and Interest: Implications for Curriculum Development and Future Research'. *Educational Psychology Review,* 13 (3): 243 – 61

Wandersman, A. (2003). 'Community science: Bridging the gap between science and practice with community centered models'. *American Journal of Community Psychology* 31(3, 4): 207–208.

Wang, X. (2003). *Education in China since 1976.* Jefferson, North Carolina: McFarland & Company.

Wassif, O.M., el-Gendy, M.F., Saleh, M.A., el-Sawaf, E.M. (1993) Effect of health education programme on knowledge about AIDS and HIV transmission in paramedical personnel working in Benha hospitals. Journal of Egypt Public Health Association 68 (1-2): 143 – 59

Webb, D. & Elliott, L., in collaboration with UK Department for International Development and UNAIDS. (2000). *Learning to Live - Monitoring and evaluating HIV/AIDS programmes for young people.* London: Save the Children Fund.

Weeks, J (1991) *Against Nature: Essays on History, Sexuality and Identity.* London: Rivers Oram Press.

Wenger, N.S., Greenberg, J.M., Hilborne, L.H., Kusseling, F., Mangotich, M., Shapiro, M.F. (1992). 'Effect of HIV antibody testing and AIDS education on communication about HIV risk and sexual behaviour. A randomised, controlled trial in college students'. *Ann Intern Med.* 117 (11): 905 -11 December

Westercamp, N. & Bailey, R.C (2007). 'Acceptability of male circumcision for prevention of HIV / AIDS in sub-Saharan Africa: A review'. *AIDS and Behavior* 11 (3): 341 - 55. (May)

Whitehead, D (2000). 'Using mass media within health-promoting practice: a nursing perspective'. *Journal of Advanced Nursing* 32(4): 807-816.

Whitehead, J and Postlethwaite, K (2000) 'Recruitment, access and retention: Some issues for secondary Initial Teacher Education in the current social context'. *Research in Education* 64: 44 – 55

Whyte, W. F. (Ed.). (1991). *Participatory action research.* Newbury Park, CA: Sage Publications.

Wicks, R. H (2005) 'Message framing and constructing meaning: An emerging paradigm in mass communication research'. *Communication Yearbook* 29: 333 – 61

Willekens, H. (2004) 'Rights and Duties of Underage Parents: a comparative approach'. *International Journal of Law Policy and the Family* 18 (3):355 – 70

Williams, F., Rice R. and Rogers, E (1988) 'Research Methods and the new media'. The Free Press: London and New York.

Wilson, D. and Halperin, DT. (2008). "Know your epidemic, know your response": a useful approach, if we get it right. Lancet, in press.

Wilson, D., Mparadzi, A., & Lavelle, E. (1992). 'An experimental comparison of two AIDS prevention interventions among young Zimbabweans'. *Journal of Social Psychology* 132 (3): 415 – 17

Winchester, H.P.M (1999). 'Interview and Questionnaire as mixed methods in population geography: the case of lone fathers in Newcastle, Australia'. *Professional Geographer* 50 (1): 60 – 67 February

Wolf, S & Webster, A. (1997) 'Subjective and objective measures of scene criticality'. In: ITU Meeting on Subjective and Objective Audiovisual Quality Assessment Methods. Turin, Italy. October

Wood, J (2006) 'Filming Fairies: Popular Film, Audience Response and Meaning in Contemporary Fairy Lore'. *Folklore* 117 (3): 279 – 96

World Bank (1994) *Adjustment in Africa: Reforms, Results, and the Road Ahead.* A World Bank Policy Research Report. Washington D.C: Oxford University Press.

World Bank. (2002) *Education and HIV: A Window of Hope.* Washington DC: USA. World Bank

World Focus (2005). *'Seventy Percent of People with AIDS Living in Sub-Saharan Africa'.* [Available: http://www.insnews.org/world/focus/1101/aids.africa.unreport.htm]. [Accessed: 2 March 2005].

World Food Programme (WFP). (2006) 'Literature Review on the Impact of Education Levels on HIV and AIDS Prevalence Rates'. Rome, Italy: World Food Programme

World Health Organisation (2001) 'Information, Education and Communication: lessons from the past; perspectives for the future' *Occasional Paper* 6, WHO: Geneva

World Health Organization (1986). *Ottawa Charter of Health Promotion.* Geneva: World Health Organization.

World Health Organization (2006). *What is a health-promoting school?* Retrieved October 31, 2006, from the World Wide Web: http://www.who.int/ school_youth health/gshi/hps/en/index.html

World Health Organization. (2003). *Skills for health. Skills-based health education, including life skills: An important component of a child-friendly/health-promoting school.* Geneva: World Health Organization.

Xia, S-C., Zhang X-W, Xu S-Y, et al.(2004) 'Creating health-promoting schools in China with a focus on nutrition'. *Health Promotion International* 2004; 19(4): 409-418.

Yates, M.E. (2000) 'What is capacity building?' *Research to Reality: A Newsletter of the Harvard Center for Children's Health* 5 (1).

Zeldin, T (2008), Lunch interview of Theodore Zeldin by John Thornhill, Finanacial Times, 9 February

Zelizer, B (2004) Taking Journalism Seriously: News and the Academy. London: Sage Publications

Zhang, X.W., Liu, L.Q., Zhang X.H., Guo, J.X., Pan, X.D., Aldinger C., Yu, SH, Jones, J. Health-Promoting School Development in a Province of China. *Health Promotion International.* doi:10.1093/her/cyn022

Zhang, Y. J. (1996) 'A survey on evaluation methods for image segmentation'. *Pattern Record* 29 (8): 1335 – 46.

Zhouying, J (2002) Driving Force of Technology Development- Principles of harmony and balance, *AI & Society* 16 (1& 2): 2 – 48.

ABOUT THE CONTRIBUTORS

Dr. Theophilus K. Gokah is Lecturer at University of Wales, Newport School of Art, Media and Design. Newport, Wales, UK. tgokah@yahoo.co.uk

Dr. William Smith is Executive Vice President of Academy for Educational Development Washington, D.C. bsmith@aed.org

Professor Gill S. Karamjit is Professor Emeritus, University of Brighton, Editor of AI & Society (Springer), and Visiting Professor, University of Wales, Newport School of Art, Media and Design, UK. kgillbton@yahoo.co.uk

Dr Waithira Gikonyo is formal Regional Training Coordinator, UNFPA Nairobi, Kenya and now Senior Learning Officer and OIC, UNICEF, New York. wgikonyo@unicef.org

Dr Isaac Obeng Quaidoo is formal Chief Technical Adviser, UNFPA Regional Population IEC Training Programme for Anglophone Africa: Nairobi, Kenya.

Alex Buertey Puplampu, MA, is Doctoral Candidate at the School of Journalism, Media and Cultural Studies, Cardiff University, UK. alex_puplampu@yahoo.co.uk

Theresa C. Norton, MBA, is Communications and Marketing Manager for the Johns Hopkins University Center for Data-Driven Reform in Education, Baltimore, Maryland, USA. theresa_norton@hotmail.com

UNICEF Innocent Research Centre is the Research Wing of the United Nations Children's Fund. Switzerland.

Dr. Carmen Aldinger is Project Director, Education Development Center, Inc. Health and Human Development Programs, Newton, MA. USA. caldinger@edc.org

Cheryl Vince Whitman, M.Ed. is Senior Vice President, Education Development Center, Inc. and Director, EDC Health and Human Development Programs Director, WHO Collaborating Center to Promote Health through Schools and Communities. Newton, MA. USA. cvincewhitman@edc.org

Dr Zhang Xin-Wei is Director Institute of Chronic Non-Communicable Disease Prevention and Control, Zhejiang Provincial Center for Disease Prevention and Control, China. dr_zhangxinwei@yahoo.com.cn

Jack Jones, MPH, is formerly School Health Focal Point, World Health Organization Headquarters. Geneva, Switzerland. jackjones_1998@yahoo.com

Peter Badcock-Walters is Director EduSector AIDS Response Trust, formerly director of the MTT on Education based at HEARD, University of KwaZulu-Natal. Durban, South Africa. peterbw@eastcoast.co.za

Prof Michael J Kelly is a retired Professor of education and member of the Jesuit Order. mjkelly@jesuits.org.zm

Marelize Gorgens-Albino is a consultant to the World Bank's Global AIDS Monitoring and Evaluation Team (writing here in her personal capacity) marelize.gorgens@gmail.com

Dr Warren Parker is Director Centre for AIDS Development, Research & Evaluation (CADRE). Johannesburg, South Africa. warrenparker@cadre.org.za

Diana DuBois, MPH, MIA, is Director Minnesota International Health Volunteers (MIHV). ddubois@mihv.org

Prof. Utpal Sharma is Dean, Faculty of Planning and Public Policy, CEPT University, Ahmedabad, India. utpalsharma2003@yahoo.com, utpalsharma@cept.ac.in

John Durant is an Institutional and Management Consultant who has worked for many multi- and bi-lateral development agencies for 25 years long-term in Africa and Asia and now does short-term missions; a former Lecturer at Open University, UK in development management. john@durant.demon.co.uk

Dr. Rajeswari Ramachandran is Deputy Director Senior Grade, Tuberculosis Research Centre (ICMR) Chennai. India. rajerama@yahoo.com

Muniyandi Malaisamy is a member of the Tuberculosis Research Centre (ICMR), Chennai, India. mmuniyandi@yahoo.com

INDEX

A

Aboriginal, 76
Abraham, 33, 369
Abramson, 268, 357
abstinence, 18, 49, 76, 77, 83, 286, 293, 296
academic, 10, 62, 68, 81, 98, 99, 118, 129, 134, 141, 146, 147, 148, 149, 158, 159, 171, 172, 175, 176, 177, 181, 185, 212, 222, 231, 268, 270, 271, 272, 280, 281, 327, 344
academic problems, 149
academic success, 177
academics, 11, 215
Academy, 15, 20, 375, 377
access, 3, 4, 6, 12, 14, 38, 39, 42, 48, 49, 72, 73, 74, 75, 87, 89, 91, 92, 97, 98, 100, 102, 107, 139, 171, 236, 248, 272, 280, 284, 287, 289, 295, 303, 304, 313, 317, 319, 320, 321, 322, 323, 326, 338, 344, 349, 374
accessibility, 4, 296, 319
accidental, 129, 132, 167
accidental injury, 129
accommodate, 69, 273, 280, 310, 311, 318, 321, 322, 325, 326
accomplices, 256
accountability, 214, 264, 332
accounting, 79, 226
achievement, 39, 141, 153, 156, 157, 171, 175, 181, 212, 333, 339, 358
Acquired Immune Deficiency Syndrome, 285
action research, 208, 209, 259, 260, 374
acute, 15, 236, 312
adaptability, 167
adaptation, 126, 214
Adgebe, 270, 349
administration, 16, 17, 106, 135
Administration, 15
administrative, 125, 174, 225, 246

administrators, 113, 118, 124, 125, 126, 127, 128, 129, 130, 131, 134, 136, 138, 141, 143, 144, 145, 146, 147, 150, 152, 155, 156, 159, 161, 162, 164, 165, 166, 167, 171, 173, 174, 175, 177, 178, 179, 180, 181
adolescence, 50, 140, 151, 154, 164
adolescent boys, 274, 275
adolescents, 14, 51, 182, 189, 238, 262, 263, 275, 283, 360, 361, 368
ADS, 84
adult, 24, 34, 79, 121, 236, 275, 278, 290, 299, 351, 368
adult education, 368
adult literacy, 24, 299
adulthood, 229, 242
adults, 18, 24, 33, 79, 102, 128, 130, 156, 236, 238, 276, 278, 357
advertisements, 16, 109
advertising, 10, 14, 19, 262, 356
advocacy, xi, 12, 90, 98, 120, 175, 221, 223, 232, 235, 245, 249, 289
Advocacy, 12, 244, 356, 372
AED, 13, 16, 17, 20
aesthetic, 82, 188, 196, 230
affordability, 18, 20, 313, 317, 329
Africa, v, xi, 9, 15, 20, 21, 22, 24, 30, 44, 45, 46, 47, 54, 55, 59, 64, 78, 79, 80, 90, 100, 120, 122, 186, 221, 223, 224, 227, 235, 236, 244, 245, 249, 250, 252, 256, 259, 260, 262, 280, 304, 346, 350, 353, 354, 355, 356, 357, 358, 359, 360, 362, 364, 365, 366, 369, 370, 371, 372, 374, 375, 377, 378
African American, 360
African continent, 223
African Union, 245
age, 13, 16, 25, 31, 36, 39, 43, 48, 61, 80, 81, 105, 120, 121, 122, 140, 146, 147, 153, 154, 171, 172, 174, 178, 189, 195, 221, 223, 224, 226, 227, 228, 229, 234, 241, 243, 251, 252, 271, 283, 284, 286, 299, 301, 302, 304, 359, 360, 362, 367, 369, 375

agent, 118, 212, 259
agents, 14, 19, 56, 91, 93, 97, 241, 291
aging, 87
aging population, 87
Agpar, 235, 253
agricultural, 55, 335, 337
agricultural sector, 335
agriculturalists, 287
agriculture, 10, 106, 240, 271, 272, 301
aid, 13, 16, 55, 64, 76, 88, 128, 129, 132, 133, 135, 136, 138, 140, 152, 153, 156, 157, 161, 162, 165, 277, 285, 302, 333, 335, 336, 338, 341
air, 72, 142, 274, 277
Airhihenbuwa, 26, 29, 70, 349
Al Gadarif, 240
Albania, 53
alcohol, 280, 363
Aldinger, 113, 114, 123, 166, 168, 349, 374, 375, 377
Alhassan, 71, 349
Allensworth, 115, 349
allies, 82
Al-Mazrou, 43, 349
alternative, 6, 10, 18, 194, 207, 216, 239, 241, 242, 256, 325, 326
alternatives, 13, 57, 346
Altheide, 70
Altman, 79, 350
aluminium, 15
Amal, 255
ambassadors, 126, 150
ambiguity, 89
ambivalence, 52
ambivalent, 51, 337
ambulances, 299
amenorrhea, 285, 286
American, 10, 74, 197, 199, 252, 357, 359, 360, 368
ammunition, 46
amorphous, 56, 61
anaemia, 234, 235
analysis, xi, 57, 59, 61, 62, 63, 64, 67, 69, 74, 75, 81, 82, 93, 124, 126, 143, 189, 222, 223, 228, 235, 252, 261, 264, 267, 268, 270, 276, 277, 278, 354, 363, 366, 371
analysts, 225
analytic, 188, 261, 273, 281
Anarfi, 79, 80, 350
ANC, 39, 42, 43
Andreason, 6, 350
anecdote, 188
Anglophone, xi, 55, 59, 64, 357, 366, 377
Anglo-Saxon, 198
Angola, 79

animals, 323
animateur, 209, 216
Anokwa, 272, 349
anthropological, 252
anthropologists, 187, 268
anthropology, 270, 354
antibody, 374
antiretrovirals, 94
antithesis, 265
Antwi-Agyei, 6
anxiety, 167
apartheid, 264
appetite, 16, 236
Appiah, 79, 80, 350, 355
Appiah-Danquah, 6
application, 7, 13, 56, 66, 68, 99, 141, 207, 210, 213, 247, 265, 266, 269
appraisals, 140, 144, 178
Apteker, 280, 350
Arabia, 230
Aranya, 307, 309, 311, 312, 313, 314, 315, 316, 317, 320, 322, 324, 325, 327, 328, 329, 373
architecture, 96, 191, 192, 194, 200, 201, 202, 203, 204, 217, 357
Ardebili, 273, 350
argument, 4, 44, 58, 71, 188, 189, 194, 199, 205, 210, 269, 328
Arimah, 272, 350
armed forces, 18
Aro, 5, 350
ART, 17, 51
articulation, 197, 204, 211
artificial, 191, 192, 204, 216, 217, 218, 365
artistic, 186, 211, 271, 276, 344
artistic movement, 271
Arusha, 230
Asante, 272, 350
Ashok, 281, 362
Asian, 331, 370
Asiimwe-Okiror, 31, 32, 50, 350
aspiration, 194, 358
assessment, 30, 63, 108, 125, 138, 144, 145, 147, 243, 256, 261, 262, 274, 333, 334, 335, 336, 341, 342, 349, 363
assessment tools, 138
assets, 58
Assiut, 240, 254
associations, 106, 107, 248, 302
assumptions, 168, 182, 194, 259, 268, 339
asylum, 246, 256
asymmetry, 214
atmosphere, 141, 145, 156, 157, 158
attacks, 12

Index

attention, ix, 4, 7, 13, 51, 69, 78, 90, 104, 116, 119, 122, 127, 130, 133, 135, 136, 137, 140, 141, 145, 146, 148, 149, 153, 156, 158, 159, 162, 164, 165, 166, 167, 169, 171, 172, 173, 174, 179, 180, 181, 195, 199, 206, 223, 237, 282
attitudes, 11, 19, 30, 33, 38, 45, 46, 70, 79, 113, 121, 123, 168, 225, 227, 230, 235, 239, 240, 242, 249, 254, 267, 340, 345, 349
audio, 274
audio visual, 274
auditing, 144
Australasia, 224
Australia, 10, 98, 224, 236, 245, 363, 364, 375
Australians, 10
authoritative, 73, 75, 232
authority, 21, 130, 132, 157, 165, 174, 277, 334
availability, 4, 6, 15, 18, 20, 97, 101, 102, 106, 107, 108, 169, 223, 288, 290, 297, 314, 328, 340, 369
avoidance, 24, 83
awareness, vii, 4, 6, 14, 17, 20, 43, 47, 48, 51, 52, 56, 63, 64, 69, 70, 76, 78, 81, 94, 101, 102, 106, 108, 109, 116, 152, 155, 231, 232, 237, 239, 240, 242, 243, 244, 245, 246, 247, 249, 254, 255, 261, 262, 263, 264, 270, 276, 277, 282, 284, 286, 289, 290, 292, 293, 301, 302, 303, 327, 345, 359, 367
Azerbaijan, 53

B

Babacar, 255
babies, 297, 299
Bacillus, 104
Backer, 119, 350
Badcock-Walters, 23, 378
Bambara, 230
bananas, 293
Bangladesh, 13, 103, 362, 364
banks, 311, 312
Banza, 255
Barbier, 58, 271, 350
Barford, 276, 350
barrier, 89
barriers, 11, 12, 71, 89, 94, 108, 302, 346
baseline, 188, 251, 361
basic needs, 56
basic research, 104
basic services, 309
basic trust, 210
Bauld, 282, 360
Bayoumi, 251
BCG, 104
Beaman, 5, 357
beautification, 156, 169
behavior, 89, 90, 91, 97, 349

behaviours, 7, 9, 16, 20, 30, 42, 70, 72, 73, 77, 78, 102, 113, 121, 123, 167, 168, 182, 196, 199
Beja, 226
beliefs, 13, 16, 19, 73, 75, 108, 185, 234, 239, 277
Bellamy, 24
Ben-Amos, 269, 351
benchmark, 52, 63, 64
beneficiaries, 6, 56, 57, 60, 61, 62, 63, 64, 65, 66, 67, 91, 186, 188, 309, 313, 314, 328
benefits, 9, 11, 12, 39, 57, 66, 90, 91, 95, 99, 128, 147, 160, 188, 231, 233, 263, 264, 292, 309, 336
Benefo, 76, 77, 85, 351
Benga, 255
Benin, 224, 226, 227, 244
Berg, 92, 351
Berger, 81, 351
Berman, 118, 351
Bersani, 76, 351
Bessinger, 351, 358
Bettina, 250, 252, 256
Bhabha, 196
Bhaskar, 273, 351
Bhola, 271, 351
bias, 52, 74, 278, 335
bicycles, 153, 284, 301
bilateral, 208, 209, 249, 340
bilateral aid, 340
binding, 3, 232, 234
bio-diversity, 195
biological, 24, 121
biology, 50, 248
biomass, 58
biomedical, 25, 26, 76, 234
birth, 104, 105, 226, 235, 237, 239, 280, 284, 285, 286, 295, 304
birth control, 104
birth weight, 235
births, 13, 14, 286
black, 79, 326, 360
black women, 79
blame, ix, 66
bleeding, 234
blocks, 110, 155, 321
blogs, 91
blood, 79, 151, 165
blood transfusions, 79
Boafo, 272, 351
Bolivia, 53
Bollinger, 250
borderline, 196
Bosk, 73, 359
Botswana, 48, 49, 50, 53, 365, 371
Botvin, 121, 352

Bown, 270, 352
boys, 46, 247, 249, 275, 278, 304
Bradbury, 186, 352, 363
Bradford, ix, 252
brain, 11
brain-drain, 11
brainstorming, 178
Brandt, 208, 211, 352, 357, 370
brass, 271
Brazil, 13, 17, 18, 22, 75, 359
Brazilian, 17, 18
breakdown, 202, 205, 207
breakfast, 152, 154
breast, 6, 79, 358
breast cancer, 358
breast feeding, 6, 79
breastfeeding, 16, 56, 94, 294, 296, 297
Brehony, 185, 352
Brighton, 208, 212, 213, 371
Britain, 10, 194
British, 71, 88, 200, 350, 352, 360
broad spectrum, 10, 340
broadcast, 71, 72, 73, 82, 84, 152, 248
broadcast media, 103
broadcasters, 7
broadcasting, 5, 71, 78, 149, 349, 364
brochures, 135, 301
Bronstein, 188, 356
Brookmeyer, 250
Brussels, 334
Bryman, 82, 83, 273, 352
Buhl, 188, 352
buildings, 321
bulletins, 69, 71, 73, 76, 81, 82, 83, 85, 91, 149, 150
Bunya, 283, 285, 290, 298, 299, 301, 305
Bunya County, 283, 298, 299, 301
bureaucracy, 73
bureaucratic, 73, 74
Burkey, 270
Burkina Faso, 41, 53, 225, 226, 227, 235, 242, 244, 245, 248, 251, 253, 255
Burkino Faso, 239
Burnham, 352
Burns, 10, 364
Burundi, 53
buses, 254
business, 13, 20, 22, 67, 197, 198, 199, 212, 269, 367
business environment, 269
business model, 199
Byrne, 77, 352

C

cables, 307, 325

Cabral, 255
CADRE, 70, 353, 378
caesarean section, 235
Cameroon, 18, 19, 45, 53, 251
campaign, 5, 10, 11, 16, 17, 56, 76, 159, 162, 271
campaigns, 10, 11, 14, 70, 78, 84, 98, 107, 132, 185, 227, 235, 237, 244, 247, 248
cancer, 355, 356
candidates, 96
cannabis, 280
capacity, 18, 19, 61, 68, 90, 115, 117, 118, 185, 192, 210, 211, 217, 239, 249, 250, 255, 263, 267, 280, 284, 288, 289, 290, 299, 303, 312, 314, 373, 375, 378
capacity building, 68, 117, 185, 249, 288, 373, 375
capital, 58, 74, 194, 287, 312, 325, 327
capital cost, 325
cardiovascular, 129
cardiovascular disease, 129
CARE, 18, 301
career development, 138, 142, 143
Caribbean, 366
carrier, 50
case study, 88, 272, 283, 287, 304, 327, 329, 370
cast, 189
catalyst, 209, 211, 212, 216, 243, 344
catalysts, 204, 216
Catholic Church, 284, 288, 290, 292, 295, 296
cattle, 322, 337
causality, 197, 358
Cavendish, 271, 352
cavities, 129
CBD, 57
CBO, 285
CDC, 128, 132, 138, 172, 175, 177, 179
CEDPA, 240, 241, 255
cell phones, 93
census, 372
Central region, 271
century-old, 199
certainty, 23, 195
certificate, 139, 153
certification, 302
cervical, 287
Chad, 53, 224, 245
Chagga, 230
Chamberlain, 124, 353
Chambers, 282, 353
Chang, 281, 353
channels, x, 4, 6, 13, 14, 18, 23, 47, 48, 49, 63, 74, 75, 76, 88, 89, 91, 95, 101, 102, 103, 104, 106, 107, 108, 109, 116, 118, 188, 189, 267, 270, 299, 302, 319, 345, 367

chart, 16, 60, 61, 301
check-ups, 132, 151, 169
chemotherapy, 104
chicken, 140, 178
chicken flu, 140, 178
child abuse, 262
child mortality, 57
child protection, 244, 254, 256
child survival, 283, 285, 305, 364
childbearing, 284, 286, 299, 302
childbirth, 94, 234, 235, 252, 253, 257
childcare, 15
childhood, 6, 56, 248, 297
children, 5, 13, 16, 17, 21, 50, 61, 79, 122, 128, 129, 134, 137, 146, 148, 149, 153, 154, 155, 156, 158, 159, 161, 164, 166, 167, 170, 171, 221, 224, 225, 233, 235, 236, 237, 243, 244, 246, 248, 249, 250, 252, 253, 254, 256, 279, 280, 281, 286, 287, 289, 290, 292, 293, 295, 296, 297, 298, 299, 304, 322, 337, 357, 358, 361
China, 7, 113, 114, 118, 122, 123, 139, 142, 143, 147, 152, 163, 168, 170, 171, 172, 173, 182, 231,
Chinese, 123, 125, 143, 145, 148, 161, 164, 172, 199, 207, 363
Chinyowa,, 268, 269, 353
Chowdhury, 185, 370
Christiansen, 271, 353
chronic diseases, 11
churches, 49, 280
cigarettes, 130
circulation, 322, 323
circumcision, 90, 91, 92, 222, 237, 250, 255, 349, 361, 365, 373, 374
citizens, 4, 9, 61, 70, 75, 156, 162, 199, 224, 236, 244
citrus, 88
civil society, 211, 232, 248, 254, 257, 354, 362
civilisation, 195
Clark, 280, 364
Clarke, 76, 79, 353, 359
classes, 135, 140, 141, 149, 157, 165, 169, 236, 238, 299
classical, 197
classified, 47, 75, 154, 278, 280
classroom, 48, 49, 51, 52, 113, 118, 121, 135, 141, 148, 149, 150, 155, 169, 238, 269, 369
classrooms, 127, 141, 156, 157
cleaning, 152, 325
clients, 18, 19, 36, 42, 43, 91, 92, 100, 292, 293, 295, 296, 297, 298, 301
climate change, 345
climatic factors, 321
clinical, 44, 70, 88, 90, 104, 218, 296

clinical trial, 44, 88, 90
clinical trials, 44, 88, 90
clinicians, 344
clinics, 14, 290, 292, 293, 296, 297
cluster model, 208, 209
clusters, 320, 322
CME, 110
coalitions, 210
codes, 126
coding, 82, 124, 126
coerced, 250, 304
cognition, 236, 361
cognitive, 23, 48, 49, 51, 73, 121, 344
cognitive tool, 344
coherence, 25, 191, 192, 193, 196, 202, 203, 204, 205, 207, 210, 217
cohesion, 204, 318
cohort, 44, 226
Coldevin, 56, 59, 354
Colditz, 10, 12, 355, 356
collaboration, 18, 93, 96, 97, 116, 119, 138, 178, 179, 191, 192, 193, 194, 197, 203, 204, 205, 208, 209, 211, 212, 213, 214, 216, 217, 219, 238, 247, 249, 292, 298, 303, 357, 374
colleague, 198
collectivism, 194
college students, 263, 264, 374
colleges, 104, 105, 110
Coll-Seck, 78
colonial, 224
commerce, 315
commercial, 12, 18, 19, 20, 21, 25, 33, 36, 37, 69, 71, 76, 80, 262, 263, 312, 314, 315, 316, 318, 319, 327
commodities, 58, 291
communication processes, vii, 259
communication strategies, 9, 103
communication technologies, 216, 355
communications, 29, 69, 71, 74, 75, 77, 78, 82, 91, 151, 261, 262, 263, 280, 292, 363, 365
Communist Party, 130, 171
communities., 268, 282
community cooperation, 133, 136
community norms, 275
community service, 122
community support, 255, 280
community-based, 3, 18, 235, 241, 248, 253, 264, 284, 285, 288, 291, 296, 297, 299, 300, 302, 360
compassion, 134, 195
compatibility, 89, 90, 99
compensation, 58
competency, 207
competition, 21, 73, 150, 156, 159, 172, 195

compilation, 114, 143, 353
complement, 16, 84, 123, 239, 242, 341
complementary, 115, 116, 173, 193, 208, 222, 246
complex systems, vii
complexity, 14, 15, 49, 89, 90, 99, 200, 201, 206, 208, 214, 217
compliance, 106, 143, 181
complications, 94, 234, 247, 253
components, 57, 108, 115, 116, 120, 123, 126, 131, 138, 167, 168, 170, 177, 178, 179, 182, 201, 262, 282, 311, 324
composite, 314
composition, 317, 328
compositions, 317
comprehension, 205
computer, 92, 139, 212, 311, 325
concentration, 15, 57, 193, 236
conception, 6, 192, 193, 195, 196, 203, 206, 207
conceptual, 3, 26, 113, 193, 205, 206, 214, 216, 269, 282, 314, 349, 360
conceptualizing, 193
concrete, 214, 222, 231, 235, 246, 270
concreteness, 345
condom, 10, 13, 14, 18, 19, 22, 33, 34, 36, 38, 44, 46, 47, 48, 55, 76, 83, 264, 265, 284, 286, 292, 297, 298, 304, 369
condom, 13, 19, 33, 35, 36, 284, 293, 363, 365, 367
condoms, ix, 10, 13, 14, 17, 19, 30, 33, 34, 47, 48, 261, 264, 284, 285, 287, 291, 293, 297, 298, 301, 303, 304, 369
confidence, 138, 141, 142, 145, 157, 166, 176, 237, 239, 269, 295
confidentiality, 125
configuration, 324
conflict, 201, 202, 204
conflict resolution, 204
confusion, 222, 236
consciousness, 75, 133, 145, 146, 152, 155, 166, 195, 198, 217, 263
consensus, 114, 116, 123, 197, 201, 238, 239, 245, 254, 270
consent, 234, 253
consolidation, 74, 75, 195, 340, 371
conspiracy, 74
conspiracy theory, 74
Constitution, 244
constraints, 91, 198, 204, 285, 294
construction, 72, 146, 188, 190, 195, 260, 307, 309, 311, 312, 313, 314, 322, 329
constructionist, 357
consultants, 304
consultation, 130, 149, 151, 169, 176, 185, 186, 228, 246, 251, 252, 253, 256, 257, 259, 277, 373

consulting, 131, 138, 160, 170
consumer choice, 14
consumers, 9, 14, 20
consumption, 6, 57, 66, 130
consumption patterns, 6
contemporary,, 188
content analysis, 81
continuing, 66, 297, 342
continuity, 243, 319
contraception, 14, 21, 97, 103, 121, 301
contraceptive, 4, 13, 14, 283, 284, 286, 287, 293, 295, 299, 301, 302, 303, 355, 363
contraceptives, 21, 57, 189, 283, 285, 287, 293, 302, 304
contractors, 96
control, 13, 14, 18, 19, 26, 33, 39, 41, 44, 46, 47, 57, 80, 101, 102, 104, 107, 130, 132, 140, 153, 166, 195, 198, 241, 276, 296, 322, 358
control group, 44, 46, 47
controlled, 57, 74, 104, 116, 264, 304, 360, 374
convention, 221, 232, 237, 252, 271
convergence, 20
conversion, 210
conviction, 245
cooking, 130, 144
Cooley, 192, 205, 206, 354
cooperative, 212, 305, 373
coordination, 194, 211, 248, 303
coping, 92, 94, 159, 362
Corbin, 124, 371
CORE Group, 287, 292, 305
corporation, 199, 350, 351
corporations, 12, 186, 352
correlation, 29, 30, 38, 39, 40, 41, 42, 51
corridors, 310
cosmopolitan, 199
cost-benefit analysis, 189
cost-effective, 62, 332, 337, 338
costs, 15, 17, 61, 202, 231, 241, 314, 325, 340
Côte d'Ivoire, 226, 227, 244, 252
Cottle, 70, 74, 354, 359
cotton, 326
Council of Europe, 245, 256
counsel, 297
counseling, 18
counselling, 44, 64, 97, 98, 115, 261, 289, 290, 302, 354
couples, 18, 286, 295, 296, 301
coverage, ix, 20, 50, 71, 73, 74, 75, 78, 83, 85, 101, 239, 333
covering, 105
Covey, 188, 354
Cowan, 270, 359

CPD, 271
CRC, 232, 233, 236, 237, 250, 253
creativity, 5, 10, 13, 18, 22, 140, 269
credibility, 52, 74, 75, 78, 278, 295, 337, 340
credit, 305
crime, 277, 278
critical thinking, 262, 263
criticism, 12, 271
cross-border, 246
cross-cultural, 191, 192, 193, 194, 195, 196, 198, 200, 201, 202, 203, 204, 205, 206, 207, 208, 209, 210, 211, 212, 213, 214, 216, 217, 219, 352, 357, 358, 370
cross-sectional, 42, 44
crying, 10
crystal, 336
cultivating, 193, 209, 216
cultivation, 197, 198, 215
cultural, vii, 5, 23, 24, 29, 55, 56, 70, 73, 75, 76, 94, 119, 186, 188, 189, 191, 192, 193, 194, 195, 196, 197, 198, 199, 200, 201, 202, 203, 204, 205, 206, 207, 208, 209, 210, 211, 212, 213, 214, 216, 217, 218, 219, 221, 229, 232, 233, 235, 241, 242, 243, 262, 265, 266, 267, 268, 269, 276, 278, 298, 304, 315, 325, 327, 345, 346, 352, 354, 357, 370
cultural differences, 193, 197, 198, 199, 200, 204, 207
cultural factors, 24
cultural identities, 196, 200
cultural influence, 29
cultural norms, 304
cultural perspective, 196, 205, 206, 262
cultural practices, 186, 232
cultural rules, 191
cultural values, 199, 233, 276
culture, 3, 5, 15, 57, 75, 105, 122, 185, 186, 187, 191, 192, 194, 196, 197, 198, 200, 201, 203, 204, 206, 210, 211, 213, 216, 217, 218, 219, 234, 244, 263, 273, 277, 278, 295, 309, 328, 344, 351, 352
cultures, 13, 56, 191, 196, 197, 198, 199, 200, 201, 202, 203, 204, 208, 210, 216, 219, 223, 236
curing, 107
currency, 189, 345
curriculum, 49, 50, 68, 118, 121, 122, 131, 361
customers, 297
cyclists, 319
cysts, 235

D

D'Angelo, 73, 354
dairy, 208, 209, 212
dairy sector, 208, 209
dance, 268, 269, 271, 272, 274, 276, 277

danger, 74, 80, 166, 202, 297
Danish International Development Agency, 283
data analysis, 126, 143
data collection, 124, 125, 294, 299
data gathering, 125, 175, 186, 267
database, 93, 96, 97, 98, 247
dating, 246
de Janvry, 271, 354
De Walque, 41, 354
Deacon, 81, 82, 354
death, ix, 10, 15, 17, 57, 102, 172, 235, 245, 252, 359
death rate, 57
deaths, 15, 79, 234, 286
debt, xi, 195
debt burden, 195
decentralization, 288, 285, 294
decision makers, 195, 333, 340
decision making, 3, 66, 185, 186, 188, 254, 255, 269, 359, 369
decision-making process, 174
decisions, 5, 23, 24, 66, 92, 174, 180, 243, 324, 333, 334, 337, 338
defects, 194
deficiency, 70, 137
definition, 5, 11, 12, 52, 72, 73, 115, 148, 160, 205, 214, 250, 272, 282, 332, 333, 339
degradation, 350
degrading, 308
degree, vii, 49, 59, 69, 73, 129, 234, 270, 290, 297, 314, 324
deinfibulation, 235
Deir el Barsha, 240, 255
Delamonica, 29, 39, 373
delivery, 9, 10, 11, 65, 77, 79, 89, 94, 97, 98, 99, 121, 235, 252, 283, 289, 296, 299, 303, 334, 335, 337, 340, 342
demand, 13, 20, 21, 78, 87, 186, 242, 283, 284, 285, 286, 296, 297, 302, 303, 312
Demery, 271, 353
Demian, 187
democracy, 202, 238, 263
democratic, 57, 58, 131, 140, 141, 188, 201, 259, 264, 368
Democratic Republic of Congo, 224
democratisation, 210
democratization, 349
Demographic, 29, 57, 223, 225, 226, 250, 251, 252, 285, 286, 355, 357, 371, 372
demographic factors, 57
demographics, 87, 118
denial, ix
dentistry, 88, 359

Denzin, 81, 275, 355, 356
Department of Education, 142
depressed, 24
depression, 121
Depression, 195
deprivation, 271
Derry, 273, 355
design, 59, 74, 88, 92, 98, 120, 122, 148, 150, 188, 189, 204, 205, 206, 207, 213, 216, 254, 264, 273, 289, 303, 307, 309, 310, 311, 314, 315, 317, 318, 319, 324, 325, 329, 358, 373
designers, 204, 207, 263
desire, 157, 171, 195, 227, 229, 280, 282, 296
destruction, 195
detection, 101, 102
detention, 245
deterministic, 194
Deuze, 75, 355
developed countries, 114
developed nations, 120
developing, 3, 6, 9, 10, 11, 12, 13, 14, 15, 21, 56, 65, 79, 88, 92, 94, 96, 97, 98, 99, 115, 117, 119, 121, 124, 127, 131, 165, 166, 167, 194, 195, 211, 222, 237, 241, 246, 268, 280, 293, 367, 371
developing countries, vii, 3, 6, 9, 11, 12, 13, 14, 15, 56, 79, 92, 195, 361
development assistance, 194, 331, 333
development policy, 337
developmental process, 191, 193
Devers, 275, 356
deviance, 274, 276, 277, 278, 279, 280
DHS, 25, 33, 38, 39, 42, 223, 224, 225, 226, 227, 228, 239, 240, 245, 250, 251, 255, 285, 286, 295, 357, 371
diagnostic, 101, 102, 206
dialogue, 66, 198, 200, 201, 204, 210, 241, 243, 246, 248, 263, 270, 282, 295, 302
diaphragm, 304
diarrhea, 106
diarrheal, 14, 15, 16, 17
diarrhoea, 294, 297
dichotomy, 4
Dictow, 6, 365
diet, x, 129, 140, 142, 152, 153, 165
dietary, 171, 172
dietary habits, 171, 172
diets, 167
diffusion, 55, 87, 88, 90, 92, 93, 97, 100, 116, 118, 210, 219, 232, 238, 359, 368
diffusion process, 232
digital television, 216
dignity, 115
Dimiter, 188, 355

Diola, 244
Diop, 253, 255
diplomas, 59
disability, 271
disadvantaged students, 134
discipline, 56, 143, 152, 194, 262, 281
discourse, x, 74, 76, 82, 189, 195, 196, 241, 270, 271, 280, 344, 357, 363, 367
discrimination, 38, 78, 109, 157, 161, 236, 249
disease, 18, 20, 69, 70, 74, 76, 77, 79, 80, 83, 84, 85, 132, 136, 147, 151, 152, 260, 277, 292, 293, 296, 371
diseases, 14, 79, 80, 140, 268
displacement, 360
disposable income, 33
disseminate, 75, 109, 150, 171, 237, 246, 277, 287
distal, 26
distance learning, 89
distress, 236
distribution, 13, 14, 18, 20, 27, 170, 222, 226, 261, 291, 299, 302, 313, 319, 320
distributive justice, 193
Divekar, 250
diversity, vii, xi, 80, 111, 119, 192, 194, 195, 201, 204, 208, 210, 211, 212, 266, 340, 346
dividends, 52
division, 104
divorce, 254
Djibouti, 224, 226, 244, 246, 247, 256
doctor, 124, 158, 206
doctors, 14, 151, 169, 226, 248, 279, 297
Dodoo, 6, 355
domestic, 10, 56, 310, 322
domestic violence, 10
dominance, 74, 195, 197
donor, 4, 60, 65, 66, 122, 185, 186, 270, 332, 333, 334, 335, 337
donors, 6, 10, 56, 67, 249, 282, 292, 296, 331, 332, 335, 336, 337, 338, 341, 342
Dorkenoo, 252, 256
DOT, 108, 109, 110
Douglas, 11, 351, 361
download, 372
draft, 45, 356
drainage, 161, 307, 308, 313, 316, 325
drama, 18, 55, 70, 268, 269, 272, 274, 276, 277, 292, 349, 358, 359
Drèze, 272, 355
Drimie, 79, 355
drinking, 132, 161, 280
drinking water, 161, 280
drought, 55, 224
drug use, 24, 30, 79, 84

drug users, 24, 30, 79
drugs, 17, 83, 104, 108, 121
dry, 270, 314
DSC, 56, 59
duality, 203
Duflo, 41
Dumas group, 277
duplication, 52, 302
duration, 27, 263, 264, 277, 334
duties, 75, 130, 280

E

earnings, 58
ears, 121, 177
earth, 156, 193
eating, 157, 161, 167, 236
ecological, 7, 192, 194
ecology, 57
economic, 3, 6, 20, 23, 24, 29, 36, 39, 55, 56, 57, 58, 61, 66, 78, 79, 83, 123, 124, 178, 192, 193, 194, 195, 202, 204, 208, 209, 210, 211, 216, 219, 224, 229, 236, 237, 247, 254, 262, 268, 271, 272, 277, 280, 287, 304, 307, 310, 311, 318, 320, 322, 326, 327, 328, 336, 350
economic activity, 272
economic change, 208
economic development, 79, 178, 208, 211, 310
economic empowerment, 254
economic globalisation, 194
economic growth, 193
economic performance, 336
economic problem, 194
economic status, 236
economic systems, 210, 219
economics, 130, 189, 195
economies, 279
economists, 12
economy, 75, 192, 193, 194, 196, 311, 324, 337
ecosystems, 195
educated women, 298
Education for All, vii, 39
education reform, 120, 173
educational, 14, 15, 20, 116, 172, 299, 350, 351, 371, 377
educational attainment, 39, 42
educational background, 59
educational institutions, 138, 315
educational psychology, 358
educational system, 171, 172
educators, 18, 19, 51, 64, 117, 122, 240, 243
efficacy, 121, 123, 287
Egypt, 53, 223, 224, 226, 227, 240, 244, 245, 246, 248, 251, 252, 254, 255, 256, 374

Egyptian, 245, 255
Eiman, 254
elder, 198, 278
elderly, 61
elders, 238, 276, 280
election, 9, 278, 357
electrical, 199
electricity, 106, 280, 287, 307, 308, 311, 316, 325
electronic, 4, 92, 97, 202, 270
electronic media, 270
electronic systems, 4
elementary school, 125, 127, 129, 131, 133, 135, 136, 139, 140, 141, 142, 143, 144, 145, 147, 148, 149, 150, 151, 153, 154, 155, 156, 157, 158, 161, 162, 163, 164, 165, 166
Elliott, 120, 374
emergency room, 288
emotional, 29, 50, 123, 148, 171, 172, 199, 235
emotional well-being, 171
emotions, 29, 166, 198, 230, 345
empirical, 189, 268
employees, 110, 199
employment, 58, 106, 142, 242, 316, 342
empowered, 67, 72, 261, 295
empowerment, 67, 101, 102, 231, 239, 265, 266, 282, 295, 365
enabling environments, 121
encouragement, 128, 153, 157
endocrine, 367
energy, 51, 149, 159, 264, 301
engagement, 196, 204, 213, 247, 250, 255, 259
English, 125, 128, 148, 160
enterprise, 200, 208, 212
entertainment, 4, 70, 76, 141, 272, 276, 281, 370
Entman, 72, 354, 355
entrepreneurial, 22, 208, 209, 212, 215
entrepreneurs, 186, 199, 207, 208, 209, 211, 216
entrepreneurship, 208, 209, 212
environmental, 12, 58, 77, 89, 91, 100, 135, 142, 144, 159, 161, 178, 194, 240, 272, 274, 276, 277, 280, 282, 308, 317, 318, 319, 325, 336, 345, 373
environmental change, 12
environmental conditions, 277
environmental degradation, 272, 276, 277
environmental factors, 100, 345
environmental impact, 325, 336
environmental movement, 77
environmental policy, 373
environmental protection, 58, 135, 178, 240
environmental threats, 282
epidemic, ix, 15, 18, 25, 27, 33, 39, 75, 76, 77, 79, 80, 83, 98, 260, 374
epidemics, 24, 25, 36, 41, 42, 359

epidemics., 24, 25, 36, 42
epidemiological, 76, 374
epidemiology, 11, 27, 365
epistemology, 355
equality, 192, 193, 211, 214, 328
equipment, 199, 274, 337
equity, 20, 193, 372
Eritrea, xi, 53, 224, 226, 227
ethical, 90, 202, 269
ethical issues, 90
ethics, 369
Ethiopia, 39, 53, 99, 223, 224, 225, 226, 227, 242, 244, 251, 352
ethnic groups, 157, 225, 226, 238
ethnicity, 224, 225
ethnographic, 186, 187, 267, 268, 269
Europe, 82, 195, 208, 212, 213, 224, 236, 245, 249, 256, 371
European, 82, 192, 207, 208, 211, 212, 213, 214, 246, 249, 256, 331, 339, 345, 352, 354, 357, 360, 370, 373
European Commission, 213, 246, 331, 339, 354, 373
European Parliament, 246, 256
European Union (EU), 207, 208, 209, 212, 214, 215, 216, 219
evaluation, 6, 16, 19, 56, 57, 59, 62, 63, 64, 66, 70, 72, 93, 99, 117, 123, 131, 143, 145, 146, 147, 165, 181, 185, 190, 215, 228, 239, 240, 249, 254, 255, 256, 289, 300, 303, 353, 354, 370, 373, 375
evening, 134, 151, 243
Everett, 10, 87, 88, 116, 355
evidence, 13, 23, 24, 25, 27, 28, 32, 33, 38, 41, 42, 43, 44, 45, 46, 47, 48, 50, 51, 52, 66, 70, 87, 94, 95, 97, 98, 99, 118, 120, 123, 182, 186, 223, 227, 230, 235, 236, 239, 243, 245, 254, 272, 280, 281, 342, 350, 363, 371
evolution, 87, 191, 195, 323
Eweland, 271
exaggeration, 52
examinations, 139, 147, 149, 151
excision, 226, 228, 230, 251
excitement, 90, 173
exclusion, 11, 222, 229, 271
excuse, 185
exercise, 64, 85, 108, 168, 169, 170, 193, 232, 252, 294, 336, 337, 338, 339, 341
exhibitions,, 105, 109
expansions, 69
experimental, 23, 44, 45, 46, 47, 273, 357, 364, 375
experimental design, 273
expert, 94, 97, 163, 199, 252, 256, 259, 280, 296, 373

expertise, 208, 209, 210, 214, 219, 243, 290, 297, 303
experts, 13, 57, 91, 93, 94, 97, 98, 114, 117, 123, 138, 143, 148, 154, 163, 164, 175, 178, 179, 264, 280, 289
explicit knowledge, 96
exploitation, 195, 255
exporter, 56
exposure, 25, 47, 70, 76, 89, 104, 121, 358
extreme poverty, 271
eye, ix, 137, 155, 198, 206
eyes, 7, 124, 151, 345
Ezra, 270, 356

F

fabric, 3, 318
facets, 56, 202
facial expression, 269
facilitators, xi, 89, 91, 206, 210, 265, 266
factual knowledge, vii
failure, 58, 66, 119, 138, 176, 185, 308, 314, 341
faith, 11, 49, 63, 99, 301
faith-based organizations, 49
family life, 242
family members, 140, 147, 155, 162, 172, 178, 229, 247, 255, 256, 287
family planning, 6, 13, 14, 55, 56, 87, 94, 96, 97, 98, 99, 103, 272, 274, 276, 277, 278, 283, 284, 285, 286, 287, 288, 289, 290, 292, 293, 294, 295, 296, 297, 298, 299, 300, 301, 302, 303, 304, 351, 356, 358, 366, 368
FAO, 305, 346, 349, 373
farm, 65, 279
farm land, 279
farmers, 212, 290, 293, 337
farming, 10, 55, 213, 279
fatigue, 48, 51
fear, ix, 78, 195, 229, 236, 246, 256, 350
fears, 104
feedback, 62, 98, 143, 144, 151, 261, 270, 277, 281, 296
feed-back, 4, 332, 341
feeding, 6, 79, 358
feelings, 155, 236, 254, 340, 341
fees, 279
feet, 272
female condom, 298, 304
females, 30, 36, 37, 124, 125
Fenn, 267, 356
fertility, 57, 63, 94, 286, 299, 303
fertility rate, 57, 286, 299
FGM, 221, 222, 223, 224, 225, 226, 227, 228, 229, 230, 231, 232, 233, 234, 235, 236, 237, 238, 239,

240, 241, 242, 243, 244, 245, 246, 247, 248, 249, 250, 251, 252, 253, 254, 255, 256, 257
fidelity, 17, 18, 76, 119, 230
field trials, 44
figure, 24, 26, 27, 28, 29, 30, 31, 32, 33, 34, 35, 36, 37, 38, 40, 41, 42, 43, 44, 45, 114, 115, 116, 117, 120
film, 105, 274, 276, 277
filters, 202
financial, xi, 6, 118, 123, 127, 136, 165, 171, 173, 176, 177, 195, 214, 216, 295, 298, 313
financial resources, 185, 336
financial support, xi, 127, 136, 165, 173, 176, 177
financing, 248, 318, 338
fines, 245
fire, 135, 136
firewood, 10
fishing, 271
focus group, 15, 263, 264, 274, 275, 278, 295, 340, 341
focus groups, 15, 264
focusing, 7, 101, 134, 147, 159, 171, 206, 208, 215, 263, 269, 309
folk media, 6, 108, 268, 270, 272, 278, 281, 282
folklore, 55, 270, 293
food, 11, 16, 115, 132, 137, 144, 149, 152, 153, 154, 156, 161, 165, 167, 169, 279
food poisoning, 132
food safety, 115
foreign policy, 369
forestry, 271
formal education, 18, 48, 51, 128, 238
formal sector, 211
forums, 70, 93, 94, 96, 97, 100, 186, 275, 278, 279, 281
framework, 27, 52, 59, 72, 108, 113, 114, 115, 116, 119, 120, 123, 124, 126, 177, 179, 180, 181, 182, 188, 189, 205, 208, 209, 211, 237, 248, 263, 265, 269, 273, 281, 282, 307, 309, 310, 357
framing, 7, 65, 72, 73, 75, 354, 374
free choice, 237
freedom, 193, 233, 328, 360
freedoms, 193
fruits, 148
frustration, 161
fuel, 282
funding, 10, 17, 91, 207, 214, 243, 299, 302, 305, 335, 337, 338
funds, 13, 65, 83, 95, 163, 165, 176, 189, 270, 288, 292, 302
fuzzy, 6, 56

G

Gachiri, 252
Galileo, 195
gambling, 132
games, 263, 292
Gangakhedkar, 250
gangs, 17
garbage, 157, 161
gauge, 277, 333
Gaza, 223
gaze, 191, 192, 193, 194, 195, 216, 219
Gbaya, 225
GCE, 39, 43
Geertz, 267
gel, 304
gender, 79, 91, 221, 222, 229, 232, 233, 239, 240, 247, 248, 271, 278, 336
gender differences, 279
gender equality, 247
gender equity, 336
gender identity, 221, 229
gender inequality, 222, 229
gender role, 279
gene, 340
general practitioner, 365
generalizations, 340
generation, 58, 77, 102, 222, 231, 240, 247, 250, 299, 301, 302, 320, 372
genetic, 280
genital mutilation, 221, 222, 223, 237, 243, 249, 250, 252, 253, 254, 256, 257
genre, 75, 270
geographic, 87, 93, 97, 222, 225, 263
geographical, 70, 71, 75, 77, 123, 272
geography, 375
Gerard, 185, 371
Gerbner, 260
geriatric, 87
Ghana, xi, 13, 41, 53, 58, 69, 71, 72, 75, 76, 78, 80, 98, 235, 244, 245, 271, 272, 275, 276, 277, 280, 349, 350, 351, 352, 355, 356, 357, 358, 362, 365, 367, 371, 372
Ghanaian, 69, 76, 80, 366
gifts, 229
Gikonyo, 4, 55, 357, 366, 377
Gill, 187, 191, 192, 193, 205, 207, 211, 357, 377
girls, 41, 46, 83, 221, 222, 223, 224, 226, 227, 228, 229, 230, 231, 233, 234, 235, 236, 237, 238, 239, 240, 241, 242, 243, 247, 248, 249, 250, 251, 252, 254, 255, 274, 275, 278, 286, 298, 304, 360
global, 76, 87, 88, 92, 94, 115, 172, 194, 195, 196, 210, 215, 216, 219, 222, 248, 250, 271, 370, 372

Global Fund, 257
global village, 216
global warming, 51
globalization, vii, 194
globally, 24, 115
goals, vii, 6, 51, 78, 79, 92, 103, 121, 122, 129, 133, 135, 136, 138, 142, 163, 271, 332
goat, 295
God, 200
Godette, 118, 359
gold, 58
goods and services, 22
governance, 58, 202, 336
government, 7, 14, 21, 33, 66, 73, 74, 75, 78, 83, 88, 110, 127, 128, 129, 135, 136, 153, 164, 165, 171, 173, 175, 177, 179, 186, 189, 232, 237, 238, 244, 245, 246, 247, 248, 249, 254, 256, 257, 285, 288, 290, 299, 302, 335, 337, 338, 340
grain, 319
grandparents, 146, 171
grants, 305
graph, 38, 83
grass, 210
grasslands, 287
grassroots, 14, 212, 239, 280, 289, 303
gravity, 222
Great Depression, 195
greed, 123
Green Revolution, 208, 212
Gregson, 24, 31, 39, 41, 42, 358, 359
gross national product, 193
group activities, 140, 178
group interactions, 198
group interests, 194
groups, 4, 5, 6, 14, 17, 18, 19, 20, 24, 39, 46, 47, 56, 57, 61, 90, 96, 102, 106, 108, 110, 119, 123, 125, 149, 152, 153, 159, 175, 188, 197, 202, 204, 225, 226, 227, 228, 230, 239, 240, 243, 246, 248, 252, 262, 263, 266, 270, 271, 272, 273, 274, 276, 277, 278, □280, 285, 290, 295, 299, 301, 302, 311, 312, 313, 314, 315, 319, 322, 328, 337, 345
growth, 6, 21, 27, 56, 66, 92, 103, 193, 262, 298, 316, 318
Gruenbaum, 252
Grunig, 60, 358
GTZ, 241, 254, 256, 257
guardian, 233
guidance, 10, 116, 124, 138, 154, 163, 164, 175, 305
guidelines, ix, 19, 45, 52, 89, 98, 118, 119, 132, 133, 138, 144, 154, 157, 168, 170, 173, 181, 296, 325, 329, 371
guiding principles, 173, 233
Guiella, 255

Guinea, ix, 53, 80, 187, 224, 225, 226, 227, 229, 239, 241, 244, 251, 252, 354, 355
Gujarat, 208, 210, 212
Gutzwiller, 10, 358
Guyana, 53

H

habitat, 189, 307, 309, 310. 315, 324
habitation, 329
Hadi, 255
haemorrhage, 235
Hailey, 185, 358
Haiti, 53
Haitian, 79
Hakim, 273, 358
Hall, 74, 262, 358, 359, 366
Hallett, 25, 31, 36, 359
Hallfors, 118, 359
Halperin, 25, 26, 32, 38, 361, 367, 374
Hammersley, 278, 359
handbags, 284, 301
handicapped, 61
handling, 6, 206
hands, 60, 104, 154, 157, 167, 186, 195, 241, 290
hanging, 290, 344, 350
happiness, 145
Harlem, 79
harm, 122, 136, 167, 186, 195, 197, 229, 231, 233, 243, 244, 249, 358, 375
harmful, 122, 130, 221, 222, 229, 232, 237, 240, 242, 244, 245, 247, 249, 250, 253, 255
harmful effects, 242
harmony, 136, 195, 197, 358, 375
harvest, 56
harvesting, 93
Hashem, 230
hate, 78
Hayibor, 6
He, 73, 76, 78, 125, 128, 141, 147, 149, 160, 163, 172, 193, 195, 196, 197, 198, 199, 205, 359
head, ix, 130, 151, 158, 252, 337
headache, 15
headmaster, 118, 128, 130, 131, 132, 133, 134, 136, 137, 139, 157, 160
headmasters, 128, 157
healing, 90, 235
health care, ix, 16, 42, 45, 70, 89, 90, 91, 92, 100, 142, 206, 207, 218, 237, 243, 247, 261, 288, 289, 290, 294, 296, 303, 351
health care professionals, 247
health care system, 90, 91, 206, 218, 261
health care workers, 16, 248, 289
health communication, 103, 104, 109

health disparities, 10
health education, 18, 107, 113, 115, 116, 119, 120, 121, 122, 126, 129, 133, 142, 143, 146, 147, 153, 155, 169, 180, 261, 368, 374, 375
health information, 16, 84, 179, 237
health problems, 11, 13, 77, 88, 129, 161, 174, 236
health psychology, 353
health services, 11, 21, 39, 99, 102, 115, 149, 151, 169, 248, 294
health status, 71
Health Survey, 123, 145, 226, 251, 285, 286, 355, 357, 363, 371, 372
healthcare, 69, 70, 100
heart, 18, 149, 151, 190, 192, 198, 203, 208
heart disease, 151
height, 272
helmets, 167
Herlund, 256
herpes, 235
herpes simplex, 235
heterosexual, 79, 80
hierarchical, 71, 199, 201, 309
hierarchy, 74, 91, 200, 254, 314, 315, 317, 318, 319, 320, 321
high pressure, 146
high school, 125, 128, 129, 135, 136, 138, 150, 157, 158, 159, 160, 162, 164, 350, 359, 369
higher education, 18, 28, 30, 31, 38, 171, 225
high-risk, 17, 23, 24, 25, 26, 30, 32, 33, 35, 36, 42, 51
Hilgartner, 73, 359
Hirsch, 281, 353
HIV infection, 24, 25, 26, 29, 32, 33, 39, 41, 42, 90, 94, 235, 262, 350, 351, 358
HIV test, 38
HIV/AIDS, v, 7, 9, 11, 13, 14, 17, 18, 19, 69, 70, 71, 72, 73, 74, 75, 76, 77, 78, 79, 80, 82, 83, 84, 85, 87, 88, 90, 92, 94, 95, 97, 98, 99, 142, 222, 247, 260, 261, 262, 271, 277, 292, 294, 296, 349, 350, 351, 353, 354, 355, 359, 360, 365, 370, 371, 373, 374
HIV-1, 250
Hofstede, 193, 198, 199, 216, 359
holiday, 156, 160
holistic, 181, 200, 207, 217, 235, 240, 248, 261, 273, 327
holistic approach, 273
holon, 187, 191, 192, 201, 202, 203, 206, 217
holonic, 192, 200, 201, 202, 203, 216
homes, 145, 243, 290, 300, 307, 317
homogeneous, 196, 317
homogenous, 263, 266
homophily, 89, 93
homophobic, 76
homosexual, 79
Honduras, 14, 15, 16, 17, 53
honesty, 157
Hopkins, 96, 261, 356, 360, 361, 371
hospital, 151, 152, 206, 288
hospitals, 234, 268, 297, 374
host, 27, 139, 224, 236, 239, 303, 344
host population, 27
House, 310, 323
household, 16, 20, 65, 228, 298, 312, 313
households, 16, 20, 64, 106, 174, 298, 311, 313, 322, 328
housing, 190, 299, 304, 307, 308, 309, 310, 311, 312, 313, 314, 321, 322, 324, 327, 328, 329, 373
HPA, 139
hub, 14, 208
Hubbard, 278, 280, 360, 368
Hulme, 271, 360
human, 6, 10, 13, 70, 83, 84, 91, 118, 189, 192, 194, 195, 197, 200, 205, 210, 212, 221, 222, 223, 225, 231, 232, 233, 235, 236, 237, 238, 239, 240, 246, 249, 250, 253, 256, 269, 309, 311, 315, 320, 322, 336, 367
human condition, 194
human development, 189, 210
human rights, 83, 91, 221, 222, 223, 225, 231, 232, 233, 235, 236, 237, 238, 239, 240, 246, 249, 250, 253, 256
hunting, 141, 142
husband, 229, 252, 292, 293
hybrid, 55, 58, 88, 92
hybrids, 87
hygiene, 16, 131, 132, 140, 142, 143, 146, 150, 152, 153, 156, 166, 167, 181, 238, 248, 301, 325
hygienic, 143, 230, 235
hyper-endemic, 42
hypothesis, 56, 208

I

IAC, 222, 249
ice, 124, 198
id, 38, 66, 143, 153, 175, 288, 372
IDA, 309, 316, 317
identification, 59, 93, 105, 113, 255, 337
identity, 5, 190, 198, 199, 201, 203, 221, 225, 229, 254, 307, 309, 315, 317, 318, 319, 322, 324, 328, 329, 355
ideologies, 69, 70, 254
ideology, 70, 72, 75, 263, 265, 355
IE&C, ix, xi, 3, 5, 6, 9, 55, 69, 71, 73, 74, 77, 78, 79, 183, 185, 186, 187, 188, 189, 267, 269, 270, 309, 357, 366, 368

IEC, ix, 5, 7, 9, 10, 18, 21, 55, 56, 58, 59, 60, 61, 62, 64, 65, 66, 67, 68, 101, 102, 107, 108, 110, 285, 349, 353, 357, 361, 362, 377
Iganga District, 283, 298
illegal encroachment, 320
illiteracy, 5, 15
illiterate, 28, 105
illusion, 216
imagery, 264
images, 186, 241, 268, 278, 357
imitation, 141, 304
immigrants, 249
immunization, 6, 14, 56, 129, 294, 295, 296, 297
immunizations, 10, 11
immunize, 9
impact assessment, 63, 64, 300
implementation, vii, 3, 16, 24, 46, 57, 59, 61, 64, 65, 66, 67, 98, 101, 103, 113, 114, 116, 118, 119, 122, 125, 126, 127, 130, 131, 132, 133, 138, 143, 144, 146, 163, 165, 166, 174, 175, 176, 177, 178, 179, 188, 189, 212, 237, 246, 257, 280, 285, 289, 302, 303, 309, 311, 314, 329, 333, 334, 335, 336, 339, 341, 342, 361
importer, 56
impoverish, 202, 271
imprisonment, 246
in transition, 210
inactive, 46
incentive, 25, 231, 287
incentives, 242, 297, 302
incidence, 25, 29, 30, 43, 47, 64, 65, 102, 223, 242, 354
inclusion, 46, 63, 97, 178, 182
incoherent, 195
income, 12, 21, 119, 193, 240, 242, 247, 295, 299, 301, 302, 311, 312, 313, 314, 315, 317, 320, 322, 327
income distribution, 313
increased workload, 159
independence, 71, 237, 271, 295
India, v, vi, ix, 13, 14, 76, 99, 101, 102, 103, 104, 105, 106, 107, 110, 111, 207, 208, 209, 212, 213, 215, 216, 219, 223, 250, 307, 308, 309, 312, 324, 346, 349, 352, 353, 355, 357, 360, 364, 365, 367, 368, 370, 371, 373, 378
Indian, 10, 76, 104, 110, 189, 199, 207, 208, 211, 212, 213, 214, 307, 310, 314, 318, 319, 325, 357, 367, 369, 370
Indiana, 352
indication, 52, 171, 337
indicators, 6, 57, 89, 111, 172, 228, 253, 331, 336, 337, 339, 340
indigenous, 276, 277, 279, 314, 352

indirect effect, 137
individual character, 320
individual perception, 274
individual rights, 233
individualism, 194, 197
individualized instruction, 148, 149
Indonesia, 53, 223
industrial, 110, 210, 311
industrialized, 14, 221, 224
industrialized countries, 221, 224
industry, 12, 75, 211, 212, 312, 356
ineffectiveness, 185
inequality, 199
infancy, 260
infant mortality, 11, 13, 14, 15, 286, 299
infant mortality rate, 286, 299
infants, 15
infection, 17, 24, 25, 26, 27, 36, 41, 51, 69, 77, 79, 80, 85, 90, 234, 235, 262
infections, 14, 24, 25, 26, 32, 39, 79, 80, 84, 94, 234, 250, 292
infectious, 6, 11, 27, 56, 88, 102, 132, 139, 152
infectious disease, 6, 27, 56, 88, 102, 132, 139, 152
inferences, 82, 271
inferiority, 232
infibulation, 226, 252
Influenza, 88
informal sector, 211, 281
information age, 344, 351, 352
Information and Communication Technologies (ICT), vii, 7, 88, 92, 93, 94, 100, 208, 209, 213, 216, 344, 351, 372
information exchange, 163
information seeking, 89, 91, 97
information sharing, 87
information systems, 92
information technology, 97, 99, 208, 351
informed consent, 90
infrastructure, 4, 11, 58, 102, 104, 111, 194, 261, 264, 276, 287, 288, 294, 307, 311, 312, 314, 315, 316, 319, 320, 322, 325, 329, 337
infrastructure design, 307, 311
Inge, 255
initiation, 19, 49, 60, 121, 241
injectables, 286, 293, 301, 304
injection, 79
injuries, 145, 167, 172
injury, 123, 146, 153, 156, 172, 176, 233, 235, 243, 245
inmates, 110
innovation, 4, 55, 87, 88, 89, 90, 91, 92, 93, 94, 95, 97, 99, 116, 188, 192, 197, 207, 208, 209, 210, 211, 212, 213, 216, 314

innovations, 88, 89, 92, 95, 97, 100, 116, 208, 209, 215, 352, 357, 370
insecticide, 20, 21, 22
insects, 22
insecurity, 51
insight, 15, 156, 193, 195, 196, 199, 200, 210, 229, 266, 268, 310
inspection, 133
inspiration, 75, 118, 327
instability, 202
institutional, 23, 47, 48, 49, 72, 74, 93, 96, 124, 206, 208, 209, 211, 213, 214, 215, 287, 303, 316, 318
institutional change, 211
institutionalisation, 213
institutions, 12, 57, 58, 67, 71, 110, 118, 199, 207, 208, 213, 214, 215, 234, 242, 243, 248, 268, 315, 332, 337, 361
instruction, 15, 16, 117, 130, 157, 163, 356
instructors, 163, 273
instruments, 123, 232, 233, 234, 236, 242, 245, 253, 270, 345
intangible, 317
integration, 9, 12, 87, 90, 96, 98, 99, 169, 260, 262, 266, 319, 362, 363, 370
integrity, 231, 233, 234, 256
intellect, 57
intelligence, 82
intensity, 122, 126, 163
intentions, 64, 115
interaction, 92, 109, 110, 191, 192, 193, 194, 196, 200, 201, 202, 203, 204, 205, 206, 207, 208, 210, 212, 216, 217, 218, 219, 260, 269, 273, 315, 317, 319, 320, 321, 369
interactions, 71, 72, 75, 94, 191, 193, 197, 198, 200, 202, 205, 206, 207, 208, 209, 216, 217, 219, 264, 269
Inter-American Development Bank, 331
interdependence, 191, 192, 197, 203, 205, 207, 210, 219
interdisciplinary, 212
interface, 97, 154, 202, 203, 205, 206, 207, 212
intergenerational, 25
international, 10, 11, 13, 17, 18, 20, 52, 96, 116, 118, 119, 120, 128, 138, 143, 164, 173, 175, 179, 194, 222, 223, 228, 232, 238, 244, 245, 246, 247, 249, 250, 256, 257, 269, 288, 294, 331, 332, 337, 345, 369, 370, 373
International Bank for Reconstruction and Development, 331
International Covenant on Civil and Political Rights, 253
International Covenant on Economic, Social and Cultural Rights, 253

International Health, 253, 283, 285, 358, 378
international relations, 269
international standards, 250, 256
internet, x, 7, 77, 89, 92, 93, 94, 97, 98, 102, 107, 128, 133, 139, 152, 154, 160, 196, 202, 216, 271, 363, 370
interpersonal communication, 4, 55, 97, 103, 109, 290
interpersonal contact, 100
interpersonal relations, 141, 156
interpersonal relationships, 141, 156
interpretation, 25, 58, 72, 126, 196, 259, 260, 266, 334, 340, 341
interpretations, 74, 260, 266
intervention, 6, 18, 38, 41, 44, 46, 56, 60, 61, 62, 90, 123, 145, 188, 202, 239, 241, 297, 300, 332, 334, 335, 336, 337, 338, 339, 340, 342, 347, 353, 359, 360
interventions, ix, 7, 9, 18, 25, 43, 45, 46, 51, 56, 60, 78, 94, 101, 113, 118, 133, 136, 137, 138, 148, 158, 159, 163, 171, 174, 177, 178, 180, 181, 225, 235, 264, 266, 270, 284, 285, 294, 297, 360, 361, 375
interview, 97, 106, 124, 125, 199, 274, 275, 276, 278, 280, 287, 355, 375
interviews, 62, 82, 93, 100, 113, 124, 125, 126, 171, 172, 175, 177, 254, 255, 274, 275, 278, 340, 341, 355
intimidating, 230
intravenous, 15, 79
intuition, 195
inversion, 260
investigative, 367
investment, 20, 21, 58, 327
Iraq, 223
IRC, vi, 221
IRESCO, 19
Islam, 230, 239, 247
Islamic, 252
island, 164
ISO, 128
isolation, 49, 242, 250, 324, 328
Israel, 305

J

Jamaica, 45
Japan, 192, 257, 372
Japanese, 192, 200, 203, 205, 207, 332
Jemmott, 121, 122, 360
jobs, 10, 12, 133, 142
John F. Kennedy, 252
Jordan, 53, 223
journalism, 70, 71, 72, 73, 74, 75, 355, 368, 371

journalists, 71, 72, 73, 74, 75, 82, 355
JoyFM, 71, 81, 85
judge, vii, 24, 75, 336
judgment, 75, 147, 332
judicious, 88
Jukes, 33, 39, 41, 360
junior high school, 125, 127, 130, 131, 133, 134, 135, 136, 137, 138, 139, 140, 141, 142, 143, 144, 146, 148, 149, 150, 151, 152, 153, 154, 155, 157, 158, 159, 160, 161, 162, 163, 164, 165, 166

K

KAP, 64, 65
Kapiriri, 11, 361
Kassala, 226, 239
Kelly, 23, 39, 48, 366, 378
Kentucky, 161
Kenya, xi, 41, 47, 53, 55, 78, 90, 186, 224, 226, 227, 235, 236, 241, 242, 244, 246, 252, 253, 254, 256, 351, 355, 365, 377
Kenyan, 224, 242
Keynes, 362, 371
Keynesian, 195
Khamis, 274, 361
Kidugavu, 363
kinship network, 244
Kinsman, 45
Kipp, 361, 366
Kippzendorff, 82
Kiragu, 361
Kirby, 43, 44, 121, 122, 361, 367
Klausner, 90, 91, 361
Klepp, 43, 45, 361
knee-jerk, 189
knowledge gaps, 196, 274
knowledge transfer, 194, 210, 357
Kols, 92, 93, 362
Konkoma., 271
Kordofan, 239
Koshal, 281, 362
Kotler, 10, 362
Kotter, 118, 362
Kpando, 271, 272
Krueger, 274, 362
Kubisch, 282, 354
Kugblenu, 71, 362
Kurdish, 223
Kyosei, 192, 207, 369

L

Labadie, 6
labour, 133, 235, 240, 247
labour force, 247
lactational amenorrhea, 286
land, 156, 307, 311, 314, 315, 316, 317, 318, 319, 322, 350, 355
land use, 315, 316, 318, 319, 322
language, 94, 125, 195, 196, 205, 219, 259, 260, 264, 269
language barrier, 94
large-scale, 11, 12, 97
Lasswell, 260
Latin America, 15, 33, 354
Latin American countries, 33
Lavelle, 121, 375
law, 230, 243, 245, 246, 253, 254, 255, 256, 345, 359
law enforcement, 255
laws, 27, 132, 237, 245, 246, 249, 256, 257
lead, 6, 15, 56, 67, 70, 74, 77, 88, 101, 175, 179, 193, 197, 207, 222, 225, 229, 236, 239, 240, 243, 245, 263, 279, 280, 304, 345
leadership, xi, 118, 127, 130, 136, 171, 173, 269, 289, 290, 295
learners, 23, 122, 273, 281
learning, vii, xi, 4, 15, 50, 51, 66, 67, 89, 108, 115, 116, 118, 121, 127, 128, 133, 140, 141, 164, 169, 172, 176, 177, 178, 181, 185, 200, 204, 205, 208, 209, 212, 236, 238, 248, 267, 269, 272, 273, 276, 277, 278, 280, 281, 282, 285, 295, 297, 303, 332, 337, 344, 346, 350, 351, 352, 355, 357, 358, 362, 363, 370
learning activity, 67, 269, 280, 282
learning environment, 51, 116, 212, 273, 346
learning process, 67, 204
legality, 27
legislation, 12, 227, 232, 237, 244, 245, 246, 247, 248, 254, 256
legislative, 250
leisure, 33, 147, 151
leisure time, 33, 147, 151
Leonard, 198
leprosy, 106
Lesotho, 42, 43, 53, 256, 355
Lewis, 78, 362, 368, 370
LFA, 338, 339, 341
liberal, 4
liberation, 5
Liberia, 224
Libya, 230, 256
life expectancy, 57
life experiences, 270
life span, 270
life style, 267, 310
lifecycle, 325

lifestyle, 149, 308, 309, 310, 314, 315, 322
lifestyles, 78, 314
light industrial, 311
likelihood, 12, 27, 39, 117, 186, 345
limitations, 66, 77, 191, 196, 207, 214, 245, 262, 265, 314, 328
linear, 29, 191, 192, 193, 195, 196, 201, 202, 216, 259, 260, 265, 319
Linear, 192, 195, 201
linear model, 202, 259
linguistic, 222, 262
linkage, 318
links, 24, 47, 51, 52, 97, 120, 202, 209, 211, 224, 244, 272, 277, 278
liquids, 17
listening, 5, 21, 108, 120, 197, 241, 270
literacy, 4, 5, 16, 23, 24, 25, 40, 48, 51, 89, 106, 238, 272, 287, 299, 301, 351, 370
literacy rates, 4, 40
literate, 5, 6, 15, 16, 188, 284, 292, 296
literature, 11, 39, 41, 52, 75, 81, 84, 87, 100, 268, 270, 281, 345, 363
Litrosol, 16, 17
living environment, 143, 157, 310, 321
loans, 242
lobby, 302
lobbying, 261, 302
local authorities, 285, 302
local community, 57, 208, 240, 262, 299
local government, 153, 290, 301, 302, 340
location, 70, 71, 77, 93, 162, 288, 314, 317, 319, 320, 325, 326, 328, 351
logistics, 102, 107, 132
Logistics, 287
long period, 345
longitudinal studies, 44
longitudinal study, 41
long-term, 12, 32, 134, 161, 176, 209, 211, 234, 235, 253, 284, 301, 334, 335, 336, 342, 378
long-term impact, 335, 336
loopholes, 245
loss of appetite, 236
love, 78, 134, 149, 156, 158, 195
Low-Beer, 47, 48, 363
lower prices, 20
low-income, 39, 322
Luganda, 287
Lupton, 78, 363
lying, 60, 272, 287
Lynagh, 116, 123, 168, 363

M

Machiavellian, 195

machinery, 58
machines, 216
Mackie, 252, 253
Maclean, 260
Madison, 351
Maendeleo Ya Wanawake, 242
magazines, 76
magnitude, 74, 80
mahila, 106
mainstream, 202
mainstream society, 202
maintenance, 119, 325, 326, 328, 345
malaria, 11, 12, 13, 20, 21, 106, 294, 296, 297
Malawi, xi, 39, 47, 48, 49, 50, 53, 356, 364
Maler, 58
males, 124, 125
Mali, 80, 224, 226, 227, 230, 242, 245, 251, 253
Malikhao, 4, 56, 369
malnutrition, 157
management, xi, 3, 20, 38, 63, 87, 88, 92, 94, 95, 96, 98, 99, 100, 102, 104, 107, 118, 128, 131, 132, 133, 134, 141, 170, 174, 185, 199, 216, 238, 247, 261, 290, 331, 332, 333, 334, 336, 337, 338, 341, 362, 378
management committee, 238
mandal, 106
Mané, 255
Maninka, 229
manipulation, 270
man-made, 58
Mann, 76, 364
Manning, 74, 364
manufacturing, 178
Manyozo, 4, 364
mapping, 216
Marahkissa, 244
Margetts, 44
marital status, 31
market, ix, 4, 12, 13, 14, 16, 20, 21, 48, 193, 199, 274, 275, 277, 278, 314
market segment, 20
marketability, 315, 317
marketing, xi, 7, 9, 10, 11, 12, 13, 14, 15, 17, 18, 19, 20, 21, 22, 280, 297, 370
markets, 10, 11, 12, 20, 110
marriage, 5, 31, 189, 229, 230, 231, 233, 236, 244, 255, 267, 344
married women, 286
mass communication, 11, 75, 78, 374
mass media, 14, 23, 55, 63, 69, 70, 76, 77, 84, 101, 103, 107, 108, 259, 365, 374
Mass Media, 14, 15, 16
masturbation, 17

maternal, 234, 235, 271, 283, 286, 294, 296, 299
maternal care, 286
mathematical, 260
mathematics, 195, 370
mathematics education, 370
matrix, 338, 343
Maurana, 280, 364
Mauritania, 226, 227, 251
Mauritius, 256
Max-Neef, 195
Mbacke, 255
Mbonye, 364
Mboum, 225
McQuail, 4
meals, 152, 153, 169
meanings, 69, 70, 265, 266, 344
measles, 14
measles,, 14
measurement, 13, 52, 195, 332, 340, 355
measures, 47, 57, 77, 80, 83, 104, 105, 115, 123, 129, 139, 143, 145, 146, 149, 152, 153, 161, 232, 233, 236, 237, 244, 245, 246, 250, 256, 315, 375
mechanism, 195, 202, 209, 215, 276, 282
mechanistic, 195, 202, 260
media messages, 70, 77, 250
media texts, 81
median, 227
mediation, 201, 202
mediators, 194, 210, 216
medical, 41, 49, 104, 234, 253, 257, 285, 290, 299, 357
medical expertise, 297
medical student, 108, 285, 297, 298
medicine, 10, 15, 16, 88, 361
Mediterranean, 368
Mehendale, 250
Mehta, 308, 309, 327, 328, 329, 330, 364
Mellanby, 43, 364
member-checking, 187
membership, 221, 229
memory, 93
men, 14, 17, 18, 19, 24, 26, 28, 29, 31, 32, 33, 35, 36, 37, 38, 47, 59, 61, 64, 79, 80, 90, 91, 189, 199, 228, 232, 237, 238, 239, 241, 243, 247, 254, 255, 275, 279, 283, 286, 287, 289, 295, 296, 297, 304, 359
menstrual, 296
menstrual cycle, 296
mental health, 115, 154, 168, 172, 178
mental model, 16
mentoring, 202
messages, ix, 3, 5, 6, 10, 12, 16, 21, 24, 25, 47, 48, 51, 56, 63, 70, 75, 76, 77, 93, 101, 103, 107, 108, 109, 152, 188, 228, 240, 241, 245, 250, 259, 260, 261, 262, 265, 272, 284, 292, 293, 294, 296, 299, 301
meta-analysis, 23, 25, 33, 44, 45, 47
metaphor, 231
methodology, 15, 52, 103, 105, 124, 189, 259, 260, 262, 263, 264, 265, 266, 272, 273, 276
micro, 58, 66, 208, 209
middle class, 10, 80
Middle East, 221, 223, 244, 245, 257
middle income, 317
middle schools, 125
midwives, 98, 226, 240, 247, 248, 288, 296, 300
migrant, 221, 243, 254
migrants, 224
migration, 224, 240, 243, 255
MIHV KPC, 287
military, 18, 152, 269
milk, 149
millennium, 77, 79, 195, 249, 257
Millennium Development Goals, 249
minerals, 58
Ministry of Education, 50, 120, 122, 128, 173, 290, 370
Ministry of Health, 19, 80, 104, 120, 122, 243, 245, 248, 285, 290, 298, 349, 352, 353, 370
minority, 11, 165, 213
Minya, 240
misconceptions, 28, 78, 104, 274, 287
misunderstanding, 72, 78
mixing, 16, 17, 37, 85
mobile, 33, 92, 102, 107, 216
mobile phone, 102, 107
mobility, 89
mobilization, 15, 120, 133, 134, 135, 175, 236, 240, 246, 255, 290, 296
modality, 78
modelling, 25, 36, 121, 201, 205, 303
models, 15, 18, 26, 137, 150, 173, 179, 194, 199, 208, 209, 210, 211, 212, 260, 262, 311, 344, 349, 374
modernisation, 197, 281
modernity, 365
Modou, 255
module, 326
modules, 238
Moldova, 54
Molly, 255
momentum, 96, 115, 249, 250
money, 21, 156, 165, 341
Mongolia, 54
monitoring, 6, 52, 56, 59, 62, 64, 108, 109, 141, 143, 144, 153, 181, 211, 228, 254, 255, 290, 299, 300

monolithic, 85
monotonous, 198, 311
mood, 144, 158
moralist, 4
morality, 130, 132, 230
morbidity, 103, 234, 283, 286, 298
Moreau, 255
Morison, 253, 254
Morita, 197
morning, 152, 153, 165, 169
Morocco, 54, 230, 247
mortality, 6, 11, 13, 14, 15, 16, 52, 56, 57, 87, 89, 103, 234, 271, 283, 286, 298, 299
mortality rate, 16, 89, 103, 234, 286, 299
mosaic, 328
mosquito bites, 20
motherhood, 247, 248, 280
mothers, 10, 15, 16, 17, 157, 166, 171, 198, 225, 228, 229, 233, 246, 251, 255, 256, 284, 286, 294, 297, 300
motion, 239, 278
motivation, 6, 56, 82, 120, 121, 159, 160, 166, 199, 230, 270, 301, 340, 345
mouthpiece, 74
movement, 15, 170, 173, 211, 239, 246, 250, 269, 271, 310, 322
Mozambique, xi, 54
Mparadzi, 121, 375
Mufune, 280, 365
multicultural, 199
multimedia, 109, 127, 208, 209, 213
multiple factors, 280
multiplicity, 191, 194
multiplier, 211
multiplier effect, 211
multivariate, 26, 31
municipal, 127, 138, 149, 171, 173, 177
Mushtaque, 185, 370
music, 82, 134, 197, 203, 269, 271
Muslim, 230, 252, 283, 298
mutuality, 191, 192, 205, 207
Muturi, 77, 78, 365
Mwangaza, 239
Mwesigye, 361
Myanmar, 98
Myhre, 70, 365
myriad, 67

N

Nahid, 254, 256, 257
Namibia, xi, 45, 46, 54, 256
Namibian, 46
Nandy, 77, 365

Narayan, 282, 365
narratives, 73, 76, 277
Narva´ez, 270
nation, 111, 118, 162, 195
national, ix, 3, 5, 6, 7, 10, 17, 18, 19, 71, 78, 89, 98, 105, 108, 110, 115, 116, 118, 119, 120, 122, 123, 138, 142, 172, 173, 175, 180, 186, 193, 195, 199, 206, 207, 208, 222, 223, 224, 225, 227, 228, 236, 237, 239, 240, 244, 245, 246, 248, 249, 257, 264, 268, 272, 298, 299, 302, 303, 334, 336, 338, 345, 366, 373
national economies, 186, 195
National Institutes of Health, 90, 365
National Service, 104, 105
natural, 13, 58, 152, 195, 278, 284, 292, 293, 295, 296, 322
natural resources, 58, 195
need-based, 108
needles, 79
negative attitudes, 296
negotiating, 189
negotiation, 121, 142, 214, 254
Negrotti, 204, 365
neighbourhood, 149, 162, 310, 319, 321
neighbourhoods, 317
neo-liberal, 195
Nepal, 54
NetMark, 20, 21
network, 14, 23, 48, 93, 95, 96, 97, 110, 191, 200, 201, 202, 207, 208, 209, 211, 212, 214, 215, 216, 234, 249, 272, 307, 311, 315, 317, 318, 319, 320, 321, 322, 325, 326
network members, 97
networking, 191, 192, 193, 196, 200, 207, 209, 210, 211, 212, 213, 215, 216, 219
networks, 4, 76, 89, 92, 93, 209, 210, 211, 244, 248, 308, 324
new media, 196, 216, 374
Newcomb, 260
news coverage, 75, 371
newsletters, 14
newspapers, ix, 47, 49, 73, 75, 76, 77, 82, 106, 128, 129, 139, 150, 174
newsroom, 75
Newton, 113, 195, 377
next generation, 146, 342
NGO, 98, 99, 237, 238, 239, 243, 246, 248, 249, 285, 331, 337, 338, 340
NGOs, 18, 83, 108, 110, 240, 246, 247, 248, 249, 257, 303, 365, 373
Nicaragua, 54
Niger, 54, 80, 224, 226, 227, 244, 251

Nigeria, 20, 45, 47, 54, 80, 98, 99, 224, 225, 227, 230, 235, 256, 335, 356, 366
Nigeria, 224, 225, 227, 230, 235, 256, 366
Nigerian, 224
nightmares, 236
NIH, 33, 104
nodes, 201, 202, 203
noise, 204, 260
Nomadic, 287
nongovernmental, 240, 269, 288, 290
nongovernmental organisations, 240, 269
non-profit, 12, 15
non-random, 45
Noo, 43
normal, 125, 143, 153, 167, 236
norms, 75, 118, 122, 170, 175, 191, 196, 214, 275, 276, 277, 281, 310, 315, 317
Norplant, 301
North Africa, 230, 252
North America, 224
Norway, 224, 248, 290
Noureddine, 250, 251
Ntozi, 366
Ntusi, 285, 303
nuclear, 280, 357
nuclear family, 280
nuclear power, 357
nurse, 164, 288, 364
nurses, 98, 169, 226, 296, 297
nursing, 110, 283, 297, 364, 374
nutrition, 115, 116, 129, 130, 131, 132, 135, 136, 139, 140, 142, 148, 150, 151, 154, 160, 163, 166, 167, 169, 172, 178, 294, 295, 296, 297, 299, 374, 375
nutrition education, 131, 137, 139, 148, 163

O

obedience, 133, 134
Obeng-Quaidoo, 4, 6, 55, 366
Obermeyer, 253
obese, 154
obesity, 10, 129, 155
objectivity, 266
obligation, 199, 229, 237
obligations, 236, 237, 254, 369
observational, 23, 44, 45, 46
observations, 125, 129, 175, 186, 187, 203, 206
occupational, 75
OCHA, 80, 366
OECD, 331, 333, 334, 366
Oman, 223
omnibus, 188
online, 139, 247

on-line, 89, 93, 94, 96, 97, 98, 100
open space, 315, 317, 318, 319, 320, 322, 323, 328
open spaces, 315, 317, 318, 319, 320, 322, 323, 328
openness, 294
operating system, 132
operator, 234
opposition, 192, 228, 289
optimism, 227, 342, 347
oral, 6, 15, 16, 17, 56, 83, 140
oral hygiene, 140
oral rehydration, 6, 56
ORC, 250, 251, 357
organic, 213, 262
organization, 17, 97, 99, 106, 124, 126, 131, 284, 285, 302, 321, 373
organizational culture, 199
organizations, 12, 13, 15, 49, 93, 94, 96, 97, 101, 102, 106, 116, 118, 199, 236, 248, 283, 302
Oriental, 198
orientation, 82, 110, 175, 178, 181, 197, 321, 322
ORS, 17
ORT, 15, 16
orthodox, 270
Ottawa, 115, 168, 178, 179, 375
outreach programs, 18
oversight, 6
overweight, 130
ownership, 119, 122, 186, 213, 280, 340
Owusu-Sarpong, 275, 366

P

packets, 15
Paget, 268, 366
pain, 234, 235, 236, 243
Paisley, 11, 367
Pakistan, 98
pamphlet, 22
pandemic, 23, 24, 47, 69, 74, 79, 85, 271
panic attack, 236
Pappoe, 6
Papua New Guinea, ix, 187, 354, 355
paradigm shift, 102, 107
paradigms, 6
paradox, 64, 229
parental support, 279
parenthood, 280
parents, 23, 61, 113, 115, 122, 124, 125, 126, 127, 128, 129, 130, 131, 133, 134, 135, 136, 137, 140, 142, 143, 144, 145, 146, 149, 151, 152, 153, 154, 155, 157, 158, 159, 160, 161, 162, 163, 166, 167, 170, 171, 172, 173, 174, 175, 177, 179, 180, 181, 221, 223, 229, 233, 235, 243, 246, 248, 279, 280, 304

Parker, 25, 26, 259, 366, 378
Parliament, 298
participatory, 4, 56, 57, 60, 63, 66, 67, 121, 140, 141, 172, 176, 177, 178, 181, 185, 188, 193, 209, 238, 240, 259, 260, 263, 270, 272, 273, 276, 283, 289, 311, 353, 360, 365, 367, 371, 373, 374
participatory research, 263
partnership, 12, 20, 32, 101, 102, 179, 240, 247, 334, 370
partnerships, 12, 32, 115, 116, 214, 216, 240, 283, 303
passive, 4, 56, 141, 161, 241
pastoral, 202
pastoralists, 287
paternity, 280
pathology, 139
patient management, 102, 107
patients, 7, 18, 101, 102, 103, 105, 107, 108, 109, 110, 284
PCM, 331, 333
PCP, 79
PE, 152
peacekeeping, 269, 369
Pearce, 58
pedagogy, 370
pedestrian, 317, 319, 322
pedestrians, 319, 320
peer, 18, 19, 44, 45, 121, 122, 234, 240, 252, 263, 264, 345, 355, 365
peer group, 264, 365
peer influence, 345
peers, 34, 48, 121, 122, 229
penalties, 170, 245
Pennsylvania, 252
people living with HIV/AIDS, 70
Per diems, 285, 302
perception, 74, 75, 128, 129, 174, 206, 228, 230, 233, 246, 247, 277, 280, 346
perceptions, 6, 59, 69, 76, 108, 123, 171, 177, 180, 197, 233, 262, 265, 274, 276, 341
performance, 7, 106, 108, 151, 196, 236, 269, 276, 278, 280, 284, 296, 311, 326, 332, 333, 334, 335, 336, 337, 338, 340, 341
performance indicator, 334
performers, 276, 278
perinatal, 235
periodic, 64, 105, 185, 286, 293, 296, 302
peripheral, 110
permeation, 193, 195
permit, 224
personal, 5, 6, 7, 23, 48, 49, 51, 92, 115, 121, 129, 137, 142, 144, 152, 153, 160, 167, 181, 197, 205, 206, 214, 215, 218, 236, 238, 245, 345, 378

personal achievements, 115
personal communication, 6
personal hygiene, 142, 152, 167
personality, 73, 279
Peru, 45, 46
Pettifor, 44, 49, 51, 366
pharmaceutical, 91
Pharos, 243, 256
phenomenology, 187
phenomenon, 70, 83, 84, 193, 222, 225, 279, 353
Philippines, 13, 45, 54, 56, 354
philosophical, 81, 351
philosophy, 194
phone, 102
photographs, 96
physical activity, 137, 142, 152, 167, 172
physical education, 115, 149, 151, 159
physical environment, 146, 169
physical exercise, 147, 149, 152, 156, 167, 169
physical health, 129, 130, 145, 152, 167, 181
physical well-being, 280
physical world, 195
physicians, 297
physiological, 192
physiotherapy, 261
pilot programs, 99, 100
pilot study, 371
planned action, 131
planning decisions, 292
plants, 156
platforms, 322, 323, 324
play, 7, 14, 20, 25, 66, 77, 78, 84, 90, 92, 101, 105, 116, 134, 198, 200, 203, 208, 216, 225, 229, 243, 244, 246, 268, 269, 272, 278, 315, 317, 322, 326, 332, 369
PLHIV, 38
pluralistic, 193, 200, 219
plurality, 193
PMTCT, 30, 97, 98
poetry, 238, 268, 269
police, 17, 136
policy, 70, 89, 98, 99, 100, 115, 117, 118, 132, 133, 150, 153, 155, 165, 168, 170, 171, 174, 175, 178, 182, 188, 189, 210, 215, 223, 246, 247, 248, 250, 252, 256, 270, 273, 282, 309, 349, 359, 367, 369, 373
policy levels, 99
policy makers, 89, 100, 215, 346
policy reform, 248, 334
policymakers, 73, 103, 116
policymaking, 98
polio, 88, 292, 364

political, 3, 10, 11, 17, 24, 29, 75, 78, 91, 130, 134, 170, 171, 172, 193, 195, 229, 246, 257, 259, 265, 271, 272, 289, 295, 333, 338, 360
political instability, 11
political leaders, 171, 289
politicians, 338
politics, 73, 272, 346
polygamous, 27, 298, 304
polygamous marriages, 27
poor, 4, 10, 12, 20, 21, 22, 50, 101, 106, 129, 134, 152, 156, 165, 186, 189, 194, 195, 236, 271, 279, 285, 287, 299, 307, 308, 310, 311, 314, 315, 324, 325, 327, 328, 329, 346
popular theatre, 269
population growth, 11, 13
population size, 340
porous, 27
Portugal, 75
positive attitudes, ix, 166
positive correlation, 38, 40, 42, 51
postal system, 4
posters, 101, 103, 105, 106, 107, 110, 135, 293, 301
Postgraduate, 213
Postlethwaite, 10, 374
postpartum, 98, 235, 253, 257, 284, 294, 296, 297, 298
postpartum period, 253
post-traumatic, 236
post-traumatic stress, 236
Potts, 24, 25, 26, 32, 33, 38, 367
poverty, 7, 156, 195, 247, 271, 272, 277, 278, 279, 280, 298, 307, 308, 337, 350, 351, 354, 360
poverty eradication, 247
poverty reduction, 7, 272, 351
power, 4, 5, 11, 25, 57, 74, 77, 78, 81, 91, 94, 136, 161, 188, 195, 196, 199, 240, 252, 254, 260, 261, 264, 265, 268, 273, 294, 345, 351
power relations, 260, 261
powerful, 73, 74, 76, 78, 196, 221, 229
powers, 304
practice, 3, 6, 60, 63, 64, 67, 68, 93, 98, 99, 114, 117, 118, 121, 122, 125, 137, 142, 144, 154, 155, 157, 175, 182, 185, 186, 187, 188, 189, 197, 205, 221, 222, 223, 224, 225, 226, 227, 228, 229, 230, 231, 232, 233, 234, 235, 236, 237, 238, 239, 240, 241, 242, 243, 244, 245, 246, 247, 248, 249, 250, 255, 256, 257, 261, 264, 267, 272, 279, 309, 325, 352, 353, 355, 356, 359, 364, 370, 372, 373, 374
Pradesh, 311, 312, 328, 355, 360, 371
pragmatic, 338, 340
prediction, 279
predictors, 100, 103
pre-existing, 73

preference, 63, 317, 322
pregnancy, 65, 79, 94, 235, 253, 257, 263, 278, 304
pregnant, 21, 30, 98, 284, 286, 293, 350
pregnant women, 21, 30, 284, 293, 350
prejudices, 232, 237
premarital, 30, 32
premature death, 172
preparation, iv, 16, 125, 236, 345, 365
preparedness, 122
prepuce, 251
pressure, 78, 89, 121, 129, 146, 159, 161, 171, 176, 221, 229, 230, 231, 232, 234, 252
pressure groups, 78
prestige, 276, 295
prevalence, 18, 24, 25, 28, 31, 36, 38, 39, 40, 41, 42, 43, 44, 47, 48, 51, 73, 76, 79, 80, 105, 223, 224, 225, 227, 228, 235, 240, 243, 251, 255, 260, 261, 284, 302, 350
prevention, ix, 14, 17, 18, 19, 23, 24, 25, 26, 30, 36, 38, 39, 45, 46, 52, 70, 71, 76, 77, 83, 84, 90, 91, 94, 120, 121, 122, 123, 130, 136, 151, 153, 169, 172, 176, 247, 249, 256, 263, 264, 280, 292, 293, 296, 350, 352, 356, 359, 360, 361, 363, 365, 366, 367, 373, □374, 375
preventive, 46, 83, 246
PRI, 110
prices, 10, 17, 313, 315, 327
primary care, 151
primary data, 81
primary school, 45, 50, 139, 140, 361
principal, 48, 118, 124, 128, 129, 130, 131, 133, 136, 138, 141, 143, 144, 145, 147, 151, 153, 154, 156, 157, 161, 164, 171, 173, 177, 222, 254, 283, 311
priorities, 10, 118, 193, 290, 302, 336
prism, 217
prisons, 268
privacy, 311, 314, 322, 325
private, 11, 12, 14, 17, 20, 21, 71, 96, 186, 242, 283, 287, 288, 297, 310, 312, 322, 323, 324, 325
private sector, 11, 12, 21, 283, 287, 288, 297
proactive, 208
probability, 121
problem solving, 121, 145
problem-solving, 238
procedure, 82, 221, 222, 223, 224, 226, 229, 230, 233, 234, 235, 236, 243, 245, 246, 252
procedures, 123, 234, 235, 270, 371
producers, 263
production, 18, 58, 59, 71, 73, 74, 108, 212, 260, 264, 276, 277, 278, 279, 281, 290, 352
productivity, 280, 335
profession, 19, 75, 297

professional, 10, 19, 72, 74, 77, 87, 89, 92, 97, 98, 122, 159, 163, 164, 177, 178, 180, 181, 186, 206, 209, 215, 247, 261, 262, 263, 327, 365
professional development, 122, 159, 163, 177, 178, 180, 181, 215
professionalism, 269, 342
professions, 199, 200, 247
profit, 200
profits, 58, 91
program, 6, 9, 11, 13, 14, 15, 16, 17, 18, 19, 33, 45, 46, 89, 94, 95, 96, 97, 98, 99, 100, 113, 114, 117, 118, 119, 121, 122, 125, 127, 128, 129, 134, 136, 138, 158, 165, 177, 178, 180, 182, 280, 289, 296, 303, 344, 349, 350, 354, 363, 368, 369
program outcomes, 114
programming, 19, 66, 67, 96, 199, 212, 285
progress reports, 64
progressive, 67, 188, 309
proliferation, 48, 51
promiscuous, 287, 304
promote, ix, 12, 14, 17, 72, 77, 96, 102, 107, 113, 114, 123, 129, 134, 137, 163, 190, 195, 223, 230, 233, 236, 237, 238, 239, 247, 248, 250, 254, 255, 256, 282, 297, 320, 350
pronouncement, 74
propaganda, 104, 105, 135, 155
property, iv, 153
prosperity, 171
prostitution, 17, 77, 278, 360
protection, 14, 24, 39, 42, 140, 155, 157, 229, 233, 237, 246, 254, 363
protective factors, 118
protocol, 124, 125
protocols, 119, 234, 345
prototype, 248
proverbs, 274, 277
proxy, 42
PSI, 13, 19
psychiatrist, 203
psychological, 36, 129, 130, 131, 137, 138, 140, 142, 143, 145, 146, 148, 149, 150, 151, 152, 154, 157, 160, 163, 164, 166, 167, 169, 170, 172, 176, 178, 222, 229, 233, 235, 236, 279
psychological development, 178
psychological health, 129, 131, 137, 138, 140, 142, 143, 145, 146, 148, 150, 154, 166
psychological problems, 151, 163, 164
psychological stress, 146
psychological well-being, 130
psychologist, 138, 160
psychology, 353
psychosocial, 120, 236
psycho-social, 146, 156, 157, 169, 181, 182

psychosomatic, 236
puberty, 50, 130, 154
public, x, 7, 9, 10, 12, 20, 21, 69, 70, 71, 73, 75, 77, 84, 87, 88, 89, 90, 91, 92, 93, 94, 97, 98, 100, 102, 107, 108, 109, 115, 122, 127, 135, 136, 137, 150, 172, 186, 193, 206, 218, 227, 228, 229, 231, 232, 235, 237, 238, 239, 241, 242, 244, 245, 246, 247, 249, 250, 260, 280, 283, 285, 288, 297, 302, 308, 310, 311, 312, 313, 314, 315, 317, 319, 321, 322, 323, 324, 338, 344, 357, 359, 362, 367, 370
public affairs, 70
public awareness, 77, 98, 235, 245, 247
public domain, x, 310
public education, 84
public finance, 338
public health, 9, 12, 20, 21, 70, 77, 87, 88, 90, 91, 92, 93, 94, 97, 100, 102, 107, 115, 127, 172, 206, 237, 280, 285, 297, 344, 362, 370
public housing, 311
public opinion, 237, 249, 357
public policy, 115
public sector, 12, 13, 20, 283, 285, 302, 308, 314
public service, 109, 186
public spaces, 310, 315, 319, 321, 322, 324
pulmonary, 104, 105
pulse, 253
punishment, 134
punitive, 244
pupils, 115, 116
Puplampu, 69, 83, 367, 377

Q

qualitative, 81, 123, 124, 126, 143, 173, 193, 194, 259, 260, 264, 266, 273, 278, 310, 311, 322, 370, 371
qualitative research, 264, 370, 371
quality control, 143
quality of life, 94, 162, 334, 344
quantitative, 26, 44, 81, 123, 193, 194, 228, 278
quantitative research, 26, 81
quantum, 84
Quena, 240
questioning, 5, 239
questionnaires, 59, 123, 125, 134, 144, 146, 155, 340, 341

R

R&D, 209, 215
radial graph, 38
radiation, 321
radical, 260

radio, 4, 5, 6, 7, 10, 15, 16, 17, 19, 23, 48, 69, 71, 72, 76, 77, 78, 82, 85, 101, 106, 109, 149, 152, 248, 265, 270, 272, 282
radio station, 71, 82, 149, 152
Rahman,, 256, 257
range, vii, ix, 13, 25, 78, 87, 97, 163, 177, 188, 222, 224, 228, 235, 236, 237, 245, 246, 253, 260, 262, 266, 268, 272, 283, 309, 311, 315, 316, 317, 320, 322, 341, 345
rape, 83, 262
rationality, 202, 206, 207
raw material, 144
raw materials, 144
RDA, 349
reading, 5, 6, 10, 142, 165, 269
real time, 108
realism, 186
reality, 5, 18, 27, 70, 72, 122, 132, 191, 192, 195, 197, 198, 200, 203, 204, 205, 206, 207, 217, 218, 234, 250, 263, 270, 303, 354, 357
reasoning, 168, 188, 273
recall, 196, 374
recitals, 231, 268, 272
recognition, 26, 61, 67, 185, 209, 215, 223, 229, 234, 254, 270, 324, 345
reconciliation, 195
recovery, 16
recreation, 115
recreational, 314, 315, 316
recreational areas, 316
recruiting, 10
redistribution, 57
redistricting, 290
reduction, 6, 14, 18, 47, 90, 91, 225, 242, 272, 316, 317, 368
reductionism, 195
reductionist, 192, 195, 202
reflection, 186, 187, 213, 231, 238, 241, 262, 263, 272
reflexivity, 187
reforms, 171, 172
refrigeration, 11
refugees, 224, 243
regional, 7, 59, 122, 194, 208, 209, 212, 213, 246, 247, 249, 304, 350
regular, 5, 20, 101, 108, 130, 131, 132, 143, 148, 151, 157, 169, 176, 177, 236, 334
regulation, 118
regulations, 130, 131, 132, 133, 135, 152, 161, 168, 173, 175, 181, 206, 315, 324
rehabilitation, 255, 284
rehearsing, 274
rehydration, 14, 15, 16, 17

reinforcement, 345
rejection, 229, 244
relationship, 9, 26, 28, 29, 33, 39, 42, 43, 56, 64, 66, 74, 76, 78, 83, 135, 136, 146, 147, 151, 157, 158, 181, 187, 192, 194, 199, 204, 205, 209, 210, 225, 235, 270, 279, 292, 295
relationships, 33, 55, 57, 58, 157, 158, 159, 162, 169, 181, 191, 192, 196, 200, 202, 205, 296, 337
relatives, 106, 233, 238, 244, 280
relevance, 121, 178, 180, 186, 233, 239, 259, 262, 265, 278, 333, 355, 366
reliability, 51, 278, 340
religions, 13, 223, 224, 230
religious, 91, 99, 106, 230, 235, 240, 246, 247, 248, 250, 254, 255, 268, 289, 320
Religious belief, 294
rent, 323
replication, 303
reporters, 73, 75
reproductive, 11, 13, 61, 64, 78, 90, 94, 99, 100, 186, 233, 239, 242, 253, 262, 264, 271, 277, 283, 284, 287, 293, 299, 300, 301, 303
reproductive age, 13, 61, 189, 283, 284, 287, 293
reproductive health, 13, 94, 262
reputation, 128, 150
researchers, 52, 81, 90, 91, 100, 187, 208, 209, 211, 213, 215, 234, 261, 268, 273, 274, 275, 276, 278, 279, 295, 344
reserves, 272
reservoir, 210
residential, 155, 312, 314, 315, 316, 318
residential plots, 315
resilience, 121
resistance, 55, 57, 90, 227
resolution, 250, 256, 265
resources, 9, 14, 58, 65, 96, 97, 98, 99, 107, 118, 119, 127, 163, 165, 168, 170, 176, 179, 186, 189, 190, 195, 204, 207, 210, 216, 261, 265, 266, 267, 271, 280, 284, 291, 292, 295, 302, 309, 311, 312, 313, 314, 336
respiration, 253
respiratory, 14
respiratory infections, 14
respondents, 59, 60, 62, 63, 64, 65, 66, 98, 126, 226, 264, 275, 277, 278, 295
responsibilities, 118, 127, 131, 153, 176, 237, 238, 294, 297, 333
restaurant, 363
retention, 24, 48, 49, 234, 374
retired, 378
revenue, 288, 315
revolutionary, 264
rewards, 170, 229

rhetoric, 7, 276, 367
rhymes, 268
rhythm, 296
rice, 56, 152, 314
right to life, 233, 234
rigidity, 214
Rio de Janeiro, 13
Risbud, 250
risk, 7, 9, 14, 17, 18, 20, 23, 24, 25, 26, 27, 28, 29, 30, 32, 33, 35, 36, 38, 39, 41, 42, 48, 51, 69, 70, 76, 77, 78, 89, 90, 91, 93, 94, 109, 118, 121, 122, 123, 153, 172, 174, 214, 223, 224, 228, 234, 235, 240, 244, 245, 248, 250, 255, 277, 286, 351, 354, 360, 365, 374
risk factors, 25, 26, 27, 28, 39, 76, 172
risk perception, 109
risks, 41, 90, 121, 122, 172, 174, 227, 231, 233, 235, 242, 245, 248
Roads, 316, 322
Rogers, 6, 56, 70, 87, 88, 92, 116, 118, 272, 368, 370, 373, 374
Roggers, 4
role-playing, 370
Roman, 200
Rosen, 3, 4, 368
Ross, 122, 305, 361, 368
rote learning, 172
rudimentary, 65, 222
Runyankole, 287
rupees, 313, 327
rural areas, vii, 14, 15, 20, 31, 99, 172, 208, 225, 272, 283, 286
rural communities, 6, 61, 64, 77, 101, 197, 268, 271, 273, 276, 278, 279, 280, 281, 282, 286
rural community, 104, 106, 107, 282
rural development, 209, 213, 272
rural people, 4, 277
rural population, 13, 15, 64
rural poverty, 350
rural women, 22, 286
Rwanda, 54, 256

S

safeguard, 58, 239, 250
safety, 10, 131, 136, 140, 142, 144, 149, 153, 156, 166, 167, 176, 181, 287
Said, 197
Saleh, 43, 368, 374
sales, 12, 13, 14, 19, 20
salts, 15, 16, 17
sample, 16, 82, 83, 99, 124, 284, 338, 340, 343
sampling, 82, 275
sanctions, 244

sanitation, 11, 116, 140, 146, 299, 315, 325
Sanyal, 269, 369
SAP, 58
SARS, 88, 140, 178
sartorial, 326
satisfaction, 126, 129, 141, 144, 166, 171
Satofuka, 192
saving lives, 189
savings, 325
sayings, 274, 277
scaling, 91, 124, 179, 240
scarce resources, 189, 309, 312, 346
scattergram, 45, 46
Scattergram, 45
scholarship, 268
Schon, 282, 369
school activities, 133
school authority, 148
school community, 48
school work, 132
schooling, 34, 133, 225, 238, 358
schools, 61, 81, 113, 114, 115, 116, 117, 118, 119, 122, 123, 124, 125, 126, 128, 129, 130, 131, 133, 134, 135, 136, 138, 139, 142, 143, 145, 147, 148, 150, 151, 152, 153, 154, 155, 156, 157, 158, 159, 160, 161, 162, 163, 164, 165, 166, 167, 168, 169, 170, 171, 172, 173, 174, 175, 176, 177, 178, 179, 181, 182, 199, 236, 268, 317, 351, 363, 371, 373, 375
Schudson, 70, 75, 369
science, 59, 194, 195, 210, 234, 248, 267, 268, 356, 363, 370, 371, 374
science education, 50, 356, 363, 371
scientific, 69, 82, 87, 89, 91, 96, 97, 100, 116, 129, 140, 143, 207, 210, 235, 273, 369
scientific community, 91
scientific knowledge, 210
scientists, 75
scores, 147, 176
scourge, 69, 85
scripts, 265
scurvy, 88
search, 93, 97
search engine, 97
searches, 96, 97, 311
searching, 128, 346
seat belt, 10
seat belt use, 10
secondary, 28, 30, 31, 39, 41, 46, 48, 50, 81, 108, 121, 122, 173, 225, 275, 278, 356, 368, 374
secondary data, 81
secondary education, 30, 31, 39, 41, 173, 225
secondary school students, 46, 48, 356

secondary schooling, 225
secondary schools, 46, 50, 368
Secretary General, 257
security, 135, 136, 146, 153, 167, 198, 309
security of tenure, 309
seed, 327
seedlings, 58
segmentation, 57, 60, 61, 62, 375
segregation, 314
selecting, 44, 188, 277
self employment, 106
self-confidence, 146, 157
self-control, 146, 166, 198
self-efficacy, 121
self-empowerment, 254
self-help, 311, 312
self-report, 52
self-study, 139
semantics, 280
semester, 131, 132, 142, 153, 158, 160
semiotics, 261, 263, 265
semi-structured interviews, 82
Sen, 193
Senegal, 20, 54, 80, 116, 223, 224, 235, 238, 239, 241, 244, 247, 248, 255, 256, 257, 372
senior citizens, 156
sensitivity, 48, 278, 340
sensitization, 108, 290
sensitizing, 14, 102
separation, 206, 214, 304, 333
septicaemia, 234
series, 15, 17, 63, 70, 123, 133, 134, 150, 243, 263, 264, 265, 321
Servaes, 4, 6, 56, 364, 369
service provider, 98, 109, 293
services, iv, vii, 10, 11, 12, 13, 18, 21, 22, 78, 87, 90, 91, 94, 96, 98, 100, 101, 102, 105, 106, 107, 109, 115, 116, 117, 120, 151, 168, 169, 186, 207, 242, 255, 257, 261, 262, 283, 284, 286, 287, 288, 289, 292, 296, 299, 301, 302, 303, 307, 309, 311, 313, 314, 315, 324, 325, 329, 334, 338
settlements, 307, 309, 310, 312, 314, 323
sewage, 316, 325, 326
sex, 17, 18, 19, 24, 25, 30, 31, 32, 33, 34, 35, 36, 37, 41, 43, 45, 46, 50, 76, 77, 80, 83, 84, 160, 161, 263, 278, 304, 352, 359, 360, 361, 362, 364
sexism, 265
sexual, 90, 96, 254, 298, 360, 369, 372
sexual abuse, 262
sexual activities, 76
sexual activity, 29, 31, 46, 65, 286, 304
sexual behavior, 351

sexual behaviour, 19, 23, 33, 44, 48, 49, 50, 264, 350, 360, 366, 374
sexual health, 98, 233, 262
sexual intercourse, 44
sexual promiscuity, 276, 277
sexuality, 278, 295, 362
sexually transmitted disease (STD), 18, 19, 33, 45, 50, 64, 262, 263, 365
sexually transmitted infections (STIs), 36, 38, 46, 250, 292, 365
shame, 222, 229, 239, 249
shape, xi, 7, 75, 194, 196, 204, 250, 270, 276
shaping, 7, 104, 270
sharing, vii, 79, 87, 92, 93, 94, 96, 97, 149, 175, 191, 200, 210, 214, 238, 270, 272, 303, 323
Sharma, 189, 307, 313
Shaw, 188, 269, 275, 369
Shell, 250, 252, 256
Shell-Duncan, 250, 252, 256
Sheperd, 250
shock, 15, 77, 231, 234, 353
shocks, 271
Shoepf, 263
short period, 161
shortage, 312, 313
short-term, 270, 284, 378
shuttles, 153
shy, 309
sick child, 15
Sierra Leone, xi, 54, 224
sign, 134, 150, 260
signs, 106, 260, 265, 297
Silverman, 83, 273, 369
similarity, 89
simplex virus, 235
Singhal, 6, 70, 370, 373
singular, 265
sites, 15, 46, 307
skills, 5, 15, 19, 23, 24, 48, 49, 50, 51, 66, 67, 99, 103, 109, 115, 116, 118, 119, 120, 121, 122, 128, 133, 135, 138, 141, 142, 145, 150, 163, 164, 170, 173, 175, 178, 237, 238, 242, 246, 254, 264, 269, 282, 289, 296, 297, 299, 311, 332, 364, 367, 375
skin, 10, 235
skin cancer, 10
slums, 307, 312
SMART, 64
smear, 102, 105
Smith, 9, 10, 124, 208, 211, 272, 355, 369, 370, 377
smoke, 121, 130, 140, 150, 157, 162, 167
smokers, 130, 178

Index

smoking, 10, 130, 132, 134, 137, 139, 140, 142, 155, 157, 161, 166, 167, 171, 172, 173, 178, 261, 280, 356, 363
smoking cessation, 172
social activities, 147, 272
social attitudes, 246
social change, xi, 7, 10, 11, 185, 186, 187, 188, 189, 238, 246, 254, 263, 268, 284, 295, 344, 345, 350, 362, 370
social cohesion, 202
social construct, 70, 186, 357, 367
social construction, 70, 357, 367
social constructivism, 186
social context, 189, 268, 271, 345, 374
social development, 57, 138, 350
social environment, 92, 157, 240, 246
social events, 273
social exclusion, 7, 229, 271
social factors, 6
social group, 275
social influence, 121
social isolation, 229
social justice, 7
social learning, 272
social learning theory, 272
social life, 236
social marketing, xi, 9, 10, 11, 12, 13, 14, 15, 17, 18, 19, 21, 280
social network, 23, 47, 49, 93, 96, 272
social norms, 12, 23, 26, 121
social problems, 13, 274, 279, 359
social roles, 199
social sciences, 192
social services, 11, 12, 316
Social Services, 240
social skills, 24, 133, 138, 141, 142
social status, 221, 222, 254
social support, 115, 244, 245, 246
social systems, 11, 91, 347
social values, 193, 242
social work, 106, 155, 280
social workers, 280
socialist, 171
socially, 122, 199, 236, 328
society, 5, 7, 9, 11, 13, 56, 58, 61, 69, 70, 74, 75, 122, 127, 128, 130, 135, 146, 156, 159, 160, 162, 165, 178, 186, 189, 191, 193, 194, 196, 197, 202, 210, 212, 219, 222, 229, 232, 238, 247, 265, 270, 273, 279, 289, 304, 313, 345
socioeconomic, 111
sociological, 71, 72, 76, 355
sociologists, 72
sociology, 71, 72, 74, 75, 85

software, 94, 126, 146, 156, 216
Sogunro, 269, 370
Sohag, 240
soil, 58, 326
solar, 321, 363
solicit, 98
solid waste, 307, 325
Solomon,, 185, 370
solutions, vii, 7, 18, 87, 92, 157, 186, 194, 202, 238, 240, 243, 250, 266, 309, 310, 324
Somali, 224, 243, 252, 253, 254
Somalia, 223, 224, 226, 230, 243, 253
songs, 82, 105, 134, 141, 234, 268, 292, 293
Sood, 76, 370
sounds, 203
South Africa, 44, 45, 46, 48, 49, 51, 52, 54, 70, 90, 120, 122, 256, 260, 262, 264, 355, 359, 360, 365, 366, 370, 371, 374, 378
South Asia, 307, 308
Southeast Asia, 368
Souza, 71, 72, 76, 370
sovereignty, 197
space, 72, 73, 191, 194, 196, 197, 200, 201, 203, 204, 206, 214, 269, 286, 292, 293, 296, 309, 310, 311, 318, 319, 320, 322, 323, 324, 326
Spain, 75
spatial, 7, 309, 314, 315, 317, 319, 321, 324
specialists, 94, 226, 261
specificity, 64
specimens, 102, 107
spectrum, 311, 344
speed, 6, 88, 92, 210, 313
spine, 319
spiritual, 195, 280
spirituality, 195
spontaneity, 311
sports, 142, 149, 152, 156, 169
SPSS, 83
sputum, 102, 105, 107
squatter, 307, 312
SRH, 90, 98, 99
Srinivasan, 282, 365
Ssembabule District, 283, 284, 286, 287, 288, 289, 296
Ssempebwa, 366
St. Leger, 119
stability, 278
staffing, 294
stages, 87, 96, 119, 120, 212, 235, 274, 281, 311, 339, 345
stakeholders, 99, 102, 103, 107, 122, 209, 212, 274, 278, 282, 283, 284, 291, 301, 303, 309, 333
standard of living, 272

standards, vii, 50, 58, 138, 142, 143, 144, 145, 147, 181, 245, 324
Stanton, 45
stars, 106
statistics, 52, 271, 286, 293
status quo, 57
sterile, 15, 90, 304
sterilization, 13
Stewart, 116, 168, 254, 371
stigma, ix, 17, 38, 78, 107, 109, 231
stigmatization, 102, 107, 225, 229, 249
stimulant, 194
stimulus, 266
stock, 14, 58, 297, 308
Stoneburner, 47, 48, 363
storage, 291
Stormshak, 278, 362
story telling, 268
strategic, 12, 108, 178, 188, 213, 352, 374
strategies, vii, 5, 6, 7, 11, 25, 56, 57, 62, 66, 67, 76, 77, 84, 88, 101, 102, 103, 104, 107, 116, 122, 138, 166, 172, 174, 176, 177, 188, 189, 221, 222, 237, 240, 246, 247, 249, 256, 274, 277, 282, 283, 285, 292, 307, 333, 354, 358, 373, 374
Strauss, 124, 371
streetwise, 17
strength, 6, 12, 215, 243
stress, 130
structural aAdjustment, 58, 372
structural modifications, 66
Stuart, 56, 59, 354
student group, 153
student motivation, 105
students, 18, 33, 46, 47, 48, 105, 106, 113, 115, 119, 121, 123, 124, 125, 126, 127, 128, 129, 130, 131, 132, 133, 134, 135, 136, 137, 138, 139, 140, 141, 142, 143, 144, 145, 146, 147, 148, 149, 150, 151, 152, 153, 154, 155, 156, 157, 158, 159, 160, 161, 162, 163,□164, 165, 166, 167, 169, 170, 171, 172, 173, 174, 175, 176, 177, 178, 179, 180, 181, 215, 248, 283, 290, 297, 301, 350, 364, 368, 370
Stuttaford, 268, 371
subgroups, 225
subjective, 214, 260, 266, 277, 341
subjective experience, 214
subjectivity, 265, 266, 335
Sub-Sahara Africa, 80
Sub-Saharan, 79, 223, 375
Sub-Saharan Africa, 20, 23, 24, 48, 79, 223, 236, 280, 350, 356, 358, 374, 375
subsidiarity, 210
subsidies, 308, 313
subsidy, 315, 327, 328

subsistence, 272
subsistence farming, 272
substance abuse, 277
substitution, 65, 272
suburban, 128, 129, 130, 134, 135, 136, 138, 140, 150, 151, 152, 153, 157, 158, 159, 160, 161, 162, 163, 164, 165, 166
success rate, 101, 102
Sudan, 223, 224, 225, 226, 230, 231, 235, 239, 242, 248, 251, 257
suffering, 83
sugar, 15, 39
suicide, 171
summer, 323
sundry, 74, 77
sunna, 230
superiority, 232
supernatural, 234
supervision, 109, 130, 296, 299, 300
supervisors, 110, 146, 158
suppliers, 284, 297
supply, 11, 20, 21, 118, 164, 165, 287, 299, 302, 308, 311, 312, 315, 316
support services, 237
surgeries, 253
surgery, 90, 367
surgical, 261, 301
surplus, 312, 327
surprise, 172, 231
surrogates, 10
surveillance, 11, 18, 80, 372
survey, 15, 98, 129, 144, 145, 146, 155, 174, 180, 225, 226, 227, 239, 245, 247, 253, 255, 257, 297, 298, 304, 312, 328, 375
surveys, 19, 20, 64, 91, 123, 129, 144, 145, 146, 147, 155, 174, 188, 224, 226, 227, 228, 293
survival, 15, 17, 24, 198, 235, 285, 290, 292, 294
surviving, 199
sustainability, 3, 12, 18, 52, 58, 59, 61, 65, 66, 122, 194, 196, 209, 211, 238, 270, 333, 335, 336, 340, 341
sustainable development, 55, 56, 58, 59, 65, 66, 208, 210, 219, 366
Swainson, 48, 49, 50
Swaziland, xi, 42
Sweden, 224, 247, 254, 301
Swedish, 248
Swikriti, 192, 193, 207
Switzerland, 224, 247, 248, 256, 257, 377, 378
symbiosis, 191, 192, 204, 205, 207, 210, 216, 217, 309, 357
symbiotic, 194, 205, 209, 210
symbolic, 36, 73, 235, 269, 346

sympathetic, 308, 310, 320, 327
symposiums, 134
symptomatics, 102, 104, 105
symptoms, 101, 102, 106, 139, 236, 279
syndrome, 4, 70
synergistic, 115, 179
synthesis, 126, 340
systematic, 3, 45, 50, 82, 88, 116, 126, 132, 186, 188, 189, 212, 239, 240, 333
systematic review, 45, 116
systemic change, 114, 117, 351
systems, 4, 10, 11, 14, 69, 70, 90, 94, 95, 114, 117, 118, 119, 127, 129, 132, 143, 161, 174, 188, 189, 192, 200, 207, 210, 212, 217, 228, 259, 260, 261, 284, 287, 288, 289, 290, 296, 299, 337, 346, 351

T

tactics, 12
Taguana, 252
Tajikistan, 54
talent, 13, 118
tangible, 261, 262, 265, 317
Tanzania, xi, 41, 45, 46, 47, 54, 224, 226, 227, 230, 236, 241, 244, 248, 351, 361, 373
Tarantola, 76, 364
target population, 118, 120, 298, 332
targets, 71, 132, 145, 188, 280, 324, 332, 337
task force, 105
tax base, 288
TBAs, 110, 284, 288, 290, 296, 297, 298, 299
teacher training, 122, 165
teaching, vii, 4, 15, 16, 50, 78, 99, 121, 122, 126, 130, 132, 133, 140, 141, 142, 143, 144, 146, 147, 148, 156, 165, 169, 172, 176, 177, 178, 181, 212, 276, 281, 350, 369
teaching experience, 147
teaching process, 133
teaching quality, 147
teaching strategies, 122
team members, 294, 296
teamwork, 153, 269
technical assistance, 118, 164, 242, 290, 331, 335, 337, 338
technical efficiency, 259
technological, 4, 194, 202, 208, 310, 314, 370
technological change, 370
technology, vii, x, 6, 7, 88, 92, 94, 97, 99, 100, 149, 193, 194, 195, 208, 210, 212, 353, 367
technology transfer, 194, 210
teenage girls, 298
teeth, 151, 155, 167
telecommunications, 287
telemedicine, 367

teleological, 195, 197
telephone, 92, 154, 260
television, 4, 6, 19, 70, 76, 77, 102, 106, 107, 109, 110, 216, 270, 272, 282, 360
tension, 233, 265, 278
tenure, 309
Teresa, 56
terminology, ix, 4, 93, 96, 214, 222, 223
terraces, 323
territory, 46, 320
tetanus, 234
textbooks, 11, 45, 133, 138, 142, 143, 299
Thailand, 13, 372
theology, 252
theoretical, 55, 58, 68, 113, 114, 121, 124, 126, 163, 167, 168, 175, 177, 179, 181, 182, 269, 344, 349, 355, 370
theory, 3, 7, 9, 10, 60, 66, 68, 74, 88, 94, 100, 113, 114, 115, 117, 118, 121, 124, 163, 182, 186, 222, 231, 238, 255, 259, 260, 263, 265, 272, 278, 282, 344, 347, 353, 354, 360, 371, 372, 373
therapeutic, 261
therapy, 15, 16, 17
think critically, 264
thinking, 6, 7, 56, 70, 96, 118, 142, 174, 181, 185, 188, 199, 263, 269, 272, 273, 281, 344, 345, 346, 351, 365
third order, 206, 207
third party, 202
Third World, 186, 362
Thomas, 271, 360, 367, 371
threat, 87, 246, 281
threatened, 140, 294
threatening, 345
threats, 57, 73, 76, 278
threshold, 267, 316, 321
timber, 58
time frame, 82, 83
timetable, 132
timing, x, 64, 177
Tlamelo, 185, 371
tobacco, 12, 130, 167, 168, 170, 172, 363
Togo, 54, 224, 244, 271
tolerance, 89
toleration, 193
Tomaselli, 259, 262, 265, 266, 371
tonic, 16
tool, 6, 16, 78, 80, 92, 96, 97, 186, 188, 189, 191, 193, 196, 204, 205, 206, 207, 219, 222, 277, 282, 296
toolkit, 81
tools, 92, 93, 96, 98, 138, 188, 189, 193, 206, 207, 208, 209, 213, 216, 221, 222, 234, 267, 296, 307

top-down, 66, 259, 289, 303
topology, 325, 328
Tostan, 238, 239, 244, 255
Toubia, 254, 256, 257
toxic, 353
tracking, 72, 102, 107, 289, 296
trade, 106, 325
trade union, 106
trade-off, 325
trading, 39
tradition, 192, 205, 212, 221, 229, 234, 243, 249, 267, 275, 319
traditional, 5, 63, 100, 117, 185, 188, 190, 194, 196, 199, 202, 209, 226, 227, 232, 233, 234, 237, 239, 240, 242, 244, 246, 249, 250, 253, 254, 255, 267, 269, 270, 271, 272, 273, 274, 276, 277, 279, 280, 288, 293, 295, 296, 300, 303, 310, 314, 329, 366
traditional healers, 110, 288, 366
traditional medicines, 234
traditional practices, 222, 223, 232, 233, 234, 237, 240, 244, 247, 249, 250, 253, 254
traffic, 135, 136, 153, 167, 317, 318, 319, 322
trainees, 7, 16
training, xi, 14, 16, 18, 59, 67, 98, 99, 103, 105, 110, 118, 119, 121, 122, 126, 128, 130, 132, 133, 134, 138, 143, 146, 148, 152, 153, 164, 165, 169, 170, 175, 176, 178, 180, 181, 208, 209, 211, 213, 237, 240, 242, 247, 248, 249, 263, 267, 269, 271, 272, 273, 289, 290, 291, 294, 295, 296, 297, 298, 299, 301, 302, 303, 311, 337, 341, 360, 365, 367, 370
training programs, 99
transcripts, 82, 97
transfer, 58, 194, 199, 207, 210, 214, 265
transference, 205
transformation, 5, 71, 76, 221, 232, 238, 270, 328
transformations, 310
transition, 241, 259, 263, 297, 310, 324
transition to adulthood, 241
translation, 196
transmission, 24, 25, 26, 27, 30, 32, 36, 38, 41, 42, 70, 78, 79, 98, 210, 222, 235, 368, 374
transport, 4, 106, 300, 301, 302
transport costs, 301
transportation, 153
Traquina, 71, 74, 371
trauma, 234, 236, 261
Trautschold, 78, 371
treatment, 15, 101
trend, 51, 82, 227, 242
trial, 41, 44, 90, 104, 354, 359, 360, 374
Trialogue, 109, 110
triangulate, 81, 125, 274
triangulation, 275, 278

tribal, 110
trickle down, 70
Trinity, 201
truancy, 280
trust, 6, 10, 17, 21, 56, 160, 241, 243, 263, 294
Tsha-Tsha, 70
tubal ligation, 301, 304
tuberculosis, 7, 104, 105, 106, 357, 365, 370, 372
Tuberculosis, v, 101, 102, 103, 104, 349, 352, 357, 365, 367, 372, 378
Tuchman, 71, 74, 372
Tunisia, 230
Turkmenistan, 54
Turner, 270
Tutu, 58, 372
TV spot, 22
twins, 342
two-way, 296

U

U.S. Agency for International Development, 14, 95, 283, 286
Uchiyama, 203, 205, 372
Uganda, vi, 31, 41, 45, 47, 48, 49, 50, 51, 54, 85, 90, 224, 241, 242, 244, 283, 286, 287, 290, 292, 296, 298, 300, 301, 303, 304, 350, 351, 352, 354, 355, 356, 358, 361, 363, 364, 365, 366, 367, 369, 371, 372
Ugandan, 224, 298
UN General Assembly, 237, 249, 254
uncertainty, 202
undemocratic, 74
UNESCO, vii, xi, 5, 116, 120, 122, 155, 271, 360, 364, 369, 372
UNFPA, xi, 55, 59, 94, 98, 120, 122, 247, 250, 257, 271, 362, 364, 369, 372, 377
unhygienic, 234
UNICEF, vi, 6, 14, 15, 16, 24, 116, 120, 121, 122, 123, 221, 224, 228, 238, 239, 240, 246, 247, 248, 250, 251, 254, 255, 256, 257, 286, 290, 296, 360, 372, 377
uniform, 266
uniformity, vii, 278
unions, 115
United Kingdom, 224, 248
United Nations (UN), 29, 79, 92, 94, 96, 116, 222, 237, 249, 251, 253, 254, 257, 286, 331, 353, 369, 372, 373, 377
United Nations Development Program (UNDP), 4, 248, 331, 334, 355, 372
United States, 13, 18, 20, 75, 115, 182, 194, 244, 253, 280, 290, 297, 305, 356, 373

United States Agency for International Development (USAID), 13, 14, 15, 18, 20, 95, 96, 97, 98, 100, 253, 257, 283, 286, 290, 293, 296, 305, 340, 372, 373
Universal Declaration of Human Rights, 253
universalist, 197
universities, 67, 207, 209, 211, 213, 216, 230
university, 18, 97, 159, 207, 208, 209, 213, 350
university students, 18
unplanned pregnancies, 261
updating, 99
upload, 97
urban, 4, 6, 18, 19, 20, 63, 102, 104, 105, 107, 127, 128, 129, 130, 131, 132, 133, 134, 135, 136, 137, 138, 139, 140, 141, 142, 143, 144, 146, 148, 149, 150, 151, 152, 153, 154, 155, 157, 158, 159, 160, 161, 162, 163, 164, 165, 166, 168, 170, 224, 225, 268, 271, 272, 282, 307, 308, 310, 311, 314, 318, 324, 328, 329, 350, 372
urban areas, 4, 102, 104, 107, 168, 225, 272
urban centers, 19
urban centres, 268, 307, 314
urban population, 307
urbanisation, 329
urbanization, 225, 307
urethra, 235
users, 33, 79, 97, 98, 197, 204, 207, 210, 217, 218, 293
Utopian, 57
Uzbekistan, 54

V

vacation, 244
vaccination, 104, 239
vaccine, 7, 10, 48, 88, 90, 91, 104, 361
vaccines, 10, 89, 104
vacuum, 4
vagina, 235
validation, 371
validity, 81, 199, 230, 278, 340
valium, 280
valorisation, 191, 192, 193, 204, 207, 210, 211, 216, 217, 219, 349
values, 5, 70, 75, 121, 122, 151, 191, 193, 196, 198, 199, 200, 210, 217, 219, 236, 242, 267, 275, 277, 281, 309, 346
van den Hove, 272, 373
Van Ginneken, 75, 373
van Grootheest, 6
variable, 48, 64, 79, 83, 225
variables, 57, 78, 83, 193
variation, 29, 224, 225, 323, 328
vasectomy, 301, 304

Vass, 84
vehicles, 167, 188, 264, 290, 291, 323
vehicular, 317, 319, 322
ventilation, 322
veranda, 323
vertical, 29, 47, 49, 79, 201, 322
victims, 237, 245, 246, 247, 255, 281, 353
video, 93, 143, 148, 149, 153, 188, 272, 274, 275, 276, 277, 278, 279, 281, 282, 301, 350
videoconference, 94
Vietnam, 54
village, 16, 104, 106, 145, 156, 185, 208, 230, 238, 239, 240, 244, 247, 255, 271, 274, 275, 276, 278, 279, 290, 294, 310, 337, 356
violence, 10, 233, 235, 239, 249, 256
virginity, 230, 239
virtual reality, 202
virus, 70, 79, 235
visible, 57, 133, 194, 199, 285, 303
vision, 117, 118, 120, 129, 172, 173, 174, 177, 191, 192, 194, 207, 210, 216
visual, 15, 82, 110, 188, 274, 278, 318
vocational, 125, 126, 128, 129, 130, 132, 134, 135, 136, 138, 140, 141, 142, 144, 145, 151, 152, 153, 156, 157, 160, 161, 162, 163, 164, 165, 166, 176
vocational schools, 125
voice, 74, 152, 198, 229, 265
Volunteers, 283, 285, 378
voting, 197
vouchers, 21
vulnerability, 39, 202, 304

W

Waithira, 6, 55, 377
Wales, 208, 211, 213, 367, 377
walking, 137, 167, 173, 298, 319
waste, 152, 186, 345
waste management, 345
wastes, 9
watch-dog, 70
water, 11, 15, 116, 155, 157, 161, 272, 280, 287, 299, 307, 308, 311, 313, 315, 316, 325, 326
watershed, 51
wealth, 60, 129, 193, 195
wear, 152
web, 97, 99, 208
web pages, 97
weight gain, 236
weight loss, 236
welfare, 64, 247, 270
wellbeing, 278
well-being, 58, 84, 130, 158, 171, 275, 277
well-being, 280, 281, 282, 292, 295, 358

West Africa, 30, 80, 247
Western, 72, 195, 198, 205, 224, 245, 252, 304, 366, 367
Western Europe, 224, 245
Westley, 260
WFP, 24, 39, 375
WHO classification, 251
wind, 156
windows, 188
winning, 150
wisdom, 25, 206, 367
witness, 202
witnesses, 301
wives, 295, 296, 304
woman, ix, 21, 83, 160, 222, 226, 228, 229, 230, 234, 236, 243, 251, 252, 279, 280, 292, 296
word of mouth, 6
workers, 16, 17, 18, 24, 33, 36, 39, 61, 77, 80, 94, 103, 106, 110, 116, 122, 173, 185, 200, 235, 237, 240, 247, 255, 263, 284, 288, 289, 290, 299, 300, 301, 302, 303
workload, 159
workplace, 44, 47, 354
World Bank, 24, 39, 58, 116, 248, 249, 257, 292, 317, 331, 335, 353, 354, 356, 360, 365, 372, 373, 375, 378
World Focus, 79, 375
World Health Organisation, 6, 252, 257, 361, 375
World Health Organization (WHO), ix, 14, 56, 79, 94, 97, 102, 113, 114, 115, 116, 118, 120, 123, 127, 128, 131, 143, 145, 160, 164, 165, 172, 173, 174, 175, 177, 179, 180, 222, 223, 234, 235, 247, 250, 251, 252, 253, 254, 257, 290, 298, 353, 372, 375, 377, 378
worldview, 191, 196
worry, 278

writing, ix, xi, 5, 71, 73, 81, 98, 110, 146, 148, 149, 150, 209, 213, 250, 378
WTO, 357
Wusuta, 268, 271, 272, 274, 275, 276, 279, 280, 281, 282

Y

yang, 192, 193, 194, 207, 216
Yates, 118, 375
Yemen, 223, 225, 226
yield, 122, 228
yin, 193, 194
Ying, 192, 207
Ylva, 250, 252, 256
Yoder, 250, 251, 252
young adults, 18, 39, 51, 262, 263
young men, 29
young people, 32, 34
young women, 28, 33, 34, 252, 360

Z

Zambia, xi, 20
Zande-N'zakara, 225
Zeldin, 199, 375
Zelizer, 71, 72, 375
Zhang, 113, 123, 166, 168, 277, 349, 374, 375, 378
Zhejiang, 113, 114, 122, 123, 124, 125, 126, 138, 139, 148, 158, 167, 168, 170, 171, 173, 176, 179, 180, 181, 182, 378
Zimbabwe, 31, 47, 54, 352, 354
zoning, 315, 324
ZOY, 71